Laboratory Management Information Systems:

Current Requirements and Future Perspectives

Anastasius Moumtzoglou
*Hellenic Society for Quality and Safety in Healthcare, Greece & P. & A.
    Kyriakou Children's Hospital, Greece*

Anastasia Kastania
Athens University of Economics and Business, Greece

Stavros Archondakis
Military Hospital of Athens, Greece

A volume in the Advances in Healthcare
Information Systems and Administration (AHISA)
Book Series

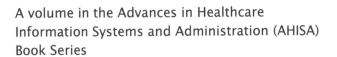

An Imprint of IGI Global

Managing Director:	Lindsay Johnston
Production Editor:	Christina Henning
Development Editor:	Erin O'Dea
Acquisitions Editor:	Kayla Wolfe
Typesetter:	Lisandro Gonzalez
Cover Design:	Jason Mull

Published in the United States of America by
Medical Information Science Reference (an imprint of IGI Global)
701 E. Chocolate Avenue
Hershey PA, USA 17033
Tel: 717-533-8845
Fax: 717-533-8661
E-mail: cust@igi-global.com
Web site: http://www.igi-global.com

Library of Congress Cataloging-in-Publication Data

Library of Congress Cataloging-in-Publication Data

Laboratory management information systems : current requirements and future perspectives / Anastasius Moumtzoglou, Anastasia Kastania, Stavros Archondakis, editors.
    p. ; cm.
Includes bibliographical references and index.
ISBN 978-1-4666-6320-6 (hardcover) -- ISBN 978-1-4666-6321-3 (ebook) -- ISBN 978-1-4666-6323-7 (print & perpetual access)
 I. Moumtzoglou, Anastasius, 1959- , editor. II. Kastania, Anastasia, 1965- , editor. III. Archondakis, Stavros, editor.
 [DNLM: 1. Clinical Laboratory Information Systems. 2. Laboratories, Hospital--organization & administration. QY 26.5]
 R858
 610.285--dc23
                                    2014017316

This book is published in the IGI Global book series Advances in Healthcare Information Systems and Administration (AHISA) (ISSN: 2328-1243; eISSN: 2328-126X)

British Cataloguing in Publication Data
A Cataloguing in Publication record for this book is available from the British Library.

For electronic access to this publication, please contact: eresources@igi-global.com.

Advances in Healthcare Information Systems and Administration (AHISA) Book Series

Anastasius Moumtzoglou
Hellenic Society for Quality & Safety in Healthcare and P. & A. Kyriakou Children's Hospital, Greece
Anastasia N. Kastania
Athens University of Economics and Business, Greece

ISSN: 2328-1243
EISSN: 2328-126X

MISSION

The **Advances in Healthcare Information Systems and Administration (AHISA) Book Series** aims to provide a channel for international researchers to progress the field of study on technology and its implications on healthcare and health information systems. With the growing focus on healthcare and the importance of enhancing this industry to tend to the expanding population, the book series seeks to accelerate the awareness of technological advancements of health information systems and expand awareness and implementation.

Driven by advancing technologies and their clinical applications, the emerging field of health information systems and informatics is still searching for coherent directing frameworks to advance health care and clinical practices and research. Conducting research in these areas is both promising and challenging due to a host of factors, including rapidly evolving technologies and their application complexity. At the same time, organizational issues, including technology adoption, diffusion and acceptance as well as cost benefits and cost effectiveness of advancing health information systems and informatics applications as innovative forms of investment in healthcare are gaining attention as well. **AHISA** addresses these concepts and critical issues.

COVERAGE

- IT Applications in Health Organizations and Practices
- Clinical Decision Support Design, Development and Implementation
- Nursing Expert Systems
- IT Applications in Physical Therapeutic Treatments
- Rehabilitative Technologies
- Management of Emerging Health Care Technologies
- Measurements and Impact of HISA on Public and Social Policy
- IT Security and Privacy Issues
- E-Health and M-Health
- Virtual Health Technologies

IGI Global is currently accepting manuscripts for publication within this series. To submit a proposal for a volume in this series, please contact our Acquisition Editors at Acquisitions@igi-global.com or visit: http://www.igi-global.com/publish/.

Titles in this Series

For a list of additional titles in this series, please visit: www.igi-global.com

Healthcare Informatics and Analytics Emerging Issues and Trends
Madjid Tavana (La Salle University, USA) Amir Hossein Ghapanchi (Griffith University, Australia) and Amir Talaei-Khoei (The University of Technology, Sydney, Australia)
Medical Information Science Reference • copyright 2015 • 325pp • H/C (ISBN: 9781466663169) • US $235.00 (our price)

Cloud Computing Applications for Quality Health Care Delivery
Anastasius Moumtzoglou (Hellenic Society for Quality and Safety in Healthcare, Greece & P. & A. Kyriakou Children's Hospital, Greece) and Anastasia N. Kastania (Athens University of Economics and Business, Greece)
Medical Information Science Reference • copyright 2014 • 342pp • H/C (ISBN: 9781466661189) • US $245.00 (our price)

Achieving Effective Integrated E-Care Beyond the Silos
Ingo Meyer (empirica, Germany) Sonja Müller (empirica, Germany) and Lutz Kubitschke (empirica, Germany)
Medical Information Science Reference • copyright 2014 • 366pp • H/C (ISBN: 9781466661387) • US $245.00 (our price)

Social Media and Mobile Technologies for Healthcare
Mowafa Househ (College of Public Health and Health Informatics, King Saud Bin Abdulaziz University for Health Sciences, Saudi Arabia) Elizabeth Borycki (University of Victoria, Canada) and Andre Kushniruk (University of Victoria, Canada)
Medical Information Science Reference • copyright 2014 • 372pp • H/C (ISBN: 9781466661509) • US $245.00 (our price)

Advancing Medical Practice through Technology Applications for Healthcare Delivery, Management, and Quality
Joel J.P.C. Rodrigues (Instituto de Telecomunicações, University of Beira Interior, Portugal)
Medical Information Science Reference • copyright 2014 • 361pp • H/C (ISBN: 9781466646193) • US $245.00 (our price)

Handbook of Research on Patient Safety and Quality Care through Health Informatics
Vaughan Michell (University of Reading, UK) Deborah J. Rosenorn-Lanng (Royal Berkshire Hospital Foundation Trust Reading, UK) Stephen R. Gulliver (University of Reading, UK) and Wendy Currie (Audencia, Ecole de Management, Nantes, France)
Medical Information Science Reference • copyright 2014 • 486pp • H/C (ISBN: 9781466645462) • US $365.00 (our price)

www.igi-global.com

701 E. Chocolate Ave., Hershey, PA 17033
Order online at www.igi-global.com or call 717-533-8845 x100
To place a standing order for titles released in this series, contact: cust@igi-global.com
Mon-Fri 8:00 am - 5:00 pm (est) or fax 24 hours a day 717-533-8661

In memory of my grandmother Eleni Liapi - A.M.

In memory of my beloved and respectable parents Nikolaos M Kastanias & Ekaterini Kastania - A.K

This book is gratefully dedicated to my mother Eleni Christoforatou Archondakis and my father Konstantinos Archondakis - S.A.

Editorial Advisory Board

Table of Contents

Detailed Table of Contents

Chapter 1

Kijpokin Kasemsap introduces the role of Total Quality Management (TQM) practices, thus explaining the introduction of Quality Management (QM) systems, the significance of TQM, the concept of TQM practices, the utilization of QM practices, and the relationship between TQM practices and quality performance. In addition, 17 TQM practices associated with quality performance (i.e., top management commitment, customer focus, training and education, continuous improvement and innovation, supplier quality management, employee involvement, information and analysis, process management, quality systems, benchmarking, quality culture, Human Resource Management (HRM), strategic planning, employee encouragement, teamwork, communication, and product and service design) are explained. This chapter serves as a valuable guideline for both researchers and practitioners to review their TQM programs in order to improve quality performance.

Chapter 2

Vincent Šoltés, Antonio José Balloni, Beáta Gavurová, and Michal Šoltés argue that there are significant disparities among the health needs of citizens and the financial resources of the health care system. Limitations of the inputs to growth of the health systems are primarily due to fiscal constraints, the demographic crisis, the degree of competitiveness of the EU, as well as the willingness of citizens to bear some degree of the tax burden. The costs of providing health care can be reduced by the proper implementation of the eHealth project, as is evidenced by the analysis of the costs and benefits of successful implementation abroad. The aim of this chapter is to evaluate the use of information and communication technologies (ICT) in medical institutions, in Slovakia, as the basis of effective strategic management, influencing the positive and negative changes in their external environment. In addition, the chapter focuses on investments in technological innovation, its determinants, and specification of the effects of the use of IS and IT in healthcare facilities. Finally, it reflects the partial outputs of the first international research GESITY/Hospitals 2011-2012 conducted in partnership with Slovakia and Brazil, in connection with the objectives of the implementation of an e-health program in Slovakia.

Chapter 3

Andrew Georgiou reviews what is currently known about the effect of the Electronic Medical Record (EMR) on aspects of laboratory test ordering, its impact on laboratory efficiency, and the contribution this makes to the quality of patient care. The EMR can be defined as a functioning electronic database within a given organisation that contains patient information. Although laboratory services are expected to gain from the introduction of the EMR, the evidence to date has highlighted many challenges associated with the implementation of the EMR, including their potential to cause major shifts in responsibilities, work processes, and practices. The chapter outlines an organisational communication framework that has been derived from empirical evidence. This framework considers the interplay between communication, temporal, and organisational factors, as a way to help health information technology designers, clinicians, and hospital and laboratory professionals meet the important challenges associated with EMR design, implementation, and sustainability.

Viroj Wiwanitkit realizes that the LIMS can be useful in all steps of the laboratory cycle (pre, intra-, and post-analytical phases). However, the present concern is on the standardization of the existing system. In this context, international collaboration to set the standards is required. Also, the multidisciplinary approach to add up the advantage and application of the technology is promising. With the more advanced computational and wireless information technology, the next step of LIMS will be a big wireless LIMS network that extends from medical laboratory and wards within the hospital to the outside unit as well as patient home. The point-of-care LIMSs are the actual future perspectives.

Po-Hsun Cheng contends that the instrument calibration is an important process within the laboratory activities. Many mobile medical devices are widely and routinely utilized for monitoring people's physiological data by home-care users. However, it is necessary to let this test data be as effective as laboratory reports and physicians can recognize as well as refer to them. Based on the ISO 15189:2012 standard, a Medical Instrument Calibration (MIC) process is proposed to let all connected instruments share and store their current calibration information in a global MIC's Database (MICDB). The MICDB provides cloud-based functions via Web Services, and also shares collaborated information that is provided by other medical instruments and vendors. A MIC process for calibrating the instrument is not only required for the laboratory, but it can also be adapted for mobile medical devices and home-care instruments.

Edison Fontes and Antonio José Balloni provide with a structured definition to develop, implement, and keep the needed regulatory—rules or principles—for an Information System Security (ISS). Also, the reader will find how to ensure the right use of this ISS, as well as regarding the authorization and protection against disaster situations such as an effective system protection when accessing, storing, using and retrieving the information in normal or contingency situations. This compound is the structure of information security policy which is based on a set of controls as described in ISO/IEC 27002:2005 NBR Norm. The definition of this structure for the information security policy is important because the Norm 27002 does not indicate nor define - or explain - what should be the structure of this policy, i.e., which are their fundamental elements and functions, which are the standards of rules for the controls and other practical issues so that the policy could be effective for the organization. The structure showed in this chapter represents a practical and useful architecture regarding the elements of the information security policy of the organization.

Chapter 7

Güney GÜRSEL gives evidence that medical laboratories are the key departments for healthcare. No matter, they are independent or part of the health center; they use an information management system. This system has to communicate and exchange data with many different organizations for many different reasons. Interoperability is the ability of two or more systems to exchange data and use that data as they are its own. As always in health information technologies, it is easy to say and hard to perform. It has some challenges. To overcome challenges, we need standard vocabularies, protocols, nomenclatures, classifications etc. In this chapter, laboratory management information system related interoperability issues are examined.

Chapter 8

Kyriacos C. Tsimillis and Sappho Michael deal with issues of quality management and quality assurance in medical laboratories. Basic terms and their role in quality assurance in laboratory examinations are analyzed and discussed. Clarifications on certification and accreditation are given with a comprehensive analysis of the procedures they refer to and their implementation for particular tasks. The implementation of the international standard ISO 15189 is presented with reference to some recent developments. The chapter has been prepared to help medical laboratories in an introductory understanding of quality assurance issues and encourage them to proceed with the implementation of the standard ISO 15189 and not as a detailed guide. Some practical considerations rising from the experience of a small country such as Cyprus are also discussed.

Chapter 9

Petros Karkalousos argues that ISO 15189:2012 is more specific to clinical laboratories as compared to the old one. The chapter emphasizes in the most important changes between the two versions of the Standard, especially in those that reveal the "spirit" of the new version. Some of these refer to ethics, quality management system, encouragement of the staff, risk management, evaluation of staff performance, purchase and withdraw of equipment, laboratory facilities, reagents and consumables, communication between the laboratory and its stakeholders, verification of the results by trained personnel, procedures of reporting the results, metrological procedures and traceability, function of Laboratory Information System, and responsibilities of the laboratory director.

Chapter 10
A Practical Approach for Implementing the Additional Requirements of the ISO 15189:2012
Fikriye Uras, Marmara University, Turkey

Fikriye Uras provides support that the accreditation standard of ISO 15189, a guidance document, provides validation that a laboratory is competent to deliver accurate and reliable test results. This international standard has been evolving since 2003. Following the second publication (2007), the standard was released as a revised and updated version in 2012 (Medical laboratories – Requirements for quality and competence). The text of ISO 15189:2012 has been approved as EN ISO15189:2012. European Union members and associate countries agreed to accord it the status of a national standard by May 2013. Any conflicting national standards need to be withdrawn by November 2015 at the latest. The purpose of this chapter is to mark the differences between the two versions of the standards and to highlight the changes and additions that have been incorporated into ISO 15189:2012. A practical approach will be helpful for laboratories to make a smooth transition to the updated standard when revising their quality and technical documentation to meet the new requirements.

Chapter 11
Stavros Archondakis, Military Hospital of Athens, Greece

Stavros Archondakis emphasizes on Quality Management concepts applied to Cytopathology laboratories and on the application of innovative information technologies in a modern cytopathology laboratory wishing to establish an effective quality management system and meet all current requirements concerning all aspects of its routine workflow (personnel, premises, environmental conditions, equipment, information systems and materials, pre-examination processes, examination processes, and the post examination phase).

Chapter 12
Innovative Architecture to Enhance Quality of Service for Laboratory Management Information
Naeem A. Mahoto, Mehran University of Engineering and Technology, Pakistan
Faisal K. Shaikh, Mehran University of Engineering and Technology, Pakistan & University
*   of Umm Al-Qura, Saudi Arabia*
B. S. Chowdhry, Mehran University of Engineering and Technology, Pakistan

Naeem A. Mahoto, Faisal K. Shaikh, B. S. Chowdhry propose an innovative architecture for the laboratory management information system to enhance the quality and management issues. The proposed architecture integrates two major fields namely: wireless technology and data mining. The wireless technology enables data collection easily and wirelessly, whilst, data mining ensures the meaningful and novel knowledge discovery from the collected data. In particular, the architecture will help management in three different ways: (1) prevention of risks/errors using technological solutions, (2) an environment to respond rapidly to adverse events, and (3) construction of a knowledge base for future guidelines.

> *Alessandro Fiori, Candiolo Cancer Institute – FPO, IRCCS, Italy*
> *Alberto Grand, Candiolo Cancer Institute – FPO, IRCCS, Italy*
> *Piero Alberto, Candiolo Cancer Institute – FPO, IRCCS, Italy*
> *Emanuele Geda, Candiolo Cancer Institute – FPO, IRCCS, Italy*
> *Francesco Gavino Brundu, Politecnico di Torino, Italy*
> *Domenico Schioppa, Politecnico di Torino, Italy*
> *Andrea Bertotti, Candiolo Cancer Institute – FPO, IRCCS, Italy & University of Torino,*
> > *Italy*

Alessandro Fiori, Alberto Grand, Piero Alberto, Emanuele Geda, Francesco Gavino Brundu, Domenico Schioppa, and Andrea Bertotti clarify that research laboratories produce a huge amount of complex and heterogeneous data. Laboratory Information Management Systems (LIMS) are software designed to support laboratory activities. For instance, LIMSs can manage the collection of samples, track laboratory procedures and store experimental data. Although many open-source and commercial LIMSs are available, it is often difficult to identify a product that is versatile enough to cover all the requirements and peculiarities of a specific research institution. To deal with this lack, their institution decided in 2011 to start a project named the Laboratory Assistant Suite (LAS), with the aim of developing a new software platform that assists researchers throughout diverse laboratory activities. The proposed system, which has been in use since May 2012, can track laboratory activities and experiments even in problematic environments (e.g., in sterile conditions). It supports the integration of heterogeneous biomedical data and helps in decision-making tasks by means of graphical tools to build complex analyses. In this chapter, we present the current architecture of the system, some real-use cases, as well as statistics about stored data and user feedback, in order to provide an overview of the functionalities and show the effectiveness of our platform in supporting research in the molecular oncology field.

> *Donovan McGrowder, The University of the West Indies, Jamaica*
> *Romeo Bishop, The University of the West Indies, Jamaica*

Donovan McGrowder and Romeo Bishop seek to find out information on the functionalities of the laboratory information systems available in medical laboratories in Jamaica and their ease of use and overall performance and satisfaction of medical technologists using them. A cross-sectional descriptive survey involving the use of a 48-item questionnaire was conducted among medical laboratories with a LIS. There was a total of 14 completed questionnaires out of 15 giving a response rate of 93.3%. The findings revealed that the majority of the laboratories have a LIS that provides a multi-level security, allows password protection at different levels, maintains a patient database, and generates records. The majority of the medical technologist agrees or strongly agrees that it was easy to use the LIS and experience improved overall performance on the job. The medical technologists clearly understand the existing features and functionality of the LIS. Additional functional features of the LIS should be customized, and adequate funding is needed especially for hospital-based laboratories.

Chapter 15

Patrizia Colangeli, Istituto Zooprofilattico Sperimentale dell'Abruzzo e del Molise "G. Caporale", Italy

Fabrizio De Massis, Istituto Zooprofilattico Sperimentale dell'Abruzzo e del Molise "G. Caporale", Italy

Francesca Cito, Istituto Zooprofilattico Sperimentale dell'Abruzzo e del Molise "G. Caporale", Italy

Maria Teresa Mercante, Istituto Zooprofilattico Sperimentale dell'Abruzzo e del Molise "G. Caporale", Italy

Lucilla Ricci, Istituto Zooprofilattico Sperimentale dell'Abruzzo e del Molise "G. Caporale", Italy

Patrizia Colangeli, Fabrizio De Massis, Francesca Cito, Maria Teresa Mercante, Lucilla Ricci assert that the Laboratory Information management System (LIMS) is recognized as a powerful tool to improve laboratory data management and to report in human health as well as in veterinary public health. LIMS plays an essential role in public health surveillance, outbreak investigations and pandemic preparedness. The chapter aims to provide an overview of LIMS use in veterinary fields as well as to report twenty years of experience of a Veterinary Public Institute in working with LIMS, illustrating the features of the LIMS currently in use in the Institute, highlighting the different aspects that should be considered when evaluating, and choosing and implementing a LIMS. In depth, it is illustrated how LIMS simplifies the accreditation path according to ISO IEC 17025 and the role in the epidemiology and veterinary public health. For this aspect, it's very important to collect clear data and for this reason, a LIMS has to activate formal checks and controls on business rules. To facilitate this issue, an interconnection between LIMS and other applications (internal or external to the laboratory) could be improved to allow automatic data exchange. At the same time, the unique data encoding at the national/international level should be used.

Foreword

It is tempting to write a book about laboratory information management systems and focus on the laboratory as one "silo" of the healthcare delivery structure. In that case, the book would target an audience of professionals involved in the laboratory services, along with information technology experts seeking to improve the efficiency of the laboratories, their appropriate use of resources, and compliance with ISO standards and other local requirements.

This is not a book about that silo.

The editors and authors of this innovative book offer us a system's perspective while focusing on the laboratory information management technologies and infrastructure. The audiences of this book are healthcare performance improvement professionals, healthcare information technology experts, and policy makers who increasingly realise that a laboratory is organically part of the entire system of delivery, and that without the appropriate communication between the various parts of that system, improving the processes and outcomes of a laboratory's performance will be akin to a case-study with little immediate impact on the improvement of the quality, safety, effectiveness, and technological leadership of the healthcare system within which a laboratory functions. In fact, a focus on the laboratory, in isolation from a hospital, a community center, a public health surveillance system, or a cloud-based, electronic medical records re-engineering within a national health care system runs the risk of adopting an academic perspective.

This is not a book about academic research or theoretical debate.

Rather, through the experience of authors from Europe, Asia Minor, and the Far East, the editors have compiled comprehensive, practice-based, and practically guided discussions about the role of a laboratory in promoting performance improvement within the health care system.

The 15 chapters of this book follow a progression of contextualization, economic implications for the use of electronic systems for data collection, storage and mining. quality improvement and its management, effectiveness and efficiency enhancement and monitoring, adoption of information technologies, use of tool and data calibration, the importance of cloud computing, the role of policy changes to promote the building of adequate communication, technology, quality improvement strategies, and the importance of standards. The inclusion of case studies strengthens the message of the authors and step-by-step validates the title of this book.

And perhaps to make the point that the topics and recommendations of this book go beyond the laboratory and in fact beyond the "human medical care systems", the last chapter shows how the topics covered by this book apply perfectly and seamlessly to laboratory information management systems in veterinary laboratories. It is a most convincing sequence of chapters showing the generic nature of the topics and their readily generalisable applicability to the roles and functions of all healthcare professionals.

This is a book of practical guidance and thoughtful recommendations for healthcare professionals who have already adopted a systems approach and are eager to learn about the interoperability of quality improvement, economic analysis and supporting technologies toward the enhancement of their health care system.

It is also a book for those who are still struggling within a silo-driven infrastructure and wonder how improved communication, electronic health and healthcare data, and adoption of international standards would incorporate the isolated silos into an organic system.

I believe this publication will convince many that such a system can be realized, and will guide the readers through the key dimensions of the process.

Vahé A. Kazandjians
Johns Hopkins University, USA

Vahé Kazandjian *is the Principal for ARALEZ HEALTH LLC, a Baltimore, Maryland-based global consulting company for healthcare performance improvement and accountability. He was the architect of the first multi-national hospital quality assessment project, the Maryland Quality Indicator Project (QIP) which he directed from 1990-2000. Dr. Kazandjian is a Professor (Adjunct) at Johns Hopkins University, Bloomberg School of Public Health, an Associate Professor (Adjunct) at the University of Maryland, School of Medicine, and a Professor (Adjunct) at the Uniformed Health Services University, School of Medicine, Maryland. Since 2002, he serves as Advisor to the World Health Organization (WHO) to assist in the hospital and healthcare systems performance assessment project in European countries. Since 2011, he has conducted evaluation programs for indicator-based programs, such as those funded by WHO in Poland, Hungary and Croatia. Dr. Kazandjian is the author of four healthcare books on quality of care improvement and author/co-author of more than 70 peer-reviewed articles and book chapters.*

Preface

Medical laboratory services are essential to patient care and include arrangements for examination requests, patient preparation, patient identification, collection of samples, transportation, storage, processing and evaluation of clinical samples, together with subsequent interpretation, reporting and advice, and safety in the medical laboratory work. ISO 15189:2012 is an international standard that can be used by medical laboratories wishing to improve their quality standards. Its requirements contain a number of general guidelines that help each laboratory to build and expand its own quality system.

Laboratory automation can offer greater productivity, lower cost, and easier integration with modern instrumental equipment. Moreover, laboratory information systems permit the laboratories to achieve maximum efficiency and significantly increase cooperation among physicians and reduce human errors. Information technology systems also provide reliable, standardized procedures for the assessment of medical laboratories (Vacata, et al., 2007).

Proper implementation of a Laboratory Management Information System (LMIS), according to the ISO 15189:2012 requirements, enhances the capacity of medical laboratories to store, organize, process, and retrieve prodigious amounts of information. In this context, the LMIS continuously improves and monitors the quality of services, monitors turnaround times and other crucial quality assurance parameters, assists research and teaching, and reduces the cost of services. Furthermore, telemedicine and e-health services shape or are affected by the ISO 15189:2012 requirements. However, there are formidable difficulties during the implementation of standards for medical laboratories, as well as ISO 15189:2012, because standards include general guidelines concerning the use of laboratory information systems with respect to electronic medical records, which require further elaboration.

During the last decade, information technology has dramatically changed the practice of clinical laboratory professionals, due to the implementation of laboratory management information systems. A Laboratory Management Information System (LMIS) is a valuable tool for medical professionals wishing to manage complex processes, ensure regulatory compliance, promote collaboration between departments of the same or independent laboratories, and generate detailed reports.

LMIS implementation in the routine laboratory workflow may present problems concerning medical data storage, security, and retrieval, as well as proper use of laboratory hardware and software by authorized and trained personnel. Medical information stored in computer systems may be lost or changed by unauthorized personnel. As a result, the laboratory has to follow strict rules in order to protect its information system from improper or unauthorized use and solve all possible problems that may be encountered.

LMIS implementation in the traditional medical laboratory workflow should also ensure continuous monitoring of prospective or retrospective, qualitative or quantitative indicators regarding the accuracy of the laboratory reports and their completeness and timeliness. LMIS should also monitor all potential telemedical or e-health medical laboratory applications, especially if they are used for quality management purposes.

ISO 15189:2012 is a powerful tool for diminishing unexpected errors or problems. The requirements of the standard for the laboratory information management include the implementation of specific measures concerning validation, documentation, protection from unauthorized access, safeguard from tampering or loss, and integrity of data. Furthermore, telemedicine procedures should follow ISO 15189:2012 requirements for quality and expertise in order to provide validated laboratory medical information. Finally, e-health services or telemedicine may help laboratories wishing to apply external quality control programs, especially in the field of proficiency testing or periodical interlaboratory comparisons.

THE CHALLENGES

The effective implementation of ISO 15189:2012 in medical laboratories demands an adequate understanding of the existing challenges. Such challenges can be classified into seven main categories:

- Development of well-written and well-implemented LIS software that can use medical data for the documentation of Quality Control (QC) measures.
- Formulation of effective security policies and procedures against the laboratory's information system improper or unauthorized use.
- Enactment of policies and procedures that will effectively monitor all available indicators regarding the accuracy of the laboratory reports, their completeness, and timeliness.
- Endowment of effective policies and procedures that will monitor all available telemedical or e-health applications.
- Establishment of effective policies and procedures that will comply with relevant regulations and guidelines edited by national or international regulatory bodies.
- Inclusion of effective policies and procedures for implementation of proper internal/external quality control measures.
- Manifestation of effective policies and procedures for the validation and verification of proper methods.

A medical laboratory should keep up quality control measures in order to detect, reduce, and correct deficiencies in laboratory diagnoses, and perform a set of procedures in order to ensure that the preparation, interpretation, and reporting of laboratory specimens meets specific quality standards. Moreover, quality assurance policy is used by a medical laboratory as a retrospective tool measuring the success of pre-, post-, and analytical methods. As a result, the laboratory should implement an effective quality control program designed to monitor and evaluate the quality of its testing methods. The quality control program implemented by a medical laboratory should be able to guarantee the accuracy, reliability, and timeliness of diagnoses.

Moreover, the laboratory may introduce electronic monitoring in order to perform quality control measures. Electronic data can be extracted and manipulated in a convenient and simple way, not demanding computer-specialists as end users. In an accredited medical laboratory, quality assurance methodologies are designed and used in order to continually improve the diagnostic accuracy and eliminate false negative diagnostic rates (Okada, 2002).

Finally, an accredited medical laboratory should electronically track QC/QA indicators, which will be computed either within the LIS and/or by exporting data from the LIS (by using common spreadsheet software).

A medical laboratory information system should monitor laboratory requisition completeness, problems documented by the accession, occurrences, and trends with any particular clinician office sending specimens to the laboratory. Identification of such problems could prompt the redesign of requisition forms while specimen rejection incidents and labeling errors should also be electronically documented, and specimen rejection frequency should be regularly reported to the offices of the physicians. Comments entered within available QA fields should be included in the final report (Okada, 2002).

Moreover, a medical laboratory information system should also monitor electronic data integrity and take all available security measures, which may include regular back up of data, password protection, data encryption, use of antiviral software, firewalls, and audit trails. It should also assign different privileges to users and allow only certain individuals to finalize and sign out abnormal medical diagnoses.

Additionally, a laboratory information system should ensure the integrity of finalized reports. Changes, where applicable, should be incorporated in the form of an addendum to the existing report. It should also use standardized diagnostic terminology and coded comments in order to ensure uniformity of the reporting language. Such coded comments allow quick data entry and rapid result reporting to the clinician. Laboratory reports using standardized language make up an efficient means to extract data, enabling calculations of diagnostic reproducibility (Okada, 2002).

Similarly, a modern medical laboratory's information system should possess the ability for remote log-in and access to ordering and reporting systems via a secure Web browser, allowing laboratories to access the LIS from distant locations. It should also allow reliable electronic signatures for data authentication. Regarding test ordering, a medical laboratory's information system should be able to provide immediate feedback to all users (Okada, 2002).

A modern medical laboratory's information system should also possess a user-friendly display of the test catalog with available alternative groupings. The laboratory's administration should periodically monitor menu consistency and complete or update them according to patient needs (Okada, 2002).

Finally, the laboratory's information system should be able to relay orders to different interfaced systems without manual intervention, so that tests ordered in one facility can enable specimens to be collected and accessioned at another location or institution.

A modern medical laboratory's information system should contain functionalities to optimize specimen collection and processing (Okada, 2002) and interface with laboratory automation management software to ensure that all the pre-analytical conditions stipulated in the ordering process are transmitted to the specimen-processing system. Likewise, the laboratory's information system should hold functionalities to optimize the analytical phase, the result entry and validation, result reporting, notification management, data mining and cross-sectional reports, method validation, and quality management by using a module supporting accreditation requirements (Okada, 2002).

SEARCHING FOR A SOLUTION

The net of accredited laboratories is globally expanding (Kubono, 2007). Many more countries will incorporate ISO 15189 requirements in their national or local regulations. Medical laboratories that will develop the most innovative and up-to-date procedures for electronic medical reporting and storage will become referral laboratories for their countries or regions (Kubono, 2007).

On the other hand, all laboratories' notices concerning the implementation of the ISO 15189:2012 are collected by an international working group, which is responsible for the revision of the standards when necessary. Problems that might be reported to this international working group are examined, and suitable solutions will be incorporated in the standard's future editions or specific guidelines (Kubono, 2007).

The ISO 15189 requirements for quality and competence concerning the electronic medical data comprise a set of general guidelines that will help each laboratory to establish and develop its quality system. However, the procedures that will eventually be performed by each laboratory during the development of an acceptable quality system may differ according to its specific needs and limitations (Kubono, 2004, 2007).

Meanwhile, the efforts of the medical community continuously aim at the creation of a secure electronic environment for medical data management, storage, retrieval, and updating, as well as decision support and quality control mechanisms (Kubono, 2004, 2007).

Procedural requirements for the implementation of high-quality electronic medical databases include the acquisition of an electronic procedure manual available to all computer users and the implementation of specific procedures aiming at the protection of electronic data from any damage caused by hardware or software failure.

System electronic security from unauthorized alterations is of paramount importance and has to be ensured by implementing strict policies concerning authorization for entering, changing, or editing electronic medical records. As a result, medical data integrity must be continuously monitored for any errors during transmission and storage processes. Specific procedures for reviewing all automatic calculations as well as the data entered in the laboratory information system must be performed in order to ensure medical data's integrity (Okada, 2002).

Specific procedures must ensure that electronic medical data will be easily retrievable by all authorized personnel. Parameters such as footnotes, interpretative comments, and uncertainty of a given measurement must be easily reproducible as part of the electronic medical report, offering the clinician the chance to interpret, with precision, laboratory medical data.

Hardware and software requirements for the implementation of high-quality electronic medical databases include the acquisition of a complete record of all preventive actions concerning computer maintenance (Vacata, et al., 2007).

Every back up must be followed by systematic verification of the software integrity. All mistakes detected during back up have to be documented, and corrective action must restore the system's proper function. Authorized personnel must verify that all programs run properly after first installation or any documented modification, and all serious computer malfunctions must be reported to an authorized laboratory's member responsible for the proper use of the medical laboratory's electronic records. System maintenance must be scheduled in such a way that it will not interrupt the patient-care service. Documented procedures for handling computer shutdown and restart will ensure medical data's integrity (Vacata, et al., 2007; Kubono, 2007).

Cooperation between the laboratory and hospital information system will be improved by the implementation of specific procedures concerning data replacement, recovery, and updating (Okada, 2002). All computer problems, such as unexpected shutdown, downtime, or breakdown, must be fully documented, and corrective action must be taken in order to avoid these problems in the future (Vacata, et al., 2007; Kubono, 2007).

The use of the electronic signature in medical reports may diminish bureaucratic problems but, on the other hand, makes the laboratory information system more vulnerable. The laboratory management has to implement specific policies that will protect medical data from unauthorized access but will not endanger the cooperation between medical and laboratory information systems (Vacata, et al., 2007).

Laboratory personnel training in informatics is necessary for ensuring the efficient function of the laboratory information system. The laboratory management has to plan personnel training in such a way that the laboratory main function will not be put in danger. Poor hardware maintenance or improper use by inadequately trained personnel may cause a laboratory information system failure. Laboratory reports may be lost or deteriorated due to malignant software (virus programs), while LIS hardware may be damaged by adverse environmental conditions, such as heat, humidity, or a possible fire, due to the vulnerability of wires and cables to unfavorable environmental conditions. Finally, medical data stored only in electronic mediums may be easily lost due to a system's unexpected failure (Vacata, et al., 2007). All these potential threats of a laboratory information system require the implementation of specific measures and policies that may have considerable economic impact, or may even prove unaffordable. The laboratory management is responsible for making an economic plan after taking into account the particular laboratory resources and needs (Okada, 2002).

Before new software or hardware is introduced in a laboratory, the risk connected with such an introduction should be assessed. The risk assessment should include identification of possible events, which may result in non-compliance, estimation of their likelihood, identification of their consequences, and ways of avoiding them, costs, drawbacks, and benefits (Vacata, et al., 2007). Good knowledge of computer software and hardware details is also essential for the maintenance, troubleshooting, and update. Medical laboratory personnel have to be periodically trained to use new computer facilities and new software products. Their training may be extremely difficult. Therefore, the laboratory director has to encourage these training sessions and continuously motivate its personnel.

Moreover, we have to take into account that computer facilities maintenance is of paramount importance in the workflow of a medical laboratory. Therefore, the laboratory personnel should take specific measures for protecting the hardware. The hardware should also be fully protected from any actual damages, and especially fire (Vacata, et al., 2007).

The provision of an uninterruptible power supply will protect the computer from crashing during power outages or from low and high voltage occurrences (Vacata, et al., 2007). A UPS is much better than a surge protector and can save the laboratory computer facilities from virtually any type of power failure (Okada, 2002).

Finally, the laboratory should also obtain a complete record of all preventive actions concerning computer maintenance (Vacata, et al., 2007), as hardware preventive maintenance is the best way to dramatically reduce all factors threatening or shortening computer life (Okada, 2002). Software preventive maintenance can be achieved by using anti-virus applications, defragmentation software, and testing utility programs (Vacata, et al., 2007).

ORGANIZATION OF THE BOOK

In Chapter 1, Kijpokin Kasemsap introduces the role of Total Quality Management (TQM) practices, thus explaining the introduction of Quality Management (QM) systems, the significance of TQM, the concept of TQM practices, the utilization of QM practices, and the relationship between TQM practices and quality performance. In addition, 17 TQM practices associated with quality performance (i.e., top management commitment, customer focus, training and education, continuous improvement and innovation, supplier quality management, employee involvement, information and analysis, process management, quality systems, benchmarking, quality culture, Human Resource Management [HRM], strategic planning, employee encouragement, teamwork, communication, and product and service design) are explained. This chapter serves as a valuable guideline for both researchers and practitioners to review their TQM programs in order to improve quality performance.

In Chapter 2, Vincent Šoltés, Antonio José Balloni, Beáta Gavurová, and Michal Šoltés argue that there are significant disparities among the health needs of citizens and the financial resources of the healthcare system. Limitations of the inputs to growth of the health systems are primarily due to fiscal constraints, the demographic crisis, the degree of competitiveness of the EU, as well as the willingness of citizens to bear some degree of the tax burden. The costs of providing healthcare can be reduced by the proper implementation of eHealth project, as is evidenced by the analysis of the costs and benefits of successful implementation abroad. The aim of this chapter is to evaluate the use of Information and Communication Technologies (ICT) in medical institutions, in Slovakia, as the basis of effective strategic management, influencing the positive and negative changes in their external environment. In addition, the chapter focuses on investments in technological innovation, its determinants, and specification of the effects of the use of IS and IT in healthcare facilities. Finally, it reflects the partial outputs of the first international research GESITY/Hospitals 2011-2012 conducted in partnership with Slovakia and Brazil, in connection with the objectives of the implementation of an eHealth program in Slovakia.

In Chapter 3, Andrew Georgiou reviews what is currently known about the effect of the Electronic Medical Records (EMRs) on aspects of laboratory test ordering, their impact on laboratory efficiency, and the contribution this makes to the quality of patient care. The EMR can be defined as a functioning electronic database within a given organisation that contains patient information. Although laboratory services are expected to gain from the introduction of the EMRs, the evidence to date has highlighted many challenges associated with the implementation of EMRs, including their potential to cause major shifts in responsibilities, work processes, and practices. The chapter outlines an organisational communication framework that has been derived from empirical evidence. This framework considers the interplay between communication, temporal, and organisational factors, as a way to help health information technology designers, clinicians, and hospital and laboratory professionals meet the important challenges associated with EMR design, implementation, and sustainability.

In Chapter 4, Viroj Wiwanitkit realizes that the LIMS can be useful in all steps of the laboratory cycle (pre-, intra-, and post-analytical phases). There are many LIMSs at present, and those LIMSs are used worldwide. The present concern is on the standardization of the existing system. In this context, international collaboration to set the standards is required. In addition, the multidisciplinary approach to add up the advantage and application of the technology is promising. With the more advanced computational and wireless information technology, the next step of LIMS will be big wireless LIMS networks that extend from medical laboratories and wards within the hospital to outside units as well as patient homes. The point-of-care LIMSs are the actual future perspectives.

In Chapter 5, Po-Hsun Cheng contends that instrument calibration is an important process within the laboratory activities. Many mobile medical devices are widely and routinely utilized for monitoring people's physiological data by home-care users. However, it is necessary to let these test data be as effective as laboratory reports, so physicians can recognize as well as refer to them. The chapter proposes a Medical Instrument Calibration (MIC) process to let all connected instruments share and store their current calibration information in a global MIC's Database (MICDB). The MICDB is based on the ISO 15189:2012 standard and provides cloud-based functions via Web Services. It also shares collaborated information that is provided by other medical instruments and vendors. A MIC process for calibrating the instrument is not only required for the laboratory, but it can also be adapted for mobile medical devices and home-care instruments.

In Chapter 6, Edison Fontes and Antonio José Balloni provide a structured definition to develop, implement, and keep the needed regulatory rules or principles for an Information System Security (ISS). In addition, the reader finds how to ensure the right use of this ISS, as well as in authorization and protection against disaster situations such as an effective system protection when accessing, storing, using, and retrieving the information in normal or contingency situations. This compound is the structure of information security policy that is based on a set of controls as described in NBR ISO/IEC 27002. The definition of this structure for the information security policy is important because the Norm ABNT does not indicate nor define—nor explain—how the structure of this policy should be (i.e., which are the fundamental elements and functions, which are the standards of rules for the controls and other practical issues) so that the policy could be effective for the organization. The structure shown in this chapter represents a practical and useful architecture regarding the elements of the information security policy of the organization

In Chapter 7, Güney Gürsel gives evidence that medical laboratories are the key departments for healthcare. It does not matter if they are independent or part of the health center; they use an information management system. This system has to communicate and exchange data with many different organizations for many different reasons. Interoperability is the ability of two or more systems to exchange data and to use the exchanged data as their own. As always in health information technologies, this is easy to say and hard to perform. It has some challenges. To conquer interoperability, we need standard vocabularies, protocols, nomenclatures, classifications, etc. In this chapter, laboratory management information system-related interoperability issues are examined.

In Chapter 8, Kyriacos C. Tsimillis and Sappho Michael deal with issues of quality management and quality assurance in medical laboratories. Basic terms and their role in quality assurance in laboratory examinations are analyzed and discussed. Clarifications on certification and accreditation are given with a comprehensive analysis of the procedures they refer to and their implementation for particular tasks. The implementation of the international standard ISO 15189 is presented with reference to some recent developments. The chapter has been prepared to help medical laboratories in an introductory understanding of quality assurance issues and encourage them to proceed with the implementation of the standard ISO 15189 and not as a detailed guide. Some practical considerations rising from the experience of a small country such as Cyprus are also discussed.

In Chapter 9, Petros Karkalousos argues that ISO 15189:2012 is more specific to clinical laboratories as compared to the old one. The present chapter emphasizes in the most important changes between the two versions of the standard, especially in those that reveal the "spirit" of the new version. Some of these refer to ethics, quality management system, encouragement of the staff, risk management, evaluation of staff performance, purchase and withdraw of equipment, laboratory facilities, reagents and consumables, communication between the laboratory and its stakeholders, verification of the results by trained personnel, procedures of reporting the results, metrological procedures and traceability, function of laboratory information system, and responsibilities of laboratory director.

In Chapter 10, Fikriye Uras provides support that the accreditation standard of ISO 15189, a guidance document, provides validation that a laboratory is competent to deliver accurate and reliable test results. This international standard has been evolving since 2003. Following the second publication (2007), the standard was released as a revised and updated version in 2012 (Medical laboratories – Requirements for quality and competence). The text of ISO 15189:2012 has been approved as EN ISO15189:2012. European Union members and associate countries agreed to accord it the status of a national standard by May 2013. Any conflicting national standards need to be withdrawn by November 2015 at the latest. The purpose of this chapter is to mark the differences between the two versions of the standards and to highlight the changes and additions that have been incorporated into ISO 15189:2012. A practical approach will be helpful for laboratories to make a smooth transition to the updated standard when revising their quality and technical documentation to meet the new requirements.

In Chapter 11, Stavros Archondakis emphasizes quality management concepts applied to cytopathology laboratories and the application of innovative information technologies in a modern cytopathology laboratory wishing to establish an effective quality management system and meet all current requirements concerning all aspects of its routine workflow (personnel, premises, environmental conditions, equipment, information systems and materials, pre-examination processes, examination processes, and the post-examination phase).

In Chapter 12, Naeem A. Mahoto, Faisal K. Shaikh, and B. S. Chowdhry propose an innovative architecture for the laboratory management information system to enhance the quality and management issues. The proposed architecture integrates two major fields, namely wireless technology and data mining. The wireless technology enables the collection of data easily and wirelessly, and data mining ensures meaningful and novel knowledge discovery from the collected data. In particular, the architecture helps management in three different ways: (1) prevention of risks/errors using technological solutions, (2) an environment to respond rapidly to adverse events, and (3) construction of knowledge base for future guidelines.

In Chapter 13, Alessandro Fiori, Alberto Grand, Piero Alberto, Emanuele Geda, Francesco Gavino Brundu, Domenico Schioppa, and Andrea Bertotti clarify that research laboratories produce a huge amount of complex and heterogeneous data typically managed by Laboratory Information Management Systems (LIMSs). Although many LIMSs are available, it is often difficult to identify a product that covers all the requirements and peculiarities of a specific institution. To deal with this lack, the Candido Cancer Institute decided to start a project, named the Laboratory Assistant Suite (LAS), with the aim of developing a new software platform that assists researchers throughout diverse laboratory activities. The proposed system can track laboratory experiments even in problematic environments, support the integration of heterogeneous biomedical data, and help in decision-making tasks. In this chapter, the authors present the current architecture of the system, some real-use cases, as well as statistics about stored data and user feedback in order to provide an overview of the functionalities and show the effectiveness of the platform in supporting research in the molecular oncology field.

In Chapter 14, Donovan McGrowder and Romeo Bishop seek to find out information on the functionalities of the laboratory information systems available in medical laboratories in Jamaica and their ease of use and the overall performance and satisfaction of medical technologists using them. A cross-sectional descriptive survey involving the use of a 48-item questionnaire was conducted among medical laboratories with a LIS. There were a total of 14 completed questionnaires out of 15, giving a response rate of 93.3%. The findings reveal that the majority of the laboratories have a LIS that provides multi-level security, allows password protection at different levels, maintains a patient database, and generates records. The majority of the medical technologists agree or strongly agree that it is easy to use the LIS and experience improved overall performance on the job. The medical technologists clearly understand the existing features and functionality of the LIS. Additional functional features of the LIS should be customized, and adequate funding is needed, especially for hospital-based laboratories.

In Chapter 15, Patrizia Colangeli, Fabrizio De Massis, Francesca Cito, Maria Teresa Mercante, and Lucilla Ricci assert that the Laboratory Information Management System (LIMS) is recognized as a powerful tool to improve laboratory data management and to report human health as well as veterinary public health. LIMS plays an essential role in public health surveillance, outbreak investigations, and pandemic preparedness. The chapter aims is to provide an overview of LIMS use in veterinary fields as well as to report 20 years of experience of a Veterinary Public Institute in working with LIMS, illustrating the features of the LIMS currently in use in the institute and highlighting the different aspects that should be considered when evaluating, choosing, and implementing a LIMS. In depth, the chapter illustrates how LIMS simplifies the accreditation path according to ISO IEC 17025 and the role in the epidemiology and veterinary public health. For this aspect, it is very important to collect clear data, and for this reason, a LIMS has to activate formal checks and controls on business rules. To facilitate this issue, an interconnection between LIMS and other applications (internal or external to laboratory) could be improved to allow automatic data exchange. At the same time, the unique data encoding at national/international level should be used.

Conclusively, *Laboratory Management Information Systems: Current Requirements and Future Perspectives* introduces the role of total quality management practices, reviews what is known about the effect of the electronic medical record on aspects of laboratory test ordering, argues that the present concern is on the standardization of the existing systems, proposes a calibration process, provides rules for information security, examines interoperability issues related to the laboratory management information system, provides support for the accreditation standard of ISO 15189:2012, proposes an innovative architecture for the laboratory management information system, and emphasizes quality management concepts applied to cytopathology laboratories.

Anastasius Moumtzoglou
Hellenic Society for Quality and Safety in Healthcare, Greece & P. & A. Kyriakou Children's
   Hospital, Greece

Anastasia Kastania
Athens University of Economics and Business, Greece

Stavros Archondakis
Military Hospital of Athens, Greece

REFERENCES

Kubono, K. (2004). Quality management system in the medical laboratory-ISO15189 and laboratory accreditation. *Rinsho Byori*, *2*(3), 274–278. PMID:15137330

Kubono, K. (2007). Outline of the revision of ISO 15189 and accreditation of medical laboratory for specified health checkup. *Rinsho Byori*, *55*(11), 1029–1036. PMID:18154036

Okada, M. (2002). Future of laboratory informatics. *Rinsho Byori*, *50*(7), 691–693. PMID:12187706

Vacata, V., Jahns-Streubel, G., Baldus, M., & Wood, W. G. (2007). Practical solution for control of the pre-analytical phase in decentralized clinical laboratories for meeting the requirements of the medical laboratory accreditation standard DIN EN ISO 15189. *Clinical Laboratory*, *53*, 211–215. PMID:17447659

Acknowledgment

We would like to thank the editorial advisory board for their invaluable advice, the reviewers for the care with which they reviewed the manuscripts, and all the authors for their diverse and outstanding contributions to this book.

Anastasius Moumtzoglou
Hellenic Society for Quality and Safety in Healthcare, Greece & P. & A. Kyriakou Children's
*   Hospital, Greece*

Anastasia Kastania
Athens University of Economics and Business, Greece

Stavros Archondakis
Military Hospital of Athens, Greece

Chapter 1
The Role of Total Quality Management Practices on Quality Performance

Kijpokin Kasemsap
Suan Sunandha Rajabhat University, Thailand

ABSTRACT

This chapter introduces the role of Total Quality Management (TQM) practices, thus explaining the introduction of Quality Management (QM) systems, the significance of TQM, the concept of TQM practices, the utilization of QM practices, and the relationship between TQM practices and quality performance. In addition, 17 TQM practices associated with quality performance (i.e., top management commitment, customer focus, training and education, continuous improvement and innovation, supplier quality management, employee involvement, information and analysis, process management, quality systems, benchmarking, quality culture, Human Resource Management [HRM], strategic planning, employee encouragement, teamwork, communication, and product and service design) are explained. This chapter serves as a valuable guideline for both researchers and practitioners to review their TQM programs in order to improve quality performance. Understanding the role of TQM practices on quality performance will significantly enhance the organizational performance and achieve business goals in the global business environments.

INTRODUCTION

Researchers have dedicated considerable efforts to examine the capacity of TQM to generate wealth, from the conceptual framework of the resource-based view (Garcia-Bernal & Garcia-Casarejos, 2014). From this approach, TQM is basically an inimitable resource that generates competitive advantages in an organization (Garcia-Bernal & Garcia-Casarejos, 2014). Both small and large businesses are required to become more efficient and cope with a competitive global market where customers' expectations continually increase (Sharabi, 2014). In addition, the systematic improvement of organizational performance should include the managers' commitment to QM, effective quality planning, and organizational learning (Delic, Radlovacki, Kamberovic, Maksimovic,

DOI: 10.4018/978-1-4666-6320-6.ch001

& Pecujlija, 2014). Quality has been typically regarded as a key strategic component of competitive advantage and the enhancement of product quality is still a matter of prime concern for firms (Li, Su, & Chen, 2011; Soltani, Azadegan, Liao, & Phillips, 2011). In highly competitive markets with escalating demands of consumers for getting better products and services (Thiagaragan, Zairi, & Dale, 2001), survival of companies in the ever-expanding marketplace (Zakuan, Yusof, Laosirihongthong, & Shaharoun, 2010), economic success of companies (Curkovic, Vickery, & Droge, 2000), improvement in productivity, customer satisfaction, profitability, and innovativeness (Sadikoglu & Zehir, 2010), changing organizational culture (Prajogo & McDermott, 2005), and globalization of world trade (Fotopoulos & Psomas, 2010), the emergence of quality plays a vital role, and has become a top priority for many companies worldwide in order to achieve the above-stated objectives and gain competitive edge. The importance of quality for company's performance in several terms and success, in the marketplace, is widely accepted in business literature and practice (Kumar, Choisne, De Grosfoir, & Kumar, 2009). In an attempt to improve the quality, numerous approaches to management of quality and continuous improvement have been pursued, most notably, and a recommended approach is the concept of TQM (Talib, Rahman, & Qureshi, 2013). A considerable body of empirical evidence suggests that TQM implementation improves quality performance of the company (Talib et al., 2013). TQM is an organization-wide process-oriented philosophy that requires changes not only in production, but also in decision-making processes, employee development, and employee involvement (Power & Sohal, 2000; Mehra, Hoffmann, & Sirias, 2001; Abdullah, Uli, & Tari, 2009).

TQM has come to be recognized as a major business driver to improve quality performance and provide customers with high quality products and services (Cai, 2009; Vecchi & Brennan, 2011).

Many companies claimed substantial benefits of implementing TQM in terms of financial results, operating performance, customer satisfaction, and employee satisfaction (Brah, Serene, & Rao, 2002; Fuentes, Montes, & Fernandez, 2006; Yang, 2006; Sila, 2007; Kumar et al., 2009). It is a holistic management approach (Hafeez, Malak, & Abdelmeguid, 2006) that seeks to manage quality; it requires development of quality strategy (Kanji & Wallace, 2000) and a framework for its implementation (Chin & Pun, 2002). TQM principles and practices have been embraced by many quality managers and practitioners from different sectors and have earned the attention of many researchers from diverse areas (Talib et al., 2013). TQM principles and practices come out with many success stories related to TQM practices (Lagrosen, 2003; Prajogo & McDermott, 2005; Karia & Asaari, 2006; Yoo, Rao, & Hong, 2006; Sila, 2007). Many researchers stated that the performance measurement is one of the most important dimensions of TQM success (Brah et al., 2002; Kaynak, 2003; Chang, 2006; Taylor & Wright, 2006). In addition, many researchers found a positive relationship between TQM and performance (Hendricks & Singhal, 2001; Prajogo & Sohal, 2003; Shenawy, Baker, & Lemak, 2007; Arumugam, Ooi, & Fong, 2008). This chapter introduces the role of TQM practices, thus explaining the introduction of QM systems, the significance of TQM, the concept of TQM practices, the utilization of QM practices, and the relationship between TQM practices and quality performance.

BACKGROUND

QM has emerged as a management paradigm for enhancing organizational effectiveness and competitiveness (Grandzol & Greshon, 1997; Dow, Samson, & Ford, 1999; Sanchez-Rodriguez & Martinez-Lorente, 2004; Sila, 2007). QM is defined and measured in empirical studies as practices of organizations that implement principles such as customer focus, continuous improvement, and teamwork to improve product and service quality (Dean & Bowen, 1994; Sousa & Voss, 2002; Prajogo & McDermott, 2005). QM has long been recognized as a source of competitive advantage and one of the most important drivers of global competition (Prajogo & Sohal, 2003). Quality, therefore, is critical if manufacturers are to achieve world class manufacturing and it has been identified as a crucial factor for sustainable development of ASEAN manufacturers (Phusavat & Kanchana, 2008). In addition, QM is a critical component to the successful management of construction projects (Abdul-Rahman, 1997). Quality and quality systems are topics which have received increasing attention worldwide (Kam & Tang, 1997; Yates & Aniftos, 1997; Tang & Kam, 1999). Several empirical studies suggest that firms achieve higher levels of profitability and organizational performance through successful implementation of QM (Powell, 1995; Easton & Jarrell, 1998; Das, Handfield, Calantone, & Ghosh, 2000; Kaynak, 2003; Yeung, Edwin Cheng, & Lai, 2006; Santos-Vijande & Alvarez-Gonzalez, 2009). The development of practices associated with QM has been instrumental in shaping management thinking and improving organizational processes (Sila, 2007; Kristal, Huang, & Schroeder, 2010; Phan, Abdallah, & Matsui, 2011). In addition, firms achieve higher levels of profitability and organizational performance through successful implementation of QM (Kaynak, 2003; Yeung et al., 2006; Carter, Lonial, & Raju, 2010; Kull & Narasimhan, 2010). QM practices have been criticized for their inability in creating a long-term competitive advantage (Soltani, Pei-Chun, & Phillips, 2008; Asif, De Bruijn, Douglas, & Fisscher, 2009). The implementation of QM techniques enables organizations to improve internal efficiencies, which is considered as a prerequisite to become competitive in global marketplace (Stading & Vokurka, 2003; Lambert & Ouedraogo, 2008). Organizations need an innovative management

methodology, such as the TQM practice, in order to achieve competitive strategy materializing toward international project management performance (Jung, Wang, & Wu, 2009).

THE ROLE OF TOTAL QUALITY MANAGEMENT PRACTICES ON QUALITY PERFORMANCE

This section introduces the introduction of QM systems, the significance of TQM, the concept of TQM practices, the utilization of QM practices, and the relationship between TQM practices and quality performance.

Introduction of Quality Management Systems

QM practices consist of not only traditional QM methods, such as quality measurement and quality control, but sets of quality programs and philosophies in TQM and ISO 9000 quality systems (Su, Li, Zhang, Liu, & Dang, 2008). Furthermore, operationalizing QM as single or multiple constructs, measuring performance in one level or multiple levels, and differences in data analysis techniques have contributed to produce mixed results in the relationship between QM and organizational performance (Kaynak, 2003; Molina, Llorens-Montes, & Ruiz-Moreno, 2007). Much has been written on the impact of QM practices on performance. Previous studies presented conflicting results on how different QM practices, specifically, infrastructure QM practices and core QM practices, affect the quality performance (Sousa & Voss, 2002). A few studies reported that only the infrastructure QM practices (i.e., executive commitment, employee empowerment, and customer focus) contribute to quality improvement, but the core QM practices (i.e., information and analysis, process improvement, benchmarking, and use of advanced manufacturing technologies) do not (Powell, 1995; Dow et al., 1999; Samson

& Terziovski, 1999). On the contrary, other studies found positive relationships between the core QM practices and performance (Forza & Flippini, 1998; Sanchez-Rodriguez & Martinez-Lorente, 2004; Rahman & Bullock, 2005), and some studies found that the infrastructure QM practices such as the role of top management, employee relations (Motwani, Mahmoud, & Rice, 1994), employee involvement, and employee development (Adam, Corbett, Flores, Harrison, Lee, Rho, Ribera, Samson, & Westbrook, 1997) are not significantly related to performance.

The categorizations of infrastructure QM practices and core QM practices vary among the studies (Ho, Duffy, & Shih, 2001; Taylor & Wright, 2006). For example, Dow et al. (1999) considered supplier relations as one of the core QM practices, whereas Rahman and Bullock (2005) categorized supplier relations as an infrastructure QM practice. The studies measure different levels of performance (Kaynak, 2003). Powell (1995) measured the financial performance, while others focused on quality performance as Forza and Flippini (1998) and Dow et al. (1999) did. Samson and Terziovski (1999) stated about performance measures to include quality performance, productivity, and employee morale. The analytical methods used to investigate relationships between quality management practices and performances differ (Sousa & Voss, 2002; Kaynak, 2003). Based on a correlation analysis (Powell, 1995; Dow et al., 1999) and multiple regression analysis (Adam et al., 1997; Samson & Terziovski, 1999), the infrastructure QM practices can enhance quality performance. These studies did not identify the direct and indirect effects of QM practices on quality performance, and hence are not adequate to draw any definite conclusions about the QM practices-quality performance relationships (Sousa & Voss, 2002; Kaynak, 2003).

The conventional QM framework has been built based on the findings of firms in the developed nations, where its applicability and generalizability should be limited to those countries (Jun, Cai, &

Shin, 2006). Whether QM practices are universal (context-free), or contingent (context-dependent) remains a controversial issue (Sousa & Voss, 2001; Rungtusanatham, Forza, Koka, Salvadora, & Nie, 2005). The results of globalization and international QM practices converge over time (Mellat Parast, Adams, Jones, Subba Rao, & Raghu-Nathan, 2006; Schniederjans, Mellat Parast, Nabavi, Subba Rao, & Raghu-Nathan, 2006). Enhancement of quality outcome and research and development (R&D) performance is the key to realize the expected effect of implementing QM practices (Su et al., 2008). QM theory and methods emerged from manufacturing plant (Su et al., 2008). Various quality control and improvement methods for manufacturing industry have been developed in the last decades (Su et al., 2008). It's relatively easy to find and resolve quality problems timely in manufacturing plants, so as to increase the ultimate quality pass rate before products are delivered to customers (Su et al., 2008). Quality gurus have put forth several approaches to improve company performance (Lakhal, Pasin, & Limam, 2006). These approaches are embodied in a set of QM practices, known as TQM (Lakhal et al., 2006). TQM is generally described as a collective, interlinked system of QM practices that are associated with organizational performance (Waldman, 1994; Madu, Kuei, & Lin, 1995). In addition, several studies have attempted to identify the key QM practices on which the success of a TQM process is based (Flynn, Schroeder, & Sakakibara, 1994; Ahire, Golhar, & Waller, 1996). Many researchers (i.e., Choi & Eboch, 1998; Terziovski & Samson, 1999; Cua, Mc Kone, & Schroeder, 2001; Douglas & Judge, 2001; Kaynak, 2003) suggested a positive relationship between TQM practices and organizational performance.

A quality system is the organizational structure, responsibilities, procedures, processes, and resources for implementing QM (Arnold, 1994). QM refers to the set of quality activities involved in producing a product, process, or service, and encompasses prevention and appraisal (Burati,

Farrington, & Ledbetter, 1992). QM is a management discipline concerned with preventing problems from occurring by creating the attitudes and controls that make prevention possible (Crosby, 1979). The core of QM encompasses methodical proceedings of the plan/do/check/act (PDCA) cycle and an orientation toward continuous improvement, often termed as TQM (Sallis, 2002; Venkatraman, 2007). Concepts of QM were first developed and implemented by large Japanese and subsequently adopted by large US organizations (Powell, 1995; Sila, 2007). Much of the academic literature has, therefore, examined the usage of QM practices in large corporations (Ghobadian & Gallear, 1997). Several studies have pointed to the importance of HRM practices and their role on effective implementation of quality programs (Asrilhant, Dyson, & Meadows, 2007; Mellat-Parast, Adams, & Jones, 2007; Sadikoglu & Zehir, 2010). Quality activities include the determination of the quality policy, objectives, and responsibilities through quality planning, quality control, quality assurance, and quality improvement, within the quality system (ASQC, 1997).

Understanding QM should be achieved through defining, analyzing and measuring specific practices associated with QM (Zu, Fredendall, & Douglas, 2008). The 13 constructs identified by Rao, Solis, and Raghunathan (1999) were considered to serve as a framework for QM:

- Top management support addresses the critical role of management in driving company-wide QM efforts (Flynn et al., 1994; Puffer & McCarthy, 1996; Ahire & O'Shaughnessy, 1998).
- Strategic quality planning incorporates the integration of quality and customer satisfaction issues into strategic and operational plans, which allow firms to set clear priorities, establish clear target goals, and allocate resources for the most important things (Barclay, 1993; Godfrey, 1993).

- Quality information availability refers to the availability of quality information for effective and efficient QM practices (Taylor & Wright, 2006). The availability of such information helps managers in making decisions.
- Quality information usage indicates how much quality information is used by managers in making decisions (Taylor & Wright, 2006).
- Employee training explains the level of continuous training as an essential part of QM (Ahire & O'Shaughnessy, 1998).
- Employee involvement relates to the involvement of employees in problem solving and decision making at all levels in the organization (Mohrman, Tenkasi, Lawler, & Ledford, 1995; Oliver, 1988).
- Product/process design indicates the implementation of product/process management techniques that reduce process variation and affect internal quality performance (Kaynak, 2003).
- Supplier quality acknowledged the importance of suppliers in achieving higher levels of quality in an organization (Deming, 1986; Flynn et al., 1994; Lascelles & Dale, 1989).
- Customer orientation refers to the extent the organization evaluates the feedback from its customers in improving quality (Doll & Vonderembse, 1991; Forza & Flippini, 1998; Schonberger, 1994).
- Quality citizenship stresses the practice of company responsibility and its social role in the community (Florida, 1996; Punter & Gangneux, 1998; Castka & Balzarova, 2008).
- Benchmarking is defined as the search for industry best practices leading to performance (Powell, 1995).
- Internal quality results determine how much QM practices have affected internal

quality measures, such as defect rates, re-processing rate, production lead time, and productivity (De Ceiro, 2003; Deming, 1986).

- External quality results refer to the improvement of external performance of the firm, which is measured by competitive market position and profitability (Deming, 1986).

Significance of Total Quality Management

TQM was conceptualized as an organizational innovation or organizational development intervention that leads firms to achieve sustainable competitive advantages (Ravichandran, 2000; Ahire & Ravichandran, 2001; Arumugam, Chang, Ooi, & Teh, 2009). TQM provides employees from all levels of the hierarchy with greater responsibility, and it applies empowerment and decentralization, which enriches their work (Luzon & Pasola, 2011). Ravichandran (2000) stated that TQM should be viewed as an administrative innovation as it comprises a set of quality practices toward the development of a quality-focused organizational system. In addition, Santos-Vijande and Alvarez-Gonzalez (2007) stated that TQM is an appropriate resource to promote organizational innovation and to increase firm's competitiveness. TQM acts as an important tool to achieve competitive advantage together with strengthening organizational competitiveness (Sila, Ebrahimpour, & Birkholz, 2006; Vanichchinchai & Igel, 2009). TQM practices result in set-up time reduction, allowing improved schedule attainment and correspondingly faster response to market demands (Flynn & Flynn, 2005). TQM application helps in synchronizing, to a greater extent, the whole supply chain (Ferdows, Lewis, & Machuca, 2004; Tutuncu & Kucukusta, 2008).

The main objective of TQM as described by Deming (1982) is to develop and sustain a competitive advantage through achieving the utmost efficiency. This quality efficiency is manifested in cost reduction and improvement of customer satisfaction (Deming, 1982). TQM achieves competitive advantage as evidenced by superior financial performance (Lemak, Reed, & Satish, 1997), improved customer satisfaction (Mehra & Agrawal, 2003), faster response to competitors (Spitzer, 1993), and improved product quality (Escrig-Tena, 2004). Reed, Lemak, and Montgomery (1996) stated that TQM has a major focus on improving the market-driven performance, and hence TQM is a business strategy. TQM application achieves customer orientation that is directed through continuous improvement and process efficiency, which are the major factors to accomplish reliable high-quality products or cost-efficient products (Reed et al., 1996). Quality or cost efficiency may lead to better firm alignment with the environment and to achieve a sustainable competitive advantage (Reed et al., 1996). To improve performance, efficient control system that is based on quality information must be applied (Young, 1992). Managers can have a clear indication of the successful component of a TQM program that together should be applied to achieve competitive advantage (Shenawy et al., 2007).

QM principle has been addressed in the management theory literature (Bowen & Schneider, 1988; Dean & Bowen, 1994; Spencer, 1994). Some of these QM practices are the extent and nature of quality training (Snell & Dean, 1992; Blackburn & Rosen, 1993) employee involvement and participation in quality improvement efforts (Oliver, 1988; Flynn et al., 1995), the important role of compensation and assessment in QM (Lawler, Mohrman, & Ledford, 1992; Lawler, 1994; Waldman, 1994; Flynn, Schroeder, & Sakakibara, 1995), empowerment among employees and in their interaction with customers (Conger & Kanungo, 1988), the growing significance of teams (Scholtes, 1988; Kumar & Gupta, 1991), process improvement methods (Modarress & Ansari, 1989; Anderson, Rungtusanatham, Schroeder, & Devaraj, 1995), the need to benchmark within and outside the industry (Camp, 1989), and various approaches to performance measurement (Dixon, Nanni, & Vollman, 1990; Oakland, 1993; Mann & Kehoe, 1994). In addition, Dean and Bowen (1994) suggested directions for theory development derived from the common focus of QM and management theory on organizational effectiveness. Spencer (1994) examined the relationship between QM and models of organizations in an effort to link quality management practice and management theory. Maiga and Jacobs (2005) found that quality performance mediates the relationships among quality control system, financial performance, and customer satisfaction. Arawati (2005) suggested that the implementations of TQM lead to the enhancement of customer satisfaction and improve the financial performance of manufacturing companies in Malaysia. Most researchers stated that there is a positive relationship between QM practices and business performance (Deming, 1986; Powell, 1995), at least for some quality actions. It will be helpful for companies to apply QM practices in R&D activities to increase innovation efficiency (Su et al., 2008). In addition, implementing QM practices in R&D will have a positive effect on R&D outcome and enhance business performance (Su et al., 2008).

Concept of Total Quality Management Practices

An extensive literature review of the previous studies on TQM has examined what constitutes TQM and what are the key practices for the success of TQM (Hafeez et al., 2006; Ju, Lin, Lin, & Kuo, 2006; Karia & Asaari, 2006; Al-Marri, Ahmed, & Zairi, 2007; Sila, 2007; Fotopoulos & Psomas, 2010; Sadikoglu & Zehir, 2010). Fotopoulos and Psomas (2010) identified leadership, strategic quality planning, employee management and involvement, supplier management, customer focus, process management, continuous improvement, information and analysis, and also knowledge

and education as a set of TQM practices forming a structural relationship with the organizational performance in ISO 9001:2000 certified Greek companies. Kumar, Garg, and Garg (2011) considered management commitment, customer satisfaction, continuous improvement, teamwork, employee's empowerment, training, feedback, and effective communication as few success factors for both manufacturing and service industries. In addition, Bayraktar, Tatiglu, and Zaim (2008) stated the following critical success factors (CSFs) of TQM: leadership, vision, measurement and evaluation, process control and improvement, program design, quality system improvement, employee involvement, recognition and award, education and training, student focus, and stakeholder's focus. CSFs for QM initiatives in small and-medium sized enterprises (SMEs) are grouped into six categories: contextualization, gradual implementation using realistic goals, involvement and training of employees, involvement of external support, management involvement, and fact-based follow-up (Assarlind & Gremyr, 2014).

Sadikoglu and Zehir (2010) developed a set of eight TQM practices. They are leadership, training, employee management, information and analysis, supplier management, process management, customer focus, and continuous improvement. Sadikoglu and Zehir (2010) investigated the effects of innovation and employee performance on the relationship between these TQM practices in Turkish firms. Talib and Rahman (2010) suggested a set of nine TQM practices for their proposed TQM model for service industries. They are top management commitment, customers focus, training and education, continuous improvement and innovation, supplier management, employee involvement, employee encouragement, benchmarking, and quality information and performance. Kanji and Wallace (2000) identified ten TQM practices: top management commitment, customer focus and satisfaction, quality information and performance measurement, HRM, employee involvement, teamwork, process management, quality assurance, zero defects, and communication. Brah, Wong, and Rao (2000) provided 11 constructs of TQM practices: top management support, customer focus, employee involvement, employee training, employee empowerment, supplier quality management, process improvement, service design, quality improvement rewards, benchmarking, and cleanliness and organization. In addition, Sila (2007) indicated six TQM practices: leadership, customer focus, information and analysis, HRM, process management, and supplier management. Through the comprehensive review of the TQM literature, Talib, Rahman, and Qureshi (2011) identified 17 TQM practices for service industries which are frequently occurring in the TQM literature. They are top management commitment, customer focus, training and education, continuous improvement and innovation, supplier management, employee involvement, information and analysis, process management, quality systems, benchmarking, quality culture, HRM, strategic planning, employee encouragement, teamwork, communication, and product and service design.

Utilization of Quality Management Practices

QM practices have been extensively investigated (Najmi & Kehoe, 2000; Zhang, Waszink, & Wijngaard, 2000; Sun, 2001; Sila & Ebrahimpour, 2002; Kaynak, 2003). QM practices have been documented in measurement studies that have developed and validated instruments capable of measuring the practices and the studies that have investigated the impacts of QM practices on performance (Kaynak, 2003). Flynn et al. (1995) stated that the seven QM practices are grouped as the core QM practices (i.e., quality information, product and service design, and process management), and the infrastructure QM practices (i.e., top management support, customer relationship, supplier relationship, and workforce management). The core QM practices and infrastructure QM practices possess different purposes and

function in continuous improvement. The core QM practices entail the use of scientific methods and statistical tools and the infrastructure QM practices create a learning and cooperative environment for QM implementation (Flynn et al., 1995; Ho et al., 2001; Sousa & Voss, 2002). Previous research in QM has revealed the importance of top management in effective implementation of QM (Wilson & Collier, 2000; Pannirselvam & Ferguson, 2001; Sharma & Gadenne, 2008). It is believed that the most decisive element in the success or failure of a QM initiative is the extent to which top managers provide personal leadership (Juran, 1994). The measure of quality performance is composed of five items (i.e., the percentage of defects at final assembly, product quality, durability, reliability, and delivery on time) based on the quality scales proposed by Dow et al. (1999) and Curkovic et al. (2000).

Relationship between TQM Practices and Quality Performance

It has been measured in various ways and found that the QM model and specific practices, which best predict performance varies across the world (Prajogo & Sohal, 2004; Arumugam et al., 2008). The research framework for QM proposed by Flynn et al. (1994) suggested that the inputs of this framework are the QM practices while quality performance represents outcomes. Furthermore, product design, process, process flow management, and top management support have significant correlation with quality performance (Flynn et al., 1995). Parzinger and Nath (2000) examined the link between TQM and software quality and found that TQM implementation improves the software quality and performance, and thus, increases customer satisfaction. Hasan and Kerr (2003) studied the relationship between TQM practices and organization performance in service organizations and discovered that TQM practices (i.e., top management commitment, employee involvement, training, supplier quality,

quality costs, service design, quality techniques, benchmarking, and customer satisfaction) lead to higher productivity and quality performance. In addition, Yang (2006) indicated that TQM practices (i.e., QM, process management, employee empowerment and teamwork, customer satisfaction management, quality goal setting and measurement, supplier's cooperation, and quality tools training) have significant effects on customer satisfaction. The adoption of TQM is an effective means by which companies can gain competitive advantage (Yang, 2006). Prajogo and Brown (2004) conducted an empirical study within Australian organizations to investigate the relationship between TQM practices and quality performance and the results indicated a strong and positive linkage. Brah and Tee (2002) examined the relationship between TQM constructs and organizational performance by measuring quality performance of companies in Singapore. Brah and Tee (2002) found that the implementation of TQM leads to quality performance and has a positive correlation between TQM and quality performance. Sanchez-Rodriguez, Dewhurst, and Martinez-Lorente (2006) stated that TQM initiatives generate significant positive gains in operation and quality performance. Sila and Ebrahimpour (2005) explored the relationships among TQM factors (i.e., leadership, strategic planning, customer focus, information and analysis, HRM, process management, supplier management) and the results from adopting such quality practices in terms of human resource, customer, finance, and organizational effectiveness. Sila and Ebrahimpour (2005) considered leadership and information and analysis as the two factors that act as the foundations of achieving favorable business results. In addition, Arumugam et al. (2008) found that the customer focus and continuous improvement are perceived as the dominant TQM practices in quality performance.

Below are the 17 TQM practices associated with the improvement in quality performance.

TOP MANAGEMENT COMMITMENT

Previous research in TQM practices emphasizes the critical role of top management commitment in driving overall TQM implementation in the organizations (Flynn et al., 1994; Teh, Ooi, & Yong, 2008; Zakuan et al., 2010). Teh et al. (2008) indicated that senior leaders and management guide the organization and assess the organizational performance. Top management commitment to quality management is an absolute precedence for preparing organizational culture before TQM practices can be implemented (Anderson et al., 1995; Antony, Leung, Knowles, & Gosh, 2002). Kanji (2001) stated that the top management commitment is the fundamental driver of business excellence. In addition, top management commitment significantly affects the quality performance (Prajogo & Brown, 2004; Arumugam et al., 2008). The importance and centrality of top management support and executive commitment in effective implementation of quality systems have been addressed in the literature (Pannirselvam & Ferguson, 2001; Sharma & Gadenne, 2008; Ogden, Wallin, & Foster, 2010). Management leadership in quality is directly related to training and employee relations (Kaynak, 2003). Through supporting, implementing and reinforcing quality practices, top management commitment has a significant effect on improving organizational quality performance (Wilson & Collier, 2000; Kaynak, 2003). Organizations with high leadership competencies are better at implementing TQM, and these organizations also produce products of higher quality (Das, Kumar, & Kumar, 2011; Laohavichien, Fredendall, & Cantrell, 2011). In addition, Perez-Arostegui, Benitez-Amado, and

Tamayo-Torres (2012) stated that leaders can facilitate staff members to achieve the expected level of customer satisfaction.

Customer Focus

Organizations must be knowledgeable in customer requirements and responsive to customer demands, and measure customer satisfaction through TQM implementation (Zakuan et al., 2010). Obtaining information about customer is one of the most widely used TQM implementation practices to improve quality performance of the organization (Hackman & Wageman, 1995). Customer focus has been described as the focal point TQM, and it is vital that leaders encourage the understanding of customer needs, build relationships with customers and fulfill their demands (Cai, 2009).

Training and Education

Training and education spread the knowledge of continuous improvement and innovation in service process to attain full benefits and business excellence (Talib et al., 2013). Talib and Rahman (2010) stated the critical role of training and education in maintaining high quality level within the service industry. In addition, there is a positive correlation between training and education, and organization performance (Vermeulen & Crous, 2000). Employees' knowledge about quality along with education and training in quality tools ensure the effectiveness of quality programs and process improvement initiatives (Phan et al., 2011). Employee training has become a key factor for achieving business success (Kaynak, 2003). Employee training and recognition have a significant impact on reducing cost of quality and improving operational performance and productivity (Ahire & Dreyfus, 2000; Kaynak, 2003). In addition, the focus on training and learning is critical in capital-intensive industries (Hales & Chakravorty, 2006).

Continuous Improvement and Innovation

Continuous improvement is the philosophy of improvement initiative that increases success and reduces failure (Juergensen, 2000). Continuous improvement and innovation, which is the most important part of services, means searching for never-ending improvements and developing processes to find new or improved methods in the process of converting inputs into useful outputs (Talib et al., 2013). Continuous improvement and innovation helped in reducing the process variability, thereby continuously improving the output performance (Sadikoglu & Zehir, 2010). Furthermore, Corbett and Rastrick (2000) stated that the best way to improve organizational performance in TQM is to continuously improve the performance activities.

Supplier Quality Management

According to Zakuan et al. (2010), an effective supply of QM can be achieved by cooperation and long term relationship with the suppliers. In addition, Zineldin and Fonsson (2000) found that developing supplier partnership and long-term relationships can increase the organizational competitiveness, and thus improve performance. Developing a long-term cooperative relationship with suppliers, regular participation in supplier quality activities, and giving feedback on the performance of suppliers' products are necessary to ensure the continuous supply of raw materials with the required quality (Zhang et al., 2000).

Employee Involvement

Deming (1986) stated that involvement and participation of employees at all level is a must to improve the quality of the current and future product or service. Even non-managerial employees can make significant contributions when they are involved in quality improvement processes, decision-making processes, and policy-making issues (Ooi, Arumugam, Safa, & Bakar, 2007a; Sadikoglu & Zehir, 2010). Employees, if they fully participate in quality improvement activities, will acquire new knowledge, realize the benefits of the quality disciplines, and obtain a sense of accomplishment by solving quality problems (Zhang et al., 2000). Organizations should utilize all employees' skill and abilities to gain business performance (Talib et al., 2013).

Information and Analysis

Ooi, Lee, Chong, and Lin (2013) considered information and analysis as a TQM practice that can support better performance. Fulfilling customer needs and expectations are considered to be the baseline of any kind of businesses (Talib et al., 2013). When customers' needs and expectations are achieved, quality performance is improved, and thus satisfaction is established. Prajogo (2005) indicated the importance of information and analysis of the TQM practices on quality performance. Information and analysis also helps an organization to ensure the availability of high quality, timely data, and information for all users like employees, suppliers, and customers (Teh, Yong, Arumugam, & Ooi, 2009).

PROCESS MANAGEMENT

Process management is a systematic approach in which all the resources of an organization are used in most efficient and effective manner to achieve desired performance (Sit, Ooi, Lin, & Chong, 2009). Process management has been frequently cited as a major dimension of QM practices (Kaynak, 2003; Mokhtar & Yusof, 2010; Kim,

Kumar, & Kumar, 2012). It is important to identify appropriate process quality improvement opportunities since they significantly influence cost reduction, quality improvement and organizational reinforcement (Ahire & Dreyfus, 2000; Mokhtar & Yusof, 2010). Motwani (2001) explained that the process management stresses the value adding to the process, increasing the productivity of every employee and improving the quality of the organization. Kohlbacher (2010) suggested that it would be interesting to determine the relationship between the level of process orientation and organizational performance with respect to quality improvement. Furthermore, many researchers (i.e., Flynn et al., 1995; Prajogo & Sohal, 2004; Cua, McKone, & Schroeder, 2011) systematically investigated the relationship between process management and quality performance.

Quality Systems

Quality systems (i.e., ISO 9000 standards, statistical process control (SPC), and other supportive qualitative tools and techniques) create an environment for quality improvement, thus implementing TQM in an organization (Curry & Kadasah, 2002). According to Abdullah, Uli, and Tari (2008), the implementation of effective quality improvement systems can improve the internal performance of electrical and electronics firms, meaning the internal functioning of organizations (i.e., increase in productivity, improvement in efficiency and reduction in costs and waste). Zu (2009) studied the quality performance in manufacturing plants as a result of QM practices, and more specifically, the quality of products and services, the process variability, the cost of waste and rework, the cycle time (from receipt of raw materials to shipment of finished products), customer satisfaction with the quality of products and services, and the equipment downtime. In addition, Lakhal et al. (2006) stated that there is a significant relationship between the use of statistical quality techniques and organizational performance.

Benchmarking

Benchmarking is the process of comparing performance information, within the organization as well as outside the organization (Talib et al., 2013). Benchmarking aims to measure organizational operations or processes against the best-in-class performers from inside or outside its industry (Sit et al., 2009). Yusuf, Gunasekaran, and Dan (2007) highlighted the usefulness of dynamic benchmarking for improving the performance of the organization and achieving competitive advantage. Organizations can compare their services and practices against peers in order to enhance performance through benchmarking (Qayoumi, 2000; Salhieh & Singh, 2003). The rapid changes in the market environment and in organizations (i.e., the changing nature of work, increased competition, specific improvement initiatives, national and international quality awards, changing internal and external demands (stakeholders), accelerated technological advancement, changing organizational roles, and the acceleration of globalization) have led to change in benchmarking of products and processes (Lockamy, 1998; Atkinson & Brown, 2001).

Quality Culture

Gore (1999) emphasized that the quality culture of an organization is a strong basis for enhancing organizational success. The culture of an organization could impact individual behavior (Bose, 2004), knowledge sharing (Ooi, Cheah, Lin, & Teh, 2012), job satisfaction (Ooi, Bakar, Arumugam, Vellapan, & Loke, 2007b). In addition, quality culture significantly contributed in

improving the performance of the organization as well as influencing the thought, feeling, and interaction among members of the organization (Yusof & Ali, 2000).

Human Resource Management

The literature acknowledges the importance of HRM practices and employee satisfaction as one of the most crucial elements of QM (Martinez-Costa, Choi, Martinez, & Martinez-Lorente, 2009; Levine & Toffel, 2010). HRM practices are reported to be the significant predictors of operational performance (De Ceiro, 2003). Deros, Yusof, and Salleh (2006) stated that the HRM is one of the most critical practices for improving business and management processes. Sanchez-Rodriguez et al. (2006) indicated that management of people is positively associated with operational performance. Yang (2006) explained that the HRM as a TQM practice significantly correlates with customer satisfaction. In addition, Teh et al. (2008) found a positive relationship between employee empowerment and role conflict in an organization.

Strategic Planning

Strategic planning incorporates the development and deployment of plans; improves relationships with customers, suppliers, and business partners; and helps in achieving long and short term goals through participative planning (Teh et al., 2009). There is a lack of empirical studies that examines the effects of strategic planning on quality performance or any other performance measure. A positive link is found between strategic planning and quality performance (Prajogo & Brown, 2004), knowledge management behavior (Ooi, Arumugam, Teh, & Chong, 2008), role conflict (Teh et al., 2009), and customer satisfaction (Sit et al., 2009).

Employee Encouragement

Employee encouragement, such as rewards and recognition, motivates employees to perform which in turn influence customer satisfaction (Zhang et al., 2000; Tari, 2005). In addition, Yusuf et al. (2007) indicated that the employee encouragement is positively related to organizational performance and employee satisfaction. Employee encouragement gives the right direction to workforce and is an essential practice in customer/public dealing industries (Yusuf et al., 2007).

Teamwork

Teamwork refers to an increase in employees' control over their work and allows them to work as a group (Ooi et al., 2007b). According to Ooi et al. (2007b), teamwork as a TQM practice is positively associated with employees' job satisfaction. Ooi et al. (2007b) found that where teamwork is perceived as a dominant TQM practice, improvements in job satisfaction levels are significant. Yang (2006) stated that the entire organization should work for improving quality and support for quality improvement activities by implementing teamwork practice.

Communication

Communication refers to the information sharing process between individual and employees of the organization (Ooi et al., 2007a). Managers and practitioners use effective communication to enlist the support of other employees toward achieving organization's objectives (Ooi et al., 2007a). In addition, effective communication influences the organization in order to systematically move toward employees' involvement and customer satisfaction and improve organizational performance (Ooi et al., 2007a; Yusuf et al., 2007).

Product and Service Design

Product and service design examines an organization's quality and service delivery performance in terms of timeliness, errors, costs of quality, responsiveness, and customer satisfaction (Brah et al., 2000). These indicators are used for measuring the product and service design quality. Bhatt and Emdad (2010) empirically investigated the relationships between IT infrastructure, product and service innovation, and business advantages. Product and service innovation is positively related to business advantages besides the two factors such as IT infrastructure and customer responsiveness (Bhatt & Emdad, 2010).

FUTURE RESEARCH DIRECTIONS

The impact of QM practices on business performance needs to investigate more extensively (Su et al., 2008). Future research directions should broaden the role of TQM practices to be utilized on firm performance in the knowledge-based organizations. QM is a complex phenomenon, and measuring the effect of QM practices on organizational performance has been a challenge for researchers (Parast, Adams, & Jones, 2011). It has been suggested that more industry-specific and cross-cultural research in QM is needed to validate the effect of QM on firm performance (Sila & Ebrahimpour, 2003). Industry-specific studies help us to better understand the determinants of performance (Garvin, 1988). It is recommended that future research should incorporate the role of organizational culture on TQM practices. Furthermore, application of structural modeling analysis can be another area to develop the causal relationship between TQM practices and quality performance, and empirically test the hypotheses.

CONCLUSION

This chapter explained the introduction of QM systems, the significance of TQM, the concept of TQM practices, the utilization of QM practices, and the relationship between TQM practices and quality performance. Furthermore, this chapter showed the 17 TQM practices (i.e., top management commitment, customer focus, training and education, continuous improvement and innovation, supplier quality management, employee involvement, information and analysis, process management, quality systems, benchmarking, quality culture, HRM, strategic planning, employee encouragement, teamwork, communication, and product and service design) associated with quality performance for the successful implementation of TQM practices to be utilized by academics, consultants, policy makers, quality practitioners, and companies. In order to facilitate quality performance and achieve the effectiveness of the whole quality management system, researchers and managers should develop and maintain their organization's TQM practices related to quality performance in organization.

REFERENCES

Abdul-Rahman, H. (1997). Some observations on the issues of quality cost in construction. *International Journal of Quality & Reliability Management*, *14*(5), 464–481. doi:10.1108/02656719710170693

Abdullah, M. M. B., Uli, J., & Tari, J. J. (2008). The influence of soft factors on quality improvement and performance: Perceptions from managers. *The TQM Journal*, *20*(5), 436–452. doi:10.1108/17542730810898412

Abdullah, M. M. B., Uli, J., & Tari, J. J. (2009). The relationship of performance with soft factors and quality improvement. *Total Quality Management and Business Excellence*, *20*(7), 735–748. doi:10.1080/14783360903037051

Adam, E. E., Corbett, L. M., Flores, B. E., Harrison, N. J., Lee, T. S., & Rho, B. H. et al. (1997). An international study of quality improvement approach and firm performance. *International Journal of Operations & Production Management*, *17*(9), 842–873. doi:10.1108/01443579710171190

Ahire, S. L., & Dreyfus, P. (2000). The impact of design management and process management on quality: An empirical investigation. *Journal of Operations Management*, *18*(5), 549–575. doi:10.1016/S0272-6963(00)00029-2

Ahire, S. L., Golhar, D. Y., & Waller, M. A. (1996). Development and validation of TQM implementation constructs. *Decision Sciences*, *27*(1), 23–56. doi:10.1111/j.1540-5915.1996.tb00842.x

Ahire, S. L., & O'Shaughnessy, K. C. (1998). The role of top management commitment in quality management: An empirical analysis of the auto industry. *International Journal of Quality Science*, *3*(1), 5–37. doi:10.1108/13598539810196868

Ahire, S. L., & Ravichandran, T. (2001). An innovation diffusion model of TQM implementation. *IEEE Transactions on Engineering Management*, *48*(4), 445–464. doi:10.1109/17.969423

Al-Marri, K., Ahmed, A. M. M. B., & Zairi, M. (2007). Excellence in service: An empirical study of the UAE banking sector. *International Journal of Quality & Reliability Management*, *24*(2), 164–176. doi:10.1108/02656710710722275

Anderson, J. C., Rungtusanatham, M., Schroeder, R. G., & Devaraj, S. (1995). A path analytic model of a theory of quality management underlying the Deming Management Method: Preliminary empirical findings. *Decision Sciences*, *26*(5), 637–658. doi:10.1111/j.1540-5915.1995.tb01444.x

Antony, J., Leung, K., Knowles, G., & Gosh, S. (2002). Critical success factors of TQM implementation in Hong Kong industries. *International Journal of Quality & Reliability Management*, *19*(5), 551–566. doi:10.1108/02656710210427520

Arawati, A. (2005). The structural linkages between TQM, product quality performance, and business performance: Preliminary empirical study in electronics companies. *Singapore Management Review*, *27*(1), 87–105.

Arnold, K. L. (1994). *The manager's guide to ISO 9000*. New York, NY: Free Press.

Arumugam, V., Chang, H. W., Ooi, H. B., & Teh, P. L. (2009). Self-assessment of TQM practices: A case analysis. *The TQM Journal*, *21*(1), 46–58. doi:10.1108/17542730910924745

Arumugam, V., Ooi, K. B., & Fong, T. C. (2008). TQM practices and quality management performance – An investigation of their relationship using data from ISO 9001: 2000 firms in Malaysia. *The TQM Magazine*, *20*(6), 636–650. doi:10.1108/17542730810909383

Asif, M., De Bruijn, E. J., Douglas, A., & Fisscher, O. A. M. (2009). Why quality management programs fail: A strategic and operations management perspective. *International Journal of Quality & Reliability Management*, *26*(8), 778–794. doi:10.1108/02656710910984165

ASQC. (1997). *Interpretive guidelines for the application of ANSI/ISO/ASQC Q9001-1994 or Q9002-1994 for owner's, designer's, and constructor's quality management systems*. Milwaukee, WI: ASQC Quality Press.

Asrilhant, B., Dyson, R. G., & Meadows, M. (2007). On the strategic project management process in the UK upstream oil and gas sector. *Omega*, *35*(1), 89–103. doi:10.1016/j.omega.2005.04.006

Assarlind, M., & Gremyr, I. (2014). Critical factors for quality management initiatives in small- and medium-sized enterprises. *Total Quality Management & Business Excellence*, *25*(3-4), 397–411. doi:10.1080/14783363.2013.851330

Atkinson, H., & Brown, J. B. (2001). Rethinking performance measures: Assessing progress in UK hotels. *International Journal of Contemporary Hospitality Management*, *13*(3), 128–135. doi:10.1108/09596110110388918

Barclay, C. A. (1993). Quality strategy and TQM policies: Empirical evidence. *Management International Review*, *33*(2), 87–98.

Bayraktar, E., Tatiglu, E., & Zaim, S. (2008). An instrument for measuring the critical factor of TQM in Turkish higher education. *Total Quality Management and Business Excellence*, *19*(6), 551–574. doi:10.1080/14783360802023921

Bhatt, G. D., & Emdad, A. F. (2010). An empirical examination of the relationship between IT infrastructure, customer focus, and business advantages. *Journal of Systems and Information Technology*, *12*(1), 4–16. doi:10.1108/13287261011032625

Blackburn, R., & Rosen, B. (1993). Total quality and human resource management: Lessons learnt from Baldrige award-winning companies. *The Academy of Management Executive*, *7*(3), 49–66.

Bose, R. (2004). Knowledge management metrics. *Industrial Management & Data Systems*, *104*(6), 457–468. doi:10.1108/02635570410543771

Bowen, D. E., & Schneider, B. (1988). Services marketing and management: Implications for organizational behavior. *Research in Organizational Behavior*, *10*, 43–80.

Brah, S. A., Serene, T. S. L., & Rao, B. M. (2002). Relationship between TQM and performance of Singapore companies. *International Journal of Quality & Reliability Management, 19*(4), 356–379. doi:10.1108/02656710210421553

Brah, S. A., & Tee, S. S. L. (2002). Relationship between TQM and performance of Singapore companies. *International Journal of Quality & Reliability Management, 19*(4), 356–379. doi:10.1108/02656710210421553

Brah, S. A., Wong, J. L., & Rao, B. M. (2000). TQM and business performance in the service sector: A Singapore study. *International Journal of Operations & Production Management, 20*(11), 1293–1312. doi:10.1108/01443570010348262

Burati, J. L., Farrington, J. J., & Ledbetter, W. B. (1992). Causes of quality deviations in design and construction. *Journal of Construction Engineering and Management, 118*(1), 34–49. doi:10.1061/(ASCE)0733-9364(1992)118:1(34)

Cai, S. (2009). The importance of customer focus for organisational performance: A study of Chinese companies. *International Journal of Quality & Reliability Management, 26*(4), 369–379. doi:10.1108/02656710910950351

Camp, R. C. (1989). *Benchmarking: The search for industry best practices that lead to superior performance.* Milwaukee, WI: ASQ Quality Press.

Carter, R. E., Lonial, S. C., & Raju, P. S. (2010). Impact of quality management on hospital performance: An empirical examination. *Quality Management Journal, 17*(4), 8–24.

Castka, P., & Balzarova, M. A. (2008). ISO 26000 and supply chains – On the diffusion of the social responsibility standard. *International Journal of Production Economics, 111*(2), 274–286. doi:10.1016/j.ijpe.2006.10.017

Chang, H. H. (2006). Development of performance measurement systems in quality management organizations. *The Service Industries Journal, 26*(7), 765–786. doi:10.1080/02642060600898286

Chin, K. S., & Pun, K. F. (2002). A proposed framework for implementing TQM in Chinese organizations. *International Journal of Quality & Reliability Management, 19*(3), 272–294. doi:10.1108/02656710210415686

Choi, T. Y., & Eboch, K. (1998). The TQM paradox: Relations among TQM practices, plant performance, and customer satisfaction. *Journal of Operations Management, 17*(1), 59–75. doi:10.1016/S0272-6963(98)00031-X

Conger, J. A., & Kanungo, R. (1988). The empowerment process: Integrating theory and practice. *Academy of Management Review, 13*(3), 471–482.

Corbett, L., & Rastrick, K. (2000). Quality performance and organizational culture. *International Journal of Quality & Reliability Management, 17*(1), 14–26. doi:10.1108/02656710010300126

Crosby, P. B. (1979). *Quality is free: The art of making quality certain.* New York, NY: McGraw-Hill.

Cua, K. O., Mc Kone, K. E., & Schroeder, R. G. (2001). Relationships between implementation of TQM, JIT, and TPM and manufacturing performance. *Journal of Operations Management, 19*(6), 675–694. doi:10.1016/S0272-6963(01)00066-3

Curkovic, C., Vickery, S., & Droge, C. (2000). Quality-related action programs: Their impact on quality performance and business performance. *Decision Sciences, 31*(4), 885–905. doi:10.1111/j.1540-5915.2000.tb00947.x

Curry, A., & Kadasah, N. (2002). Focusing on key elements of TQM – Evaluation for sustainability. *The TQM Magazine, 14*(4), 207–216. doi:10.1108/09544780210429816

Das, A., Handfield, R. B., Calantone, R. J., & Ghosh, S. (2000). A contingent view of quality management – The impact of international competition on quality. *Decision Sciences*, *31*(3), 649–690. doi:10.1111/j.1540-5915.2000. tb00938.x

Das, A., Kumar, V., & Kumar, U. (2011). The role of leadership competencies for implementing TQM: An empirical study of Thai manufacturing industry. *International Journal of Quality & Reliability Management*, *28*(2), 195–219. doi:10.1108/02656711111101755

De Ceiro, M. D. (2003). Quality management practices and operational performance: Empirical evidence for Spanish industry. *International Journal of Production Research*, *41*(12), 2763–2786. doi:10.1080/0020754031000093150

Dean, J. W., & Bowen, D. E. (1994). Management theory and total quality: Improving research and practice through theory development. *Academy of Management Review*, *19*(3), 392–418.

Delic, M., Radlovacki, V., Kamberovic, B., Maksimovic, R., & Pecujlija, M. (2014). Examining relationships between quality management and organisational performance in transitional economies. *Total Quality Management & Business Excellence*, *25*(3-4), 367–382. doi:10.1080/14783363.2013.799331

Deming, W. E. (1982). *Quality, productivity, and competitive position*. Cambridge, MA: Center for Advanced Engineering Studies, Massachusetts Institute of Technology.

Deming, W. E. (1986). *Out of crisis*. Cambridge, MA: MIT Center for Advanced Engineering Study.

Deros, B. M., Yusof, S. M., & Salleh, A. M. (2006). A benchmarking implementation framework for automotive manufacturing SMEs. *Benchmarking: An International Journal*, *13*(4), 396–430. doi:10.1108/14635770610676272

Dixon, J. R., Nanni, A. J., & Vollman, T. E. (1990). *The new performance challenge: Measuring operations for world-class competition*. Homewood, IL: Business One Irwin.

Doll, W., & Vonderembse, M. A. (1991). The evolution of manufacturing systems: Towards the post-industrial enterprise. *Omega*, *19*(5), 401–411. doi:10.1016/0305-0483(91)90057-Z

Douglas, T. J., & Judge, W. Q. (2001). Total quality management implementation and competitive advantage: The role of structural control and exploration. *Academy of Management Journal*, *44*(1), 158–169. doi:10.2307/3069343

Dow, D., Samson, D., & Ford, S. (1999). Exploding the myth: Do all quality management practices contribute to superior quality performance? *Production and Operations Management*, *8*(1), 1–27. doi:10.1111/j.1937-5956.1999.tb00058.x

Easton, G. S., & Jarrell, S. L. (1998). The effects of total quality management on corporate performance: An empirical investigation. *The Journal of Business*, *71*(2), 253–307. doi:10.1086/209744

Escrig-Tena, A. B. (2004). TQM as a competitive factor: A theoretical and empirical analysis. *International Journal of Quality & Reliability Management*, *21*(6-7), 612–637. doi:10.1108/02656710410542034

Ferdows, K., Lewis, M. A., & Machuca, J. A. D. (2004). Rapid-fire fulfillment. *Harvard Business Review*, *82*(11), 104–110.

Florida, R. (1996). Lean and green: The move to environmentally conscious manufacturing. *California Management Review*, *39*(1), 80–105. doi:10.2307/41165877

Flynn, B. B., & Flynn, E. J. (2005). Synergies between supply chain management and quality management: Emerging implications. *International Journal of Production Research*, *43*(6), 3421–3436. doi:10.1080/00207540500118076

Flynn, B. B., Schroeder, R. G., & Sakakibara, S. (1994). A framework for quality management research and an associated instrument. *Journal of Operations Management, 11*(4), 339–366. doi:10.1016/S0272-6963(97)90004-8

Flynn, B. B., Schroeder, R. G., & Sakakibara, S. (1995). The impact of quality management practices on performance and competitive advantage. *Decision Sciences, 26*(5), 659–691. doi:10.1111/j.1540-5915.1995.tb01445.x

Forza, C., & Flippini, R. (1998). TQM impact on quality conformance and customer satisfaction: A causal model. *International Journal of Production Economics, 55*(1), 1–20. doi:10.1016/S0925-5273(98)00007-3

Fotopoulos, C. V., & Psomas, E. L. (2010). The structural relationships between total quality management factors and organizational performance. *The TQM Journal, 22*(5), 539–552. doi:10.1108/17542731011072874

Fuentes, M. M. F., Montes, F. J. L., & Fernandez, L. M. M. (2006). Total quality management, strategic orientation and organizational performance: The case of Spanish companies. *Total Quality Management, 17*(3), 303–323.

Garcia-Bernal, J., & Garcia-Casarejos, N. (2014). Economic analysis of TQM adoption in the construction sector. *Total Quality Management & Business Excellence, 25*(3-4), 209–221. doi:10.1080/14783363.2012.728848

Garvin, D. (1988). *Managing quality: The strategic and competitive edge*. New York, NY: Free Press.

Ghobadian, A., & Gallear, D. (1997). TQM and organization size. *International Journal of Operations & Production Management, 17*(2), 121–163. doi:10.1108/01443579710158023

Godfrey, A. B. (1993). Ten areas for future research in total quality management. *Quality Management Journal, 1*(1), 47–70.

Gore, E. W. (1999). Organizational culture, TQM, and business process reengineering: An empirical comparison. *Team Performance Management: An International Journal, 5*(5), 164–170. doi:10.1108/13527599910288993

Grandzol, J. R., & Greshon, M. (1997). Which TQM practices really matter: An empirical investigation. *Quality Management Journal, 4*(4), 43–59.

Hackman, J. R., & Wageman, R. (1995). Total quality management: Empirical, conceptual, and practical issues. *Administrative Science Quarterly, 40*(2), 309–342. doi:10.2307/2393640

Hafeez, K., Malak, N., & Abdelmeguid, H. (2006). A framework for TQM to achieve business excellence. *Total Quality Management, 17*(9), 1213–1229. doi:10.1080/14783360600750485

Hales, D. N., & Chakravorty, S. S. (2006). Implementation of Deming's style of quality management: An action research study in a plastics company. *International Journal of Production Economics, 103*(1), 131–148. doi:10.1016/j.ijpe.2005.05.020

Harvey, L., & Stensaker, B. (2008). Quality culture: Understandings, boundaries and linkages. *European Journal of Education, 43*(4), 427–442. doi:10.1111/j.1465-3435.2008.00367.x

Hasan, M., & Kerr, R. M. (2003). The relationship between TQM practices and organizational performance in service organization. *The TQM Magazine*, *15*(4), 286–291. doi:10.1108/09544780310486191

Hendricks, K. B., & Singhal, V. (2001). The long-run stock price performance of firms with effective TQM programs. *Management Science*, *47*(3), 359–368. doi:10.1287/mnsc.47.3.359.9773

Ho, D. C. K., Duffy, V. G., & Shih, H. M. (2001). Total quality management: An empirical test for mediation effect. *International Journal of Production Research*, *39*(3), 529–548. doi:10.1080/00207540010005709

Ju, T. J., Lin, B., Lin, C., & Kuo, H. J. (2006). TQM critical factors and KM value chain activities. *Total Quality Management*, *17*(3), 373–393. doi:10.1080/14783360500451614

Juergensen, T. (2000). *Continuous improvement: Mindsets, capability, process, tools and results.* Indianapolis, IN: The Juergensen Consulting Group.

Jun, M., Cai, S., & Shin, H. (2006). TQM practice in Maquiladora: Antecedents of employee satisfaction and loyalty. *Journal of Operations Management*, *24*(6), 791–812. doi:10.1016/j.jom.2005.09.006

Jung, J. Y., Wang, Y. J., & Wu, S. (2009). Competitive strategy, TQM practice, and continuous improvement of international project management - A contingency study. *International Journal of Quality & Reliability Management*, *26*(2), 164–183. doi:10.1108/02656710910928806

Juran, J. M. (1994). The upcoming century for quality. *Quality Progress*, *27*(8), 29–37.

Kam, C. W., & Tang, S. L. (1997). Development and implementation of quality assurance in public construction works in Singapore and Hong Kong. *International Journal of Quality & Reliability Management*, *14*(9), 909–928. doi:10.1108/02656719710186830

Kanji, G. K. (2001). Forces of excellence in Kanji's business excellence model. *Total Quality Management*, *12*(2), 259–272. doi:10.1080/09544120120025311

Kanji, G. K., & Wallace, W. (2000). Business excellence through customer satisfaction. *Total Quality Management*, *11*(7), 979–998. doi:10.1080/09544120050135515

Karia, N., & Asaari, M. H. A. H. (2006). The effects of total quality management practices on employees' work-related attitudes. *The TQM Magazine*, *18*(1), 30–43. doi:10.1108/09544780610637677

Kaynak, H. (2003). The relationship between total quality management practices and their effects on firm performance. *Journal of Operations Management*, *21*(4), 405–435. doi:10.1016/S0272-6963(03)00004-4

Kim, D. Y., Kumar, V., & Kumar, U. (2012). Relationship between quality management practices and innovation. *Journal of Operations Management*, *30*(4), 295–315. doi:10.1016/j.jom.2012.02.003

Kohlbacher, M. (2010). The effects of process orientation: A literature review. *Business Process Management Journal*, *16*(1), 135–152. doi:10.1108/14637151011017985

Kristal, M. M., Huang, X., & Schroeder, R. G. (2010). The effect of quality management on mass customization capability. *International Journal of Operations & Production Management*, *30*(9), 900–922. doi:10.1108/01443571011075047

Kull, T. J., & Narasimhan, R. (2010). Quality management and cooperative values: Investigation of multilevel influences on workgroup performance. *Decision Sciences*, *41*(1), 81–113. doi:10.1111/j.1540-5915.2009.00260.x

Kumar, R., Garg, D., & Garg, T. K. (2011). Total quality management success factors in North Indian manufacturing and service industries. *The TQM Journal*, *23*(1), 36–46. doi:10.1108/17542731111097470

Kumar, S., & Gupta, Y. (1991). Cross functional teams improve manufacturing at Motorola's Austin plant. *Industrial Engineering (American Institute of Industrial Engineers)*, *23*(5), 32–36.

Kumar, V., Choisne, F., De Grosfoir, D., & Kumar, U. (2009). Impact of TQM on company's performance. *International Journal of Quality & Reliability Management*, *26*(1), 23–37. doi:10.1108/02656710910924152

Lagrosen, S. (2003). Exploring the impact of culture on quality management. *International Journal of Quality & Reliability Management*, *20*(4), 473–487. doi:10.1108/02656710310468632

Lakhal, L., Pasin, F., & Limam, M. (2006). Quality management practices and their impact on performance. *International Journal of Quality & Reliability Management*, *23*(6), 625–646. doi:10.1108/02656710610672461

Lambert, G., & Ouedraogo, N. (2008). Empirical investigation of ISO 9001 quality management systems' impact on organisational learning and process performances. *Total Quality Management and Business Excellence*, *19*(10), 1071–1085. doi:10.1080/14783360802264244

Laohavichien, T., Fredendall, L. D., & Cantrell, R. S. (2011). Leadership and quality management practices in Thailand. *International Journal of Operations & Production Management*, *31*(10), 1048–1070. doi:10.1108/01443571111172426

Lascelles, D. M., & Dale, B. G. (1989). A review of the issues involved in quality improvement. *International Journal of Quality & Reliability Management*, *5*(5), 76–94. doi:10.1108/eb002920

Lawler, E. E. (1994). Total quality management and employee involvement: Are they compatible? *The Academy of Management Executive*, *8*(1), 68–76.

Lawler, E. E., Mohrman, S. A., & Ledford, G. E. (1992). *Employee involvement and total quality management*. San Francisco, CA: Jossey-Bass.

Lemak, D., Reed, R., & Satish, P. (1997). Commitment to quality management: Is there a relationship with firms' performance? *Journal of Quality Management*, *2*(1), 77–86. doi:10.1016/S1084-8568(97)90022-5

Levine, D. I., & Toffel, M. W. (2010). Quality management and job quality: How the ISO 9001 standard for quality management systems affects employees and employers. *Management Science*, *56*(6), 978–996. doi:10.1287/mnsc.1100.1159

Li, L., Su, Q., & Chen, X. (2011). Ensuring supply chain quality performance through applying the SCOR model. *International Journal of Production Research*, *49*(1), 33–57. doi:10.1080/00207543.2010.508934

Lockamy, A. (1998). Quality-focused performance measurement systems: A normative model. *International Journal of Operations & Production Management, 18*(8), 740–766. doi:10.1108/01443579810217440

Luzon, M. D. M., & Pasola, J. V. (2011). Ambidexterity and total quality management: Towards a research agenda. *Management Decision, 49*(6), 927–947. doi:10.1108/00251741111143612

Madu, C. N., Kuei, C. H., & Lin, C. (1995). A comparative analysis of quality practice in manufacturing firms in the US and Taiwan. *Decision Sciences, 26*(5), 621–635. doi:10.1111/j.1540-5915.1995.tb01443.x

Maiga, A. S., & Jacobs, F. A. (2005). Antecedents and consequences of quality performance. *Behavioral Research in Accounting, 17*(1), 111–131. doi:10.2308/bria.2005.17.1.111

Mann, R., & Kehoe, D. (1994). An evaluation of the effects of quality improvement activities on business performance. *International Journal of Quality & Reliability Management, 11*(4), 29–44. doi:10.1108/02656719410057935

Martinez-Costa, M., Choi, T. Y., Martinez, J. A., & Martinez-Lorente, A. R. (2009). ISO 9000/1994, ISO 9001/2000 and TQM: The performance debate revisited. *Journal of Operations Management, 27*(6), 495–511. doi:10.1016/j.jom.2009.04.002

Mehra, S., & Agrawal, S. P. (2003). Total quality as a new global competitive strategy. *International Journal of Quality & Reliability Management, 20*(8-9), 1009–1026. doi:10.1108/02656710310500824

Mehra, S., Hoffmanm, J. M., & Sirias, D. (2001). TQM as a management strategy for the next millennia. *International Journal of Operations & Production Management, 21*(5-6), 855–876. doi:10.1108/01443570110390534

Mellat-Parast, M., Adams, S. G., & Jones, E. C. (2007). An empirical study of quality management practices in the petroleum industry. *Production Planning and Control, 18*(8), 693–702. doi:10.1080/09537280701630759

Mellat Parast, M., Adams, S. G., Jones, E. C., Subba Rao, S., & Raghu-Nathan, T. S. (2006). Comparing quality management practices between the US and Mexico. *Quality Management Journal, 13*(4), 36–49.

Modarress, B., & Ansari, A. (1989). Quality control techniques in US firms: A survey. *Production and Inventory Management Journal, 30*(2), 58–62.

Mohrman, S. A., Tenkasi, R. V., Lawler, E. E., & Ledford, G. G. (1995). Total quality management: Practice and outcomes in the largest US firms. *Employee Relations, 17*(3), 26–41. doi:10.1108/01425459510086866

Mokhtar, S. S. M., & Yusof, R. Z. (2010). The influence of top management commitment, process quality management and quality design on new product performance: A case of Malaysian manufacturers. *Total Quality Management, 21*(3), 291–300. doi:10.1080/14783360903553198

Molina, L. M., Llorens-Montes, J., & Ruiz-Moreno, A. (2007). Relationship between quality management practices and knowledge transfer. *Journal of Operations Management, 25*(3), 682–701. doi:10.1016/j.jom.2006.04.007

Motwani, J. G. (2001). Critical factors and performance measures of TQM. *The TQM Magazine, 13*(4), 292–300. doi:10.1108/13683040010362300

Motwani, J. G., Mahmoud, E., & Rice, G. (1994). Quality practices of Indian organizations: An empirical analysis. *International Journal of Quality & Reliability Management, 1*(1), 38–52. doi:10.1108/02656719410049493

Najmi, M., & Kehoe, D. F. (2000). An integrated framework for post-ISO 9000 quality development. *International Journal of Quality & Reliability Management, 17*(3), 226–258. doi:10.1108/02656710010300117

Oakland, J. S. (1993). *Total quality management.* Oxford, UK: Butterworth-Heineman.

Ogden, J. A., Wallin, C., & Foster, S. T. (2010). On Baldrige core values and commitment to quality. *Quality Management Journal, 17*(3), 21–34.

Oliver, N. (1988). Employee commitment and total quality control. *International Journal of Quality & Reliability Management, 7*(1), 21–29.

Ooi, K. B., Arumugam, V., Safa, M. S., & Bakar, N. A. (2007a). HRM and TQM: Association with job involvement. *Personnel Review, 36*(6), 939–962. doi:10.1108/00483480710822445

Ooi, K. B., Arumugam, V., Teh, P. L., & Chong, A. Y. L. (2008). TQM practices and its association with production workers. *Industrial Management & Data Systems, 108*(7), 909–927. doi:10.1108/02635570810897991

Ooi, K. B., Bakar, N. A., Arumugam, V., Vellapan, L., & Loke, A. K. Y. (2007b). Does TQM influence employees' job satisfaction? An empirical case analysis. *International Journal of Quality & Reliability Management, 24*(1), 62–77. doi:10.1108/02656710710720330

Ooi, K. B., Cheah, W. C., Lin, B., & Teh, P. L. (2012). Total quality management practices and knowledge sharing: An empirical study of Malaysia's manufacturing organizations. *Asia Pacific Journal of Management, 29*(1), 59–78. doi:10.1007/s10490-009-9185-9

Ooi, K. B., Lee, V. H., Chong, A. Y. L., & Lin, B. (2013). Does TQM improve employees' quality of work life? Empirical evidence from Malaysia's manufacturing firms. *Production Planning and Control, 24*(1), 72–89. doi:10.1080/09537287.2011.599344

Pannirselvam, G. P., & Ferguson, L. A. (2001). A study of the relationships between the Baldrige categories. *International Journal of Quality & Reliability Management, 18*(1), 14–34. doi:10.1108/02656710110364468

Parast, M. M., Adams, S. G., & Jones, E. C. (2011). Improving operational and business performance in the petroleum industry through quality management. *International Journal of Quality & Reliability Management, 28*(4), 426–450. doi:10.1108/02656711111121825

Parzinger, M. J., & Nath, R. (2000). A study of the relationships between total quality management implementation factors and software quality. *Total Quality Management, 11*(3), 353–372. doi:10.1080/0954412006874

Perez-Arostegui, M. N., Benitez-Amado, J., & Tamayo-Torres, J. (2012). Information technology-enabled quality performance: An exploratory study. *Industrial Management & Data Systems, 112*(3), 502–518. doi:10.1108/02635571211210095

Phan, A. C., Abdallah, A. B., & Matsui, Y. (2011). Quality management practices and competitive performance: Empirical evidence from Japanese manufacturing companies. *International Journal of Production Economics, 133*(2), 518–529.

Phusavat, K., & Kanchana, R. (2008). Future competitiveness: Viewpoints from manufacturers and service providers. *Industrial Management & Data Systems, 109*(2), 191–207. doi:10.1108/02635570810847572

Powell, T. C. (1995). Total quality management as competitive advantage: A review and empirical study. *Strategic Management Journal, 16*(1), 15–37. doi:10.1002/smj.4250160105

Power, D., & Sohal, A. S. (2000). Strategies and practices in Australian just-in-time environments. *International Journal of Operations & Production Management, 20*(8), 932–958. doi:10.1108/01443570010332953

Prajogo, D. I. (2005). The comparative analysis of TQM practices and quality performance between manufacturing and service firms. *International Journal of Service Industry Management, 16*(3), 217–228. doi:10.1108/09564230510601378

Prajogo, D. I., & Brown, A. (2004). The relationship between TQM practices and quality performance and the role of formal TQM programs: An Australian empirical study. *Quality Management Journal, 11*, 31–43.

Prajogo, D. I., & McDermott, C. M. (2005). The relationship between TQM practices and organizational culture. *International Journal of Operations & Production Management, 25*(11), 1101–1122. doi:10.1108/01443570510626916

Prajogo, D. I., & Sohal, A. S. (2003). The relationship between TQM practices, quality performance, and innovation performance: An empirical examination. *International Journal of Quality & Reliability Management, 20*(8), 901–918. doi:10.1108/02656710310493625

Prajogo, D. I., & Sohal, A. S. (2004). The multidimensionality of TQM practices in determining quality and innovation performance – An empirical examination. *Technovation, 24*(6), 443–453. doi:10.1016/S0166-4972(02)00122-0

Puffer, S. M., & McCarthy, D. J. (1996). A framework for leadership in a TQM context. *Journal of Quality Management, 1*(1), 109–130. doi:10.1016/S1084-8568(96)90008-5

Punter, L., & Gangneux, D. (1998). Social responsibility: The most recent element to ensure total quality management. *Total Quality Management, 9*(4-5), 197–199. doi:10.1080/0954412988893

Qayoumi, M. (2000). Benchmarking and organizational change. Alexandria, VA: The Association of Higher Education Facilities Officers (APPA).

Rahman, S., & Bullock, P. (2005). Soft TQM, hard TQM, and organizational performance relationships: An empirical investigation. *Omega, 33*(1), 73–83. doi:10.1016/j.omega.2004.03.008

Rao, S. S., Solis, L. E., & Raghunathan, T. S. (1999). A framework for international quality management research: Development and validation of a measurement instrument. *Total Quality Management, 10*(7), 1047–1075. doi:10.1080/0954412997226

Ravichandran, T. (2000). Swiftness and intensity of administrative innovation adoption: An empirical investigation of TQM in information systems. *Decision Sciences, 31*(3), 691–724. doi:10.1111/j.1540-5915.2000.tb00939.x

Reed, R., Lemak, D., & Montgomery, J. (1996). Beyond process: TQM content and firm performance. *Academy of Management Review, 21*(1), 173–202.

Rungtusanatham, M., Forza, C., Koka, B. R., Salvadora, F., & Nie, W. (2005). TQM across multiple countries: Convergence hypothesis versus national specificity arguments. *Journal of Operations Management, 23*(1), 43–63. doi:10.1016/j.jom.2004.10.002

Sadikoglu, E., & Zehir, C. (2010). Investigating the effects of innovation and employee performance on the relationship between TQM practices and firm performance: An empirical study of Turkish firms. *International Journal of Production Economics, 127*(1), 13–26. doi:10.1016/j.ijpe.2010.02.013

Salhieh, L., & Singh, N. (2003). A system dynamics framework for benchmarking policy analysis for university system. *Benchmarking: An International Journal, 10*(5), 490–498. doi:10.1108/14635770310495528

Sallis, E. (2002). *Total quality management in education.* London, UK: Kogan.

Samson, D., & Terziovski, M. (1999). The relationship between total quality management practices and operational performance. *Journal of Operations Management*, *17*(4), 393–409. doi:10.1016/S0272-6963(98)00046-1

Sanchez-Rodriguez, C., Dewhurst, F. W., & Martinez-Lorente, A. R. (2006). IT use in supporting TQM initiatives: An empirical investigation. *International Journal of Operations & Production Management*, *26*(5), 486–504. doi:10.1108/01443570610659874

Sanchez-Rodriguez, C., & Martinez-Lorente, A. R. (2004). Quality management practices in the purchasing function: An empirical study. *International Journal of Operations & Production Management*, *24*(7), 666–687. doi:10.1108/01443570410541984

Santos-Vijande, M. L., & Alvarez-Gonzalez, L. I. (2007). Innovativeness and organizational innovation in total quality-oriented firms: The moderating role of market turbulence. *Technovation*, *27*(9), 514–532. doi:10.1016/j.technovation.2007.05.014

Santos-Vijande, M. L., & Alvarez-Gonzalez, L. I. (2009). TQM's contribution to marketing implementation and firm's competitiveness. *Total Quality Management and Business Excellence*, *20*(2), 171–196. doi:10.1080/14783360802622953

Schniederjans, M. J., Mellat Parast, M., Nabavi, M., Subba Rao, S., & Raghu-Nathan, T. S. (2006). Comparative analysis of Malcolm Baldrige National Quality Award criteria: An empirical study of India, Mexico, and the United States. *Quality Management Journal*, *13*(4), 7–21.

Scholtes, P. R. (1988). *The team handbook: How to use teams to improve quality*. Madison, WI: Joiner Associates.

Schonberger, R. J. (1994). Human resource management lessons from a decade of total quality management and reengineering. *California Management Review*, *36*(4), 109–123. doi:10.2307/41165769

Sharabi, M. (2014). Today's quality is tomorrow's reputation (and the following day's business success). *Total Quality Management & Business Excellence*, *25*(3-4), 183–197. doi:10.1080/14783363.2013.858877

Sharma, B., & Gadenne, D. (2008). An empirical investigation of the relationship between quality management factors and customer satisfaction, improved competitive position and overall business performance. *Journal of Strategic Marketing*, *16*(4), 301–314. doi:10.1080/09652540802264181

Shenawy, E. E., Baker, T., & Lemak, D. J. (2007). A meta-analysis of the effect of TQM on competitive advantage. *International Journal of Quality & Reliability Management*, *24*(5), 442–471. doi:10.1108/02656710710748349

Sila, I. (2007). Examining the effects of contextual factors on TQM and performance through the lens of organizational theories: An empirical study. *Journal of Operations Management*, *25*(1), 83–109. doi:10.1016/j.jom.2006.02.003

Sila, I., & Ebrahimpour, M. (2002). An investigation of the total quality management survey based research published between 1989 and 2000: A literature review. *International Journal of Quality & Reliability Management*, *19*(7), 902–970. doi:10.1108/02656710210434801

Sila, I., & Ebrahimpour, M. (2003). Examination and comparison of the critical factors of total quality management (TQM) across countries. *International Journal of Production Research*, *41*(2), 235–268. doi:10.1080/0020754021000022212

Sila, I., & Ebrahimpour, M. (2005). Critical linkages among TQM factors and business results. *International Journal of Operations & Production Management*, *25*(11), 1123–1155. doi:10.1108/01443570510626925

Sila, I., Ebrahimpour, M., & Birkholz, C. (2006). Quality in supply chains: An empirical analysis. *Supply Chain Management: An International Journal*, *11*(6), 491–502. doi:10.1108/13598540610703882

Sit, W. Y., Ooi, K. B., Lin, B., & Chong, A. Y. L. (2009). TQM and customer satisfaction in Malaysia's service sector. *Industrial Management & Data Systems*, *109*(7), 957–975. doi:10.1108/02635570910982300

Snell, S. A., & Dean, J. W. (1992). Integrated manufacturing and human resources management: A human capital perspective. *Academy of Management Journal*, *34*(1), 60–85.

Soltani, E., Azadegan, A., Liao, Y., & Phillips, P. (2011). Quality performance in a global supply chain: Finding out the weak link. *International Journal of Production Research*, *49*(1), 269–293. doi:10.1080/00207543.2010.508955

Soltani, E., Pei-Chun, L., & Phillips, P. (2008). A new look at factors influencing total quality management failure: Work process control or workforce control? *New Technology, Work and Employment*, *23*(1-2), 125–142. doi:10.1111/j.1468-005X.2008.00207.x

Sousa, R., & Voss, C. A. (2001). Quality management: Universal or context dependent. *Production and Operations Management*, *10*(4), 383–404. doi:10.1111/j.1937-5956.2001.tb00083.x

Sousa, R., & Voss, C. A. (2002). Quality management re-visited: A reflective review and agenda for future research. *Journal of Operations Management*, *20*(1), 91–109. doi:10.1016/S0272-6963(01)00088-2

Spencer, B. A. (1994). Models of organization and total quality management: A comparison and critical evaluation. *Academy of Management Review*, *19*(3), 446–471.

Spitzer, R. D. (1993). TQM: The only source of sustainable competitive advantage. *Quality Progress*, *26*(6), 59–65.

Stading, G. L., & Vokurka, R. J. (2003). Building quality strategy content using the process from national and international quality awards. *TQM & Business Excellence*, *14*(8), 931–946. doi:10.1080/1478336032000090851

Su, Q., Li, Z., Zhang, S. X., Liu, Y. Y., & Dang, J. X. (2008). The impacts of quality management practices on business performance - An empirical investigation from China. *International Journal of Quality & Reliability Management*, *25*(8), 809–823. doi:10.1108/02656710810898621

Sun, H. (2001). Comparing quality management practices in the manufacturing and service industries: Learning opportunities. *Quality Management Journal*, *8*(2), 53–71.

Talib, F., & Rahman, Z. (2010). Critical success factors of total quality management in service organization: A proposed model. *Services Marketing Quarterly*, *31*(3), 363–380. doi:10.1080/15332969.2010.486700

Talib, F., Rahman, Z., & Qureshi, M. N. (2011). An interpretive structural modeling approach for modeling the practices of total quality management in service sector. *International Journal of Modeling in Operations Management*, *1*(3), 223–250. doi:10.1504/IJMOM.2011.039528

Talib, F., Rahman, Z., & Qureshi, M. N. (2013). An empirical investigation of relationship between total quality management practices and quality performance in Indian service companies. *International Journal of Quality & Reliability Management*, *30*(3), 280–318. doi:10.1108/02656711311299845

Tang, S. L., & Kam, C. W. (1999). A survey of ISO 9001 implementation in engineering consultancies in Hong Kong. *International Journal of Quality & Reliability Management, 16*(6), 562–574. doi:10.1108/02656719910249810

Tari, J. J. (2005). Components of successful total quality management. *The TQM Magazine, 17*(2), 182–194. doi:10.1108/09544780510583245

Taylor, W. A., & Wright, G. H. (2006). The contribution of measurement and information infrastructure to TQM success. *Omega, 34*(4), 372–384. doi:10.1016/j.omega.2004.12.003

Teh, P. L., Ooi, K. B., & Yong, C. C. (2008). Does TQM impact on role stressors? A conceptual model. *Industrial Management & Data Systems, 108*(8), 1029–1044. doi:10.1108/02635570810904596

Teh, P. L., Yong, C. C., Arumugam, V., & Ooi, K. B. (2009). Does total quality management reduce employees' role conflict? *Industrial Management & Data Systems, 109*(8), 1118–1136. doi:10.1108/02635570910991337

Terziovski, M., & Samson, D. (1999). The link between total quality management practice and organizational performance. *International Journal of Quality & Reliability Management, 16*(3), 226–237. doi:10.1108/02656719910223728

Thiagaragan, T., Zairi, M., & Dale, B. G. (2001). A proposed model of TQM implementation based on an empirical study of Malaysian industry. *International Journal of Quality & Reliability Management, 18*(3), 289–306. doi:10.1108/02656710110383539

Tutuncu, O., & Kucukusta, D. (2008). The role of supply chain management integration in quality management system for hospitals. *International Journal of Management Perspectives, 1*(1), 31–39.

Vanichchinchai, A., & Igel, B. (2009). Total quality management and supply chain management: Similarities and differences. *The TQM Magazine, 21*(3), 249–260. doi:10.1108/17542730910953022

Vecchi, A., & Brennan, L. (2011). Quality management: A cross-cultural perspective based on the GLOBE framework. *International Journal of Operations & Production Management, 31*(5), 527–553. doi:10.1108/01443571111126319

Venkatraman, S. (2007). A framework for implementing TQM in higher education programs. *Quality Assurance in Education, 15*(1), 92–112. doi:10.1108/09684880710723052

Vermeulen, W., & Crous, M. J. (2000). Training and education for TQM in the commercial banking industry of South Africa. *Managing Service Quality, 10*(1), 61–67. doi:10.1108/09604520010307058

Waldman, D. A. (1994). The contributions of total quality management to theory of work performance. *Academy of Management Review, 19*(3), 510–536.

Wilson, D. D., & Collier, D. A. (2000). An empirical investigation of the Malcolm Baldrige National Quality Award causal model. *Decision Sciences, 31*(2), 361–390. doi:10.1111/j.1540-5915.2000.tb01627.x

Yang, C. C. (2006). The impact of human resource management practices on the implementation of total quality management. *The TQM Magazine, 18*(2), 162–173. doi:10.1108/09544780610647874

Yates, J. K., & Aniftos, S. C. (1997). International standards and construction. *Journal of Construction Engineering and Management, 123*(2), 127–137. doi:10.1061/(ASCE)0733-9364(1997)123:2(127)

Yeung, A. C. L., Edwin Cheng, T. C., & Lai, K. (2006). An operational and institutional perspective on total quality management. *Production and Operations Management*, 15(1), 156–170.

Yoo, D. K., Rao, S. S., & Hong, P. (2006). A comparative study on cultural differences and quality practices: Korea, USA, Mexico and Taiwan. *International Journal of Quality & Reliability Management*, 23(6), 607–624. doi:10.1108/02656710610672452

Young, S. (1992). A framework for successful adoption and performance of Japanese manufacturing practices in the United States. *Academy of Management Review*, 17(4), 677–700.

Yusof, A. A., & Ali, J. (2000). Managing culture in organization. *Malaysian Management Review*, 35(2), 60–65.

Yusuf, Y., Gunasekaran, A., & Dan, G. (2007). Implementation of TQM in China and organizational performance: An empirical investigation. *Total Quality Management*, 18(5), 509–530. doi:10.1080/14783360701239982

Zakuan, N. M., Yusof, S. M., Laosirihongthong, T., & Shaharoun, A. M. (2010). Proposed relationship of TQM and organizational performance using structured equation modeling. *Total Quality Management*, 21(2), 185–203.

Zhang, Z., Waszink, A., & Wijngaard, J. (2000). An instrument for measuring TQM implementation for Chinese manufacturing companies. *International Journal of Quality & Reliability Management*, 17(7), 730–755. doi:10.1108/02656710010315247

Zineldin, M., & Fonsson, P. (2000). An examination of the main factors affecting trust/commitment in supplier dealer relationships: An empirical study of the Swedish wood industry. *The TQM Magazine*, 12(4), 245–265. doi:10.1108/09544780010325831

Zu, X. (2009). Infrastructure and core quality management practices: How do they affect quality? *International Journal of Quality & Reliability Management*, 26(2), 129–149. doi:10.1108/02656710910928789

Zu, X., Fredendall, L. D., & Douglas, T. J. (2008). The evolving theory of quality management: The role of Six Sigma. *Journal of Operations Management*, 26(5), 630–650. doi:10.1016/j.jom.2008.02.001

ADDITIONAL READING

Albacete-Saez, C. A., Fuentes-Fuentes, M. M., & Bojica, A. M. (2011). Quality management, strategic priorities and performance: The role of quality leadership. *Industrial Management & Data Systems*, 111(8), 1173–1193. doi:10.1108/02635571111170758

Anh, P. C., & Matsui, Y. (2011). Relationship between quality management information and operational performance - International perspective. *Management Research Review*, 34(5), 519–540. doi:10.1108/01409171111128706

Bell, M., & Omachonu, V. (2011). Quality system implementation process for business success. *International Journal of Quality & Reliability Management*, 28(7), 723–734. doi:10.1108/02656711111150814

Chen, J. K., & Lee, Y. C. (2009). A new method to identify the category of the quality attribute. *Total Quality Management and Business Excellence*, 20(10), 1139–1152. doi:10.1080/14783360902781832

Dick, G. P. M. (2009). Exploring performance attribution - The case of quality management standards adoption and business performance. *International Journal of Productivity and Performance Management*, 58(4), 311–328. doi:10.1108/17410400910950991

Evans, J. R., & Lindsay, W. M. (2011). *The management and control of quality*. Mason, OH: South-Western Cengage Learning.

Fons, L. A. S. (2011). Measuring economic effects of quality management systems. *The TQM Journal, 23*(4), 458–474. doi:10.1108/17542731111139527

Fotopoulos, C. B., & Psomas, E. L. (2009). The impact of soft and hard TQM elements on quality management results. *International Journal of Quality & Reliability Management, 26*(2), 150–163. doi:10.1108/02656710910928798

Fotopoulos, C. B., Psomas, E. L., & Vouzas, F. (2010). Investigating total quality management practices' inter-relationships in ISO 9001:2000 certified organizations. *Total Quality Management & Business Excellence, 21*(5), 503–515. doi:10.1080/14783363.2010.481512

Gadenne, D., & Sharma, B. (2009). An investigation of the hard and soft quality management factors of Australian SMEs and their association with firm performance. *International Journal of Quality & Reliability Management, 26*(9), 865–880. doi:10.1108/02656710910995064

Hariharan, S., & Dey, P. K. (2010). A comprehensive approach to quality management of intensive care services. *International Journal of Health Care Quality Assurance, 23*(3), 287–300. doi:10.1108/09526861011029352 PMID:20535901

Holschbach, E. (2013). Comparison of quality management for externally sourced business services. *International Journal of Quality & Reliability Management, 30*(5), 530–570. doi:10.1108/02656711311315503

Holschbach, E., & Hofmann, E. (2011). Exploring quality management for business services from a buyer's perspective using multiple case study evidence. *International Journal of Operations & Production Management, 31*(6), 648–685. doi:10.1108/01443571111131980

Hur, M. H. (2009). The influence of total quality management practices on the transformation of how organisations work. *Total Quality Management and Business Excellence, 20*(8), 847–861. doi:10.1080/14783360903128306

Iden, J. (2012). Investigating process management in firms with quality systems: A multi-case study. *Business Process Management Journal, 18*(1), 104–121. doi:10.1108/14637151211215037

Khanna, V. K. (2009). 5 "S" and TQM status in Indian organizations. *The TQM Journal, 21*(5), 486–501. doi:10.1108/17542730910983407

Kull, T. J., & Wacker, J. G. (2010). Quality management effectiveness in Asia: The influence of culture. *Journal of Operations Management, 28*(3), 223–239. doi:10.1016/j.jom.2009.11.003

Kumar, U., Kumara, V., De Grosfois, D., & Choisnea, F. (2009). Continuous improvement of performance measurement by TQM adopters. *Total Quality Management, 20*(6), 603–616.

Kureshi, N., Qureshi, F., & Sajid, A. (2010). Current health of quality management practices in service sector SME – A case study of Pakistan. *The TQM Journal, 22*(3), 317–329. doi:10.1108/17542731011035541

Lagrosen, Y., Backstrom, I., & Wiklund, H. (2012). Approach for measuring health-related quality management. *The TQM Journal, 24*(1), 59–71. doi:10.1108/17542731211191221

Laosirihongthong, T., The, P. L., & Adebanjo, D. (2013). Revisiting quality management and performance. *Industrial Management & Data Systems*, *113*(7), 990–1006. doi:10.1108/IMDS-02-2013-0058

Leonard, D. (2010). Quality management practices in the US homebuilding industry. *The TQM Journal*, *22*(1), 101–110. doi:10.1108/17542731011009658

Lin, C., Kuei, C. H., & Chai, K. W. (2013). Identifying critical enablers and pathways to high performance supply chain quality management. *International Journal of Operations & Production Management*, *33*(3), 347–370. doi:10.1108/01443571311300818

Mady, M. T. (2009). Quality management practices - An empirical investigation of associated constructs in two Kuwaiti industries. *International Journal of Quality & Reliability Management*, *26*(3), 214–233. doi:10.1108/02656710910936708

Mellat Parast, M. (2013). Convergence theory in quality management: Evidence from the petroleum industry. *International Journal of Quality & Reliability Management*, *30*(2), 177–196. doi:10.1108/02656711311293580

Miller, W. J., Sumner, A. T., & Deane, R. H. (2009). Assessment of quality management practices within the healthcare industry. *American Journal of Economics and Business Administration*, *1*(2), 105–113. doi:10.3844/ajebasp.2009.105.113

O'Mahony, K., & Garavan, T. N. (2012). Implementing a quality management framework in a higher education organization - A case study. *Quality Assurance in Education*, *20*(2), 184–200. doi:10.1108/09684881211219767

Papadimitriou, A., & Westerheijden, D. F. (2010). Adoption of ISO-oriented quality management system in Greek universities - Reactions to isomorphic pressures. *The TQM Journal*, *22*(3), 229–241. doi:10.1108/17542731011035488

Psomas, E. L., Fotopoulos, C. B., & Kafetzopoulos, D. P. (2011). Core process management practices, quality tools and quality improvement in ISO 9001 certified manufacturing companies. *Business Process Management Journal*, *17*(3), 437–460. doi:10.1108/14637151111136360

Psychogios, A. G., Wilkinson, A., & Szamosi, L. T. (2009). Getting to the heart of the debate: TQM and middle autonomy. *Total Quality Management and Business Excellence*, *20*(4), 445–466. doi:10.1080/14783360902781949

Pun, K. F., & Jaggernath-Furlonge, S. (2012). Impacts of company size and culture on quality management practices in manufacturing organizations - An empirical study. *The TQM Journal*, *24*(1), 83–101. doi:10.1108/17542731211191249

Qui, Y., & Tannock, J. D. T. (2010). Dissemination and adoption of quality management in China - Case studies of Shanghai manufacturing industries. *International Journal of Quality & Reliability Management*, *27*(9), 1067–1081. doi:10.1108/02656711011084846

Salaheldin, S. I. (2009). Critical success factors for total quality management implementation and their impact on performance of SMEs. *International Journal of Productivity and Quality Management*, *58*(3), 215–237.

Salaheldin, S. I., & Mukhalalati, B. A. (2009). The implementation of TQM in the Qatari healthcare sector. *Journal of Accounting-Business and Management*, *16*(2), 1–14.

Sayeda, B., Rajendran, C., & Lokachari, P. S. (2010). An empirical study of total quality management in engineering educational institutions of India - Perspective of management. *Benchmarking: An International Journal*, *17*(5), 728–767. doi:10.1108/14635771011076461

Talib, F., Rahman, Z., & Qureshi, M. N. (2011). A study of total quality management and supply chain management practices. *International Journal of Productivity and Performance Management*, *60*(3), 268–288. doi:10.1108/17410401111111998

Talib, F., Rahman, Z., Qureshi, M. N., & Siddiqui, J. (2011). Total quality management and service quality: An exploratory study of management practices and barriers in service industries. *International Journal of Services and Operations Management*, *10*(1), 94–118. doi:10.1504/IJSOM.2011.041991

Thawesaengskulthai, N. (2010). An empirical framework for selecting quality management and improvement initiatives. *International Journal of Quality & Reliability Management*, *27*(2), 156–172. doi:10.1108/02656711011014285

Wickramasinghe, V. (2012). Influence of total quality management on human resource management practices - An exploratory study. *International Journal of Quality & Reliability Management*, *29*(8), 836–850. doi:10.1108/02656711211270324

Wong, C. H., Sim, J. J., Lam, C. H., Loke, S. P., & Darmawan, N. (2010). A linear structural equation modeling of TQM principles and its influence on quality performance. *International Journal of Modelling in Operations Management*, *1*(1), 107–124. doi:10.1504/IJMOM.2010.035257

Wu, S. J., Zhang, D., & Schroeder, R. G. (2011). Customization of quality practices: The impact of quality culture. *International Journal of Quality & Reliability Management*, *28*(3), 263–279. doi:10.1108/02656711111109883

Xiaofen, T. (2013). Investigation on quality management maturity of Shanghai enterprises. *The TQM Journal*, *25*(4), 417–430. doi:10.1108/17542731311314890

Zeng, J., Anh, P. C., & Matsui, Y. (2013). Shop-floor communication and process management for quality performance - An empirical analysis of quality management. *Management Research Review*, *36*(5), 454–477. doi:10.1108/01409171311327235

KEY TERMS AND DEFINITIONS

Performance: The accomplishment of a given task measured against standards of accuracy, completeness, cost, and speed.

Quality Improvement: The systematic approach to reduction or elimination of waste, rework, and losses in production process.

Quality Management System: A system by which an organization aims to reduce and eliminate nonconformance to specifications, standards, and customer expectations in the most cost effective and efficient manner.

Quality Management: Management activities and functions involved in determination of quality policy and its implementation through quality planning and quality assurance.

Quality Planning: The systematic process that translates quality policy into measurable objectives and requirements, and lays down a sequence of steps for realizing them within a specified timeframe.

Quality Policy: Top management's expression of its intentions, directions, and aims regarding quality of its products and processes.

Quality System: Aggregate of the organizational activities, policies, procedures, processes, and the infrastructure required in formulating and implementing a total quality management approach.

Quality: A measure of excellence or a state of being free from defects, deficiencies, and significant variations.

Total Quality Management (TQM): A holistic approach to long-term success that views continuous improvement in all aspects of an organization as a process.

Chapter 2
Economic Aspects of a Health System Electronization

Vincent Šoltés
Technical University of Košice, Slovakia

Beáta Gavurová
Technical University of Košice, Slovakia

Antonio José Balloni
Centro de Tecnologia da Informação Renato Archer (CTI), Brazil

Michal Šoltés
Technical University of Košice, Slovakia

ABSTRACT

There are significant disparities among the health needs of citizens and the financial resources of the healthcare system. Limitations of the inputs to growth of the health systems are primarily due to fiscal constraints, the demographic crisis, the degree of competitiveness of the EU, as well as the willingness of citizens to bear some degree of the tax burden. The costs of providing healthcare can be reduced by the proper implementation of eHealth project, as is evidenced by the analysis of the costs and benefits of successful implementation abroad. The aim of this chapter is to evaluate the use of Information and Communication Technologies (ICT) in medical institutions, in Slovakia, as the basis of effective strategic management, influencing the positive and negative changes in their external environment. In addition, the chapter focuses on investments in technological innovation, its determinants, and specification of the effects of the use of IS and IT in healthcare facilities. Finally, it reflects the partial outputs of the first international research GESITY/Hospitals 2011-2012 conducted in partnership with Slovakia and Brazil, in connection with the objectives of the implementation of an eHealth program in Slovakia.

INTRODUCTION

An aging population, higher incidence of chronic diseases and financial cost of the new procedures are global trends that cause increase of expenditures in healthcare. Together with the growing demands of patients, it is clear that, for achievement of long-term sustainability of the system, an efficient and stable system of financing is needed. The volume of resources in the Slovak healthcare is determined by two factors. First, the development of macro-economic situation, which is not directly influenced by government through direct state intervention, social, fiscal and other policies. Exactly in these interventions we can find an explanation for the lack of money in the system.

DOI: 10.4018/978-1-4666-6320-6.ch002

The Government through the tax-contributions policy determines the amount of health insurance contributions, which constitute the most important component of income. While the economically active population has to pay 14% of their salary, the State pays for a defined group of people (pensioners and unemployed) only 4% of the minimum wage. The number of subsidized persons is increasing due to population aging, and older people need financially demanding healthcare services. The State low fixed rate contributes significantly to the formation of the deficit in the finance sector. Slovak health expenditures are represented with an estimate 8% of GDP, which is in percentage and per capita more than the other V4 countries (WHO, 2011). The larger amount of money in the system is not reflected in higher wages, quality or lower price of medicinal products. Compared to the average of OECD country, Slovakia spends 13% more of medical products (OECD, 2010), while staff salaries are still lower than in neighbouring countries (Morvay, 2009; Romanová, Ivančová & Klepáková, 2013). The health status of the population in Slovakia is significantly worse in many parameters compared to more developed countries of the European Union (EU). In Slovakia, health needs of the population are not yet mapped properly. If we add the lower cost of hospital treatment (WHO, 2011) and a lower quality of service than in the Czech Republic, Poland and surroundings (Szalay, 2009) it is clear that the Slovak health system has significant problems with the allocation and efficient transformation of resources (Harkovotová, 2011). This fact was also confirmed by several studies (Balloni, 2011; Soltes, Gavurova, Balloni & Pavlickova, 2012). Estimates show that health expenditures (20 to 50%) are spent inefficiently (WHO, 2010; Harkovotová, 2011; PWC, 2010). The most important factors that reduce the effectiveness of the Slovak healthcare are demotivated staff, inefficient use of beds and staff, unnecessary prescription of antibiotics, lack of generic medical products, corruption, lack of transparency, overpriced purchases

and administrative complexity. These problems are a reflection of many systematic errors which should be changed. One of them is the weak flow of information.

In Slovakia, there is no single system that collects information about patients. This deficit of information allows and often causes duplication of diagnostics and prescription of medical products that affect the resource usage efficiency. Problematic is the lack of information flow in the relation to healthcare providers. Lack of communication is weakening the negotiating power of hospitals with health insurance companies and thus reduces their attractiveness from the perspective of the private sector. Therefore, the flow of information is a critical factor influencing the efficiency of the whole system. Solving this problem will help to create an online eHealth platform that will work on European basis (PWC, 2011; PWC, 2010). This will allow a higher level of specialization and use of beds; thereby supporting the reduction of the average cost of treatment. Assumptions for further development of Slovak Health to 2020 are affected by an aging population, increasing incidence of difficult diagnoses, shortening of the medicinal products life cycle, increasing expenditures in the sector by 30% - 70%. Therefore, necessary priority will be to focus on the following aspects: pressure for effective treatment, elimination of inadequate flow of information and the creation of a vision and strategy for Slovak healthcare.

BACKGROUND

The changing paradigm of healthcare, as well as the new challenges, requires constant updating of state health policy. This should reflect the economic status of the country based on the challenges for the healthcare, current data of the population´s health status as well as providers of healthcare (Benčo & Kuvíková, 2011; Klepáková, 2010). It has to clearly define the vision, strategic targets, priorities and methods to achieve those objectives and regulatory instruments and position of the state. Its update should be based on the current information on the population´s health status and its trends (Nemec, Ochrana & Šumpíková, 2008). It is the primary role of the eHealth program, which lags behind leading countries in the eHealth program in the EU about ten years. Slovakia has in a time of fiscal crisis problems to ensure adequate resources for eHealth; therefore, our country takes the risk that the expected benefits shall be reached (Janke & Prídavok, 2012; Závadská, Závadský & Sirotiaková, 2013). It is important to ensure the partial resources in the state budget and strict prioritization in eHealth for the potential of health and economic benefits. Table 1 declares SWOT analysis of eHealth in Slovak healthcare.

Economic and social determinants of the development of Pan European area of healthcare

The European Union constantly pushes for the emergence of a Pan European area of healthcare, which brings many opportunities, but also potential risks. We can mention a potential financial collapse in the public health insurance system because of the lack of regulation resulting from the wide use of healthcare abroad. Also, citizens of other member countries which are using our healthcare can due to low prices and state subsidies to healthcare cause deepening of the financial problems. Last but not least there is a major obstacle to the development of the Pan European area of healthcare; language skills and absent semantic interoperability. Document of the World Economic Forum (Global Risk Report, 2010) specifies a group of global risks that can occur and can cause a phase transition in the form of disasters, of unforeseeable great impact on the society and at the same time on the health system, not only within the country, but in the EU or all over the world. The on-going destabilization of the euro area, followed by economic and political as well as the social impact on Slovakia and its economy is another actual risk of the EU.

Moreover, the disruption of the economies of neighbouring countries should have on our export-oriented economy a negative influence (Szabo et al., 2013; Hejduková & Klepáková, 2013), which would have a direct negative impact on the decrease of funds in the healthcare system. Other facts are the negative effects of climate change, which may cause a short-term negative trajectory of rising food prices, through the risk and unmanageable mass migration from the worst affected countries into the EU, followed by socio-economic as well as significant health impact (Ivančík, 2012; Janke & Prídavok, 2012). The above mentioned unfavourable findings with impact on the healthcare system are not depleted; it is only the most visible calculation. In this conceptual framework and intentions of globalization with an emphasis on ensuring the function of the healthcare system in Slovakia is necessary:

… stop the growth of hidden debt due to obsolescent infrastructure promote energy efficient and cost-effective areas to invest in it and correctly set the minimum network of PZS in terms of ownership (State vs. private sector), forms (stock company, contributory company, non-profit company) and structure (hospital, clinic, primary healthcare, laboratories, ADOS, etc.) (Danilák, 2011)

Figure 1 depicts selected economic and social determinants impacting, to a significant extent, on the health system in Slovakia.

An important instrument to eliminate the negative effects of the mentioned economic and social determinants is quality monitoring with exact outcomes from analyses and effective feedback, essential for the design and implementation of systemic measures in the State Health Policy. Important role in creating a Pan European area in healthcare also plays an eHealth implementation. Its development and using are in individual countries very different, caused by many socio-economic, political and cultural determinants. Mapping its specifics, as the basis of comparison of

Table 1. SWOT analysis of eHealth in Slovakia based on Health System Electronization

Strengths	Weaknesses
• eHealth Support from Government. • eHealth Support from the Ministry of Health. • Good availability and quality of Internet • connection. • Interest in technologies and information • technologies in healthcare. • The high number of good quality infrastructure suppliers, HW and SW. • Reasonable price level of available • HW and SW. • The completed first phase of building • IS in most hospitals. • Computerisation of all ambulances of general practitioners - secure collection of • healthcare data from all citizens, • Introduction of modern hospital IS. • - The existence of medical records.	• Scepticism of the public towards eHealth based on past results. • Lack of successful pilot eHealth applications. • Minimum investment in existing eHealth. • Failure to meet existing plans and tasks in eHealth. • Inadequate legislative support. • Low rate of connection to Internet in ambulances. • Underdeveloped secured infrastructure. • Lack of eHealth standards (for EHR, EDS...) • Limited interoperability of systems.
Opportunities	**Threats**
• Reduce healthcare costs by increasing efficiency, removing duplicates, errors and their impacts. • Reduce the cost in healthcare by inserting data into system in the place where a data (digital) picture emerges. • Increase the interest of citizens in care of their health. • Increase the awareness of all participants of healthcare through the National Health Portal. • More effective pressure of public healthcare on citizens, especially in the field of prevention of civilization diseases. • Restrict the use of the older generation of medical systems and implement the latest technology. • Increase the attractiveness of provided healthcare in the SR and for the citizens from other EU countries and thus obtain additional funding. • Active participation in EU initiatives in eHealth. • The possibility to use EU funds for eHealth. • Mobility of healthcare in the SR and the EU. • The introduction of an electronic identifier for the policyholders and healthcare professionals. • The possibility to provide new medical services. • The ability to create active and dynamic real-time changing picture of the health status of the population. • Ensuring input data in real time and natural form in the first contact places with the patient and establish traceability of dynamic data at all levels of the proposed data model and all cooperating components in real time, not only in time-delayed statistics evaluations. • Possibilities of improving prevention, diagnostics and treatment of chronic non-infectious diseases, increase the success of care in acute life-threatening conditions and also epidemic infectious diseases. • In economic assessment to cross the shadow of current understanding of saving resources to maximize benefits for health condition of the population in a defined financial framework.	• Failure to provide adequate financial coverage of infrastructure and eHealth projects. • Improperly designed infrastructure. • Inefficient use of funds for eHealth. • Underestimating the legislative and standardization process. • Underestimating the importance of data collection in already built infrastructure of general physicians. • Incomplete architecture of eHealth and data model for inclusion of infrastructure of general practitioners. • Inadequate level of data protection. • Lack of funding for IS of healthcare providers. • Limited interoperability of healthcare IS in Slovakia due to missing required standards. • Limited interoperability of healthcare IS with the EU due to the absence of EU standards. • Reduced effectiveness of some activities by their inconsistent informatization. • Dehumanization of healthcare. • Excessive unfulfilled expectations of public from eHealth. • The risk of corruption by entities participating in the allocation and use of resources for eHealth.

Source: processed based on: http://www.ezdravotnictvo.sk/Documents/Strategicke_ciele/priloha_1.pdf

Figure 1. Selected economic and social determinants of healthcare system in the Slovak Republic
Source: own elaboration

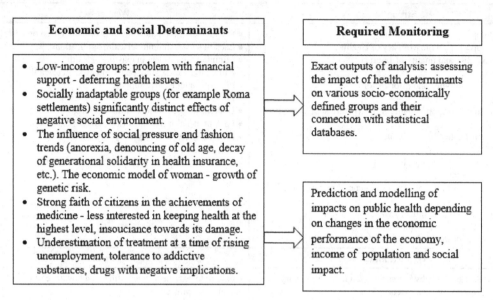

the IT and IS platforms in individual countries was the main ambition of the international research. We present the partial results in the following subsections.

Specification of the Effects from the Use of IS and IT

Effects of the use of IS and IT can be viewed from its content, divided into several groups, respectively types of effects. Each of these groups is suitable for different size and orientation of healthcare provider. In this subchapter, we focus more on economic effects, customer effects, effects from increased procedural efficiency of the healthcare provider, effects from increased analytical performance and quality management and personnel effects.

- **Economic Effects:** Of informatics could be understood as differences in current economic indicators of the organization, resulting from the application of information technologies. Those are monitored in natural or financial terms, and they reflect the dif-

ferences in indicators before the introduction of appropriate application or service and after its introduction. The examples are cost indicators, indicators of the labour productivity and so on. The problem in this group of effects represents how exactly determine whether the effect (i.e. positive difference in the values of the monitored variable) was achieved by the given informatics application, service, or other organizational and personal factors, by environmental factors change, or in a shift in demand of customers, or by the changes in offer of competition.

- **Custom Effects:** Customer orientation and most accurate knowledge of all customer needs, analysis of the activities and interests of customers (e.g. communication with business websites) are currently the focus of attention of many organizations in a competitive environment. They also document the use of specialized applications for customer relationship management (CRM - Customer Relationship Management, CLTV - Customer Life Time Value, etc.). Customer effects are currently mainly linked to the specific types of applications and technologies, and therefore their detection is easier and more accurate than in other groups of effects.

- **Improving Operational Performance of the Organization:** It can be generally seen as reducing the time and financial difficulties of the processes in the organization and also increases its flexibility – i.e. flexible responses to customer - patient conditions. Among the important characteristics of this group of effects can be included the reduction of waiting times, reducing length of healthcare, etc. A prerequisite for achieving effects in process performance is providing more comprehensive reengineering projects in the organization. Interest in shortening the intermediate times of processes in the organization is changing the approaches and priorities of organization management in the management and application of information technologies. This reinforces the expansion of applications and technologies for managing organizational performance (CPM - Corporate Performance Management).

- **Increasing Analytical Performance and Quality Management:** We can state it as a working title for the overall improvement of the quality and accuracy of decision-making processes, for determining and achieving an effective number and structure parameters for analysis, planning and other managerial activities and in particular to provide the necessary number and internal structure (dimensions), on the basis of which it is possible to analyse individual variables and plan. Currently, the main carriers of these effects are applications and Business Intelligence technologies. These applications bring other effects, as they ensure the evaluation of monitored hospital indicators; they analyse these indicators under different dimensions and combinations; they monitor developments over time; this means they create time series and different types of

indexes, they provide analysis, reports and overviews on a consolidated basis, without duplicities and differences in the various reports of organisation and so on.

- **Personal Effects:** For example, increasing the skill level of employees thanks to the use of computer applications based on the latest management techniques and economic models, enhancing the level of formal internal communication and communication with the external partners. A specific indicator of this group is, like in the customer group, the level of customer satisfaction. This is followed by internal surveys among users and user departments on the basis of a defined range of values and usually focuses on the quality of the provided functionality of the applications, the availability of technical resources and other resources of information technology.

RESEARCH IN HEALTHCARE FACILITIES IN SLOVAKIA: THE GESITI PROJECT

The objective of the international research "An Evaluation of the Management of the Information Systems (IS) and technology (IT) in Hospitals" (GESITI-Hospitals) in the Slovak Republic was to map management information systems (IS) and information technologies (IT) in hospitals in Slovakia, analyse and evaluate their current situation and thus identify the specific needs and requirements for development of the region's hospitals. Research was conducted on the basis of cooperation agreements between the Center of information technologies in Brazil with the Faculty of Economics, the Technical University of Kosice, as the only participant from Slovakia. The outcome of the research is the Integrated Research Report (IRR), which should help managers of hospitals to support decision-making processes and increase their competitiveness. To obtain the data, we used a form of personal interviews through a structured questionnaire" Prospective Questionnaire" (PQ) containing more than 200 open and closed questions. The research questionnaire was divided into several strategic areas: "Human Resources, Strategic Management, Research and Development and Technology innovation, Competitiveness of hospitals, Availability of information technologies, Electronic commerce, Telemedicine, Access to the clients, Rapid prototyping of health, Waste management." (Balloni, 2011).

The project is emphasizing several main directions: "knowledge society", "the challenges and considerations" and research and dissemination of best management practices". Currently the outputs of the project in Slovakia acquire an importance in connection with accepting a special law no. 153/2013 about the National Health Information System (NHIS), which regulates the status, rights and obligations defined by the National Health Information Center (NHIC) as its operator, the rights and obligations of other entities in relation to NHIC.

Database and Methods

Consequently, the next subchapter proposes partial results of the research that are oriented on development of innovation potential in the medical institutions on the basis of the research outputs. Our researched sample represents approximately 50% of all the hospitals in a given area (ŠÚ SR, 2009). Twelve (12) of these hospitals are situated in the Košice region, and eight (8) of these hospitals are in the Prešov region. Figure 2 illustrates the structure of researched sample of the hospitals on the basis of their law statues (on the left) and according to their ownership form (on the right).

We used statistical methods except of descriptive statistics and graphic illustrations to evaluate the data. We also used the analysis of variance (ANOVA) in order to compare the specifications of various types of hospitals from the point of view of their legal and ownership status. . The core of the ANOVA method is a reduction of the total sum of square variances (SS) to two components – sum of squares of inner-level (residual) variances (SSE) and sum of squares of semi-level variances (SST). In addition, we used contingency coefficients as well as other statistical characteristics by using the SAS software in order to analyse the qualitative variables. Their importance is in determining the strength of association of row and column variables in contingency tables.

Solutions and Recommendations

In the following subchapters, we focus on partial results of the research, while prior orientation was on aspects of computing equipment use (PC) in the hospitals as well as their use of technological innovations.

Figure 2. Analysed hospitals according to the law form (in the left) and according to the ownership form (in the right)

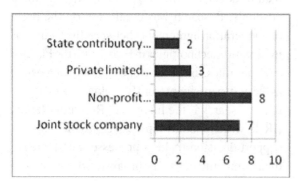
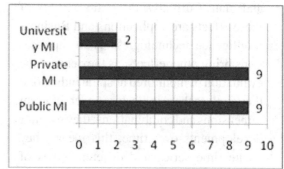

PC Equipment Use

The number of computers that are used in hospitals depends on their size and structure according to the results of the survey. Seventy five percent (75%) of all the computers have access to the Internet and almost ninety five percent (95%) of computers have access to the LAN network.

We found out that the standard deviation is significantly higher than the middle value in case of the number of PCs. This indicates the fact that there exist clear differences between hospitals, where hospitals with a low number of computers occur similarly as hospitals, which have a higher number of computers. Hospitals with a minimum number of computers include only 5 computers. On the other hand, the largest hospital has had 1350 computers. We may conclude that most of the computers are connected to LAN network.

The possible relation between the number of PCs in the hospital and law status or ownership status of a hospital (19 hospitals provided relevant data) was analysed by means of ANOVA. The fundamental assumption of ANOVA method shows dispersion homogeneity. The results proposed in Table 2 show that zero hypotheses may be accepted, and ANOVA may be used. This indicates that the dispersion of individual groups is the same. It means that the dispersion sizes within individual groups are approximately the same. However, it does not evoke error occurrence in calculations of the ANOVA method. We did not observe any statistical differences, while observing the hospitals from the point of view of private/public/university ownership. We deepened the analysis of differences among hospitals of different legal status by the Bonferroni test, which confirmed the significant differences between state allowance organizations and other legal status. Table 4 illustrates that the largest differences are especially against the allowance organizations. State contributory organizations own more computers than other hospitals of different legal status. However, it should be noted

that the sample included only two contributory organizations. These hospitals are the biggest hospitals in the analyzed region considering the number of doctors and beds. Therefore, we expect that the number of computers will be primarily related with the size of hospitals and not with their legal status. This fact about the sample size of contributory organizations clearly contributed to the accuracy of measurement, but due to the low proportion of contributory organizations between hospitals in the analyzed region, we cannot assume that we could reach their higher number. If we focus on the form of ownership, we find out that the problem of the comparison arises in university hospitals, where we have identified only two hospitals. It justifies the fact that between the university hospitals may also be classified smaller hospitals and therefore there was not significant differentiation by computers. An important part of hardware architecture is the printer. The laser printers are the most frequently used printers (Table 1 – mean maximum value). Ink Jets are used to a limited extent in spite of the fact that they are the most frequent types of printers in the world. The use of printers is significantly related to the bureaucratic system of hospital management. We estimated that the dot printers are used to a lesser extent due to the absence of graphic pictures in printing. It especially includes the patient's statements that exclusively consist of texts. Laser printers are used in outputs, where graphics occurs without graphics resolution. The need of graphics resolution is rarely indicated. We also identified during this research that a part of outputs are given to compact discs that significantly decrease the costs for result illustration. It includes the results of computer tomography examinations (CT) and magnetic resonance (MR). In this case, the electronic version is preferred, as it is easily readable, and also other doctors may use it. The previously used prints and outputs given in roentgen films are not used anymore. Forty percent (40%) of analyzed hospitals consider the need to invest in technical equipment and tools the next two years,

Table 2. Descriptive statistics of pc and printers

	Mean Value	Standard Variance	Minimum	Maximum
PC number	262	334.8	5	1 350
PC number with access to the Internet	197	197.2	4	7 70
Number of PC with access to LAN	251	287.4	0	1 100
Number of LaserJets	155	149.1	5	5 50
Number of InkJets	13	14.6	0	50
Number of dot printers	23	71.7	0	315
PC number with multimedia	86.2632	131.40	0	500

Source: own elaboration

fifty five percent (55%) of hospitals consider this fact as a medium importance fact. Consequently, IT innovation is very important for them. The next section presents a detailed view on investments in technological innovation.

Investments in Technological Innovation

It is important to follow the size of investments, which is a critical factor in the process of implementation of technological innovation besides the assumed impact and income from of the implementation from technological innovations.

Considering the financial resources of medical institutions, it is not possible to predict their view to the implementation of innovation. The necessity and planning of innovation primarily lead strategic planning. In several organizations, we encountered the fact that, in planning, they are speculating to implement innovation and technological innovation.

Figure 3 shows that only in a single hospital, they could not answer whether they are or are not considering in their strategic planning the investments in technological innovation. However, the rest of the hospitals declare that the strategic plan contains besides interest in innovation also

Figure 3. Investments in innovation technologies are involved in strategic plan
Source: own elaboration

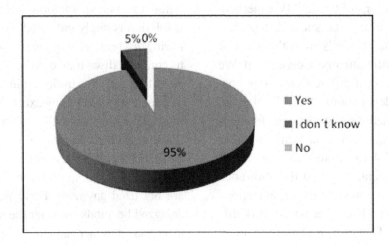

proper planning of investments that are necessary for implementation and provision of innovation.

Within the questionnaire, we focused on the investments of hospitals into the sphere of ICT during the past three years as well as in the future. First of all, each of analyzed hospitals had included the intention to invest in innovation technologies into their strategic and business plan. Within the past three years, only one hospital has invested more than 4% of revenues, 35% of hospitals invested between 3-4% of revenues and one hospital invested between 2-3% and 1-2%, and the rest of hospitals invested less than 1% (Figure 4). Significant association was found by the Fisher exact test (p=0.011) among aggregated relative volumes (up to 3% and more than 3%) of innovation investments and hospital legal forms. The significance is due to the difference between non-profit and private companies.

We used the Chi-square test, while observing the statistic dependence of this answer of the type of hospital from the point of view of its property (private, public, university). In this case, we identified that the dependency was not confirmed on the level of 5% importance, as we could not reject the zero hypothesis of non-dependency of these variables (p-value 0.3762) and therefore

with probability of 37,62% we would permit a mistake of rejecting a true hypothesis. Hence, we consider the zero hypotheses $H_0 : \rho = 0$ for true and, therefore, we cannot consider the existence of dependency between these variables.

Subsequently, we decided to analyse the structure of hospitals according to their answers in this question. The result is shown through the following categories. We found out that, in the group of hospitals that marked the amount of investments on the level of 1%, we could see that university hospitals are there. Private hospitals are investing more in technology investment. Three to four percent share of investment in innovative

Table 3. Output of SAS Software – type of hospital vs. investment capacity

Statistic	DF	Value	Prob
Chi-Square	8	8.6111	0.3762
Likelihood Ratio Chi-Square	8	9.3227	0.3158
Mantel-Haenszel Chi-Square	1	0.0246	0.8754
Phi Coefficient		0.6562	
Contingency Coefficient		0.5486	
Cramer's V		0.4640	

Source: own elaboration

Figure 4. Volume of investments in innovation technologies
Source: own elaboration

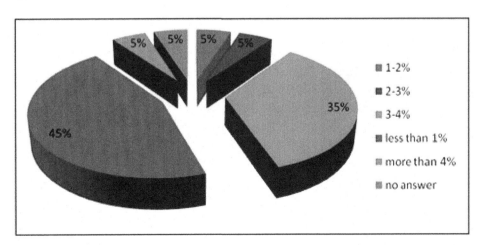

Table 4. Output of SAS Software – t-test comparisons of medium values of the employees' number

	Analysis Variable: A12				
	Mean	Std Dev	Minimum	Maximum	N
Private hospitals	247.22	107.22	33.00	379.00	9
Public hospitals	348.78	378.37	55.00	1248.00	9
T-Tests					
Variable	Method	Variances	DF	t Value	Pr > |t|
Number	Pooled	Equal	8	-0.76	0.4665
Number	Satterthwaite	Unequal	4.86	-0.76	0.4800
Equality of Variances					
Variable	Method	Num DF	Den DF	F Value	Pr > F
Number	Folded F	4	4	9.18	0.0541

Source: own elaboration

technologies is not indicated by any University Hospital (Figure 5). We may assume that the private hospitals are more oriented on investments than public ones.

Larger hospitals are primarily represented by public hospitals. Table 4 - Output of SAS Software – average number of employees according to a hospital type. On the basis of the average number of personnel, the divergence between private and public hospitals is not significant. It is confirmed by the result of the t-test, comparing the average number of personnel.

We cannot reject the zero hypothesis, which assumes that the average number of personnel in private or public hospitals has statistically distinguished p-values which is 0.4665, significantly higher than 0.05. We determine that the p-value of the consonance dissipation test is 0.0541, and hence we cannot reject the zero hypotheses about the dissipation agreement of primary files

Figure 5. MI according to their ownership and volume of investments in innovation technologies
Source: own elaboration

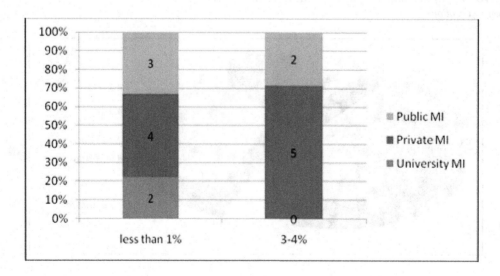

$H_0 : \sigma_1^2 = \sigma_2^2$. We also considered the "Pooled" test to verify the zero hypotheses $H_0 : \mu_1 = \mu_2$. Therefore, we could evaluate the portion of investments as comparable. We may state that, for private hospitals, the investments are reasonably important which had not been confirmed. It could be also caused by the fact that these hospitals are not bounded on budget of other organizations, and hence a potential negative financial result is not able to be compensated from external sources that are, on the other hand, possible in cases of public hospitals. In present economic situation, we may not clearly expect this kind of behaviour from the side of the founder even though this kind of action occurred in the past by upraising of financial problems directly or through transmission of a given facility to another organization.

In the last verification of dependency existence, we measured the relation between the portion of the capacity investments that was measured through the questions E11 and also by the amount of personnel in a hospital. We found out that the dependency is not statistically important even though the correlation coefficient reaches the value of -0.46. In a given sample, we had identified a negative dependency when, in increasing number of personnel, a decreasing portion of investments is recorded. In this case, we may predict that the capacity of investments is not developing linearly according to the number of personnel, which reflects a negative dependency and hence the relative capacity of investments is decreasing. By monitoring the capacity of investments in absolute formulation, we should be able to record a dependency as the rising amount of personnel probably leads to growth of capacity of investments in an absolute formulation.

Technological Innovation Use

Healthcare infrastructure of the Slovak hospitals is technically, economically and operationally outdated, which significantly affects the efficiency of its management. The average age of Slovak hospitals is 34.5 years. The layout of the hospitals is characterized by the distribution of multiple objects within the complex. General hospitals have an average of 30 buildings in one hospital; some hospitals have up to 81 buildings. Table 5 indicates the number of healthcare providers, the number of professional services and the corresponding number of beds.

The use of technological innovations concerning the knowledge of many authors may be considered as a significant element that encourages the development of individual procedures. In the

Table 5. Bedspread of healthcare facilities for 2009

	Number of Healthcare Providers	Number of Professional Service Units	Number of Beds Up to 31.12.2009
Slovak republic	147	1345	35520
Bratislava region	24	148	5294
Trnava region	9	95	2568
Trenčín region	12	125	3135
Nitra region	16	141	4154
Žilina region	13	162	4276
Banská Bystrica region	25	193	4376
Prešov region	25	215	5998
Košice region	23	226	5729

Source: National Centre for Health Information, 2010

field of the health system, we may improve the procedures and processes of the medical institutions, within this process. Significance of technological innovations affects all spheres of economy and especially producers. The implementation of new technologies represents a possibility of improving the present state and identification of improvements that form better assumptions for high-grade service provision. The medical institution may achieve a competitive advantage towards other subjects on the market of healthcare providers by means of new technologies.

We have identified the medical institutions knowledge on the basis of realized research towards other reasons of technological innovation implementation. In this case, we may observe that the highest number of reasons of technological innovation implementation is due to quality improvement (Figure 6). Seven medical institutions presented cost reduction as the main reason of technological innovation implementation. Image improvement is also very important for a health facility that is connected with doctor's free choice and also with the rise of competition among medical institutions. In this case, the patient may decide which medical institutions/he chooses. This is connected with the possible decrease of

performances and also with lower transaction from the health insurance companies' side. Therefore, the medical institutions struggle for the improvement of their image by means of examination and operation activities provision, while using the up-to-date technologies and technical equipment. This may be related to subsequent shortening of recovery length, which has a positive influence on other costs of health insurance companies, but also employees, or their employers.

Productivity increase is closely connected with modern technology use as well as cost reduction. In this case, it is the realization of the higher number of performances (analyses) during a specified and observed time interval, or lower need of corrections or technical layoffs after a chosen number of repetitions. The representatives of the medical institution consider this result differently from the possibility of cost reduction.

We found out that this division does not have the essential influence on perception of technological innovation contribution. It was found out on the basis of given data from the point of view of the medical institutions (public, private, university). Similarly, we found out that, in all cases, we did not reject the non-existence of a relation between indication of given option (to choose a given

Figure 6. Reasons of technological innovation implementation
Source: own elaboration

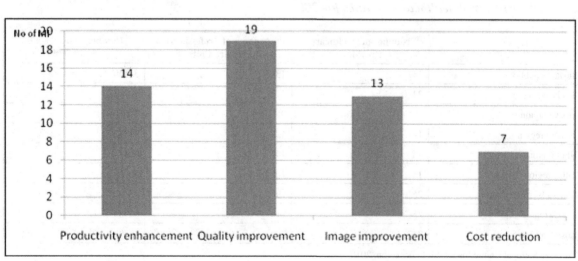

contribution) and medical institutions type, while analysing. In the case of productivity increase, we have determined the p-value of 0.7090.

A similar result was noticed in the case of the second option, i.e. "quality improvement". In this case, we observed that the p-value is lower; however, it is always relatively distant from the 0.05 level under which the zero hypotheses have been rejected. Therefore, the probability of zero hypothesis refusals is higher; however, there is always a risk of true hypothesis rejection error that is even higher than the boundary of accepted 5%. In the case of image improvement analysis, we found out that there exists a possible relation between the hospital type and perception of the contribution of the technological innovation implementation, which is the lowest. The given result is confirmed by the p-value of Chi-Square test of independence that has a value of 0.7287.

In this case, it may be considered as a fact that some hospitals are situated in the regions, where there is no existing competition. As a result, they are not forced to primarily observe their image, and so this factor does not represent a motive force that would force them to implement the technological innovations.

We may not draw a conclusion from the given data that hospitals which represent the only providers of healthcare in the region have not been focusing on technological innovations. However, image improvement does not represent a sufficient motivation of such implementation for them. In this case, there prevail economic factors that especially include cost savings, productivity increase of work or quality improvement. These factors reach minimum downtimes and reduction of cost or material consumption. All these aspects are reflected in economic indicators for hospitals. Even the public medical institutions are forced to behave as private enterprises, as they do not have unlimited budgets. In such a case, the medical institution is established and financed by means of towns' or municipalities' budgets. As a result, they do not have a good financial situation

concerning tax income and, therefore, they limit their financial fees for these organizations in their founder's competency.

We also found out, on the basis of the given analyses that the contribution of technological innovation implementation does not differ by hospital type. We may not assume that the private medical institution was more focused on contribution achievement in the field of cost reduction by means of technological innovation implementation, or image improvement. Also, other aspects of technological innovation implementation, such as quality improvement, or productivity increase are common for all three types of hospitals that are analyzed in this research. In the next research, it would be possible to focus on individual aspects of these innovations and to analyse contributions of individual areas of economic and operating hospitals activities. On the other hand, we may assume that the influence may also be observed in the field of management types, which is possible to be determined in the analysis of hospital management or analysis of a strategy of a medical institution.

CONCLUSION

The health system in Slovakia is marked by permanent indebtedness, while, in this sector, it is not possible to accurately quantify the extent of structural debt. This includes the current problems related to the project realization of changing the system of public health insurance, problems associated with reducing the volume of purchased care from health insurance companies with an unchanged demand, thereby reaching a difficult moral dilemma when healthcare facilities reach the limits. This caused many negative subsequent processes, such as doctors leaving abroad, waiting for the realization of performance, growth of corruption, increasing dissatisfaction of medical staff and patients, unwillingness to accept over-limit. As well as results from a recent research (Gavurová et al. 2013) it is urgently necessary to define the price of performance for hospitals, because price lists of performance do not correspond to reality, one aspect of indebtedness. Effective implementation of eHealth in close cooperation with health insurance companies, as well as representatives of primary healthcare and focus on areas with defined potential high benefits should be examined. Informatization in this process reaches a crucial point and influences the strategy for hospitals. The legal status and content of hospitals strategy significantly depends on the type and ownership. As shown by research results, the most important barrier to the adoption of technological innovations in hospitals is the lack of financial and personnel resources. This is also reflected in the inadequate use of e-commerce, which is not determined by the price of the product or the size of the hospital, but by the skills of managers. From the analysed hospitals, only one currently uses telemedicine, and eight other hospitals are planning to use it in the near future. Hospitals invest most resources into informatization of economic and management processes and to health information systems, which is related to the requirements of current legislation and the objectives of the project eHealth. International research outputs from which the chapter presents only partial findings, provide a valuable platform for national and international benchmarking of informatization development in healthcare facilities, allow identifying potential development opportunities of healthcare facilities and flexibly respond to the challenges of Project 2020 and the opportunity to complementary adapt the strategy programs to eHealth.

Based on the results of the research in 20 Slovak hospitals, we can conclude that the use of ICT is very diverse and inadequate. As declared by the results for investments in ICT, only in one hospital they exceeded 4% of their income, in half of the analyzed hospitals it is under 1%. Their investments are directed primarily to management processes and information systems, which helps to adapt to the rapid pace of IT development.

Another negative fact is that the systems dealing with human resource management, ERP systems, logistics and application solutions, solutions for process management (BPM), as well as systems for customer relationship management (CRM), are in our healthcare facilities used minimally. This greatly affects the efficiency of management, as well as limits the successful implementation of eHealth. Slovak hospitals must primarily move from rigid, long-existing organizational structures and norms of behaviour towards flexible and easily changeable forms and integrating and interconnected networks. If the growth in the quantity and quality of interaction processes of the hospital is not regulated and controlled, it will cause chaos.

REFERENCES

Ash, J. S., Gorman, P. N., Seshadri, V., & Hersh, W. R. (2004). Computerized physician order entry in U.S. hospitals: Results of a 2002 survey. *Journal of the American Informatics Association*, *11*, 95–99. doi:10.1197/jamia.M1427 PMID:14633935

Balloni, A. J. (2011). *GESITI Project, "An Evaluation of the Management Information System and Technology in Hospitals" (GESITI/HOSPITALS)*. Retrieved October 12, 2013, from http://repositorio.cti.gov.br/repositorio/bitstream/10691/246/3/GESITI_Project_INGL_22.pdf

Bashshur, R. L. (1997). Telemedicine and the healthcare system. In R. L. Bashshur, J. H. Sanders, & G. W. Shannon (Eds.), Telemedicine theory and practice (pp. 5–36). Academic Press.

Benčo, J., & Kuvíková, H. (Eds.). (2011). Economics of public services. Banská Bystrica: Ekonomická fakulta UMB, 333.

Bjorn-Andersen, N., Eason, K., & Robey, D. (1986). *Managing Computer Impact: An International Study of Management and Organization*. Norwood, NJ: Ablex.

Danilák, M. (2011). *Challenges for Health and possible eHealth solutions.* Košice: LYNX.

Gavurová, B., Šoltés, V., Kafková, K., & Černý, Ľ. (2013). *Selected aspects of the Slovak health efficiency. Day-healthcare and its development in the Slovak Republic. Košice.* Technical University.

Global Risk. (2010). *A Global Risk Network Report.* World Economic Forum. Retrieved October 08, 2013, from http://www3.weforum.org/docs/WEF_GlobalRisks_Report_2010.pdf

Harkovotová, S. (2011). *According to the OECD Slovaks are inefficient in healthcare.* Retrieved October 02, 2013, from http://aktualne.centrum.sk/domov/zdravie-skolstvospolocnost/clanek.phtml?id=1223847

Hejduková, P., & Klepáková, A. (2013). *The Issue of Healthcare Financing in Selected Countries.* WSEAS Press.

Ivančík, R. (2012). Globalization and the global economy. Vedecký Obzor, 4(1), 27-45.

Janke, F., & Prídavok, M. (2012). B2B network performance: Practical Aspects Of Network Supply Adequacy Indicator. In *Proceedings of IDIMT-2012, ICT Support For Complex Systems.* Jindrichuv Hradec, Czech Republic: Schriftenreihe Informatik.

Kaplan, B. (1991). Models of change and information systems research. In H.E. Nissen, H.K. Klein, & R. Hirschheim (Eds.), Information Systems Research: Contemporary Approaches and Emergent Traditions, (pp. 593–611). Academic Press.

Klepáková, A. (2010). Information cluster for subjects of Slovak public health insurance market. In *Clusters, bi and global economy (international aspects).* Poland: Serve & Bonus Liber.

Kling, R. (1980). Social analyses of computing: Theoretical perspectives in recent empirical research. *Computing Surveys, 12,* 61–110. doi:10.1145/356802.356806

Leifer, R., & McDonough, E. F. (1985). Computerization as a predominant technology effecting work unit structure. In *Proceedings 6th Annual Conference on Information Systems,* (pp. 238–248). Academic Press.

Markus, M. L. (1983). Power, politics, and MIS implementation. *Communications of the ACM, 26,* 430–444. doi:10.1145/358141.358148

Markus, M. L., & Robey, D. (1988). Information technology and organizational change: Causal structure in theory and research. *Management Science, 34,* 583–598. doi:10.1287/mnsc.34.5.583

Moehr, J. H. (2002). Special issue: Evaluation in health informatics. *Computers in Biology and Medicine, 32,* 11–236.

Morvay, K. (2009). *"Relative price" of doctor in Slovakia is growing in a domestic and international scale.* Health Policy Institute. Retrieved from http://www.hpi.sk/hpi/sk/view/3536/relativna-cena-lekara-v-sr-rastie-v-nbsp-domacom-nbsp-aj-nbsp-medzinarodnom-meradle.html

National Centre for Health Information. (2010). Retrieved October 12, 2013, from http://www.nczisk.sk/en/Statistical_Findings/Pages/default.aspx

Nemec, J., Ochrana, F., & Šumpíková, M. (2008). Czech and Slovak Lessons for Public Administration Performance Evaluation, Management and Finance. *Ekonomicky Casopis, 56*(4), 353–369.

OECD. (2010). OECD Health at Glance 2010. OECD Publishing.

Olson, M. H. (1982). New information technology and organizational culture. *Management Information Systems Quarterly, 6,* 71–92. doi:10.2307/248992

Pfeffer, J. (1982). *Organizations and Organization Theory.* Marshfield, MA: Pitman.

PriceWaterhouseCoopers (PWC). (2010). *The price of excess: Identifying waste in healthcare spending*. London: PriceWaterhouseCoopers.

PriceWaterhouseCoopers (PWC). (2011). *Pharma (2020): Supplying the future*. London: PriceWaterhouseCoopers.

Romanová, D., Ivančová, L., & Klepáková, A. (2013). The requirements for competence for quality management entities. *Ekonomické spectrum, 8* (3), 4 - 13.

Soltes, V., Gavurova, B., Balloni, A.J. & Pavlickova, V. (2012). *Website*. Retrieved October 12, 2013, from http://www.cti.gov.br/images/stories/cti/gesiti/relatorios_de_pesquisa/Research_report_Gavurova_TUKE_Eslovaquia_2012.pdf

Soltes, V., Gavurova, B., Balloni, A. J., & Pavlickova, V. (2013). *ICT in Medical Institutions in Selected Regions of the Slovak Republic. Research report of the GESITI Project: An Evaluation of the Management of the Information Systems (IS) and Technologies (IT) in Hospitals*. Brasil: Center for Information Technology Renato Archer – Ministry of Science, Technology and Innovation.

Štatistický Úrad Slovenskej Republiky (ŠÚ SR). (2013). *Regionálna databáza*. Retrieved October 22, 2013, from http://portal.statistics.sk/showdoc.do?docid=96

Strategic Objectives. (2012). Retrieved October 22, 2013, from http://www.ezdravotnictvo.sk/Documents/Strategicke_ciele/priloha_1.pdf

Szabo, K. Z., Šoltés, M., & Herman, E. (2013). Innovative Capacity & Performance of Transition Economies: Comparative Study at the Level of Enterprises. *E+M Ekonomie a Management, 16*(1), 52-69.

Szalay, T. (2009*). Ranking of health systems from a consumer perspective*. Retrieved from http://www.hpi.sk/hpi/sk/view/3703/slovensko-v-europe-sieste-od-konca.html

World Health Organization. (2010). *The world health report: health systems financing: The path to universal coverage*. Geneva: World Health Organisation. Retrieved October 22, 2013, from http://www.who.int/health_financing/Health_Systems_Financing_Plan_Action.pdf

World Health Organization. (2011). *World Health Statistics 2011*. Geneva: World Health Organisation. Retrieved October 22, 2013, from http://www.who.int/whosis/whostat/2011/en/

Zákon č. 153. (2013). *O Národnom zdravotníckom informačnom systéme (NZIS)*. Retrieved October 22, 2013, from: http://epredpisy.sk/predpisy-vo-vlade/2520028-o-narodnom-zdravotnickom-informanom-systeme

Závadská, Z., Závadský, J. & Sirotiaková, M. (2013). Process model and its real application in the selected management areas. *E+M Ekonomie a Management, 16* (1), 113-127.

KEY TERMS AND DEFINITIONS

Efficiency: Known as effectiveness or productivity, generally refers to the efficiency of the used resources and the utility obtained by them. It is a ratio of inputs and outputs of an activity or a system. In terms of organizational management, it is a ratio of quantity or quality of final products and the amount of the resources invested into the production process. Thus, it is the use of such resources, which maximize the volume and quality of the services.

eHealth/Electronic Healthcare: Through information and communication technologies provides the right information at the right time in the right place in all phases and processes of healthcare, which will significantly contribute to improve healthcare and thus to improve the quality of life of citizens.

Healthcare: Is defined as a social set of professional knowledge institutions, establishments and authorities, workers and their corresponding activities, serving specifically to providing healthcare with an appropriate order to promote, preserve and restore health. It is a range of activities and measures leading to prolonged and sustained life of individuals, to improve the quality of life and its protection, the promotion, strengthening, improving, restoring health, alleviation of suffering or health assessment of a person associated with disease or disease state, and directed to better health for future generations.

Informatics and ICT Management: Is an area that includes, in practice, all management methods and analytical techniques, whose topic is information, data or information and communication technologies management, day to day operations, development, implementation of new information technologies, data security and information, and software development. Partially it extends into knowledge management. Informatics in the enterprise cannot be separated from the overall organizational architecture and its needs - it must be measurable costs and benefits (utility) for the customer and the functioning of the organization.

Innovation Management: Contains thematically all that is related to innovation in organizations and businesses. Without innovation, business, organizations or companies do not make any progress. The ability to manage innovation is a natural ability which helps to introduce new or improved goods, services, processes, procedures and other things. Innovation is closely linked to quality management, because quality improvement also brings innovation and therefore the mentioned methods overlap each other considerably.

Strategic Management: Is a management field focusing on long-term planning and the direction of the organization. Strategic management in an organization ensures that things do not happen randomly but according to pre-planned, long-term plans. It serves, on one hand, the transmission of the owners' requirements to the management of the organization, and, on the other hand, the organizational management for the organization, unifies and directs the behaviour of all people in all parts of the organization. It formulates operating rules, priorities and direction in the long term, including the direction the organization wants to go.

System of Healthcare: We understood it as the provision of health services. Is one component of healthcare and health policy is determined by the state. A healthcare system consists of all individuals and organizations, which contribute to improve the health of its members, what is the main objective of healthcare.

Chapter 3
The Impact of the Electronic Medical Records (EMRs) on Hospital Pathology Services:
An Organisational Communication Perspective

Andrew Georgiou
University of New South Wales, Australia

ABSTRACT

This chapter reviews what is currently known about the effect of the Electronic Medical Records (EMRs) on aspects of laboratory test ordering, their impact on laboratory efficiency, and the contribution this makes to the quality of patient care. The EMR can be defined as a functioning electronic database within a given organisation that contains patient information. Although laboratory services are expected to gain from the introduction of the EMRs, the evidence to date has highlighted many challenges associated with the implementation of EMRs, including their potential to cause major shifts in responsibilities, work processes, and practices. The chapter outlines an organisational communication framework that has been derived from empirical evidence. This framework considers the interplay between communication, temporal, and organisational factors, as a way to help health information technology designers, clinicians, and hospital and laboratory professionals meet the important challenges associated with EMR design, implementation, and sustainability.

INTRODUCTION

The chapter reviews what is currently known about the effect of the electronic medical record (EMR) on aspects of laboratory test ordering, its impact on laboratory efficiency and the contribution this makes to the quality of patient care. The

chapter identifies the key challenges associated with the introduction of the EMR and the organisational context in which it is used in pathology laboratories. It examines how communication is undertaken within the laboratory and its effect on the way that work is carried out. Particular consideration is given to key concepts such as:

DOI: 10.4018/978-1-4666-6320-6.ch003

a) the synchronicity of communication required within sections of the laboratory (e.g., real time communication between the laboratory and clinicians versus asynchronous messages and notes); b) the role of feed-back mechanisms which provide confirmation of the receipt of information; and c) considerations of what (and how much) information is needed by different recipients. The chapter also incorporates an examination of temporal and spatial factors, particularly as they relate to where work is carried out, how it is allocated, prioritised and coordinated. The objective of the chapter is thus to outline an empirically-derived organisational communication framework, which can be used to help enhance the design, implementation and sustainability of EMR systems and hospital pathology services.

BACKGROUND

Hospital laboratory services are involved in the examination of clinical and pathologic data which are incorporated into a broader context and used to provide meaningful information to physicians and patients(Deeble & Lewis-Hughes, 1991). In the last few decades, this important task has become increasingly reliant on sophisticated information technology systems to assist in the management, storage and communication of data(Pantanowitz, Henricks, & Beckwith, 2007).

The EMR can be defined as a functioning electronic database that contains patient information within a given organisation (Aller, Georgiou, & Pantanowitz, 2012). EMRs can encompass a wide range of systems including computerised provider order entry (CPOE) systems that allow clinicians to place orders directly into computers (Birkmeyer, Lee, Bates, & Birkmeyer, 2002). They may also incorporate clinical information databases, which can be used to provide decision support to assist diagnosis, or to help understand

and interpret laboratory results (Georgiou, Williamson, Westbrook, & Ray, 2007). The EMR is therefore more than just a replacement for the previous paper-based medical record system, it has the potential to expand modes of communication and improve access to information and knowledge across the hospital and the wider community (Aller et al., 2012).

There is an expanding body of literature which has identified many benefits associated with the EMR, including the ability to provide timely access to patient information and electronic decision support to enhance clinical decision-making and the delivery of quality care(Buntin, Burke, Hoaglin, & Blumenthal, 2011). Nevertheless, there remain major international reservations about the slow pace of EMR diffusion amid concerns about the failure of the existing evidence base to clearly demonstrate benefits (Black et al., 2011). Literature reviews continue to point to the need to improve our knowledge of why some EMR implementations succeed and others do not(Jones, Rudin, Perry, & Shekelle, 2014). This has led to a growing international imperative to examine and improve our understanding of the context of EMR system implementations, particularly as regards the circumstances that may (or may not) contribute to their success and sustainability (Aarts, Ash, & Berg, 2007).

THE IMPACT OF THE EMR ON HOSPITAL LABORATORY SERVICES

Hospital pathology services are widely seen as an area where information and communication technologies (ICT) like the EMR can have a major impact on the efficiency and effectiveness of service delivery. Pathology laboratories are information-intense bodies that provide services across primary, secondary and tertiary care. It is estimated that pathology laboratory services are responsible for leveraging 60-70% of all critical decision-making involving admittance, discharge and medication (Forsman, 1996). Within this context the EMR has been identified as an important means to:

- Improve the efficiency and effectiveness of laboratory services.
- Increase the utilisation of evidence-based test ordering.
- Enhance the quality and safety of patient care.

Improve the Efficiency and Effectiveness of Laboratory Services

One of the most regularly used indicators of laboratory performance is the measure of turnaround times (TATs). TATs can be measured either from the time a test is ordered, a sample is taken, or the time the sample is presented at the laboratory reception area for processing, right up to the time a verified result has been issued and seen(A Georgiou, M Williamson, et al., 2007). TATs can influence how the quality of the pathology service is judged by clinicians (Hawkins, 2007). Research evidence has shown that EMR ordering (utilising a Computerised Provider Order Entry component) has contributed to significant reductions in TATs (Georgiou, Prgomet, et al., 2013; A Georgiou, M Williamson, et al., 2007). For instance, a 2002 study showed a 25% shorter laboratory TAT (measured from the time of receipt of a specimen in the laboratory to the electronic posting of the result) in a medical Intensive Care Unit (ICU) (Mekhjian et al., 2002). In 2006, a controlled before and after study in an Australian teaching hospital reported a significant average decrease of 15.5 minutes/test assay in laboratory TAT across intervention wards which used a CPOE system. This improvement in TAT was not found in the non-intervention wards (J.I. Westbrook, Geor-

giou, Dimos, & Germanos, 2006). Other studies have shown that these improvements have been consistent over time(J.I. Westbrook, Georgiou, & Rob, 2009) and across hospitals(J.I. Westbrook, Georgiou, & Lam, 2009).

Increase the Utilisation of Evidence-Based Test Ordering

Evidence-based medicine has meant a shift in the culture of health provision away from decisions based on opinion, past practices and precedent, towards a system that utilises science, research and evidence to guide decision making (Sackett, Rosenberg, Gray, Haynes, & Richardson, 1996). For pathology this has inspired greater emphasis on its role in the whole patient journey beginning with asking the right clinical questions, selecting the most appropriate test or investigation needed to diagnose the problem, across to providing appropriate clinical advice and treatment to encompass the whole spectrum of specialties involved in the patient pathway. The EMR can be seen as an important clinical aid, helping to provide the "end-to-end connectivity" to deliver effective order communication(Georgiou, Lang, Rosenfeld, & Westbrook, 2011; J.I. Westbrook et al., 2006) and decision support based on the linking of laboratory test results with evidence-based guidelines. Prior research in this area has provided potent examples of how guideline-based reminders can improve guideline compliance,(Overhage, Tierney, Zhou, & McDonald, 1997) or contribute to sustained and significant decreases in the proportion of troponin I test ordered in an Emergency Department in Melbourne, Australia(Georgiou, Lam, Allardice, Hart, & Westbrook, 2012). Even electronic prompts for basic information (e.g., specifying whether a gentamicin or vancomycin sample is random, peak or trough (J.I. Westbrook et al., 2006) or whether a patient is on heparin or warfarin when coagulation testing is undertaken(A

Georgiou et al., 2011) can improve the efficiency and effectiveness of pathology services and their contribution to quality patient care.

Evidence-based test ordering is particularly relevant to issues concerning the volume of pathology test orders. The past few decades have seen a massive growth in pathology services with many more people receiving laboratory tests than previously, leading to a considerable increase in the volume of laboratory tests performed(Legg & Cheong, 2004). This has raised major concerns about excessive and redundant test ordering and the financial burden this may impose on health care resources. It also carries serious implications for patient safety, threatening to increase the number of false-positive test results associated with unnecessary and time-consuming diagnostic examinations(Axt-Adam, 1993).

Enhance the Quality and Safety of Patient Care

The World Health Organization's World Alliance for Patient Safety has highlighted the importance of pathology services to the global patient safety agenda, emphasising the role of the laboratory in ensuring that reliable and accurate results are delivered in a timely fashion to inform clinical management decisions (The World Alliance For Patient Safety Drafting Group et al., 2009). The main sources of laboratory errors have been shown to arise within the pre-analytic (doctor's test order) and post-analytic (laboratory report to the doctor) phases of the laboratory test order process (Bonini, Plebani, Ceriotti, & Rubboli, 2002). These are areas where the EMR can have a major positive impact. The addition of decision support functions can assist physicians to alleviate problems with test requisitions, for example, ordering incorrect tests, inaccurately specifying aspects of the test order, or neglecting a test altogether. The EMR may also help to promote appropriate test requests where there is a clear clinical question for which the result will provide an answer leading to the

initiation of appropriate treatment (Price, 2003). For instance, a 1999 study carried out in the Brigham and Women's Hospital in USA, provided a powerful example where the introduction of electronic reminders about apparent redundant tests led to significantly improved performance (27% in the intervention v 51% in the control) in the rate of redundant tests (Bates et al., 1999).

EMR: THE CHALLENGES ASSOCIATED WITH DESIGN, IMPLEMENTATION AND SUSTAINABILITY

Although laboratory services are expected to gain significantly from the introduction of the EMR, the evidence to date has also highlighted problems and inconsistencies (J. Callen, Paoloni, Georgiou, Prgomet, & Westbrook, 2010; J. L. Callen, Braithwaite, & Westbrook, 2008; Georgiou, Greenfield, Callen, & Westbrook, 2009; Andrew Georgiou et al., 2007; Georgiou, Morse, Timmins, Ray, & Westbrook, 2008; Georgiou & Westbrook, 2007; A Georgiou, J.I. Westbrook, et al., 2007; Georgiou, Westbrook, Callen, & Braithwaite, 2008; Johanna I. Westbrook, Georgiou, & Rob, 2008). One of the major limitations of the existing evidence base relates to the generalisability of existing research findings, along with concerns about the applicability of the findings to hospitals internationally (Black et al., 2011; Chaudhry et al., 2006). In part this has been linked to the preponderance of US-centred studies in the evidence base, (often from the same three or four hospitals), and the inclusion of a large number of early studies based on home grown applications prior to the worldwide proliferation of commercial "off-the-shelf" systems (Ash, Stavri, Dykstra, & Fournier, 2003; A Georgiou, M Williamson, et al., 2007).

Another major concern about the existing evidence base relates to the overwhelming focus on measures of process rather than patient care outcomes (Georgiou, Prgomet, et al., 2013).

Measures of patient outcome usually involve the consideration of multiple and complex factors that can be difficult to identify and measure (A Georgiou, M Williamson, et al., 2007). Most studies that have considered the impact of electronic pathology ordering on indicators such as patient length of hospital stay, mortality or even readmission rates to ICU, report no significant changes (A Georgiou, M Williamson, et al., 2007). The generation of research evidence regarding clinical outcomes will likely need to employ more sophisticated statistical techniques to account for the many factors involved in considerations of patient outcome(J.I. Westbrook, Georgiou, & Lam, 2009; Johanna I. Westbrook et al., 2008).

The evidence also highlights major problems with implementing and sustaining electronic decision support features. There are often difficulties achieving agreement about standards (e.g., commonly agreed laboratory order sets or diagnostic algorithms relevant for specified patient conditions) (Bobb, Payne, & Gross, 2007). There is also the possibility of clinical resistance to particularly features of the EMR that may be related to problems with the usability of the system, its compatibility with existing applications or even a failure to complement the way that clinical and laboratory work is performed (A Georgiou, J.I. Westbrook, et al., 2007; L. Peute, Aarts, Bakker, & Jaspers, 2009; L. W. P. Peute & Jaspers, 2007).

FUTURE RESEARCH DIRECTIONS

Many health informatics researchers have noted that while information technology systems like the EMR can be designed and implemented, socio-material infrastructures (involving work processes, spatial locations and existing social settings) are hardly ever designed; instead they are generated dynamically and organically (Bygstad, 2010). In this way innovation associated with information technology should not be seen as a product of a single intervention, but part of a collective or-

ganisational and communication change process incorporating numerous stakeholders (e.g., care providers, patients, institutions, vendors, regulatory agencies) within tightly coupled clinical and social settings(Greenhalgh & Russell, 2010). The success or otherwise of the EMR should, therefore, be considered through a *multi-dimensional and system-oriented perspective* that takes into account the perspectives of the numerous stakeholders involved in the process (e.g., pathologists, laboratory scientists, doctors, nurses, patients, hospital managers etc.)(Georgiou, Westbrook, Braithwaite, & Iedema, 2005; A Georgiou, J.I. Westbrook, et al., 2007).

Generally, our understanding of the mechanisms by which information technology drives work practice change and improvements in service performance has been underdeveloped(Menou & Taylor, 2006). This is because many of the changes introduced by information technologies are undefined, complex or dynamic(Organisation for Economic Co-operation Development, 2011). While the EMR may be designed to facilitate improvements, evidence has shown that people may also decide not to use them, or may find their lack of integration with current work patterns difficult to handle, leading to situations where the full potential of the system is not realised(Clegg et al., 1997). Traditionally, information system research approaches have focused on the technological application, and struggled to appreciate the informational, organisational and communications infrastructure that underpins how work is performed (Chen, 1990).

As a consequence of widespread concerns about the applicability, sustainability and safety of the EMR and health information technology more generally, the US Committee on Patient Safety and Health Information Technology, Institute of Medicine has drawn attention to the critical importance of socio-technical factors involved in the adoption of information technology(Committee on Patient Safety and Health Information Technology; Institute of Medicine, 2011). Socio-technical approaches view social aspects (culture, values and politics) and technical elements (equipment, procedures and technology) as interdependent and interrelated (Coiera, 2004; J.I. Westbrook et al., 2007; Whetton & Georgiou, 2010).

Organisational Communication Framework

This chapter concludes by considering some of the key socio-technical factors identified by the Committee on Patient Safety and Health Information Technology(Committee on Patient Safety and Health Information Technology; Institute of Medicine, 2011) particularly in regards to the communication infrastructure that underpins each organisation. The chapter describes an organisational communication framework (see Figure 1) which considers the interplay between communication, temporal factors and organisational

functions drawing heavily on empirical findings of the impact of the EMR on hospital laboratory services.

Organisational communication approaches emphasise the essential (constitutive) role that communication processes play in the make-up and functioning of an organisation (Putnam, Nicotera, & McPhee, 2009). The management of every organisation usually involves some combination of the classic tasks related to the planning, organising, staffing and controlling of how work is performed(Fayol, 1967). Each of these functions is connected to a communication and temporal dimension (Georgiou, Westbrook, & Braithwaite, 2012). In order to *plan*, it is important to obtain information with which to organise future activities. The *organisation* of work requires people and resources to be set out according to specified communication networks. *Staffing* includes communication required for the management of

Figure 1. Diagrammatic conceptualisation of an organisational communication framework

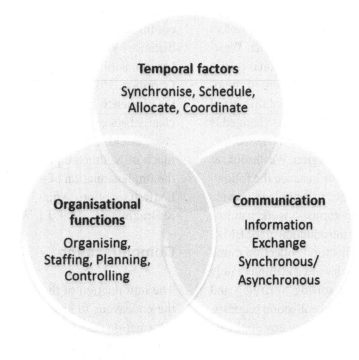

human resources and *controlling* involves the coordination of resources using the exchange of information. The viability and eventual success of an EMR are therefore contingent on its suitability and fit within the particular organisational and communication setting in which it is installed (A. Georgiou et al., 2012).

Temporal Factors

One of the most challenging features of ICT systems is their effect on the *temporal landscape* that is how time is conceived, structured and organised, and the impact this has on how work is carried out (Adam, 2004). EMR systems are widely believed to facilitate major increases in the pace and volumes of data transfer, allowing for linkage and storage of information across multiple sites. They also have the ability to deliver efficiency gains that are often related to the speed and timeliness of information exchange and its effect on organisational output.

There is a general presumption that new technologies lead to an increase in the pace of activities, increasing reliance on some practices (e.g., computer entry) to the hindrance of others (e.g., manual tasks)(Georgiou, Tariq, & Westbrook, 2013). However, this supposition is overly simplistic because technologies, in and of themselves, are not necessarily the cause of this speed up (Wajcman, 2008). Often, what has changed is the way that work is *allocated, prioritised, sequenced* or *coordinated*(Georgiou, Westbrook, & Braithwaite, 2011). Take for instance the following example of the changes to pathology service blood collectors' (phlebotomists) work patterns that came about with the introduction of the EMR. In the past, the blood collectors' collection round involved their visiting each ward and immediately setting out on the task of sorting, verifying and validating each ward's blood collection requests. This task also involved identifying any duplicate blood collection requests that may have been made for the same patient. Once the EMR was implemented, practices changed dramatically to

the point that the blood collector's job now started in the Central Specimen Reception area where a print-out was obtained that had all collection tasks already listed and included the identification of all duplicate requests. Aside from the obvious time savings involved, the new work practice procedure significantly altered the way that the blood collector's work was allocated, sequenced and coordinated (A. Georgiou et al., 2008; A Georgiou, JI Westbrook, & J Braithwaite, 2010).

The influence that temporal factors have on the EMR and organisations is complex and can be difficult to identify(Poole, 2004). For instance, in the past, "space" and "place" usually meant you were in the same place as the person with whom you needed to work with. However, information technology has fostered relations between people without face-to-face interaction(Giddens, 1990). This means that preparation for the introduction of the EMR needs to include an awareness of how the system may change the way that work is organised between professionals, departments and even within the community (A. Georgiou et al., 2011). For instance, will information exchange continue to happen in the same place or across distance? Will the exchange involve major shifts in responsibility among professionals?(Fernando, Georgiou, Holdgate, & Westbrook, 2009). Will the sequence of activity and allocation of tasks change between key professionals? Often it is these changes and shifts in responsibility which underpin much of healthcare professionals concern about the implementation of new technologies like the EMR (Georgiou, Ampt, Creswick, Westbrook, & Braithwaite, 2009; J.I. Westbrook et al., 2007)

Communication

The introduction of the EMR is associated with the endeavour to ensure that the right data and information are provided to the right person when needed. Achieving these tasks can be much harder than expected. Communication across the "laboratory–hospital ward" interface can take on different forms, either as synchronous or asynchronous exchange. It is also linked to a complex array of actions involving many different groups and processes (Gorman, Lavelle, & Ash, 2003). Sometimes it is not easy to identify the right data or information needed, let alone when it is needed and by whom. Problems with communication across the hospital are often identified as a major cause of substandard quality of care. This is because the reasons for an adverse event (from a simple mishap to a more serious patient-related safety incident), are generally related to the role that communication plays in how things are planned and organised(Kuziemsky et al., 2009; Sutcliffe, Lewton, & Rosenthal, 2004).

The constitutive role that communication plays in how things are organised is illustrated by a case study of the Blood Bank. The Blood Bank provides compatible blood components for patients along with a range of tests (e.g., blood grouping, antibody screening and identification and pre-transfusion testing). Unlike other pathology laboratory departments, the Blood Bank does more than issue results; it also dispenses blood products(A. Georgiou et al., 2009). These tasks involve a large number of work processes and interrelationships across numerous professions (e.g., haematologists, laboratory scientists, physicians, nurses and technical officers). All these relationships are coordinated through the *synchronous* and coordinated exchange of vital information involving urgent patient-care situations (A. Georgiou et al., 2011).

The Blood Bank provides a valuable example of the importance of *synchronous* information to the safety and quality of care. In contrast, the Microbiology Department offers empirical evidence about *asynchronous* communication and the role that relevant patient information plays in the laboratory's processing and interpretation of test requests. A study that examined the impact of the EMR on the provision of information to the laboratory showed a significant improvement

in the provision of relevant patient information that came about from: a) the laboratory's use of the EMR to access clinically relevant information about a patient's reason for admission; and b) improvements in the volume and nature of clinical information entered by physicians into the EMR (Georgiou, Prgomet, Toouli, Callen, & Westbrook, 2011).

CONCLUSION

There are many challenges for hospital laboratory services associated with the implementation and utilisation of the EMR. As a health technology, the EMR has the potential to bring about major shifts in responsibilities, procedures and even work practices (A Georgiou, J Westbrook, & J Braithwaite, 2010). The success or otherwise of EMR implementations are contingent on the conditions and circumstances in which they are placed. The EMR has to be negotiated and refined within each social and technical setting. Frameworks, like the organisational communications framework, derived from existing empirical evidence, provide an important theoretical lens which can help health information technology designers, clinicians and hospital and laboratory professionals deal with the important challenges associated with the implementation of the EMR.

REFERENCES

Aarts, J., Ash, J., & Berg, M. (2007). Extending the understanding of computerized physician order entry: Implications for professional collaboration, workflow and quality of care. *International Journal of Medical Informatics*, 76(Supplement 1), S4–S13. doi:10.1016/j.ijmedinf.2006.05.009 PMID:16798068

Adam, B. (2004). *Time*. Cambridge, MA: Polity.

Aller, R., Georgiou, A., & Pantanowitz, L. (2012). Electronic Health Records. In L. Pantanowitz, J. M. Tuthill, & U. G. Balis (Eds.), *Pathology Informatics Theory and Practice* (pp. 217–230). Canada: American Society for Clinical Pathology.

Ash, J. S., Stavri, P. Z., Dykstra, R., & Fournier, L. (2003). Implementing Computerized Physician Order Entry: the importance of special people. *International Journal of Medical Informatics, 69*(2-3), 235–250. doi:10.1016/S1386-5056(02)00107-7 PMID:12810127

Axt-Adam, P., van der Woulden, J. C., & van der Does, E. (1993). Influencing behaviour of physicians ordering laboratory tests: a literature study. *Medical Care, 31*(9), 784–794. doi:10.1097/00005650-199309000-00003 PMID:8366680

Bates, D., Kuperman, G., Rittenberg, M., Teich, J., Fiskio, J., & Ma'luf, N. et al. (1999). A randomized trial of a computer-based intervention to reduce utilization of redundant laboratory tests. *The American Journal of Medicine, 106*(2), 144–150. doi:10.1016/S0002-9343(98)00410-0 PMID:10230742

Birkmeyer, C. M., Lee, J., Bates, D. W., & Birkmeyer, J. D. (2002). Will electronic order entry reduce health care costs? *Effective Clinical Practice, 5*(2), 67–74. PMID:11990214

Black, A., Car, J., Pagliari, C., Anandan, C., Cresswell, K., & Bokun, T. et al. (2011). The Impact of eHealth on the Quality and Safety of Health Care: A Systematic Overview. *PLoS Medicine, 8*(1). doi:10.1371/journal.pmed.1000387 PMID:21267058

Bobb, A. M., Payne, T. H., & Gross, P. A. (2007). Viewpoint: controversies surrounding use of order sets for clinical decision support in Computerized Provider Order Entry. *Journal of the American Medical Informatics Association, 14*(1), 41–47. doi:10.1197/jamia.M2184 PMID:17068352

Bonini, P., Plebani, M., Ceriotti, F., & Rubboli, F. (2002). Errors in laboratory medicine. *Clinical Chemistry, 48*(5), 691–698. PMID:11978595

Buntin, M., Burke, M., Hoaglin, M., & Blumenthal, D. (2011). The benefits of Health Information Technology: A review of the recent literature shows predominantly positive results. *Health Affairs, 30*(3), 464–471. doi:10.1377/hlthaff.2011.0178 PMID:21383365

Bygstad, B. (2010). Generative mechanisms for innovation in information infrastructures. *Information and Organization, 20*(3-4), 156–168. doi:10.1016/j.infoandorg.2010.07.001

Callen, J., Paoloni, R., Georgiou, A., Prgomet, M., & Westbrook, J. (2010). The rate of missed test results in an Emergency Department. *Methods of Information in Medicine, 49*(1), 37–43. PMID:19893851

Callen, J. L., Braithwaite, J., & Westbrook, J. I. (2008). Contextual Implementation Model: A Framework for Assisting Clinical Information System Implementations. *Journal of the American Medical Informatics Association, 15*(2), 255–262. doi:10.1197/jamia.M2468 PMID:18096917

Chaudhry, B., Wang, J., Wu, S., Maglione, M., Mojica, W., & Roth, E. et al. (2006). Systematic review: impact of health information technology on quality, efficiency, and costs of medical care. *Annals of Internal Medicine, 144*(10), 742–752. doi:10.7326/0003-4819-144-10-200605160-00125 PMID:16702590

Chen, H. (1990). *Theory-driven evaluations*. Newbury Part, California: Sage Publications.

Clegg, C., Axtell, C., Damodaran, L., Farbey, B., Hull, R., & Lloyd-Jones, R. et al. (1997). Information technology: a study of performance and the role of human and organizational factors. *Ergonomics, 40*(9), 851–871. doi:10.1080/001401397187694

Coiera, E. (2004). Four rules for the reinvention of health care. *British Medical Journal, 328*(7449), 1197–1199. doi:10.1136/bmj.328.7449.1197 PMID:15142933

Committee on Patient Safety and Health Information Technology; Institute of Medicine. (2011). *Health IT and Patient Safety: Building Safer Systems for Better Care*. Washington, DC, USA: National Academies Press.

Davidson, E. J. (2005). *Evaluation Methodology Basics*. Thousand Oaks: Sage Publications.

Deeble, J., & Lewis-Hughes, P. (1991). *Directions for pathology*. Melbourne: National Health Strategy.

Fayol, H. (1967). *General and Industrial Management*. London: Pitman.

Fernando, S., Georgiou, A., Holdgate, A., & Westbrook, J. (2009). Challenges associated with electronic ordering in the emergency department: A study of doctors' experiences. *Emergency Medicine Australasia, 21*(5), 373–378. doi:10.1111/j.1742-6723.2009.01214.x PMID:19840086

Forsman, R. W. (1996). Why is the laboratory an afterthought for managed care organizations? *Clinical Chemistry, 42*(5), 813–816. PMID:8653920

Georgiou, A., Ampt, A., Creswick, N., Westbrook, J., & Braithwaite, J. (2009). Computerized provider order entry - what are health professionals concerned about? A qualitative study in an Australian hospital. *International Journal of Medical Informatics, 78*(1), 60–70. doi:10.1016/j.ijmedinf.2008.09.007 PMID:19010728

Georgiou, A., Greenfield, T., Callen, J., & Westbrook, J. (2009). Safety and efficiency considerations for the introduction of electronic ordering in a Blood Bank. *Archives of Pathology & Laboratory Medicine, 133*(6), 933–937. PMID:19492886

Georgiou, A., Lam, M., Allardice, J., Hart, G. K., & Westbrook, J. I. (2012). Troponin testing in the emergency department: a longitudinal study to assess the impact and sustainability of decision support strategies. *Journal of Clinical Pathology, 65*(6), 546–550. doi:10.1136/jclinpath-2011-200610 PMID:22412052

Georgiou, A., Lang, S., Alvaro, F., Whittaker, G., Westbrook, J. I., & Callen, J. (2007). Pathology's front line - a comparison of the experiences of electronic ordering in the Clinical Chemistry and Haematology departments. In J. Westbrook, E. Coiera, & J. Callen (Eds.), *Information Technology in Health Care; Socio-technical approaches* (pp. 121–132). Sydney, Australia: IOS Press.

Georgiou, A., Lang, S., Rosenfeld, D., & Westbrook, J. I. (2011). The Use of Computerized Provider Order Entry to Improve the Effectiveness and Efficiency of Coagulation Testing. *Archives of Pathology & Laboratory Medicine, 135*, 495–498. PMID:21466368

Georgiou, A., Morse, W., Timmins, W., Ray, S., & Westbrook, J. I. (2008). The use of performance metrics to monitor the impact of CPOE on pathology laboratory services. In S. K. Andersen, G. O. Klein, S. Schulz, J. Aarts & M. Cristina Mazzoleni (Eds.), *eHealth Beyond the Horizon - Get IT There; Proceedings of MIE2008* (pp. 291-296). Amsterdam: IOS Press.

Georgiou, A., Prgomet, M., Paoloni, R., Creswick, N., Hordern, A., Walter, S., & Westbrook, J. (2013). The Effect of Computerized Provider Order Entry Systems on Clinical Care and Work Processes in Emergency Departments: A Systematic Review of the Quantitative Literature. *Annals of Emergency Medicine, 61*(6), 644–653. doi:10.1016/j.annemergmed.2013.01.028 PMID:23548404

Georgiou, A., Prgomet, M., Toouli, G., Callen, J., & Westbrook, J. (2011). What do physicians tell laboratories when requesting tests? A multi-method examination of information supplied to the Microbiology laboratory before and after the introduction of electronic ordering. *International Journal of Medical Informatics*, *80*(9), 646–654. doi:10.1016/j.ijmedinf.2011.06.003 PMID:21757400

Georgiou, A., Tariq, A., & Westbrook, J. I. (2013). The temporal landscape of residential aged care facilities-implications for context-sensitive health technology. In M.-C. Beuscart-Zéphir, M. W. M. Jaspers, & C. Kuziemsky (Eds.), *Context Sensitive Health Informatics: Human and Sociotechnical Approaches* (Vol. 194, pp. 69–74). Amsterdam, Netherlands: IOS Press.

Georgiou, A., Westbrook, J., & Braithwaite, J. (2010). Computerized provider order entry systems–Research imperatives and organizational challenges facing pathology services. *Journal of Pathology Informatics*, *1*, 11. doi:10.4103/2153-3539.65431 PMID:20805962

Georgiou, A., Westbrook, J., & Braithwaite, J. (2010). What effect does electronic ordering have on the organisation dynamics of a hospital pathology service?. In C. Safran, H. Marin & S. Reti (Eds.), *Partnerships for Effective eHealth Soultions 13th World Congress on Medical and Health Informatics (Medinfo 2010)* (pp. 223-227). Cape Town, South Africa: IOS Press.

Georgiou, A., Westbrook, J., Braithwaite, J., & Iedema, R. (2005). Multiple perspectives on the impact of electronic ordering on hospital organisational and communication processes. *Health Information Management Journal*, *34*(4), 130–134. PMID:18216417

Georgiou, A., & Westbrook, J. I. (2007). Computerised Physician Order Entry systems and their effect on pathology laboratories. *Hospital Information Technology Europe*, *2007*(Autumn), 40–41.

Georgiou, A., Westbrook, J. I., & Braithwaite, J. (2011). Time matters - a theoretical and empirical examination of the temporal landscape of a hospital pathology service and the impact of e-health. *Social Science & Medicine*, *72*, 1603–1610. doi:10.1016/j.socscimed.2011.03.020 PMID:21497430

Georgiou, A., Westbrook, J. I., & Braithwaite, J. (2012). An empirically-derived approach for investigating health information technology: the elementally entangled organisational communication (EEOC) framework. *BMC Medical Informatics and Decision Making*, *12*(1), 68. doi:10.1186/1472-6947-12-68 PMID:22788698

Georgiou, A., Westbrook, J. I., Braithwaite, J., Iedema, R., Ray, S., & Forsyth, R. et al. (2007). When requests become orders - A formative investigation into the impact of a Computerized Physician Order Entry system on a pathology laboratory service. *International Journal of Medical Informatics*, *76*(8), 583–591. doi:10.1016/j.ijmedinf.2006.04.002 PMID:16702022

Georgiou, A., Westbrook, J. I., Callen, J. L., & Braithwaite, J. (2008). Electronic test management systems and hospital pathology laboratory services. In N. Wickramasinghe, & E. Geisler (Eds.), *Encyclopaedia of Healthcare Information Systems* (Vol. II, pp. 505–512). Hershey, PA: Medical Information Science Reference. doi:10.4018/978-1-59904-889-5.ch064

Georgiou, A., Williamson, M., Westbrook, J., & Ray, S. (2007). The impact of computerised physician order entry systems on pathology services: a systematic review. *International Journal of Medical Informatics*, *76*(7), 514–529. doi:10.1016/j.ijmedinf.2006.02.004 PMID:16567121

Giddens, A. (1990). *The consequences of modernity*. Stanford, CA: Stanford University Press.

Gorman, P. N., Lavelle, M. B., & Ash, J. S. (2003). Order creation and communication in healthcare. *Methods of Information in Medicine*, *42*(4), 376–384. PMID:14534637

Greenhalgh, T., & Russell, J. (2010). Why Do Evaluations of eHealth Programs Fail? An Alternative Set of Guiding Principles. *PLoS Medicine*, *7*(11), e1000360. doi:10.1371/journal.pmed.1000360 PMID:21072245

Hawkins, R. C. (2007). Laboratory turnaround time. *The Clinical Biochemist. Reviews / Australian Association of Clinical Biochemists*, *28*, 179–194. PMID:18392122

Jones, S. S., Rudin, R. S., Perry, T., & Shekelle, P. G. (2014). Health Information Technology: An Updated Systematic Review With a Focus on Meaningful Use. *Annals of Internal Medicine*, *160*(1), 48–54. doi:10.7326/M13-1531 PMID:24573664

Kuziemsky, C., Borycki, E., Purkis, M., Black, F., Boyle, M., & Cloutier-Fisher, D. et al. (2009). An interdisciplinary team communication framework and its application to healthcare 'e-teams' systems design. *BMC Medical Informatics and Decision Making*, *9*(1), 43. doi:10.1186/1472-6947-9-43 PMID:19754966

Legg, M., & Cheong, I. (2004). *A Study of the Impact of the Use of General Practice Computer Systems on the Ordering of Pathology*. Retrieved from http://www.nhhrc.org.au/internet/main/publishing.nsf/Content/qupp-qupp-reports.htm

Mekhjian, H. S., Kumar, R. R., Kuehn, L., Bentley, T. D., Teater, P., & Thomas, A. et al. (2002). Immediate benefits realized following implementation of physician order entry at an academic medical center. *Journal of the American Medical Informatics Association*, *9*(5), 529–539. doi:10.1197/jamia.M1038 PMID:12223505

Menou, M. J., & Taylor, R. D. (2006). A "grand challenge": Measuring information societies. *The Information Society*, *22*(5), 261–267. doi:10.1080/01972240600903904

National Coalition of Public Pathology. (2012). *Encouraging Quality Pathology Ordering in Australia's Public Hospitals*. National Coalition of Public Pathology.

Organisation for Economic Co-operation Development. (2011). *OECD Guide to Measuring the Information Society 2011*. OECD.

Overhage, J. M., Tierney, W. M., Zhou, X.-H., & McDonald, C. J. (1997). A randomized trial of "corollary orders" to prevent errors of omission. *Journal of the American Medical Informatics Association*, *4*(5), 364–375. doi:10.1136/jamia.1997.0040364 PMID:9292842

Pantanowitz, L., Henricks, W. H., & Beckwith, B. A. (2007). Medical laboratory informatics. *Clinics in Laboratory Medicine*, *27*(4), 823–843. doi:10.1016/j.cll.2007.07.011 PMID:17950900

Peute, L., Aarts, J., Bakker, P., & Jaspers, M. (2009). Anatomy of a failure: A sociotechnical evaluation of a laboratory physician order entry system implementation. *International Journal of Medical Informatics*. PMID:19640778

Peute, L. W. P., & Jaspers, M. W. M. (2007). The significance of a usability evaluation of an emerging laboratory order entry system. *International Journal of Medical Informatics*, *76*(2-3), 157–168. doi:10.1016/j.ijmedinf.2006.06.003 PMID:16854617

Poole, M. S. (2004). Central Issues in the study of change and innovation. In M. Poole, & A. Van de Ven (Eds.), *Handbook of Organizational Change and Innovation* (pp. 3–31). New York: Oxford University Press.

Price, C. P. (2003). Application of the principles of evidence-based medicine to laboratory medicine. *Clinica Chimica Acta, 333*(2), 147–154. doi:10.1016/S0009-8981(03)00179-7 PMID:12849898

Putnam, L., Nicotera, A., & McPhee, R. (2009). Introduction - Communication Constitutes Organization. In L. Putnam, & A. Nicotera (Eds.), *Building Theories of Organization - The Consitutive Role of Communication* (p. 222). New York: Routledge.

Sackett, D. L., Rosenberg, W. M., Gray, J. A., Haynes, R. B., & Richardson, W. S. (1996). Evidence based medicine: what it is and what it isn't. *British Medical Journal, 312*(7023), 71–72. doi:10.1136/bmj.312.7023.71 PMID:8555924

Scriven, M. (1991). *Evaluation Thesaurus* (4th ed.). Newbury, CA: Sage.

Sutcliffe, K. M., Lewton, E., & Rosenthal, M. M. (2004). Communication failures: an insidious contributor to medical mishaps. *Academic Medicine, 79*(2), 186. doi:10.1097/00001888-200402000-00019 PMID:14744724

The World Alliance For Patient Safety Drafting Group. (2009). Towards an International Classification for Patient Safety: the conceptual framework. *International Journal for Quality in Health Care, 21*(1), 2–8. doi:10.1093/intqhc/mzn054 PMID:19147595

van Walraven, C., & Raymond, M. (2003). Population-based study of repeat laboratory testing. *Clinical Chemistry, 49*(12), 1997–2005. doi:10.1373/clinchem.2003.021220 PMID:14633870

Wajcman, J. (2008). Life in the fast lane? Towards a sociology of technology and time. *The British Journal of Sociology, 59*(1), 59–77. doi:10.1111/j.1468-4446.2007.00182.x PMID:18321331

Westbrook, J. I., Braithwaite, J., Georgiou, A., Ampt, A., Creswick, N., Coiera, E., & Iedema, R. (2007). Multimethod evaluation of information and communication technologies in health in the context of wicked problems and sociotechnical theory. *Journal of the American Medical Informatics Association, 14*(6), 746–755. doi:10.1197/jamia.M2462 PMID:17712083

Westbrook, J. I., Georgiou, A., Dimos, A., & Germanos, T. (2006). Computerised pathology test order-entry reduces laboratory turnaround times and influences tests ordered by hospital clinicians: a controlled before and after study. *Journal of Clinical Pathology, 59*(May), 533–536. doi:10.1136/jcp.2005.029983 PMID:16461564

Westbrook, J. I., Georgiou, A., & Lam, M. (2009). Does computerised provider order entry reduce test turnaround times? A before-and-after study at four hospitals. In K.-P. Adlassnig, B. Blobel, J. Mantas, & I. Masic (Eds.), *Medical informatics in a united and healthy Europe: proceedings of MIE 2009* (pp. 527–531). Amsterdam: IOS Press.

Westbrook, J. I., Georgiou, A., & Rob, M. (2009). Test turnaround times and mortality rates 12 and 24 months after the introduction of a computerised provider order entry system. *Methods of Information in Medicine, 48*, 211–215. PMID:19283321

Westbrook, J. I., Georgiou, A., & Rob, M. I. (2008). Computerised order entry systems: sustained impact on laboratory efficiency and mortality rates?. In S. Andersen, G. Klein, S. Schulz, J. Aarts & M. Mazzoleni (Eds.), *eHealth Beyond the Horizon Get IT There; Proceedings of MIE 2008 IOS Press Amsterdam* (pp. 345-350). Goteborg, Sweden: IOS Press.

Whetton, S., & Georgiou, A. (2010). Conceptual challenges for advancing the socio-technical underpinnings of health informatics. *The Open Medical Informatics Journal*, *4*, 221. doi:10.2174/1874325001004010221 PMID:21594009

ADDITIONAL READING

Aller, R., Georgiou, A., & Pantanowitz, L. (2012). Electronic Health Records. In L. Pantanowitz, J. M. Tuthill, & U. G. Balis (Eds.), *Pathology Informatics Theory and Practice* (pp. 217–230). Canada: American Society for Clinical Pathology.

Ash, J. S., Berg, M., & Coiera, E. (2004). Some unintended consequences of information technology in health care: the nature of patient care information system-related errors. *Journal of the American Medical Informatics Association*, *11*(2), 104–112. doi:10.1197/jamia.M1471 PMID:14633936

Barley, S. (1988). On technology, time, and social order: technically induced change in the temporal organization of radiological work. In F. Dubinskas (Ed.), *Making time: ethnographies of high-technology organizations* (pp. 123–169). Philadelphia: Temple University Press.

Bates, D. W., Boyle, D. L., Rittenberg, E., & Kuperman, G. J., Ma'Luf, N., Menkin, V., . . . Tanasijevic, M. J. (1998). What proportion of common diagnostic tests appear redundant? *The American Journal of Medicine*, *104*(4), 361–368. doi:10.1016/S0002-9343(98)00063-1 PMID:9576410

Berg, M. (2001). Implementing information systems in health care organizations: myths and challenges. *International Journal of Medical Informatics*, *64*(2-3), 143–156. doi:10.1016/S1386-5056(01)00200-3 PMID:11734382

Berg, M., Aarts, J., & van der Lei, J. (2003). ICT in health care: sociotechnical approaches. *Methods of Information in Medicine*, *42*(4), 297–301. PMID:14534625

Callen, J. L., Braithwaite, J., & Westbrook, J. I. (2008). Contextual Implementation Model: A Framework for Assisting Clinical Information System Implementations. *Journal of the American Medical Informatics Association*, *15*(2), 255–262. doi:10.1197/jamia.M2468 PMID:18096917

Coiera, E. (2003). *Guide to Health Informatics* (2nd ed.). London: Oxford University Press. doi:10.1201/b13618

Coiera, E. (2004). Four rules for the reinvention of health care. *British Medical Journal*, *328*(7449), 1197–1199. doi:10.1136/bmj.328.7449.1197 PMID:15142933

Connelly, D., & Aller, R. (1997). Outcomes and informatics. *Archives of Pathology & Laboratory Medicine*, *121*(11), 1176–1182. PMID:9372745

Dighe, A. S., Soderberg, B. L., & Laposata, M. (2001). Narrative interpretations for clinical laboratory evaluations: an overview. *American Journal of Clinical Pathology*, *116*(8), S123–S128. PMID:11993697

Friedman, B. A., & Mitchell, W. (1991). Using the laboratory information system to achieve strategic advantage over the competitors of hospital-based clinical laboratories. *Clinics in Laboratory Medicine*, *11*(1), 187–202. PMID:2040141

Friedman, C. P. (2013). What informatics is and isn't. *Journal of the American Medical Informatics Association*, *20*(2), 224–226. doi:10.1136/amiajnl-2012-001206 PMID:23059730

Georgiou, A. (2001). Health informatics and evidence based medicine - more than a marriage of convenience? *Health Informatics Journal*, *7*(3-4), 127–130. doi:10.1177/146045820100700303

Georgiou, A. (2002). Data information and knowledge: the health informatics model and its role in evidence-based medicine. *Journal of Evaluation in Clinical Practice*, *8*(2), 127–130. doi:10.1046/j.1365-2753.2002.00345.x PMID:12180361

Georgiou, A., Ampt, A., Creswick, N., Westbrook, J., & Braithwaite, J. (2009). Computerized provider order entry - what are health professionals concerned about? A qualitative study in an Australian hospital. *International Journal of Medical Informatics*, *78*(1), 60–70. doi:10.1016/j.ijmedinf.2008.09.007 PMID:19010728

Georgiou, A., Callen, J., Westbrook, J., Prgomet, M., & Toouli, G. (2007). Information and communication processes in the microbiology laboratory - implications for Computerised Provider Order Entry. In K. Kuhn, J. Warren & L. Tze-Yun (Eds.), *12th World Congress on Health (Medical) Informatics Medinfo 2007* (Vol. 2, pp. 943-947). Amsterdam: IOS Press.

Georgiou, A., Greenfield, T., Callen, J., & Westbrook, J. (2009). Safety and efficiency considerations for the introduction of electronic ordering in a Blood Bank. *Archives of Pathology & Laboratory Medicine*, *133*(6), 933–937. PMID:19492886

Georgiou, A., Lam, M., Allardice, J., Hart, G. K., & Westbrook, J. I. (2012). Troponin testing in the emergency department: a longitudinal study to assess the impact and sustainability of decision support strategies. *Journal of Clinical Pathology*, *65*(6), 546–550. doi:10.1136/jclinpath-2011-200610 PMID:22412052

Georgiou, A., Lang, S., Rosenfeld, D., & Westbrook, J. I. (2011). The Use of Computerized Provider Order Entry to Improve the Effectiveness and Efficiency of Coagulation Testing. *Archives of Pathology & Laboratory Medicine*, *135*, 495–498. PMID:21466368

Georgiou, A., Prgomet, M., Paoloni, R., Creswick, N., Hordern, A., Walter, S., & Westbrook, J. (2013). The Effect of Computerized Provider Order Entry Systems on Clinical Care and Work Processes in Emergency Departments: A Systematic Review of the Quantitative Literature. *Annals of Emergency Medicine*, *61*(6), 644–653. doi:10.1016/j.annemergmed.2013.01.028 PMID:23548404

Georgiou, A., Westbrook, J., & Braithwaite, J. (2010). Computerized provider order entry systems–Research imperatives and organizational challenges facing pathology services. *Journal of Pathology Informatics*, *1*, 11. doi:10.4103/2153-3539.65431 PMID:20805962

Georgiou, A., Westbrook, J. I., & Braithwaite, J. (2011). Time matters - a theoretical and empirical examination of the temporal landscape of a hospital pathology service and the impact of e-health. *Social Science & Medicine*, *72*, 1603–1610. doi:10.1016/j.socscimed.2011.03.020 PMID:21497430

Georgiou, A., Westbrook, J. I., & Braithwaite, J. (2012). An empirically-derived approach for investigating Health Information Technology: the Elementally Entangled Organisational Communication (EEOC) framework. *BMC Medical Informatics and Decision Making*, *12*(1), 68. doi:10.1186/1472-6947-12-68 PMID:22788698

Georgiou, A., Westbrook, J. I., Braithwaite, J., Iedema, R., Ray, S., & Forsyth, R. et al. (2007). When requests become orders - A formative investigation into the impact of a Computerized Physician Order Entry system on a pathology laboratory service. *International Journal of Medical Informatics*, *76*(8), 583–591. doi:10.1016/j.ijmedinf.2006.04.002 PMID:16702022

Georgiou, A., Williamson, M., Westbrook, J., & Ray, S. (2007). The impact of computerised physician order entry systems on pathology services: a systematic review. *International Journal of Medical Informatics*, *76*(7), 514–529. doi:10.1016/j.ijmedinf.2006.02.004 PMID:16567121

Kim, J. Y., Kamis, I. K., Singh, B., Batra, S., Dixon, R. H., & Dighe, A. S. (2011). Implementation of computerized add-on testing for hospitalized patients in a large academic medical center. *Clinical Chemistry and Laboratory Medicine*, *49*(5), 845–850. doi:10.1515/CCLM.2011.140 PMID:21303296

Kuperman, G. J., Teich, J. M., Gandhi, T. K., & Bates, D. W. (2001). Patient safety and computerized medication ordering at Brigham and Women's Hospital. *Joint Commission Journal on Quality and Safety*, *27*(10), 509–521. PMID:11593885

Leonardi, P. M., & Barley, S. R. (2008). Materiality and change: Challenges to building better theory about technology and organizing. *Information and Organization*, *18*(3), 159–176. doi:10.1016/j.infoandorg.2008.03.001

Pantanowitz, L., Henricks, W. H., & Beckwith, B. A. (2007). Medical laboratory informatics. *Clinics in Laboratory Medicine*, *27*(4), 823–843. doi:10.1016/j.cll.2007.07.011 PMID:17950900

Pantanowitz, L., Tuthill, J. M., & Balis, U. G. (Eds.). (2012). *Pathology Informatics - Theory & Practice*. Canada: American Society for Clinical Pathology.

Peute, L., Aarts, J., Bakker, P., & Jaspers, M. (2009). Anatomy of a failure: A sociotechnical evaluation of a laboratory physician order entry system implementation. *International Journal of Medical Informatics*. PMID:19640778

Peute, L. W. P., & Jaspers, M. W. M. (2007). The significance of a usability evaluation of an emerging laboratory order entry system. *International Journal of Medical Informatics*, *76*(2-3), 157–168. doi:10.1016/j.ijmedinf.2006.06.003 PMID:16854617

Putnam, L., Nicotera, A., & McPhee, R. (2009). Introduction - Communication Constitutes Organization. In L. Putnam, & A. Nicotera (Eds.), *Building Theories of Organization - The Consitutive Role of Communication* (p. 222). New York: Routledge.

Putnam, L., & Pacanowsky, M. E. (1983). *Communication and organizations, an interpretive approach* (Vol. 65). Sage Publications, Inc.

Westbrook, J. I., Georgiou, A., Dimos, A., & Germanos, T. (2006). Computerised pathology test order-entry reduces laboratory turnaround times and influences tests ordered by hospital clinicians: a controlled before and after study. *Journal of Clinical Pathology*, *59*(May), 533–536. doi:10.1136/jcp.2005.029983 PMID:16461564

Westbrook, J. I., Georgiou, A., & Lam, M. (2009). Does computerised provider order entry reduce test turnaround times? A before-and-after study at four hospitals. In K.-P. Adlassnig, B. Blobel, J. Mantas, & I. Masic (Eds.), *Medical informatics in a united and healthy Europe: proceedings of MIE 2009* (pp. 527–531). Amsterdam: IOS Press.

Westbrook, J. I., Georgiou, A., & Rob, M. I. (2008). Computerised order entry systems: sustained impact on laboratory efficiency and mortality rates?. In S. Andersen, G. Klein, S. Schulz, J. Aarts & M. Mazzoleni (Eds.), *eHealth Beyond the Horizon Get IT There; Proceedings of MIE 2008 IOS Press Amsterdam* (pp. 345-350). Goteborg, Sweden: IOS Press.

Whetton, S., & Georgiou, A. (2010). Conceptual challenges for advancing the socio-technical underpinnings of health informatics. *The Open Medical Informatics Journal*, *4*, 221. doi:10.2174/1874325001004010221 PMID:21594009

KEY TERMS AND DEFINITIONS

Commercial System: System software purchased from a software developer (also referred to as an "off-the-shelf" system).

Computerised Provider Order Entry: Computer systems that allow physicians (or other authorised staff) to electronically issue orders, e.g., laboratory tests, medical imaging, diets, medications.

Electronic Decision Support System: Electronically-stored knowledge which can be used to aid health care decisions.

Electronic Medical Record (EMR): Computerised medical record which is found in an organisation that provides health care. The EMR encompasses tasks related to the storage, retrieval and modification of record.

Evaluation: To determine the merit, worth, or value of something, or the product of that process (Scriven, 1991).

Home-Grown System: Systems developed within the hospital or clinical setting in which they are used.

Impact: Change or (sometimes) lack of change caused by an evaluand (that which is being evaluated). Can also mean outcome or effect (Davidson, 2005).

Organisational Communication: A theoretical perspective which emphasises the essential (constitutive) role that communication processes play in the makeup of an organisation (Putnam et al., 2009).

Test Appropriateness: While there are many pathology tests that are conducted repeatedly in order to monitor a condition or treatment, when a repeat test is ordered within a brief time frame there is a high likelihood that it will be redundant and provide no additional information (National Coalition of Public Pathology, 2012; van Walraven & Raymond, 2003).

Turnaround Times (TAT): Can be defined as the time of physician order request to when the physician views the result (Total TAT), or the time a request and accompanying specimen arrive at the laboratory, to the time a result is dispatched (Laboratory TAT)(A Georgiou, M Williamson, et al., 2007; Hawkins, 2007).

Chapter 4
Overview of Requirements and Future Perspectives on Current Laboratory Information Management Systems

Viroj Wiwanitkit
Hainan Medical University, China & University of Nis, Serbia

ABSTRACT

The chapter argues that a Laboratory Information Management System (LIMS) is the application of computational technology in laboratory medicine. This is an advanced technology that can support the general work in medical laboratories. The LIMS can also be useful in all steps of the laboratory cycle (pre-, intra-, and post-analytical phases). There are many LIMSs at present, and those LIMSs are used worldwide. The present concern is on the standardization of the existing system. In this context, international collaboration to set the standards is required. In addition, the multidisciplinary approach to add up the advantage and application of the technology is promising. With the more advanced computational and wireless information technology, the next step of LIMS will be big wireless LIMS networks that extend from medical laboratories and wards within the hospital to outside units as well as patient homes. The point-of-care LIMSs are the actual future perspectives.

INTRODUCTION

"Information" is an important thing in scientific work. In biomedical work, there is information, which is considered as important data for diagnosis and treatment of the patients. In laboratory medicine, the information also exists and becomes an important concern. By definition, laboratory medicine deals with any steps and aspects of

medical laboratory. This includes both intra- and extra- medical laboratory processes. The laboratory information means any data that exist within the intra- and extra- medical laboratory processes. For the specific medical laboratory, the laboratory information is called "medical laboratory information". Those data can be the direct laboratory analytical information or indirectly related information.

DOI: 10.4018/978-1-4666-6320-6.ch004

As already mentioned, the medical laboratory information can be generated in any step, directly and indirectly related to the analysis, hence, there is a heap of data in routine medical laboratory work. It can be seen that the medical laboratory information is an important thing in medical laboratory service activity. Hence, the management of medical laboratory information has a direct interrelationship with the medical laboratory management process (Wiwanitkit, 2000).

To help the reader better understand the medical laboratory information and the interrelation with the laboratory cycle, the author will hereby describe the details for each step. First, the medical laboratory information in pre-analytical phase means any medical laboratory information that is generated within the pre-analytical phase of the laboratory cycle. The good examples include patient identification data (name, surname, hospital number, age, diagnosis, financial information, laboratory request, etc.) Second, the medical laboratory information in the analytical phase means any medical laboratory information that is generated within the analytical phase of the laboratory cycle. The good examples include laboratory results (either qualitative or quantitative ones), quality control data (either internal or external controls), picture from microscopic examination, etc. Third, the medical laboratory information in post-analytical phase means any medical laboratory information that is generated within the post-analytical phase of the laboratory cycle. The good examples include laboratory reports, notification, etc. Hence, when one would like to manage the medical laboratory information, one must focus on all phases within the laboratory cycle.

In the medical laboratory, there are several data. Those data can be easily classified into three groups: a) textual data (examples: patient name and surname, laboratory request, pathological description, seroreaction result) b) numeric data (examples: hospital number, laboratory number, laboratory price, biochemistry analytical results values) and c) figure data (usually from micro-scopic examination such as blood smear picture, the histological picture). It can be seen that these data are considered as primary data, which means these data are directly generated within the process of laboratory analysis, from patient requesting to interpretation of the laboratory result. To properly manage these data is very important. The good practice is required for data acquisition, recording, reporting and storage. First, data acquisition is the first step of the process. The examples are acquisition of laboratory request form from a medical ward, acquisition of payment slip of laboratory charge, etc. Second, data recording means the process of creating data within the laboratory. This covers the generations of the barcodes for laboratory investigation, recording of results from the analysis of the specimen, recording of the quality control result, etc. Third, reporting is the next step of the process. This is an important process transferring the data from the laboratory to the ward. A good example is the reporting of the result via the laboratory result report form. Fourth, the final step is the storage. This step is the backing up of the data for tracing back and future referencing. This is a very important but usually forgotten step. Without data storage, the accountability of the laboratory cannot be done, and this means no quality due to non-traceability or no transparency.

BACKGROUND

There are many kinds of information within medical laboratory. Both direct and indirect information can be seen in routine daily medical laboratory work (Table 1). There is no doubt that the medical laboratory has to put great effort to effectively manage the information. To manage the information in the medical laboratory is usually an important issue to be discussed in laboratory medicine. Successful management of information in medical laboratory means a) effectively receiving information from the outside laboratory, b) effectively providing

Table 1. Examples of medical laboratory information

Types of Information	Intra-Laboratory	Extra-Laboratory
Direct information Indirect information	Laboratory result, Quality control data Patient identification	Laboratory request record Patient identification, financial data

information to outside laboratory, c) systematic recording of the information, d) effectively, on - time and correct, circulating of information e) allowing rechecking of past information and e) keeping information secret. To reach these aims, there must be a good system. Several ways are proposed for successfully managing the medical laboratory information. A classical way proposed by the College of American Pathology (1965) is the implementation of good quality control and assigning specific medical personnel to monitor and manage the information. This method was widely used in the past, and it can still be seen in some medical laboratory at present. However, this method was challenged by the introduction of the new electronic – computational system for management of medical laboratory information (Scalfani and Ramkissoon, 1983). In fact, the new method can give be faster with less possibility for error. However, it requires higher cost for implementation. Scalfani and Ramkissoon (1981) noted that it required at least four years to recover the cost for implementation of the new technology. In addition, some experts such as Friedman (1989) mentioned the need for highly educated medical laboratory personnel for using the new computational system. Therefore, some laboratories still do not use the new system. However, other experts mentioned for the opposite idea. For example, Ariotti et al. (1986) mentioned that computationally based technology, if it was a simple one, could be usable without the need of special training. In the author's idea, a good system seems to be using an information

management system. The main reason is due to the ability of computers to decrease the problem of human error, which is a common problem that can lead to a serious problem in laboratory medicine (Wiwanitkit, 2001). To adjust details of specifications of the computations to fit with user in each setting is not a problem and can be simply done with health information technology specialist (McDonald et al., 1985).

At present, to manage medical laboratory information by applying an information management system is widely used in medical laboratory. The use of the laboratory information management system can be a useful tool for dealing with increased laboratory information in the present day. The system becomes a basic apparatus in medical laboratory. The topic that should concern on the use of the system in the present day is the "quality" of using. Due to the increased volume of usage, the standardization of the system is required. Also, continuous improvement of the system or more advanced systems is needed. These topics are rarely mentioned in the literature. The implementation of the new technology does not mean reducing the role of medical laboratory personnel. However, the medical laboratory and its personnel have to modify their role to correspond to the rapidly changing medical laboratory technology (Friedman and Mitchell, 1992). In the present chapter, the author hereby briefly summarizes and discusses the requirements and future perspectives of the laboratory information management system (LIMS). The controversies and existing problems of the presently available LIMS will be discussed, and the possible solutions will be recommended. Finally, the expected future direction of LIMS will be mentioned.

Issues, Controversies, Problems

Since the data storage is very important step, the author will hereby further discuss in depth this step. There are many methods for data storage. In the classical way, the human registration system is used. In the past, the hand writing in the record book was done. But this is usually time consuming and the problem of poor handwriting can be expected. When more advanced technique of typing is available, the use of typing for data storage is done. And when the most advanced technique, computational technique is available, the use of computer to help storage of the information. At present, information can be kept or stored in hard disks, floppy disks, removal disks or on the Internet. There is no doubt that the computational technology is a necessary tool for management of medical laboratory information at present. Focusing on its usefulness, using computational technology can help a) reduction of the workforce requirement b) shorten the required turnaround time, c) reduction of the unnecessary process or consolidation of the workflow, d) increase the effectiveness of the activity and e) reduce the pitfall or error in the process (especially the problem due to human beings). As already mentioned, there is a lot of information within the medical laboratory cycle. To manage data requires good management. The management can be done by several ways (Wiwanitkit, 2000; Wiwanitkit, 2011). As previously discussed, the classical management by human being is widely used. This technique makes use of laboratory staff to take the responsibility for the laboratory management process. This might be low cost in terms of the requirement of no additional tool. However, it is time consuming and not effective. The human error can be expected, and this can be a big problem in the era of decreased doctor and patient relationship. The alternative use of computer management should be considered. This is the application of computational technology for the management of medical laboratory information. The process can be fast and can save the human workforce and materials. It requires no space for data storage. The computational approach for medical laboratory management is the good example of using computer technology for medical purposes (Agthong and Wiwanitkit, 1998; McDowall, 1993;

Nararuk, 1998; Wiwanitkit, 2000; Wiwanitkit, 2011). LIMS is the application of computational technology in laboratory medicine. This is an advanced technology that can support the general work in a medical laboratory. Also, the LIMS can also be useful in all steps of the laboratory cycle (pre-, intra- and post- analytical phases). LIMS is the use of a connection to a networking system to manage the information within the medical laboratory.

This system has been introduced for a half century. It was firstly mentioned in the era of pioneering development of computer. The first attempt was tested in USA. The concurrent development of intranet and internet make the development of LIMS faster. The "network" is the core concept of the LIMS. The details of the network will be hereby discussed. Network is a term in computer science implying using a computational technique. The examples of networks are intranet and internet. The connection in the past required wire connection, but it is already wireless in the present day. Wireless LIMS is presently available and becomes the exact advancement in laboratory medicine. Focusing on the network, the basic parts include a) server, b) client and c) linkage. First, the server is the main computer acting as a center for control of the communication within the network system. It requires experienced personnel to be on duty for control of the communication. Second, client is the computer that acts as the member of the network system. The client can communicate with the server and under supervision or suggestion by the server. Also, there can be many clients and those clients can communicate. Third, the linkage is an important part. Without a linkage, the communication or traffic cannot occur. The linkage is the way to bridge between service and client, as well as client and client. As already mentioned, bridging can make use of wire or wireless technology.

For the medical laboratory, LIMS follows the basic concept of computer network. There are some specific features of LIMS:

1. The whole system is a kind of computer network.
2. The server is required. There must be a computer assigned to be the server of the LIMS.
3. The linkage is required and can be either wire or wireless connection. At first, the intra-laboratory communication usually uses the wire connection. This aims at communication on internal laboratory analytical process. For the extra-laboratory communication, the wire system can be used if the wire route is available within the hospital setting. However, the use of the wireless system can better serve the communication to the remote area that the wire track cannot reach. The wireless linkage is developed after the wire linkage. A useful application of the wireless linkage is the application to the point of care testing system.
4. The client is required. There must be computer(s) acting as a member to the network. Generally, the client is usually placed at each work station within the medical laboratory.
5. The connection can be between computers or between computers and medical laboratory analyzers. The advanced signal modification technique is required in the later category to help transfer the data between the computer and the medical laboratory analyzer.
6. There can also be specially designed software to help manipulate the communication within the LIMS.
7. The backing up and storage system is still required. This must be assigned in any LIMS network.
8. The LIMS can connect with other networks. The basic connection is the connection between LIMS and hospital information management system (HIS).

Table 2. Comparison between manual and computational assisted concepts for medical information management

Aspects	Manual Concept	Computational Assisted Concept
Workforce Turnaround time Material cost Simplicity Error	Requires high workforce Time consuming Requires material cost for regular running of the system (such as paper, etc.) Very simple Human error is very common	Requires low workforce Not time consuming Requires material cost for the first implementation of the computation system Requires knowledge on computer science Error can be reduced by computer

Since LIMS is widely used at present, hence, there is no doubt that the knowledge on LIMS is the basic requirement for any personnel working in the field of laboratory medicine. One cannot refute the computational application for helping facilitate the routine work. Not only the LIMS but also the other network systems such as HIS are widely used, and it is a requirement of the practitioner to update the knowledge on these new advents. As a conclusion, "computer information technology is widely used technology in the present day. A laboratory information management system is an application of this technology used in medicine. Based on the concepts of network and database, the system is very useful in every phase of laboratory process (Wiwanitkit, 2000)."

There are many LIMSs at present, and those LIMSs are used worldwide (Agthong and Wiwanitkit, 1998; McDowall, 1993; Nararuk, 1998; Wiwanitkit, 2000; Wiwanitkit, 2011). Those LIMS systems require a good computational database and IT for success in operation. The database is the basic computational application for data storage. The database has been continuously developed since the introduction of computer. The main aim of the database is the storage of data. The database is the databank. There are many softwares for manipulating databases. The software can be applied in the network for functioning as data storage part. Focusing on IT, the application of new technology helps develop both "Local Area Network (LAN)" within the unit and "Wide Area Network (WAN)" among different units. The successful data management requires both effective database and IT parts. As previously mentioned, data is important in medical laboratory activity. In the past, when there is no computational assisted approach, the management of information is usually time consuming and at risk for error. Using the database and IT techniques in the present day is the solution of those problems. Considering the workflow of the laboratory, the computer, can help in each step. First, the physician can request the laboratory via the HIS and the requested information will be further transferred into the LIS. When the laboratory gets the information from LIS, further process on barcode generation and preparation for specimen collection can be done. The computer can also help identify the patient and collected sample. At the same period, the computer can help communicate with the financial unit for dealing with laboratory charge and payment. After the pre-analytical step, the computer can take part in the laboratory analysis. The computer can help distribute the collected specimen to correct work stations. Then the analysis of specimen starts and the results are derived. At the same time, the computer can help quality control and validation of the laboratory results. The approved results will be computationally modified and transferred from the laboratory analyzer to LIMS. Then the final process of laboratory reporting can be done. The back transferring of laboratory results from LIMS to HIS to reach the physician for interpretation and using is the final step. The final results can be printed out from the system and backed up into the storage database at the same time. The control of the whole process can be done by using

passwords for safety protection, and stratification of the corresponding person can also be applied.

Nevertheless, there are some aspects of the LIMS to be mentioned. Those aspects are existed problems for using LIMS in the present day. First, the security of the system must be considered. Although the security system of the LIMS can be available, the problem of security can be expected (Gostin et al., 1995; Ulirsch et al., 1990). Ulirsch et al. (1990) noted that there are many etiologies of harmfulness or non-safety for the LIMS. Ulirsch et al. (1990) argued "various forces may act to compromise this information including (1) accidents, such as fire, floods, or earthquakes; (2) human error; and (3) deliberate acts, such as sabotage or theft of information." Ulirsch et al.(1990) concluded that "to safeguard against the potential catastrophic loss of information, a formal information resource management policy must be adopted within the clinical laboratory and directed by a specific individual, under the guidance of the director of pathology ." The concern of the privacy must be kept in the first rank in priorities setting (Gostin et al., 1995; Ulirsch et al., 1990). Iversen et al. (1995) said that "complex aspects of security, privacy, effectiveness, and user friendliness" must be considered in the implementation of the system. In USA, the security and privacy of health information are seriously considered. "The Health Insurance Portability and Accountability Act (HIPAA)" has already been proposed (Boothe, 2000). This specific Act covers "substantial handling of health information by establishing national standards for electronic transactions, data privacy, and data security (Boothe, 2000)". The first standards according to this Act were first published August 17, 2000, and the next version was launched on Winter 2000 (Boothe, 2000). Boothe (2000) noted "implementation of data security and data privacy provisions will bring sweeping changes to laboratory service providers." Based on the mentioned standards, the protection of health information including medical laboratory information is improved (DeMuro et al., 2001). Nulan (2001) concluded that HIPAA is "a real world perspective." To meet the requirement, the focus on the standards for security of the system is an important key point.

The second concern is on "error". In fact, error is totally unwanted event in medicine but it is commonly found. The error is totally unwanted episode and can result in many adverse events (in the worst case; it can result in patient's death). In laboratory medicine, the error is also common and can be problematic. According to the study of Wiwanitkit (2001)], the high rate of error can still be seen despite the laboratory has already been accredited. The common error is usually related to the human cause and exists in the pre-analytical phase (Wiwanitkit, 2001). As already mentioned, the application of LIMS can help reduce the error within the process. This is due to the reduction of the manual work and all things are controlled by a single computer. However, it should be noted that the error can still be expected in case there is still a part that has to be done manually. In some settings where there is no complete total computational process, manual work might be seen in the sample request or registration or manual gathering of results from the laboratory analyzer for further reporting and the error can still be detected. McDowall (1988) discussed on how to maximize the benefits of a LIMS and mentioned for system integration with the analytical instrumentation in the laboratory. McDowall (1988) concluded "this provides on-line data capture or transfer of results for matching with the corresponding sample records held within the database, which reduces transcription error checking and ensures data integrity." As already noted, the application of computational technology can help decrease error [13 – 16] (Dito et al., 1992; Hammaod, 1993; McDowall, 1988; Tilzer and Jones, 1988). A good example is the transferring tool for modification results from the laboratory analyzer into the format that can be carried by the LIMS (McDowall, 1988). Hammond et al. (1993)

noted that "a data hub that makes it feasible to use one instrument interface line from the LIS to acquire data from instruments" can be the solution to reduce the error during transferring of data derived from the laboratory analyzer to the result reporting section. Without such a hub, the error can still be detectable despite there is the LIMS in other parts (Wang and Ho, 2004). Wang and Ho (2004) concluded "a direct interface of the instruments to the laboratory information system showed that it had favorable effects on reducing laboratory errors." The other example is the use of the computational barcode for reducing the error in specimen collection (Tilzer and Jones, 1988). Tilzer and Jones (1988) argued "the incorporation of this technology into laboratory information systems offers a streamlining of specimen workflow never before achievable in a laboratory environment." Dito et al. (1992) mentioned that implementing the barcode system was cost effective since it could help personnel savings. In addition, Dito et al. (1992) proposed "hardware costs should be recovered in 2 years." A similar report by Sivic et al. (2009) also reported a similar conclusion. Sivic et al. (2009) studied the result from implementing of a LIMS in a clinical setting and found "shorter time in treatment of patients by 7%, reduced consumption of essential medicines by 8%, costs of treatment in medical facilities are down by 5%." Sivic et al. (2009) concluded "substantial savings in radio and laboratory diagnostics procedures have been achieved by reducing time for doing lab reports, savings in materials and through minimizing human error."

Cost of implementation of the LIMS became a big concern and obstacles in many settings (Cannavo, 1990). To implement, a laboratory administrator might think that the implementation cost is high. However, the system can help cut cost in several ways (Anonymous, 1995; Cianciotto, 1990). Park et al. (2005) reported an interesting study on "association between the implementation of the laboratory information system and the revenue of a general hospital" and found that the implementation was "significantly associated with higher outpatient and inpatient revenues." In another observation by Workman et al. (2000), it was concluded "this system's financial return is several times that of the information system investment." Finally, the consideration of the routine maintenance of the system has to be mentioned. The LIMS required regular maintenance similar to any other medical tool. The preparation for any problem due to temporally shut down is required. Some new computational applications can also help notify the need for maintenance of LIMS and analyzer within the laboratory (Roberts et al., 1982; Winsten, 1992). To implement the LIMS in any setting, the general rules for the implementation of new tools in medical laboratory should be followed. The basic concept for implementation of a new LIMS (Greenes et al., 1969; McDowall et al., 1988; Nold, 1003; Weilert, 1991; Wiwanitkit, 2000; Wiwanitkit, 2011) includes:

1. There must be a self-analysis. This means the need for laboratory situation analysis on all present aspects (workplaces, workforce, workload, existed laboratory analyzer, turnaround time, budget, etc.) The information from self-analysis can be useful for further planning for implementation of the new LIMS. With the available data from self-analysis, the administrator of the laboratory can decide to implement based on the information on a) limitation of space of the laboratory, b) daily workload, c) medical laboratory analyzer, d) workforce (experienced and non-experienced ones).

2. If there are identified problems, there must be corrective actions to solve the existing problem to make the whole situation proper for the implementation in the future.

3. When the basic requirements are fulfilled for further implementation, the laboratory head must be the one who leads the team. The policy making must be done, and the clarification of the vision and mission is needed.

There must also be the interdisciplinary talk with the other units (such as nursing unit, physician, etc.). Agreement between units must be signed.

4. The education and training of the staff to fit with the new system to be implemented is needed. It is the role of the laboratory head to lead the staff to understand and accept the usefulness of the system.

5. The trial implementation is needed and required. In the case that there is an identified problem during the trial, the solution should be followed.

6. After completeness of the trial, the real launch of the system starts. This is the actual implementation.

7. The post implementation following up is required. Regular maintenance of the system is needed as previously mentioned. Continuous monitoring of the efficacy, effectiveness and the unwanted incidence must also be performed. This is the way for continuous quality improvement. McDowall et al. (1988) noted that "once installed the LIMS must be validated and in the event of hardware or software changes, should undergo partial or full re-validation."

To implement the system, the requirements include a) computer hardware, b) computer software and c) linkage tool. The computer hardware is similar to the general computer that is used worldwide. The computer software is usually specifically designed to use in LIMS. The system can be commercially available. However, in the resource limited countries, there are several attempts to create a locally made software for the management of the LIMS. The use of locally made software can be useful in cost reduction. However, the concern is about the efficacy and effectiveness. The locally made software usually faces the problem of under standardization. Sometimes, a hybrid between the locally made and commercially available software is used.

The decision making to use any alternative usually depends on a) the size of the laboratory, b) the structure of the laboratory, c) the budget of the laboratory, d) the knowledge on computer science of the staff in the laboratory and e) the ability to link HIS and laboratory analyzers. In case that the commercially available software is used, the following points should be focused and considered: a) the cost for implementation of the software and the cost for the connection or linking HIS and laboratory analyzers; b) the service and charge in maintenance and correction of the problem after implementation of the software; c) the charge for updating of the laboratory tool and system in the future and d) the feasibility for actual use in real clinical practice.

Solutions and Recommendations

According to the recent publication by Sepulveda and Young (2013), specific suggestions for improving the function of LIMS cover these aspects "(a) Information Security, (b) Test Ordering, (c) Specimen Collection, Accessioning, and Processing, (d) Analytic Phase, (e) Result Entry and Validation, (f) Result Reporting, (g) Notification Management, (h) Data Mining and Cross-sectional Reports, (i) Method Validation, (j) Quality Management, (k) Administrative and Financial Issues, and (l) Other Operational Issues ." The requirement on the information security was already mentioned in the previous heading. In fact, the security is a key factor in quality accreditation (Chousiadis et al, 2002; Fielder et al., 1993; Sepulveda and Young, 2013; Tazawa, 2004; Tomlinson et al., 2006; Tzelepi et al., 2002). This point is an important consideration according to the recommendation of CAP, "establishment of a laboratory management program and laboratory techniques to assure the accuracy and improve the overall quality of laboratory services" (Tazawa, 2004). According to the concept of Good Laboratory Practice, security of data collection and storage is also an important point to be man-

aged (Fielder et al., 1993). The management on security must be continuously and actively done (Chousiadis et al, 2002).

For the test ordering, the role of the classical LIMS is usually limited. However, the newly developed system usually covers this aspect. It can help decrease incorrect requests (Tarkan et al., 2011). Tarkan et al. (2011) noted that the good LIMS must be able to "(1) define a workflow management model that clarifies responsible agents and associated time frame, (2) generate a user interface for tracking that could eventually be integrated into current electronic health record (EHR) systems, (3) help identify common problems in past orders through retrospective analyses ." Janssens (2010) noted that the good LIMS system was the solution to the problem of improper ordering. Janssens (2010) suggested using LIMS in concordant with "a reimbursement system based on the diagnosis-treatment combination and the allocation of the laboratory budget to those requesting laboratory services" as the best method for solving the mentioned problem. Levick et al. (2013) also reported their experience in using LIMS for reduction of unnecessary testing and showed the effectiveness in a reduction of cost. Levick et al. (2013) proposed that ability to manage test ordering was an important requirement for LIMS.

For specimen collection, accessioning, and processing, the role of the classical LIMS is also usually limited. However, similar to the issue of test ordering, the newly developed system usually covers this aspect. In fact, the pre-analytical phase is usually forgotten in laboratory medicine despite this phase is the first determinant of the analysis and the problem in the analysis usually occur in this phase. To manage the pre-analytical phase by LIMS is very interesting. The use of LIMS can increase safety. (Minato et al., 2011). Detection of error in pre-analytical phase can be possible (Chmura, 1987). Vaught et al. (2011) noted that a good information management system had to correspond to the biomedical specimen collection process. Da Rin (2009) reported "the implementation of advanced information technology and robotics in the pre-analytical phase (specimen collection and pre-analytical sample handling) have improved accuracy, and clinical efficiency of the laboratory process." For the accessioning and processing of the specimen, the tracking for traceability can also be derived by implementation of LIMS (Easler and Moore, 1999; Emmerich et al., 1998). The new version of commercially available LIMS usually has the ability for specimen collection, accessioning, and processing. A good example is the modular work cells (Felder, 1998). Felder noted that "proper standardization" is the requirement for any new LIMS (Felder, 1998).

Focusing on analytic phase, all LIMSs are required for their ability to manage all processes (both analysis and quality control) in this phase. The new version of LIMS must focus on the linkage between the laboratory analyzer to LIMS that can help directly transfer the data (Hammond, 1993). Chou (1996) mentioned that a good hub that can help interface between laboratory analyzer and LIMS is the basic requirement of the present LIMS. In fact, this point is the basic requirement according to the standards for automated laboratory systems developed by the NCCLS Subcommittee on Communications between Automation Systems (Kataoka, 2000). The standards focusing on interfaces by NCCLS have been proposed since 1996 (Tao, 2000). Similarly, the JCCLS, in Japan, has also proposed similar standards since 1997(Tao, 2000). In the present era that the automated laboratory analyzer is widely used in medical laboratories, the focus on those requirements is very important in considering a LIMS. This aspect was also an important concern in the checklist for accreditation according to the ISO15189 system (Freeman et al., 2006).

Focusing on result entry and validation, the LIMS has a lot of things to deal with. Concerning result entry, Ulma and Schlabach (2005) noted "use of an LIMS through a web browser allows a person to interact with a distant application, pro-

viding both remote administration and real-time analytical result delivery from virtually anywhere in the world." The technical consolidation for result entry is an important requirement of LIMS (Ulma and Schlabach, 2005). For the validation, Klein (2003) said that "thorough and accurate validation" is an important process, and this is the basic requirement for LIMS. This seems to be a critical point to consider in the implementation of the new LIMS (Bund et al, 1998; Klein, 2003).

For the result reporting, the LIMS has to cover this property, as well. In fact, result reports deal with both LIMS and HIS. The laboratory results have to be transferred from LIMS to HIS for further usage by physician in charge. According to Good Automated Laboratory Practices (GALP) and National Environmental Laboratory Accreditation Conference (NELAC) documents, the result reporting is the thing to be considered for all LIMS (Turner et al., 2001). According to Health Level Seven (HL7), a Japanese standard for medical informatics exchange between healthcare providers, test result reporting is an important issue to be monitored (Kimura, 1999) . Protocol definitions for HIS-LIS data exchange according to HL7 can be well applied in all laboratories using LIMS (Kimura, 1999).

For notification management, the GALP and NELAC documents also pay attention to this process. The notification is an important requirement. This can be the way to call for attention. "Alerts containing information" can be useful and should be provided for all critical laboratory results (Hysong et al., 2011). Hysong et al. (2011) noted that setting of "policies and procedures related to test result notification" is the basic requirement in any laboratory using LIMS.

For data mining and cross-sectional reports, this is the application of the LIMS in data storage and statistical aspect. The LIMS that is applied in genomics work requires the good property in this aspect (Grandjean et al., 2011; Thallinger et al., 2002).

For validation, the LIMS can help this operation. The validation must focus on both the laboratory analyzer and LIMS. Some new systems can help additional decision after validation (Carmona-Cejudo et al., 2012). For specific LIMS software validation, the ISO/IEC 9126 checklist can be applied (Palamas et al., 2001).

For quality management, the LIMS must be able to correspond to this process. There are many guidelines on this aspect (such as ISO, CAP, etc.) (Otter et al., 2013; Srenger et al., 2005). Ota et al. (2012) recently reported the successful use of LIMS to cover quality management in their laboratory and mentioned for the final accreditation by ISO 15189. However, as Wiwanitkit (2001) reported, the ISO accreditation does not mean there is quality. The actual quality management must be by good practice of the laboratory staffs. Focusing on administrative and financial issues, the LIMSs have to cover this aspect [63]. According to "Chapter 4: management requirement" of ISO15189, the specific process for administrative and financial issues by LIMS is needed (Shitara, 2009). Friedman (1996) concluded that the four things on administrative and financial issues for further improvement of existing LIMS include "(a) organizational integration of departmental information systems such as a laboratory information system; (b) weakening of the best-of-breed approach to laboratory information system selection; (c) the shift away from the centralized laboratory paradigm; and (d) the development of rule-based systems to monitor and control laboratory utilization."

It can be seen that there are several requirements for the present LIMSs. The present concern is on the standardization of the existing LIMS. Some international laboratory standards such as ISO15189 and CAP can be applied for use in quality management of the LIMS. However, the international collaboration to set the standards is recommended.

FUTURE PERSPECTIVES AND DIRECTIONS

As noted, there are several requirements that the present LIMSs should fulfill. There are also several future perspectives on medical laboratory information management system. First, the setting of international standards that are specific for LIMS usage is required as already mentioned. In fact, there are some attempts but those attempts are usually limited in regional level (Barbarito et al., 2012) or not for general laboratory but research laboratory (Briscoe, 2011). Second, the continuous improvement of the existing systems can be expected. The multidisciplinary approach to add up the advantage and application of the technology is promising. In fact, this is not a new approach. The application of the financial concept into LIMS for the management of the financial aspect is a good example.

Finally, based on the more advanced computational and wireless information technology, the next step of LIMS should be the worldwide wireless LIMS network. Such network can extend from the medical laboratory and wards within the hospital to outside units as well as patient home. This concept is concordant with the concept of point of care testing and the combination between the two concept results in POCT-LIMS (Jani and Peter, 2013; O'Kane, 2013). The POCT-LIMSs are the actual future perspectives. At present, the starting point of this combined concept can be seen. Several POCT analyzers can presently connected to LIMS. A good example is the case of LIMS for POCT glucometer (Park et al., 2006; Yoo et al., 2006). The wireless data transmission is the core method for the operation of POCT-LIMS (Toffaletti, 2000). A recent study by Park et al. (2006) showed that the laboratory staff had high satisfaction with the new approach and decreased turnaround time. Park et al. (2006) also noted the further development of quality control system for POCT-LIMS.

CONCLUSION

There are many LIMSs at present, which are used worldwide. The present concern is on the standardization of the existing systems. The international collaboration to set the standards is necessary. Also, the multidisciplinary approach to add up the advantage and application of the technology is promising. With the more advanced computational and wireless information technology, the next step of the LIMS will be a big wireless LIMS network that extends from medical laboratory and wards within the hospital to outside units as well as patient home. The point-of-care LIMSs are the future.

REFERENCES

Agthong, S., & Wiwanitkit, V. (1999). Cyberspace in medicine. *Chulalongkorn Medical Journal*, *43*(1), 5–14.

Anonymous, . (1995). Understanding and implementing hospital information systems. *Health Devices*, *24*(2), 71–83. PMID:7737881

Barbarito, F., Pinciroli, F., Mason, J., Marceglia, S., Mazzola, L., & Bonacina, S. (2012). Implementing standards for the interoperability among healthcare providers in the public regionalized Healthcare Information System of the Lombardy Region. *Journal of Biomedical Informatics*, *45*(4), 736–745. doi:10.1016/j.jbi.2012.01.006 PMID:22285983

Turner, E., & Bolton, J. (2001). Required steps for the validation of a Laboratory Information Management System. *Quality Assurance*, *9*(3-4), 217-24.

Boothe, J. F. (2000). Implementation of data security and data privacy provisions will bring sweeping changes to laboratory service providers. *Clinical Leadership & Management Review*, *14*(6), 301–305. PMID:11210219

Briscoe, C. (2011). Laboratory and software applications for clinical trials: the global laboratory environment. *Bioanalysis*, *3*(21), 2381–2384. doi:10.4155/bio.11.246 PMID:22074278

Cannavo, M. J. (1990). Integrated information and image management systems for the 90s. *Hospital Technology Series*, *9*(21), 1–11. PMID:10110925

Carmona-Cejudo, J.M., Hortas, M.L., Baena-García, M., Lana-Linati, J., González, C., Redondo, M, & Morales-Bueno, R. (2012). DB4US: A Decision Support System for Laboratory Information Management. *Interactive journal of medical research*, *1*(2), e16.

Chmura, A. (1987). Measurement of physician specimen-handling errors and its contribution to laboratory information system quality. *Journal of Medical Systems*, *11*(2-3), 95–103. doi:10.1007/BF00992345 PMID:3668410

Chou, D. (1996). Integrating instruments and the laboratory information system. *American Journal of Clinical Pathology*, *105*(4 Suppl 1), S60-4.

Chousiadis, C., Georgiadis, C.K., & Pangalos, G. (2002). Integrating the lightweight authentication protocol (LAP) with access control mechanisms in wireless health care information systems. *Studies in Health Technology and Informatics*, *90*, 697-701.

Cianciotto, J.P. (1990). On-line, on time: A centralized laboratory information system speeds the results. *Health Progress*, *71*(8), 32-4.

College of American Pathology. (Ed.). (1965). *Laboratory management: Symposium on Computer-Assisted Pathology (1964 Miami)*. Chicago: College of American Pathologists.

Da Rin, G. (2009). Pre-analytical workstations: a tool for reducing laboratory errors. *Clinica Chimica Acta*, *404*(1), 68–74. doi:10.1016/j.cca.2009.03.024

DeMuro, P.R., & Gantt, W.A. 3rd. (2001). HIPAA privacy standards raise complex implementation issues. *Health Financial Management, 55*(1), 42-7.

Palamas, S., Kalivas, D., Panou-Diamandi, O., Zeelenberg, C., & van Nimwegen, C. (2001). Design and implementation of a portal for the medical equipment market. *MEDICOM, 3*(4), E32.

Dito, W.R., McIntire, .S, & Leano, J. (1992). Bar codes and the clinical laboratory: adaptation perspectives. *Clinical Laboratory Management Review, 6*(1), 72-6, 78-80, 82-5.

Easler, J. W., & Moore, J. F. (1999). Specimen information tracking system: information management in the laboratory support environment. *American Clinical Laboratory, 18*(9), 10. PMID:10623323

Emmerich, K. A., Quam, E. F., Bowers, K. L., & Eggert, A. A. (1998). The combination of specimen tracking with an advanced AutoLog in a laboratory information system. *Journal of Medical Systems, 22*(3), 137–145. doi:10.1023/A:1022659631904 PMID:9604781

Felder, R. A. (1998). Modular workcells: modern methods for laboratory automation. *Clinica Chimica Acta, 278*(2), 257–267. doi:10.1016/S0009-8981(98)00151-X

Fielder, F.G., Eleuteri, B.A., & Gross, E.M. (1993). Quality assurance responsibilities as defined by the EPA Good Automated Laboratory Practices (GALPs). *Quality Assurance, 2*(1-2), 175-9.

Freeman, K. P., Bauer, N., Jensen, A. L., & Thoresen, S. (2006). Introduction to ISO 15189: a blueprint for quality systems in veterinary laboratories. *Veterinarian Clinical Pathology, 35*(2), 157–171. doi:10.1111/j.1939-165X.2006.tb00109.x

Friedman, B. A. (1989). The laboratory information system as a tool for implementing a strategic plan. *American Journal of Clinical Pathology, 92*(4Suppl 1), S38–S43. PMID:2801622

Friedman, B. A. (1996). The challenge of managing laboratory information in a managed care environment. *American Journal of Clinical Pathology, 105*(4Suppl 1), S3–S9. PMID:8607459

Friedman, B.A., & Mitchell, W. (1992). The deployment of information technology in clinical laboratories and its impact on professional roles. *Clinical Laboratory Management Review, 6*(1), 87-8, 90-3.

Gostin, L. O., Turek-Brezina, J., Powers, M., & Kozloff, R. (1995, Winter). Privacy and security of health information in the emerging health care system. *Health Matrix Clevel., 5*(1), 1–36. PMID:10141742

Grandjean, G., Graham, R., & Bartholomeusz, G. (2011). Essential attributes identified in the design of a Laboratory Information Management System for a high throughput siRNA screening laboratory. *Combinatorial Chemistry & High Throughput Screening, 14*(9), 766–771. doi:10.2174/138620711796957152 PMID:21631413

Greenes, R. A., Pappalardo, A. N., Marble, C. W., & Barnett, G. O. (1969). Design and implementation of a clinical data management system. *Computers and Biomedical Research, an International Journal, 2*(5), 469–485. doi:10.1016/0010-4809(69)90012-3 PMID:11697375

Hammond, J. E. (1993). The laboratory workstation: a data management model for a small laboratory section. *Journal of Medical Systems, 17*(5), 299–307. doi:10.1007/BF01008531 PMID:8113634

Hysong, S. J., Sawhney, M. K., Wilson, L., Sittig, D. F., Esquivel, A., Singh, S., & Singh, H. (2011). Understanding the management of electronic test result notifications in the outpatient setting. *BMC Medical Informatics and Decision Making, 11*, 22. doi:10.1186/1472-6947-11-22 PMID:21486478

Jani, I. V., & Peter, T. F. (2013). How point-of-care testing could drive innovation in global health. *The New England Journal of Medicine, 368*(24), 2319–2324. doi:10.1056/NEJMsb1214197 PMID:23758238

Janssens, P. M. (2010). Managing the demand for laboratory testing: options and opportunities. *Clinica Chimica Acta, 411*(21-22), 1596–1602. doi:10.1016/j.cca.2010.07.022

Kataoka, H., Nishida, M., & Sugiura, T. (2000). Communications among components of automated clinical laboratory systems. *Rinsho Byori, 48*(Suppl 114), 59-65.

Kimura, M. (1999). Outline of Health Level Seven (HL7) standard. *Rinsho Byori, 47*(12), 1165-9.

Klein, C.S. (2003). LIMS user acceptance testing. *Quality Assurance, 10*(2), 91-106.

Levick, D. L., Stern, G., Meyerhoefer, C. D., Levick, A., & Pucklavage, D. (2013). Reducing unnecessary testing in a CPOE system through implementation of a targeted CDS intervention. *BMC Medical Informatics and Decision Making, 13*, 43. doi:10.1186/1472-6947-13-43 PMID:23566021

(1986). Management of a clinical pathology laboratory using a record system on personal computer data base. *Medica (Stuttgart), 77*(9-10), 289–296.

McDonald, J. M., & Smith, J. A. (1995). Value-added laboratory medicine in an era of managed care. *Clinical Chemistry, 41*(8 Pt 2), 1256–1262. PMID:7628116

McDonald, C.J., Wheeler L.A., Glazener, T., & Blevins, L. (1985). A data base approach to laboratory computerization. *American Journal Clinical Pathology, 83*(6), 707-15.

McDowall, R. D. (1988). Laboratory Information Management Systems in practice. *Journal of Pharmaceutical and Biomedical Analysis, 6*(6-8), 547–553. doi:10.1016/0731-7085(88)80068-2 PMID:16867320

McDowall, R.D. (1993). An update on laboratory information management systems. *Journal of Pharmaceutical and Biomedical Analysis, 11*(11 - 12), 1327 – 30.

McDowall, R. D., Pearce, J. C., & Murkitt, G. S. (1988). Laboratory Information Management Systems--part II. Implementation. *Journal of Pharmaceutical and Biomedical Analysis, 6*(4), 361–381. doi:10.1016/0731-7085(88)80002-5 PMID:16867403

Iversen, K.R., Heimly, V., & Lundgren, T.I. (1995). Implementing security in computer based patient records clinical experiences. *Medinfo, 8*(Pt 1), 657–660. PMID:8591292

Minato, H., Nojima, T., Nakano, M., & Yamazaki, M. (2011). Safety management in pathology laboratory: from specimen handling to confirmation of reports. *Rinsho Byori, 59*(3), 299–304. PMID:21560413

Nararuk, N. (1998, May). Internet. *Chula Med J, 42*(5), 385–394.

Nold, E. G. (1993). Preparing to implement an information system. *American Journal of Hospital Pharmacy, 50*(5), 958–964. PMID:8506877

Nulan, C. (2001). HIPAA--a real world perspective. *Radiology Management, 23*(2),29-40.

O'Kane, M. J. (2013). Observations from the archives: the evolution of point-of-care testing. *Annals of Clinical Biochemistry, 50*(1), 91–92. doi:10.1177/0004563212472794 PMID:23417446

Ota, Y., Ide, H., Tsukamoto, T., Koga, M., Higaki, K., & Takano, H. (2012). From the position of a private sector hospital: ISO 15189 acquisition by a clinical laboratory, and quality management system deployment in the whole hospital. *Rinsho Byori*, *60*(7), 677–682. PMID:22973730

Otter, M., & Domas, G., & membres des groupes de travail de la SFIL. (2013). Guidelines for quality management of laboratory information systems. *Annales de biologie clinique (Paris)*, *71*(1), 257-74.

Park, A. J., Kim, H. R., & Lee, M. K. (2006). Networking Experience of Point-of-Care Test Glucometer. *The Korean Journal of Laboratory Medicine*, *26*(4), 294–298. doi:10.3343/kjlm.2006.26.4.294 PMID:18156741

Park, W.S., Yi, S.Y., Kim, S.A., Song, J.S., & Kwak, Y.H. (2005). Association between the implementation of a laboratory information system and the revenue of a general hospital. *Archive of Pathology and Laboratory Medicine*, *129*(6), 766-71.

Roberts, B.I., Mathews, C.L., Walton, C.J, & Frazier, G. (2009). A computer-based maintenance reminder and record-keeping system for clinical laboratories. *Clinical Chemistry, 28*(9), 1917-21.

Scalfani, J., & Ramkissoon, R. A. (1981). Acquisition of a laboratory information system. *Journal of Medical Systems, 5*(4), 281–303. doi:10.1007/BF02222146 PMID:7320664

Scalfani, J., & Ramkissoon, R. A. (1993). Acquisition of a laboratory information system. *Medical Electronics*, *14*(5), 97–109.

Ulirsch, R.C., Ashwood, E.R., & Noce, P. (1990). Security in the clinical laboratory. Guidelines for managing the information resource. *Archives of Pathology & Laboratory Medicine*, *114*(1), 89–93. PMID:2294872

Sepulveda, J. L., & Young, D. S. (2013). The ideal laboratory information system. *Archives of Pathology & Laboratory Medicine*, *137*(8), 1129–1140. doi:10.5858/arpa.2012-0362-RA PMID:23216205

Shitara, M., Umezu, S., & Katsuno, H. (2009). Effects of the ISO15189 accreditation on clinical laboratory. *Rinsho Byori*, *57*(6), 521–526. PMID:19621783

Sivic, S., Gojkovic, L., & Huseinagic, S. (2009). Evaluation of an information system model for primary health care. *Studies in Health Technology Informatics*, *150*, 106-10.

Srenger, V., Stavljenić-Rukavina, A., Cvoriscec, D., Brkljacić, V., Rogić, D., & Juricić, L. (2005). Development of laboratory information system-quality standards. *Acta Medica Croatica*, *59*(3), 233–239. PMID:16095197

Tarkan, S., Plaisant, C., Shneiderman, B., & Hettinger, A. Z. (2011). Reducing missed laboratory results: defining temporal responsibility, generating user interfaces for test process tracking, and retrospective analyses to identify problems. In Proceedings of *AMIA* (pp. 1382–1391). AMIA.

Tazawa, H. (2004). CAP quality management system in clinical laboratory and its issue. *Rinsho Byori*, *52*(3), 266–269. PMID:15137328

Thallinger, G. G., Trajanoski, S., Stocker, G., & Trajanoski, Z. (2002). Information management systems for pharmacogenomics. *Pharmacogenomics, 3*(5), 651–667. doi:10.1517/14622416.3.5.651 PMID:12223050

Tilzer, L.L., & Jones, R.W. (1988). Use of bar code labels on collection tubes for specimen management in the clinical laboratory. *Archive Pathology and Laboratory Medicine, 112*(12), 1200-2

Toffaletti, J. (2000). Wireless POCT data transmission. *Medical Laboratory Observer, 32*(6), 44-8, 50-1.

Tomlinson, J.J., Elliott-Smith, W., & Radosta, T. (2006). Laboratory information management system chain of custody: Reliability and security. *Journal of Automated Methods and Management in Chemistry, 74907.*

Tzelepi, S., Pangalos, G., & Nikolacopoulou, G. (2002, September). Security of medical multimedia. *Medical Informatics and the Internet in Medicine, 27*(3), 169–184. doi:10.1080/14639230210153730 PMID:12507263

Ulma, W., & Schlabach, D.M. (2005). Technical Considerations in Remote LIMS Access via the World Wide Web. *Journal of Automated Methods and Management in Chemistry,* 217-22.

Vaught, J. B., & Henderson, M. K. (2011). Biological sample collection, processing, storage and information management. *IARC Scientific Publications,* (163): 23–42. PMID:22997855

Wang, S., & Hom, V. (2004). Corrections of clinical chemistry test results in a laboratory information system. *Archives of Pathology and Laboratory Medicine, 128*(8), 890-2

Weilert, M. (1991). Implementing information systems. *Clinics in Laboratory Medicine, 11*(1), 41–51. PMID:2040148

Winsten, D.I. (1992). Taking the risk out of laboratory information systems. *Clinical Laboratory Management Review, 6*(1), 39-40, 42-4, 46-8.

Wiwanitkit, V. (2000). Laboratory information management system: an application of computer information technology. *Chulalongkorn Medical Journal, 44*(11), 887–891.

Wiwanitkit, V. (2001). Types and frequency of preanalytical mistakes in the first Thai ISO 9002:1994 certified clinical laboratory, a 6-month monitoring. *BMC Clinical Pathology, 1*(1), 5. doi:10.1186/1472-6890-1-5 PMID:11696253

Wiwanitkit, V. (Ed.). (2011). *Medical laboratory information management system.* Bangkok: Chulalongkorn University.

Workman, R.D., Lewis, M.J., & Hill, B.T. (2000). Enhancing the financial performance of a health system laboratory network using an information system. *American Journal of Clinical Pathology, 114*(1), 9-15.

Yoo, E.H., Cho, H.J., Ki, C.S., & Lee, S.Y. (2006). Evaluation of COSMO sensor Glucose Monitoring System. *Korean Journal of Laboratory Medicine, 26*(1), 1-8.

KEY TERMS AND DEFINITIONS

Information: Data.

Laboratory: A way to systematically test and assess something.

Management: A way to properly deal with something.

Problem: Something that brings difficulty.

Requirement: Something that is required.

Solution: A way to solve the problem.

System: A group of things in proper order.

Chapter 5
An Extensible Cloud-Based Medical Instrument Calibration Mechanism

Po-Hsun Cheng
National Kaohsiung Normal University, Taiwan

ABSTRACT

To obtain effective data from a medical instrument, instrument calibration, an important process within the laboratory activities, is required. Many mobile medical devices are widely and routinely utilized for monitoring people's physiological data by home-care users. However, it is necessary to let these test data be as effective as laboratory reports, so physicians can recognize as well as refer to them. The chapter proposes a Medical Instrument Calibration (MIC) process to let all connected instruments share and store their current calibration information in a global MIC's Database (MICDB). The MICDB is based on the ISO 15189:2012 standard and provides cloud-based functions via Web Services. It also shares collaborated information that is provided by other medical instruments and vendors. A MIC process for calibrating the instrument is not only required for the laboratory, but it can also be adapted for mobile medical devices and home-care instruments.

INTRODUCTION

In order to obtain effective data from a medical instrument, instrument calibration, an important process within the laboratory activities, is required. Most of the calibration process can be documented by hand, even created as electronic forms, for further reference. Based on most quality management standards, the documentation is required for clinical laboratories. However, it is too cumbersome for a technician to take care of

the document's lifecycle. It is time to propose a manageable information technology (IT) supported procedure to simplify the quality manager's life in the laboratory (Neumann, 2013).

A simplification of the quality management life cycle might promote laboratory productivity. It seems an advantageous part for laboratory managers and might be worth while well-establishing it. Conversely, do the laboratory reports be trusted by physicians, if we follow the present procedures of laboratory quality management? Although the

DOI: 10.4018/978-1-4666-6320-6.ch005

impact factors for the laboratory reports can be numerated, none of the technicians can say very confidently that the report is one hundred percent correct for a specific medical instrument. Anyhow, the quality of the laboratory report is one of the key indexes to let physicians trust the report contents (Chien, 2012).

Some of the laboratory reports are doubted by the physicians, let alone the data that is created from the cheap mobile instruments such as blood glucose, blood pressure. Further, some engineers proposed similar intelligent visions for people to promote the home-care services by connecting many inexpensive, effective and portable medical devices as well as routinely collecting people's physiological data. Although the physiological data is collected, it seems that not all physicians treat it as official reports and even refer to it. It is so wasteful for healthcare resources; hence it is necessary for engineers to adjust some IT parts to pull the direction to the right way. Fortunately, one of the directions we can solve is to establish a global medical equipment calibration mechanism and let most medical instruments refer to the standardization data bank and calibrate themselves before we use these instruments.

BACKGROUND

To understand the importance for the research topic of our proposed mechanism, this section illustrates the following topics: ISO/IEC 15189:2012 standard, ISO-related standards, equipment calibration, and global computing.

ISO/IEC 15189:2012 Standard

As we knew, the International Organization for Standardization (ISO) is a worldwide federation of national standards organization. The ISO works closely with the International Electrotechnical Commission (IEC) on most of the electrotechnical standardizations. Because the ISO/IEC standards

are trustable, most countries follow and adapt these standards as their national standards. For example, the ISO 9001 and the ISO/IEC 15189.

The ISO/IEC 15189 is an important revised international standard and mainly illustrates medical laboratories of particular requirements for quality and competence (ISO/IEC, 2012). Medical laboratory services are fundamental tasks to patient care. Healthcare enterprises engaged in the medical laboratory can utilize this standard as the basis for their routine processes. Anyhow, this standard discloses several particular requirements for clinical laboratory quality and competence, including 15 management requirements and 10 technical requirements. Table 1 illustrates the details.

Because of our research interests, our research team focuses on one of the particular and important quality processes, the medical instrument calibration and its affiliated contents. Inside the ISO/IEC 15189 standard (ISO/IEC, 2012), at least eight sections mention the related terms of the calibration that is listed in Table 2.

In summary, the expressions of the calibration-related sections of the ISO/IEC 15189:2012 standard, most of the definitions or descriptions emphasize that a clinical laboratory shall implement a feasible procedure to routinely execute appropriate instrument calibration processes and even record necessary data for preventive calibration usage. Likely, there are some ISO-related standards, which mention calibration process, and we explain them in the following sections.

ISO Related Standards

As the introduction section of the ISO/IEC 15189:2012 standard expressed, its content is based upon the ISO/IEC 17025 and the ISO 9001 standards. Therefore, these related standards are illustrated below.

First, the ISO/IEC 17025:2005 is a revised international standard and illustrates general requirements for the competence of testing and

Table 1. List of requirements in ISO/IEC 15189:2012

\Chapter Section	4. Management Requirements	5. Technical Requirements
1	Organization & management responsibility	Personnel
2	Quality management system	Accommodation and environmental conditions
3	Document control	Laboratory equipment, reagents and consumables
4	Service agreements	Pre-examination processes
5	Examination by referral laboratories	Examination processes
6	External services and supplies	Ensuring quality of examination results
7	Advisory services	Post-examination processes
8	Resolution of complaints	Reporting of results
9	Identification and control of nonconformities	Release of results
10	Corrective action	Laboratory information management
11	Preventative action	
12	Continual improvement	
13	Control of records	
14	Evaluations and audits	
15	Management review	

Table 2. List of calibration term in the sections of the ISO/IEC 15189:2012

Chapter	Chapter Name	Related Sections
4.2	Quality Management System	4.2.5
4.3	Document Control	4.3.1
4.6	External Services and Supplies	4.6.3
4.9	Identification and Control of Nonconformities	4.9.1
4.13	Quality and Technical Records	4.13.3
5.3	Laboratory Equipment	5.3.1.4, 5.3.2, 5.3.4, 5.3.7, 5.3.9, 5.3.13
5.5	Examination Procedures	5.5.3
5.6	Assuring Quality of Examination Procedures	5.6.2, 5.6.3, 5.6.4

calibration of laboratories (ISO/IEC, 2005). Its preceded standard is the ISO/IEC 17025:1999 standard that is based on the ISO/IEC Guide 25:1990. The ISO/IEC 17025 standard emerges the spirit of the ISO 9001 standard and revises some contents by referring to ISO 9001:2008 standard. Meanwhile, it is an extended standard of laboratory calibration requirements for the ISO/IEC 15189 standard and provides an amount of detailed guidelines.

Fundamentally, the ISO/IEC 17025 standard divides descriptions into two parts: management requirements and technical requirements. The management requirement is mentioned in chapter 4 and at least includes 15 needs. Also, chapter 5 includes nine requirements, which belong to technical requirements. The section outlines these two requirements, which are listed in Table 3.

The ISO 9001 standard is one of the documents of the well-known ISO 9000 series standards

Table 3. List of requirements in ISO/IEC 17025:2005

\Chapter Section	4. Management Requirements	5. Technical Requirements
1	Organization	Personnel
2	Management system	Accommodation and environmental conditions
3	Document control	Test and calibration methods and method validation
4	Review of requests, tenders, and contracts	Equipment
5	Subcontracting of testing and calibrations	Measurement traceability
6	Purchasing services and supplies	Sampling
7	Service to the customer	Handling of test and calibration items
8	Complaints	Assuring the quality of test and calibration results
9	Control of nonconforming testing and/or calibration work	Reporting the results
10	Improvement	
11	Corrective action	
12	Prevention action	
13	Control of records	
14	Internal audits	
15	Management reviews	

and describes the requirements for the quality management systems (ISO, 2008). This standard is divided into five parts: (1) quality management system, (2) management responsibility, (3) resource management, (4) product realization, and (5) measurement, analysis and improvement. Because the ISO/IEC 17025 standard adopts the spirit of the ISO 9001 standard, it is also necessary to understand and refer to the ISO 9001 contents carefully. For example, section 7.6 of the ISO 9001 standard provides five requirements for measuring equipment, and two of them directly relate to the calibration process.

Equipment Calibration

By definition for the information technology field, the calibration is a process to align the instrument parameters to locate within the normal and appropriate measurement range, before measuring (Giusca, 2013). Calibration is one of the core parts to promote the laboratory quality. Meanwhile,

based upon the explanation of the ISO/IEC 15189 and 17025 standards, the laboratory quality is one of the ultimate goals. Accordingly, the equipment calibration is so important that the technician shall rigorously execute the calibration procedure before every laboratory test. That is; the medical instrument calibration process is a required step to guarantee the laboratory test results are within the acceptable range and keep the laboratory quality.

In order to keep promoting the laboratory quality, it is necessary to clarify the calibration requirements and improve the known calibration disadvantages. For example, most of the medical instrument calibration parameters are provided by the manufacturers. Commonly, these calibration parameters are fixed and can be referred only by specific medical instruments such as TaiDoc's YD-3250C device. That is; these parameters lack global on-line reference capability.

Further, every medical instrument shall be calibrated before every measurement. However, such a mechanism is not executed by every test and laboratory managers can provide a dozen of explanations such as money wasting, time consumption and test performance. Hence, most technicians execute medical instrument calibration procedures using specific calibration frequency. Nevertheless, it might result in incorrect test results in case that the technician forgets to execute the calibration procedure.

If the technician rigorously executes the calibration procedure using specific calibration frequency, the calibration procedure can be adjusted locally. That is, the calibration procedure does not provide global adjustment capability. It seems that the calibration data cannot be shared globally for further utilization. After executing the calibration procedure, the result from the calibration data is recorded by the technician or saved locally in the electronic medical instrument. That is, the calibration results cannot be shared for global reference via online network. Even if these data can be shared; there is no standardized database to store them and provide further utilization functions.

Global Computing

The mobile device can be carried by hand and be used to communicate via a specific wireless communication protocol with each other. Originally, the performance of the mobile device is limited by its transmission rate and processing throughput (Peng, 2005). However, up to now, most of the mobile devices have a high transmission rate (such as a minimum data rate of 2Mbit/s for walking user in 3G environment) and processing throughput (such as a 1.9GHz four-core Qualcomm Snapdragon 600 CPU in the HTC Butterfly smart phone). Thus, the user can transmit an amount of data in a couple of time periods. Hence, most mobile devices can simply process the multimedia data by their own computing capability and resource.

Yet, most mobile devices are connected via the Internet and some pioneer vendors, such as Google, start to pull user's working behaviors from local storage to the Internet (Gkatzikis, 2013). Meanwhile, mobile users also start to share their information and resources on the Internet. Then, most vendors push their computing facilities to the cloud side and treat these facilities as open services. These facilities include applications (a.k.a. software as a service, SaaS), system platforms (a.k.a. platform as a service, PaaS) and infrastructures (a.k.a. infrastructure as a service, IaaS) (Miller, 2009).

Based on the cloud computing concept, the specific resource can be treated as a service and shared via the Internet (Hsieh, 2012). However, most computing capabilities are not efficiently integrated for healthcare usage and users need to discover the possible solutions from the online users (Rada, 2011). Therefore, it is time to propose a feasible mechanism and empower the medical instrument calibration quality by integrating mobile computing and cloud computing functionalities (Cheng, 2010).

MEDICAL INSTRUMENT CALIBRATION QUALITY

As the ISO/IEC 17025 standard described, the laboratory quality can be promoted by appropriately adjusting the calibration process. That is, the calibration requirements have to be cared and improved for effectually promoting the whole laboratory management quality. First of all, the local calibration procedure can be diligently executed. However, these procedures are limited inside the local area and cannot be accessed by other sites (Melo, 2012). If there is a network sharing mechanism, these local calibration data can be extended into a global calibration reference requirement.

Further, if all calibration data are shareable inside a trustable public network, these data have to be routinely executed using a specific calibration frequency, and an efficient synchronous mechanism must be executed simultaneously.

In order to achieve standardization, an approach is required that provides reliable transfer of the measurement values from the highest hierarchical level to methods, which are routinely used in the clinical laboratories (Panteghini, 2009). Hence, the correction rate of the medical instrument calibration will be promoted.

Reliability for Instrument Calibration

The reliability of the medical reports shall be trusted by physicians and physicians not care which laboratory creates these reports. However, some of the physicians do not fully trust all laboratory reports that are created by some medical laboratories. This situation means that specimen tests have to be redone if the physician does not trust the original laboratory reports. In addition, the laboratory resource waste and previous laboratory reports are almost useless.

Likely, if these laboratory reports are created by a known medical instrument with reliable calibration procedure that is shared via trustable networks, then the reports' reliability might be increased for physicians. The savings of the medical instrument resource will also increase. Note that the calibration procedure can be designed to integrate with the Internet and to fit for global adjustment. Further, the global adjustment is not only suitable for the general medical instrument in the healthcare enterprise but also fits for the portable healthcare instruments at home.

Isolation of Historical Calibration Data

The calibration records can be saved from a local side to the global site in case that the medical instrument calibration process is executed via the Internet. The more local medical instruments execute their calibration procedures on the Inter-

net;, the higher reliable calibration reference will be obtained from the global calibration records. That is, the isolation of the historical calibration data for a local medical instrument will be broken and start to share its calibration data with others.

Are Our Laboratory Reports Trustworthy?

Hence, it is necessary to let these calibration data be as effective as laboratory reports and physicians can recognize as well as refer to them via the Internet. The physicians' trust of a laboratory report can follow the quality of the calibration levels of the data, even if it is marked as the report quality of the specific medical instrument. The more global calibration data provided, the higher quality will be confirmed. Note that it can be designed as a competitive mechanism and let the quality of laboratory reports be promoted by specific global calibration procedures.

Difficult to Promote Tele-Care Instruments

How can global calibration procedures benefit from our proposed mechanism? The answer is also disclosed from one of the telemedicine researches (Gulla, 2010), and it is difficult to promote the tele-care instruments without effectually integrating the network capability. However, the information technology is one of the key elements to promote the healthcare quality, and it is necessary for engineers and technicians to analyze the practical environment before further execution (Helms, 2011). If the sharing concept of tele-care instruments is not accepted by clinical physicians, then the test data from the portable or semi-portable medical instrument is only for fun, not for official utilization.

Globalize Calibration Solution

Based on the spirit of the ISO/IEC 15189:2012 standard, a Medical Instrument Calibration (MIC) process is proposed. Figure 1 illustrates the MIC procedure through an activity diagram by the Unified Modeling Language (Vasilakis, 2010). Note that the MIC process also follows the continual quality improvement spirit in the section 4.12 of the ISO/IEC 15189 standard. Meanwhile, the MIC procedure permits all connected instruments share and store their local calibration information in a global MIC's Database (MICDB).

The MICDB provides cloud-based functions via Web Services, and also shares collaborated information that is provided by other medical instruments and laboratories. Note that such a cloud-based mechanism also follows the guidelines in section 4.13 (Control of records) in the ISO/IEC 15189 standard. That is, the sharable information in the MICDB at least includes the instrument vendor, instrument model, test item, test method, reagent, calibration date, calibration value, measurement unit, and calibration user. Therefore, a class diagram of the MICDB is drawn in Figure 2.

An experimental scenario is executed by using our proposed MIC process and is shown in Figure 3. It proves that the mobile medical devices can exchange extra calibration information via cloud-based MICDB during the MIC process (Chen, 2013). The related instrument calibration information can also be documented by utilizing the standardized Electronic Healthcare Records (EHR) formats, such as Clinical Document Architecture (CDA), for further reference by clinical staffs. If all the fixed and portable medical instruments can be grouped in a global network, then a

Figure 1. Activity diagram of the medical instrument calibration process

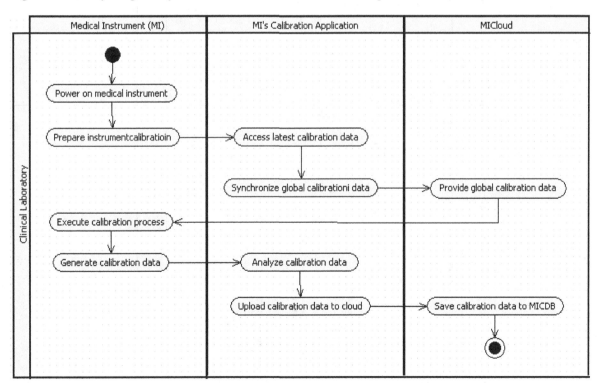

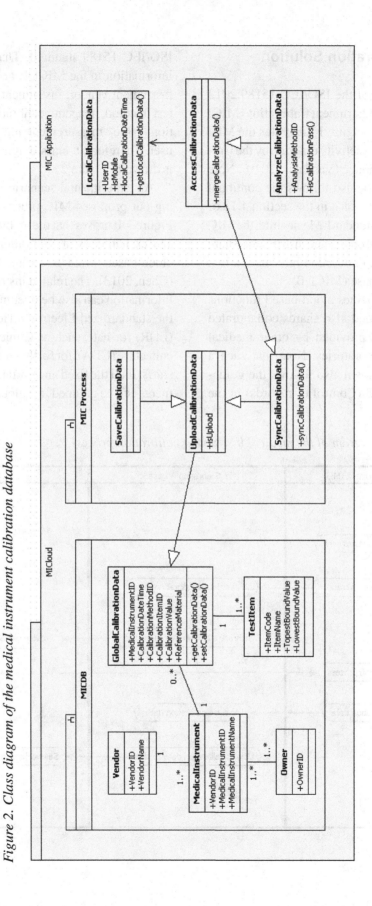

Figure 2. Class diagram of the medical instrument calibration database

Figure 3. Screen snapshot of test data in HTC smart phone via Bluetooth wireless connection

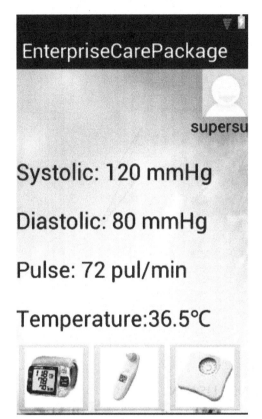

medical instrument calibration cloud (MICloud) will be generated and can facilitate all the physicians and patients in this world.

Figure 4 illustrates a system architecture diagram of the MICloud. Both Electronic Medical Records (EMR) cloud and EHR cloud can be treated as either two heterogeneous clouds or one migrated cloud. However, they can communicate with MICloud for referring to the MICDB data to understand the calibration correction rate of the specific medical instrument. Note that the connection quality is another big challenge for executing the calibration process through MICloud. At the same time, our research team also proposes a tunnel solution by using the Stream Control Transmission Protocol (SCTP) to achieve seamless wireless transmission between both Wi-Fi and 3G connections (Cheng, 2013).

FUTURE RESEARCH DIRECTIONS

To achieve the comparability of medical instrument calibration between the calibration procedures is quite significant, so it is necessary to harmonize the calibration data and interchange via the Internet. Although there is a dozen of challenges and future research directions, three of them are more important and correlated to our research topic. They are described as follows.

Before establishing our proposed mechanism, there is a task in order to simplify the subsequent tasks. That is, vendors and experts have to coordinate global calibration data at first. If possible, consistent commitment for the ISO standardization shall be executed. Then, all further works will be more feasible.

It is essential for software engineers to implement a dozen of the mobile applications that can connect all the mobile instruments. Meanwhile, the calibration procedure shall be implemented as a public component of a Web Service, which provides the fundamental MIC process. The more established connections between medical instruments and MICloud, the more vendors, will open their secured calibration specification and even share their connection protocols to the public. The more vendors join the MICloud connections, the much more healthcare budget saved for further utilization.

Then, the global MICDB shall be reconfigured for providing efficient amounts of medical instruments' reference in the MICloud. Furthermore, people who utilize the mobile medical devices can join the global medical instruments without extra setup effort and the generic healthcare data

Figure 4. System architecture diagram of the medical instrument calibration cloud

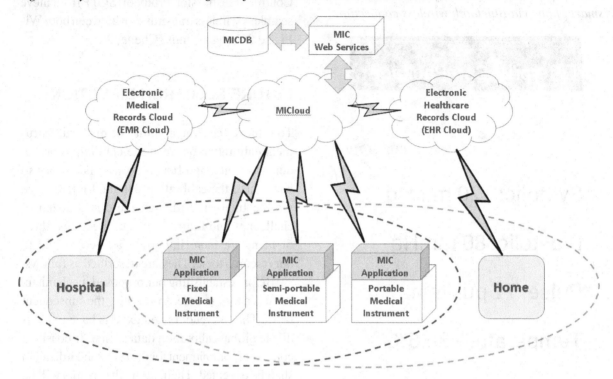

that is stored for a specific user can be accessed by physicians, not for own use. Anyhow, it depends upon the patient's authority, whether he/she wants to share his/her personal healthcare reports with physicians. In addition, the MICDB can tell the physician whether his/her patient utilizes a specific medical instrument and he/she cares of him/herself.

The more fixed and portable medical instrument's calibration data is stored in the MICloud;, the bigger data is generated for healthcare research use. Hence, the trend of the public health promotion can be effectively predicted and controlled via the big data analysis and mining of the MICloud data bank. The effective use of big data has a great potential to support a new wave of clinical discovery, leading to early detection and prevention of a wide range of medical conditions (McGregor, 2013). Therefore, quality can be possibly moved into the prevention phase through the impressive big data.

CONCLUSION

The collected data without correct instrument calibration is worthless for further utilization. A MIC process for calibrating the instrument is not only obligatory for a laboratory, but also can be adapted for mobile medical devices and home-care instruments. We believe that the MIC process will be broadly adapted in most mobile medical devices in the future. It will promote both report quality and physician trusty of patient's physiology data between home care and healthcare enterprises. A well-formed medical instrument calibration cloud will be created for real-time calibration. As a consequence, the more calibration data for medical instruments opened in a public place, the much higher reliability and quality of healthcare will be achieved. Then the vision of high quality of health society is reachable.

REFERENCES

Chen, G. Z., Chang, J. Y., Su, X. Y., & Cheng, P. H. (2013). Enterprise e-care package. *Transactions of Japanese Society for Medical and Biological Engineering, 51*(Supplement), U-15.

Cheng, P. H., Chen, H. S., Lai, F., & Lai, J. S. (2010). The strategic use of standardized information exchange technology in a university health system. *Telemedicine Journal and e-Health, 16*(3), 314–326. doi:10.1089/tmj.2009.0080 PMID:20406119

Cheng, P. H., Lin, B. S., Yu, C., Hu, S. H., & Chen, S. J. (2013). A seamless ubiquitous telehealthcare tunnel. *International Journal of Environmental Research and Public Health, 10*(6), 3246–3262. doi:10.3390/ijerph10083246 PMID:23917812

Chien, T. N., Hsieh, S. H., Cheng, P. H., Chen, Y. P., Chen, S. J., & Luh, J. J. et al. (2012). Usability evaluation of mobile medical treatment carts: Another explanation by information engineers. *Journal of Medical Systems, 36*(3), 1327–1334. doi:10.1007/s10916-010-9593-x PMID:20852921

Giusca, C., & Leach, R. K. (2013). Calibration of the scales of areal surface topography measuring instruments: part 3. Resolution. *Measurement Science & Technology, 24*(10), 105010. doi:10.1088/0957-0233/24/10/105010

Gkatzikis, L., & Koutsopoulos, I. (2013). Migrate or not? Exploiting dynamic task migration in mobile cloud computing systems. *IEEE Wireless Communications, 20*(3), 24–32. doi:10.1109/MWC.2013.6549280

Gulla, V. (2010). How can telemedicine benefit from broadband technologies? In K. Khoumbati, Y. Dwivedi, A. Srivastava, & B. Lal (Eds.), *Handbook of Research on Advances in Health Informatics and Electronic Healthcare Applications: Global Adoption and Impact of Information Communication Technologies* (pp. 91–107). Hershey, PA: Medical Information Science Reference. doi:10.4018/978-1-60566-986-1.ch121

Helms, M. M., Moore, R., & Ahmadi, M. (2011). Information Technology (IT) and the Healthcare Industry: A SWOT Analysis. In J. Tan (Ed.), *Developments in Healthcare Information Systems and Technologies: Models and Methods* (pp. 65–83). Hershey, PA: Medical Information Science Reference.

Hsieh, S. H., Hsieh, S. L., Cheng, P. H., & Lai, F. (2012). E-Health and healthcare enterprise information system leveraging service-oriented architecture. *Telemedicine Journal and e-Health, 18*(3), 205–212. doi:10.1089/tmj.2011.0100 PMID:22480301

ISO IEC 17011. (2004). Conformity assessment — General requirements for accreditation bodies accrediting conformity assessment bodies. Geneva, Switzerland: ISO Press.

ISO IEC 17025. (2005). General requirements for the competence of testing and calibration laboratories. Geneva, Switzerland: ISO Press.

ISO IEC 15189. (2012). Medical laboratories -- Requirements for quality and competence. Geneva, Switzerland: ISO Press.

ISO 9001. (2008). *Quality management systems -- Requirements.* Geneva, Switzerland: ISO Press.

McGregor, C. (2013). Big data in neonatal intensive care. *Computer*, *46*(6), 54–59. doi:10.1109/MC.2013.157

Melo, R., Barreto, J. P., & Falcao, G. (2012). A New Solution for Camera Calibration and Real-Time Image Distortion Correction in Medical Endoscopy–Initial Technical Evaluation. *IEEE Transactions on Bio-Medical Engineering*, *59*(3), 634–644. doi:10.1109/TBME.2011.2177268 PMID:22127990

Miller, H. G., & Veiga, J. (2009). Cloud Computing: Will Commodity Services Benefit Users Long Term? *IT Professional*, *11*(6), 57–59. doi:10.1109/MITP.2009.117

Neumann, M. (2013). Quality management in hospital laboratory. European Hospital, 22(3/13), 8-9.

Panteghini, M. (2009). Traceability as a unique tool to improve standardization in laboratory medicine. *Clinical Biochemistry*, *42*(4-5), 236–240. doi:10.1016/j.clinbiochem.2008.09.098 PMID:19863912

Peng, W. C., & Chen, M. S. (2005). Query processing in a mobile computing environment: exploiting the features of asymmetry. *IEEE Transactions on Knowledge and Data Engineering*, *17*(7), 982–996. doi:10.1109/TKDE.2005.115

Rada, R. (2011). E-patients empower healthcare: discovery of adverse events in online communities. In J. Tan (Ed.), *Developments in Healthcare Information Systems and Technologies: Models and Methods* (pp. 232–240). Hershey, PA: Medical Information Science Reference.

Vasilakis, C., Lecnzarowicz, D., & Lee, C. (2010). Application of unified modelling language (UML) to the modelling of health care systems: An introduction and literature survey. In J. Rodrigues (Ed.), *Health Information Systems: Concepts, Methodologies, Tools, and Applications* (pp. 2179–2191). Hershey, PA: Medical Information Science Reference. doi:10.4018/978-1-61692-002-9.ch019

KEY TERMS AND DEFINITIONS

Calibration: A set of the processes that establish the relationship between the values of quantities.

Cloud Computing: The distributed computing implemented over the Internet.

Global information Collection: The database implemented to collect specific information via the Internet, which offers access to authenticated users.

Instrument Calibration Database: The database implemented to store the instrument calibration parameters.

Instrument Calibration: The process defined by instrument vendors to align the instrument parameters before instrument utilization.

Medical Instrument: The equipment designed and manufactured by medical vendors, which provides specific medical treatment and/or medical tests.

Metrological Traceability: The property with the value from the calibration data that it can be related to some known references via a series of comparisons.

Mobile Device: The device implemented for mobile users with wireless communication; enough computation and power supply capabilities.

Software as a Service: The software implemented using the Web Services methodology; open execution via the Internet.

ENDNOTE

This research is sponsored by National Science Council, Taiwan, under grants: NSC102-2218-E017-003.

Chapter 6
Information Security Policy:
The Regulatory Basis for the Protection of Information Systems

Edison Fontes
Faculdade de Informática e Administração Paulista (FIAP), Brazil

Antonio José Balloni
Centro de Tecnologia da Informação Renato Archer (CTI), Brazil

ABSTRACT

In this chapter, the reader finds a structured definition to develop, implement, and keep the needed regulatory rules or principles for an Information System Security (ISS). In addition, the reader finds how to ensure the right use of this ISS, as well as in authorization and protection against disaster situations such as an effective system protection when accessing, storing, using, and retrieving the information in normal or contingency situations. This compound is the structure of information security policy that is based on a set of controls as described in NBR ISO/IEC 27002 (ABNT, 2005). The definition of this structure for the information security policy is important because the Norm ABNT (2005) does not indicate nor define—nor explain—how the structure of this policy should be (i.e., which are the fundamental elements and functions, which are the standards of rules for the controls and other practical issues) so that the policy could be effective for the organization. The structure shown in this chapter represents a practical and useful architecture regarding the elements of the information security policy of the organization.

INTRODUCTION

This chapter describes a structure for the information security policy with the objective of facilitating the elaboration of a set of regulations of the organization which comprises this policy. So, this information security policy structure aims to facilitate the development of this set of regulation.

The NBR ISO/IEC 27002 (ABNT, 2005) (Information Technology (Security Techniques) Practice Code for Information Security Management) requires the need of information security policy, but the Norm does not indicate how the regulation or regulations, which make up this policy, should be structured.

It is desirable that the directions of the organization establishes a clear political guidance aligned with the business goals, and demonstrate support and commitment with the information security

DOI: 10.4018/978-1-4666-6320-6.ch006

through the publication and maintenance of an information security policy for the entire organization. (ABNT, 2005)

To prepare an information security policy is a difficult task for the organizations. A tangible example was recorded in organizations that deal with health data, and which do not yet have their policies for information security in spite of their executives understanding of the importance of regulations for information security. Albertin and Pinochet (2010) in their research "Cycle of continuous monitoring for the development of information security policy in hospital organizations", described the survey in five hospitals in the State of San Paolo, Brazil, where in all of them, in a direct or indirect way, the managers declare the importance of information security, but none of them had an appropriate information security policy. Declarations from managers of such hospitals demonstrate the difficulty that these organizations have to generate an information security policy:

The hospital has a serious lack in developing information security policy. (Albertin and Pinochet, 2010).

The managers, in their majority, consider there is a lack of knowledge regarding how to map the needs to develop a formal information security policy. (Albertin and Pinochet, 2010).

The hospital has clear shortcomings in developing information security policy due to lack of guidance from the Secretary (of State) and the board of health. (Albertin and Pinochet, 2010).

According to Picovsky (2012), it is, therefore, necessary the proper and suitable use of information systems, aiming to improve the quality and safety of health care at lower cost. Yet, according to Morales (2007), all of the information that a physician may need should be available in the

charts of the patient and, therefore, it is necessary to guarantee security in obtaining this information. This shows clearly the issue and need of a security system -information security policy-.

A survey conducted by Consultancy PriceWaterhouseCoopers (2011), CIO Magazine and CSO Magazine shows policies for information security is an ongoing concern. This study represents a unified data analysis regarding the information provided by more than 12,800 executives, among CEOs, CFOs, CIOs, CSO, and vice presidents, directors of IT and information security officers from medium, large and giant enterprises from 135 countries and all sectors. About 500 of these executives were from Brazil.

In spite of the world crises regarding information security (as described in the survey), the PriceWaterhouseCoopers (2011) document also presents a compliance with the organization internal policies for information security and the resources with information security process as one of the five most important factors. The other factors were identified as: economic conditions, business continuity/disaster recovery, company reputation and regulatory compliance.

The authors believe the investment in information security is dragged/pulled by five items above mentioned: the information security policy requires the organization to implement actions in such a way that the organization is in compliance with the security rules. In this way, the compliance with the policy and other organizational internal rules becomes a driver/(give directions) towards the spending of resources in information security.

In the year 2013, the PricewaterhouseCoopers (2013) carried out a new research. This time there were 575 executives from Brazil and 9,300 executives from others countries. The survey showed 68% of respondents understand the major challenge of an organization is the establishment of a Security Corporative Strategy. This research indicates that executives need structures which guide them how to implement an information security process; i.e. the executives need guidance on how to distribute, how to prioritize and how to make the controls which will materialize (make real) the information security process.

In a specific situation, Terra and Bax (2003) observes "The analysis of the current situation of Portugal clinical information systems shows that the policies and mechanisms for the security throughout Portugal National Health System (SNS) are not adequate". This indicates the difficulty for establishing policies and norms of information security.

With the objective of facilitating the development of organizational policies and norms for information security, the Court of Accounts of the Union (TCU Brazil) has developed a Document of Best Practices in Information Security (PSI) and guides in relation to the documents elaboration. However this document does not explain the hierarchical structure from this set of documents which will comprise the Information Security Policy:

In addition, when the organization finds it is convenient and necessary that its PSI be more comprehensive and detailed; it is suggested the creation of other documents which specify practices and procedures that describe in more detail the rules of use of information technology. These documents are usually available on more specific rules, which detail the users, managers and auditors responsibilities and, typically, are updated with greater frequency. The PSI is the first of many documents with increasingly detailed information about procedures; practices and standards to be applied in certain circumstances, systems or resources. (TCU, 2007)

However, the lack of guidance on how these documents should be prepared and how should be its structure becomes evident, when in the year 2010 the TCU published the book "Summary Executive Book (Survey of IT Governance" a survey carried out in three hundred and fifteen (315) government agencies from the Federal Public Administration. This survey indicated only 37% of these agencies had a Security Policy. It should be noted that in this survey was not evaluated the quality of the documents that make up these policies of these 37% agencies. (TCU, 2010).

The necessity of existence of guidance on how it should be the set of regulations that will comprise the Information Security Policy is evident.

At first, in this chapter the information security dimensions based on NBR ISO/IEC 27002 (ABNT, 2005) (Information Technology (Security Techniques) Practice Code for Information Security Management) are presented. In this chapter, the information security policy is presented as one of these dimensions. Next it is presented, according to the norm ISO/IEC 27001 (ABNT, 2006), as the political dimension of security is addressed by Information Security Management Systems. Then practical situations for elaboration of information security policies and presented some normative instructions given by the Brazilian government are presented.

After these considerations, a structure for the standards and policies for information security is presented. It is important to mention that has been taken into account that there are a few guidelines published on the matter and so, the intrinsic difficulty for the preparation of a structure for the information security policy.

Finally, considerations regarding futures work, taking as guideline the content of this chapter, are presented.

AN ARCHITECTURE MODEL FOR AN INFORMATION SYSTEM SECURITY (ISS)

The previous model of the information architecture of the organization (Balloni, 2004, 2006; Balloni, Azevedo & Silveira, 2012, Oliveira, Balloni, Oliveira & Toda, 2012) has been modified to take into consideration Information System Security (ISS), (Figure 1). This proposed model

Figure 1. The Architecture Model of an Information System Security (AMISS)" deals with the particular project of a security ecosystem towards a chain or specific information security concerns. The AMISS comprise both, the Information Technology (IT) hardware and the Information System (IS) in the organizational structure. Details from this figure have been explained in the beginning of the section "The Architecture Model of an Information System Security" (ISS), items a – f. This figure has been adapted (Balloni, 2004, 2006; Balloni, Azevedo & Silveira, 2012, Oliveira, Balloni, Oliveira & Toda, 2012), by inserting the concepts of ISS.

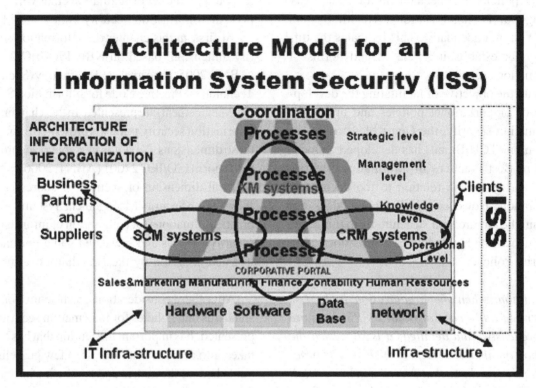

"Architecture Model of an Information System Security (AMISS)" complies (see Figure 1) with:

1.   The processes and the organizational levels (strategic, management, knowledge and operational) that allow the definition of the use of the information by the organization, and

2.   The information systems (Supply Chain Management (SCM), Customer Relationship Management (CRM) and Knowledge Management (KM)), which support the organizational processes assuring the organization uses the information to meet the business objectives.

3.   The IT infrastructure which represents the platform on which the organizations can construct specific IS (the hardware, software and the connections between the systems).

4.   The Information System Security (ISS), which stands for information security activity monitoring for all managerial levels of the enterprise. It is important to make clear that, in the original figure, (Balloni, 2004,

2006; Balloni, Azevedo & Silveira, 2012, Oliveira, Balloni, Oliveira & Toda, 2012), the BAM (business activity monitoring) has been replaced by the ISS with a similar function, standing for an information system activity monitoring for all managerial levels of the enterprise.

5. The strategic level in the Figure 1 is concerned with the "Information Security Main Policy", as will be presented in Figure 3. Yet, the Management Level of Figure 1 is also concerned with the "Logical Access, Email message & Internet, Development and Systems Acquisition, Physical Access, Continuity Plan, Information Backup & Retrieval and Information Classification", as also presented in Figure 3.

6. Finally, according to Balloni (2006), the Corporative Portal represented in Figure 1, allows the enterprise to have access and to modify the corporation information. It provides the user with a single gateway to get information for decision making. The access and interactivity with the corporation data and information through this Corporative Portal occur in a safe and protected form, for example, through the public keys cryptography system, employed to authenticate the user.

Therefore, for a correct operationalization of all the above systems (the organizational levels & the information systems) towards the security concerns, the model proposed by Figure 1 complies with a transversal Information System Security (ISS), regarding all other systems previously mentioned. So, the definition is necessary on how this ISS interacts with all the business processes (Process in Figure 1), which uses the information towards the business goals (business partners, suppliers and clients in Figure 1).

So, regarding the Information System Security (ISS) the existence of policies and norms are mandatory. They must define how the accuracy of the information controls may meet and deliver a trustful requirement of the needs of the organization, such as:

- Authorized users.
- Accountability for the users' authorization.
- Continuity of the use of the information.
- Compliance to: the legal and corporation requirements.

Therefore, in light of the above explanation, the Information System Security (ISS), Figure 1, exists as a third element that makes the inter-relationship among the information of the organization (their businesses processes) and the information technology systems (SCM, CRM, KM).

POLICY FOR THE INFORMATION SECURITY AND THE ORGANIZATION

For an effective, efficient and continued information protection, there are policies to be followed (among other controls) as presented below:

The information security is got from the implementation of a set of appropriate controls, including policies, processes, procedures, organizational structures and software & hardware functions (ABNT, 2005).

These controls, whenever needed, must be established, implemented, monitored, critically analyzed and improved, to ensure the objectives of the organizational business and security issues are met. (ABNT, 2006).

For a better understanding, Fontes (2008) organized these controls in functions of dimensions as presented in the Figure 2, the security policy and their dimensions.

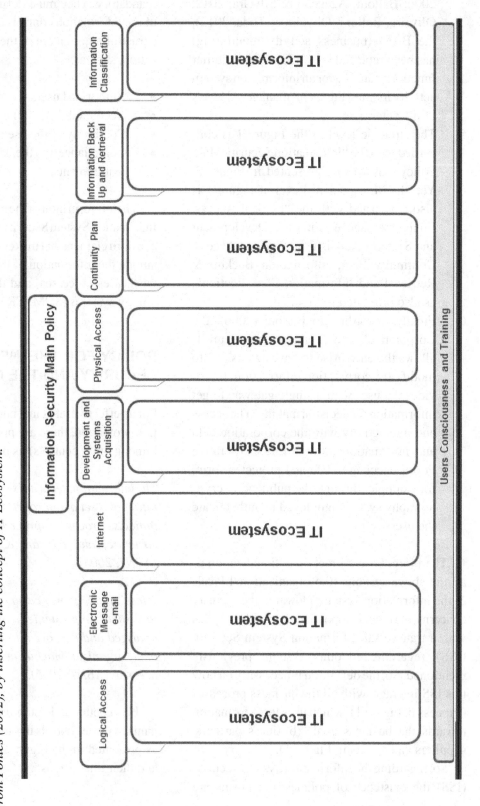

Figure 3. Architecture of the Information Security Policy presenting a Set of Regulations (such as: Logical Access, electronic Message e-mail etc.), which should comprise the rules of an information security system. According to Balloni, Azevedo and Silveira (2012), the IT Ecosystem deals with the particular project of an ecosystem towards a chain or specific niche of market. To maximize the benefits of the IT Ecosystem is necessary to plan the AMISS Architecture (Figure 1) of this IT Ecosystem and, this is the great managerial challenge, i.e., to create a uniform sociotechnical system in which everyone is using similar processes and information: integration of key business processes of this IT Ecosystem and improvement of the ISS coordination, efficiency and decision making in all managerial levels of Figure 1. The Figure 3 has been adapted from Fontes (2012), by inserting the concept of IT Ecosystem.

Figure 2. This figure presents the ten dimensions form the information security

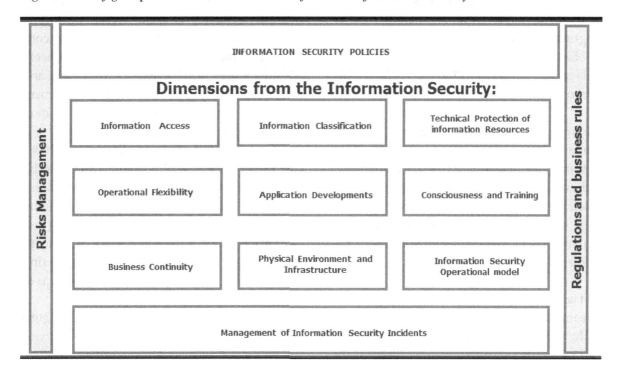

This structure has been based on International Standard NBR ISO/IEC 27002 (ABNT, 2005). Source: Fontes (2008).

However, this NBR ISO/IEC 27002 (ABNT, 2005) Norm mentioned in Figure 2 do not present how the controls should be structured. It only defines the purpose of the policy (such as information access, information classification, technical protection of information resources etc) and suggests the organization must support these actions. This is also presented by the item 5.1 in the Brazilian Norm NBR ISO/IEC 27002 (ABNT, 2005), as is presented below:

5.1 - Information Security Policy
Objective: Providing the managers a guidance and support regarding the information security in compliance with the business requirements, the laws and the relevant regulations.

The managers should establish a clear policy aligned with the business goals as well, to demonstrate their support and commitment regarding the security of the information by publishing and maintaining information security policy for the entire organization.

Regarding the Brazilian Norm NBR ISO/IEC 27002 (ABNT, 2005) above described, we could affirm the business goals mentioned in its second paragraph could be part of the business processes (and the respective managerial levels) presented in Figure 1. The Information System Security (ISS) stands for the information security activity monitoring all managerial levels of the enterprise (Strategic, Management, Knowledge and Operational)

However, the importance of an information security policy and an effective information security program has been highlighted by Peltier (2004, 2005) as:

The policy is a directive from the executive management who aims to create an information security program, to establish the goals and to define accountabilities. With the policy implementation process, the organization takes control of its destiny. (Peltier 2004)

The first and most important aspect of information security is the security policy issues. If the security of the information were a human being, so the security policy would be its nervous system. Politics is the basis of the information security, since it provides the structure and defines the goals of all other aspects of information security. (Peltier 2005).

The statement above (Peltier, 2005) is in agreement with the model proposed in the Figure 1: the ISS stands for the information security activity monitoring all managerial levels of the enterprise (Strategic, Management, Knowledge and Operational) (so secure policies are indeed the core for the proposed Architecture Model of an Information System Security (AMISS)) Figure1.

The norm ISO/IEC 27001 (ABNT, 2006) is another regulatory element. According to this norm the security policy should take into consideration the PDCA model (Plan, Do, Check, Act) regarding the Management of System and Information Security (MSIS) (this management should be carried out through the Information Security System) ISS, Figure 1.

According to Dartmouth (Dartmouth, 2008) the PDCA cycle is a methodology which may be applied aiming the improvement of any process or system. Balloni and Holtz (Balloni & Holtz, 2008) proposed the use of the PDCA cycle (associated with other methodologies), as a way to make feasible the Business Process Reengineering (BPR) towards the IT Sociotechnical Concerns & Human Relationship & Synergy.

As previously mentioned the ISS, Figure 1, stands for the information security activity monitoring all managerial levels of the enterprise. Regarding the PDCA, Table 1 presents its description towards the security management which is clearly concerned with sociotechnical aspects of the enterprise (Figure 1), its synergism and the ISS continuous improvement.

Table 1. PLAN, DO, CHECK, ACT (PDCA) towards the Management of Systems and Information Securities (MSIS). Source: NBR ISO/IEC 27001(ABNT, 2006) and 02/IN01/DSIC/GSIPR (DSCI, 2008)

PLAN: Establishment of the MSIS	To establish a policy, goals, process and procedures for the Management of System and Information Security. These are relevant for the risk management and the improvement of the information security. It aims to generate results according to the policies and global objectives of the organization. These policies are established by the Strategic level, Figure 1.
DO: Implementing and functioning the MSIS	To implement and accomplish the policies, controls, processes and procedures for the Management of System and Information Security (MSIS). These policies are implemented by the Managerial level of Figure 1.
CHECK: Monitoring and critical analysis from the MSIS	To assess and when possible, to measure the performance of the process regarding the policy, objectives and practical experience of the Management of System and Information Security (MSIS). To present the results for the managerial critical analysis, which should be carried out by the Knowledge level in compliance with the Managerial and Strategic levels, Figure 1.
ACT: To keep and generate improvement in MSIS	To prevent and improve actions based on the Management of System and Information Security (MSIS) internal auditing and a managerial critical analysis (or any other pertinent information), aiming for continuous improvement in the MSIS. This internal auditing and critical analysis should be carried out in compliance with the Knowledge level, Figure1.

Therefore, this security PDCA cycle process (Table 1) should be applied constantly from top to bottom through all managerial levels, Figure 1, establishing the politics for information security of the organization.

For the reasons above, the organization must have a policy regarding its security of information to ensure the process of information security can be developed, implemented and maintained according to the security *PLAN, DO, CHECK, ACT* (PDCA cycle) as presented in Table 1. This policy will define the guidelines, the limits and directions regarding the controls that will be implemented for the protection of the information from the organization. (ABNT, 2005; Vianez, Segobia and Camargo, 2008)

By virtue of the legislation (Sarbanes-Oxley Law), the financial segment of organizations and also large corporations from the United States, which have shares in Stock Exchanges, have already been forced to draw up their policies for information security. Other organizations have decided to follow this structured Corporative Governance, including Brazil, and so they are also constrained to develop and implement policies for information security. So, since a few years ago, many organizations have already their security policies and have also made revisions and practical adjustments to these security policy regulations.

However, other organizations are not (yet) qualified regarding their information protection through a more formal and structured manner. This lack of capability from these organizations happens because they provide services for larger organizations and the larger organizations are required to have their own structure of information security. Nowadays these organizations have understood their suppliers (small organizations as being part of their business supply chain) must have the same degree and security infrastructure of information as have larger organizations. This was in harmony with the proposed Architecture Model of an Information System Security (AMISS), Figure 1, which has presented an integrated vision of all

business supply chains: the Information System Security (ISS) standing for an information security activity monitoring all enterprises in the chain.

In other situations, such as aiming at the business sustainability, there are the entrepreneur awareness and/or the mature attitude from the shareholders. These required the organization to make use of the best security practices by having the appropriate organizational controls for information security.

Many health organizations do not have -yet- their policies for information security aiming the protection of their data, even though their executives have understood the importance of safety regulations of information. Albertin and Pinochet (2010) have presented in the paper "Cycle of continuous monitoring for the development of information security policy in hospital organizations" that in all the five hospitals from their survey (in the State of San Paolo, Brazil), the hospitals' managers have declared that, in spite of their understanding regarding the importance of information security, none of the hospitals has an appropriate policy for information security. Occasionally, they have some rules for supervising the access to the computing environment. Based on statements by the hospital managers, it becomes clear that the difficulty of these organizations relates to the generation of an information security policy:

The hospitals have shortcomings in developing information security policy and most of their manager's state there is a lack of knowledge regarding how to map out, develop and implement a hospital information security policy; there is a lack of guidance from Board of Health and State Secretary. (Albertin & Pinochet, 2010).

When the hospital organization seeks to develop an information security policy, it will be faced with a large amount of requirements described in the Brazilian Norm ISO/IEC 27002 (ABNT, 2005). In this NBR norm, these requirements are addressed in an egalitarian way, pointing out that a possible policy should contain all those requirements. Besides, the NBR norm does not provide information how this set of regulation or requirements should be structured. In the section, "Structure for the Information Security Policy", this set of regulations is presented in its Figure 3.

In a pilot research carried out in 118 hospitals distributed around 7 countries (Management of System and Information Technology in Hospitals (GESITI)), (GESITI, 2013) it has been found that several controls for Information System Security (ISS) have not been implemented such as, to highlight the research, the following essential control: Identification and Access Management Software. Table 2 presents the results from this pilot research regarding the ISS of countries and hospitals surveyed.

The non-existence of an information system security (such as Identification and Access Management Software) may signify there is not any security policy, or if it exists, its application is not happening as it should. Whatever the option, it indicates that the existence and implementation of an information security policy are not an easy task.

According to Fontes and Balloni (2007) "The security in information systems must contemplate not only the technical aspects. The social aspects related to the organization environment and the people also have importance and must be considered". The information security policy interacts directly with people since it is the instrument by which the organization shows the organization information security. This policy needs to be well thought out, very well structured and easy for communication to meet the social aspect of the information security process from the organization. Fontes and Balloni (2007) explain this characteristic as follows:

4. SOCIAL ASPECTS

4.1 – Regulations

The regulations (politics, norms and procedures) provide the definitions and make explicit what must be considered as a standard behavior. The

Table 2. GESIT health pilot project and some security information system vs. countries and number of hospitals surveyed. Source: GESITI (2013).

COUNTRIES and Amount of Hospitals: Information System Security (ISS):	SLOVAKIA 20	CZECH REPUBLIC 3	BRAZIL 76	PERU 5	PORTUGAL 7	BULGARIA 4	MÉXICO 4
Security System Management Software	2	2	18	-	5	1	-
Firewall	17	2	49	3	7	3	4
Net Security Software	10	1	36	1	4	2	4
Intrusion Detection System	6	-	23	-	6	1	-
Identification and Access Management Software	7	2	26	-	4	1	4
Antivirus	20	3	64	5	7	4	4
SSO (Single Sign-On)	-	-	38	-	5	1	-

people must follow these regulations; otherwise they will be breaking the organization coexistence rules. The existence of these explicit rules is very important for the social environment. (Edison & Balloni, 2007).

As we have showed, through this chapter, the characteristic, above mentioned, was in harmony with the concepts presented in the Figure 1 (Architecture Model of an Information System Security (AMISS)), where all managerial levels are responsible for the rules of the organizational coexistence (also presented in Table 1, PDCA security cycle) regarding the business process reengineering (BPR), as previously discussed.

STRUCTURE FOR THE INFORMATION SECURITY POLICY

For the development of regulations (policies, standards and procedures) that will comprise the information security policy it is necessary to structure a set of regulations to facilitate the understanding. Figure 3 presents the Architecture of the Information Security Policy with a Set of Regulations.

Peltier (2004) considers the Policy as the highest level of statement an organization believes and wants. These levels of statement from all organizations are known as functional areas of business organization. Figure 1 presents the main and more important functional areas from an organization (Human resources, Finance etc).

So, the policy is a directive from the executive board (or strategic level from Figure 1) to create a program of information security, establish goals and define all responsibilities which must be drilled up (detailed) to all functional areas. This executive board must be aware of the description of PDCA (Table 1) regarding the management of systems and information securities and which is clearly concerned with sociotechnical aspects of the enterprise (Figure 1), its synergism and the

ISS continuous improvement. The PDCA cycle process should be applied constantly from top to bottom through all managerial levels for establishing the politics for the information security of the organization.

Policy and Security Policy definitions:

A policy is a general guide for the action. It delineates an action and not a moment for that action. It is a definition of purpose from a company, and it establishes guidelines and limits for the individual actions which are responsible for its implementation. The policies are principles that establish rules for action and contribute the successful achievement of objectives. (Chiavenato, 2010).

Regarding the above Chiavenato statement, the rules for the actions mentioned are aligned with the PDCA security cycle process (Table 1), which should be applied constantly from top to bottom through all managerial levels, Figure 1, establishing the politics for information security of the organization.

Security Policy is a general guideline set intended to manage the protection that will be given to information assets. (Caruso & Steffen, 1999)

Security Policy is a set of rules and standards regarding what must be done to ensure the information could receive a convenient protection guarantying its confidentiality, integrity and availability. (Barman, 2002).

The policies are guidelines that indicate the limits or restrictions regarding what you want to achieve. (Albertin and Pinochet, 2010)

The Court of Accounts of the Union (Brazil) presents its definition of Security Policy:

The Information security Policy is a set of principles that govern the management of information security, which must be followed by the technical

and managerial staff and internal and external users. The established policy guidelines must be followed by the institution in order to be assured their computing resources and information -guaranteed protection by the policy guideline-. (TCU, 2012).

Again, the definition from the Court of Accounts of the Union (Brazil can be delineated from the PDCA security cycle process) Table 1.

The Document 03/IN01/DSIC/GSIPR of 30 June 2009 (DSIC, 2009) Guidelines for the preparation of the Information Security Policy and Communications in Government Agency and Entities from the Federal Public Administration, (from the Department of Communication and Security Information, Office of Institutional Security of the Brazilian Republic Presidency) states: "the commitment from the high level directions of the organization with views to provide strategic guidelines, responsibilities, skills and support to implement the communication and information security management in the Government Agency or Entities from direct and indirect Federal Public Administration."

However, the NBR ISO/IEC 27002 (ABNT, 2005) Norm (Information Technology (Security Techniques) Practice Code for Information Security Management), and no other norm from the ISO/IEC 27000 Family, defines the set of documents that constitute the Information Security Policy, as well as, in which way these documents will be divided.

The Information Security Best Practices Manual, from the Court of Accounts of the Union (TCU, 2012) cites some topics that should be considered in the Information Security Policy. However, this TCU/Manual does not define the composition of these topics. This Manual presents the following:

The Information Security Policy (ISP) may be composed of several inter-related policies, such as the policy of passwords, backup, recruitment and installation of equipment and software. Furthermore, when the institution finds that it is convenient and necessary the ISP should be more comprehensive and detailed, so it suggested the creation of other documents which specify practices and procedures describing in more detail the rules of using information technology. (TCU, 2012)

This TCU (2012) Best Practices Manual mentioned above is in agreement with the survey presented in Table 2: Security Information System vs. Countries and Number of Hospitals Surveyed. It can be seen from this table, regarding the Security Information System that, in all 76 Brazilians Hospitals surveyed, we have only 64 with antivirus protections, only 49/firewall, 38/SSO etc). This observation has generated a new research proposal outlined in the section "future research direction".

In relation to the elements that compose the Information Security Policy, the Document 03/IN01/DSIC/GSIPR of 30 June 2009 (DSIC, 2009) (Guidelines for the preparation of an Information Security Policy and Communications in Government Agency and Entities from the Federal Public Administration, from the Department of Communication and Security Information, Office of Institutional Security of the Brazilian Republic Presidency) points out that at least the followings topics should be considered:

1. Handling of Information;
2. Handling of Network Incidents;
3. Risk Management;
4. Management of Continuity;
5. Auditing and Compliance;
6. Access Controls;
7. Using e-mail; and
8. Internet Access

Therefore, for the elaboration of a set of regulations (presented in Figure 3) which comprises the information security policy, the existence of architecture is required, which must settle how linked are these set of regulations. This architecture enables the Organization to understand and plan (before having the set of regulations), the set of documents which comprises the rules of information security that should be complied by all. Figure 2 Dimensions from the Information Security presents how linked are these set of regulations. Figure 3 and Figure 1 as well the PDCA Security cycle Table 1 are intertwined regarding the "Structure for the Information Security Policy".

Taking into consideration the norm NBR ISO/IEC 27002 (ABNT, 2005), Fontes (2012) recommends that the structure of the regulations (rules to be applied in the organization), must be divided into at least three levels of specifications. Fontes (2012) has identified the following levels of details (rules to be applied in the organization) as described below.

Level 1: Guideline Document or Main Policy

This document (Guideline or Main Policy) contains the basic controls for the information security of the organization. It does not detail how these controls will be implemented and, nor it presents how or in which time and restrictions will these controls happen. In short, this document describes the philosophy of the organization in connection to information security. It presents the principles which should be followed by all users (employees, trainees, service providers, visitors and etc) of the organization. This organization philosophy must be the basis for the documents which will contain the detailed rules for each dimension of the information security. Table 1 should be extensively considered in the generation of the main policy document.

This Guideline or Main Policy of Information Security must be devised as a strategic planning document which does not need to be changed in the next five to ten years. As this strategic document contains the Basic Principles (the controls the organization wants (their guidelines)), and which explicitly states the organization philosophy, so very hardly the defined controls from this document will be changed over time. A specific technology should never be presented in the guideline document since this technology will be obsolete in a couple of years. Rather this guideline document should mention the IT ecosystem as in Figure 3. This guideline document must also be generated by the security process coordination (the strategic level of the organizations, as presented in Figure 1).

This Guideline or Main Policy (which must be aligned with the organization's guidelines), must also be signed by the president of the organization or must be approved by the Board of Directors of the Organization, with the final decision making formally registered in the Board´s minutes meeting.

This main policy should present what is requested from the information security, i.e., what are the macro controls the organization must implement to protect its information. However, this policy does not describe how the macro controls will be implemented. This will be described in detail in the documents of levels 2 and 3.

The approval by the Board of Directors becomes indispensable if the Counselors make use of an information system and receive an identification and authentication code for the information access. In general, for the information architecture of the organization, as proposed in the Figure 1, the organization has its Corporative Portal, which provides the infrastructure means for such transaction (in whatever place it could be located by the Board of Director members). Example of control described in the Guideline or Main Policy Document => The identification of each user is nontransferable (which guarantees the information veracity).

Level 2: Document Norm or Policy Dimension

The documents that will compose Level 2 from the Structure of the Information Security Policy of the Organization shall define the basic rules (basic controls) for each Information Security Dimension.

The basic controls of the documents for Level 2 must be consistent with the structural controls (organization philosophy) as explained in the second paragraph of "a) – Level 1", and begin to detail how the controls should be implemented.

The controls defined in these Level 2 Norms should be detailed in such a way as to present how they should be developed and implemented. For the specific situation of existing distinct environments which requires different controls for its implementation, Level 2 controls should not go in detail and must clarify the basic rules for the specific Information Security Dimension. For this specific situation, the details must be left to Level 3" Action Procedure or Technical Guidance Document.

At least there should be a quantity of Level 2 documents which are identical to the quantity of Information Security Dimensions (ten) and are considered in the Process of Information Security of the Organization. Figure 2 presents the ten Dimensions from the Information Security. Example of control described in the Norm or Policy Dimension. => When the authentication is performed by using a password; it must be kept secret and within the exclusive knowledge of the owner. Not even the headship should request the password of another user.

Level 3: Action Procedure or Technical Guidance Document

This document sets out in detail the actions that must be performed, or the content that must exist in the documentation or the technical detail which must be followed to ensure that the controls (as defined in Dimension Norm or Policy Dimension or the Main Policy Guideline), can be developed and implemented in the organization.

The documents prepared for this level and levels below, are of great detail. These documents complement and will allow the organization has the settings for the operationalisation of its controls and, in this way develop, implement and keep the success from its Information Security Policy, which is the basis for its Information Security Organizational Process.

The Next Levels

For a formal effect of architecture, the definition will be up to Level 3 (Action Procedure or Technical Guidance Document). In short: the three levels already presented allow the understanding of the structure, so whenever this is necessary more detailed level of definitions (level higher than 3) regarding the organization information security regulation may be carried out. Example of controls described in the Procedure for Action Document or Technical Specification Document. => When forgetting the password in the computational environment the user must ask his manager to send an email to the security support in order to give him a new password.

Structure: Visualization of the Information Security Policy Architecture

According to Fontes (2012), Figure 3 presents the structuring of the Information Security Policy Architecture. This figure presents three levels, respectively:

1. The first level (Information Security Main Policy) must be a Guideline or Main Policy document.
2. The second level presents the eight structuring Dimensions of Norm (Logical Access, Electronic Message, Email, Internet, etc).

For each of these structuring Dimensions of the Norm there are the corresponding ten dimensions as has been described in Figure 2 (Information Access, Information Classification, Technical Protection etc).

3. Finally, in the third level of Figure 3 (IT Ecosystem), documents with a detailed description of the actions must exist, presenting technical standards or documentation registration (IT ecosystem) regarding the concerned Dimensions of the Norm (level 2).

ELEMENTS OF THE ARCHITECTURE/STRUCTURE FROM THE INFORMATION SECURITY POLICY

According to Fontes (2008) the Political Dimension of Information Security (Figure 2) deals with controls from other dimensions of the process of information security. Therefore, the elements that make up the Structure of the Information Security Policy correspond to the Dimensions of Information Security. This Structure of Information Security Policy is formed by the following levels of controls:

Main Guideline or Policy: Level 1

This document sets out the basic rules and the foundations for the information security process of the organization. Everything that has been written in this document should be described with more detail in documents of Levels 2 and/or 3 and, by showing how it should be done.

Each one of the information security dimensions Figure 2 must be considered in this document so that the organization directions explain the basic rules and guiding questions for each dimension and must exist only as one Guideline Document or an Information Security Main Policy document. This document must be signed by the President of the Organization or must be approved by the Board of Directors of the Organization or approved by another body-person who has hierarchical power to ensure that all the people who will read the document will understand that these rules are serious, are for all users and are mandatory Table 1.

The Dimension Norm or Dimension Policy: Level 2

1. Logical Access

This document details the basic principles of information security defined in the Main Policy in relation to logical access of information. It should be detailed controls and rules that are common to all the technology environments. The detail of each technology environment must be defined in a document of logical access for each environment, standard Level 3 in the Architecture of Information Security Policy Figure 3.

You must set user id, user authentication, access logging, access authorization, access limitations (time, scheduling, dates), information manager, manager of the user, inclusion/change/deletion of user identification.

2. Physical Access

This document details the basic principles of information security defined in the Main Policy in relation to the physical access that contains information resources. It should be detailed controls and rules that are common to all physical environments. The specific controls for each physical environment must be defined in a document of physical access of each environment, standard Level 3 in the Architecture of Information Security Policy.

You must set user id, user authentication, access logging, access authorization, access limitations (time, scheduling, dates), information manager, manager of the user, inclusion/change/deletion of user identification.

3. Electronic Mail

This document details the basic principles of information security policy defined in the Main Document in relation to the use of electronic mail by users. It should be detailed controls and rules that are common to all types of electronic mail used by users of the Organization. Specific controls of information security for each type of electronic mail should be defined in an e-mail document (a specific tool, standard Level-3 in the Architecture of Information Security Policy).

You must set: electronic address identification, types of users that will have access to electronic mail, authorizer for user access electronic mail, responsibility for the user inclusion and exclusion in electronic mail, rules for professional use of corporate mail, rules use of personal mailbox.

4. Internet

This document details the basic principles of information security defined in the Main Policy in relation to the use of the general environment of the Internet. It should be detailed controls and rules that are common to the general environment of the Internet used by users of the Organization.

For the construction of the information security controls of this regulation, the organization should identify what activities are and are not allowed by the user when using the Internet. The laws of the country where the organization is, the contracts with customers and the business rules should be considered in the definition of these controls. The necessity of the use of the Internet for conducting the business of the organization should be considered as priority -business goals-. The controls must be explicitly defined, without leaving doubts in its interpretation.

5. Social Networks

This document details the basic principles set out in the information security in the Main Policy in relation to the use of tools of social network by users. This issue can be included in the Internet Dimension, but possessing specific characteristics. A separate document for this subject, thus facilitating its maintenance is recommended. See Table 1 and discussion earlier above to that table.

It should be detailed controls and rules that are common to all types of social networking tools used by users of the Organization. Specific controls of information security for each type of social networking tools should be defined in a document of social network -specific tool, standard Level-3 in the Architecture of Information Security Policy.

The use of social networks by using the organization's resources should consider two situations. The first is the use of these social networks for the official presence of the organization in the corporate world of the digital environment. In reality, the rules of the organization's exposure must exist for this digital environment as for the conventional environment. The organization must be present in social networks to communicate with their customers, with the market and also for the corporate positioning in this digital world. The second situation is the presence of the user as an individual, as a person in this social network. For the two situations described corporative or individual presence, the organization must define information security controls for using the social networks. Consideration of legislation, contractual and which affect the organizational climate should be considered when defining the information security controls of this regulation. The controls must be explicitly defined, without leaving doubts in its interpretation.

6. Information Technology Equipment

This document details the basic principles of information security defined in Main Policy in relation to the use of information technology equipment by users.

It should be detailed controls and rules that are common to all types of information technology equipment used by the users of the Organization. Specific Controls for information security for each type of information technology should be defined in a specific document of technology equipment, standard Level 3 in the Architecture of Information Security Policy, Figure 3.

The performance of each user with the digital world happens with the use of equipment. Currently there is a great diversity of types of equipment, as well as a diversity of operating systems which control equipment. Another issue is in relation to the equipment when the users have their own equipment with better quality and more modern than those supplied by the organization. In such cases, users want to use their personal equipment in the digital environment of the organization (BYOD - Bring Your Own Device). In the light of this huge variety of options for use of equipment, the organization needs to define what information security controls are required to follow. This regulation must set the rules how the information technology equipment will be allowed and used by users.

For the controls, the definition and positioning of the area of information technology are fundamental. Why? Because the maturity of the organization, the technical possibilities available and the capacity of the technical area to control and to protect the digital environments, will determine the rigidity of controls to be defined and implemented. According to the continuous and rapid updating of equipment, this regulation will be one which will be more frequently updated. The controls must be explicitly defined, without leaving doubts in its interpretation.

7. Classification of the Pattern of Information Secrecy

This document details the basic principles of information security defined by the Main Policy in relation to the pattern of secrecy of information, that is, classification of information.

It should be detailed controls and rules that are common to the information standard secrecy used by the users of the Organization. This means that this document should contain what procedures define the pattern of secrecy of information and must also contain the controls that should be implemented in relation to information, after the same is classified in relation to their pattern of secrecy.

Before elaborating this regulation of information classification, the organizations must analyze and assess their needs in relation to the information confidentiality. Once the organization needs are identified, the levels of information confidentiality are identified, that is, where each level has rules for the use of classified information. This requires new responsibilities for the managers of the organization specifically for the information managers, because the managers have an obligation to carry out the information confidentiality classification. With the existence of this regulation, presenting the levels of information confidentiality, the information of the organization must be classified based on this classification, and the procedures for maintaining the confidentiality of information may be defined and implemented. The controls must be explicitly defined, without leaving doubts in the interpretation.

8. Development, Implementation, and Maintenance of Applications Systems

This document details the basic principles of information security defined in the Main Policy in relation to the development, implementation and maintenance of application systems.

It should be detailed controls and rules that are common to all types of applications developed and implemented for the organization. Specific controls of information security for each type of application must be defined in a document for the development, implementation and maintenance - System application, standard Level-3 in the Architecture of Information Security Policy, Figure 3.

The implementation of information security controls in the process of development and maintenance of application systems of information technology is dependent on the existence of a methodology for systems development that consider the participation of the information security area. It is necessary the security controls described in this regulation be considered in the beginning of the development or maintenance process of applications. The organization must be determined to require the security controls definitions on each of the applications. For the implementation of the regulation of each control of information security, it is a must have the participation of business areas, while also considering the information and user managers. It is important to note that typically the business areas do not participate in these definitions of information protection. This regulation will help to change the organization culture in relation to the responsibilities concerned with information security. The controls must be explicitly defined, without leaving doubts in the interpretation.

9. Continuity Business Plan

This document details the basic principles of information security, as defined in Main Policy in relation to the use of information resources required for the business continuity, unavailability of information resources.

It should be detailed controls and rules that are common to all types of business continuity plans used by the organization. Specific controls of information security for each type of business continuity plan should be defined in a continuity plan - specific situation, standard Level 3 in the Architecture of Information Security Policy.

Business continuity is the responsibility of all areas of the organization. With the existence of the digital environment, this responsibility has migrated to the technology area; which is an ongoing mistake. The technology area will implement solutions to meet the needs of business and/or administrative areas. Therefore, it is a must be very well defined and explicit to the business and/or administrative areas their responsibility to define the requirements for recovery, such as time and limit of financial impact, operational and image, when the occurrence of a situation of unavailability. There is another important issue which, in spite of being valid for all other regulations of information security, it is critical to this regulation: the control definitions must be endlessly tested at a frequency consistent with the size of the organization and business type. This regulation deals with the business existence after adverse situations and so; it must be explicitly approved by the organization executive manager: the rigidity of this regulation controls will generate financial costs and impact on people's time. The controls must be explicitly defined, without leaving doubts in the interpretation.

10. Security Copies: Backup Copy

This document details the basic principles of information security defined in the Main Policy in relation to the use of security copies of the organization.

It should be detailed controls and rules that are common to all types of security copies used by the business areas of the organization. Specific controls of information security for each type of security should be defined in a document of backup -specific system, standard Level 3 in the Architecture of Information Security Policy, Figure 3.

For the elaboration of this regulation, it is a must the involvement from the business and administrative areas. Backup copies exist to meet the legal, information technology, historical and care for audit needs. Except for the information technology, other needs must be defined by business and administrative areas: this is a situation where these areas are not commonly used to be involved i.e., in practice, because all the information is in a digital environment; the responsibility has been left for the information technology area. The information technology area should develop actions to meet the backup needs from the business and administrative areas. This regulation will allow the existence of a business continuity plan since it will make possible the existence of the information backup in alternate locations, even if the original information has been destroyed. This regulation affects the organization culture in relation to the responsibilities concerned with information security processing. The controls must be explicitly defined, without leaving doubts in the interpretation.

11. Risk Management

This document details the basic principles of information security defined in the Main Policy in relation to the Risk Management. It should be detailed controls and rules that are common to all types of risk management used by the organization. Specific controls of information security for each type of risk management should be defined in a document of risk management -specific situation, standard Level 3 in the Architecture of Information Security Policy, Figure 3.

The information security risk management implementation is the responsibility of the area of information security which should involve other organizational areas concerned with each aspect of information security. The controls defined in this regulation shall indicate the manager responsible for the risk management. The business and administrative areas must be involved (this does not occur in most of the organizations). Therefore, it is necessary the responsibilities be well defined and

the security control of this regulation ensures its implementation. For organizations which already have implemented some risk management, the development and implementation of this control should be much easier. For organizations in which this theme is not common, there will be greater difficulty in the development and especially in the implementation of risk management in information security. In this latter case, the true participation of the executive direction of the organization will be crucial. The risk management interacts with all aspects of information security and indicates the effectiveness of the controls of other regulations. In short: the more effective the risk management, more effective will be the information security of the organization.

FUTURE RESEARCH DIRECTIONS

The following future studies on policies and standards for information security are recommended:

1. To apply the structure presented in this chapter in organizations of various sizes and, also to conduct a survey evaluating the difficulty of implementation and easiness of maintenance of elements of security policy.
2. To make a research in a large number of organizations, questioning the elements presented in this chapter, regarding the structure of information security policy, need for other elements?
3. Search for the comparison of the effectiveness between organizations that have implemented this structure -presented in this chapter- to the information security policy and organizations of size and type of business equivalent that do not have implemented this structure, or other equivalent structure.
4. Take into consideration other information security structures, other than those presented by the norms of the family ISO/IEC 27000 family.

5. Regarding the results presented in Table 2 (*GESIT Health Pilot Project and some Security Information System VS. Countries and Number of Hospitals Surveyed, GESITI (2013)*), a future research could be the investigation of correlations between the low implementation of information security controls and the existence of the Information Security Policy in the 118 organizations (hospitals surveyed). Another research could be the investigation of the organizations pointed out by the TCU as organizations which do not comply (do not have) an Information Security Policy. The investigation question could involve the following: after the security policy has been enforced by organizations mentioned by the TCU would they implement the policies? We understand the implementation of an Information Security Policy as well its respective operational controls, are a vast research field, which could indicate how the organizations behave regarding their security and policies issues.

CONCLUSION

The development of the information security policy for the organization has too much to be researched when it comes to contemplate the controls of the process of information security.

The Family norms ISO/IEC 27000 are dedicated to the topic of information security controls and present this very well. The difficulty occurs when the information security professional intends to transform the concept of information security policy for the organization. How to divide the elements? How to separate the granularity of the guidelines? What issues should be considered in each regulations block?

To these questions there is not a single truth. The structure presented here is a solution to facilitate the development and implementation of the Political Dimension of Information Security -Figure 2.

The approach of "how to do" is little explored, and consequently little publicized. But, it is believed that the more this topic is explained, the more experiences are gathered. All this with the aim of ensuring the organization has an effective security policy; i.e.; effective, efficient and over time.

REFERENCES

ABNT. (2005). *NBR ISO/IEC 27002 - Tecnologia da informação – Técnicas de segurança - Código de prática para a gestão da segurança da informação*. Rio de Janeiro: Associação Brasileira de Normas Técnicas.

ABNT. (2006). *ABNT-NBR ISO/IEC 27001 Tecnologia da informação – Técnicas de segurança – Sistema de Gestão de segurança da informação – Requisitos*. Rio de Janeiro: Associação Brasileira de Normas Técnicas.

Albertin, A. L., & Pinochet, L. H. C. (2010). *Política de Segurança de Informações, página 275*. Rio de Janeiro: Elsevier Editora.

Balloni, A. J. (2004). Why Management in System and Information Technology? In Virtual Enterprises and Collaborative Networks, (vol. 149, pp. 291-300). Springer. Retrieved October 15, 2013, from http://repositorio.cti.gov.br/repositorio/bitstream/10691/238/3/WHY%20MANAGEMENT%20IN%20SYSTEM%20AND%20INFORMATION%20TECHNOLOGY.pdf

Balloni, A.J. (2006). *Por que GESITI? - Por que gestão em Sistemas e Tecnologias de Informação.* São Paulo: Editora Komedi. Retrieved October 15, 2013, from http://upload.wikimedia.org/ wikipedia/commons/2/21/LIVRO_POR_QUE_ GESITI_CENPRA.pdf

Balloni, A. J., Azevedo, A. M. M., & Silveira, M. A. (2012). Socio-technical management model for governance of an ecosystem. *International Journal of Managing Information Technology (IJMIT)*. Retrieved October 15, 2013, from http:// airccse.org/journal/ijmit/papers/4312ijmit01.pdf

Balloni, A. J., & Holtz, S.V. (2008). *Aspectos sociotécnicos das TI & Relacionamento Humano & Sinergia.* Revista Iérica de Sistemas e Tecnologias de Informação (RISTI). Retrieved October 15, 2013, from http://repositorio.cti.gov.br/ repositorio/bitstream/10691/250/1/Aspectos%20 sociot%c3%a9cnicos%20das%20TI%20%26%20 Relacionamento.pdf

Balloni, A. J., Levy, S. N., Nemer, G. I. C. T., Freire, J. M. B., Júnior, J. C. L., Pereira, D. A., & Monteiro, B. L. F. (2014). *Por que GESITI? Gestão de Sistemas e Tecnologias da Informação em Hospitais: panorama, tendências e perspectivas em saúde.* Brasília, Brasil: Ministério da Saúde. Retrieved June 06, 2014,from bvsms.saude.gov. br/bvs/publicacoes/por_que_gesiti_gestao_sistemas.pdf

Barbará de Oliveira, S., Balloni, A. J., Barbará de Oliveira, F. N., & Toda, F. A. (2012). Information and Service-Oriented Architecture & Web Services: Enabling Integration and Organizational Agility. *Procedia Technology, 5*, 141–151. Retrieved October 15, 2013 doi:10.1016/j. protcy.2012.09.016

Barman, S. (2002). *Writing Information Security Polices.* Indianapolis, IN: New Riders.

Caruso, C., & Steffen, F. D. (1999). *Segurança em Informática e de Informações, página 49.* São Paulo: Editora SENAC.

Chiavenatto, I. (2010). *Administração – Teoria, Processo e Prática, página 173.* Rio de Janeiro: Elsevier Editora.

Dartmouth. (2008). *The PDCA Cycle.* Dartmouth Medical School - Office of Community-Based Education and Research - The Clinician's Black Bag of Quality Improvement Tools. Retrieved October 15, 2013, from http://www.aha.org/advocacy-issues/workforce/nww/nww-res-s5c.pdf

DSIC. (2008). *Metodologia de gestão de segurança da informação e comunicações. 02/IN01/ DSIC/GSIPR.* Brasília: Gabinete de Segurança Institucional da Presidência da República. Retrieved June 6, 2014, from http://dsic.planalto. gov.br/documentos/nc_2_metodologia.pdf

DSIC. (2009). *Diretrizes para elaboração de política de segurança da informação e comunicações nos órgão e entidades da administração pública federal. 03/IN01/DSIC/GSIPR.* Brasília: Gabinete de Segurança Institucional da Presidência da República. Retrieved June 6, 2014, from http:// dsic.planalto.gov.br/documentos/nc_3_psic.pdf

Fontes, E. (2008). *Praticando a segurança da informação.* Rio de Janeiro: Editora Brasport.

Fontes, E. (2012). *Políticas e normas para a segurança da informação.* Rio de Janeiro: Editora Brasport.

Fontes, E. L. G., & Balloni, A. J. (2007). Security In Information Systems: Sociotechnical Aspects. In Innovations and Advanced Techniques in Computer and Information Sciences and Engineering (pp. 163-166). Springer. Retrieved October 15, 2013, from http://repositorio.cti.gov.br/repositorio/bitstream/10691/256/1/Security.pdf

GESITI. (2013). *Management of System and Information Technology in Hospitals (GESITI)*. CTI Renato Acher – Campinas/SP – Brasila.

GESITI Health Repository of Indexed Scientific Publications. (n.d.). Retrieved October 15, 2013, from http://repositorio.cti.gov.br/repositorio/simple-search?query=hospital

Moraes, I. H. S. d., & Gomez, M. N. d. (2007). Informação e informática em saúde: Caleidoscópio contemporâneo da saúde. *Ciênc. Saúde Coletiva., 12*(3), 553-565.

Peltier, T. (2005). *Information Security Fundamentals*. Auerbach.

Peltier, T. (2004). *Information Security Policies and Procedures*. Auerbach.

Picovsky, J. (2012). *Análise de Gestão de Riscos e Impactos da Tecnologia da Informação nos Negócios Hospitalares*. São Paulo: XIII – Congresso de Informática na Saúde.

PriceWaterhouseCoopers. (2011). *Pesquisa Global de Segurança da Informação 2011*. São Paulo: PricewaterhouseCoopers.

PriceWaterhouseCoopers. (2011). *Pesquisa Global de Segurança da Informação 2013*. São Paulo: PricewaterhouseCoopers.

TCU. (2007). *Tribunal de Contas da União*. Brasília: Manual de Boas Práticas em Segurança da Informação.

TCU. (2010). Brasília: Tribunal de Contas da União, Levantamento de Governança de TI.

TCU. (2012). *Tribunal de Contas da União. Boas práticas em segurança da informação*. Brasília: TCU, Secretaria de Fiscalização de Tecnologia da Informação.

Terra, J. C., & Bax, M. P. (2003). Portais corporativos: Instrumento de gestão de informação e de conhecimento. In *A Gestão da Informação e do Conhecimento*. Belo Horizonte.

Vianez, M. S., Segobia, R.H., & Camargo, V. (2008). Segurança de Informação: Aderência à Norma ABNT NBR ISO/IEC N. 17.799:2005. *Revista de Informática Aplicada, 4*(1).

KEY TERMS AND DEFINITIONS

Backup Copy: It is a copy of information (audio, video and data) which can be used for restoring the original information when it has been lost or destroyed.

Business Activity Monitoring (BAM): It is a tool that provides real time access to the critical indicators of business performance, improving the business operations in a more efficient and effective way. Depending on the business and from the BAM applications, these events can vary from.

Contingency Situations: Are situations that make an information (or other resource) unavailable. Such situations may be concerned with the nature (rain, lightning, and earthquake) or by human action (theft, outrage, error).

Conventional Environment: It is the physical environment. The information in this conventional environment is available in several situations such as: in a piece of paper, written in table, and chalkboard or in other physical media.

Digital Environment: It is the environment that uses technology to represent the information in digital format. The information is stored in an Information Resource and is available for retrieval through information technology hardware and software.

Information Confidentiality Level: Indicates the kind of handling which must be given to the information regarding the possibility of accessing it. We may have a more rigid or less rigid handling of information in relation to the possibility of its access. For example, information classified as public does not need be destroyed after its use. Otherwise, confidential information must be handled carefully and, sometimes must be destroyed in such a way that may not be recovered.

Information Manager: It is the person who authorizes or denies the information access. This authorization or denial is an assessment function that the manager makes regarding the need of accessing that information.

Information Resource: They are elements that store, process, transmit or deal with the information. These elements could be technological discs, tapes and equipment or could even include the environment such as: conventional paper or our minds.

Information Security Process: It is the organizational process which aims to allow and enable organizations reach their objectives regarding the correct use of information and information resources.

Manager´s User: It is a person, usually the headmaster, which has the responsibility to indicate that the user, which performs tasks in the organization, is a real person. sweeping a bar code, up to an Information Security System threat (ISS -Figure 1 and item d, page 4-), and then correlating these events with relevant data inside a context or organizational environment.

User: It is the person who uses the information both in the digital environment as in conventional environment.

Chapter 7
Interoperability in Laboratory Management Information Systems

Güney Gürsel
Gülhane Military Medical Academy, Turkey

ABSTRACT

Medical laboratories are the key departments for healthcare. It does not matter if they are independent or part of the health center; they use an information management system. This system has to communicate and exchange data with many different organizations for many different reasons. Interoperability is the ability of two or more systems to exchange data and to use the exchanged data as their own. As always in health information technologies, this is easy to say and hard to perform. It has some challenges. To conquer interoperability, we need standard vocabularies, protocols, nomenclatures, classifications, etc. In this chapter, laboratory management information system-related interoperability issues are examined.

INTRODUCTION

Medical laboratories are the key departments for healthcare. The tests done in medical laboratories give important information that constitutes the basis for the diagnosis and treatment. The term "Medical laboratories" is commonly used for Pathology, Microbiology and Biochemistry. Genetics and Hematology can also be understood. Medical laboratories may be independent, or part of a healthcare institute such as hospital or health center. They may belong to private sector or government. In all cases, they employ highly compli-

cated information systems, called as Laboratory Management Information Systems (LAMIS).

If the medical laboratory is part of a hospital, LAMIS used in it may be a component of the Hospital Information System (HIS), it has the same database and application platform. In this case, it can exchange data with the other information system components such as order entry, accounting etc. natively. Alternatively, LAMIS may be a third party product independent of the HIS, having different database and application platform. In this scenario, it does not have a chance to communicate with the other HIS components

DOI: 10.4018/978-1-4666-6320-6.ch007

natively. A communication application is needed. If the medical laboratory is independent then this need is inevitable. Because the LAMIS used are different from the systems of the sites, it needs a separate communication application to manage the communication. The notion "Interoperability" has arisen from this need of communication with other information systems.

Healthcare Information and Management Systems Society (HIMSS, 2013) defines interoperability as "In healthcare, interoperability is the ability of different information technology systems and software applications to communicate, exchange data, and use the information that has been exchanged". The Institute of Medicine of the National Academies (IOM,2004) defines interoperability as "the ability of systems to work together, in general through the adoption of standards. Interoperability refers not only to the ability to exchange health information, but also to the need to understand the information that has been exchanged".

Figure 1 presents the communication needs of LAMIS. LAMIS' are to communicate

- With auto analyzer laboratory devices used within the laboratory,
- With public health departments about the mandatory reporting of the infectious diseases and other important data,
- With wearable and portable devices used by patients,
- With insurance companies for accounting,
- With patient provider healthcare institutes.

Figure 1. LAMIS communication needs

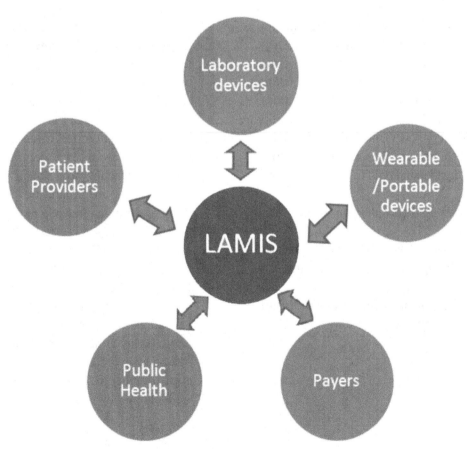

The term "interoperable" is used to explain that an information system has the ability to communicate with the necessary systems and devices.

BACKGROUND

Patient providers of the independent laboratories are the clinicians, may be working in a hospital center or working privately. Although most hospitals have their own laboratories, they need services from independent laboratories in the tests that are not studied frequently, and/or in the tests whose kits are not available temporarily. If the LAMIS used in the hospital laboratory is not part of the HIS, which means it is a third party product, then its providers are the clinical departments of the hospital.

No matter who is the provider, interoperability between laboratories and providers, improve clinical care by giving clinicians better access to patients' longitudinal test results, eliminating errors associated with verbally reporting results, optimizing ordering patterns by making test cost information available to clinicians, and making testing more convenient for patients(CITL, 2004).

Two potential cost savings in interoperability between patient providers and independent laboratories reported by the Center for Information Technology Leadership (CITL, 2004)

- Computer-assisted reduction of redundant tests.
- Reduction of delays and costs associated with ordering and reporting of results.

The most outstanding benefit of public health interoperability will certainly have gains from (CITL, 2004);

- Earlier recognition of emerging disease outbreaks, and

- Bio-surveillance, as it becomes easier by interoperability to identify warning signs and trends by data collected from many sources.

Interoperability Levels

Interoperability levels were defined in the work done at the Virginia Modeling Analysis & Simulation Center, Levels of Conceptual Interoperability Model (LCIM), by Tolk, Diallo and Turnitsa (2008), first proposed in 2003 and finalized in 2008. Figure 2 describes the LCIM.

Authors define LCIM as the model developed to cope with different layers of interoperability in modeling and simulation applications. Seven levels of interoperability in this model can be explained briefly as;

- **Level 0 (No Interoperability):** Stand-alone systems having no interoperability (Tolk, Diallo & Turnitsa, 2008).
- **Level 1 (Technical Interoperability):** This level stands for exchanging data between systems. On this level, communication network is available that allows exchanging bits and bytes (Tolk, Diallo & Turnitsa, 2008).
- **Level 2 (Syntactic Interoperability):** This level introduces a common defined message structure to exchange information. On this level, data are documented using a common reference model based on a common ontology clearly defined. The exchanged data will be in human readable format (Aguilar, A. 2005).
- **Level 3 (Semantic Interoperability):** This level brings a usage of common information exchange reference model. The participating systems are able to use information acquired automatically with equivalent meaning to their own data, as if they were entered by own users directly (Iroju,

Figure 2. Levels of Conceptual Interoperability Model (LCIM) (Tolk, Diallo & Turnitsa, 2008)

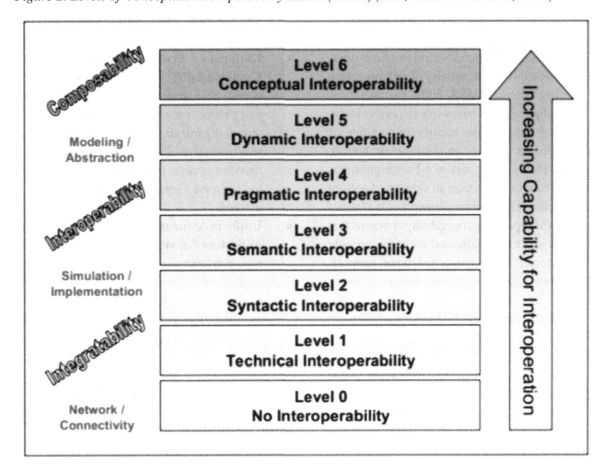

Soriyan, Gambo, & Olaleke, 2013). The exchanged data will be in computer processable format (Aguilar, A. 2005).

- **Level 4 (Pragmatic Interoperability):** In this level, the interoperating systems are aware of the methods and procedures that each other are employing. The use of the data or the context of its application is understood by the participating systems; the context in which the information is exchanged is clearly defined (Tolk, Diallo & Turnitsa, 2008).

- **Level 5 (Dynamic Interoperability):** If systems have reached Dynamic Interoperability, they are able to understand the state changes occurring in the assumptions and constraints that each other

is making over time, and are able to take advantage of those changes(Tolk, Diallo & Turnitsa, 2008).

- **Level 6 (Conceptual Interoperability):** This is the highest level of interoperability. This level requires conceptual models be documented based on engineering methods enabling their interpretation and evaluation by other engineers (Tolk, Diallo & Turnitsa, 2008).

Interoperability Dimensions

The HIMSS Integration and Interoperability Steering Committee (I&I) was formed in September 2004. The purpose is to provide oversight across the integration and interoperability-related activities. I&I wanted to provide additional precision in the ways that systems need to work together to create an interoperable solution. To accomplish this, I&I created a deeper description of interoperability that explains the activity of interoperation in six dimensions (HIMSS, 2005).

Each dimension is necessary to perform total interoperability, but the relative importance of any dimension depends on the problem solved. Interoperability in support of e-Prescription has different requirements than in support of patient health record. The six dimensions provide a framework for the type of interoperability concerns that are supposed to be addressed and then provide interconnected information solutions supporting various aspects of the healthcare delivery (HIMSS, 2005).

The interoperability dimensions of I&I are (HIMSS, 2005):

- **Uniform Movement of Healthcare Data:** Clinical or operational purpose and meaning of the data is preserved and unchanged.
- **Uniform Presentation of Data:** Enabling different stakeholders to use different systems to have a consistent presentation of data.
- **Uniform User Controls:** Stakeholders have a variety of underlying systems, in all participating systems, the contextual information and navigational controls should be presented consistently and provide for consistent actions. We can give as an example; "the controls that enable the user to log off of the application would look and behave the same across all applications, enabling caregivers to easily sign off when they are finished, and in so doing, respect patient privacy by properly closing patient records they are no longer viewing."
- **Uniform Safeguarding Data Security and Integrity:** The data is exchanged between systems and only authorized users and programs may view, manipulate, create, or alter the data.
- **Uniform Protection of Patient Confidentiality:** The exchanged data between healthcare systems have sensitive and private patient contents; users in different organizations gain access to these sensitive data. In order to prevent unauthorized access, there must be regulations to preserve patient confidentiality and privacy.
- **Uniform Assurance of a Common Degree of System Service Quality:** Stakeholders who rely on a set of interoperable systems want to be sure about the trustworthiness of the overall system in the concepts such as reliability, availability, responsiveness, consistency, speed etc.

INTEROPERABILITY IN LAMIS

Interoperability Mistakes to Avoid in LAMIS

Although there are numerous benefits of interoperability between LAMIS' and their dependent systems given in Figure 1, the task of interoperability is not easy. There are still many problems faced in the interoperability solutions such as (Beckwith, Aller, Brassel, Brodsky, & Baca 2013)

- Truncated results.
- Not displayed comments.
- Unaccepted Results because of the unmatched patient identifiers.
- Results mapped to incorrect tests.
- Undetected errors because of the unmonitored error logs.

The common mistakes to avoid in LAMIS interoperability are grouped into four categories and defined by the College of American Pathologists (CAP) in the white paper about the Laboratory Interoperability (Beckwith et al., 2013):

- Data harmonization and standardization.
  - Having no standardized test definitions.
  - Having unsynchronized test catalogs.
  - Having not uniquely identified test names using Logical Observation Identifiers Names and Codes (LOINC).
- Networking.
  - Underestimation of establishment of a secure electronic connection.
- Validation processes.
  - Having no thorough testing plan.
  - Not giving enough importance to result display.
  - Not recognizing challenges associated with patient identifiers.
- Report delivery and display.
  - Not considering all results delivery situations.
  - Not anticipating that results may be passed through multiple EHRs.
  - Assuming that EHRs can properly display complex reports.

Brief explanations of some critical mistakes to avoid in LAMIS interoperability are given below (Beckwith et al., 2013).

Having No Standardized Test Definitions

For a successful interoperability application, participating systems must speak the same language and understand the same thing from the same concept. The laboratory and its interoperating partner must determine a set of possible tests and associated results (catalog). Instead of using mapping tables between systems, it is more affordable to have a worldwide standard providing

the opportunity of reusability and plug and play applications. In the following sections, the standards used for interoperability will be discussed.

Having Unsynchronized Test Catalogs

Using same set of test catalog is not enough alone, the interoperability partners should be very careful about the synchronization of the catalog. If the definition of any member of the catalog changes in the site, the other site must be aware of the change. Otherwise the data exchange related to the changed test fails. Manual change of the tracking system is proposed to handle the unexpected definition changes.

Not Uniquely Identifying Test Names Using LOINC

LOINC is the system that provides universal names and codes for laboratory and clinical test results. Instead of using test names not known and understood by other systems, it is better to use worldwide the LOINC standard. LOINC will be discussed in the Medical nomenclatures section.

Underestimation of Establishment of a Secure Electronic Connection

Secure connection is not considered when interoperability is discussed. Establishing a virtual private network (VPN), using antivirus, firewall, other protective software; regular patching of the operating system; and upgrading to current versions of software when vulnerabilities are identified in older versions may be some helpful advices to secure the connection.

Having No Thorough Testing Plan

Directors of laboratories should ensure critical functionality is present and stable. To ensure this functionality, accreditation checklists should be constituted.

Not Giving Enough Importance to Result Display

Result display is an important quality measure in laboratory interoperability. Data presented in the display results should be logical, legible, and intuitive manner, not to confuse clinicians where to look.

Not Recognizing Challenges Associated with Patient Identifiers

Test request originates from different patient providers, using different Healthcare Information System (HCIS) and different patient identifiers. This is a big challenge for LAMIS interoperability. One way to handle this problem is to treat each specimen independently, and leave the request provider system to associate with patient; this time the laboratory will lose the ability to use prior results of the same patient. A well-known aspect of the patient (such as national id number) should be better to use as a unique identifier.

Communication Standards and Protocols Used in LAMIS Interoperability

ISO/IEEE 11073 Standard for Medical Devices

Medical devices are becoming an indispensable part of life with the rapidly developing technology. Some of them are worn by patients and collect data, measure parameters for a specific purpose while the patients go on their daily living. In Figure 3. one of the interoperability need given is with the wearable/portable devices.

These collections of wearable devices on the patient form a Body/Personal Area Network (BAN/PAN) (Martínez et al., 2008). With the complementary devices to BAN/PAN for monitoring patients with limited mobility, such as presence detectors, movement sensors etc. a Home Area Network (HAN) is formed (Martínez et al., 2008).

The devices that form HAN and BAN/PAN should be interoperable with the system that is supposed to use the collected data for diagnosis or prognosis.

The ISO/IEEE11073 Point-of-Care (is also called as X73-PoC), internationally harmonized family of standards, is co-produced by manufacturers, institutions and IEEE Institute, to bring a standard *(Martínez et al., 2008)*.

It is not possible to examine this family of standards in detail. But we can say, related to our subject, according to X73, interoperability in the wearable medical devices can be solved by connecting all of them to a central element acting as the main connection point with the data requesting system (LAMIS or HCIS). Figure 3 summarizes this design.

IEEE 11073 attempts to address every aspect of medical device communication instead of using available standards such as TCP, what makes it hard to apply and understand (Hoffman, 2007).

Digital Imaging and Communication in Medicine (DICOM)

For imaging systems, DICOM specifies a set of network protocols, message syntax and semantics, media storage services and medical directory structure (Hoffman, 2007). DICOM Standards Committee manages the standard. For the proof of DICOM compatibility of trademark products,

Figure 3. Wearable/Portable Devices Interoperability

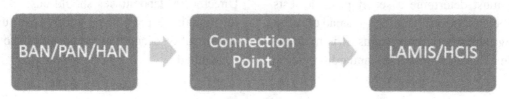

DICOM Conformance Statement is used. Medical imaging devices, such as Magnetic Resonance Imaging, PET, and Computed Tomography called as Modality, use DICOM to communicate with picture archiving and communication system (PACS). The services of the DICOM are given below.

- **DICOM Worklist:** To send data related to patient and imaging request from HCIS to the Modalities' worklist, this service is used. The imaging modality technician does not have to enter this data again, and he knows the type of imaging requested and some data of the patient he needs. This service facilitates eliminating the possible human errors in data entering and decrease in work load of the imaging technician.
- **DICOM Storage:** When the imaging process in the modality is over, the image and concatenated patient data is sent to PACS and stored using this service.
- **DICOM Modality Performed Procedure Steps (MPPS):** Modality imaging details such as the modality information of the imaging, beginning and ending time of imaging, radiation dose etc is captured by the help of this service.
- **DICOM Query/Retrieve:** Making queries from PACS about the patient's images and retrieval to the modality is the facility of this service.
- **DICOM Print:** Printing the image stored in PACS is the facility of this service. DICOM printer is needed.

DICOM services in the modalities (called as DICOM Options) are not provided with the modality. In purchasing duration of medical imaging modality, the DICOM options must be considered, and licenses should also be purchased if a PACS is employed in the healthcare institution.

Unlike the 11073 standard, DICOM employs existing standards, such as TCP/IP and JPEG, instead of re-defining new standards and does not constrain the hardware or implementation details. Instead; it constrains data to store, its configuration, and the messages that should be used for exchanging information between systems (Hoffman, 2007). That is why it is a common worldwide standard.

HL7 Messaging Standard

In interoperability applications, to exchange data between different systems, messaging is used. In the past, the messaging methods were application specific. This technique is not manageable as the number of interoperability need increases; new effort was spent to produce a new application each time. As the healthcare informatics develops, and the number of communications increase, a manageable, plug and play standard is needed for communication of different systems. A standard communication language need has arisen like TCP/IP standard. You do not need to make or purchase a new application for plugging your new computer to the existing network. Making a minor configuration, specific to that network, is sufficient. To meet this need, HL7 was developed and has become the most adopted worldwide standard. It arranges the communication messages between two or more systems about health data. 7 means it is operated in the application level (uses 7th level of the network architecture of OSI). If a healthcare system is HL7 compliant, then to exchange data with another HL7 compliant system is done by minor configurations. Most systems use a function such as HL7 engine, used for packing HL7 messages to send and decompose the received ones. It is not as easy as TCP/IP, but much easier when compared to past. It is managed by HL7 International organization.

HL7 employs a Reference Information Model (RIM). It is an object model for the messages used to exchange data. These RIM objects are grouped into templates for specific contexts, patient administration, order entry, financial management, observation reporting (especially for lab data), medical records, and hospital room scheduling (Hofmann, 2007). HL7 uses Extensible Markup Language (XML) in the messages.

For transferring patient data, the Clinical Document Architecture (CDA) is developed by HL7 (Hofmann, 2007). CDA uses RIM for specifying the structure and semantics of clinical documents, encoded as human-readable XML (Hofmann, 2007), and is commented to have a powerful representation of medical record data (Hofmann, 2007).

Extensible Markup Language (XML) Messaging Standard

XML is used to identify, exchange, and process distributed data in different applications, proposed by the World Wide Web Consortium (W3C) (Zisman, 2000). XML is a data description language which separates content from formatting and describes the structure of the text within a document, containing explicit rules to determine where specific document structures begin and end. (Zisman, 2000). XML separates the data presentation from the content, enabling data portability (Catley & Frize, 2002).

The HL7 board is actively working with XML through its SGML/XML special interest group (North, 2009). CDA and RIM were mentioned before. HL7 is also working on a standard for electronic submission for CDA Public Health Case Reporting (PHCR) to state and local public health departments (North, 2009). XML became an important technical component for HL7 as the standards are becoming mature. As an example; an XML architecture for exchange of clinical documents based on XML Document Type Definitions (DTDs) is defined by the first version of the CDA, that is included in the specification with semantics defined using the HL7 RIM and HL7 registered coded vocabularies (North, 2009).

XML is used for semantic interoperability in healthcare. It is becoming the integration glue for biomedical information interoperability, by leading to improvements in pharmaceuticals, genomic-based clinical research, and personalized medicine, by serving individuals concatenating their longitudinal electronic health records (Shabo, Rabinovici-Cohen, & Vortman, 2006).

A small XML file is given in Figure 4, as an example. In this example, we see a document used by the Windows operating system for media connection.

Medical Vocabularies That LAMIS Interoperability Based On

The importance of speaking the same language in interoperability was emphasized before. Constructing agreed catalogs are an example of the efforts for speaking the same language. Standard Medical Nomenclatures and Classifications are the advanced form of these "agreed catalogs". Drawing from the literature, medical classification can be defined as a system organizing medical terms,

Figure 4. XML example

```
<?xml version="1.0" ?>
- <scpd xmlns="urn:schemas-upnp-org:service-1-0">
  - <specVersion>
      <major>1</major>
      <minor>0</minor>
    </specVersion>
  </scpd>
```

according to shared properties, into categories and groups. Nomenclature is completely different from the classification. No category or group is available in nomenclature; each item is identified separately. Again by drawing from literature Medical nomenclature can be defined as a catalog having the systematic list of names for medical terms. Many institutions, both governmental and private, sometimes the mixture, have special interest groups for constructing and managing medical nomenclatures and classifications. In this part, the nomenclatures and classifications related to LAMIS interoperability will be examined.

Logical Observation Identifiers Names and Codes (LOINC)

Laboratories and patient providers (hospital clinics or private) use HL7 commonly to exchange laboratory orders and results electronically (McDonald, Huff, Mercer, Hernandez, & Vreeman, 2011). If these HL7 messages contain internal codes for the test, the receiving partner cannot fully understand the results they receive unless they adopt the sender's laboratory codes (that is impossible) (McDonald et al., 2011). Then we need something ubiquitous, universal to use and understand for every system. LOINC is our ubiquitous system to use in this field, managed by Centers for Medicare & Medicaid Services (CMS) of United States Department of Health and Human Services (DHHS).

LOINC provides universal names and codes for laboratory and clinical test results. For operational laboratory systems, it presents a universal database of standard test names and codes. It is not intended to transmit all possible information about a test or observation using LOINC, but to identify the test result or clinical observation (McDonald et al., 2011). Other parts give some detail such as identity of the laboratory and information about the sample (McDonald et al., 2011).

Each LOINC record corresponds to a single test or test panel (Hammond, 2008). A LOINC record has six fields that give (Hammond, 2008):

- Component name (analytic)
- Property measured
- Timing
- Type of sample
- Type of scale
- Method (where relevant)

The LOINC database contains fields for each of the six parts and also contains short names, related words, synonyms, and comments for all observations (McDonald et al., 2011).

Because LOINC is a complex and rich system, it requires some background and education for proper use (Beckwith et al., 2013). LOINC's website has instructional material to support all levels, from beginner to expert, of LOINC proficiency (Beckwith et al., 2013).

Systematized Nomenclature of Medicine (SNOMED)

While LOINC is used for laboratory tests, SNOMED is used for coding and exchanging clinical data. SNOMED is a collection of systematic, computer-processable medical terms, in human and veterinary medicine, providing codes, terms, synonyms and definitions covering anatomy, diseases, findings, procedures, microorganisms, substances, etc. (Wikipedia, 2013).

SNOMED Clinical Terms (CT) is the most used version of SNOMED, which is created by the College of American Pathologists (CAP) and since April 2007, owned and managed by the International Health Terminology Standards Development Organization (IHTSDO), a nonprofit organization in Denmark (National Library of Medicine, NLM). SNOMED CT is a comprehensive clinical terminological resource providing clinical content which can be used to code, retrieve, and analyze clinical data, reliably and reproducibly (International Health Terminology Standards Development Organization, IHTSDO user guide, 2013).

The purpose is to represent clinically relevant information, used to support multidisciplinary delivery of effective healthcare to individuals and populations (IHTSDO editorial guide, 2013).

Unlike the other nomenclatures, SNOMED CT is a hierarchical (multi-axis) system. Multi axing gives flexibility to define relations but also makes the system complex. For this reason, using SNOMED is not an easy task.

International Classification of Diseases (ICD)

ICD is a classification system rather than a nomenclature. It classifies diseases, injuries and causes of death (Kagadis, Langer, Sakellaropoulos, Alexakos, & Nagy, 2006). It was developed collaboratively by the World Health Organization (WHO) and ten international bodies (Kagadis, Langer, Sakellaropoulos, Alexakos, & Nagy, 2006). This classification system is a member of the World Health Organization Family of International Classifications, a set of integrated classification systems that share similar features, and can be used singularly or jointly, for different aspects of healthcare systems (WHO, 2011). s

WHO defines ICD as "a system of categories to which morbid entities are assigned according to established criteria", states the purpose of the ICD, as "to permit the systematic recording analysis, interpretation and comparison of mortality and morbidity data collected in different countries or areas and at different times (WHO, 2011). It translates diagnoses of diseases and other health problems from words into an alphanumeric code, which permits easy storage, retrieval and analysis of the data" (WHO, 2011). ICD is a widely used international standard having 10 versions; the current version in use is ICD-10. By adding additional

details or rearranging the ICD, special purpose classifications are derived such as International Classification of Diseases to Dentistry and Stamotology (ICD-DA), International Classification of Diseases to Rheumatology and Orthopedics (ICD-R&O), International Classification of Musculoskeletal Disorders (ICMSD) etc.

The most common purpose of ICD is coding the pro-diagnosis or final diagnosis of the patient. The part related to the LAMIS is; the pro-diagnosis of the patient sent to the LAMIS via the interoperability facility.

Unified Medical Language System (UMLS)

The Unified Medical Language System (UMLS), "is a set of files and software that brings together many health and biomedical vocabularies and standards to enable interoperability between computer systems" (NLM, 2013). UMLS can be briefly defined as the mapping source between different vocabularies (including nomenclatures and classification systems).

The UMLS has three tools, called as the Knowledge Sources (NLM, 2013):

- **Metathesaurus:** Terms and codes from many vocabularies, including ICD-10, LOINC, SNOMED CT.
- **Semantic Network:** Broad categories (semantic types) and their relationships (semantic relations)
- **SPECIALIST Lexicon and Lexical Tools:** Natural language processing tools

The Metathesaurus contains more than two millions concepts from more than 130 source vocabularies. Each concept is assigned to a concept unique identifier (CUI). Cross-mappings between different vocabularies are made via CUI (Kim, Coenen, & Hardiker, 2012).

Metathesaurus has a considerable rate of complexity. The semantic network is used for reducing the complexity of the Metathesaurus, which groups concepts according to the semantic types that have been assigned to them (NLM, 2013). The UMLS semantic groups have been established for need of certain purposes, which are a smaller and coarser-grained set of semantic type groupings.

Integrating the Healthcare Enterprise (IHE) Laboratory Framework

IHE is an organization of healthcare professionals and industry representatives working to improve information exchange between HCIS'. It provides a framework to develop solutions to enable the interoperability of HCIS and their communication gaps (Siemens, 2013). In this section of the chapter, the laboratory framework of IHE will be examined briefly.

IHE brings users and developers of healthcare information technology together in an annually periodic four-step process (Radiological Society of North America (RNSA), 2013):

- Definition of critical use cases by clinical and technical experts for information sharing.
- Optimization of established standards, for communication among systems, by detailed specifications (IHE Profiles).
- Implementation of IHE Profiles into the healthcare IT systems by vendors.
- Testing the vendors' systems at IHE Connectathon, a carefully planned and supervised event.

IHE has 12 domains that are (IHE, 2013);

- Anatomic Pathology
- Cardiology
- Dental
- Eye Care
- IT Infrastructure
- Laboratory
- Patient Care Coordination

- Patient Care Devices
- Pharmacy
- Quality, Research and Public Health
- Radiation Oncology
- Radiology

The IHE Laboratory domain deals with information sharing and workflow related to diagnostic testing in clinical laboratories (IHE, 2013). The domain (The Laboratory Planning and Technical Committee) develops and publishes IHE Laboratory Technical Framework.

IHE integration profiles based on the HL7 standards for LAMIS are (IHE, 2013):

- **Laboratory Testing Workflow (LTW):** LTW integrates the:
  - ○ Ordering,
  - ○ Scheduling,
  - ○ Processing,
  - ○ Result reporting activities,
  of the tests done by clinical laboratories in healthcare institutions.
- **Laboratory Device Automation (LDA):** LDA covers the exchanges between LAMIS and a set of automated Laboratory Devices to run the tests on the given specimens and retrieve the results.
- **Laboratory Point of Care Testing (LPOCT):** LPOCT handles running and collecting the results of in-vitro testing at the laboratory or patient's bedside. It requires surveillances such as clinical validation of results, Quality Control, point of care devices surveillance etc.
- **Laboratory Code Set Distribution (LCSD):** LCSD is responsible for sharing common nomenclatures among systems involved in laboratory workflows such as LOINC, SNOMED etc.
- **Laboratory Specimen Barcode Labeling (LBL):** It arranges the labeling integration between auto analyzers and order labeling in the context of laboratory test requests.

- **Sharing Laboratory Reports (XD-LAB):** XD-LAB addresses laboratory reports sharing by describing the content (both human and machine readable) of an electronic clinical laboratory report.

Interoperability in Medical Laboratories: Requirements for Quality and Competence Standard (ISO 15189:2012)

ISO 15189:2012 is the standard of the International Organization for Standardizations' Technical Committee 212 (ISO/TC 212), 2012 version, which arranges the requirements for competence and quality that are particular to medical laboratories (Wikipedia, 2013).

In neither versions of the 15189 interoperability is addressed directly. In some parts, interoperability requirements are/may be mandatory for the competence. In this section of the chapter, the parts indirectly related to the notion of interoperability will be examined.

The section 4.1.2.4, "Quality objectives and planning" requires Laboratory management to establish quality objectives, including meeting the needs and requirements of the users (International Accreditation New Zealand (IANZ), 2013). In the view of Figure 1, one of the requirements of the medical laboratory users is said to be interoperability. One of the parts that 15189:2012 addresses interoperability indirectly is this section.

The section 5.4.3, "Request form information", can be interpreted as another section that addresses interoperability indirectly. It arranges the details of the request form or its electronic equivalent; these details were specified as "shall" where in 2007, they were specified as "should" (International Accreditation New Zealand (IANZ), 2013). That means these details are mandatory in

the current version and most of which can be got from the patient providers' information system via interoperability.

The section 5.6.3, "Interlaboratory comparisons" part may have a sub-requisite as interoperability comparison with the other compared laboratories.

The section 5.8.3 "Report content" arranges the contents of the report (International Accreditation New Zealand (IANZ), 2013) some of which, e.g. patient identification and location should be taken via data exchange with the patient provider's information systems to eliminate the user errors.

The section 5.10.3, "Information system management" has statements that point interoperability without naming it such as "The laboratory is required to verify that all examinations results received into external information systems can be accurately reproduced. When a new examination or automated comment is implemented, the laboratory is also required to verify that the changes are accurately reproduced." (International Accreditation New Zealand (IANZ), 2013).

It seems that, although 15189 does not address interoperability directly, there are parts that interoperability is required to comply with the regulations.

FUTURE RESEARCH DIRECTIONS

As the medical laboratories become private, and the number of patient providers increases, interoperability will be crucial. The most important future work about LAMIS interoperability can be its inclusion in ISO 15189 standard. It can take part in the standard as subsections of the parts related to the interoperability given in the previous section, or can be a separately dedicated part. Anyway, a standard that organizes the quality measures of a medical laboratory should contain and emphasize the requisites for interoperability of LAMIS with the other information systems.

CONCLUSION

In the era of science and technology we live, health informatics is rapidly growing and evolving together with advances in healthcare. In this situation, interoperability is becoming a must attribute of HCIS, not a luxury or additionally preferred feature. In this chapter, the basics of the interoperability, its need and benefits to the healthcare, the challenges, standards and vocabularies it relies on for LAMIS are mentioned. Finally, the chapter refers to the IHE framework and ISO standard that organizes the medical laboratories.

Designing interoperable systems have endless and undeniable benefits such as; integration of patient information for effective decision making, universal information distribution, real time statistics collection (Beckwith et al., 2013).

The industry is seeking better ways, standards and protocols to perform the interoperability in a more qualified and easy to manage way. It seems as the systems get better, the quality of the interoperability will also be better.

REFERENCES

Aguilar, A. (2005, December). *Semantic Interoperability in the context of eHealth*. Paper presented at the HP/DERI/CIMRU Research Seminar. Galway, Ireland.

Aspden, P., Corrigan, J. M., Wolcott, J., & Erickson, S. M. (Eds.). (2004). Patient safety: Achieving a new standard for care. National Academy Press.

Beckwith, B.A., Aller, R.D., Brassel, J.H., Brodsky B.V., & Baca M.E. (2013). *Laboratory Interoperability Best Practices*. College of American Pathologists. Retrieved February 02, 2014, from http://www.cap.org/apps/docs/committees/informatics/cap_dihit_lab_interop_final_march_2013.pdf

Catley, C., & Frize, M. (2002, October). *Design of a health care architecture for medical data interoperability and application integration*. Paper presented at the Engineering in Medicine and Biology, 2002. New York, NY..

Center for Information Technology Leadership, Partners Healthcare System (CITL), Healthcare Information, & Management Systems Society. (2004). *The value of healthcare information exchange and interoperability*. Healthcare Information and Management Systems Society. Retrieved February 02, 2014, from http://www.partners.org/cird/pdfs/CITL_HIEI_Report.pdf

Hammond, W. E. (2008). *An Introduction to LOINC: Logical Observation Identifier Name and Codes*. Retrieved February 02, 2014, from http://www.hcup-us.ahrq.gov/datainnovations/clinical-data/FL20LOINCIntroductionHammond.pdf

Healthcare Information and Management Systems Society. (2013). *What is Interoperability*. Retrieved July 27, 2013, from http://www.himss.org/library/interoperability-standards/what-is

Healthcare Information and Management Systems Society (HIMSS). (2005). *Interoperability definition and background*. Retrieved July 25, 2013, from http://www.himss.org/files/HIMSSorg/content/files/AUXILIOHIMSSInteroperabilityDefined.pdf

Hofmann, R. M. (2007). *Modeling medical devices for plug-and-play interoperability*. (Unpublished Doctoral Dissertation). Massachusetts Institute of Technology, Cambridge, MA.

Integrating the Healthcare Enterprise. (2013). Retrieved 27 June 2013 from http://www.ihe.net/ Laboratory/

International Accreditation New Zealand. (2013). *Implementing ISO 15189:2012*. Retrieved 26 September, 2013 from https://go.promapp.com/ ianz/view/Documents/View/Open?displayType= document&documentId=e0196d0e-49e8-4962- 94ee-b1b437d93970.

International Health Terminology Standards Development Organization. (2013). *SNOMED CT® User Guide July 2013 International Release*. Retrieved September 13 from http://ihtsdo.org/ fileadmin/user_upload/doc/download/doc_User- Guide_Current-en-US_INT_20130731.pdf

Iroju, O., Soriyan, A., Gambo, I., & Olaleke, J. (2013). Interoperability in Healthcare: Benefits, Challenges and Resolutions. *International Journal of Innovation and Applied Studies*, *3*(1), 262–270.

ISO 15189. (2013). In *Wikipedia*. Retrieved September 25, 2013, from http://en.wikipedia. org/wiki/ISO_15189

Kagadis, G. C., Langer, S. G., Sakellaropoulos, G. C., Alexakos, C., & Nagy, P. (2006). Overview of Medical Imaging Informatics. In A. B. Wolbarst, R. G. Zamenhof, W. R. Hendee, & I. P. Smith (Eds.), *Advances in Medical Physics* (pp. 160–169). Madison, WI: Medical Physics Publishing.

Kim, T. Y., Coenen, A., & Hardiker, N. (2012). Semantic mappings and locality of nursing diagnostic concepts in UMLS. *Journal of Biomedical Informatics*, *45*(1), 93–100. doi:10.1016/j. jbi.2011.09.002 PMID:21951759

Martínez, I., Escayola, J., Martínez-Espronceda, M., Serrano, L., Trigo, J., Led, S., & García, J. (2008, August). Standard-based middleware platform for medical sensor networks and u-health. In *Proceedings of Computer Communications and Networks*, (pp. 1-6). IEEE.

McDonald, C., Huff, S., Mercer, K., Hernandez, J. A., & Vreeman, D. J. (2004). *Logical observation identifiers names and codes (LOINC®) users' guide*. Retrieved February 02, 2014 from http:// loinc.org/downloads/files/LOINCManual.pdf

National Library of Medicine (NLM). (2013). *SNOMED Clinical Terms*. Retrieved September 25, 2014 from http://www.nlm.nih.gov/research/ umls/Snomed/snomed_main.html

National Library of Medicine (NLM). (2013). *Unified Medical Language System® (UMLS®)*. Retrieved September 25, 2013 from http://www. nlm.nih.gov/research/umls/quickstart.html

North, K. (2009). *Healthcare's XML Heartbeat*. Retrieved September 23, 2013 from http://www. ibm.com/developerworks/data/library/dmmag/ DMMag_2009_Issue2/Industry/

Radiological Society of North America. (2013). *Integrating the Healthcare Enterprise*. Retrieved 27 July 2013 from https://www.rsna.org/ihe.aspx

Shabo, A., Rabinovici-Cohen, S., & Vortman, P. (2006). Revolutionary impact of XML on biomedical information interoperability. *IBM Systems Journal*, *45*(2), 361–372. doi:10.1147/sj.452.0361

Siemens. (2013). *Integrating the Healthcare Enterprise*. Retrieved 27 July, 2013 from http://www. healthcare.siemens.com/services/it-standards/ ihe-integrating-the-healthcare-enterprise

Systematized Nomenclature of Medicine. (2013). In *Wikipedia*. Retrieved August 5, 2013, from http://en.wikipedia.org/wiki/Snomed

Tolk, A., Saikou, D., & Turnitsa, C. D. (2008). Applying the levels of conceptual interoperability model in support of integratability, interoperability, and composability for system-of-systems engineering. Journal of Systemics. *Cybernetics and Informatics.*, *5*(65), 65–74.

Walker, J., Pan, E., Johnston, D., Adler-Milstein, J., Bates, D. W., & Middleton, B. (2005). The value of health care information exchange and interoperability. *Health Affairs*, *24*, W5. PMID:15659453

World Health Organization. (2011). *International Statistical Classification of Diseases and Related Health Problems 10th revision.* Retrieved September 01, 2013 from http://www.who.int/classifications/icd/ICD10Volume2_en_2010.pdf

Zisman, A. (2000). An overview of XML. *Computing & Control Engineering Journal*, *11*(4), 165–167. doi:10.1049/cce:20000405

ADDITIONAL READING

Alkraiji, A. I., Jackcon, T. W., & Murray, I. (2012). The Role of Health Data Standards in Developing Countries. *Journal of Health Informatics in Developing Countries*, *6*(2).

Benson, T. (2012). *Principles of health interoperability HL7 and SNOMED.* Springer. doi:10.1007/978-1-4471-2801-4

Boone, K. W. (2011). Codes and Vocabularies. In *The CDA TM book* (pp. 81–84). Springer London. doi:10.1007/978-0-85729-336-7_8

Chávez, E., Krishnan, P., & Finnie, G. (2010). A taxonomy of e-health standards to assist system developers. In Information Systems Development (pp. 737-745). Springer US.

Friedlin, J., & McDonald, C. J. (2010). An evaluation of medical knowledge contained in Wikipedia and its use in the LOINC database. *Journal of the American Medical Informatics Association*, *17*(3), 283–287. PMID:20442145

Garde, S., Knaup, P., Hovenga, E. J., & Heard, S. (2007). Towards Semantic Interoperability for Electronic Health Records--Domain Knowledge Governance for open EHR Archetypes. *Methods of Information in Medicine*, *46*(3), 332–343. PMID:17492120

González, C., Blobel, B., & López, D. M. (2010). Ontology-based interoperability service for HL7 interfaces implementation. *Studies in Health Technology and Informatics*, *155*, 108–114. PMID:20543317

Goverdhan, D. M. (2011). Why PHR when EHR is the record of future? *Sri Lanka Journal of Bio-Medical Informatics*, *1*, 27.

Huff, S. M. (2011). Ontologies, vocabularies, and data models. Clinical Decision Support: The Road Ahead, 307.

Jayaratna, P., & Sartipi, K. (2012). HL7 v3 message extraction using Semantic Web techniques. *International Journal of Knowledge Engineering and Data Mining*, *2*(1), 89–115. doi:10.1504/IJKEDM.2012.044699

Jones, S., & Groom, F. M. (Eds.). (2011). *Information and communication technologies in healthcare.* CRC Press. doi:10.1201/b11696

Kaminker, D. (2010). HL7 Clinical Document Architecture Ambassador Briefing. In 11th International HL7 Interoperability Conference, Rio de Janeiro, Brazil.

Khan, W. A., Hussain, M., Khattak, A. M., Amin, M. B., & Lee, S. (2012). Saas based interoperability service for semantic mappings among health-care standards. In 8th International Conference on Innovations in Information Technology.

Lin, M. C., Vreeman, D. J., McDonald, C. J., & Huff, S. M. (2011). A characterization of local LOINC mapping for laboratory tests in three large institutions. *Methods of Information in Medicine*, *50*(2), 105–114. doi:10.3414/ME09-01-0072 PMID:20725694

Meyer, R., Tschopp, M., & Lovis, C. (2010). Interoperability in hospital information systems: a return-on-investment study comparing CPOE with and without laboratory integration. *Swiss Medical Informatics*, *26*(69), 3–7.

Mogli, G. D. (2012). Why PHR when EHR is the record of future? *Sri Lanka Journal of Bio-Medical Informatics*, *2*(2), 75–83. doi:10.4038/sljbmi.v2i2.2246

Mouttham, A., Kuziemsky, C., Langayan, D., Peyton, L., & Pereira, J. (2012). Interoperable support for collaborative, mobile, and accessible health care. *Information Systems Frontiers*, *14*(1), 73–85. doi:10.1007/s10796-011-9296-y

Nagy, M., Preckova, P., Seidl, L., & Zvarova, J. (2010). Challenges of interoperability using hl7 v3 in czech healthcare. *Studies in Health Technology and Informatics*, *155*, 122–128. PMID:20543319

Ozbek, M. E., Kara, A., & Atas, M. (2010, April). Software technologies, architectures and interoperability in remote laboratories. In Information Technology Based Higher Education and Training (ITHET), 2010 9th International Conference on (pp. 402-406). IEEE.

Sheide, A., & Wilson, P. S. (2013). Reading up on LOINC. Journal of AHIMA/American Health Information Management Association, 84(4), 58-60.

Tang, T., Liu, Y., Ning, B., Li, K. C., & Yuan, L. (2012, January). Method of the Laboratory Interoperability Test for the Onboard Equipment of CTCS-3 Train Control System. In Proceedings of the 1st International Workshop on High-Speed and Intercity Railways (pp. 345-354). Springer Berlin Heidelberg.

Vreeman, D. J., McDonald, C. J., & Huff, S. M. (2010). Representing patient assessments in LOINC®. []. American Medical Informatics Association.]. *AMIA ... Annual Symposium Proceedings / AMIA Symposium. AMIA Symposium*, *2010*, 832. PMID:21347095

Walker, J., Pan, E., Johnston, D., Adler-Milstein, J., Bates, D. W., & Middleton, B. (2005). The value of health care information exchange and interoperability. *HEALTH AFFAIRS-MILLWOOD VA THEN BETHESDA MA*, *24*, W5. PMID:15659453

Zarcone, P., Nordenberg, D., Meigs, M., Merrick, U., Jernigan, D., & Hinrichs, S. H. (2010). Community-driven standards-based electronic laboratory data-sharing networks. *Public Health Reports*, *125*(Suppl 2), 47. PMID:20521375

Zunner, C., Bürkle, T., Prokosch, H. U., & Ganslandt, T. (2013). Mapping local laboratory interface terms to LOINC at a German university hospital using RELMA V. 5: A semi-automated approach. *Journal of the American Medical Informatics Association*, *20*(2), 293–297. doi:10.1136/amiajnl-2012-001063 PMID:22802268

KEY TERMS AND DEFINITIONS

Body/Personal Area Network (BAN/PAN): The collection of medical sensors worn by patient that collects biological data about patient.

Home Area Network (HAN): The network composed of the BAN/PAN and the devices used to monitor the patient.

Interoperability: It is the ability of two or more systems to exchange data, and use that data as they are its own.

Medical Classification: The system that organizes the medical terms, according to the shared similar properties, into categories and groups.

Medical Nomenclature: It is a catalog having the systematic list of names for medical terms.

Native Information Exchange: In this form of information exchange, no tool is needed to connect and communicate between two communicating bodies.

Patient Confidentiality and Privacy: The principle that ensures, the patient data is not exposed to public access and only the people who are entitled according to law and the consented by the patient can access the patient data.

Virtual Private Network: A VPN is an encrypted connection between a network and an outside device.

Chapter 8
Quality Management and Quality Assurance in Medical Laboratories

Kyriacos C. Tsimillis
Cyprus Accreditation Body, Cyprus

Sappho Michael
Ministry of Health, Cyprus

ABSTRACT

This chapter deals with issues of quality management and quality assurance in medical laboratories. Basic terms and their role in quality assurance in laboratory examinations are analyzed and discussed. Clarifications on certification and accreditation are given with a comprehensive analysis of the procedures they refer to and their implementation for particular tasks. The implementation of the international standard ISO 15189 is presented with reference to some recent developments. The chapter has been prepared to help medical laboratories in an introductory understanding of quality assurance issues and encourage them to proceed with the implementation of the standard ISO 15189 and not as a detailed guide. Some practical considerations rising from the experience of a small country such as Cyprus are also discussed.

INTRODUCTION

Quality can be defined as the degree to which the characteristics of a product, a service or a procedure satisfy set requirements and expectations. Legal and other requirements, reflecting the specific needs in each area, create the framework within which relevant activities are planned, implemented, monitored, controlled and assessed. Is there "good" and "bad" quality? Would it not be better if we referred to "adequate" or "non-adequate" quality instead? In any case, we need to describe the criteria for this consideration.

All services, regardless of their nature, need to be organized in an appropriate way using appropriate and documented procedures, properly trained and competent personnel, properly maintained and calibrated equipment, and to be operated with clear quality tasks.

DOI: 10.4018/978-1-4666-6320-6.ch008

Medical (or, clinical) laboratories represent an important infrastructure in every society. The services they provide are of decisive importance for the health of people and the quality of life, thus constituting an important and illustrative indicator of the level of development in society. As a result, provision of reliable services by medical laboratories is of high priority.

Quality management and quality assurance can be evaluated by accreditation or certification, depending on the nature of the particular activity. For many activities certification is adequate; however, the key element which needs to be ensured in medical laboratories is their technical competence and accreditation is the only tool to apply. Basic aspects of quality management and quality assurance in medical laboratories are presented and discussed in this chapter.

To this end the requirements of the international standard ISO 15189 which is the main document for quality management and technical competence in medical laboratories are analyzed.

BACKGROUND

In most economic activities quality and productivity issues are usually discussed in figures reflecting economic and quality indicators. A lot of aspects may be of a similar or an analogous relevance in all sectors. However, in the medical sector as well as in cases related to health and safety, the quality of services provided has quite a different significance.

There is very often a discussion on the cost of quality; the higher cost of high quality is considered as a disadvantage; however, what about the high cost of non-quality? Experience clearly illustrates that this cost is much higher even when corrective actions are possible, realistic and adequately efficient. To this end, a simplified approach "high quality or low cost?" seems to be the wrong question which may lead to a wrong answer, especially in times of economic recession. The

cost of failure and lack of reliability in medical laboratories cannot be estimated in figures and statistics. Although the economic aspects play their important and decisive role in the medical sector as well, the reliability of the results from medical laboratories is a must and a task for which no compromise can be allowed.

Laboratories in general represent the most widely known institution in the quality infrastructure in a country; other bodies, namely certification and inspection bodies are also important parts of the quality infrastructure. They all come under the title of "conformity assessment bodies" since they all contribute to the named task. Laboratories focus on two main activities, testing and calibration, the latter being an activity of high importance to all conformity assessment bodies since it contributes to the documentation of the metrological traceability, thus providing the basis for the "common measuring language" required in all measuring applications.

Measurements are carried out by laboratories. In almost all cases, measurements of various parameters and other factors are necessary. You can neither make an assessment nor an evaluation of compliance to set criteria without carrying out appropriate measurements. In the case of measurements, the meaning of quality includes reliability:

- What about the reliability of the measurement?
- What about the cost of non-reliable measurements?

In Europe, the European cooperation for Accreditation (EA) is the network of national accreditation bodies, one in each member state. All national accreditation bodies operate in compliance with both the ISO 17011 and the Regulation (EC) No 765/2008 of the European Parliament and of the Council setting out the requirements for accreditation and market surveillance relating to the marketing of products and repealing Regulation (EEC) No 339/93 [2008] OJ L 218/30.

Further to its requirement for the operation of a sole national accreditation body, the Regulation provides for no cross border accreditation except under clearly described conditions. However, the equal reliability of all national accreditation bodies is ensured via peer evaluation in which all bodies contribute regardless of their size and the size of the country where they operate. One of the committees of the European cooperation for Accreditation is dealing with the accreditation of laboratories. A Working Group, named "Healthcare", operating under it is focused on medical laboratories. The International Laboratory Accreditation Cooperation (ILAC) is globally active and covers all regional networks. The two organizations publish technical documents both mandatory and advisory to facilitate the implementation of all accreditation standards and, in the case of medical laboratories, the ISO 15189; they also provide a framework of requirements and guidance to support the harmonized operation of the accreditation bodies and the provision of accreditation services. The European and the International Federations of Clinical Chemistry have direct communication with the accreditation organizations with regard to healthcare and medical laboratories.

Accreditation and certification are two terms which are often wrongly considered equivalent. Accreditation is the assessment by an authorized body that a laboratory or other conformity assessment body is technically competent to carry out specific tasks. The legal basis for accreditation is provided in the relevant European Regulation (2008). Accreditation is considered to represent the highest level of recognition of activities within quality infrastructure. Certification refers to the approval by a body that a product, a service or a person conforms to specified requirements. This is based on the auditing of the relevant activity but does not deal with the technical competence.

QUALITY MANAGEMENT IN MEDICAL LABORATORIES

Quality management is implemented with a quality management system which consists of the following components:

- A Quality Manual, where the policies for compliance with set requirements e.g. as described in a standard.
- A series of operational procedures, which illustrate how these policies are implemented.
- Working instructions to facilitate the implementation of the procedures.
- Templates and forms to keep relevant records.
- External documents (legislative, technical and others).

The efficiency of the management system can be monitored through some questions, mainly:

- Does the Quality Manual address all necessary aspects?
- Do appropriate operational procedures exist?
- Are they in written form?
- Are they efficiently implemented?
- What happens when they are not considered functional and effective?

The answers to these questions are given in practice, during the actual operation of the activity, through quality assurance which provides the means to continuously monitor the implementation of the set procedures. In principle, these aspects can be served by certification of the activity according to the standard ISO 9001 (2008). However, this could be fit for purpose in hospitals but not in medical laboratories.

Medical laboratories should prepare and implement a quality management system as described in either the standard ISO 9001 or Chapter 4 of the standard ISO 15189 (Note: In what follows, ISO 15189 will be referred to as the "Standard"). This does not impose the need for certification. However, these elements are not adequate. The laboratory needs to demonstrate its competence and the reliability of its results. To this end, further to the management system, it needs to ensure that all factors contributing to the reliability of the measurements are properly considered. They refer to the

- Technical competence of personnel.
- Adequacy of infrastructure (premises, equipment, metrological traceability).
- Appropriateness of the methodology.

Uncertainty of measurements should be estimated and taken into consideration in the evaluation of the results of the examination for diagnosis. Although this parameter may still not be well conceived by the users of the reports, it is indeed evidence of reliability! Results always include uncertainty! It is a matter of competence for the laboratory to estimate it and consider it as appropriate. It is worth noting that, in the medical sector, samples under examination are unique by their nature and often the results need to be available in a short time to be used for the diagnosis and treatment of the patient.

The above mentioned are the main technical elements to be dealt with in the quality management system; this makes it necessary for a laboratory to be accredited.

The Accreditation Standard ISO 15189 for Medical Laboratories

Accreditation is globally recognized as the highest level of assessment of the competence and reliability of laboratories. The international standard ISO 15189 represents the main tool for the accreditation of medical laboratories. When this standard was first published in 2003, there were some reservations from those familiar with ISO/IEC 17025 which had been implemented for some years in all types of laboratories; they were, to some extent, reluctant to shift to the new standard. Ten years later, the second revision of the ISO 15189 (2012) is already available. The new edition introduces a number of changes which will need a transient period, ending before March 2016, for its implementation by all interested parties, namely the medical laboratories and the accreditation bodies as well as other stakeholders. Even now, the question whether a medical laboratory may prefer to follow the ISO/IEC 17025, which is generally applicable to all testing laboratories, arises. The accreditation body is expected to provide the service requested by the applicant laboratory. However, after more than ten years of coexistence of the two standards, it is doubtless that ISO 15189 can better meet the needs of the medical laboratory, both regarding the terminology used and the description of various steps in the operation of the laboratory. One of the main elements in the said standard is the definition of the medical laboratory which clearly puts boundaries to the extent that this standard could be used.

Regardless of the developments in the operation of the National Health System or other relevant infrastructure in each country, it is expected that accreditation will gradually be more widely used as a pre-requisite for medical laboratories in order to be part of the social insurance system, thus upgrading the reliability of medical laboratory results.

The starting point for medical laboratories trying to establish reliability is the preparation and implementation of a quality management system. A tool to address the management requirements for this task is either ISO 9001 or (more appropriate due to fitness for purpose) ISO 15189 (Chapter 4) where all management issues are addressed. This step does not impose the need for certification and does not document the competence of the laboratory; to this end, the technical requirements could be addressed only with ISO 15189.

ISO 15189 presents some differences compared to ISO 17025; the most important of them are the following:

- The term patient is used instead of customer.
- No reference is made to subcontracting.
- Examination by referral laboratories is included.
- A detailed description of three phases, namely pre-examination, examination and post-examination, is included.
- Reference is made to ethical issues which is quite an important issue in medical laboratories.
- Detailed reference is made to the laboratory information system.

The Structure of the Standard

The structure of the Standard facilitates a direct correlation with the quality management certification standard ISO 9001. The accreditation standard ISO 15189 classifies the main requirements in two categories, namely the ones related to management issues (Chapter 4) and the ones related to technical competence issues (Chapter 5). This is advantageous because it facilitates an easy correspondence of Chapter 4 to the issues addressed by ISO 9001. Although the certification is not of any added value for laboratories, it may be the case that a medical laboratory operating in a hospital which is certified as appropriate may need to demonstrate that its accreditation status meets the needs of ISO 9000, as well. This is indeed reflected in a statement on the accreditation certificate, after a decision by ISO, ILAC and IAF; according to the IAF-ILAC-ISO Joint Communiqué (2009) "This laboratory is accredited in accordance with the recognized International Standard ISO 15189:2007. This accreditation

demonstrates technical competence for a defined scope and the operation of a laboratory quality management system".

Point-of-Care Testing

A particular activity refers to the point-of-care-testing (POCT). The standard ISO 22870 (2006) specifies it as the testing that is performed near or at the site of a patient with the result leading to possible change in the care of the patient. This is an activity provided by medical laboratories either within the boundaries of their own organization or to external organizations i.e. another legal entity. The assessment of these activities has to be made against the international standards ISO 22870 and ISO 15189.

SOME BASIC QUESTIONS ABOUT ACCREDITATION

Who Can Accredit?

The responsibility and authority for the assessment for accreditation lies with the accreditation bodies. In Europe, the Regulation 765/2008 specifies that only one national accreditation body can operate in a member state. This is not the case in all other regions. However, in all cases, the accreditation body has to fully comply with the relevant international standard ISO/IEC 17011 (2004) which specifies all necessary requirements for the competence of the accreditation bodies which are periodically evaluated for their compliance with the said standard, in both their operation and the provision of accreditation services according to regional and international rules.

Can a Hospital Be Accredited?

The objective of accreditation is the assessment of the technical competence of conformity assessment bodies. Bearing this in mind, could hospitals, clinics and other institutions be accredited? Only the laboratories operating in these institutions can be accredited. For the institutions as a whole, the main need is for the compliance with management issues; thus certification is the appropriate procedure preferably based on an integrated management system where all relevant quality, environmental, occupational health and safety as well as information management aspects should be included. These elements are covered by relevant standards, namely ISO 9001 (2008), ISO 14001 (2004), OHSAS 18001 (2007) etc. There are cases of hospitals and clinics holding accreditation certificates issued by private companies based on own standards. These certificates do not justify an accreditation status due to the absence of both the correct basis i.e. the ISO 15189 and the authorization for accreditation which lies only with accreditation bodies. To this end the use of the term accreditation for hospitals and clinics is not appropriate and not correct at all!

Accreditation or Certification for Medical Laboratories?

For a long time there was confusion between certification and accreditation with regard to laboratories. The two terms and their different objectives may have not been clearly understood. In practice they present similarities referring to the audit-based nature of the procedures followed and the fact that they both conclude on the compliance with specified standards. However they also present significant differences as a result of their different tasks illustrated in their definitions (Tsimillis, 2010; ILAC, 2013).

Further to the management aspects, medical laboratories need to demonstrate their technical competence in order to ensure reliable results upon which diagnosis and medical treatment, whenever necessary, can be based. Technical competence is assessed only through Accreditation (ISO 15189). The Standard includes both management (Chapter 4) and technical requirements (Chapter

5). Therefore an accredited medical laboratory demonstrates both its technical competence for a range of activities and the implementation of an appropriate organized management system.

HOW TO IMPLEMENT THE STANDARD: THE MANAGEMENT REQUIREMENTS

The Scope of Accreditation

A laboratory may apply for accreditation for only part of the examinations it performs; therefore, the scope of accreditation, appearing on the accreditation certificate, will include only this part. In any case, the management system and the management issues in particular are implemented for the whole range of activities. It is expected that the scope of accreditation will gradually be extended to cover all examinations performed by the laboratory. The accreditation certificate granted by the accreditation body clearly illustrates the exact scope of accreditation at the time of issue, usually as an annex which is an integral part of the certificate (ILAC, 2010).

The Quality Management System

The implementation of the Standard requires that the laboratory drafts its quality management system. It comprises of a series of documents, addressing the provisions of the Standard and, at the same time, describing what the laboratory does in its everyday work. The laboratory is not expected to describe what it is intended to do or what it should do but only what it is really doing. The whole set of documents is not kept static but it is periodically reviewed and further developed to reflect the changing needs and demands using also the experience gained during its implementation and monitoring. The International Laboratory Accreditation Cooperation has recently prepared a guide for the medical laboratories accreditation

(ILAC, 2012); the Working Group "Healthcare" operating under the Laboratory Committee of the European cooperation for Accreditation elaborates on specific issues, in cooperation with European and International Federations for Clinical Chemistry and other institutions. Eurachem has published a Guide for the accreditation of microbiological laboratories, covering medical ones as well (Eleftheriadou & Tsimillis, 2013) after the revision of the relevant document published by the European cooperation for Accreditation (2002).

The Quality Management System is the "Bible" for a medical laboratory. Its basic elements are the following:

- The quality manual.
- The standard operational procedures.
- Working instructions.
- Forms and templates.
- The examination methods.

Further to the above which are internal documents prepared by the laboratory, a series of external documents are maintained and implemented as appropriate. They are mainly pieces of legislation, standards, methods, manuals of equipment, codes of practice, publications by national, regional and international bodies, scientific institutions and networks and other documents from the bibliography. All these documents are taken into consideration when drafting documents describing the methods implemented as well as other documents addressing specific technical aspects. Forms and templates filled in as appropriate represent records of the laboratory which are part of the management system.

Organization and Management Responsibility

The organization structure needs to be well defined reflecting all main activities, as well as the relations with the parent organization (if applicable).

Key personnel, mainly the technical manager and the quality manager and, depending on the case, heads of the departments need to have their deputies appointed. All members of the staff need to be aware of the tasks of the management system and all relevant documentation, according to their assignments and authorization. The structural links between various roles are illustrated in the organizational chart of the laboratory. The laboratory management shall describe the quality policy of the laboratory and establish measurable quality objectives consistent to this policy. Effective communication with the staff needs to be ensured as well as between the laboratory and its stakeholders. The relevant clause also includes provisions for ethical conduct which refer to the non-involvement in activities that would diminish confidence in the laboratory's competence, impartiality, judgment and integrity, the freedom from any undue pressures and influences, the need to declare any potential conflict, the availability of appropriate policy and procedures for the treatment of samples and remains and the confidentiality of information.

Document Control

The laboratory needs to ensure that all members of the staff are aware of the management system, its tasks and objectives and how these are being respected through the operation of the laboratory. To this end the various components/ elements of the management system are distributed to the members of the staff, either in electronic or hardware copies, according to the individual roles, authorization and responsibility allocated to them as appropriate. It is quite important to ensure that the status of all documents, both internal and external, is followed. In the case of the internal documents this is important in order to ensure their harmonized and appropriate use; in the case of external documents, this is necessary to ensure that new requirements, if any, are reflected in the internal documents and implemented.

Service Agreements

The policies and procedures on how to review contracts need to be documented; these should refer to the methods required, the capabilities of the laboratory and the confirmation of the availability of necessary skills. These aspects need to be discussed between the medical laboratory and the customer; the latter could be the requesting physician, the hospital or clinic, the patient. The task is to ensure that the laboratory is aware of what the customer is expecting, the examinations to be carried out, the reporting procedure, the turnaround time and the resulting cost and confirm that the laboratory is capable of providing a particular service. In the case of laboratories operating within hospitals and clinics, the contract review is included in service agreements. National legislative requirements are also taken into consideration and respected as appropriate.

Subcontractors

Contrary to the standard ISO/IEC 17025 (2005), the standard ISO 15189 (2007) did not provide for subcontracting. However there may be a need for subcontracting part of the examinations for various reasons either occasionally e.g. due to workload, technical problems with equipment, absence of competent personnel or on a permanent basis e.g. lack of expertise in case of new tasks. According to the new edition of the Standard ISO 15189 (2012), the laboratory is expected to consider subcontractors as referral laboratories.

Referral Laboratories

Initially the term was used only for external laboratories to which samples are submitted for a second opinion (ISO 15189:2007); as already mentioned, the new edition of the Standard widens the scope of the term to cover laboratories to which samples may be submitted even for routine examinations which cannot be carried out in the laboratory. In any case, referral laboratories need to be selected and evaluated against certain criteria. Furthermore, the policies for reporting the results and the inherent responsibilities need to be defined.

External Services and Supplies

Supplies and services make up a very important factor affecting the performance of the medical laboratory; they refer to equipment, reagents, control samples, kits and calibrators, proficiency testing schemes, calibration services, consultancy, software etc. The laboratory should evaluate suppliers of critical reagents, supplies and services against well described criteria, both initially and periodically.

Advisory Services

The medical laboratory is expected to document the way of communicating with both the requesting physicians and the patients. The latter mainly refers to guidance provided by the laboratory to patients regarding their preparation prior to primary sample collection.

Complaints

Clinicians, patients, laboratory staff and other parties may submit complaints to the laboratory; a documented procedure needs to exist and be followed for the management of the complaints. Relevant records shall be maintained.

Nonconformities

Whatever represents a failure of the management system or a deviation from the written procedures or an incident resulting in a complaint by the requesting physicians or the patients is considered as a nonconformity. Such nonconformities could be raised:

- Internally, during the monitoring of everyday work or the internal audit or after a complaint is received.
- During an external assessment by the accreditation body.

In the medical laboratory, the most crucial nonconformities refer to non-reliable results. This is due to the fact that a corrective action might not always be possible and, at the same time, the sample might be unique.

Corrective and Preventive Actions

Regardless of the origin of nonconformities, the laboratory is obliged to implement effective corrective actions which are audited for their efficiency after being implemented. Relevant records need to be retained for a pre-determined period. Further to this, the laboratory needs to analyze the root of the nonconformity and try to implement appropriate and efficient preventive measures to avoid its recurrence. The analysis of all nonconformities over a period of time e.g. annually may lead to useful conclusions for their trend, if any. Is there a need for further training, is it just an isolated incident, are the written procedures clear or do they need some revision for improvement?

Continual Improvement

In all quality management systems, continual improvement is a major task; a number of reasons during the implementation of the management system may initiate efforts for improvement. To this end the use of quality indicators is very useful; some examples of indicators refer to the outcome of surveys among patients and physicians, the number of nonconformities and complaints, the participation in proficiency testing schemes, etc.

Records

The medical laboratory needs to retain records of its activity for a specified period of time; retaining period depends on the nature of the records and the particular needs as well as the national and other legislative requirements. Records include results and reports, documentation for the training of the staff, calibration of equipment and nonconformities and corrective actions, reports from internal audits, minutes of the management review meetings, contracts, monitoring of suppliers, results of examinations, data related to referral laboratories, reports from external quality assessment schemes etc.

Internal Audits

All activities of the laboratory, including management and technical issues, need to be audited periodically, preferably annually, according to an appropriate plan by trained and competent personnel. The plan may be spread all over the year. Further to the competence of the internal auditors, it is required that their independence of the activity to be audited is adequately documented. This role mainly belongs to the Quality Manager and his/her deputy. However, other competent persons could be involved depending on the variety of activities and the methods implemented by the laboratory. The competence of the internal auditors is ensured by their training on the relevant standard ISO 19011 (2002).

Management Review

The management of the laboratory needs to carry out management reviews, preferably once a year to review all aspects regarding the operation and further improvement of the laboratory. This annual meeting does not eliminate the need for continuous interaction of the management with the staff during the year, both within departments and as a whole. According to the provisions of the Standard, the management review meeting should deal with reports by managerial staff, the outcome of the internal audit and external assessment i.e. the ones of the accreditation body, nonconformities with relevant trends illustrating the root of the problems, new demands and training needs, results from the participation in proficiency testing activities, budgetary issues, feedback from customers and partners, analysis of quality indicators etc. All key personnel should attend the meeting and present reports relevant to their role in the System. The minutes of these meetings are kept as records and are reviewed with regard to the implementation of appropriate actions within a defined time schedule as specified by the decisions taken.

HOW TO IMPLEMENT THE STANDARD: THE TECHNICAL REQUIREMENTS

Personnel

The technical competence of the staff needs to be documented based on the academic background, the experience and continuous training. Furthermore, appropriate documentation for the familiarization with relevant methodology, use of equipment and successful participation in proficiency testing schemes or other comparisons are necessary. Last but not least, national and regional legislative requirements need to be considered prior to authorization of personnel. Authorization is required for all activities in the laboratory including carrying out the examinations, maintenance/calibration of equipment (if applicable), reviewing of results, signing and releasing the reports.

Accommodation and Environmental Conditions

It is quite important to ensure adequate environmental conditions. This refers to all factors which might affect the integrity of the samples and the appropriate implementation of the examinations e.g. temperature, humidity, storage, electromagnetic interference, the safety in the workplace, separation of sections where incompatible activities are carried out, ventilation, prevention of contamination etc. Further to the proper planning for the location arrangements, the laboratory needs to monitor its efficiency and take appropriate actions when required. Management and safe disposal of samples, reagents and other materials is of high importance; national legislation applies for the waste management. Requirements for safe practices in the medical laboratory are specified in ISO 15190 (2003).

Laboratory Equipment, Reagents, and Consumables

The laboratory should be furnished with all appropriate equipment to carry out the whole range of examinations for which it is intended to provide services as well as the equipment necessary for all preparatory and supporting work. Each item of equipment should be uniquely identified and should be operated by authorized personnel in a safe and appropriate working condition. The capability and the performance of the equipment should be monitored to ensure that it is still fit for the purpose. To this end appropriate preventive maintenance and calibration need to be carried out as specified in time-schedules. In the case of equipment found to be defective, it shall be labeled accordingly and remain out of service. Following appropriate repair, there should be a confirmation that the equipment is again fit for purpose. The provisions of the relevant clause of the Standard applies to instruments, reference materials, reagents, consumables, analytical systems and computer software included in laboratory equipment.

Metrological traceability needs to be documented for all equipment used including supporting equipment monitoring the environmental conditions. Thus all equipment e.g. thermometer, balances, incubators, pipettes have to be calibrated according to plan at a documented frequency while in other cases control samples traceable to SI units have to be used. The instruments, the equipment, the reagents, the control materials, the calibrators and the diagnostic kits are covered by the Directive 98/79/EC of the European Parliament and of the Council on *in vitro* diagnostic medical devices [1998] OJ L 331/1. The Directive provides for these devices to be CE marked; in the case of calibrators and control materials, it also provides for their traceability to SI units, although, in practice, this is not always possible or relevant.

Pre-Examination Processes

The pre-examination phase is considered as the most important one. It starts from the primary sample collection and is related to factors not always under the control of the laboratory, even unknown in some cases, resulting in the highest percentage of failure of the results. The pre-examination phase starts from the primary sample collection to the examination phase. The integrity of the sample is related to the interval and the conditions during its transfer to the laboratory. Before this, the proper preparation of the patient is another crucial factor. The laboratory should prepare and use the primary sample collection manual. This manual contains all necessary information and instructions regarding all examinations offered e.g. patient preparation, primary sample collection, identification, transfer and storage of primary samples etc. The whole

trip from the collection location to the laboratory needs to be monitored with regard to the appropriate conditions for each case. Upon reception at the laboratory, all samples need to be registered accompanied by details of who collected/received them and when. The laboratory should ensure that samples are stored under appropriate conditions so that repetitive or additional examination could be carried out if needed. In case the patient receives any medication, this is recorded by the laboratory and is taken into consideration when the results are discussed.

Examination Processes

The laboratory needs to use appropriate procedures to provide the services required. Therefore, it is preferable to use widely recognized methods, published in textbooks and scientific journals. If this is the case, the laboratory needs to verify the method used, i.e. to confirm that it can perform the method in a satisfactory way, according to its published features. In case of in-house procedures and methods or modifications made by the laboratory, it has to carry out an appropriate validation for the intended use. Relevant documentation needs to be retained. A document should be prepared by the laboratory based on the instructions provided by the published information. This refers also to the use of kits for which the information provided by the supplier should be checked for changes and confirmed for on-going suitability. The documentation for an examination needs to be properly identified and included in the document control. It shall include, among others, the purpose and the principles of the procedure used, the performance specifications, the type of primary sample, the type of container and additives, equipment and reagents to be used, calibration and quality control procedures, interferences and cross reactions, the principle for calculation of the results and the expression of the uncertainty, biological reference intervals, alert/critical values, safety precautions, laboratory interpretation etc.

Biological reference intervals should be periodically reviewed taking into account any changes as well as the possibility of some differentiation for the reference population.

The laboratory needs to estimate the uncertainty of results in the cases this task is relevant and possible. All sources of uncertainties i.e. sampling, reagents, calibrators, reference materials, environmental conditions and other inputs, which could be critical for the diagnosis should be taken into account. Uncertainty of measurement should be reported upon request especially in case it might be critical for the diagnosis and curing or treatment.

Ensuring Quality of Examination Results

The laboratory needs to take specific measures to attain and document quality assurance in the implementation of the examination procedures. To this end it should use a combination of actions including the following:

Internal Quality Control

This refers to the monitoring of the performance of the laboratory. For each examination, daily measurement is carried out on controls (certified reference materials). Deviations of the results from the assigned values in correlation to pre-determined acceptance limits, variation from day to day and inherent trends provide the basis for corrective and/or preventive actions if considered necessary. Bearing in mind that all necessary equipment and materials (reagents, kits, controls and calibrators) are usually provided by the same supplier, it is difficult to identify systematic errors which may occur; therefore the need for an external quality assurance system is imperative.

External Quality Assessment

The participation in proficiency testing schemes and other interlaboratory comparisons is a requirement for the medical laboratory. The Standard specifies that proficiency testing schemes should substantially agree with the accreditation standard for this activity. As from February 2012 when ISO/IEC 17043 (2010) was fully implemented, the easy way to meet this requirement is the accreditation of the particular scheme against the said standard. If this is not the case, it is upon the laboratory itself to assess the scheme. Based on the results of this participation, the laboratory takes corrective actions in case deviations are higher than the acceptable limits; furthermore it detects the trends and takes preventive actions as appropriate. All personnel authorized for specific tasks should participate, in rotation, in the respective schemes.

Post-Examination Processes

This phase refers to the evaluation of the results of the examinations by competent personnel who authorize the release of the results. Further to this, the storage of primary samples after examination has to be in line with established policy while their management and disposal after a certain period has to follow local regulations and other codes of practice.

Reporting of Results

A report of the results of the examination should include reference to all details of the identification and location of the patient, the name of the requester, the examination carried out, the biological reference intervals, the date and time of the primary sample collection, the time of its receipt by the laboratory, the name of the person authorizing the release of the report, interpretation and other comments, uncertainty of measurement upon request. The results should be reported in SI units or units traceable to SI units, where applicable. The laboratory should have documented its policy on the communication of the results, considering the protection of data, the correction of the report already issued, if this is considered necessary and the authorization of the person checking or releasing the report. National and regional regulations may provide for additional requirements. Results of accredited and non accredited examinations should be clearly indicated on the report.

Laboratory Information System

The need to safeguard the results and all information produced by the laboratory is one of the main priorities. As yet, this issue was referred to in the Standard in an informative Annex. However, in the new version of the Standard, requirements on the management of the laboratory information system have been upgraded, included under one of its clauses. This means that this issue has been given higher emphasis and is considered as significant as it really is. To this end, it needs to be addressed by the laboratory in a more systematic way. The main aspects refer to the procedures and the appropriate environment for the proper maintenance of the results and information, their entry and storage, retrieval and use both in hardware and software. A detailed presentation of the main aspects to be dealt with has been recently published (Archondakis, Stathopoulou, & Sitaras, 2011).

FUTURE DEVELOPMENTS

Standards are not static tools; they are reviewed periodically, usually every five years, in order to ensure that they meet existing and additional needs, based on the experience gained during their implementation. The new standard represents a chal-

lenge for medical laboratories, both the accredited and the ones in the process towards accreditation. The transient period for its full implementation by all interested parties, i.e. the laboratories and the accreditation bodies, ends before March 2016. A synopsis of the main changes it introduces is the following (Hubca et al., 2013):

- Definitions are referred to ISO 9000 (2005), ISO/IEC 17000 (2004) and ISO/IEC Guide 99 (2007).
- *Shall* is used instead of *should*, thus making relevant provisions stronger.
- More detailed text regarding e.g. organization and management responsibility, internal audits, management review, accommodation and environmental conditions, equipment, pre-examination, examination, assuring quality.
- Subcontractors could be dealt with under referral laboratories.
- The title of some clauses is changed; service agreements is used instead of contract review, evaluation and audits instead of internal audits, processes instead of procedures.
- Some provisions have been moved to other clauses; in other cases, new sub-clauses are included.
- The reference to the Laboratory Information Systems, previously included in an informative Annex, becomes part of the Standard, thus a requirement and not a recommendation.
- The issue of Ethics, previously included in an informative Annex, is now dealt in a more comprehensive way in the main text, thus becoming normative.

It is expected that international and regional accreditation organizations as well as national accreditation bodies will further elaborate on issues referring to the interpretation of the new provisions and providing training of assessors and awareness material to medical laboratories in order to ensure the smooth transition to the new standard and its harmonized implementation.

PROBLEMS, SOLUTIONS, AND RECOMMENDATIONS

In Cyprus, there are quite a few accredited medical laboratories, most of them operating as independent ones in the private sector. For some years now, there is an on-going discussion regarding the need to establish a National Health System which is expected to provide, among others, for the accreditation of medical laboratories. Despite the delay in fulfilling this task, accreditation of medical laboratories which started at the beginning of the previous decade represents a challenge for medical laboratories. Although the number of the accredited medical laboratories is still rather small, namely approximately twenty five out of more than 150, they represent the largest group among other accredited bodies. Further to a number of private sector laboratories, which initially proceeded to accreditation, significant interest for accreditation has recently been shown by hospital laboratories in the public sector. In some cases, the scope of activity of new applicants introduced interesting challenges in new areas and specialized techniques. It is worth noting that in such a small country, more than 130 private medical laboratories are operating. Inevitably, their size, in most cases, is small with only 1-5 members of staff. This creates some difficulties when trying to implement the Standard which are being faced without deviation from the requirements of the Standard.

The most frequently occurring findings during the assessment of the laboratories towards their accreditation are related to the small size and therefore the whole set-up of the private medical laboratories (Tsimillis & Michael, 2011). In particular:

- Management issues - key personnel with multiple roles, no deputies, internal audits and management review, code of ethics.
- Documentation and monitoring of corrective measures.
- Health and safety issues.
- Quality assurance of the samples - sampling, sample transport conditions.
- Metrological traceability.
- Supporting services: suppliers, referral laboratories or sub-contractors.
- Best use of the participation in proficiency testing schemes.

The Cyprus Accreditation Body (CYS-CYS-AB) has extensively contributed to the increase of awareness on quality assurance and accreditation having organized a number of training and other events for more than fifteen years now, in some cases with invited speakers from abroad. In 2011 CYS-CYSAB became a signatory to the Multilateral Agreement of the European cooperation for Accreditation for testing (including medical) and inspection and signed the Mutual Recognition Arrangement, thus becoming a Full Member of the International Laboratory Accreditation Cooperation. This development was of additional support for all accredited bodies in Cyprus.

The preparation of the Standard ISO 15189 was oriented to serve the needs of hospital laboratories; however, the Standard can be implemented by small private laboratories as well. From the Cyprus experience some examples are illustrative:

- In a small laboratory with only two or three members of staff, one of them can be designated for more than one key roles in the management system. Then, how can the laboratory meet the requirement for independence of the internal auditor of the activities being audited? In such a case, an external partner could undertake this role, provided he/she is competent for the particular task.

- In a laboratory with two members of the staff authorized for a particular examination, the internal audit for this examination is carried out by one of them with the other being witnessed; in case only one person is authorized, an external competent partner has to be invited to undertake the role of the internal auditor for the said task.
- In case an appropriate proficiency scheme is not available, what can the laboratory do? Exchange of samples with another laboratory may serve the need provided that a protocol is drafted to describe the framework for this comparison and how to use its outcome.
- A laboratory operating in a hospital, is supported by the parent organization with regard to a series of services, e.g. supplies, maintenance, management of environmental conditions, information system, accounts department, receipt of complaints, primary sample collection etc. In such a case, a service agreement should be signed between the parent organization, namely the management of the hospital and the laboratory director providing, on the one hand, for the conditions under which the specified support and services are ensured and, on the other hand, the responsibilities of the laboratory to provide reliable results. To this end the hospital and its services are considered as suppliers in the meaning of the Standard and are evaluated according to its requirements.
- Medical laboratories operating in hospitals which have already been implementing a management system in compliance with ISO 9001 or, preferably, integrated management system, may find it easier to proceed with their preparation towards accreditation due to the fact that they already implement the requirements of ISO 9001 which as already mentioned are the same as the management requirements in

Chapter 4 of the accreditation standard. However, their system is to be assessed by the accreditation body. No need for the certification body to audit this part, no added value for this.

CONCLUSION

The benefits of accreditation for all involved are multiple and of great significance; they refer to the patients, the regulators, the medical laboratories themselves (ILAC, 2013). They could be summarized in the following:

- According to the Standard the patients' welfare is paramount. It provides for a fair and non-discriminatory treatment of all patients.
- Accreditation is patient-focused, impartial and objective; it provides a mechanism for measuring quality improvement and supports consistency in the quality of care.
- The increase in confidence on the results allows for the reduction of risks and the minimization of repetitive examinations and duplication
- The reliability of the examination results provides the basis for correct and efficient diagnosis and further treatment.

The reliability of measurements in medical laboratories is undoubtedly of critical importance. Quality assurance takes into consideration all phases, namely the pre-examination, the examination and the post-examination. The implementation of a management system including all relevant aspects, both management and technical, provides the appropriate framework for the operation of medical laboratories. Accreditation provides the third party attestation of the overall competence of the laboratory. Accreditation is the main tool to demonstrate reliability of medical laboratories. In a number of countries, including Cyprus, the competent authorities have introduced, or consider introducing, requirements for the mandatory accreditation of medical laboratories.

REFERENCES

Archondakis, S., Stathopoulou, A., & Sitaras, I. (2011). ISO 15189:2007: Implementation in a laboratory information system. In A. Moumtzoglou & A. Kastania (Eds.), E-Health Systems Quality and Reliability: Models and Standards (pp 64-72). Hershey, PA: IGI Global.

Eleftheriadou, M., & Tsimillis, K. C. (Eds.). (2013). *Accreditation for microbiological laboratories* (2nd ed.). Retrieved February 2, 2014, from www.eurachem.org

European cooperation for Accreditation. (2002). *EA-4/10 G: Accreditation for microbiological laboratories.* Retrieved February 2, 2014, from www.european-accreditation.org

European Cooperation for Accreditation. (2008). *EA-4/17 M: EA position paper on the description of scopes of accreditation of medical laboratories.* Retrieved February 2, 2014, from www.european-accreditation.org

Hubca, A., Koniotou, R., Gligic, L., Noten, V., Zdilna, P., Kastrop, P., & Greven, I. (2013, June). *Comparison ISO 15189:2007 vs ISO 15189:2012.* Paper presented at the meeting of the EA WG "Healthcare". Frankfurt, Germany.

International Accreditation Forum - International Laboratory Accreditation Cooperation - International Organization for Standardization IAF-ILAC-ISO Joint communiqué on the management systems requirements of ISO 15189:2007. (2009). Retrieved February 2, 2014, from http://www.ilac.org

International Laboratory Accreditation Cooperation. (2001). *ILAC B9: ISO 15189 Medical laboratory accreditation.* Retrieved February 2, 2014, from http://www.ilac.org

International Laboratory Accreditation Cooperation. (2010). *ILAC G18: Guideline for the formulation of scopes of accreditation for laboratories.* Retrieved February 2, 2014, from http://www.ilac.org

International Laboratory Accreditation Cooperation. (2012). *ILAC-G26: Guidance for the Implementation of a medical laboratory accreditation system.* Retrieved February 2, 2014, from http://www.ilac.org

International Laboratory Accreditation Cooperation. (2013). *ILAC B5: Securing testing, measurement or calibration services - The difference between accreditation and certification.* Retrieved February 2, 2014, from http://www.ilac.org

International Organization for Standardization. (2002). *ISO 19011: Guidelines for quality and/or environmental management systems auditing.* Geneva: ISO.

International Organization for Standardization. (2003). *ISO 15190: Medical laboratories – Requirements for safety.* Geneva: ISO.

International Organization for Standardization. (2004). *ISO 14001: Environmental management systems - Requirements with guidance for use.* Geneva: ISO.

International Organization for Standardization. (2005). *ISO 9000: Quality management systems - Fundamentals and vocabulary.* Geneva: ISO.

International Organization for Standardization. (2006). *ISO 22870: Point-of-care testing (POCT) - Requirements for quality and competence.* Geneva: ISO.

International Organization for Standardization. (2007). *ISO 15189: Medical laboratories - Particular requirements for quality and competence.* Geneva: ISO.

International Organization for Standardization. (2008). *ISO 9001: Quality management systems – Requirements.* Geneva: ISO.

International Organization for Standardization. (2012). *ISO 15189: Medical laboratories - Requirements for quality and competence.* Geneva: ISO.

International Organization for Standardization / International Electrotechnical Committee. (2004a). *ISO/IEC 17000: Conformity assessment- Vocabulary and general principles.* Geneva: ISO/IEC.

International Organization for Standardization / International Electrotechnical Committee. (2004b). *ISO/IEC 17011: Conformity assessment - General requirements for accreditation bodies accrediting conformity assessment bodies.* Geneva: ISO/IEC.

International Organization for Standardization / International Electrotechnical Committee. (2005). *ISO/IEC 17025: General requirements for the competence of testing and calibration laboratories.* Geneva: ISO/IEC.

International Organization for Standardization / International Electrotechnical Committee. (2007). *ISO/IEC Guide 99: International vocabulary of metrology - Basic and general concepts and associated terms* (VIM 3rd ed). Retrieved February 2, 2014, from http://www.bipm.org/vim

International Organization for Standardization / International Electrotechnical Committee. (2010). *ISO/IEC 17043: Conformity assessment - General requirements for proficiency testing.* Geneva: ISO/IEC.

The Occupational Health and Safety Advisory Services. (2007). *OHSAS 18001: Occupational Health and Safety Management.* London: OHSAS.

Tsimillis, K. C. (2010). Accreditation or certification for laboratories? In B. W. Wenclawiak, M. Koch, & E. Hadjicostas (Eds.), *Quality assurance in Analytical Chemistry* (2nd ed., pp. 73–93). Heidelberg, Germany: Springer. doi:10.1007/978-3-642-13609-2_4

Tsimillis, K. C., & Michael, S. (2011, March). *Frequently occurring findings in the accreditation of medical laboratories.* Paper presented at the 5th Congress of Clinical Chemistry. Limassol, Cyprus.

KEY TERMS AND DEFINITIONS

Accreditation: An attestation by a national accreditation body that a conformity assessment body meets the requirements set by harmonized standards and, where applicable, any additional requirements including those set out in relevant sectoral schemes, to carry out a specific conformity assessment activity (Regulation (EC) No 765/2008).

Certification: Third-party attestation related to products, processes, systems or persons (ISO/IEC 17000:2004).

Conformity Assessment: The process demonstrating whether specified requirements relating to the product, process, system, person or body have been fulfilled (Regulation (EC) No 765/2008).

Conformity Assessment Body: A body that performs conformity assessment activities including calibration, testing, certification and inspection (Regulation (EC) No 765/2008).

Medical (or, Clinical) Laboratory: Laboratory for the biological, microbiological, immunological, chemical, immunohaematological, haematological, biophysical, cytological, pathological, genetic or other examination of materials derived from the human body for the purpose of providing information for the diagnosis, management, prevention and treatment of disease of human beings or the assessment of their health; such examination may provide a consultant advisory service covering all aspects of laboratory investigation including the interpretation of results and advice on further appropriate investigation (ISO 15189:2012).

Metrological Traceability: The establishment of a correlation of all measurements to SI units or to a natural constant or other stated reference through a documented unbroken chain of comparisons all having stated uncertainties. This chain of comparisons is achieved either by a calibration laboratory documenting the traceability of its measurements or by certified reference materials/controls which are accompanied by a stated value traceable to SI units.

Quality Assurance: Part of quality management focused on providing confidence that quality requirements will be fulfilled (ISO 9000:2005).

Quality Management System: Management system to direct and control an organization with regard to quality (ISO 9000:2005).

Quality Management: Coordinated activities to direct and control an organization with regard to quality (ISO 9000:2005).

Quality: Degree to which a set of inherent characteristics fulfils requirements (ISO 9000:2005).

Chapter 9
Differences of ISO 15189:2012 and ISO 15189:2007

Petros Karkalousos
Technological and Educational Institute of Athens, Greece

ABSTRACT

The new version of the ISO 15189:2007 Standard was published in 2012, and it is called ISO 15189:2012. The new version is more specific to clinical laboratories as compared to the old one. The present chapter emphasizes in the most important changes between the two versions of the standard, especially in those that reveal the "spirit" of the new version. Some of these refer to ethics, quality management system, encouragement of the staff, risk management, evaluation of staff performance, purchase and withdraw of equipment, laboratory facilities, reagents and consumables, communication between the laboratory and its stakeholders, verification of the results by trained personnel, procedures of reporting the results, metrological procedures and traceability, function of laboratory information system, and responsibilities of laboratory director.

INTRODUCTION

The new version of the ISO 15189:2007 Standard isn't a copy of ISO15189:2007 neither can be used as a substitute. The laboratories interested to apply for ISO 15189:2012 should procure a valid copy of the new version. The purpose of this chapter is to help laboratories to "transfer" their quality system from ISO 15189:2007 to the new ISO 15189:2012. For these laboratories, it wishes to be useful and comprehensible guideline serving actually as a manual.

The new version of the ISO 15189 will be presented a paragraph per paragraph summarizing mostly in tables the differences and similarities with the version of 2007. The most important parts of the two documents are presented, which must always be considered during the writing process of the quality manual and its accompanying documents. It is underlined that the described paragraphs and sentences are only summaries of the original documents since the intention is to only present the correspondence. The readers are advised to procure the two versions, ISO 15189:2012 and ISO 15189:2007 for further reading and understanding.

This chapter is also addressed to the laboratory personnel who have in their possession either ISO

DOI: 10.4018/978-1-4666-6320-6.ch009

15189:2012 either ISO 15189:2007. In order to satisfy both readers, we comprised in this chapter quite enough documents from ISO 15189:2012 in order to help laboratories with ISO 15189:2007 Standard to understand every pairing between paragraphs of both Standards. We comprise on purpose the minimum document of ISO15189:2012 in order not to violate the copyright.

The chapter contains a lot of tables which pair the paragraphs between ISO 15189:2012 and ISO 15189:2007. The readers shall have in mind that these pairs have not always the same meaning, and many times are only informative. They should consider the authentic ISO 15189:2012 and ISO 15189:2007 for further information.

The old Standard for medical laboratories (ISO 15189:2007) was based upon the international Standards ISO/IEC 17025 and ISO 9001. The same is happening with the new Standard ISO 15189:2012. It is based on these two Standards and also on ISO 15189:2007. It has been written by the Technical Committee ISO/TC 2012 with the collaboration of the International Electro-technical Commission (IEC) and the German Institute for Standardization (DIN).

Although the new Standard has the same number of chapters, and almost the same number of paragraphs it has many differences and new sub-paragraphs, thus it must be considered as a totally new Standard. It is true that the new Standard is much clearer and well written as compared to the old one. This conclusion is based on the following remarks:

- The annexes of ISO15189:2007 have been included in the main body of the new Standard. Ethics and laboratory information security are now mandatory.
- Almost all the paragraphs of the Standard have become mandatory (the "should" has been replaced by "shall").

- All paragraphs, new and old, their title and the general structure of the new Standard correspond much more to the actual structure of modern clinical laboratory.

The main differences between the two versions of the Standard (ISO 15189: 2007, ISO 15189: 2012) focus on chapters 4 and 5 and the appendixes at the end of the document. These two chapters, 4 and 5, include all the requirements of the Standard. The smallest chapters 1, 2 and 3 include the scope (chapter 1), the normative references (chapter 3) and a comprehensive vocabulary (chapter 3). At the end of the Standard 3 tables include the differences between ISO 9001, ISO 17025 as well as between ISO 15189:2007 and ISO 15189:2012.

BACKGROUND

The new standard ISO 15189:2012 is more compatible with the real work in medical laboratories than the old one. The first ISO standard which was specific for the clinical laboratories was ISO 15189:2003 (eJFCC, 2004). It was based on the ISO 17025:1999 and ISO 9000: 2000. It was the first attempt to create a specific standard for the laboratories dealing with biological samples. At the beginning, the two standards were quite similar and for this reason the laboratories were free to choose which ISO Standard to follow.

The most important changes were based on the following:

- The ISO 15189 was specific to patient care in spite of the ISO 17025. For that reason, ISO 15189 has always special requirements for sampling, reports of results, ethics etc.
- The ISO 15189 had special requirements for the personnel. For example, the laboratory director should be a medical doctor or

other scientist who can have the same role. The requirements of personnel training are more demanding.

- The ISO 15189 gives much attention to laboratory safety not only for the samples, the laboratory personnel but also for the patients.
- The first ISO 15189 standard (ISO 15189:2003) did not give so much attention to the measurement of uncertainty. The truth is that it was considered that the measurement of uncertainty was not mandatory for the medical laboratories. Now that has been changed. In ISO 15189:2012 the measurement of uncertainty is mandatory for all the tests which are been provided. Nonetheless, the medical laboratories are not obliged to inform their customers (patients, doctors) for the uncertainty of their results.
- The ISO 15189 has more demanding rules of internal and external quality control. For example, it demands the estimation and application of critical/alert levels and the establishment of specific reference values for different gender, ages etc.

In the next ISO 15189 standards (ISO 15189:2007 and ISO 15189:2012) the previous differences are wider. Nonetheless, each new ISO 15189 standard is based on the previous ISO 9001 and ISO 17025 standards (Kawai, 2010).

But why ISO 15189 is developing all these years?

The reason is that ISO 15189 is trying to become more and more different from its "maternal" standards. ISO 15189 keeps the management requirements of ISO 9001 and the technical requirements of ISO 17025. The crucial is that all

these requirements are becoming more and more "medical". So, ISO 15189 has achieved to replace many local and national medical laboratories requirements (Li & Adeli, 2009). For instance, the Greek Health Care ministry demands from all the referral laboratories of Greece to have the certification ISO 15189. This is not mandatory for the rest of laboratories but if they did not have this certification they are obliged to suffice strict national directions and a lot of bureaucracies with different documentation and questionnaires.

Some of the unique requirements of ISO 15189 which make it very useful for patients and doctors are (ILAC 2011):

- Ethics.
- Requirements about sampling and pre-analytical errors (Kubano, 2004).
- Risk management.
- Requirements about internal and external quality control. Both are mandatory for all rests (Kawano, 2005).
- Requirements about the report of results.
- Requirements about informatics and protection of data.

Medical laboratories are the key partners in patient safety. Laboratory results influence 70% of medical diagnoses (Guzel & Guner, 2009). More and more countries make this standard mandatory for their medical laboratories. With this way, the medical laboratories are inspected by qualified scientists instead from a non-qualified public service.

On the contrary, with other papers with the same topic (NATA, 2013) this chapter shows all the differences and similarities paragraph per paragraph and sentence per sentence.

DIFFERENCES OF ISO 15189:2012 VS. ISO 15189:2007

Chapter 4: Management Requirements

Paragraph 4.1 Organization and Management Responsibility

Paragraph 4.1.1.2 Legal Entity

The chapter "Management requirements" starts with a new paragraph about the legal entity: "the laboratory is legally responsible for all its activities …".

Paragraph 4.1.1.3 Ethical Conduct

The almost new paragraph with the title "Ethical conduct" (4.1.1.3) refers to the confidence to the laboratory ethical integrity. It declares: "the laboratory must have arrangements to ensure that the laboratory must have no any commercial … or

other pressure and influence that may affect the quality of its work. It also shall treat carefully and … to the human samples and patient's information. In general the new paragraph "Ethical conduct" has replaced the paragraphs 4.1.4, 4.1.5.a, and 4.1.5.d and the Annex C "Ethics in laboratory medicine" of the ISO 15189:2007.

Paragraph 4.1.1.4 Laboratory Director

The new chapter "laboratory director" includes everything about the duties of the laboratory director and is related to the paragraphs 5.1.3 and 5.1.4 of ISO 15189:2007.

"The laboratory director can be any person with the competence and skills of this important position". Elsewhere the Standard mentions the specificity of the laboratory director (i.e. medical doctor or any other health care provider). The duties of the laboratory director are too many. In fact, he is responsible for everything in the laboratory".

Table 1. Pairing of paragraphs between ISO 15189:2012 and ISO 15189:2007 for the duties of laboratory director

	ISO 15189:2012	ISO 15189:2007
Short description of duties	**4.1.1.4**	**5.1.3, 5.1.4**
General duties	a	Introductory paragraph
Corporation with scientific community	b	c
Sufficient staff's number and competence	c	g
Safe laboratory environment	d	m
Contributing with medical …	f	b
Clinical advice for the results	g	-
Choosing of suppliers	h	-
Selection of referral laboratories	i	l
Laboratory staff's motivation	j	h, o
Quality Standards	k	d
Work monitoring	l	f
Addressing of complaints and suggestions	m	n
Emergency plans	n	-
Research and Development	o	k

Paragraph 4.1.2 Management Responsibility

Paragraph 4.1.2.1 Management Commitment

In ISO 15189:2012 a new paragraph named "Management commitment" functions as a catalog in which each sentence leads to a whole new paragraph. For instance, there is the sentence "… establishing the quality policy" which leads to the paragraph "4.1.2.3 Quality policy".

In general, this paragraph includes all the commitments which the management must undertake according to quality policy, like the establishment of quality objectives and plans, the defining of responsibilities (appointing a quality manager is mandatory) of the personnel, the ensuring of the availability of human and material resources for any laboratory work and others.

Paragraph 4.1.2.3 Quality Policy

One of the duties of the lab management is to establish the quality policy of the laboratory. The ISO 15189:2012 devotes a specific paragraph on it.

On the opposite, the references to the quality policy were included mostly in the subparagraph 4.2.3.

Paragraph 4.1.2.4 Quality Objectives and Planning

An almost new paragraph has added the "quality objectives and planning". "The laboratory shall:

1. Establish objectives which are measurable and …
2. Ensure the planning of the quality management system
3. Ensure the integrity of the quality management system and any changes are planned ….

Paragraph 4.1.2.5 Responsibility, Authority, and Interrelationships

Totally new paragraph. "Laboratory management shall ensure that responsibilities, authorities and … are defined … and communicated within the laboratory organization. This shall include the appointment of person(s) responsible for each one … laboratory functions".

Table 2. Pairing of paragraphs between ISO 15189:2012 and ISO 15189:2007 for management commitments

	ISO 15189:2012	ISO 15189:2007
Short description of management commitments	**4.1.2.1**	**4.1.5, 4.1.6**
Communicating to laboratory personnel about customers needs and …	a	4.1.6
Establishment the quality policy	b	Introductory paragraph
Ensuring quality objectives	c	-
Defining responsibilities ….of all personnel	d	f
Establishing communication processes	e	4.1.6
Appointing quality manager	f	i
Conducting management reviews	g	-
Ensuring the competence of lab personnel	h	a, b, c, d, g
Ensuring of adequate lab resources to enable the conduct of pre-examination … activities	i	h

Table 3. Pairing of paragraphs between ISO 15189:2012 and ISO 15189:2007 about the quality policy

	ISO 15189:2012	ISO 15189:2007
Short description of quality policy ensuring	**4.1.2.3**	**4.2.3**
Effectiveness for the purpose of the organization	A	a
Commitment to good laboratory practice	B	e
Establishing and reviewing of quality objectives	C	c
It is communicated and understood within the organization	D	Introductory paragraph
Reviewing of continuing suitability	E	-

Paragraph 4.1.2.6 Communication

This paragraph corresponds to the paragraph 4.1.6 of ISO 15189:2007. "Laboratory management shall have effective means for communicating with staff and its stakeholders. Every communication … must be record".

Paragraph 4.1.2.7 Quality Manager

An almost new paragraph has added the "quality manager". The quality management duties include:

a. Ensuring the processes needed for the quality management system are established …
b. Reporting to laboratory management everything about … the quality management system and …,
c. Ensuring the promotion of awareness of users' needs and requirements throughout the laboratory organization.

Paragraph 4.2 Organization and Management Responsibility

Paragraph 4.2.1 General Requirements

Although there is a paragraph named quality management system in both standards ISO 15189:2012 and ISO 15189:2007 the paragraph of "general requirements" is totally new.

So the laboratory shall establish and maintain a quality management system and continually improve its effectiveness in accordance with ISO 15189:2012.

"The laboratory shall:

a. Determine the processes needed for the quality management system and ensure … throughout the laboratory,
b. Determine the sequence and … of these processes and monitor and …,
c. Determine criteria and … needed to ensure that both operation and control of these processes are effective and ensure the availability of resources and information necessary to support the operation … of these processes."

Paragraph 4.2.2 Document Requirements

Totally new paragraph. It functions as a list of contents of many paragraphs which follow. It includes a short list of what "the quality management system documentation" must include:

a. Statements of a quality policy and ….
b. A quality manual.
c. Procedures and … required by ISO 15189:2012.

Table 4. Pairing of paragraphs between ISO 15189:2012 and ISO 15189:2007 about quality manual

	ISO 15189:2012	ISO 15189:2007
The laboratory shall establish and maintain a quality manual that includes:	**4.2.2.2**	**4.2.4**
The quality policy	a	c
A description of the scope of the quality management system	b	4.2.3.a
A presentation of the organization and ...	c	b
A description of the roles and responsibilities of laboratory management for ...	d	-
A description or the structure and relationships of the documentation ...	e	Introductory paragraphs
The documented policies established for the quality management system and reference to the managerial and technical activities that support them	f	a, d - w

d.　Documents and records determined by the laboratory to ensure the effective planning ... of its processes".

Paragraph 4.2.2.2 Quality Manual

This short paragraph of ISO 15189:2012 has replaced the paragraph 4.2.4 of ISO 15189:2007. It contains the following sentences in Table 4.

Paragraph 4.3 Document Control

The paragraph 4.3 Document control of ISO 15189:2012 exists almost alike in ISO 15189:2007.

Paragraph 4.4 Service Agreements

Paragraph 4.4.1 Establishment of Service Agreements

The paragraphs about the establishment of service agreements are a new addition to the Standard ISO 15189. According to these: "the laboratory shall have documented procedures for the establishment and review of agreements for providing medical laboratory services ... all the following conditions shall be met when the laboratory enters into an agreement to provide medical laboratory services.

1.　The requirements of the customers and users, and of the provider of the laboratory services, including the examination processes to be used, shall be defined ...
2.　The laboratory shall have the capability and ... to meet the requirements.
3.　Laboratory personnel shall have the skills and ... for the performance of the intended examinations.
4.　Examinations procedures selected shall be appropriate and ...
5.　Reference shall be made to any work referred by the laboratory from the agreement that ..."

Paragraph 4.4.2 Review of Service Agreements

The paragraph "review of service agreements" is also a new addition to the ISO 15189. It says that any amendment of the laboratory agreement with its customers (patients, doctors, other laboratories) must be recorded.

Table 5. Pairing of paragraphs between ISO 15189:2012 and ISO 15189:2007 about what the document control

	ISO 15189:2012	ISO 15189:2007
The laboratory shall establish and maintain a quality manual that includes:	**4.3**	**4.3**
The laboratory shall control documents required by the quality management system and shall ensure …	Introductory paragraph	4.3.2.a
All documents, including those maintained in a computerized system, issued as part of the quality management system are reviewed and approved by …	a	a
All documents are identified to include: - A title - A unique identifier on each page - The date of the current edition/edition number - Page number to total number - Authority of issue	b	4.3.3 Not exist: Page number to total number
Current authorized editions and their distribution are identified by means of a list …	c	-
Only current, authorized editions of applicable documents are available at points of use	d	c
Where a laboratory's document control system allows for the amendment of documents by hand, this and all the amendments shall be clearly marked …	e	d
Changes to documents are identified	d	f
Documents remain legible	g	-
Documents are periodically reviewed and updated at a frequency that ensures that they remain fit for purpose	h	d
Obsolete controlled documents are dated and …	i	f
At least one copy of an obsolete controlled document is retained for a specific time period …	j	-

Paragraph 4.5 Examination by Referral Laboratories

Paragraph 4.5.1 Selecting and Evaluating Referral Laboratories and Consultants

The paragraphs of "Examination by referral laboratories" have much more details in ISO 15189:2012 than in ISO 15189:2007. The Table 6 describes all these details.

Paragraph 4.5.2 Provision of Examination Results

This paragraph is almost new even though many of its requirements exist in ISO 15189:2007.

Paragraph 4.6 External Services and Supplies

The paragraph "External services and supplies" exists also in ISO 15189:2012 and ISO 15189:2007. Table 8 presents more details.

Paragraph 4.7 Advisory Services

The paragraph "Advisory services" exists also in ISO 15189:2012 and ISO 15189:2007.

Paragraph 4.8 Resolution of Complaints

The paragraph "Resolution of complaints" exists also in ISO 15189:2012 and ISO 15189:2007 and

Table 6. Pairing of paragraphs between ISO 15189:2012 and ISO 15189:2007 about selecting and evaluating laboratories and consultants

	ISO 15189:2012	ISO 15189:2007
Recommendations about the examination of referral laboratories	**4.5.1**	**4.5**
The laboratory shall have a documented procedure for selecting and evaluating referral laboratories and …	Introductory paragraph	4.5.1
The laboratory, with the advice of user of laboratory services where appropriate, is responsible for selecting the referral laboratory and referral consultants, monitoring the quality of performance and …	a	4.5.1
Arrangements with referral laboratories and consultants are reviewed and …	b	4.5.2.a
Records of such periodic reviews are maintained.	c	4.5.3
A register of all referral laboratories and consultants from … are sought is maintained.	d	4.5.3
Requests and results of all samples referred are kept for a … period.	e	-

Table 7. Pairing of paragraphs between ISO 15189:2012 and ISO 15189:2007 about the provision of examination results

	ISO 15189:2012	ISO 15189:2007
Recommendations about the provision of examination results	**4.5.1**	**4.5.4**
Unless otherwise specified in the agreement, the referring laboratory shall be responsible for ensuring that examination results of the referral laboratory …	First paragraph	First paragraph
When the referring laboratory prepares the report, it shall include all essential elements of the results reported by the referral laboratory …	Second paragraph	Third paragraph
The author of any additional remarks shall be clearly identified.	Third paragraph	Third paragraph
Laboratories shall adopt the most appropriate means of reporting referral laboratories, taking in mind turnaround times ….	Fourth paragraph	-

Table 8. Pairing of paragraphs between ISO 15189:2012 and ISO 15189:2007 about the external services and supplies

	ISO 15189:2012	ISO 15189:2007
Recommendations about the external services and supplies	**4.6**	**4.6**
The laboratory shall have a documented procedure for the selection and … of external services, equipment, … that affect the quality of its service	First paragraph	4.6.1
The laboratory shall select and approve suppliers based on their ability to supply external services ... However, it may be necessary to collaborate with other organizational departments or …	Second paragraph	4.6.1 New addition: " it may be necessary to collaborate with other organizational departments"
A list of selected and approved suppliers shall be maintained.	Third paragraph	4.6.3
Purchasing information shall describe the requirements for the product or … to be purchased	Fourth paragraph	4.6.2
The laboratory shall monitor the performance of suppliers to ensure that purchased services … meet the stated criteria	Fifth paragraph	4.6.2

Table 9. Pairing of paragraphs between ISO 15189:2012 and ISO 15189:2007 about the advisory services

	ISO 15189:2012	ISO 15189:2007
The laboratory shall establish arrangements for communicating with users on the following:	**4.7**	**4.7**
Advising on choice of examinations and use of the services …	a	First paragraph
Advising on individual clinical cases	b	First paragraph
Professional judgments on the interpretation of the results of examinations	c	-
Promoting the effective utilization of laboratory services	d	-
Consulting on scientific and logistic means such as instances of failure of sample(s) to meet … criteria	e	-

it is almost the same "the laboratory shall have a documented procedure for the management of complaints …".

Paragraph 4.9 Identification and Control of Nonconformities

The paragraph "Identification and control of nonconformities" exists also in ISO 15189:2012 and ISO 15189:2007. Table 10 compares them.

Paragraph 4.10 Corrective Actions

This paragraph exists also in ISO 15189:2012 and ISO 15189:2007. Table 11 compares them.

Paragraph 4.11 Preventive Actions

The paragraph "Preventive action" exists also in ISO 15189:2012 and ISO 15189:2007. Table 12 compares them.

Table 10. Pairing of paragraphs between ISO 15189:2012 and ISO 15189:2007 about identification and control of nonconformities

	ISO 15189:2012	ISO 15189:2007
The laboratory shall have a documented procedure to identify nonconformities. The procedure shall ensure that:	**4.9**	**4.9**
The responsibilities and authorities for handling nonconformities are designated	a	a
The immediate actions to be taken are defined	b	b
The extent of nonconformity is determined	c	c
Examinations are halted and … withheld as necessary	d	d
The medical significance of any nonconforming examinations is considered … the requesting person for using the results is informed	e	e
The results of any nonconforming or … already released are recalled, if it is necessary	f	f
The responsibility for authorization of the resumption of examination is defined	g	g
Each episode of nonconformity is documented and recorded	h	h

Table 11. Pairing of paragraphs between ISO 15189:2012 and ISO 15189:2007 about corrective action

	ISO 15189:2012	ISO 15189:2007
The laboratory shall have a documented procedure for:	**4.10**	**4.10**
Reviewing nonconformities	a	4.10.1
Determining the root causes of nonconformities	b	4.10.1
Evaluating the need for corrective action to ...	c	4.10.2
Determining and implementing corrective action needed	d	4.10.3
Recording the results of corrective action taken	e	4.10.2
Reviewing the effectiveness of the corrective action taken	f	4.10.3

Table 12. Pairing of paragraphs between ISO 15189:2012 and ISO 15189:2007 about preventive actions

	ISO 15189:2012	ISO 15189:2007
The laboratory shall have a documented procedure for:	**4.11**	**4.11**
Reviewing laboratory data and ... to determine where potential nonconformities exist	a	-
Determining the root causes of nonconformities	b	4.11.1
Evaluating the need for preventive action to prevent ...	c	4.11.1
Determining and implementing preventive action needed	d	-
Recording the results of preventive action needed	e	-
Reviewing the effectiveness of the preventive action taken.	f	4.11.2

Paragraph 4.12 Continual Improvement

The paragraph "Continual improvement" exists also in ISO 15189:2012 and ISO 15189:2007 but it has been changed a lot.

Paragraph 4.13 Control of Records

The paragraph "Control of records" exists also in ISO 15189:2012 and ISO 15189:2007 but with slightly different content.

Paragraph 4.14 Evaluation and Audits

Paragraph 4.14.1 General

The paragraphs of "4.14 Evaluation and audits" are almost new. Only a small part ("Internal audit") existed also in ISO 15189:2007. The first part is called "General" and it is introductory to the rest. Its main sentences are the following and don't exist in ISO 15189:2007:

"The laboratory shall plan ... the evaluation and internal audit processes needed to:

1. Demonstrate that the examinations... are being conducted in a manner that meets and requirements of users.
2. Ensure conformity to the ... system
3. Continually improve the effectiveness of the ... system".

Paragraph 4.14.2 Periodic Review of Requests, and Suitability of Procedures and Sample Requirements

This is a new paragraph. It requires that "authorized personnel and periodically review examinations

Table 13. Pairing of paragraphs between ISO 15189:2012 and ISO 15189:2007 about continual improvement

	ISO 15189:2007
Continual improvement	**4.12**
The laboratory shall continually improve the effectiveness of the quality management system through the use of management reviews ...	4.12.1
Improvement activities shall be directed at areas of highest priority based on risk assessments.	-
The effectiveness of the actions taken shall be determined through a focused review ...	4.12.3
Laboratory management shall ensure that the laboratory participates in continual improvement activities.	4.12.4
When the continual improvement program identifies opportunities for improvement, laboratory management shall address them ...	-
Laboratory shall communicate to staff improvement plans and related goals.	-

provided by the laboratory to ensure that they are clinically appropriate ... ensure that the sample is properly collected to preserve the measurement".

Paragraph 4.14.3 Assessment of User Feedback

This is a new paragraph. "The laboratory shall seek information relating to user perception as to whether the service has met the needs and requirements of the users. ... Records shall be kept of information collected and actions taken".

Paragraph 4.14.4 Staff Suggestions

This is a new paragraph. "Laboratory management shall encourage staff to make suggestions ... of any aspect of a laboratory service"

Paragraph 4.14.5 Internal Audit

This introductory paragraph corresponds to the paragraph 4.14 of the ISO 15189:2007. It asks as shown in Table 15.

Paragraph 4.14.6 Risk Management

Totally new paragraph. "The laboratory shall evaluate the impact of work processes and potential failures on examination results as they affect patient safety. Relative records shall be maintained".

Paragraph 4.14.7 Quality Indicators

Totally new paragraph. "The laboratory shall establish quality indicators to monitor and evaluate performance ..."

Paragraph 4.14.8 Reviews by External Organizations

Totally new paragraph. "When reviews by external organizations indicate the laboratory has nonconformities or potential nonconformities the laboratory shall take appropriate immediate actions..."

Paragraph 4.15 Management Review: 4.15.1 General

This introductory paragraph corresponds to the paragraph 4.15.1 of the ISO 15189:2007. ISO 15189:2012 says: "laboratory management shall review the quality management system at planned intervals ...."

Paragraph 4.15.2 Review Input

The paragraph "Review input" exists also in ISO 15189:2012 and ISO 15189:2007 but with slightly different content. The corresponding paragraph in ISO 15189:2007 is called "Management review".

Table 14. Pairing of paragraphs between ISO 15189:2012 and ISO 15189:2007 about control of records

	ISO 15189:2012	ISO 15189:2007
	4.13	**4.13**
The laboratory shall have a document for identification, collection, indexing, access, storage, maintenance, amendment and safe disposal of quality and technical records.	1st paragraph	4.13.1
Records shall be created concurrently with performance of each activity that effects the quality of the examinations	2nd paragraph	4.13.2
The date and where relevant, the time of amendments to records shall be captured along with the identification of personnel	3rd paragraph	-
The laboratory shall define the time period that various records pertaining to the quality management system are to be retained...	4th paragraph	4.13.3
Facilities shall provide a suitable environment for storage of records ...	5th paragraph	4.13.4
Records shall include at least the following:	**4.13**	**4.13**
Supplier selection and performance and changes to the approved supplier list.	a	-
Staff qualifications.	b	p
Request for examination.	c	a
Records of receipt of samples.	d	-
Information on reagents and materials.	e	n
Laboratory workbooks or worksheets.	f	e
Instrument printouts and retained data and information.	g	c
Examination results and reports.	h	b
Instrument maintenance records, including internal and external calibration records.	i	m
Calibration functions and conversion factors.	j	g
Quality control records.	k	h
Incident records and action taken.	l	o
Risk management records.	m	-
Nonconformities identified ... or corrective action taken.	n	-
Preventive action taken.	o	-
Complaints and action taken.	p	i
Records of internal and external audits.	r	
Interlaboratory comparisons ...	s	k
Records of quality improvement activities.	t	
Minutes of meetings that record decisions made about quality system.	u	
Records of management reviews.	v	

Table 15. Pairing of paragraphs between ISO 15189:2012 and ISO 15189:2007 about internal audits

	ISO 15189:2012	ISO 15189:2007
Requirements for internal audits	**4.14.5**	**4.14**
The laboratory shall conduct internal audits at planned intervals to determine whether all activities conform to the requirements of ISO15189:2012 ...	1st paragraph	4.14.1
Audits shall be conducted by personnel trained...	2nd paragraph	4.14.2
Selection of auditors and conduct of audits shall ensure objectivity and impartiality of the audit process ...	3rd paragraph	4.14.2
The laboratory shall have a documented procedure to define the responsibilities and requirements for planning and conducting audits ...	4th paragraph	4.14.3
Personnel responsible for the area being audited shall ensure that appropriate action ...	e	4.14.2

Differences and similarities are synopsized in Table 16.

Paragraph 4.15.3 Review Activities

This paragraph corresponds partially to the 4.15.3 of ISO 15189:2007 but it is a little rephrased: "The laboratory shall analyze the input information for causes of nonconformities... The review shall include assessing these opportunities for improvement ...".

Paragraph 4.15.4 Review Output

This paragraph corresponds partially to the 4.15.4 of ISO 15189:2007. "The output from the management review shall ... into a record that documents any decisions ... during management review related to:

1. Improvement of the effectiveness of the quality management system ...
2. Improvement of services to ...
3. Resource needs.

New addition: "Laboratory management shall ensure that actions arising from management review are completed within a defined timeframe".

Chapter 5: Technical Requirements

Paragraph 5.1 Personnel

All the relevant paragraphs about personnel have been changed a lot. The old paragraphs of ISO 15189:2007 have been divided into smaller, clearer and more detailed paragraphs.

Paragraph 5.1.2 Personnel Qualifications

This is a new paragraph even though some of its requirements also exist in ISO 15189:2007.

Paragraph 5.1.3 Job Descriptions

This paragraph corresponds to 5.1.3.c of ISO 15189:2007 "the laboratory shall have job descriptions that describe responsibilities, authorities and tasks of the personnel".

Table 16. Pairing of paragraphs between ISO 15189:2012 and ISO 15189:2007 about review input

	ISO 15189:2012	ISO 15189:2007
The input to management review of requests shall include information from the results of evaluations of at least the following:	**4.15.2**	**4.15.2**
The periodic review of requests ...	a	-
Assessment of user feedback.	b	-
Staff suggestions.	c	-
Internal audits.	d	d
Risk management.	e	-
Use of quality indicators.	f	-
Reviews by external organizations.	g	e
Results of participation in interlaboratory programmes.	h	f
Monitoring and resolution of complaints.	i	h
Performance of suppliers.	j	m
Identification and control of nonconformities	k	j
Results of continual improvement including current status of corrective and preventive actions.	l	b
Follow-up actions from ... reviews.	m	a
Changes in the volume and scope of work ... that could affect the quality management system.	n	g
Recommendations for improvement, including ...	o	-

Table 17. Pairing of paragraphs between ISO 15189:2012 and ISO 15189:2007 about personnel qualifications

	ISO 15189:2012	ISO 15189:2007
Personnel qualifications	**5.1.2**	**5.1**
Laboratory management shall document personnel qualifications for each position... demonstrated skills needed for each task	1st paragraph	5.1.1
The personnel making judgments with reference to examinations ...	2nd paragraph	5.1.12

Paragraph 5.1.4 Personnel Introduction to the Organizational Environment

Totally new paragraph. It includes the following requirement: "the laboratory shall have a programme to introduce new staff to the organization...".

Paragraph 5.1.5 Training

This paragraph corresponds to the 5.1.4 of ISO 15189:2007.

Paragraph 5.1.6 Competence Assessment

This paragraph corresponds to 5.1.11 of ISO 15189:2007 but it has much more details. "Following appropriate training, the laboratory shall access the competence of each person ... Reassessment shall take place at regular intervals. Retraining shall occur when necessary".

Table 18. Pairing of paragraphs between ISO 15189:2012 and ISO 15189:2007 about personnel's training

	ISO 15189:2012	ISO 15189:2007
The laboratory shall provide training for all personnel which includes the following areas	**5.1.5**	**5.1**
The quality management system.	a	5.1.6
Assigned work processes and procedures	b	-
The applicable processes and procedures	c	-
The applicable information system	d	5.1.8/?[1]
Health and safety, including the prevention or containment of the effects of adverse incidents	e	-
Ethics	f	Annex C
Confidentiality of patient information	g	Annex C (C6)
Personnel that are undergoing training shall be supervised at all times	2nd paragraph	-
The effectiveness of the training programme shall be periodically reviewed	3rd paragraph	5.1.11

Paragraph 5.1.7 Reviews of Staff Performance

Totally new paragraph. "The laboratory shall ensure that reviews of staff performance consider the needs of the laboratory and the individual in order to maintain or improve the quality of service given to the users and encourage productive working relationships".

Paragraph 5.1.8 Continuing Education and Professional Development

This paragraph corresponds to 5.1.12 of ISO 15189:2007 but with the addition "a continuing education program shall be available to personnel who participate in managerial and technical processes. Personnel shall take part in continuing education which effectiveness shall be periodically reviewed".

Paragraph 5.1.9 Personnel Records

This paragraph corresponds to 5.1.2 of ISO 15189:2007 but with many additions.

Paragraph 5.2 Accommodation and Environmental Conditions

The old group of paragraphs has been rewritten. New paragraphs and details have been added.

Paragraph 5.2.1 General

This introductory paragraph corresponds to 5.2.1 of ISO 15189:2007. "The laboratory shall have space allocated for the performance of its work … and shall evaluate and determine the sufficiency and adequacy of the space allocated for the performance of the work."

Table 19. Pairing of paragraphs between ISO 15189:2012 and ISO 15189:2007 about personnel records

	ISO 15189:2012	ISO 15189:2007
The laboratory shall provide training for all personnel which includes the following areas	**5.1.9**	**5.1.2**
The quality management system.	a	5.1.6
Assigned work processes and procedures	b	-
The applicable processes and procedures	c	-
The applicable information system	d	5.1.8/?²
Health and safety, including the prevention or containment of the effects of adverse incidents	e	-
Ethics	f	-
Confidentiality of patient information	g	-
Personnel that are undergoing training shall be supervised at all times	2ⁿᵈ paragraph	-
The effectiveness of the training programme shall be …reviewed	3ʳᵈ paragraph	5.1.11

The new addition is: "Where applicable; similar provisions shall be made for primary sample collection and examinations at sites other than the main laboratory premises, for example,, point-of-care testing under the management of the laboratory".

Paragraph 5.2.2 Laboratory and Office Facilities

This is a new paragraph. It describes the requirements about the laboratory facilities and other areas which affect the laboratory operation like office,

computer room. The corresponding paragraphs of ISO 15189:2007 are shown in Table 20.

Paragraph 5.2.3 Storage Facilities

This is a new paragraph. It describes the requirements about the storage facilities and it corresponds to the paragraphs as shown in Table 21.

Paragraph 5.2.4 Staff Facilities

This is a new paragraph with no corresponding paragraph to ISO 15189:2007. It says: "there shall be adequate access to washrooms, to the supply

Table 20. Pairing of paragraphs between ISO 15189:2012 and ISO 15189:2007 about laboratory and office facilities

	ISO 15189:2012	ISO 15189:2007
The laboratory and associated office facilities shall provide an environment suitable for the tasks to be undertaken, to ensure the following conditions are met	**5.2.2**	**5.2**
Access to areas affecting the quality of examinations controlled.	a	5.2.7
Medical information … are safeguarded from unauthorized access.	b	5.2.7
Facilities for examination allow for correct performance of examinations (energy sources, waste disposal e.t.c.).	c	5.2.4
Communication systems within the laboratory are appropriate to the size and complexity of the facility to ensure the efficient transfer of information …	d	
Safety facilities and devices are provided, and their functioning regularly verified …	e	-

Table 21. Pairing of paragraphs between ISO 15189:2012 and ISO 15189:2007 about storage facilities

	ISO 15189:2012	ISO 15189:2007
Storage facilities	**5.2.3**	**5.2**
Storage space and conditions shall be provided that ensure the continuing integrity of sample materials ... that could affect the quality of examination results.	1st sentence	5.2.9
Clinical samples and materials used in examination processes shall be stored in a manner to prevent cross contamination.	2nd sentence	5.2.6
Storage and disposal facilities for dangerous material shall be appropriate to the hazards of the materials, and as specified by applicable requirements.	3rd sentence	5.2.10

of drinking water and to facilities for storage of personal protective equipment and clothing".

Paragraph 5.2.5 Staff Facilities

This is a new paragraph, and it corresponds to the paragraph 5.2.2 of ISO 15189:2007. It says: "patient sample collection facilities shall have separate reception/waiting and collection areas. Consideration shall be given to the accommodation of patient privacy, comfort and needs. Sample collection facilities shall be undertaken in a manner that does not affect the quality of the examination".

Paragraph 5.2.6 Facility Maintenance and Environmental Conditions

This paragraph corresponds to the paragraph 5.2.4, 5.2.5 and 5.2.6 of ISO 15189:2007.

Paragraph 5.3 Laboratory Equipment, Reagents, and Consumables

In ISO 15189:2012 the corresponding paragraph 5.3 Equipment of ISO 15189:2007 has been divided into two different paragraphs the 5.3.1 Equipment and 5.3.2 Reagents and consumables.

Paragraph 5.3.1 Equipment – 5.3.1.1 General

This paragraph corresponds to the paragraph 5.3.1 of ISO 15189:2007. In general, it says: "the laboratory shall be furnished with all equipment needed for the provision of services .... Where the laboratory needs to use equipment outside its permanent control, laboratory management shall ensure that the requirements of ISO 15189:2012

Table 22. Pairing of paragraphs between ISO 15189:2012 and ISO 15189:2007 about facility maintenance and environmental conditions

	ISO 15189:2012	ISO 15189:2007
Storage facilities	**5.2.5**	**5.2**
Laboratory premises shall be maintained in a functional and reliable condition ...	1st sentence	5.2.4
The laboratory shall monitor, control and record environmental conditions ...	2nd sentence	5.2.5
There shall be effective separation between laboratory sections in which there are incompatible activities...	3rd sentence	5.2.6

are met. The laboratory shall replace equipment as needed to ensure the quality of examination results."

The paragraph "5.3.1.2 Equipment acceptance testing"

This paragraph corresponds to the paragraph 5.3.2 of ISO 15189:2007. In general, it says: "the laboratory shall be verified upon installation and before use that the equipment of achieving the necessary performance ….".

Paragraph 5.3.1.3 Equipment Instructions for Use

This paragraph corresponds mostly to the paragraph 5.3.2 (third sentence) of ISO 15189:2007.

Paragraph 5.3.1.4 Equipment Calibration and Metrological Traceability

This is almost new paragraph. Some of its sentences correspond to 5.3.4 second paragraph and to 5.3.9.

"The laboratory shall have a documented procedure for the calibration or equipment that directly or indirectly affects examination results. This procedure includes:

a. Taking into account conditions of use and the manufacturer instructions.
b. Recording the metrological traceability of the calibration Standard …
c. Verifying the required measurement accuracy and the functioning of the measuring system …

d. Recording the calibration status and date of recalibration.
e. Ensuring that … calibration factors are correctly updated.
f. Safeguard adjustments or tampering that might invalidate examination results.

Metrological traceability shall be to reference material or reference procedure of a higher metrological order available…"

Paragraph 5.3.1.5 Equipment Maintenance and Repair

This paragraph corresponds to the paragraph 5.3 of ISO 15189:2007.

Paragraph 5.3.1.6 Equipment Adverse Incident Reporting

Totally new paragraph. "Adverse incidents and accidents than can be attributed directly to specific equipment shall be investigated and reported to the manufacturer and appropriate authorities as required."

Paragraph 5.3.1.7 Equipment Records

This paragraph corresponds to the 5.3.4 of ISO 15189:2007.

Paragraph 5.3.2 Reagents and Consumables

This is almost a new paragraph. The next table describes it and any correspondence to ISO 15189:2007.

Table 23. Pairing of paragraphs between ISO 15189:2012 and ISO 15189:2007 about equipment instructions for use

Equipment instructions for use	5.3.1.3	5.3
Equipment shall be operated at all times by trained and authorized personnel …	1st sentence	5.3.2
Current instructions on the use … shall be readily available.	2nd sentence	5.3.2.c
The laboratory shall have procedures for safe handling, storage, prevent from contamination e.t.c	3rd sentence	5.3.12

Table 24. Pairing of paragraphs between ISO 15189:2012 and ISO 15189:2007 about equipment maintenance and repair

Equipment maintenance and repair	5.3.1.3	5.3
The laboratory shall have a documented programme of preventive maintenance …	1st sentence	-
Equipment shall be maintained in a safe working condition andworking order. This shall include an examination of electrical safety …	2nd sentence	5.3.6
The laboratory shall take reasonable measures to decontaminate equipment before use … and provide personal protective equipment.	3rd sentence	5.3.7
When equipment is removed from the direct control of the laboratory, the laboratory shall ensure that its performance is verified …	4th sentence	-

Table 25. Pairing of paragraphs between ISO 15189:2012 and ISO 15189:2007 about equipment records

	ISO 15189:2012	ISO 15189:2007
Records shall be maintained for each item or equipment…. These records shall include, but not be limited to, the following:	5.3.1.7	5.3.4
Identify of the equipment	a	a
Manufacturer's name, model and serial number …	b	b
Contact information for the supplier or the manufacturer …	c	c
Date of receiving and date of entering into service.	d	d
Location	e	e
Condition when received …	f	f
Manufacturer's instructions	g	g
Records that confirmed the equipment's initial acceptability for use	h	-
Maintenance carried out and the schedule for preventive maintenance	i	i
Damages, malfunctions, modifications etc	j	j

Paragraph 5.4 Pre-Examination Processes

This paragraph corresponds to the paragraphs 5.5 of ISO 15189:2007 but has many new requirements divided into new paragraphs.

Paragraph 5.4.2 Information for Patients and Users

This is a totally new paragraph. It says that "the laboratory shall have information available for patients and users of the laboratory services:

a. The location of the laboratory
b. Types of clinical services offered by the laboratory …
c. Opening hours of the laboratory
d. The examinations offered by the laboratory …
e. Instructions for completion of the request form
f. Instruction for preparation of the patient
g. Instructions for patient-collected samples
h. Instructions for transportation of samples …

Table 26. Pairing of paragraphs between ISO 15189:2012 and ISO 15189:2007 about reagents and consumables

	ISO 15189:2012	ISO 15189:2007
	5.3.2	**5.3**
Reception and storage. Where the laboratory is not the receiving facility, it shall verify that the receiving location has adequate storage … to maintain the purchased items …. The laboratory shall store reagents and consumables according to the manufacturer's specifications.	5.3.2.2	-
Acceptance testing Each new kit, or a lot, or shipment shall be verified for performance before use in examinations.	5.3.2.3	-
Inventory management The laboratory shall establish an inventory system for reagents and consumables … which segregate uninspected and unacceptable items …	5.3.2.4	-
Instructions for use All instructions for the use and consumables shall be readily available	5.3.2.5	-
Adverse incident warming. Adverse incidents and accidents that can be attributed directly to specific reagents or consumables shall be investigated and reported to the manufacturer	5.3.2.6	-
Records Records shall include but not be limited to the following:	**5.3.2.7**	**5.3.4**
Identify the reagent or consumable	a	a
Manufacturer's name, model and serial number …	b	b
Contact information for the supplier or the manufacturer.	c	c
Date of receiving and date of entering into service.	d	d
Condition when received (e.g. new, used)	e	f
Manufacturer's instructions	f	g
Records that confirmed the reagents or consumable's initial acceptance for use	h	-
Performance records that confirm the reagent's or consumable's acceptance for use	j	h
Where the laboratory uses reagents prepared in-house records shall include reference to the persons undertaking their preparation and the date of preparation.	Last sentence	-

i. Any requirements of patient's consent …
j. The laboratory criteria for accepting and rejecting samples …
k. A list of factors known to affect … the results
l. Availability of clinical advice on ordering of examinations and on interpretation of them
m. Laboratory policy on protection of personal information
n. Laboratory's complaint procedure"

Paragraph 5.4.3 Request Form Information

This paragraph corresponds to the paragraph 5.4.1 of ISO 15189:2007.

Paragraph 5.4.4 Primary Sample Collection and Handling

All this group of paragraphs corresponds to many different paragraphs and subparagraphs of 5.4 paragraphs of ISO 15189:2007. For that reason, we will present them in one table.

Table 27. Pairing of paragraphs between ISO 15189:2012 and ISO 15189:2007 about request form information

	ISO 15189:2012	ISO 15189:2007
The request form or an electronic equivalent shall allow space for the inclusion of, but not be limited to the following.	5.4.3	5.4.1
Patient identification, including gender, date of birth, patient health number etc	a	a
Name of other unique number of clinician ... or other person legally authorized ...	b	b
Type of primary sample and, where relevant, the anatomic site of origin	c	c
Examinations requested	d	d
Clinically relevant information about the patient ...	e	e
Date and time of primary sample collection	f	f
Date and time of sample receipt	g	g
The laboratory shall have a documented procedure concerning verbal requests for examinations	2nd paragraph	-
The laboratory shall be willing to cooperate with users ..... in clarifying the user's request	3rd paragraph	-

Paragraph 5.4.5 Sample Transportation

This paragraph corresponds to the paragraph 5.4.6 of ISO 15189:2007.

Paragraph 5.4.6 Sample Reception

This is a new paragraph that corresponds to many different paragraphs 5.4. of ISO 15189:2007.

Paragraph 5.4.7 Pre-Examination Handling, Preparation and Storage

This paragraph corresponds to the paragraph 5.4.14 of ISO 15189:2007. "Laboratory shall have procedures and appropriate facilities for securing patient samples and avoiding deterioration, loss or damage during pre-examination activities and during handling .... There shall be time limits for requesting additional examinations or further examinations on the same primary sample".

Paragraph 5.5 Examination Processes

This group of paragraphs corresponds to the paragraphs 5.5 of ISO 15189:2007. Like the previous groups of paragraphs (equipment, pre-examination processes) the paragraphs 5.5 has been divided into smaller groups which make the studying and application of that paragraph clearer and easier.

The Paragraph 5.4.7 Pre-Examination Handling, Preparation, and Storage, 5.5.1.1 General

Totally new paragraph which requires: "the laboratory shall select examination procedures which have been validated for their intended use... The specified requirements (performance specifications) ... shall be related to the intended use of that examination".

Table 28. Pairing of paragraphs between ISO 15189:2012 and ISO 15189:2007 about primary sample collection and handling

	ISO 15189:2012	ISO 15189:2007
General principles The laboratory shall have:	**5.4.4.1**	**5.4**
Documented procedures for the proper collection and handling of primary samples…	1st paragraph	5.4.4
Where the user requires any deviations they shall be recorded ….	2nd paragraph	-
Instructions for pre-collection activities They shall include the following:	**5.4.4.2**	**5.4.3**
Completion of request form or electronic request.	a	5.4.3.c.1
Preparation of the patient.	b	5.4.3.b.1
Type and amount of the primary sample	c	5.4.3.c.2
Special timing of collection, where needed.	d	5.4.3.c.3
Clinical information relevant to or affecting sample collection.	e	5.4.3.c.6
Instruction of collection activities They shall include the following:	**5.4.4.3**	**5.4.3**
Determination of the identity of the patient from whom a primary sample is collected.	a	5.4.3.c.7
Verification that the patient meets pre-examination requirements …	b	5.4.3.b.1
Instructions for collection of sample with descriptions about containers and any necessary additives.	c	5.4.3.c.4
Where the primary sample is collected as part of clinical practice ….	d	-
Instructions for labeling of primary samples ….	e	5.4.3.c.5
Identity of the person collecting the primary sample and the collection date and time when needed.	f	-
Proper storage conditions …	g	5.4.3.d.1
Safe disposal of materials used in the collection.	h	5.4.3.c.9

Paragraph 5.5.1.2 Verification of Examination Procedures

This paragraph corresponds to the paragraph 5.5.2 of ISO 15189:2007. According to that "Validated

Table 29. Pairing of paragraphs between ISO 15189:2012 and ISO 15189:2007 about sample transportation

	ISO 15189:2012	ISO 15189:2007
The laboratory shall have a documented procedure for monitoring the transportation of samples to ensure the following:	**5.4.5**	**5.4.6**
Within a time frame appropriate to the nature of the requested examinations and the laboratory discipline concerned	a	a
Within a temperature interval specified for sample collection and handling and with the … proper preservatives	b	b
In a manner that ensures the integrity of the sample and the safety for the carrier …	c	c

Table 30. Pairing of paragraphs between ISO 15189:2012 and ISO 15189:2007 about sample reception

	ISO 15189:2012	ISO 15189:2007
The laboratory's procedure for sample reception shall ensure that the following conditions are met:	**5.4.6**	-
Samples are unequivocally traceable, by request and labeling	a	-
Laboratory-developed and documented criteria for acceptance or rejection of samples …	b	5.4.8
Where there are problems with the patient or sample identification or any other problem with the sample …. the final report shall indicate the nature and … the required caution when interpreting the result.	c	-
All samples received are recorded in the accession book .. or any other comparable system. Whenever possible the identity of the person receiving the sample shall also be recorded.	d	5.4.7
Authorized personnel shall evaluate received samples ...	e	5.4.10
Where relevant, there shall be instructions for the receipt, labelling, processing, reporting of samples specifically marked as urgent ...	f	5.4.11
All portions of the primary sample shall be unequivocally traceable to the original primary sample	Last paragraph	5.4.12

examination procedures used without modification shall be subject to independent verification by the laboratory being introduced into routine use … the laboratory shall document the procedure used for the verification …"

Paragraph 5.5.1.3 Verification of Examination Procedures

This paragraph corresponds to the paragraph 5.5.1 of ISO 15189:2007. "The laboratory shall validate examination procedures derived from:

a. Non-Standard methods
b. Laboratory designed or developed methods
c. Standard methods used outside their intended scope
d. Validated methods subsequently modified

The validation shall be as extensive as is necessary … and shall be documented …"

Paragraph 5.5.1.4 Measurement Uncertainty of Measured Quantity Values

This paragraph corresponds to the paragraph 5.6.2 of ISO 15189:2007. "The laboratory shall determine uncertainty for each measurement procedure

… The laboratory shall define the performance requirements uncertainty of the measurement procedure. The laboratory, upon request, shall make the uncertainty available to laboratory users."

Paragraph 5.5.2 Biological Inference Intervals or Clinical Decision Values

This paragraph corresponds to the paragraph 5.5.5 of ISO 15189:2007. "The laboratory shall define the biological reference intervals or clinical decision values … of its population and it shall change them if the examination/pre-examination procedure or the population has been changed."

Paragraph 5.5.3 Documentation of Examination Procedures

This paragraph corresponds to the paragraph 5.5.3 of ISO 15189:2007.

Paragraph 5.6 Ensuring Quality of Examination Results

This paragraph corresponds to the paragraph 5.6 of ISO 15189:2007 but has been totally changed. New titles and subtitles have been added like in

Table 31. Pairing of paragraphs between ISO 15189:2012 and ISO 15189:2007 about documentation of examination procedures

	ISO 15189:2012	ISO 15189:2007
Documentation shall include the following	**5.5.3**	**5.5.3**
Purpose of the examination	a	a
Principle and method of the examination procedures	b	b
Performance characteristics	c	c
Type of sample	d	d
Patient preparation	e	-
Type of container and additives	f	e
Required equipment and reagents	g	-
Environmental and safety controls	h	-
Calibration procedures	i	g
Procedural steps	j	-
Quality control procedures	k	-
Interferences (e.g. lipaemia, haemolysis)	l	-
Principle of procedure for calculation results	m	k
Biological reference intervals …	n	l
Reportable interval of examination results	o	m
Instructions for determining quantitative results when a result in not within the measurement interval	p	-
Alert/critical values	q	n
Laboratory clinical interpretation	r	-
…. sources of variation	s	q
References	t	-

many paragraphs before and the whole meaning has become clearer, richer and more understood.

Paragraph 5.6.1 General, 5.6.2 Quality Control. General

This is a new paragraph although it corresponds to the paragraph 5.6.1 of ISO 15189:2007. "The laboratory shall ensure the quality of examinations … the laboratory shall not fabricate any results". "…. Quality control procedures shall verify the attainment of the intended quality of results".

Paragraph 5.6.2.2 Quality Control Materials

Totally new paragraph. "The laboratory shall use quality control materials that react … like patient samples and they shall be periodically examined … to diminish any harm to the patient from an erroneous result".

Paragraph 5.6.2.3 Quality Control Data

Totally new paragraph. "The laboratory shall have a procedure to prevent the release of patient results in the event of quality control failure …. Quality control data shall be reviewed at regular intervals to detect trends in examination performance …".

Paragraph 5.6.3 Interlaboratory Comparisons

This paragraph is divided into many subparagraphs which set the requirements of any aspect of interlaboratory comparisons.

Paragraph 5.6.3.1 Participation

This paragraph corresponds to the paragraph 5.6.4 of ISO 15189:2007. "The laboratory shall participate in an appropriate interlaboratory comparison program (certified by ISO/IEC 17043)". The control materials of interlaboratory comparison scheme shall mimic patient samples and the laboratory shall establish performance criteria"

Paragraph 5.6.3.2 Alternative Approaches

This paragraph corresponds to the paragraph 5.6.5 of ISO 15189:2007. "Whenever an interlaboratory comparison is not available … the laboratory shall develop other approaches …"

Paragraph 5.6.3.3 Alternative Approaches

This paragraph corresponds partially to the paragraph 5.6.5 of ISO 15189:2007. It explains how the laboratory shall treat interlaboratory comparison samples. "The laboratory shall integrate interlaboratory comparison samples into the routine workflow … like patient samples … Interlaboratory comparison samples shall be examined by personnel who routinely examine patient samples … the laboratory shall not communicate with other participants … the laboratory shall not refer interlaboratory comparison samples for confirmatory examinations".

Paragraph 5.6.3.4 Evaluation of Laboratory Performance

This paragraph corresponds partially to the paragraph 5.6.7 of ISO 15189:2007. "The performance in interlaboratory comparisons shall be reviewed and discussed with relevant staff … which shall do and record any preventive action".

Paragraph 5.6.4 Comparability of Examination Results

Totally new paragraph. "There shall be a defined means of comparing procedures … This is applicable to the same or different procedures, equipment, different sites … The laboratory shall notify users of any differences in comparability of results … The laboratory shall document, record … the results of the comparisons …."

Paragraph 5.7 Post Examination Processes

Paragraph 5.7.1 Review of Results

This paragraph corresponds to the paragraph 5.7.1 of ISO 15189:2007. "The laboratory shall have procedures to ensure that authorized personnel review the results … When there is automated selection … review criteria shall be established …".

Paragraph 5.7.2 Storage, Retention and Disposal of Clinical Samples

This paragraph corresponds to the paragraph 5.7.2 and 5.7.3 of ISO 15189:2007.

Paragraph 5.8 Reporting of Results

Paragraph 5.8.1 General

This paragraph corresponds partially to the paragraph 5.8.11 of ISO 15189:2007.

Table 32. Pairing of paragraphs between ISO 15189:2012 and ISO 15189:2007 about storage, retention and disposal of clinical samples

	ISO 15189:2007
Storage of primary samples ... shall be in accordance with approved policy.	5.7.2
Safe disposal of samples ... shall be carried out in accordance with local regulations ...	5.7.3

The results of each examination shall be reported accurately ....

The laboratory shall define the format and medium of the report ...

The laboratory shall have a procedure to ensure the correctness of the transcription of laboratory results ...

Reports shall include all the information necessary ...

The laboratory shall have a process for notifying the requester when an examination is delayed ...

Paragraph 5.8.2 Report Attributes

Totally new paragraph. "The laboratory shall ensure that the following report attributes effectively communicate laboratory results and meet the user's needs:

Comments on sample quality ...

Comments regarding sample suitability ...

Critical results ...

Interpretive comments on results ..."

Paragraph 5.8.3 Report Content

This paragraph corresponds to the paragraphs 5.8.3 of ISO 15189:2007.

Paragraph 5.9 Release of Reports

Paragraph 5.9.1 General

This paragraph corresponds partially to the paragraphs 5.8.5, 5.8.7, 5.8.8 and 5.8.9 of ISO 15189:2007.

Paragraph 5.9.2 Automated Selection and Reporting of Results

Totally new paragraph. "If the laboratory implements a system for automated selection and reporting of results it shall establish a documented procedure to ensure that:

a. The criteria for automated selection and reporting are defined ....and understood by the staff

b. The criteria are validated for proper functioning ...

c. There is a process for indicating the presence of sample interference ....

d. There is a process for incorporating analytical warning messages ...

e. Results selected for automated reporting shall be identifiable ...

f. There is a process for rapid suspension of automated selection and ..."

Paragraph 5.9.3 Revised Reports

This paragraph corresponds partially to the paragraph 5.8.15 of ISO 15189:2007."When an original report is revised there shall be written instructions regarding the revisions ...

The revised report is clearly identified as a revision ...

The user is made aware ...

The revised record shows the time/date ...

An original report remains in the record ..."

Table 33. Pairing of paragraphs between ISO 15189:2012 and ISO 15189:2007 about report content

	ISO 15189:2012	ISO 15189:2007
The report shall include, but not to be limited to the following	**5.8.3**	**5.8.3**
A clear unambiguous identification of the examination ...., where appropriate, the examination procedure	a	a
The identification of the laboratory that issued the report	b	b
Identification of all examinations that have been performed by a referral laboratory	c	-
Patient identification and ... on each page	d	c
Name or other unique identifier of the requester and the requester's contact details	q	d
Date of primary sample collection (and time when available and relevant to patient care)	f	e
Type of primary sample	g	g
Measurement procedure, where appropriate	h	-
Examination results reported in SI or .. other units	i	h
Biological reference materials	j	i
Interpretation of results, where appropriate	k	j
Other comments ...	l	k
Identification of examinations undertaken as part of a research program	m	-
Identification of the person(s) reviewing the results ...	n	l
Date of the report and date of the release	o	-
Page number to total number of pages	p	-

Table 34. Pairing of paragraphs between ISO 15189:2012 and ISO 15189:2007 about release of results

	ISO 15189:2012	ISO 15189:2007
The laboratory shall establish documented procedures for the release of examination results ...:	**5.9.1**	**5.8**
When the quality of the primary sample received is unsuitable for examination ... this is indicated in the report	a	5.8.5
When examination results fall within established "alert" or "critical" intervals ...: - A physician is notified ... - Records are maintained of action taken ...	b	5.8.7, 5.8.8
Results are legible, without mistakes in transcription	c	-
When results are transmitted as an interim report, the final report is ... forwarded to the requester	d	5.8.9
There are processes for ensuring that results distributed by telephone or .... reach only authorized recipients .... Results provided orally shall be followed by a written report ...	e	5.8.14

Paragraph 5.10 Laboratory Information Systems

Totally new paragraph. All the requirements concerning the laboratory information systems (LIS) have been totally revised. In ISO 15189:2007 the requirements about LIS were reported in the paragraph 5.3.11 and the Annex B (informative). In ISO 15189:2012 there are new paragraphs which set new mandatory requirements.

Paragraph 5.10.1 General

This paragraph corresponds to the paragraph 5.3.11.c of ISO 15189:2007. "The laboratory shall have access to the data ... and shall have a documented procedure to ensure the confidentiality of ..."

Paragraph 5.10.2 Authorities and Responsibilities

This paragraph corresponds to the paragraph B.5.8 (Annex B) of ISO 15189:2007. "The laboratory shall define the authorities and responsibilities of all personnel .... Access ..., enter ..., change ... and authorize patient data".

Paragraph 5.10.3 Information System Management

This paragraph corresponds to many different paragraphs of Annex B of ISO 15189:2007.

CONCLUSION

The laboratories which will change their quality Standard from ISO 15189:2007 to ISO 15189:2012 have surely a lot of work to do. The new standard has much more requirements than the old one but also a strong advantage: it is more understood and more compatible to the modern medical laboratories and the laboratory science and management. I wish this guide will help the medical laboratories in their future accreditation.

Table 35. Pairing of paragraphs between ISO 15189:2012 and ISO 15189:2007 about information system management

	ISO 15189:2012	ISO 15189:2007
The laboratory shall establish documented procedures for the release of examination results ...:	**5.9.1**	**5.8**
validated by the supplier and verified by the laboratory ...	a	5.8.5
documented ... including that for day to day functioning of the system	b	B.8 Annex B
protected from unauthorized access	c	5.8.7, 5.8.8, B.4 Annex B
Safeguarded against tampering or ...	d	5.8.14, B.2, B.4 Annex B
operated in an environment that complies with supplier specifications ...	e	B.2 Annex B
Maintained in a manner that ensures the integrity of the data ...	f	5.8.9, B.5 Annex B
... in compliance with national or ... requirements ..."	g	-
The laboratory shall verify that the results of examinations ... are accurately reproduced ... When a new examination ... are implemented ... the laboratory shall verify ... that the changes are accurately reproduced	2nd paragraph	B.6 Annex B
The laboratory shall have documented contingency plans to maintain services in the event of failure ...	3rd paragraph	B.8 Annex B
.... laboratory management shall be responsible for ensuring that the provider ... with all applicable requirements of	4th paragraph	B.7 Annex B

REFERENCES

Guzel & Guner. (2009). ISO 15189 accreditation: Requirements for quality and competence of medical laboratories, experience of a laboratory. *Clinical Biochemistry*, *42*(4-5), 274–278. PMID:19863920

Hong Kong Accreditation Service. (2004). Practical application of ISO 125189 by accrediatation bodies. *EJIFCC*.

ILAC. (2011). *The ISO 15189 Medical Laboratory Accreditation*. Author.

ISO/CEN. (2012). *Medical laboratories – Requirements for quality and competence* (EN ISO 15189:2012). Author.

ISO/CEN. (2012). *Medical laboratories – Particular requirements for quality and competence* (EN ISO 15189:2012). Author.

Kawai, T. (2007). Evaluation of clinical laboratories-assurance of their quality and competence. *Rinsho Byori*, *55*(1), 59–62. PMID:17319492

Kawai, T. (2010). History of ISO 15189 and its future perspective. *Rinsho Byori*, *58*(1), 64–68. PMID:20169946

Kawano. (2005). External quality assessment with reference to the certification/accreditation of medical laboratories. *Rinsho Byori, 53*(4), 319-23.

Kubono. (2004). Quality management system in the medical laboratory-ISO15189 and laboratory accreditation. *Rinsho Byori, 52*(3), 274-8.

Li, A. (2009). Laboratory quality regulations and accreditations standards in Canada: External quality assessment with reference to the certification/accreditation of medical laboratories. *Clinical Biochemistry*, *42*(4-5), 249–255. doi:10.1016/j.clinbiochem.2008.09.006 PMID:19863915

NATA. (2013). *Gap Analysis of ISO 15189:2012 and ISO 15189:2007 in the field of Medical Testing*. Australia Accreditation Body.

KEY TERMS AND DEFINITIONS

Analyzers: Automatic machines which perform simultaneously many different chemical reactions based on chemical, informative and robotics technology.

Clinical Laboratory: Any chemical, microbiological or cytological laboratory which analyzes human samples.

Error: The difference between the result of a laboratory determination and the true value.

Interlaboratory Comparison: A statistical method for estimating the accuracy of chemical or physical measures by comparing them with their consensus means value.

ISO 15189: The special international standard for the clinical laboratories which is based on the ISO 9001:2008 and ISO 17025:2005.

Kit: A small package which contains all the necessary materials and instructions for a chemical determination.

Laboratory Information System (LIS): All the information systems of a clinical laboratory including the software, the hardware, the network materials and all the connections from/to laboratory analyzers and the other information systems of the medical organization.

Quality Manual: An electronic or hardcopy book which contains all the quality policy, the quality procedures and a list including detailed information of all the quality instructions and files of a company or organization.

Statistical Quality Control: Statistical procedures which identify random and systematic errors in automatic processes like chemical analyses in automatic analyzers.

Uncertainty: A statistical measure which refers to the dispersion of the values around the theoretical true value and it is estimated taking in mind all the possible sources of dispersion.

ENDNOTES

[1] Not exactly with the same meaning.
[2] Not exactly with the same meaning.

Chapter 10
A Practical Approach for Implementing the Additional Requirements of the ISO 15189:2012 Revision

Fikriye Uras
Marmara University, Turkey

ABSTRACT

Medical laboratory services have a critical role as an integral component of patient care. The accreditation standard of ISO 15189, a guidance document, provides validation that a laboratory is competent to deliver accurate and reliable test results. This international standard has been evolving since 2003. Following the second publication (2007), the standard was released as a revised and updated version in 2012 (Medical laboratories – Requirements for quality and competence). The text of ISO 15189:2012 has been approved as EN ISO15189:2012. European Union members and associate countries agreed to accord it the status of a national standard by May 2013. Any conflicting national standards need to be withdrawn by November 2015 at the latest. The purpose of this chapter is to mark the differences between the two versions of the standards and to highlight the changes and additions that have been incorporated into ISO 15189:2012. A practical approach will be helpful for laboratories to make a smooth transition to the updated standard when revising their quality and technical documentation to meet the new requirements.

INTRODUCTION

There is a need for diagnostic tests which can identify illness, isolate causes and subsequently check the effectiveness of treatment. In order to achieve reliability and consistency of results a comprehensive laboratory quality management system is called for (Peter T.F., 2010). The ac-

creditation standard of the International Organization for Standardization (ISO) 15189 provides for this. It promotes 'best practice' globally and makes for comprehensive harmonisation of lab practices in the field.

The standard of ISO 15189 has been implemented in over 140 countries, in most cases voluntarily although it is mandatory in some countries,

DOI: 10.4018/978-1-4666-6320-6.ch010

Australia, the Canadian province of Ontario, Iran, and some European countries (e.g. France and Latvia) (Ford A., 2008; ENAC, 2011).

ISO first published its 15189 standard in 2003, "Medical laboratories— Particular requirements for quality and competence for clinical laboratory testing and in vitro diagnostic test systems", for use in medical laboratories worldwide (2003). It was reformulated in 2007, which is to be superseded by a third- technically revised 2012 version (ISO, 2007 and 2012). Currently, it is closely aligned with the requirements for 'testing and calibration laboratories' (ISO 17025).

A cross-reference, including the itemizing of the clauses, between the second and third editions of this International Standard is provided as Annex B in the updated version (ISO, 2012). There have been several important changes to the content of ISO 15189:2012. The purpose of this chapter is to mark the differences between the two versions of the standards, and to highlight the changes and additions that have been incorporated into the ISO 15189:2012.

BACKGROUND

The text of ISO 15189:2012 has been approved by the European Committee for Standardization (CEN) as EN ISO 15189, as it stands on 31 October 2012 (Austrian Standards Institute, 2013). CEN members are legally required to observe the CEN/CENELEC Internal Regulations, which imposes this as a basis for a common European standard. This has to be incorporated into national law as it stands, without modification. Accordingly, it had to be given the status of a national standard by issuing an identical text or by endorsement, by May 2013, and any conflicting national standards have to be withdrawn by November 2015 at the latest. By the CEN/CENELEC Internal Regulations, the national standards organisations of the European Union (EU) member and associate countries are bound to implement this European Standard.

The International Laboratory Accreditation Cooperation (ILAC) organisation has agreed a transition period of three years four months for the implementation of ISO 15189:2012 (ILAC, 2012). Henceforward, all accredited medical laboratories must demonstrate their conformity to the new standard and have up-dated accreditation certificates issued by March 2016.

Using the ISO 15189 standard the College of American Pathologists (CAP) now offers a new laboratory accreditation programme, 'CAP 15189', which is available for US-based medical laboratories. Laboratories applying for the accreditation to CAP 15189 must be CAP accredited by the CAP's Laboratory Accreditation Program (CAP, 2012). ISO 15189 accreditation is voluntary in the United States.

In the UK, UKAS (United Kingdom Accreditation Service) is currently managing the transition of all CPA (Clinical Pathology Accreditation) accredited laboratories to the standard ISO 15189:2012. UKAS and CPA made an early decision to carry out transition assessments against the 2012 version of ISO 15189 rather than the 2007 version, with initial accreditation scheduled for July 2014 (CPA, 2012). They have provided summarised information regarding the new, additional, requirements of the updated version in their web pages (UKAS, 'Potential' and 'Summary').

Some national and regional accreditation organizations have prepared their transition plans and given detailed information for the main changes in practice to provide guidance and practical steps for managing the transition from ISO 15189:2007 to ISO 15189:2012. These are: The National Association of Testing Authorities (NATA)(2013), Irish National Accreditation Board (INAP) (2013), International Accreditation New Zealand (IANZ) (IANZ, n.d.), South African National Accreditation Services Accreditation Service (SANAS), The Southern African Development Community (SADCAS) (2013), Malaysian Accreditation Body (SAMM) (2013), Dutch Accreditation Council (RVA) (RVA, n.d.), Hong Kong Laboratory Accreditation Scheme (HOKLAS) (2013), and Quality Management Program—Laboratory Services (QMP-LS) (QMP-LS, n.d.).

DIFFERENCES BETWEEN ISO 15189: 2012 AND ISO 15189: 2007 - SECTION 4: MANAGEMENT REQUIREMENTS

4.1 Organisation and Management Responsibility

4.1.1 Organisation

4.1.1.1 General

Now ISO 15189 Standard covers medical laboratories working at remote sites in temporary or mobile facilities. 'Mobile facilities' has been added to this clause, where laboratory work is performed.

4.1.1.2. Legal Entity

According to the updated version, the laboratory must be 'legally responsible' for its performance whereas previously it was merely 'legally identifiable'. The laboratory must demonstrate in which ways any legal obligations and responsibilities are to be met. This requirement covers the contract details to lay down legal accountability.

4.1.1.3 Ethical Conduct

Some sub-clauses from the previous version (4.1.4, 4.1.5b- 4.1.5d) have been moved or consolidated under this sub-clause and amended. Where there are potential conflicts, they must be openly stated. Such relationships with other organisations and departments must be defined clearly. The laboratory must identify conflicts of interest and relationships between personnel and departments. One new item has been added: It is now a requirement for the handling and treatment of human samples, tissues or remains, in accordance with relevant local regulations.

4.1.1.4 Laboratory Director

The laboratory director is responsible for ensuring ongoing compliance with the ISO 15189 Standards and implementing the requirements. Specific responsibilities of the laboratory director have been outlined by the addition of new sections: implementing the quality policy; selecting and monitoring laboratory supplies; designing and implementing a 'contingency plan' for unexpected or emergency circumstances; and, addressing any 'complaint, request or suggestion from personnel and/or users of laboratory services'. The director must have the qualifications, authority and resources to fulfil all these responsibilities effectively [(a) to (o) inclusive].

4.1.2 Management Responsibility

4.1.2.1 Management Commitment

The laboratory management must demonstrate its commitment to establish the quality policy, implement a quality management system, and conduct management review. How this is to be achieved is specified, with an extra focus on the role of management in this clause. Since the Management System has been based on 'continual improvement' methodology, management commitment to effective implementation of continual improvement must be demonstrated. This can be achieved by carrying out self-assessments and management reviews. They can be realised by collecting data, analysing information, setting objectives, and implementing corrective and preventive actions [(a) to (i) inclusive]. The personnel must be competent to perform their assigned duties to carry out their work in accordance with ISO 15189 Standard and local regulations. The management system needs to be customised to ensure the quality of laboratory services.

4.1.2.2 Needs of the User

Keeping patients and clinicians satisfied is a priority for management. The laboratory must be able to demonstrate that the services provided are adequate to satisfy the needs of patients, clinicians, and those using the laboratory services. There must be a procedure to measure and monitor satisfaction levels from all services, including appropriate advisory and interpretative services. All the records of clinician/patient satisfaction surveys or complaint rates must be retained. The laboratory must demonstrate that the results of findings were reviewed, and necessary actions taken where the medical laboratory is a permanent facility, or, if not, in sites remote from its permanent facilities, or temporary or mobile facilities.

4.1.2.3 Quality Policy

The aims of the laboratory's quality management system must be defined as 'quality policy' and reviewed periodically for 'ongoing suitability'.

4.1.2.4 Quality Objectives and Planning

This new sub-clause is focused on details of establishing quality objectives in the quality management programme. Measurable targets should be agreed with all key staff. These should be clearly communicated to those involved in its implementation by all relevant functions within the organisation. Management needs to ensure there is an appropriate change management procedure to enable that the integrity of the whole system is maintained, during periods of change (staff, substances, technology, processes, and location). The indicators of the objectives must be realistic and measurable, taking into consideration the requirements of the users.

4.1.2.5 Responsibility, Authority and Interrelationships

Some sub-clauses (4.1.5 a, e, f, and j) in the 2007 version have been consolidated and amended. The laboratory must ensure that 'responsibilities,

authorities and interrelationships are all defined, documented and communicated within the organisation'.

4.1.2.6 Communication

This clause emphasises the responsibility of management for establishing clear communication between managers and employees in all areas. Communication is a key factor for providing laboratory services efficiently and accurately. This should be appropriate for the size and scope of the organisation. The lines of communication within the organisation and with its stakeholders need to be open and effective. There must be a procedure for communicating information between personnel when responsibility is handed over from one person to another (a change in shift, pending specimens and tests). Records of communications and meetings must be kept available for the assessors from the accreditation body.

4.1.2.7 Quality Manager

Now the quality manager's responsibilities have been expanded. The extra role of the quality manager is to promote the awareness of users' needs and requirements throughout all parts of the laboratory.

4.2 Quality Management System

4.2.1 General Requirements

This clause has been substantially rewritten. The general aims, however, remain. The laboratory must have a documented quality management system and implement this system to continually improve the quality and effectiveness of the service provided in accordance with ISO 15189:2012 and local regulations. Documents must include the quality policy; quality objectives and plans;

a quality manual; the laboratory's operational processes and procedures; quality indicators; records of management review and actions taken.

4.2.2 Documentation Requirements

4.2.2.2 Quality Manual

The contents of a quality manual have been simplified. There is a significant change to the editorial, "the quality manual shall include descriptions of integral elements of the quality management system, laboratory management and documented policies". It must also include 'all relevant policies' in sufficient detail to form a basis for any procedural documentation and records.

4.3 Document Control

This clause has been amended with new additions. Document control is the management of all documents (paper or electronic), including policies, procedures, instructions and forms. There must be a system governing how all documents are initiated or revised, approved, reviewed, maintained, and discontinued. The updated version of ISO 15189 emphasises an effective document control procedure ensuring that any changes to the system are reflected in their documentation. It must be demonstrated that the documents are readily available, are periodically reviewed for current validity and removed when obsolete. Changes to documents must be identified. A copy of external documents such as national or local regulations relating to laboratory issues must be kept. All documents must now also include a page number to the total number of pages (e.g. page 2 of 5) rather than just the number of pages.

The following has been deleted from ISO 15189:2007: "procedures are established to describe how changes to documents maintained in computerised systems are to be made and controlled".

4.4 Service Agreements

The clause has been substantially reordered and reformulated. The general aims, however, remain the same. Test orders once accepted by the laboratory must be considered binding agreements. There must be a procedure to create and maintain agreements that establish the detail of laboratory service to be provided, and also the actual documentary record of the agreements.

4.5 Examination by Referral Laboratories

4.5.1 Selecting and Evaluating Referral Laboratories and Consultants

This clause has been amended to bring it into line with 4.5.1-4.5.3 in the earlier standard. Now the requirements have been expanded to cover documented procedures for recruitment of consultants to give opinions and interpretation for complex testing. It relates to consultants within all relevant disciplines, not just for cytology, histopathology and related disciplines. The clause has also been extended to say that "a register of all referral laboratories and consultants from whom opinions are sought is maintained". Performance of referral laboratories services must be monitored, reviewed periodically, and all the records must be retained.

The following have been removed: "details concerning what is required to be reviewed", [4.5.2 (a) to (d)], and "A duplicate of the laboratory report shall be retained in both the patient record and in the permanent file of the laboratory".

4.5.2 Provision of Examination Results

The clause 4.5.4 in the 2007 version has been amended so that the laboratory now has the option to specify in the agreement whether the referral laboratory will be responsible for providing results directly to the person requesting the tests. An additional requirement is that the report must indicate which examinations were performed by a referral laboratory or interpreted by an outside consultant.

4.6 External Services and Supplies

This clause has been significantly edited and some parts in the 2007 version moved to 4.13 (Control of records) and 5.3.2 (Reagents and consumables).

When selecting a supplier to fulfil the laboratory's needs, the laboratory must have detailed criteria and procedures to ensure that equipment, reagents or services provide accurate and reliable results. A list of selected and approved suppliers and services must be retained. The performance of suppliers must be monitored and reviewed to make sure the items provided consistently meet the stated criteria.

4.7 Advisory Services

Now 'advisory services' has been expanded. The laboratory must promote the efficient streamlining and effective utilisation of laboratory services (e.g. choice and frequency of examinations). The responsible staff must provide advice or interpretation of test results and/or logistical matters such as the failure of samples to meet acceptance criteria, to the users of the laboratory services.

A portion has been deleted: "There should be regular documented meetings of professional staff with the clinical staff regarding the use of the laboratory services and for the purpose of consultation on scientific matters. The professional staff should participate in clinical rounds, dispensing advice on effectiveness in general as well as in individual cases".

4.9 Identification and Control of Nonconformities

This clause has been amended from 4.9.1-4.9.3 in the 2007 version. There must be procedures for identifying and managing 'nonconformities'. The practical impact of the nonconformity is to be clearly explained. The procedures must take into account the medical significance of nonconformities under consideration and for the clinician making the request to be informed about this. Corrective and/or preventive actions must be taken and documented even if it is merely the suspicion of the reappearance of nonconformity or there is uncertainty concerning compliance with the management system.

The results of any examinations already released are to be recalled and appropriately identified, where necessary. Nonconforming examinations or activities can be identified from: checking of quality control results; calibrations; clinician complaints; staff comments; laboratory management reviews, and internal and external assessments.

4.10 Corrective Action

Some sub-clauses (4.10.1-4.10.4 inclusive) in the 2007 version have been combined: "The laboratory shall take corrective action to eliminate the cause(s) of nonconformities". A procedure must be established to find out the underlying causes of the problem, to resolve it, and to record the review of nonconformities. Laboratories must perform root cause analysis of any nonconformity. The results and effectiveness of any corrective action need to be submitted for laboratory management review.

The clause 4.10.4 in the previous version has been removed: "The requirement to assess areas where doubt is cast on the compliance with policies and procedures".

4.11 Preventive Action

This clause has been amended from the previous clauses of 4.11.1 and 4.11.2. Now a number of additional criteria have been added to the documented procedure for preventive action. A system needs to be put in place to identify potential nonconformities: action plans must be established, implemented and monitored to reduce the likelihood of the re-occurrence of such nonconformities. Records of the root cause analyses and other activities performed for preventive action activities must be retained.

4.12 Continual Improvement

A new requirement focuses on risk assessment based approaches for continuous improvement activities, which are to be directed to the areas of highest priority.

The clause 4.12.4 in the 2007 version has been amended such that "the laboratory must have a procedure to communicate personnel improvement plans and any related goals". The records of any communication concerning the information of improvement plans from management to staff must be retained.

The clause of 4.12.5 in the previous version has been removed: "Laboratory management shall provide access to suitable educational and training opportunities for all laboratory personnel and relevant users of laboratory services not specifically mentioned".

4.13 Control of Records

The name of the clause has been altered, all subclauses (4.13.1 to 4.13.3) from the previous version have been integrated into a single clause in the latest version, and 4.6.3 and 4.6.4 have been moved to this clause.

The list of records to be reviewed is now mandatory, rather than optional. In this clause a detailed list has been given [(a) to (v) inclusive]. It now includes additional quality related records (e.g. selection and performance of suppliers, minutes of meetings that record decisions etc.). These must be reviewed periodically by management.

Previously, 'record retention limits' was defined by the nature of the examination or specifically for each record. Now the retention time may vary, based on a number of factors. However, reported patient test results must be maintained in a retrievable condition for as long as medically relevant or as required by regulation. Records may be stored on any appropriate medium (paper or electronic) in compliance with national or local legal requirements.

Further new requirements have been added. Records must be created to monitor the performance of each activity that affects the quality of the examination. There must be total traceability throughout all processes in the laboratory to see who collected the sample, who made the analysis, and what the quality control results were, for the examination, including issuing of the report. The date and, where relevant, time, of amendments must be noted, and the identity of staff amending them.

4.14 Evaluation and Audits

The name of the clause has been changed.

4.14.1 General

Now this requirement is recast and extended to include other areas of evaluation, not merely internal audits.

4.14.2 Periodic Review of Requests, and Suitability of Procedures and Sample Requirements

It has been amended so that the examinations provided by the laboratory are to be reviewed periodically by authorised personnel to ensure they are clinically appropriate for the requests received.

Now there is a new requirement to review this sample collection procedure on a regular basis. The laboratory must ensure that all pre-analytical steps are up-to-date (sample collection devices, volume and preservatives of samples). Neither insufficient nor excessive amounts of sample are to be collected and the "measurand" (analyte) is to be reserved.

4.14.3 Assessment of User Feedback

Previously laboratories were 'encouraged' to seek positive and negative feedback from the 'users' of laboratory services, physicians, patients, and caregivers. Now obtaining users' feedback is required as an important component of the laboratory management. There must be a documented procedure for users to cooperate and relay concerns about quality and safety to management. Complete confidentiality must be maintained with regard to all users. This feedback information must be regularly reviewed by management. Records must be retained, and any actions based on it.

4.14.4 Staff Suggestions

The new requirement is that laboratories must implement and maintain a staff suggestion system providing a constant flow of ideas for continual improvement. Ideas should be elicited from staff at all levels. They must be evaluated and implemented as appropriate, and feedback provided to the staff. Records of suggestions and action taken by the management must be retained.

4.14.5 Internal Audit

There is now a greater focus on the internal assessment programme since internal audits play a crucial role in risk management and continuous improvement. As a note to this clause suggests, the cycle of internal assessments should normally be completed within one year. The assessment programme must be organised so as to provide observations about the conformity of the laboratory with the requirements of ISO 15189. The assessment must be objective and impartial (at least two auditors), and wherever resources permit, auditors from a different part of the department/laboratory. These assessments are to be conducted by personnel specially trained to conduct assessments. They can be performed as a series of 'mini-audits' with different frequencies for different processes. Not all technical procedures need to be assessed, but the procedure should cover all critical processes. Personnel responsible for the area being audited must ensure that appropriate action is promptly undertaken when nonconformities are identified and documented.

4.14.6 Risk Management

A new requirement focuses on risk management and quality improvement for patient safety. The laboratory must have a documented system to gather problems involving the laboratory services (complaints from patients, clinicians or nurses; incidents and accidents).

The laboratory must investigate any problem that could potentially interfere with patient care or safety and identify all potential failures on test results insofar as they affect patient care. It must modify processes to reduce or eliminate these risks. The records must be retained to demonstrate that appropriate risk-reduction activities are performed, based on root cause analysis.

4.14.7 Quality Indicators

The laboratory must develop, monitor, and periodically review relevant quality indicators for all stages of its performance (pre-examination, examination and post-examination). When developing quality indicators, laboratories must ensure the following: that they are objective and measurable; the laboratory is able to measure them; acceptable limits are decided in advance; how to interpret the information; action plans for problems, and when to stop measurement.

"Turnaround times" required for each examination has been moved from "Reporting" in the previous version to "Evaluation" in the 2012 version. The laboratory must periodically evaluate turnaround times by comparing the established limits, as a key performance indicator of their service.

4.14.8 Reviews by External Organisations

Laboratories must respond to nonconformity or potential nonconformities identified by external assessments to ensure ongoing compliance. There must be immediate action, and, as appropriate, corrective or preventive actions with root cause analysis. The records of evaluation and all activities including external reviews, corrective or preventive actions taken and reviews of the effectiveness of such actions must be kept. They are objective evidence of compliance.

4.15 Management Review

4.15.1 General

This clause has been reformulated and expanded to include review input (4.15.2), activities (4.15.3) and output (4.15.4). "The expected interval for conducting management review" has been moved to a note as a suggestion. ISO standards understand the word 'review' to mean 'team studies', not merely that of one individual. This team evaluates the input and then creates the output plan.

4.15.2 Review Input

The inputs are actual records which have been produced since the previous management review meeting. The number of inputs has been expanded to cover Section 4 activities including a list [(a) to (o) inclusive]. The periodic review of requests

from doctors, and suitability of procedures and sample requirements (see 4.14.2) is added to the list of material for management review. Also, management review must take account of risk management (see 4.14.6), staff suggestions (see 4.15.4), performance of suppliers (see 4.6), and recommendations for improvement, including technical requirements.

4.15.3 Review Activities

This clause has been amended so that management must analyse the input information for causes of nonconformities, trends and patterns that indicate any process problems. The scope of the review, an opportunity for improvement, should be comprehensive, though not all elements within it need to be reviewed at once. Review of the policy, objectives, and procedures should be carried out. This process needs to take place over a period of time at variable frequencies based upon the level of risk.

4.15.4 Review Output

Records of management review must cover decisions made, and actions taken relating to the improvement of the effectiveness of the management system and its processes; improvement of services to users; and resource demands. Actions arising from management review are to be completed within a defined timeframe. For each action, there must be included the following: action item or task; person responsible; due date; stating whether corrective or preventive action. 'Review output' is a list of operations decided on based on the review input.

5.1 Personnel

5.1.1 General

The clause has been subjected to significant editorial changes to consider staff requirements under different headings (qualifications, job descriptions, introductions, training, competency, staff performance, continuing education and records). The requirement covering the responsibilities of the laboratory director has been moved to sub-clause 4.1.1.4.

5.1.2 Personnel Qualifications

Personnel policies, job descriptions including qualifications and duties for each position must be documented by laboratory management.

5.1.4 Personnel Induction to the Organizational Environment

A new clause indicates that a programme for staff inductions is required. Induction has to be designed to provide new staff with practical information on how the organisation operates and is a vital process to ensure that the new staff will be productive from the start. This programme must include the terms and conditions of employment, staff facilities, safety and security requirements (fire and emergency), and occupational health services. It should assist in inducting new staff into the 'culture' of the management system in the new organisation.

5.1.5 Training

This section 5.1.5 (a combination of 5.1.6 and 5.1.10 from the 2007 version) lays down the responsibilities of the laboratory in staff training. These have been changed to help improve the organisation's quality, including health and safety, and ethics. Personnel, who are undergoing training, must be supervised at all times. Measures of training effectiveness can be performance-based, or by written or oral test. They must be periodically reviewed. Evidence as to how competence has been verified, and training confirmed as effective is to be documented.

"Authorisation and responsibilities for the management of information systems" has moved to the new section 5.10.

5.1.6 Competence Assessment

The laboratory must assess the competence of the individual after training, in respect of assigned managerial or technical tasks, according to established criteria. This must cover retraining and reassessment. It needs to be documented that all technical personnel have satisfactorily completed initial training on all instruments before the person performs patient testing. Notes 1 and 2 to this clause suggest examples of approaches to assessment.

5.1.7 Review of Staff Performance

Review of staff performance is an opportunity to maintain and continually improve laboratory services. For this reason, in addition to the assessment of technical competence, the laboratory must consider the needs of the laboratory and also the personnel. As a note to this clause suggests, "staff performing reviews should receive appropriate training".

5.1.8 Continuing Education and Professional Development

In the earlier version of ISO 15189, 'continuing education program' was to be made available to staff at 'all levels'. In the updated version, it requires for 'managerial and technical' personnel, including that the effectiveness must be periodically reviewed.

5.1.9 Personnel Records

The number of personnel records required to be maintained has been expanded [(a) to (k) inclusive] to include the following: induction of new staff; reviews of staff performance; accidents and exposure to occupational hazards; competence assessments; immunisation status, where relevant to assigned duties. This is now mandatory in ISO 15189:2012 whereas it was optional in 2007. These are not required to be stored in the laboratory but are to remain accessible when needed.

5.2 Accommodation and Environmental Conditions

This clause has been divided into five sub-clauses which emphasises that the laboratory must be adequate to perform duties safely and accurately including having adequate space, adequate storage areas, clean areas, and acceptable temperature/humidity.

5.2.1 General

Adequacy of allocated working space for point-of-care testing under the laboratory's management is now a consideration.

5.2.2 Laboratory and Office Facilities

Now, there are additional requirements for safety facilities and devices. Their functioning must be regularly monitored and verified. Some of these facilities are operation of 'emergency release' of staff from the laboratory in emergency situations; intercom and alarm systems for cold rooms; accessibility of emergency showers and eyewash, etc.

The laboratory should provide efficient transfer of information to outside bodies. Medical information, patient samples and laboratory resources should be safeguarded against unauthorised access.

5.2.3 Storage Facilities

There is an additional requirement concerning clinical samples and biological material used in the laboratory. It is required to handle and store such materials in such a manner as prevents cross-contamination. All hazardous material must be managed in accordance with local or national regulations. Laboratories are responsible for proper handling, storage, transportation and removal of all hazardous waste in accordance with regulations.

5.2.4 Staff Facilities

The new requirement is to manage the risks and mitigate the hazards so as to maintain a safe environment for staff. The following must be easily accessible by staff: "washrooms, drinking water and areas storing personal protective equipment and clothing". Where possible, laboratories should provide space for staff activities such as meetings and private study and a rest area.

5.2.5 Patient Sample Collection Facilities

This sub-clause subsumes 5.2.2, 5.2.3, and 5.2.4 from the previous version. There is a new requirement for separation of the areas of reception, waiting and collection. Also, all sample collection facilities must include first aid facilities. Some facilities may need equipment appropriate for resuscitation: local regulations may apply.

5.2.6 Facility Maintenance and Environmental Conditions

The monitoring of environmental conditions has been extended to cover the welfare of staff.

Examination procedures must be carried out in a way which is safe for the staff. Care must be taken to prevent cross-contamination. Ambient temperature and humidity must be controlled, and all records must be retained.

5.3 Laboratory Equipment, Reagents, and Consumables

5.3.1 Equipment

Parts of 4.6 from the previous version have been subsumed into clause 5.3 in the 2012 version.

5.3.1.1 General

Editorial re-arrangement of what was previously 4.6.1and 5.3.1 covers procedures for the management of equipment, including selection and purchase. Also, the laboratory must monitor and review equipment to ensure the quality of examination results.

Deleted: "A previous requirement concerning the energy efficiency and future disposal of equipment (care of the environment) has been deleted".

5.3.1.2 Equipment Acceptance Testing

A note to this clause suggests that the requirement covers equipment used in the laboratory, on loan or used in associated or mobile facilities or by others authorised by the laboratory. Each item of equipment must be uniquely labelled, marked or otherwise identified. There must be documentation that the equipment is adequately tested and verified for proper functioning when first installed.

5.3.1.3 Equipment Instructions for Use

This requirement has been expanded to include that staff must be trained and authorised for operating equipment before using.

5.3.1.4 Equipment Calibration and Metrological Traceability

This new requirement emphasises the importance of the calibration of equipment. The laboratory must have a documented procedure for this. Where the laboratory examination procedures require the calibration of the instruments, there must be information relating to the metrological traceability of the material used in the calibration. It must be demonstrated in that the traceability of materials used in the validation processes has been taken into account (including those used by the manufacturers) in the laboratory review of validation/verification. This should be to a reference material or reference procedure of the higher metrological order, where possible. Where this is not possible or relevant, other means for providing confidence must be applied. Equipment that could affect the result and which requires calibration must have evidence of a traceable calibration being completed and all the records kept. It also needs to be proved that the calibration data have been reviewed by the laboratory to establish that the equipment is fit for purpose. Metrological traceability for physical measurements such as thermometers is to be demonstrated in an ISO 17025 accredited calibration laboratory, or else internally.

5.3.1.5 Equipment Maintenance and Repair

A number of clauses from the 2007 version (5.3.2, 5.6.3, 5.3.6-5.3.9, 4.6.2) have been subsumed into a single clause.

5.3.1.6 Equipment Adverse Incident Reporting

This new requirement is that equipment-related adverse incidents and accidents must be investigated and reported to the manufacturer and appropriate authorities, when it is linked to directly to specific equipment. This includes equipment in all areas in the laboratory and devices used for specimen collection.

5.3.1.7 Equipment Records

Equipment records are no longer required to include the recommended replacement date. Previous clauses 5.3.3 and 5.3.4 have been combined and amended. Now the laboratory must keep copies of reports/certificates of all calibrations and/or verifications. Previously this was merely a recommendation in the 2007 version.

Records must be kept for each item of equipment that contributes to the conduct of examinations. Equipment records must include the following: verification results; contact information of the supplier; condition of the equipment when received (e.g. whether new or second hand); date of receipt and entrance of equipment into service; manufacturer's instructions. This clause provides a detailed list concerning what an equipment record must include [(a) to (k) inclusive].

Copies of reports/certificates of all calibrations and/or verifications must include dates; adjustments; times and results; the acceptance criteria, and the anticipated date of the next calibration or verification. All these records must be retained for the lifespan of the equipment or afterwards (see 4.13).

5.3.2 Reagents and Consumables

5.3.2.1 General

The previous 4.6.1 has been re-edited: "Documented procedures are required for the reception, storage, acceptance testing and inventory management of reagents and consumables".

5.3.2.2 Reagents and Consumables: Reception and Storage

The new requirement is for those laboratories lacking a reception facility. The laboratory must ensure that the receiving location has adequate storage conditions to prevent damage or deterioration. All reagents and consumables must be stored in accordance with manufacturer's specifications.

5.3.2.3 Reagents and Consumables: Acceptance Testing

The laboratory must verify the performance of each new formulation of examination kits, where there have been changes in reagents or procedures, or else a new batch of kits, before use.

5.3.2.4 Reagents and Consumables: Inventory Management

A new addition is that uninspected or rejected reagents and consumables must be kept remote from those accepted for use.

5.3.2.5 Reagents and Consumables: Instructions for Use

A new requirement covers instructions concerning the use of reagents and consumables, including manufacturer's instructions. They must be easily accessible at all times.

5.3.2.6 Reagents and Consumables: Adverse Incident Recording

A new clause is that adverse incidents and accidents must be investigated and reported to the manufacturer and appropriate authorities, when there are attributed to directly to specific reagents and consumables, as the case may be.

5.3.2.7 Reagents and Consumables: Records

The previous 4.6.3 has been expanded to include the records required to be retained, relating to reagents and consumables. Where the laboratory uses reagents prepared or completed in-house, there must be a record of the staff member who prepared them together with the date of preparation.

Records must be retained for each reagent and consumable that influences the analytical performance. These must include the batch code/lot number; reception and expiry dates; manufacturer's name; contact information of the supplier; where applicable, verification and acceptability records or the date of taken out of service; condition received in (acceptable or damaged); instructions of the manufacturer.

5.4 Pre-Examination Processes

This clause has been subjected to editorial changes. Now "pre-analytical processes" is divided into: seven sub-clauses, viz.: 5.4.1 to 5.4.7.

5.4.1 General

The laboratory must have procedures for standardisation of pre-examination /pre-analytical steps to maintain the validity of examination results.

5.4.2 Information for Patients and Users

Alterations have been made to the information which is to be made available for the patients and users of the laboratory services [(a) to (n) inclusive]. Now the laboratory must provide more information covering types of clinical services by the laboratory; examinations referred to other laboratories, and the opening hours. Also, it must include a list of factors affecting the examination or the interpretation of the results, and instructions concerning patient collected samples.

5.4.3 Request form Information

Now the requisition requirements have been made explicit and mandatory where previously they were optional (paper or electronic). Their number has been expanded and includes adequate information to identify the right patient correctly [(a) to (g) inclusive]. The location or contact information of the patient and the date of sample collection are a requirement; however the time of specimen collection is only required if appropriate. The new requirement is "The laboratory shall be willing to cooperate with users or their representatives in clarifying the user's request".

5.4.4 Primary Sample Collection and Handling

Critical requirements in this clause have been segregated into three sub-clauses.

5.4.4.1 General

Now, the laboratory must record the extra situations where the user requires variations from, or additions to, the documented sample collection procedure. This information must be kept in all records through to patient report. Also, the laboratory must communicate these to the appropriate staff.

The laboratory must give a more detailed explanation to patients for special procedures. In some cases, written consent must be received from patients, including invasive procedures or those with an increased risk of complications (e.g. stimulation tests). In an emergency situation, when it is not practicable to get consent, the laboratory needs to carry out any necessary procedures in what is deemed to be in the patient's best interest.

5.4.4.2 Instructions for Pre-Collection Activities

An addition to this requirement is that instructions must cover any necessary additives to primary sample containers.

5.4.4.3 Instructions for Collection Activities

The new requirement is for collecting specimens when they are taken by clinical personnel (e.g. during invasive clinical activities). Instructions for the proper collection and transfer of specimens must be made available to anyone collecting biological materials from patients. This information is to be communicated to the clinical personnel.

5.4.5 Sample Transportation

Detail of the packaging of samples for transportation must now be included in the procedure of sample transportation to closely control maintaining specimen integrity. These include specimen temperature and transport time. The laboratory must package and transport biological material safely in accordance with applicable regulations.

5.4.6 Sample Reception

The previous clauses from 5.4.7- 5.4.12 inclusive have been combined. Now, the date and time that the specimen was received by the laboratory must be recorded as a part of tracking system. The identity of the person receiving the sample must also be recorded, where possible.

5.4.7 Pre-Examination Handling, Preparation and Storage

When the clinician requests additional tests on the same primary sample, the laboratory only must accept these requests within pre-agreed time limits. Now the requirement emphasises that the laboratory procedures must indicate these time limits clearly. The procedures and operation must provide a secure system for patient samples, including protection from deterioration, loss or damage. Refrigerator and freezer temperatures must be checked and recorded (e.g. daily).

5.5 Examination Processes

The clause on analytical testing (examination) processes has been rewritten, and it is now apportioned into three sub-clauses (5.5.1 to 5.5.3 inclusive). The term "examination" is defined in the ISO 15189 as "set of operations having the object of determining the value or characteristics of a property" together with a note saying "in some countries and disciplines (e.g. microbiology) examination is the total activity of a number of tests, observations or measurements". In this chapter, the term "examination" is used in place of 'analytical' to cover steps of pre-examination, examination and post-examination.

5.5.1 Selection, Verification and Validation of Examination Procedures

5.5.1.1 General

This requirement has been amended so that the identity of personnel performing examination activities must be recorded.

5.5.1.2 Verification of Examination Procedures

Previously the laboratory was required to 'evaluate' methods and procedures before putting them into service. Now, verification within the laboratory is mandatory for validated examination procedures used without modification. Verification is a process to check the performance characteristics of a method measured within the laboratory versus the values of the manufacturer. The laboratory must perform analyses and statistical activities to obtain the values of accuracy, precision, specificity, sensitivity, linearity and etc. Then, these values need to be compared with the information obtained from the manufacturer. Only authorised staff within assigned roles and responsibilities can review the verification results and approve them. This must be done prior to the test system being put into service, and all the records must be retained.

5.5.1.3 Validation of Examination Procedures

The amended clause covers the situations in which validation of examination procedures is required. Validation involves determining the performance specifications of newly developed methods by the laboratory. According to this clause, it must be "as extensive as necessary and confirm that specific requirements for the intended use of the examination have been fulfilled". It is mandatory for non-standard methods; laboratory- developed methods; standard methods used outside their intended scope; and modified methods. When changes are made to a validated examination procedure, the influence of such changes must be documented by a re validation. Nonc but authorised personnel should approve the validation results as meeting pre-defined criteria for acceptability. As evidence, all the records of validation studies together with the identity of the authorised person must be retained and made available to the assessors from the accreditation body.

Allowable limits of analytical performance vary within individual countries. The CLIA (Clinical Laboratory Improvement Amendments) from US, RiliBÄK *(Guidelines of the German Federal Medical Society)*, and RCPA (Royal College of Pathologists of Australasia), and others have been developed as a set of specifications for analytical limits. All these and others may contribute to the decision to accept the validation results.

5.5.1.4 Measurement Uncertainty of Measured Quantity Values

In the 2007 version of ISO 15189 Standard, the laboratory should determine the uncertainty of the results, "where relevant and possible", but now, in the updated version it becomes mandatory for all tests. 'Measurement uncertainty' values must be estimated for all test procedures and the periodic review of these estimates should be documented. When interpreting quantitative values, the impact of these measurement uncertainty values on the interpretation of the test result must be taken into account. The laboratory must make measurement uncertainty estimates available to laboratory users on request.

Some test results can be reported verbally (e.g. positive or negative) based on the numerical values obtained at the end of the analysis. Even in this situation, the laboratory should calculate the measurement uncertainty where it has a practical effect on the reported result.

5.5.2 Biological Reference Intervals or Clinical Decision Limits

An amended requirement is that the laboratory must document and communicate to users the reference resources on which the biological reference intervals or clinical decision values are taken. When pre-analytical or analytical changes occur, consideration must be given as to whether it could affect reference intervals and clinical decision values.

5.5.3 Documentation of Examination Procedures

In the 2007 version, including the information about the documentation of examination procedures was optional. It is now mandatory in the 2012 version. The following information must also be included, in addition to 'document control identifiers', when applicable to the examination procedure: patient preparation; instructions for performing the quantitative tests where the result is not within the measurement interval; environmental and safety controls; calibration procedures (with metrological traceability); and reference resources. A detailed list has been given in this sub-clause [(a) to (t) inclusive].

Examination procedures must be documented in user-friendly language by staff in the laboratory and be kept readily available. Furthermore, the laboratory must now, if it is intended to change an existing examination procedure which might significantly alter results, explain to users its significance after validation.

5.6 Ensuring Quality of Examination Results

The clause name has been changed, subjected to significant editorial arrangement and divided into two sub-clauses.

5.6.1 General

This requirement has emphasised general demands concerning the quality of examination results. The laboratory must perform examinations under defined conditions with standardised pre- and post-examination processes. The laboratory must not change any actual results intentionally.

5.6.2 Quality Control

5.6.2.2 Quality Control Materials

This requirement has been amended focusing on the nature of Quality Control (QC) materials. These materials must be chosen to perform within the examining system in a manner conforming as nearly as possible to patient samples. The laboratory must periodically check QC materials with a frequency depending on the stability of the examination procedure and the risk from an erroneous result.

5.6.2.3 Quality Control Data

The new requirement emphasises the importance of quality assurance. The laboratory must have a documented procedure for checking QC data and, if need be, suspending the release of patient results. When the quality control system has a problem,

patient results must be rejected. Relevant patient samples must be re-examined together with QC material after the problem has been resolved. The laboratory must also re-evaluate all the results from patient samples that were examined after the last successful quality control event.

The laboratory must have a documented QC procedure including number and frequency of QC, establishing tolerance limits for QC, regular review by authorised staff, and corrective actions relating to QC system failures.

If untoward trends are observed, preventive actions must be taken and recorded. A note included in this clause explains the importance of techniques and technology for process control, to continuously monitor examination system performance. Using an integrated Laboratory Information System (a computerized system) makes internal QC monitoring much easier. A completely automated QC system also needs to minimise patient risk because of unreliable test results. This data management system identifies trends, instrument errors or reagent issues as soon as they arise, assuring the validity and increasing confidence in the accuracy of results. It minimises false rejections whilst maintaining high error detection through the use of multi-rule QC procedures (see 5.9.2).

5.6.3 Interlaboratory Comparisons

5.6.3.1 Participation

In the updated version of the standard, the requirement for interlaboratory comparison programmes has been changed that they should substantially fulfil the relevant requirements of ISO/IEC 17043.

The new requirement is that there must be a detailed documented procedure for participation in interlaboratory comparison programmes (external quality assessment or proficiency testing) including responsibilities and instructions for participation. This procedure must also indicate any other performance criteria for evaluation if the laboratory uses different criteria from the general. The results of the interlaboratory comparison programme(s) must be monitored and reviewed. Corrective actions must be taken when 'predetermined performance criteria' are not fulfilled.

Some of the content of 5.6.3 in the 2007 version, relating to calibration for measuring systems, is now included in 5.3.1.4.

5.6.3.2 Alternative Approaches

This sub-clause includes some alternative ways where an interlaboratory comparison programme is not available.

5.6.3.3 Analysis of Interlaboratory Comparison Samples

This new clause gives specific details for analysis of interlaboratory comparison samples. These samples must be treated within the general workflow in a manner that reflects the handling of patient samples. They must also be analysed by the same personnel who analysed the patient samples using the same procedures. The laboratory must not divulge the results of samples to other labs until final submission by all participating labs. Also, the laboratory must not use confirmatory analytical methods prior to the submission of data, even if this would be done for patient samples in daily routine.

5.6.3.4 Evaluation of Laboratory Performance

The new requirement is that the reports of interlaboratory comparisons must be reviewed and discussed with any relevant staff. When a defined performance level is missed, the 'relevant staff', not the management, is required to take ameliorative action and check it for effectiveness. When trends indicate potential nonconformities, preventive action must be taken.

5.6.4 Comparability of Examination Results

The new requirement is for the situations where the laboratory uses different procedures, equipment or different test sites for the same test parameter (defined as "measurand" in the ISO standard). In these cases, the details of analytical specifications must be defined for the comparability of test results. The laboratory must communicate to users of laboratory services whether patient results have any clinically significant differences owing to a change of methodology.

5.7 Post-Examination Processes

5.7.1 Review of Results

This clause has been amended covering review criteria for automatic selection and reporting where the laboratory has an autoverification system. In this case, the documented procedure to review results must include established criteria for autoverification (see 5.9.1). Test results must be evaluated against available clinical information and previous test results prior to release. It is essential to not report patient results until the QC system is successfully evaluated and accepted.

5.7.2 Storage, Retention and Disposal of Clinical Samples

A procedure for management of biological samples must be documented, including identification, collection, transport, storage and safe disposal. Also, the procedure must define how long the clinical samples will be retained depending on the nature of the sample, the examination and any applicable requirements.

5.8 Reporting of Results

Clause 5.8 in the previous version has been divided into three sub-clauses in the latest version.

5.8.1 General

It is the duty of the laboratory to decide on the report format, medium (paper or electronic), content and the manner. A documented procedure must cover all tests performed by the local lab or referral laboratories. The reports must be clear, concise, complete, clinically relevant, accurate, and including pertinent information required for interpretation. The amended clause emphasises communicating with those making requests when an examination result may be delayed, if this would compromise patient care.

5.8.2 Report Attributes

Previously, this was included under 5.8.3k and 5.8.5. By 'editorial changes', the updated version bears on how the report effectively communicates laboratory results and meets the users' needs. Now critical results and interpretive comments are to be included in the final report, even if the laboratory employs an autoverification system (see 5.9.1). The inclusion of detection limits and measurement uncertainty in reports is no longer a consideration.

5.8.3 Report Content

Now, in the updated version, the content of reports has been described in extended detail [(a) to (p) inclusive]. Some of them are the following:

- Identification of all tests performed by a referral laboratory;
- Patient name, unique identification, and contact information on each page;
- Name of clinician making request;
- A clear description of the examination including, where appropriate, the examination procedure;
- Identification of examinations performed as part of a research;
- Page number to total number of pages (e.g., 'Page 2 of 4' etc.);
- The date of sample collection;
- The date of the report; the time of release (This information should be readily accessible, if not on the report)
- Type, and conditions of specimen which may limit adequacy of testing

The time of receipt into the laboratory is no longer to be noted. The signature of the person checking or releasing the report is no longer a requirement. However, the identity of the person(s) reviewing the results and authorising the release of the report, if not contained in the report is required to be readily accessible.

5.9 Release of Results

This clause incorporates some clauses from 5.8 in the 2007 version and includes some additional requirements.

5.9.1 General

Seven sub-clauses in the 2007 version (5.8.3, 5.8.5, 5.8.7, 5.8.9, 5.8.10, 5.8.13, 5.8.14) have been merged into one clause emphasising the importance of patient confidentiality. There must be documented procedures for the release of examination results, including details of personnel authorised to release results and persons authorised to receive them. A result distributed by telephone or electronic means must reach only authorised recipients. Where results were communicated orally in emergency (e.g. critical results), this must be recorded and retained, including who received the result, who gave the information from laboratory, and date and time. Also, a written report must be prepared.

5.9.2 Automated Selection and Reporting of Results

This new clause covers requirements and criteria [(a) to (f) inclusive], where the laboratory has implemented a system for the automated selection and reporting of results. To use an autoverification system for reporting patient results is not mandatory for laboratories. A procedure of autoverification, if used, must be implemented, readily available and understood by the personnel. It must be documented that the system was validated initially, and is re-tested (verified) whenever there is a change to the system that could affect their function.

In this system, patient results generated from instruments are sent directly to a Laboratory Information System (LIS). There, they are automatically evaluated and compared against closely defined acceptance parameters set by the laboratory. If the results are acceptable, they are automatically converted into patient reporting formats. In this process, there is no additional laboratory staff intervention except to define the acceptance criteria. The criteria and logic must be established, documented, and tested by the medical staff of the laboratory.

A key point is that applicable quality control samples have been run within an appropriate time period, with acceptable results. The computer system must automatically check quality control status prior to verification. When QC has not been run within the required time interval or QC results are unacceptable, there must be a procedure for the instant suspension of automated selection and reporting.

The laboratory's stated QC interval limits must be accurately reflected in the LIS (see 5.6.2.3).

Any sample interferences (e.g. haemolysis, icterus, lipaemia) must be indicated, if present. The acceptable range of results must be defined for all patient tests. Analytical warning messages generated from the instruments must be incorporated into the reporting criteria, where necessary and relevant. Any automated reporting system must identify the time of review before release and include date and time of selection.

If patient results are outside the defined criteria, these must be evaluated and verified by authorised personnel prior to reporting.

5.9.3 Revised Reports

Where changes are needed to a patient's report produced previously, which has already been released, there must be written instructions governing how the changes will be reported in the revised version. The revised report must include the following: reference to the date and patient's identity in the previous report; the time and date of the change and the name of the person responsible for the change. The revised version must be labelled as a "Revised report" (paper or electronic).

The revised reports must be available for a clinical decision by the end user of the results. All revised reports must also be communicated to the clinician in good time (telephone call, message to mobile devices etc.).

When the reporting system does not have the facility to make alterations or to prepare a revised report or keep changes, a record noting this must be kept in the laboratory.

5.10 Laboratory Information Management

This clause, laboratory information management, is now mandatory whereas before it was optional (Annex B in the 2007 version). The term "information system" usually refers to a computer-based system, but in the ISO 15189 Standard, "information system" includes the management of data and information not only using computer-based but also non-computerised systems. For this reason, some of the requirements may apply to computerised systems but others to non-computerised systems. Computer-based systems may include those which integrate records of laboratory equipment automatically or stand-alone systems which require manual entry of test results.

5.10.1 General

There must be an information management system which is available to access the data and information needed to provide a laboratory service meeting the needs and requirements of the user. As well as this, there must be a documented procedure to ensure confidentiality of patient information at all times.

5.10.2 Authorities and Responsibilities

Editorial arrangements have been made in B.4 of Annex B in the 2007 version. This requirement concern unauthorised users. The laboratory must clearly define who is responsible for various functions, operation, and maintenance of the data. There must be explicit documented procedures describing the authorities and responsibilities of staff concerning; which staff have exclusive access to patient data, and who are authorised to enter and alter patient results as well as release of reports. Only authorised staff can be allowed to access patient data using 'security codes' for computerised systems.

5.10.3 Information System Management

5.3.11, B2, B3, B5, B6-B8 from the previous version have been combined and amended as a requirement focusing on the system(s) used for the collection, processing, recording, reporting, storage, or retrieval of examination data and information. The laboratory must ensure that the information system is able to send patient results and other patient-specific information accurately and reliably.

Before initiating this information system in routine work, it must be validated by the supplier and the laboratory must be documented that this system is adequately tested (verified) for proper functioning. A note has been included with this clause to make clear what are 'validation and verification'. Also, verification process must be performed after any modifications.

The procedure must include verification of the integrity of the system after restoration of data files. When a hardware or software problem is resolved, verification must be repeated. In the records of any review, either a real patient report or a sample 'dummy' report needs to be kept as evidence of re-verification. Integrity, retrieval and preservation of the data must be maintained consistent with regulatory requirements.

Also, there must be instructions for routine operations appropriate to the level of use.

The system must be secure for the confidentiality of patient data, and protected against unauthorised access and alterations. Computer facility and equipment must be operated in an environment that complies with supplier specifications, and includes appropriate environmental controls and safety elements. In the case of non-computerised systems, conditions must safeguard the accuracy of manual recording and transcription.

In the event of a failure of laboratory information system, there must be comprehensive contingency plans in place to maintain the continuity of laboratory work. In the case of system failures, these must be recorded together with appropriate immediate and corrective actions.

Accurate transmission of data across instrument interfaces and interfaces with external systems such as hospital information systems, and other output devices must be provided. When a new examination or automated comment system is implemented, it must be verified that the changes are accurately implemented in the chain of interfaces, information systems external to the laboratory (such as hospital information systems or personal web devices).

When the system is managed off-site or subcontracted to an alternative provider, the laboratory must be responsible for ensuring the provider meets all applicable requirements of the updated ISO 15189 standard.

CONCLUSION

This chapter, which provides a practical approach a comparison between old and new, will be helpful for laboratories to consider their own gaps and make a smooth transition to the updated standard when revising their quality and technical documentation to meet the new requirements.

REFERENCES

Austrian Standards Institute. (2013). *ÖNORM EN ISO 15189*. Medical Laboratories — Requirements for Quality and Competence. Retrieved September 21, 2013, from https://shop.austrian-standards.at/Preview.action;jsessionid=99230A509647A240137A2C589CF5C872?preview=&dokkey=468411&selectedLocale=en

CAP, College of American Pathologists, Commission on Laboratory Accreditation, Laboratory Accreditation Program. (2012, December 25). *Laboratory General Checklist*. Retrieved December 21, 2013, from http://www.pathologie-online.de/wordpress/wp-content/uploads/2012/11/laboratory_general_checklist.pdf

CPA, Clinical Pathology Accreditation. (2012, December 12). Transition of CPA accredited medical laboratories to ISO 15189 accreditation by UKAS. *Clinical Pathology Accreditation News Letter*. Retrieved September 21, 2013, from http://www.cpa-uk.co.uk/files/CPA_News_28.pdf

ENAC, Entidad Nacional de Acreditación. (March, 2011). *Survey on: Accreditation of medical laboratories within EA*. Retrieved November 1, 2013, from http://www.cskb.cz/res/file/zapisy-vyboru-cskb/2011/13/13-P7.pdf

Ford A. (2008 November). Labs on the brink of ISO 15189 approval. *CAP TODAY*. Retrieved September 22, 2013, from http://www.cap.org/apps/cap.portal?_nfpb=true&cntvwrPtlt_actionOverride=%2Fportlets%2FcontentViewer%2Fshow&cntvwrPtlt%7BactionForm.contentReference%7D=cap_today%2F1108%2F1108_ISO_15189_approval_02.html&_pageLabel=cntvwr

HOKLAS, Hong Kong Laboratory Accreditation Scheme. (2013 April). *016 Assessment / Reassessment Questionnaire (Medical Laboratories) (based on HOKLAS 015 5th edition)*. Retrieved December 8, 2012, from http://www.itc.gov.hk/en/quality/hkas/doc/hoklas/HOKLAS016.pdf

IANZ, International Accreditation New Zealand. (n.d.). *Implementing ISO 15189:2012*. Retrieved September 21, 2013, from https://go.promapp.com/ianz/view/Documents/View/Open?displayType=document&documentId=e0196d0e-49e8-4962-94ee-b1b437d93970

ILAC, International Laboratory Accreditation Cooperation. (2012, October 26). *Adopted Resolutions 16th ILAC GA*. Retrieved November 1, 2013, from https://www.ilac.org/documents/Adopted%20Resolutions%2016th%20ILAC%20GA%2026%20Oct%202012.pdf doc

INAP, Irish National Accreditation Board. (2013, April 10). *Summary of changes in ISO 15189:2012 compared to the 2007 version.* Retrieved September 21, 2013, from http://inab.ie/media/Summary%20of%20changes%20for%20ISO%2015189.pdf

ISO 15189:2003. (2003). *Medical laboratories — Particular requirements for quality and competence. International Organization for Standards.* Geneva, Switzerland: ISO.

ISO 15189:2007. (2007). *Medical laboratories – Particular requirements for quality and competence. 2nd ed. International Organization for Standards.* Geneva, Switzerland: ISO.

ISO 15189:2012. (2012). *Medical laboratories – Requirements for quality and competence. 3rd ed. International Organization for Standards.* Geneva, Switzerland: ISO.

NATA, National Association of Testing Authorities. (2013, May). *Gap analysis of ISO 15189:2012 and ISO 15189:2007 in the field of medical testing.* Retrieved September 21, 2013, from http://www.nata.asn.au/phocadownload/publications/Guidance_information/checklist-worksheets-site-notification-forms/Gap-analysis-15189.pdf

Peter, T. F., Rotz, P. D., Blair, D. H., Khine, A. A., Freeman, R. R., & Murtagh, M. M. (2010). Impact of Laboratory Accreditation on Patient Care and the Health System. *American Journal of Clinical Pathology, 134,* 550-555. doi:10.1309/AJCPH1SKQ1HNWGHF.

QMP-LS, Quality Management Program—Laboratory Services. (n.d.). *Gap analysis between ISO 15189:2007 and ISO 15189:2012 – Items that affect laboratory practice.* Retrieved November 1, 2013, from http://www.qmpls.org/Portals/0/OLA/PDFs/Transition%20to%20ISO%2015189%202012.pdf

RVA, Dutch Accreditation Council. (n.d.). *Comparison ISO 15189:2007 and ISO 15189:2012.* Retrieved September 21, 2013, from http://www.rva.nl/uri/?uri=AMGATE_10218_1_TICH_R12156407044799&xsl=AMGATE_10218_1_TICH_L155999126

SADCAS. (2013, September 9). *Policy – ISO 15189:2012 Transition (Document No: SADCAS TR 10; Issue No: 2).* Retrieved September 21, 2013, from http://www.sadcas.org/doc/sadcas_tr10.pdf

SAMM, Malaysian Accreditation Body. (2013). *ISO 15189:2012 Migration. SAMM Circular (NO.1 / 2013).* Retrieved September 21, 2013, from http://www.standardsmalaysia.gov.my/documents/10179/427212/SAMM%20Circular%20(No.%202013)%20-%20Migration%20to%20ISO%2015189%2016072013%20(1).pdf

UKAS, United Kingdom Accreditation Service. (n.d.). *Potential gap/difference in focus between CPA and UKAS assessment.* Retrieved November 13, 2013, from http://www.ukas.com/Library/Services/CPA/Assessment_Focus-Differences.pdf

UKAS, United Kingdom Accreditation Service. (n.d.). *Summary of ISO 15189 additional requirements.* Retrieved September 30, 2013, from http://www.ukas.com/Library/Services/CPA/Summary%20of%20Idifferences%20betwen%20ISO%2015189%20&%20CPA.pdf

ADDITIONAL READING

Burnett, D. (2013). A Practical Guide to ISO 15189 in Laboratory Medicine. Association of Clinical Biochemistry and Laboratory Medicine (UK). Retrieved November 1, 2013, from http://www.acbstore.org.uk

Guidance for Laboratory Quality Manuals. QM-PLS. Retrieved January 2013 from http://www.qmpls.org

ISO/TR 22869, Technical Report: Medical laboratories – Guidance on laboratory implementation of ISO 15189:2003 (Published 2005-02-15).

Lippi, G., Chance, JJ., Church, S., Dazzi, P., Fontana, R., Giavarina, D., Grankvist, K., Huisman, W., Kouri, T., Palicka, V., Plebani, M., Puro, V., Salvagno, GL., Sandberg, S.,Sikaris, K., Watson, I., Stankovic, AK., Simundic, AM. (2011). Preanalytical Quality Improvement: From Dream to Reality, *Clinical Chemistry and Laboratory Medicine, 49*(7), 1113-26. doi: 10.1515/CCLM.2011.600. Epub 2011 Apr 25; Retrieved January 2013 from http://www.ncbi.nlm. nih.gov/pubmed/21517699 .

Mario Plebani. (2012). Quality Indicators to Detect Pre-Analytical Errors in Laboratory Testing, *The Clinical Biochemist Reviews, 33*(3), 85–88; Retrieved January 2013 from http://www.ncbi.nlm.nih.gov/pmc/articles/PMC3428256

PLUS. 15189 (2nd ed. pub. 2010) - The ISO 15189:2007 essentials - A practical handbook for implementing the ISO 15189:2007 standard for medical laboratories. Retrieved January 2013 from http://shop.csa.ca

Practical application of ISO 15189 by accreditation bodies- A Comparison with ISO/IEC 17025, Bella Ho. Retrieved January 2013 from http://www.ifcc.org/ifccfiles/docs/150412200403.pdf

KEY TERMS AND DEFINITIONS

Accreditation: Formal recognition by a third party qualified to the relevant specific standards.

Automated Selection and Reporting of Results: A customized computer system integrated in the laboratory information system to review and verify test results based on acceptance criteria as defined by the laboratory.

Clinical Chemistry: Clinical Biochemistry, an area of clinical pathology.

Harmonization: Obtaining test results that fall within agreed parameters.

ISO 15189: International Organization for Standardization 15189, accreditation standard for medical laboratories – Requirements for quality and competence.

Laboratory Management: Person(s) responsible for managing or directing laboratory activities, synonymous with 'top management' in ISO 9000.

Laboratory Medicine: Medical laboratory, clinical laboratory.

Nonconformity: Non-fulfilment of a requirement, ISO 9000 (synonymous with: accident; adverse event; error; event; incident and occurrence).

Point-of-Care Testing (POCT): Near-patient testing, tests performed in the presence of the patient.

Process: Set of activities transforming inputs into outputs, in accordance with ISO 9000.

Turnaround Time: Period for two points between pre-analytical (examination) and post-analytical (examination) processes.

Chapter 11
The Use of Information Systems in a Modern Cytopathology Laboratory

Stavros Archondakis
Military Hospital of Athens, Greece

ABSTRACT

Over the last decade, cytopathology laboratories wishing to achieve an automated and seamless work-flow process, to diminish turnaround times, and to improve their diagnostic accuracy have successfully adopted information technologies and automation. New types of cameras and microscopes connected to computers made possible image capture and transmission (telecytology). New innovative information technologies, including e-health and telemedical applications, constitute a valuable tool for interlaboratory collaboration and quality improvement. New applications are expected to enhance the opportunities for improvement in the field of cytological data management and sharing. In this chapter, the authors emphasize quality management concepts applied to cytopathology laboratories and the application of innovative information technologies in a modern cytopathology laboratory wishing to establish an effective quality management system and meet all current requirements concerning all aspects of its routine workflow (personnel, premises, environmental conditions, equipment, information systems and materials, pre-examination processes, examination processes, and the post-examination phase).

INTRODUCTION

During the last decades, medical data deriving from the analysis of patient samples was stored in medical laboratories and was provided to physicians manually (Brerider-Jr-McNai, 1996). The absence of an integrated laboratory information system was making medical data transfer extremely slow and potentially ineffective, while results correction and quality control were proved time and money consuming process (Kubono, 2004).

Over the last decade, the wide implementation of laboratory information systems became a necessity dictated by the need of real-time results and the increasing role of laboratory medicine in therapeutic decisions (Georgiou & Westbrook, 2007).

Laboratory information systems have been implemented in many medical laboratories wishing to improve their quality standards. A laboratory information system (LIS) is a valuable tool for medical professionals in order to achieve

DOI: 10.4018/978-1-4666-6320-6.ch011

regulatory compliance, manage interlaboratory or intra laboratory collaboration, deliver detailed reports, and develop the laboratory networking capabilities. The result is better data management and sharing between the laboratory and its customers (either laboratories or clinicians) (Brerider-Jr-McNai, 1996).

Cytopathology laboratory services are crucial to patient care and have to meet the scientific or regulatory requirements concerning examination requests, patient preparation, patient identification, samples collection and handling (transportation, storage and processing), specimen's evaluation, clinical interpretation and reporting, as well as personnel's working safety (Okada, 2002).

The main cytological examination, the well-known Papanicolaou test consists a widely applied, cost-effective screening method for the early detection of cervical dysplasia and cancer. Well-written and well-implemented LIS software can implement emerging technologies aiming to improve the diagnostic accuracy of the method. Pap smears screening, and cytological diagnosis provision for the large majority of the female population requires a large number of skilled cytotechnologists and cytopathologists. Since the number of these professionals is still inadequate, the development of automated laboratory instruments and screening systems may give practical and satisfactory solutions. Laboratory informatics consists nowadays an essential tool of laboratory's quality assurance and improvement by playing a key role in the preanalytical, analytical and post analytical, diagnostic phases. A well-written and well-implemented LIS software can use medical data for the documentation of quality control (QC) measures (Okada, 2002).

In the past, manual methods of data storage in cytopathology laboratories were including logs and card files organized by patient name, date, specimen number or interpretation. During the last ten years, information technology has dramatically influenced the clinical laboratory practice, due to laboratory management information systems wide implementation. A laboratory management information system (LMIS) implementation in the routine laboratory workflow has to overcome serious problems concerning medical data and laboratory hardware and software protection. The medical laboratory has to take measures against laboratory's information system improper or unauthorized use.

LMIS can also monitor all available indicators of the laboratory reports accuracy, completeness and timeliness. LMIS can also monitor effectively all available telemedical or e-health applications, especially when used for quality management purposes (Okada, 2002).

The management of laboratory information systems has nowadays to meet the requirements of relevant quality standards, applied for accreditation purposes. Accreditation is the process by which a certified organization or agency recognizes that a facility or service meets specific pre-established standards (Pantanowitz et al., 2009). ISO 15189:2012 is an international quality standard, mainly used by medical laboratories. ISO 15189:2012 can diminish significantly unexpected errors or problems. ISO 15189:2012 requirements for laboratory information systems suggest the implementation of specific measures concerning environmental conditions, system security, data entry control, medical reports, data retrieval and storage, and finally system's hardware and software maintenance (Kubono, 2004).

During the last decade, there is an ongoing demand by regulators, laboratory accreditation bodies and customers for implementation of more effective measures that could increase confidence in cytological laboratories performance. ISO 15189:2012 specific requirements improve the cytopathology laboratories' capacity to store, organize, process, and retrieve large amounts of information, to monitor turnaround times and other crucial quality assurance parameters. ISO 15189:2012 requirements include the implementation of specific measures concerning documentation, protection from unauthorized access, validation, safeguard from tampering or loss, and data integrity. Telemedical applications should follow ISO 15189:2012 requirements and can help laboratories wishing to implement external quality control programs.

During the last decade, there is an ongoing demand for telecytological applications. Telecytology is the process of diagnostic cytopathology performed on digital images, transferred via telecommunication networks. Telecytological diagnosis can be achieved with the application of either dynamic or static telecytological systems.

Cloud computing is changing the way enterprises, institutions and people understand, perceive and use current software systems. By means of cloud computing technology, cytopathologists can efficiently manage imaging units by using the latest software and hardware available without having to pay for it at non affordable prices. Cloud computing systems used by cytopathology departments can function on public, modern, hybrid, or community models. Using cloud applications, infrastructure, storage services, and processing power, cytopathology laboratories can avoid huge spending on maintenance of costly applications and image storage and sharing. Cloud computing allows imaging flexibility and may be used for creating a virtual mobile office. Security and privacy issues have to be addressed in order to ensure cloud computing wide implementation in the near future.

The purpose of this chapter is to present our own experience on the application of Quality Management concepts to Cytopathology laboratories, on the application of commonly used quality management system standards, and on the possible ways Information Systems can encourage or facilitate the wide implementation of these standards specific requirements.

Furthermore, we examine the feasibility of applying e-health and telemedical solutions for laboratory information systems data sharing and handling, for medical interlaboratory comparisons and proficiency testing and for validating the accuracy of cytological diagnoses.

We also examine the role of modern laboratory information systems and applications for providing or enhancing the existing laboratory capabilities for educational training and other research activities.

Finally, we give clear and comprehensive guidance concerning various financial, legal, professional, and ethical problems in this field.

BACKGROUND

Laboratory automation can offer greater productivity, lower cost and easier integration with modern instrumental equipment (Vacata et al., 2007). Laboratory information systems permit the laboratories to achieve maximum efficiency (Westbrook et al., 2008; Vacata et al., 2007), and can improve cooperation with physicians and reduce significantly all human errors. Information technology systems can provide reliable standardized procedures for the assessment procedure of medical laboratories (Vacata et al., 2007). Medical laboratory information systems can also help the laboratory's administration to prepare and administer the management handbook and standard operation procedures, to train the laboratory's personnel, to provide and archive documents via intranet, to create customer databases, to evaluate test results and to contact with customers.

Verification is the confirmation that specified requirements have been fulfilled. Computing system monitoring, user acceptance testing, and code reviews are some verification tools. Validation is the confirmation that the requirements for the specific use are fulfilled. Electronic records contain any combination of digital data that is created, modified, archived, or distributed by a computer system. Electronic records must be protected from exposure to accidental or malicious alteration or destruction (record security).

Computing systems may be open or closed. In closed computing systems, individuals responsible for the content of the electronic records control access to medical archives. On the contrary, in open computing systems, people not responsible for the content of the electronic records (Vacata et al., 2007) control access to medical archives.

The computing systems software may be used for testing, calibration and sampling purposes (testing software) or for managing document control (document software) (Vacata et al., 2007). The integrity of electronic records must be checked periodically (file integrity check), while the computing system must be tested periodically in order to determine if it meets specific requirements (acceptance test). Finally, according to the European Federation of National Associations of Measurement (2006), the software of the laboratory computing system must be tested in such a way that the internal workings of the item being tested are known (white-box testing) or unknown by the tester (black-box testing).

The ISO 15189:2012 requirements cover all aspects of the laboratory activities, including the laboratory information system (LIS) (Vacata et al., 2007). Clause 5.10 of ISO 15189:2012 suggests specific measures for the protection of laboratory electronic records. The measures proposed in clause 5.10 of ISO 15189: 2012 comprise a valuable tool for quality improvement in the field of electronic documentation of medical records.

In the field of cytopathology, laboratory information systems have enabled cytotechnologists and cytopathologists to achieve efficient, streamlined workflows, regulatory compliance, and superior reporting capabilities. A well-written and well-implemented cytopathology LIS, when integrated to EMRs can provide full lab automation through connections to instrumentation and clinicians offices, minimize human errors and achieve detailed test order entry and efficient results retrieval.

Early software programs in the field of Cytopathology included reporting, data storage, and elementary data mining. During the past ten years, laboratory information systems capabilities have been dramatically increased by automated enhancements, such as specimen tracking, barcode labeling, reflex testing, automated and customized report delivery and billing system interfaces.

Laboratory information systems in the field of Cytopathology may be autonomous or may be a part of an integrated anatomic pathology system, or a part of a larger hospital information system.

National or international regulatory agencies are nowadays specifying the minimum period of time cytopathology laboratories should record and retrieve specimen information and patient reports. The information system applied, should permit easy access to all cytology reports and, if possible, to related surgical pathology reports, in order to make possible cytologic/histologic correlation. Older records should be archived and stored offsite as long as retrieval does not hinder patient care or delay regulatory inspections. Laboratory information systems should be able to correlate or merge records when there is an alteration in patient identifiers without altering the data in the original records. It is advisable for laboratory information systems in cytopathology departments to use unique identifiers, such as the patient's record number, in order to achieve more accurate matching.

A well-written and well-implemented LIS in a cytopathology laboratory should assign a unique accession number for each sample. All demographic data required by national or international regulatory agencies should be entered at accessioning. The unique accession number enables cytopathology department personnel to track of the case during pre-analytic (accessioning and specimen preparation,) analytic (screening and interpretation,) and post-analytic (reporting, and quality assurance follow up) phases. Slides labelling may also be generated by the LIS as part of accessioning. Cytopathology laboratories should be encouraged to use bar coded labels in order to increase the efficiency and accuracy of this process.

Confidentiality is a sine qua non for a well-written and well-implemented cytopathology LIS. Access to laboratory records should be strictly limited to authorized individuals. The implementation of security codes is essential for preserving electronic systems integrity; prevent corruption of computer software or release of results by unauthorized individuals. All reports that are stored in electronic format should be electronically signed. Since the use of electronic signature is still debated, the laboratory should adopt a specific procedure assuring the identification of the person who is responsible for the case and the approval of the content of the report.

Diagnostic terminology in a well-written and well-implemented Cytopathology LIS should adopt the Standardized Terminology (The Bethesda System or other comparable system) proposed by national or international scientific societies. A well-written and well-implemented LIS should also dispose free-text capabilities in case of rare or unusual interpretations or for comments that are not routine.

Precise transfer of clinical information and interpretive data to the report may be achieved by using optical mark readers interfaced with the LIS, or entering the data manually into the LIS. The laboratory's Quality Assurance Program should monitor the accuracy of the clinical information stored. Cytopathology laboratory information systems (LIS) may also generate billing statements or transfer data to billing systems, clinician offices, hospital computer systems, and other third party payers. Cytological reports should be linked to procedure codes, hospital procedure and billing codes and Current Procedural Terminology (CPT) codes may be required for billing purposes. Cyto-

logical reports should also be linked to SNOMED (Systematized Nomenclature of Medicine) for pure statistical purposes.

Laboratory cytological diagnoses should be retrievable for quality assurance purposes. The laboratory's Quality Assurance Program should be able to generate statistical reports required by regulatory agencies and accrediting bodies within the retention period indicated. The laboratory's Quality Assurance Program should be able to monitor the interpretive categories reported by each individual. This individual cytological diagnosis should be available and retrievable for further comparisons with the laboratory's or with the proficiency testing provider's average.

It is highly indicated for the LMIS to permit easy selection of cases initially screened as negative for random and directed re screening. The laboratory's Quality Assurance Program should not permit the release of results until the completion of re screen examination. Cytological diagnoses of re screening should be retrievable for calculation of false negative proportions or other measures of performance within the retention period prescribed by state or international accreditation bodies, cytological scientific societies or applicable local, national or international regulations. Cytological /histological correlation information needs to be available for review (again within the retention period described by applicable regulations.) The data management system should permit cytopathologists to follow-up premalignant and malignant lesions and monitor unsatisfactory rates by clinician.

A well-written and well-implemented LIS in the field of Cytopathology should have the capacity to apply case numbers to each case. The Cytopathology LIS should also have the capacity to automatically produce labels for each specimen for tracking purposes throughout processing and storage. Mislabeling errors caused by manually labeling requisitions, specimens and slides should be avoided by implementing barcoding or radiofrequency identification in the laboratory. Barcoding also provides a tracking mechanism of orders, specimens and slides in the workflow process.

After cytological samples processing and staining, the cytotechnologist can screen a given case and enter his own diagnosis directly, either by typing directly within the software's window or through voice recognition software. The Cytopathology laboratory may use Image Guided screening or manual screening methods; in both cases the LIS software should permit slide notation through shortcuts or voice recognition with feedback.

All negative cases can be signed out by the cytotechnologist or the cytopathologist and the reports can be distributed to the client. A certain percentage of these normal cases will automatically be flagged out for internal quality control measures. Some software applications permit cytopathology laboratories to define re screen rates per employee, for new employees' evaluation and training purposes, especially for employees identified as having a need for further training. Some cytopathology laboratories permit patients or clinicians direct access to negative results through secure web portal access.

Positive for malignancy or atypia cytological cases should be automatically sent to the cytopathologist for review. Well-written and well-implemented laboratory software should permit the cytopathologist to edit or keep the diagnosis set by the cytotechnologist, allowing report generation and delivery to the ordering physician.

A well-written and well-implemented cytopathology laboratory software should comply with relevant regulations and guidelines edited by bodies such as CMS, FDA, CAP and CLIA. For these purposes, each employee's performance should be constantly monitored by means of unique user accounts provision based upon access rights for each individual.

A well-written and well-implemented cytopathology laboratory information system, when

interfaced to laboratory equipment can help laboratory avoid all errors associated with manual data entry. If the orders from clinicians can be placed via the Internet or the Intranet, then the LIS may automatically have access to all necessary information needed for rapidly processing the examination required. Furthermore, the LIS may deliver the cytological diagnosis electronically back to physicians requesting the exam. The physicians, or their departments, will also be able to track the progress of the cytological examination via the secure login.

A report indicating all the results of the cytological examinations ordered should be distributed to clinicians, daily. The reporting format should meet the clinicians and patients demands. Each physician may have special preferences concerning the format, the time and the way cytological reports are distributed to his office (electronically, directly to an EMR, faxed, or printed directly within the clinician's office). Customized reporting is a feature of a good cytology laboratory information system that can improve patients and clinicians satisfaction and may play a major role in developing and maintaining a good relationship between the lab and its customers.

Well-written and well-implemented LIS software should be able to store and look up patient history, providing the cytopathologist an accurate picture of patient health status. The LIS software should be able to store patient's history for long periods of time (five years, ten years, etc.), in order to provide helpful information to ordering clinicians and to the members of the Cytopathology Department.

The Cytopathology Department LIS should meet the needs and specifications dictated by the laboratory's workflows by increasing efficiencies, ensuring regulatory compliance, and providing a complete report on patient health. The Cytopathology Department LIS, when integrated with laboratory instrumentation will permit automated processes to reduce errors caused by manual data entries. The Cytopathology Department LIS can also reduce errors by implementing electronic order entry, barcode requisition, and sample scanning.

Quality control defines service's quality, imparting to it the credibility needed for its intended purpose, while quality assurance activities measure the degree to which desired outcomes are successful (Wiener et al., 2012). Quality control may be internal or external. Quality control in the field of cytology is mainly achieved by slide re screening or clinical-histological correlation of cytological diagnoses (Wiener et al., 2012). Many slide re screening procedures have been proposed for quality assurance purposes, such as rapid reviewing of smears initially reported as negative or inadequate, rapid preview/prescreening of all smears, random re screening, targeted re screening of specific patient groups, seeding abnormal cases into the screening pools, retrospective re screening of negative cytology specimens from patients with a current high grade abnormality and automated re screening of smears initially reported as negative. The laboratory manager is responsible for choosing the most appropriate method for quality assurance purposes, according to the specific needs of his own laboratory.

Proficiency testing (PT) is a process for checking actual laboratory performance usually by means of interlaboratory comparisons. Results from proficiency testing are an indication of a laboratory's competence and are an integral part of the assessment and accreditation process. According to ISO 15189, all accredited laboratories must participate in proficiency testing schemes according to their normal patient testing and reporting procedures (Pantanowitz et al., 2009).

Telecytology is a novel process that can be used for obtaining expert opinions on difficult cases from distant laboratories (Archondakis et al., 2009). Telecytological diagnosis can be achieved either by dynamic or static telecytological systems (Archondakis et al., 2009)..The static telecytology systems have the advantage of considerably lower cost, but they only allow the capture of a selected subset of microscopic fields (Pantanowitz et al., 2009).The dynamic telecytology systems permit evaluation of the cytological material present on the slide. These systems may be hampered by high network traffic and their high cost of purchasing and maintaining may be unaffordable by small laboratories wishing to participate in proficiency testing programs (Thrall et al., 2011).

A small number of studies have focused, so far, on the use of telecytology for diagnostic and consultation purposes in the everyday workflow (Archondakis et al., 2009).

The use of digital images in quality control/assurance programs eliminates the need for glass slides retrieval from the laboratory's registry (at least at the point of examination), allows annotations to be added to the image, enhances the ability to rapidly transmit and remotely share images electronically for several purposes (telecytology, conferences, education, quality assurance, peer review) and protects more efficiently patients anonymity (Archondakis et al., 2009).

Moreover, the use of digital images for quality assurance programs is more practical and less time consuming although some additional time has to be spent during glass slides conversion to digital images.

Static telecytology systems are preferred due to their low cost by laboratories that cannot afford the high cost of buying and maintaining dynamic systems (Archondakis et al., 2009).

The limitations and diagnostic errors related to telecytology that are already mentioned by some authors may cause misinterpretation of digital images by less experienced participants (Briscoe et al., 2000). Appropriate field selection, sufficient image quality, and especially diagnostic expertise are the most crucial parameters ensuring the proper function of a static telecytological system (Archondakis et al., 2009).

The most common manifestations of interobserver discrepancy are upgrading of the telecytological diagnosis to a definitive carcinoma diagnosis or downgrading of a suspicious telecytological diagnosis to a rather benign lesion because of image deficiencies (Archondakis et al., 2009).

My own laboratory was the first modern cytological laboratory in Greece, which was officially certified according to ISO 15189:2012. In less than four years and collaboration with colleagues from public hospitals, the laboratory has constructed an electronic library of more than 45.000 representative digital images of histologically confirmed specimens of gynecological and non-gynecological cytology. This electronic database is currently used for interlaboratory diagnostic comparisons while the whole project is scheduled to be certified as an individual proficiency testing provider in the near future. Participants experience in making telecytological diagnoses is constantly recorded for further evaluation in the near future. Statistical parameters are continuously recorded while practical problems that may be encountered contribute to continuous self-improvement of this pilot program.

Cloud computing consists an innovative concept of creating a computer grid using the Internet facilities aiming at the shared use of resources such as computer software and hardware. Cloud-based system architectures provide many advantages in terms of scalability, maintainability and massive data processing. Cloud computing, when integrated into the daily workflow, can provide exceptional consultation opportunities to distant cytopathology laboratories. Cloud computing infrastructures can improve the professional skills of the participating medical staff and make them feel more confident in their daily work (Rosenthal et al., 2010).

Nowadays, cloud computing is not widely used for the various tasks related to cytopathology; however, there are numerous fields that are possible to be applied. The envisioned advantages for the everyday practice of laboratories workflow and eventually for the patients are significant (Rosenthal et al., 2010).

Cloud computing, in the field of cytopathology, may provide a precious web-based service, which may be incorporated in the Laboratory Information System and become part of a web-based Electronic Health Record (Rosenthal et al., 2010). The modeling of this cloud system, maintained by one organization/institution may be of the SaaS, IaaS, or PaaS type, and can provide valuable services to the end users (cytopathologists, clinicians and patients).

The main components of Cloud computing in the field of Cytopathology are the following:

- **Applications:** Cloud applications may be run as software as a service (SaaS), software plus service or data as a service. In Cloud applications, used by cytopathologists, the end users take advantage of some kind of "Software as a Service" for image reviewing, creating diagnostic reports, or patient billing.

- **Client:** A Cloud client, in the field of Cytopathology, is the medium which cytopathologists use to access the Cloud via the Internet. Cloud client may be a computer or a Smartphone.

- **Infrastructure:** Cloud infrastructure, in the field of Cytopathology, includes computer hardware and servers used for software running and data storage.

- **Platform:** In the field of Cytopathology, a well-designed platform is an essential parameter for efficient application of laboratory's Cloud applications.

- **Service:** A cloud service, in the field of Cytopathology, can be, without having to be limited to, either a web-based image archiving system or a web-based image gallery.

- **Storage:** Cloud computing, in the field of Cytopathology, enables, for example,, the storage of large medical laboratory databases in the form of documents and image libraries, instead of physical storage at site (hospital or imaging center) which is much more expensive and difficult to maintain.

- **Processing Power:** Cloud computing, in the field of Cytopathology can provide infinite processing power to all cytopathology laboratories at a very low cost.

A cytopathology laboratory wishing to store a large amount of images and patient information files is nowadays obliged to install one or more servers and accompanying disk arrays, having poor or no earlier experience in its upkeep. A possible server crash may result to severe data loss. Furthermore, the server may require constant upgrades. These two reasons are good enough for a modern cytopathology laboratory to shift its data to the Cloud (Rosenthal et al., 2010). By doing this, the laboratory reduces dramatically all costs related to server software and hardware, as well as the costs for maintenance and licenses. Here the cloud acts as LIS, telecytology software, and billing unit. A patient may perform a cytological examination at a hospital ora private laboratory. Representative images of the case may be stored on a hybrid Cloud (Rosenthal et al., 2010). If the patient performs another cytological examination after some time, in another facility (and possibly distant), he can provide the reporting cytopathologists direct access to the images stored in the Cloud. The cytopathologists can retrieve and merge the images on his/her workstation. The cytopathologists can make their final diagnosis after having reviewed the images of the first cytological examination (Rosenthal et al., 2010).

Cloud computing, when applied in the field of cytopathology, has some main benefits, such as innovative dashboard for easy use, report formatted custom for each participant's lab with images, automatic versioning history, secure access to records that remove backup concerns, faster cytopathologist approval process, easy to use browser-based system (SaaS), automatic spell-checking, images insertion into reports, faster "voice-to-file" process, HL7 interface availability, safe storage, safe records transmission, low cost of record retrieval, labor, copying, filing and storage, easy

PDF documents production for easy integration to EMR systems and use of digital signatures for document control and compliance with standards (Rosenthal et al., 2010).

A modern cytopathology laboratory should take advantage of cloud computing technology and in close collaboration with colleagues from public and private hospitals incorporate cloud computing technology in proficiency testing telecytological applications. A modern cytopathology laboratory, in collaboration with local and national scientific societies and professionals practicing cytopathology in private or public laboratories, should aim, at the construction of a cloud based information platform where all cytological diagnoses will be stored, distributed and monitored by highly trained personnel for quality assurance purposes. Statistical parameters should be continuously recorded while practical problems that may be encountered should contribute to continuous self-improvement of this pilot program.

THE IMPLEMENTATION OF ISO 15189:2007 AND ISO 15189:2012 IN LABORATORY INFORMATION SYSTEMS

The ISO 15189:2007 requirements for quality and competence concerning the electronic medical data constitute a set of general guidelines that will help each laboratory to establish and develop its quality system (Kubono, 2004; Kubono, 2007). The procedures that will eventually be implemented by each laboratory during the development of an acceptable quality system may differ according to its specific needs and limitations (Kubono, 2004; Kubono, 2007). Meanwhile, the efforts of the medical community continuously aim at the creation of a secure electronic environment for medical data management, storage, retrieval and updating as well as decision support and quality control mechanisms (Kubono, 2004; Kubono, 2007). According to clause 3.5, the capability of the laboratory is affected by the information resources available for the tests in question. Post-test procedures, such as authorization for release, reporting, and transmission of the results has a dramatic impact on laboratory quality improvement (clause 3.10). Therefore, specific policies and procedures must ensure the protection of confidential information (clause 4.1.5 c). Moreover, adequate laboratory personnel must be trained regarding the LIS (clause 4.1.5 g), and adequate communication processes carried out by the LIS should be established (clauses 4.1.6 and 4.2.1). Written policies related to LIS should be described in the laboratory quality manual (clause 4.2.4 f, g, r, w), while controlled documents may be maintained in electronic media. Procedures and policies for controlling all types of documents should be defined. This definition might apply to a LIS for the controlling of documents as well (clause 4.3.1). Furthermore, specific procedures should be established for describing documents control and changes in computerized systems (clause 4.3.2 h).

Requirements referring to the selection of hardware, software and services for maintenance, troubleshooting, update, peripherals and consumables (for example storage devices) have to be documented (clause 4.6). Concerning LIS, the laboratory has to evaluate suppliers of critical equipment, consumables and services and maintain records for this evaluation and approval (clause 4.6). LIS should be able to halt results of nonconforming work, recall already released nonconforming tests, define the authority or the resumption of examinations, record and review root causes of non-conformity incidents (clauses 4.9, 4.10, 4.11). Systematic monitoring of the laboratory contribution to patient care through quality indicators should include the use of LIS (clause 4.12). In case the laboratory chooses to or has to (subject to legal requirements) implement electronic media for the storage of quality and technical data, its facilities have to be suitable in order to prevent loss, deterioration or unauthorized

access (clause 4.13.2). LIS may be used for the maintenance of personnel records, while special care has to be taken for authorized access to records of exposure to occupational hazards and records of immunization status (clause 5.1.2). The confidentiality of information regarding patients has to be safeguarded also from external risks, coming from the LIS and its external communication (web, remote access and other options) (clause 5.1.13). Environmental conditions (temperature, electrical supply, electromagnetic interference, Wi-Fi should have to be taken into consideration in case of the existence of an integrated LIS system (clause 5.2.5). The use of the LIS for the implementation of internal communication, as well as the efficiency of the message transfer, has to be documented (clause 5.2.8), and space and conditions appropriate for the storage of electronic media and relevant LIS equipment have to be provided (clause 5.2.9).

In clause 5.3 (except 5.3.11 and 5.3.14) general requirements for laboratory equipment are given. Those requirements include:

- Use of energy and future disposal (environmental care).
- Qualification of hardware and software equipment during installation.
- Regular performance verification through established requirements.
- Labeling of equipment.
- Record keeping.
- Operation by authorized personnel.
- Check of non-conformity work because of defected equipment.

In clause 5.3.11, reference is made to:

- Validation of software.
- Procedures for protection of data integrity.
- Proper maintenance and proper conditions for LIS equipment.
- Protection for unauthorized alteration of software.

Protection of equipment from adjustments or invalidation of test results should be provided (clause 5.3.14) The use of electronic request form and the way the request is communicated to the laboratory should be selected after discussion with the laboratory clients (clause 5.4.1). All primary samples should be recorded by the LIS (clause 5.4.7), and the use of electronic manuals for the documentation of working procedures is acceptable at the workstations. Use of intranet web pages could be examined as an alternative to a card files system for use as a quick reference option at the work station (clause 5.5.3) Use of electronic signature or a traceable system of authorization through the LIS should be examined where possible (clause 5.8.3). The way and the time reported results would be stored in a LIS system should be carefully selected in order to assure prompt retrieval as well conformity with legal requirements (clause 5.8.6). LIS and electronic media could be used for immediate notification of "alert" or "critical" results (clause 5.8.7). The issue of alteration of reports, availability of the original report, and traceability at the alteration, time and responsible person is referred in clause 5.8.15 of the standard. Many options are provided through a LIS system and document control software, and requirements for the organization of revised reports and file keeping system are given in clause 5.8.16.

The ISO 15189: 2007 requirements for electronic archives concern environmental conditions, procedures in use, system's electronic security, hardware and software integrity and system's maintenance. Environmental requirements for the implementation of high quality electronic medical database include proper maintenance of computer facilities, accessibility to firefighting equipment, dependable protection of wires and cables, provision of an uninterruptible power supply and protection from unauthorized access

Procedural requirements for the implementation of high quality electronic medical database cover the acquisition of an electronic procedure manual, available to all computer users and the implementation of specific procedures aiming at the protection of electronic data from any damage caused by hardware or software failure.

System's electronic security from unauthorized personnel alterations is of paramount importance and has to be ensured by implementing strict policies concerning authorization for entering, changing or editing electronic medical records. Medical data integrity must be continuously monitored for any errors during transmission and storage process. Specific procedures for reviewing all automatic calculations as well as the data entered in the laboratory information system must be implemented, in order to ensure electronic medical data's integrity.

Specific procedures must ensure that electronic medical data will be easily retrievable by all authorized personnel. Parameters such as footnotes, interpretative comments and uncertainty of a given measurement must be easily reproducible as part of the electronic medical report, offering the clinician the chance to interpret, with precision, laboratory medical data. The specific needs of each laboratory will determine the time, during which medical data will remain electronically.

Hardware and software requirements for the implementation of high quality electronic medical database cover the acquisition of a complete record of all preventive actions concerning computer maintenance (Vacata et al., 2007).

Every back-up must be followed by systematic verification of the software integrity. All mistakes detected during back-up have to be documented, and corrective action must restore the system's proper function., while every modification of the system hardware and software must be documented and verified (Vacata et al.,2007; Kubono, 2007). Authorized personnel must verify that all programs run properly after first installation or any documented modification, and all serious computer malfunctions must be reported to an authorized laboratory's member, responsible for the proper use of medical laboratory's electronic records

(Vacata et al., 2007; Kubono, 2007). System's maintenance must be scheduled in such a way that it will not interrupt the patient-care service. Documented procedures for handling computer's shutdown and restart will ensure medical data's integrity (Vacata et al., 2007; Kubono, 2007). Cooperation between laboratory and hospital information system will be improved by the implementation of specific procedures concerning data replacement, recovery and updating. All computer problems, such as unexpected shutdown, downtime or breakdown, must be fully documented, and corrective action must be taken in order to avoid these problems in the future (Vacata et al., 2007; Kubono, 2007).

The laboratory must also adopt a documented program of preventive maintenance.(clause 5.3). The laboratory must maintain a record containing the hardware's identity, manufacturer's name date of receiving and date of entering into service, manufacturer's instructions, maintenance carried out, hardware's and software's performance and repair diary(clause 5.3).

Clause 5.10 is explaining in detail the current requirements for medical laboratories information management.

According to clause 5.1, the medical laboratory must adopt a documented procedure to ensure the confidentiality of patient information. .

According to clause 5.2, the medical laboratory must adopt a documented procedure to define the authorities and responsibilities of all personnel who use the laboratory information system, for accessing patient data and information, entering or altering patient data and examination results,

According to clause 5.3, all systems used for the collection, processing, recording, reporting, storage or retrieval of examination data and information must be validated by the supplier and verified for functioning by the laboratory before introduction to the laboratory workflow. All these systems must also be protected from unauthorized access, safeguarded against tampering or loss, operated in an environment that complies with

supplier specifications, maintained in a manner that ensures the integrity of the data and includes the recording of system failures and the appropriate immediate and corrective actions.

STATIC TELECYTOLOGICAL APPLICATIONS FOR PROFICIENCY TESTING PROVIDING PURPOSES

In a modern cytopathology laboratory, selected cytology slides with histological confirmation are retrospectively selected from the laboratory's registry or donated by cooperating cytology labs. The slides collected for the production of the digital material from the Cytology Laboratory's registries are coming from already histologically confirmed cases (Pantanowitz et al., 2009).The histological examination consists the best way cytology slides can be validated. Inadequate validation of test slides could lead to indiscriminate failure of qualified, competent personnel participating in external quality control programs (Pantanowitz et al., 2009).

A modern cytopathology laboratory's managerial and technical personnel have all necessary education; resources and technical competence required (Thrall et al., 2011).The minimum levels of qualification and experience necessary for the key positions within their organization should be clearly defined. Contracted or additional technical personnel may be used. The laboratory's director should authorize specific personnel to:

- Operate specific equipment (microscopes and cameras mounted on them).
- Prepare handle and distribute proficiency test items (digital cytological images).
- Conduct statistical analysis of telecytological diagnoses.
- Select appropriate proficiency test items (cytology slides and digital cytological images).
- Plan proficiency testing schemes.

- Evaluate the participants diagnostic performance.
- Give opinions and interpretations on participants telecytological diagnoses.
- Authorize the issue of interlaboratory comparisons reports.

The laboratory should ensure that:

- There are appropriate facilities and equipment for proficiency test item manufacturing, handling and storage.
- The environmental conditions do not compromise the proficiency testing scheme's quality.
- The methods and equipment used to confirm the content, homogeneity and stability of proficiency testing items (digital cytological images) are appropriately validated and maintained.
- Processes which directly affect the quality of the proficiency testing scheme are carried out in accordance with prescribed procedures.
- There are appropriate facilities and equipment for data processing and communications integrity.

The laboratory should maintain up-to-date records of authorizations, qualifications, training, skills, competence, and experience of all technical personnel in a professional testing scheme organization. The effectiveness of training activities should be evaluated and described in detail (Thrall et al., 2011).

The laboratory director should ensure that there are appropriate facilities and equipment for cytology images capturing and storage, for data processing, for communications, and for retrieval of materials and records (Khurana, 2012).

The laboratory director should ensure that the environmental conditions do not compromise the quality of the proficiency testing scheme. All environmental conditions should be continuously monitored.

The laboratory should have access to the necessary technical expertise and experience in the field of Cytopathology and Statistics and should establish an advisory group in order to:

- Plan specific requirements.
- Identify and resolve any difficulties expected in the preparation and maintenance of the proficiency testing scheme.
- Prepare instructions for participants.
- Make comments on any technical difficulties observed in previous proficiency testing rounds.
- Provide advice in evaluating the participants performance.
- Make comments on the results and performance of participants.
- Respond to feedback from participants.
- Plan and participate in technical meetings with participants.

The laboratory should give detailed instructions to all participants, concerning the following:

- The necessity to treat digital cytological images in the same manner as the majority of routinely tested samples.
- The procedure for viewing the digital images and writing down their final diagnosis.
- The procedure for recording and reporting test results and associated uncertainties.

The laboratory should provide expert commentary on the performance of participants with regard to the overall performance against prior expectations, the interobserver and intra observer variability, and comparisons with any previous proficiency testing rounds, the possible sources of error and suggestions for improving performance, as well as advice and educational feedback to participants.

The proficiency testing reports should include the following information (Stewart et al., 2007):

- The name and contact details for the proficiency testing provider and the coordinator.
- The date of issue and status of the report.
- The report number and identification of the proficiency testing scheme.
- A description of the proficiency test items used (digital cytological images).
- The participants' results.
- Comments on participants' performance by the proficiency testing provider and technical advisors.
- Statistical data and procedures used to statistically analyze the data.
- Comments or recommendations, related to the outcomes of the proficiency testing round.

The laboratory should also provide to all participants details about (Stewart et al., 2007):

- The application procedure.
- The scope of the proficiency testing scheme.
- The fees for participation.
- The eligibility criteria for participation.
- The confidentiality arrangements.

All information supplied by a participant to the laboratory should be treated as confidential. The laboratory should ensure that the identity of participants is known only to persons involved in the proficiency testing scheme. Participants can waive confidentiality for mutual assistance or scientific discussion purposes. The laboratory should implement specific policies and procedures to ensure valuable information's safety during electronic storage and transmission (Stewart et al., 2007).

The laboratory's managerial and technical personnel should be free from any commercial or financial bias that could adversely affect the quality of their work. The laboratory's managerial and technical personnel should have the authority and the resources required for the implementation and improvement of the management system. The laboratory's managerial and technical personnel is also responsible to identify any departures from the management system and to initiate preventive actions. The laboratory implements specific policies and procedures to avoid personnel's involvement in any activities that might diminish confidence in its competence or impartiality. The laboratory director should ensure that all employees are aware of their activity's importance, provides adequate supervision to all technical staff, has appointed one quality manager for ensuring that the management system is implemented and followed at all times. Finally, the laboratory director should appoint deputies for key managerial personnel (Stewart et al., 2007).

The laboratory should retain records of all data relating to each telecytology proficiency testing round for a defined period, including:

- Instructions to participants.
- Participants original responses.
- Data for statistical analysis.
- Final reports.

The laboratory should periodically review its proficiency testing activities. More specifically, it reviews:

- Changes in the volume and type of work.
- Advisory group or participant feedback.
- The outcome of recent internal or external audits.
- Corrective and preventive actions.
- Complaints and appeals.

CLOUD COMPUTING TELEMEDICAL APPLICATIONS FOR QUALITY ASSURANCE PURPOSES IN A MODERN CYTOPATHOLOGY LABORATORY

A cytopathology laboratory is dealing mainly with images as the routine cytological examinations are performed via the use of glass slides and analysis with the microscope.

A modern cytopathology, laboratory, is also performing additional examinations based on molecular techniques and immunocytochemistry methods. A modern cytopathology laboratory is equipped with numerous modalities capable of performing medical tests and exchanging data via networks. A modern cytopathology laboratory is equipped with imaging systems capable of creating digital pictures of the slides or even virtual slides, which are complete slides in electronic format.

Cloud-based software for digital cytology may enable image and data sharing, scientific collaboration and automated analysis of whole slide images via web browsers. The power of cloud computing combined with the convenience of web applications can improve significantly the collaboration among cytology labs participating in image or data sharing quality assurance programs (Rosenthal et al., 2010).

Storing, archiving and accessing images in the cloud allow a modern cytopathology laboratory to manage data more efficiently and cost-effectively (Rosenthal et al., 2010).

The cloud enables a modern cytopathology laboratory to efficiently handle large bandwidth images, to use non-proprietary, standards-based, vendor-neutral architecture, to expand or contract storage capacity easily as needed, to manage authentication, encryption and security protocols, to conduct efficient system-wide application upgrades and finally to extend the life of existing infrastructure/investments (Rosenthal et al., 2010).

As the pressure to reduce costs is constantly raising, many laboratories nowadays are exploiting virtualization capabilities that are basic characteristics of cloud computing. In addition to cost reduction, the set-up and configuration time for a laboratory wishing to adopt a new LIS is minimal. Therefore, a cytopathology laboratory that does not have a LIS, but wants to start using a Cloud-based LIS may purchase a LIS system hosted in the cloud, configure it according to the needs, train the users and launch the application within a short time (Rosenthal et al., 2010). Using a community Cloud, many hospitals can share standard software and save large amounts of money.

The servers applied for image or data sharing quality assurance programs will have to support most digital slide formats and to be easily integrated with various scanners for single-click slide upload for on-premises deployment (Rosenthal et al., 2010).

A cloud-based infrastructure for digital cytology can analyze whole slides on special image servers from each professional's web browser with just few mouse clicks.

All professionals, although possessing different scanners, microscopes and cameras, will be able to use cloud-based software in order to integrate seamlessly with imaging hardware. Cloud-based software permits the digital slide to be uploaded to the user workspace via the cloud server automatically (Rosenthal et al., 2010).

A modern cytopathology laboratory and the network of cooperating cytopathology laboratories have no obligation to conform to any single unified corporate IT policy. A modern cytopathology laboratory and the network of cooperating cytopathology laboratories can use a variety of computers, operating systems and browsers. The special web interface can work with all the technology – Windows, Mac, iPad and android tablets – without exceptions. Each professional (whether cytotechnologist or cytopathologist) can view digital slides online without having to download, install or update anything. A simple log on to the browser is enough for making the connection with the cloud platform (Rosenthal et al., 2010).

An integrated, flexible Database module can create a powerful knowledge database from each cytopathologist's digital slide collection. Cloud-based software can use flexible attributes, quick tags, comments and attachments for cases and slides to organize images and keep track of all available medical data.

Cytopathology professionals should be able to separate shared and modern images. A modern cytopathology laboratory and the network of co-operating cytopathology laboratories can invite collaborators and share digital slides via email, by using cloud-based software.

No need to mention once more that digital cytology images storage and transmission must follow strict regulations in order to avoid any unauthorized alteration or improper use. Current standards of electronic medical data handling are still informative, but the need for secure electronic environment, continues to grow.

Quality assurance in the field of Cytopathology is achieved mainly by monitoring diagnostic discrepancies, through cytological and histological correlation. The improvement of information systems and LIS in most pathology laboratories, allows such correlations to be performed just immediately after the release of the examination results. Additionally, data mining either on-line or in a later stage may produce important knowledge for trends and problematic areas in the processes and therefore to initiate corrective actions for quality improvement. Additionally images based systems to evaluate the quality of classification systems such as the Bethesda System 2001 for reporting the results of cervical cytology have already been reported in the literature. The cloud obviously can be of help for QC & QA as the related application may be developed and operated for such an envi-

ronment; storage and application load will not be an issue and additional benefits may be obtained as the QC & QA application can be shared among numerous laboratories and rare cytological cases can be used by all participating labs.

A modern cytopathology laboratory should establish a system wherein images and virtual slides are available online and all cytopathologists can report remotely. By using the laboratory' server, the users experienced many difficulties because of frequent LAN disruptions within the local network. By shifting the data to the Cloud, the cytopathologists are now able to access web-based cytopathology software. Here, the Cloud enables a telecytology and implementation of teleconsultation applications.

A modern cytopathology laboratory may need to cooperate in real time with a cytopathology laboratory in a remote location. In order to send or receive images in real time, a modern cytopathology laboratory can push the images into the Cloud, enabling the cytopathologists to review images at nodal centers, without having to buy additional software and hardware. Here, the Cloud works as a gateway to the peripheral center wherein all its information is available on the Cloud.

A modern cytopathology laboratory may use cloud computing for making the entire medical record of a patient accessible for review by a remote cytopathologist. All cytopathologists can review admission notes for all cases, can seek prior data from other laboratories that are mentioned in these notes and can review all available imaging material in order to make all applicable correlations.

Further evaluation and development of intelligent cloud based search engines exploiting artificial intelligence appears worthwhile.

Another aspect of primary diagnosis is related to homeworker cytopathologists. Virtual slide technology enables the digitization of complete slides; thus the diagnostic data can be now stored and transmitted. The barrier, in this case, is the large amount of data. Eventually cloud computing provides endless storage and fast communication channels, in this aspect, remote primary diagnosis could be a reality (Rosenthal et al., 2010).

THE USE OF LABORATORY INFORMATION SYSTEMS FOR QUALITY CONTROL PURPOSES IN A MODERN CYTOPATHOLOGY LABORATORY

A modern cytopathology laboratory should maintain quality control measures in order to detect, reduce, and correct deficiencies in cytological diagnoses accredited according to ISO 15189:2012.

The laboratory should implement a set of procedures in order to ensure that the preparation, interpretation, and reporting of cytology specimens meets specific quality standards. Quality assurance policy is used by a cytopathology laboratory as a retrospective tool measuring the success of pre-, post- and analytical processes. A cytopathology laboratory should implement an effective quality control program designed to monitor and evaluate the quality of its testing processes.

The quality control program implemented by a cytopathology laboratory should be able to ensure the accuracy, reliability and timeliness of cytological diagnoses. A modern cytopathology laboratory may introduce electronic monitoring in order to perform quality control measures. Electronic data can be extracted and manipulated in a convenient and simple way, not demanding computer-specialists end users. In a modern cytopathology laboratory, Quality Assurance methodologies are designed and used in order to continually improve the diagnostic accuracy and to eliminate false negative diagnostic rates.

The electronic database kept in a modern cytopathology laboratory has numerous advantages, such as simple and efficient qualitative and quantitative data analysis, standardization of reporting formats, efficient and fast transmission of information, efficient integration of many health records, and rapid billing transactions.

In a modern cytopathology laboratory data is retrieved and stored by using relational databases. Basic spreadsheets allow the existing data to be charted, sorted, and organized into tables. A cytopathology laboratory is using simple and inexpensive spreadsheet applications (Microsoft Excel). Moreover, it should have constructed simple but efficient relational databases, offering many valuable opportunities for further statistical analyses and graphs generation.

A cytopathology laboratory should have electronically tracking of QC/QA indicators, which can be done either within the LIS and/or by exporting data from the LIS (by using common spreadsheet software).

A cytopathology laboratory information system should be monitoring laboratory requisition completeness, problems documented by the accession, occurrences and trends with any particular clinician office sending specimens to the laboratory. Identification of such problems could prompt the redesign of requisition forms. Specimen rejection incidents and labeling errors are also electronically documented and specimen rejection frequency is regularly reported to all physicians' offices. Comments entered within available QA fields are included in the final cytological report. Electronic monitoring of lost specimens is accomplished with a simple spreadsheet log.

A cytopathology laboratory information system should be monitoring electronic data integrity and be taking all available security measures, which may include regular back up of data, password protection, and data encryption, use of antiviral software, firewalls, and audit trails. A modern cytopathology laboratory information system should be assigning users different privileges and allows only certain individuals to finalize and sign out abnormal cytological diagnoses. A cytopathology laboratory information system should be ensuring the integrity of finalized reports. Changes, where applicable, should be incorporated in the form of an addendum to the existing report.

A cytopathology laboratory information system should be using standardized diagnostic terminology and coded comments, in order to ensure uniformity of the reporting language. Such coded comments allow quick data entry and rapid result reporting to the clinician. In other types of cytological specimens, such as fine needle aspiration biopsies and no gynecologic specimens, a cytopathology laboratory should be using a more flexible diagnostic terminology. Cytological reports using standardized language consist an efficient means to extract data, enabling calculations of diagnostic reproducibility, for the entire laboratory, or for individual cytopathologists.

In a cytopathology laboratory, mandatory cntrics may include the following parameters: specimen adequacy statement, name of the cytopathologist and final diagnosis. In a cytopathology laboratory, reports cannot be issued until the completion of all mandatory fields. In a modern cytopathology laboratory, the primary diagnostic code should remain assigned to the case.

In a cytopathology laboratory, turnaround times are an excellent indicator of laboratory's workflow management. Special reports are constantly generated to calculate turnaround time, identify outliers, investigate the cause of a delay, and implement corrective actions.

In a cytopathology laboratory, a predetermined number of cases is randomly selected from the previous month and checked for timely retrieval, appropriate storage, and reporting accuracy. All errors are documented, and procedures are reevaluated or even revised. In a cytopathology laboratory, all negative Pap tests for the last five years for which current cases are diagnosed with high grade squamous intraepithelial lesion (HSIL) or above (i.e. cancer) are retrospective reviewed.

The author's cytology laboratory software is designed to search for cases of abnormal cytology (e.g. Pap test interpretation of LSIL or higher) during a specific time period and then identify any cytology specimen has occurred since that designated period.

The author's cytology LIS database records workloads for individual cytopathologists. This is done by evaluating diagnostic accuracy as it compares to productivity.

A modern cytopathology laboratory information system prohibits the screening of more than 200 conventional slides over a 8 - hour period. No gynecologic and gynecologic liquid-based preparation slides also count as half-slides in such daily counts. A cytopathology laboratory information system should have implemented software solutions which can be used to ensure that workload limits are not exceeded.

Random rescreening is mandated or has been implemented as a measure of QA in screening Pap tests in many countries. A cytopathology laboratory should implement a 10% random rescreen of negative cytology specimens. The Rapid prescreening method is considered more efficient at detecting false negative rates. A cytopathology laboratory's software allows adjustments of the number of cases pulled for quality control review, according to individual screeners. This is very useful for closer inspection of work quality, as a tool for remedial training, or for new cytopathologists monitoring and assessing. A cytopathology laboratory's software often has data entries that allow the degree of error to be defined (e.g. minor disagreement or major disagreement).

In a modern cytopathology laboratory, pivot tables, created after downloading data into spreadsheets, are useful tools to cross reference diagnoses by cytopathologists and for analyzing diagnostic correlations and discrepancies. In a cytopathology laboratory, software systems allow for individual cases to be easily retrieved for continuing education purposes.

Additional performance monitors that can be tracked by the laboratory information system include the rates for frequencies of diagnostic categories which can be tabulated on a monthly, quarterly, and/or six month basis for each cytopathologist and compared against the department as a whole. The laboratory's director may need to take remedial actions if an individual average exceeds a predetermined variance from the normal.

In a cytopathology laboratory, the ASC-US HPV DNA positivity rate serves as a useful quality indicator. Performance beyond two standard deviations (SDs) of the mean, for HPV-positive rates in ASC-US Pap tests, prompts reassessment of diagnostic criteria used in the evaluation of Pap tests.

For quality control purposes, a cytopathology laboratory compares cytological and biopsy reports (if available) and determines the cause of any discrepancies. Such cytologic-histologic correlation is compiled at annual intervals.

In a modern cytopathology laboratory, such correlations are accomplished by using the LIS through QC/QA software tools.

THE USE OF LABORATORY INFORMATION SYSTEMS FOR ACCREDITATIONAL PURPOSES IN A MODERN CYTOPATHOLOGY LABORATORY

A modern cytopathology laboratory's information system:

- Should be secured from unauthorized internal and external access and preserves the confidentiality of health records according to national law and regulations. Different levels of security are available.
- Should possess the ability for remote log-in and access to ordering and reporting systems via a secure Web browser, allowing laboratories to access the LIS from distant locations. A modern cytopathology laboratory's information system should also allow reliable electronic signatures for data authentication. Regarding test ordering, a modern cytopathology laboratory's information system should be able to provide immediate feedback to all users.

- Should have documented policies which are guiding clinicians how to order the appropriate cytological examinations. The clinicians are allowed and encouraged to directly enter the order in the system.
- Should be able to receive inputs from clinicians that have to include the following information: Ordering physician information (name, specialty, address, contact media for routine notification, contact information for critical result notification). Patient information (patient identification, patient demographics, including date of birth/age, sex, patient location, results of laboratory and nonlaboratory tests, medications, medical procedures applied to the patient, gynecologic and obstetric information, other pertinent clinical information).
- Should possess a user-friendly display of the test catalog with available alternative groupings. A modern cytopathology laboratory's administration should periodically monitor menus consistency and complete or update them, according to patient needs.
- Should be able to relay orders to different interfaced systems without manual intervention, so that tests ordered in one facility can enable specimens to be collected and accessioned at another location or institution. A modern cytopathology laboratory's information system should keep a list of the reference laboratories available to the ordering provider. A modern cytopathology laboratory's information system should be able to generate a report with sender, receiver, and shipping information.
- Should be able to split clinicians' orders, tracks the progress and reports the status of each component separately less than 1 order.

- Should possess functionalities to optimize specimen collection and processing, such as:
  - Specimen collection lists as appropriate to laboratory operation.
  - Printed and electronic guidelines to the specimen collectors with a comprehensive display of proper specimen collection instructions.
  - List of pending laboratory orders.
  - Automatic generation of unique barcoded labels.
  - Automatic recording of patient information, location, date and time of collection, and collector identity.
- Should allow deviations of the sequence of specimen processing described above, according to laboratory's policy, for example, specimens received in the laboratory without an order or accession, but with appropriate patient identifiers should be acknowledged by the system.
- Should interface with laboratory automation management software to ensure that all the preanalytical requirements stipulated in the ordering process are transmitting to the specimen-processing system.
- Should track the specimen location throughout the preanalytical, analytic, and post analytic phases, including transportation to various sections of the laboratory or external sites, and management of specimen storage.
- Should possess functionalities to optimize the analytical phase, such as:
  - Tracking and association with individual testing records of all the components necessary for testing.
  - Generation of printed and electronic versions of appropriate standardized operating procedures for each test upon request by the cytopathologist.
  - Generation of laboratory-specific workload lists.

- Generation of "Incomplete lists" of tests that have been accessioned but not completed, highlighting those that have exceeded the stated time for the category of the request.
- Generation of lists of incomplete or unfulfilled orders.
- Should possess functionalities to optimize the result entry and validation, such as:
  - Ability to record results in various data formats.
  - Automated and manual entry and correction of results of tests, with appropriate security levels applied.
  - Application of different levels of result certification.
  - Reception of results in a variety of formats from other laboratories, including external reference laboratories, through electronic interfaces.
  - Utilization of advanced expert decision support for auto validation of results. Inputs used to arrive at an auto validation decision include comparison with results of previous tests in the patient record, comparison with results of other related tests in the same or closely related specimens, statistical data on result distribution.
- Should possess functionalities to optimize result reporting, such as:
  - Report generation which includes both laboratories and recipients (clinicians, patients) of the test information.
  - Report generation available by user-configurable automated secure faxing and e-mailing.
  - Sophisticated graphing of laboratory results.
  - Ability to incorporate in result comments hyperlinks to pages containing further test information.

- ○ Ability to append appropriate interpretative comments on test results.
- Should possess functionalities to optimize notification management, such as:
  - ○ Possession of a sophisticated "significant result" notification system that includes multiple tiers of urgency for significant result notification.
  - ○ Utilization of dynamic rules in order to determine whether a result is critical.
  - ○ Utilization of a rule-based notification of appropriate third parties.
  - ○ Rapid update and notification about any changes or corrections to laboratory results.
- Should possess functionalities to optimize data mining and cross-sectional reports, such as:
  - ○ Ability to perform queries into the laboratory and clinical databases.
  - ○ Search functions for combinations of laboratory results and clinical information.
  - ○ Production of laboratory testing turnaround time reports with the ability to consolidate or split the various components.
  - ○ Online reporting of surveillance data to public health agencies in their required format, using the appropriate standards.
- Should possess functionalities to optimize method validation, by using the module with the ability to guide and record intra-observer and inter-observer concordance.
- Should take measures to optimize Quality management, by using a module supporting accreditation requirements. This module should include the following functionalities:
  - ○ Quality control protocols and alerting mechanisms which use thresholds for acceptability.

- ○ Linkage of each patient test result to the relevant quality control results in an easily retrievable record.
- ○ automated alerts to appropriate staff to perform quality control tasks.
- ○ Active quality control rules and reports are customizable by test.
- ○ Ability to document corrective actions resulting from quality control failure in real time.
- ○ Ability to remove outliers and erroneous results from quality control calculations.
- ○ Ability to provide user-definable quality control summary reports for review by supervisory and management staff.
- ○ Ability to manage proficiency-testing (PT) programs, from inventory control of PT materials to documenting PT results and investigation of PT failures.
- ○ Ability to manage accreditation requirements online, including preparation of appropriate documents.
- Should aim at incorporating advanced administrative and financial functionalities, including the following:
  - ○ Ability to generate and transmit the necessary forms and notifications for reimbursement of tests.
  - ○ Intelligent generation of online and printed regulatory forms associated with laboratory testing, billing, compliance, and accreditation.
  - ○ Tracking of costs of laboratory operation.
  - ○ Analysis of profitability, pricing and outreach client management capabilities.
  - ○ Ability to produce periodic reports of laboratory productivity and management efficiency, by using aggregate

numbers and individual cost and productivity analysis per test.

○ Automated ordering from selected suppliers and real-time tracking of budget.

○ Tracking of human resource databases, labor-cost accounting, and credentials, competency, continuing education training, and performance appraisals.

Issues, Controversies, Problems

The implementation of ISO 15189:2012 guidelines in medical laboratories information systems presents some problems that need further analysis. Medical data that is stored and retrieved from the laboratory information system contains valuable information that needs to remain confidential. The widespread use of computers makes access to classified documents easier than ever. The use of electronic signature in medical reports may diminish bureaucratic problems but, on the other hand, makes the laboratory information system more vulnerable. The laboratory management has to implement specific policies that will protect medical data from unauthorized access, but will not endanger the cooperation between medical and laboratory information systems (Vacata et al., 2007).

Laboratory personnel training in informatics is necessary for ensuring efficient function of the laboratory information system. The laboratory management has to plan personnel training in such a way that the laboratory main function will not be put in danger (Vacata et al., 2007). Poor hardware maintenance or improper use by inadequately trained personnel may cause a laboratory information system failure. Laboratory reports may be lost or deteriorated due to malignant software (virus programs), while LIS hardware may be damaged by adverse environmental conditions, such as heat, humidity or a possible fire, due to the vulnerability of wires and cables to unfavorable environmental conditions (Vacata et al., 2007). Finally, medical data stored only in electronic mediums may be easily lost due to a system's unexpected failure (Vacata et al., 2007). All these possible threats of a laboratory information system require the implementation of specific measures and policies that may have considerable economic impact, or may even prove non-affordable. The laboratory management is responsible for making an economic plan, after taking into account the specific laboratory resources and needs.

The implementation of cloud computing technology in medical laboratories information systems presents some problems that need further analysis. The main threats for cloud computing technology in the field of Medical Informatics are:

- New threats of data security and privacy, these threats, may be anticipated by data encryption during storage and transfer and connecting with the server using encryption protocols.
- Unauthorized access may be anticipated by passwords and password control mechanisms and via mandatory biometric checks.
- Database safety and long-term archival process in case of emergencies and natural disasters have to be discussed with the Cloud computing service provider in detail.
- Server failures may be avoided by maintaining mirror servers.
- Efficiency of service, related to broadband speed may be ensured by the hospital cooperation with multiple Internet service providers to prevent disruption of service.
- Increased load can be easily handled by adding more processing power to existing virtual servers and/or by splitting the application to run on multiple servers, either via load balancing or by the exploitation of multi-tier architectures and splitting to one or more separate application servers and database servers.

The implementation of telemedical applications for proficiency testing purposes in medical laboratories wishing accreditation presents some problems that need further analysis. In conventional cytology, specific diagnostic criteria and pitfalls are already described. During static telecytological diagnosis, the cytopathologist has to use the same diagnostic criteria and to avoid the same pitfalls. What makes the telecytological diagnosis more demanding is uncertainty about the real specimen's adequacy or the representativity of the selected images (Archondakis et al., 2009). Static digital images suffer from representing only limited portions of the specimen and hence there may be a potential bias of the image acquisition process. The inability of focusing and image manipulation (contrast, brightness, and color) may cause additional problems (Khurana, 2012).

Cytology slides used for digital images capture must be validated in order to make sure that the initial cytological diagnosis was correct and did not differ significantly from the final histological diagnosis.

Reporting terminology is well established for some categories of cytological specimens such as thyroid fine needle aspiration specimens and cervicovaginal smears. Still cytological diagnosis for the majority of specimens remains descriptive, and no specific diagnostic categories have been established and implemented in the everyday laboratory practice. The absence of a universally accepted and adopted reporting terminology is a serious problem for the correct statistical elaboration of cytological diagnoses provided by participants in a proficiency testing scheme. A widely accepted reporting terminology would make easier the implementation of scoring systems, validating participants' performance and improvement.

Participation in proficiency testing programs is still poor. Many large cytological departments are reluctant to implement such practices as a measure of continuous improvement and quality assurance. Even when a proficiency testing program is ordered, only one or two certified cytopathologists are participating.

Last but not least, digital images storage and transmission must follow strict regulations in order to avoid any unauthorized alteration or improper use. Current standards of electronic medical data handling are still informative, yet the need for secure electronic environment, especially in the field of static telecytology, continues to grow.

Solutions and Recommendations

Before new software or hardware is introduced in a laboratory, the risk connected with such an introduction should be assessed (Vacata et al., 2007). The risk assessment should include identification of possible events, which may result in non-compliance, estimation of their likelihood, identification of their consequences, and ways of avoiding them, costs, drawbacks, and benefits (Vacata et al., 2007). Good knowledge of computer software and hardware details is also essential for the maintenance, troubleshooting and update. Medical laboratory personnel have to be periodically trained to use new computer facilities and new software products. Their training may be extremely difficult. Therefore, the laboratory director has to encourage these training sessions and continuously motivate its personnel.

Moreover, we have to take into account that computer facilities maintenance is of paramount importance in the workflow of a medical laboratory. Therefore, the laboratory personnel should take specific measures for protecting the hardware. These measures should be documented in specific procedures, including:

- The way a computer should be turned off.
- The way data should be stored.
- The way the top and rear of the PC monitor should be kept clean and clear of debris.

- The way to avoid excessive heating of the computer facilities.
- The way to clean the inner surfaces of the PC.
- How often hard disks should be scanned and defragmented.
- How many MBs should be kept free in the hard disk.
- The way peripherals should be plugged or unplugged from the computer.
- How many programs should load up when the computer starts.
- What firewall program should be used in case the computer facilities are connected to the Internet.
- How often and what type of virus checker should be used.
- What programs should be installed.
- How often should the antivirus programs be updated.
- How often should the Internet cache be emptied.
- How often should unnecessary files be cleaned up from the hard drives.

The hardware should also be fully protected from any actual damages, and especially fire (Vacata et al., 2007). The measures should be documented in specific procedures, and might include:

- Smoke alarms installation and periodical testing.
- Flammable items storage and use.
- Storage and use of heating sources.
- Control of electrical wires.
- Installation of fire extinguishers.

Wires and cables of the computer facilities should also be fully protected. Procedures might include:

- Identification and maintenance of underground cables.
- Cables maintenance.
- Record keeping to determine the position of underground cables.
- Looping, linking and servicing connections.
- Maps or computer databases for all cable installations.

The provision of an uninterruptible power supply will protect the computer from crashing during power outages, or from low and high voltage occurrences (Vacata et al., 2007). A UPS is much better than a surge protector and can save the laboratory computer facilities from virtually any type of power failure.

Medical records and computer facilities should also be well protected from unauthorized access (Vacata et al., 2007). The laboratory should establish guidelines for the protection of medical data from unauthorized access, which should:

- Protect all laboratory data and information.
- Analyze access methods based on standards.
- Use the standard application methods wherever possible.
- Designate individuals responsible for the integrity of specific data sets.
- Restrict access to data and information to authorized individuals only.
- Restrict writing, updating, and deleting data.

The laboratory should also obtain a complete record of all preventive actions concerning computer maintenance (Vacata et al., 2007). Hardware preventive maintenance is the best way to dramatically reduce all factors threatening or shortening computer's life. The laboratory should implement specific procedures referring to many issues, such as:

- Excessive heat prevention.
- Dust removal.
- Magnetism, radiated electromagnetic interference and static electricity prevention.
- Power surges, incorrect line voltage, and power outages handling.
- Water and corrosive agents prevention.

Finally, software preventive maintenance is achieved by using anti-virus applications, defragmentation software and testing utility programs (Vacata et al., 2007). The laboratory should/must implement specific procedures referring to many issues, such as:

- Computers cleaning and defragmenting.
- Periodical virus check.
- Back-up, followed by systematic verification of the software's integrity. All mistakes detected during back-up should be documented, and a corrective action should restore the system's proper function.
- Every modification of the system hardware and software should be documented and verified. Authorized personnel should verify that all programs run properly after the first installation or any documented modification.
- All serious computer malfunctions should be reported to an authorized laboratory's member.
- System's maintenance should be scheduled in such a way that it will not interrupt patient-care service.
- Documented procedures for handling computer's shutdown and restart.
- Implementation of specific procedures concerning data replacement, recovery and updating.
- All computer problems, such as unexpected shutdown, downtime or degradation should be fully documented.

- A corrective action must be taken in order to avoid these problems in the future.

In the field of telecytology,, the role of the person appointed to picture capture and transmission is of paramount importance for the success of a static telecytology system. The person appointed to capture and transmit the digital images should be already certified cytopathologist or cytotechnologist with adequate experience in conventional cytological diagnosis. Less specialized personnel, such as inexperienced screeners, may endanger the acquisition of representative images from each cytological slide (Archondakis et al., 2009).

Besides histological examination, other measures for cytology slides validation must be adopted in order to avoid possible indiscriminate failure of qualified, competent personnel (Nagy et al., 2006). Such measures may be the verification of cytological diagnosis by board certified, well trained, scientific personnel, the establishment of specific scoring system and reporting terminology for all kinds of cytological specimens and finally the capturing of a significant number of representative images by certified, well trained personnel (Nagy et al.,2006).

The scoring system and reporting terminology may be simplified and possibly inappropriate and unfair for certain cytological specimens. Specific scoring systems and reporting terminologies should be established for each kind of cytological specimens in order to ensure that the cytological diagnoses reflect the clinical implications associated with this terminology in modern practice, particularly regarding recommended follow-up.

Static telecytological systems are affordable by all cytopathology departments and give the opportunity to all scientific personnel to participate in proficiency testing programs, even when there is a significant time difference among participating laboratories (Thrall et al., 2011).

Cytology scientific societies should focus on cytology proficiency testing particularities and define special technical aspects such as images size and analysis, suggested testing intervals, diagnostic categories and methodology used for statistical evaluation of the proficiency testing results (Nagy et al., 2006).

Laboratory management should encourage personal participation of all scientific personnel in such proficiency testing programs. Laboratory management must have in mind that proficiency testing programs proffered on the basis of static digital images can improve the professional skills of the participating medical staff and make them feel more confident in their daily work.

Proficiency testing providers should ensure that the personnel appointed to picture capture and transmission has adequate experience in both conventional and image-based diagnosis. Previous experience in that field should be well documented and recorded (Nagy et al., 2006).

FUTURE RESEARCH DIRECTIONS

The net of accredited laboratories is globally expanding (kubono 2007). Many more countries will incorporate ISO 15189 requirements in their national or local regulations. Medical laboratories that will develop the most innovative and up to date procedures for electronic medical reporting and storage will become referral laboratories for their countries or regions (Kubono 2007).

All laboratories notices concerning the implementation of the ISO 15189:2012 are collected by an international working group, which is responsible for the revision of the standards, when necessary. Problems that might be reported to this international working group are examined, and suitable solutions will be incorporated in the standard's future editions or specific guidelines (Kubono 2007).

Considering the future of telecytology, we estimate that the telecytology, when integrated into the daily workflow, can provide exceptional consultation and professional testing opportunities to distant laboratories. Static telecytology systems are preferred due to their low cost by laboratories that cannot afford the high cost of buying and maintaining dynamic systems (Thrall et al., 2011). In any case, the cost of participation in a running telecytology program is inexpensive for small cytopathology labs (Archondakis et al., 2009; Nagy et al.,2006). Provincial hospitals where immediate scientific collaboration and support is necessary can take advantage of this great opportunity in order to improve their cytology services (Archondakis et al., 2009).

Future research must focus on the details of the implementation of a static telecytological application for proficiency testing purposes, that is, determining the required testing interval, elucidating the validation criteria applied to electronic material used for proficiency testing purposes and possibly changing the focus of the test from individuals to laboratory level testing (Thrall et al., 2011).

The diagnostic reliability of static telecytology makes possible its use for further amelioration of the laboratory services, by producing digital educational material for use in web-based training systems (Stergiou et al.2009). These programs can improve the professional skills of the participating medical staff and make them feel more confident in their daily work (Khurana, 2012).

Considering the future of Cloud Computing in Cytopathology, It is expected that Cloud computing will be further exploited by cytopathology laboratories wishing to improve their quality standards. One of the major challenges of Cloud computing will be to resolve possible problems regarding data safety and security. A possible solution could be a multi-cloud approach with a key sharing mechanism and patient identification cross reference numbers.

In the distant future, it is expected that the cytopathology departments will witness a large-scale migration to Cloud-based LIS due to ease of availability and low cost of ownership and maintenance.

In relation to the research activities, as sequencing costs are continuously becoming lower, nowadays it is not only possible but extremely easier for genomics researchers to have large amounts of data. The increasing availability of computational power according to Moore's law and the falling overhead for data storage, give to the scientists the opportunity not only to create and store large genetic data sets over the course of their research, but it is possible to process them. However, the majority of the laboratories has already become or will soon become, oversubscribed and underpowered in relation to the exploitation of data. Unavailable software and lack of computational power to run exhaustive search algorithms, eventually, will lead many researchers towards cloud computing to conduct their research. Alternatively, much of the minable information may remain untouched, underutilized and not properly explored. As a bonus cloud computing provides the means for data sharing among research teams, thus larger data sets can be exploited, more robust results and conclusions related to rear diseases can be obtained.

In the near future cytopathology, laboratory information systems will be able to record large datasets and interface with legacy systems to capture historical laboratory data, with the goal of storing lifelong results on each patient. Capabilities for handling large genomic data sets will be increasingly necessary for future LIS.

In the near future cytopathology laboratory information systems will have to capture industry standards for coding, billing, document generation, and interface formats, such as CDC, HL7 CDA1/2, XML, ASC X12, LOINC, SNOMED-CT, ICD-9, or ICD-10, as appropriate for each data type. The user interface and navigation will become friendlier. The LIS will minimize the number of keystrokes required for all activities and will be uniform for similar tasks within the software.

In the near future, all screens and reports will be printed and exported in appropriate document texts, spreadsheet, or graphic formats, while fully functional text editors will be used in text entry fields.

In the near future cytopathology, laboratory information systems will use interfaces that will be flexible in data formats and fully functional with appropriate routines available for testing the functionality of the interfaces before use in order to meet end-user expectations.

The cytopathology laboratory information systems will be able to integrate instant messaging, forum, online meeting, and social-networking capabilities. The cytopathology laboratory information systems will also be able to perform multiple functions simultaneously with imperceptible impact on their speed.

In Greece, the accreditation of a small number of private and public cytopathology laboratories according to ISO 15189:2007 is already completed by the National Accreditation Board. Digital material from histologically confirmed cases continues to be collected in cooperation with many cytology departments and the first static telecytology program will soon apply for accreditation as an individual proficiency testing provider. By the end of the year, this first proficiency testing program on clinical cytology is expected to have given many answers to many unresolved problems in healthcare, while scientific support and collaboration by local and distant cytology labs is expected (Thrall et al., 2011).

The author's cytopathology laboratory in close collaboration with the Hellenic Society of Clinical Cytology, and colleagues from the private and the public sector are elaborating a laboratory information system that will meet the specific needs of a modern cytopathology laboratory and will use all available new technologies, such as e-learning, telecytology and cloud computing facilities in order to improve quality control standards, create educational opportunities and finally create a large professional database that will eventually cover and monitor all private and public cytopathology laboratories.

CONCLUSION

The standard ISO 15189:2007 and its new edition (ISO 15189:2012) include direct and indirect references to the requirements concerning the implementation of laboratory information systems in medical laboratories. These requirements constitute a powerful tool for medical laboratories wishing to improve the quality of their laboratory information system because they diminish dramatically the possibility of human error or unexpected hardware or software failure. Laboratories should only specify the procedures to be followed according to their needs.

Laboratory informatics is critical to meet current and future challenges. Many of these challenges can be met by advancing technologies, such as improving the integration of disparate information systems, automation, specimen tracking, electronic document management systems, and streamlining procedures.

Telecytology can be used as an economical method for the implementation of quality assurance programs in the everyday laboratory practice, provided that representative images are taken, standard diagnostic criteria are applied, and the participants have already acquired sufficient experience in the evaluation of digital images. The use of static telecytology systems for proficiency testing provision is possible, and the first steps towards this direction are already taken in Greece.

Cloud computing promotes the concept of bedside cytopathology, point-of-care cytopathology, and instant cytopathology. It gives the cytopathologists, pathologists, physicians, and even patients the possibility to review images and medical data on any display device with a simple Internet connection. Emerging information technologies are expected to provide flexibility to all cytopathology services and will undoubtedly revolutionize the way cytopathology data is stored, accessed, and processed in a modern laboratory environment.

REFERENCES

Archondakis, S., Georgoulakis, J., Stamataki, M., Anninos, D., Skagias, L., & Panayiotides, I. et al. (2009). Telecytology: a tool for quality assessment and improvement in the evaluation of thyroid fine-needle aspiration specimens. *Telemedicine Journal and e-Health, 5*(7), 713–717. doi:10.1089/tmj.2009.0037 PMID:19694595

Brerider-Jr-McNai, P. (1996). User requirements on the future laboratory information systems. *Computer Methods and Programs in Biomedicine, 50*(2), 87–93. doi:10.1016/0169-2607(96)01738-Q PMID:8875016

Briscoe, D., Tellado, M. V., Buckner, S. B., Rosenthal, D. L., & O'Leary, T. J. (2000). Telecytologic diagnosis of breast fine needle aspiration biopsies. *Acta Cytologica, 44*, 175–180. doi:10.1159/000326357 PMID:10740603

Georgiou, A., & Westbrook, J. I. (2007). Computerized order entry systems and pathology services — a synthesis of the evidence. *The Clinical Biochemist. Reviews / Australian Association of Clinical Biochemists, 27*, 79–87.

Khurana, K. K. (2012). Telecytology and its evolving role in cytopathology. *Diagnostic Cytopathology, 40*(6), 498–502. doi:10.1002/dc.22822 PMID:22619124

Kubono, K. (2004). Quality management system in the medical laboratory-ISO15189 and laboratory accreditation. *Rinsho Byori, 2*(3), 274–278.

Kubono, K. (2007). Outline of the revision of ISO 15189 and accreditation of medical laboratory for specified health checkup. *Rinsho Byori, 55*(11), 1029–1036. PMID:18154036

Nagy, G. K., & Newton, L. E. (2006). Cytopathology proficiency testing: Where do we go from here? *Diagnostic Cytopathology*, *34*, 257–264. doi:10.1002/dc.20361 PMID:16544329

Okada, M. (2002). Future of laboratory informatics. *Rinsho Byori*, *50*(7), 691–693. PMID:12187706

Pantanowitz, L., Hornish, M., & Goulart, R. A. (2009). The impact of digital imaging in the field of cytopathology. *CytoJournal*, *6*, 6. doi:10.4103/1742-6413.48606 PMID:19495408

Rosenthal, A., Mork, P., Li, M. H., Stanford, J., Koester, D., & Reynolds, P. (2010). Cloud computing: a new business paradigm for biomedical information sharing. *Journal of Biomedical Informatics*, *43*(2), 342–353. doi:10.1016/j.jbi.2009.08.014 PMID:19715773

Stewart, J. III, Miyazaki, K., Bevans-Wilkins, K., Ye, C., Kurtycz, D. F., & Selvaggi, S. M. (2007). Virtual microscopy for cytology proficiency testing: are we there yet? *Cancer*, *111*(4), 203–209. doi:10.1002/cncr.22766 PMID:17580360

Thrall, M., Pantanowitz, L., & Khalbuss, W. (2011). Telecytology: Clinical applications, current challenges, and future benefits. *Journal of Pathology Informatics*, *2*, 51. doi:10.4103/2153-3539.91129 PMID:22276242

Vacata, V., Jahns-Streubel, G., Baldus, M., & Wood, W. G. (2007). Practical solution for control of the pre-analytical phase in decentralized clinical laboratories for meeting the requirements of the medical laboratory accreditation standard DIN EN ISO 15189. *Clinical Laboratory*, *53*, 211–215. PMID:17447659

KEY TERMS AND DEFINITIONS

Accreditation: Procedure by which an authoritative body gives formal recognition that a body or person is competent to carry out specific tasks.

Cytopathology: Medical Specialty based on microscopic evaluation of cells from various human organs.

Telecytology: The process of diagnostic cytopathology performed on digital images, transferred via telecommunication networks from one site to another.

Proficiency Testing: Evaluation of participant performance against pre-established criteria by means of interlaboratory comparisons. The term may include a quantitative scheme, qualitative scheme, sequential scheme, simultaneous scheme, single occasion exercise, continuous scheme, sampling or data transformation and interpretation.

IS0: (The International Organization for Standardization) Is a worldwide federation of national standards bodies (ISO member bodies). The work of preparing International Standards is normally carried out through ISO technical committees.

Quality Management: Management activities and functions involved in the determination of quality policy and its implementation through quality planning and quality assurance (including quality control).

Laboratory Information System: It is a software-based laboratory and information management system that offers workflow and data tracking support, flexible architecture, and smart data exchange interfaces.

Chapter 12
Innovative Architecture to Enhance Quality of Service for Laboratory Management Information Systems

Naeem A. Mahoto
Mehran University of Engineering and Technology, Pakistan

Faisal K. Shaikh
Mehran University of Engineering and Technology, Pakistan & University of Umm Al-Qura, Saudi Arabia

B. S. Chowdhry
Mehran University of Engineering and Technology, Pakistan

ABSTRACT

Technological improvements have changed the life style in the modern era, where communication has become easier compared with olden days. Technological solutions have been deployed in every sector including business, education, and health services. Although a number of solutions are proposed for improvements in the healthcare sector, the complexity and growing interest in this sector have created new approaches. This chapter proposes an innovative architecture for the laboratory management information system to enhance the quality and management issues. The proposed architecture integrates two major fields, namely wireless technology and data mining. The wireless technology enables the collection of data easily and wirelessly, and data mining ensures meaningful and novel knowledge discovery from the collected data. In particular, the architecture helps management in three different ways: (1) prevention of risks/errors using technological solutions, (2) an environment to respond rapidly to adverse events, and (3) construction of knowledge base for future guidelines.

DOI: 10.4018/978-1-4666-6320-6.ch012

INTRODUCTION

The Information Technology (IT) has taken great attention since last few decades, and it has altered the lifestyle. Healthcare agencies are one of the examples that have taken fruits from emerging technological solutions (Kushniruk, 2013; Tongsiri, 2013). For instance, Health Information Technology (HIT) using hardware and software maintains and analyzes information of health data. However, poor design may risk the patient's safety (Jha, 2009; Kushniruk, 2013). Electronic Health Records (EHRs), being part of HIT, are cost effective in comparison with manually and paper-based systems (Wang, 2003). EHRs significantly improve health services for health providers (Jha, 2009; Wu, 2006). Furthermore, health is an essential element in human's life, and it needs to be taken care, because the lack of immediate care can cause a problem for a long time in life. Developed nations draw great attention towards health on priority. For example, by allocating higher percentage of the annual budget on health.

The growing increase in interest and complexity of healthcare has caused new approaches as the center of attention for researchers (Bates, 2003). Every day, hospital management using HIT solutions store a large amount of hospital data having records about patients, disease diagnosis, statistics about medical tests and many more. Information management is a fundamental factor for healthcare providers (Chassin, 1998). The key issue in healthcare domain is the procedure to collect the medical data (i.e., hospital data) and then interpretation of the collected data. Firstly, the collection of data is resolved using computerized solutions e.g., HIT solutions for monitoring the laboratory information system. Regular and continuous human monitoring is inherently boring and unsuitable (Bates, 2003). Instead, wireless technology can be exploited to facilitate hospital management. For example, healthcare data can be collected with the help of wireless sensors for the ease, and computerized applica-

tions can generate reports and other calculations inquired by management. The literature reports that hospital computerized physician order entry (CPOE) caused reduction in medication errors by 81% (Koppel, 2005). To maximize the efficiency of huge electronic data resources available in hospitals, the electronic surveillance system has been suggested (Freeman, 2013). Hence, use of sensors in collecting hospital data would significantly facilitate hospital management. Secondly, the large collections of data can profitability be analyzed using data mining techniques to extract meaningful and important information (Mahoto, 2013). The derived information can help in managing hospital resources, as well as care guidelines. Several techniques and methods are proposed to extract valuable knowledge from healthcare data (Baralis, 2010; Antonelli, 2012; Antonelli, 2013a; Antonelli, 2013b).

The availability of wearable and implantable sensors that are parts of networks known as *wireless body area networks* (WBANs) significantly help to collect the vital signs of the humans, which can be very useful for the laboratory management information system, where data is fed to the system. WBAN is a new dimension of Wireless Sensor Networks (WSNs) and have evolved in recent years due to significant innovation in sensor miniaturization, embedded computing, and wireless technologies. WBAN has received tremendous interest from academia, industry, and consumer device manufacturers due to their novel defense and commercial applications. During the past decade, the drivers for WSN research were applications of surveillance, monitoring, tracking, and automation, but the drivers behind WBAN growth are applications that directly impact on quality of human life, including telemedicine, ubiquitous health care, laboratory management, sports, and entertainment. Furthermore, because of a sedentary lifestyle and lack of exercises, the society is moving toward a disastrous situation, and life-threatening diseases are being diagnosed in almost every family. The traditional healthcare systems were not designed to cater to the huge flow of patients and are inadequate in current scenarios.

In simple words, a WBAN is a network of multiple interconnected low-power, lightweight, intelligent nodes that may be inside the body, on the body, or near the body, and perform sensing, processing, and communication. With the emerging intriguing application of WBANs, they will have a significant impact on our lifestyle and will change the concept of how humans can use information technology for saving human life, improving its quality, and making health care affordable and accessible for everyone. As depicted in Figure 1, WBAN is deployed on the human body in order to collect details about their vital signs such as heart rate, blood pressure, ECG, temperature etc. Here, S1, S2 and S3 are the sensing nodes. These vital signs are then routed to the central node, G1, which is also called the Gateway. Gateway is generally a personal device such as mobile phone, PDA etc. The Gateway sends the collected data to the medical health centre (MHC) through a third party carrier, for instance a laptop connected to the internet (PC1). After the data reaches the MHC, the doctor can analyze the data and prescribe the medicine for the patient accordingly (Latré, 2011) and instruct the laboratories for further tests and diagnosis. However, ongoing research area is the usage of actuators. The data can also be sent back to the appropriate device, which has to start the action (e.g., inject the medication).

With the existence of WBANs, a huge amount of data is generated and collected for post processing at MHC and laboratories. The large collections of data can profitability be analyzed by exploiting data mining techniques to uncover meaningful and important information (Mahoto, 2013). The discovered knowledge can help in managing hospital resources, as well as care services. A number of techniques and methods are proposed to extract valuable knowledge from healthcare data (Baralis, 2010; Antonelli, 2012; Antonelli, 2013a; Antonelli, 2013b). For example, Cluster analysis has been carried out in (Antonelli, 2013b) by means of clustering – a data mining technique. Frequent medical pathways are derived by means of sequential pattern mining in Baralis (2010). Moreover, knowledge management helps decision-making activities with the provision of

Figure 1. WBAN scenario

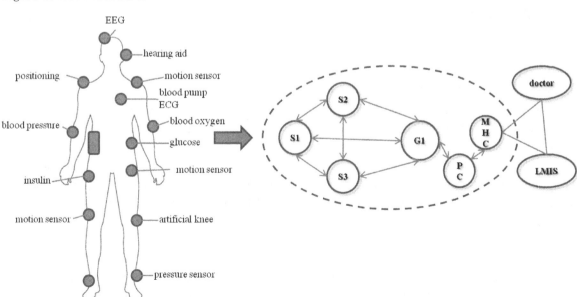

sophisticated techniques, application tools and methods (Wickramasinghe, 2013).

The proposed architecture in this chapter is an innovative concept that integrates the wireless technology (i.e., WBANs) and data mining techniques to increase the Quality of Service (QoS) in hospitals. Particularly, the architecture can help to reduce the risks and error rates of the laboratory information system in three different ways: (1) preventing risks/errors by deploying technological solutions. For example, necessary proactive actions would be taken to prevent possible risks/ errors based on previous known patterns, (2) facilitating with a rapid response to adverse events, and (3) building a knowledge domain for future guidelines by tracing and getting feedback from adverse events.

The rest of the chapter is organized as follows. Section *Background* presents the wireless technology and data mining techniques used in healthcare services. The details of the proposed architecture are described in *Innovative Architecture* section, which also contain the possible *Applications and Limitations*. Further, *Future Research Directions* are given, and finally conclusions are drawn in the *Conclusion* section.

BACKGROUND

The design of the Laboratory information management systems (LIMS) helps the analytical laboratory research with the optimal instrumental access (Prasad, 2012). Initially, LIMS has been used for Quality Control and Quality Assurance in pharmaceutical and other relevant industries. Later its usage has been expanded to many sectors like agriculture, environment, and manufacturing etc. (Prasad, 2012). The organizations get fruits from Management Information Systems (MIS) by significantly effective management.

Hospitals, especially intense care units, produce a huge amount of data every day. To manage such data effectively, Clinical Information Systems (CIS) are implemented, which provide accuracy in data entry and the monitoring issues (Plenderleith, 2013). Additionally, data mining allows uncovering new knowledge for decision-making in several application domains including healthcare. The data mining algorithms for several different techniques such as classification, clustering and association rule mining used for biomedical data and healthcare data are presented in Yoo (2012). Clinical pathways analysis is addressed in Huang (2012) by means of process mining, which aims at finding patterns of the clinical pathways from workflow logs. An approach is proposed in (Buczak, 2012) that focuses on data mining activities to design a patient care model. Furthermore, clustering is performed on the patient care model to group together similar patients. To develop a decision support system, analysis of medical data, in particular, dialysis patients using data mining techniques is reported in Yeh (2011).

The ongoing WBAN research is mostly concentrated on the telehealth applications since it is gaining social acceptance in this area due to the ability to provide ubiquitous and pervasive monitoring of physiological and biochemical parameters in an unobtrusive manner. In addition, sedentary lifestyle has introduced life-threatening diseases, and the existing means of diagnosis and treatment of these types of diseases are inadequate and costly. The current monitoring system cannot capture transient abnormalities and other momentary events. They are based on qualitative observation, whereas WBANs provides quantitative data collection through real-time sensing, extending health care beyond the confines of geographical limits. In traditional health care, the life-threatening disorders get undetected; however, WBANs will provide long-term trend analysis and handle transient abnormalities, emergency alerting, and improved comfort (Patel, 2010).

The HealthPAL™ (Alhere, 2013) from MedApps is a portable and dedicated remote monitoring device that provides vital biometric data. It seamlessly gathers and sends patient readings to their electronic medical record for access by care providers. Another device is NanoSonic's new EKGear™ sensor shirt that measures heart rate and EKG and wirelessly transmits the information to a remote display and storage unit (Rademakers, 2013). Industry giants like Philips have launched products that that will monitor physiological states without restricting movements such as the Telehealth Solutions (Wang, 2007) which specified the potential uses of WBANs in health care.

In Chung (2008), sensor devices and server based architecture for health care monitoring is proposed. To provide services for the elderly people, components based system architecture of health care monitoring is designed in Bourouis (2011). The system monitors location and health status using Bluetooth and smartphone with accelerometer. In Osmani (2012), different sensor placements techniques are applied for analyzing the efficiency of WBAN.

A hospital environment is considered in the CodeBlue project (Shnayder, 2005) using the Zigbee standard. The publish-subscribe model is used to exchange the data among patients and the MHC. There is no centralized database or server involved for data storage and is stored in a P2P manner (Sahar, 2013). The Advanced Health and Disaster Aid Network (AID-N) is developed at Johns Hopkins University (Gao, 2007) for mass casualty incidents where RFID tags are deployed on the victims. In order to facilitate the communication between WBAN and MHC servers additional wireless capabilities are utilized such as WiFi or GSM networks. The Wearable Health Monitoring Systems (WHMS) is being developed at the University of Alabama (Milenković, 2006) and target a larger-scale telemedicine system for ambulatory health status monitoring.

INNOVATIVE ARCHITECTURE

The proposed architecture is innovative, since, it proposes two major fields to be integrated to get fruits in a laboratory management information system. Both fields have been beneficial to make ease and comfortable the life of humans. The architecture would not only provide the macro level information about healthcare services but also provides the micro level details for further procedures. Figure 2 shows an innovative architecture for the laboratory information system to improve Quality of Service (QoS). Mainly, it comprises of two blocks WSN/BAN Module and Data Mining Module, which are described in the following.

Components of Architecture

The architecture contains two blocks, which in turn comprise of several other components. Each block is addressed, in details, as below.

WBAN Module

The WBAN module is responsible for retrieving the data from the patient body and sends it towards doctors and laboratories for further investigations. The WBAN module is further divided into several layers to properly acquire and send the data across the network.

Topology Control Layer

This layer is responsible for maintaining and managing the WBAN topology on the human body such that appropriate data can be obtained for further processing at medical centers and laboratories. For WBANs three possible topologies

Figure 2. Architecture of the laboratory information system

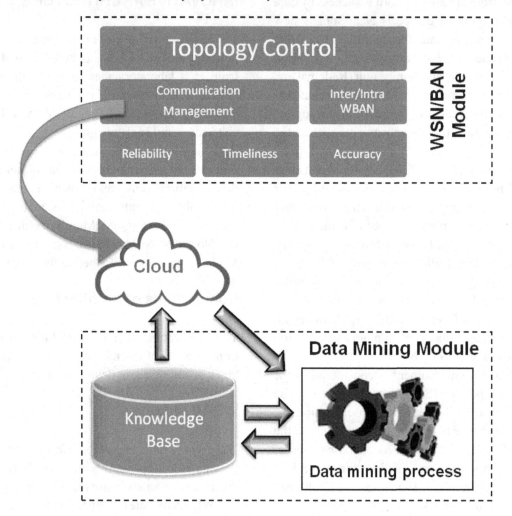

can be established, i.e., star, multihop and mesh topology as shown in Figure 3. Depending on the application requirement and the current network scenario the topology control layer switches across these topologies or can choose a combination of them for proper communication. The topology control layer switches the power levels of the nodes to manage the topology.

Communication Management Layer

The role of this layer is to select the appropriate communication standard for communicating between the WBAN and the cloud environment

for storing the collected data of the patient. Currently there are many communication standards available for WBANs.

1. **IEEE 802.11:** This standard is used in WLANs, having a large form factor and is power hungry.
2. **IEEE 802.15.1:** Bluetooth standard is less flexible and utilizes high-power consumption.
3. **IEEE 802.15.4:** The ZigBee supports low-power devices and delivery of periodic and repetitive data. ZigBee is a fast, scalable, and low-power option for WBANs.

Figure 3. Possible WBAN topologies

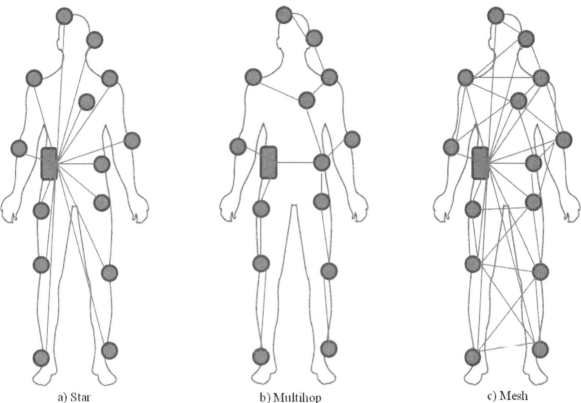

a) Star   b) Multihop   c) Mesh

4. **Ultra Wideband:** The energy consumption of WBANs cannot be met by Bluetooth/ZigBee and, so UWB offers a better low-cost integrated solution. The complexity is shifted in the receiver so that the transmitter is ultra low power.

Inter/Intra WBAN Layer

There are two different infrastructures (Ullah, 2012), i.e., managed and autonomous WBANs as shown in Figure 4. The managed WBAN (also called as Inter WBAN) has a long-range connection such as a GSM network to send an alert message to the closest hospital via the cloud environment. On the contrary, in autonomous WBANs (also called as Intra WBAN), has no connection with the long-range network; it is more intelligent and has

been programmed to take decisions autonomously, e.g., if the glucose level goes high; the actuator can inject insulin. Furthermore, the basic types of WBANs can be categorized as stand-alone WBANs and interconnected WBANs. According to Wang and Pei (Wang, 2007), stand-alone WBAN is a network with sensor nodes in or in the immediate vicinity of the bearer. The stand-alone WBAN can be connected to the Internet. The data can be raw or locally processed and sent in real time. The service provider or health-care provider can send feedback/alert/instructions accordingly.

Accuracy Layer

The accuracy layer is responsible for the accurate data acquisition from WBAN sensors. Accurate data collection is important for correct decision

Figure 4. Inter/Intra WBAN architectures

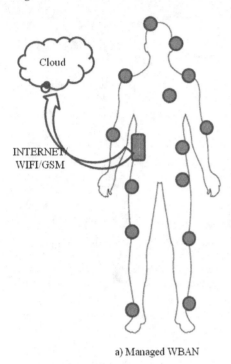

a) Managed WBAN

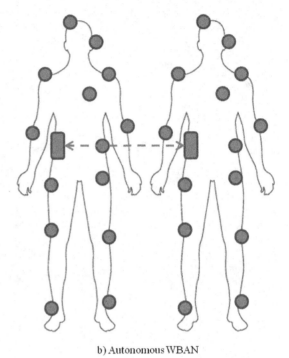

b) Autonomous WBAN

making at the healthcare provider end. This layer provides mechanisms and procedures for accurate data extraction and also provides solutions to overcome errors in obtained data.

Timeliness Layer

Generally medical data require to be made available to the application with some time bounds. Accordingly, the timeliness layer provides mechanisms to send data by fulfilling the latency requirements of the application.

Reliability Layer

The main objective is to assure and maximize the end-to-end reliability of data transfer. Generally, the data loss is due to poor links, perturbations, movement of body and congestion in the network. The reliability layer provides various acknowledgement mechanisms and retransmissions techniques to ensure reliable data delivery.

Data Mining Module

The data-mining module of the architecture performs data mining techniques and algorithms to find out meaningful knowledge from the data stored in the cloud by WAS/BAN Module. The laboratory data is retrieved from the clouds for the mining process, which includes a set of activities such as preprocessing, transformation for converting data into a suitable format for the mining process.

Preprocessing

This step performs cleaning, and segmentation of the data and selection of the data is processed for further actions. For example, the stored data contain records of resources, management staff and patients being diagnosed. The preprocessing step selects the subset of data and removes unnecessary and additional data to further activities.

Transformation

This step converts preprocessed data into the format, which is suitable for the data-mining algorithm being applied to get knowledge.

Mining Process

This step actually extracts knowledge from the transformed data. A number of data mining algorithms are introduced for knowledge extraction, such as sequential pattern mining (Agrawal, 1995), association rule discovery (Agrawal, 1993) and frequent items (Agrawal, 1994) etc. These well-established algorithms could profitably be exploited in the laboratory management information system.

Evaluation

In the evaluation step, the derived knowledge is accessed and validated by the domain expert (i.e., medical expert). The evaluated knowledge could be utilized in several domains like medical guidelines enhancement, resource management, and decision-making.

After important hospital and resources information is extracted from the raw data, it is stored into the local knowledge domain. The copy of the knowledge domain results is also stored into the cloud, which facilitates the management personnel to easily access it and get fruits from the mined results. The technological equipment would monitor the events as well as store and send such data to the data mining module for knowledge discovery. The WBANs devices can automatically warn the laboratory management personnel for any undesired event by getting feed on knowledge base. The knowledge base would keep on increasing day-by-day and would help in decision-making issues, as well. For instance,

several risks could be prevented based on historical information extracted from the knowledge base.

Applications and Limitations

The proposed architecture would be beneficial for the public as well private healthcare/laboratory management sectors. It allows collecting sparse hospital data with ease and monitor hospital activities effectively and easily without continuous human monitoring. The continuous data is automatically collected through sensors and accessible to laboratory management. The use of knowledge base would increase the quality of healthcare services as well as help in managing resources significantly. For example, medical experts would be able to predict the complications and possible symptoms of a certain disease condition based on knowledge contained in the knowledge base. Moreover, healthcare treatments can also be updated on a timely basis, since medical science is an evolving process. Sensors would indicate the adverse events and management could tackle such situations rapidly. The micro level details of data will be available for in-depth analysis in the laboratory. Precisely, the innovative architecture would help management not only tackle the management issues efficiently but also increase the quality in health services effectively. The knowledge base, a central hub available in the cloud, would work as an expert system to respond to the queries in solving both management and health services issues. This knowledge base simultaneously can be accessed by different locations of healthcare providers.

The architecture still needs improvements to manage the constraints that are inherent in the integrated architecture. For example, the noise in sensory data and optimal use of the batteries used for sensors. Furthermore, network security is an open issue that needs to be addressed properly.

FUTURE RESEARCH DIRECTIONS

The future directions will investigate the distributed issues in the healthcare data collection and accessing to get useful knowledge in a distributed environment. Particularly, the aspects of sharing the information between heterogeneous terminals working for the same pathology will be addressed. For example, different operating systems would be allowed to access the information stored in the knowledge domain located somewhere on the web. Further, network issues of the wireless network technology (i.e., WSNs and WBANs) will be addressed to ensure the security and privacy of laboratory data. Besides, accuracy of the sensory data, being one of the challenging issues in wireless body area networks (WBANs), will also be investigated.

CONCLUSION

The innovative architecture proposed in this chapter emphasized on integration of wireless technology and data mining in order to get easy access to the hospital data. The electronic records of patients, as well as equipment used in the laboratory, can profitably be used in decision-making and prediction exploiting data mining techniques to enhance Quality of Service (QoS) in hospitals. The implementation of the proposed architecture will reduce the risks and error rates as well as increase the efficiency by reducing time and cost of the laboratory management information system. Particularly, the architecture offers three different mechanisms to improve the laboratory management information system: 1) deployment of technological solutions to prevent risks/errors, 2) facilitating management to react rapidly to adverse events, and 3) building a central knowledge system (knowledge base), which comprises of extracted knowledge from collected data by means of data mining techniques. The health care management can get benefits in terms of effectively utilizing human resources, medical equipment and providing quality healthcare services with the help of knowledge extracted from data (i.e., knowledge base).

ACKNOWLEDGMENT

This research work is partially supported by Mehran University of Engineering and Technology, Jamshoro, Pakistan, National ICT R&D Fund, Ministry of Information Technology, Pakistan under National Grassroots ICT Research Initiative and by grant number 10-INF1236-10 from the Long-Term National Plan for Science, Technology and Innovation (LT-NPSTI), the King Abdul-Aziz City for Science and Technology (KACST), Kingdom of Saudi Arabia. We also thank the Science and Technology Unit at Umm Al-Qura University for their continued logistics support.

REFERENCES

Agrawal, R., Imieliński, T., & Swami, A. (1993). Mining association rules between sets of items in large databases. *SIGMOD Record, 22*(2), 207–216. doi:10.1145/170036.170072

Agrawal, R., & Srikant, R. (1994). Fast algorithms for mining association rules. In *Proc. 20th Int. Conf. Very Large Data Bases, VLDB* (Vol. 1215, pp. 487-499). ACM.

Agrawal, R., & Srikant, R. (1995). Mining sequential patterns. In *Proceedings of Data Engineering,* (pp. 3-14). IEEE.

Antonelli, D., Baralis, E., Bruno, G., Cerquitelli, T., Chiusano, S., & Mahoto, N. A. (2013b). Analysis of diabetic patients through their examination history. *Expert Systems with Applications, 40*(11), 4672–4678. doi:10.1016/j.eswa.2013.02.006

Antonelli, D., Baralis, E., Bruno, G., Chiusano, S., Mahoto, N. A., & Petrigni, C. (2012). Analysis of diagnostic pathways for colon cancer. *Flexible Services and Manufacturing Journal, 24*(4), 379–399. doi:10.1007/s10696-011-9095-2

Antonelli, D., Baralis, E., Bruno, G., Chiusano, S., Mahoto, N. A., & Petrigni, C. (2013a). Extraction of Medical Pathways from Electronic Patient Records. In I. Association (Ed.), *Data Mining: Concepts, Methodologies, Tools, and Applications* (pp. 1004–1018). Hershey, PA: Information Science Reference.

Baralis, E., Bruno, G., Chiusano, S., Domenici, V. C., Mahoto, N. A., & Petrigni, C. (2010). Analysis of medical pathways by means of frequent closed sequences. In *Knowledge-Based and Intelligent Information and Engineering Systems* (pp. 418–425). Springer. doi:10.1007/978-3-642-15393-8_47

Bates, D. W., & Gawande, A. A. (2003). Improving safety with information technology. *The New England Journal of Medicine, 348*(25), 2526–2534. doi:10.1056/NEJMsa020847 PMID:12815139

Bourouis, A., Feham, M., & Bouchachia, A. (2011). Ubiquitous Mobile Health Monitoring System for elderly (UMHMSE). *International Journal of Computer Science and Information Technology, 3*(3). doi:10.5121/ijcsit.2011.3306

Buczak, A. L., Moniz, L. J., Feighner, B. H., & Lombardo, J. S. (2009, March). Mining electronic medical records for patient care patterns. In *Proceedings of Computational Intelligence and Data Mining,* (pp. 146-153). IEEE.

Chassin, M. R., & Galvin, R. W. (1998). The urgent need to improve health care quality. *Journal of the American Medical Association, 280*(11), 1000–1005. doi:10.1001/jama.280.11.1000 PMID:9749483

Chung, W. Y., Lee, Y. D., & Jung, S. J. (2008, August). A wireless sensor network compatible wearable u-healthcare monitoring system using integrated ECG, accelerometer and SpO<inf>2</inf>. In *Proceedings of Engineering in Medicine and Biology Society,* (pp. 1529-1532). IEEE.

Freeman, R., Moore, L. S. P., García Álvarez, L., Charlett, A., & Holmes, A. (2013). Advances in electronic surveillance for healthcare-associated infections in the 21st century: A systematic review. *Journal of Hospital Infection, 84*(2), 106–119.

Gao, T., Massey, T., Selavo, L., Crawford, D., Chen, B. R., & Lorincz, K. et al. (2007). The advanced health and disaster aid network: A light-weight wireless medical system for triage. *IEEE Transactions on* Biomedical Circuits and Systems, *1*(3), 203–216.

Alhere Healthpal. (2013). Retrieved from http://alereconnect.com/solutions/alere-healthpal/

Huang, Z., Lu, X., & Duan, H. (2012). On mining clinical pathway patterns from medical behaviors. *Artificial Intelligence in Medicine, 56*(1), 35-50

Jha, A. K., DesRoches, C. M., Campbell, E. G., Donelan, K., Rao, S. R., & Ferris, T. G. et al. (2009). Use of electronic health records in US hospitals. *The New England Journal of Medicine, 360*(16), 1628–1638. doi:10.1056/NEJMsa0900592 PMID:19321858

Koppel, R., Metlay, J. P., Cohen, A., Abaluck, B., Localio, A. R., Kimmel, S. E., & Strom, B. L. (2005). Role of computerized physician order entry systems in facilitating medication errors. *Journal of the American Medical Association, 293*(10), 1197–1203. doi:10.1001/jama.293.10.1197 PMID:15755942

Kushniruk, A. W., Bates, D. W., Bainbridge, M., Househ, M. S., & Borycki, E. M. (2013). National efforts to improve health information system safety in Canada, the United States of America and England. *International Journal of Medical Informatics, 82*(5), e149–e160.

Latré, B., Braem, B., Moerman, I., Blondia, C., & Demeester, P. (2011). A survey on wireless body area networks. *Wireless Networks, 17*(1), 1–18. doi:10.1007/s11276-010-0252-4

Mahoto, N. A. (2013). *Data mining techniques for complex application domains*. (Doctoral dissertation). Politecnico di Torino, Torino, Italy.

Milenković, A., Otto, C., & Jovanov, E. (2006). Wireless sensor networks for personal health monitoring: Issues and an implementation. *Computer Communications, 29*(13), 2521–2533. doi:10.1016/j.comcom.2006.02.011

Osmani, A. (2012). Design and Evaluation of New Intelligent Sensor Placement Algorithm to Improve Coverage Problem in Wireless Sensor Networks. *Journal of Basic and Applied Scientific Research, 2*(2), 1431–1440.

Patel, M., & Wang, J. (2010). Applications, challenges, and prospective in emerging body area networking technologies. *IEEE Wireless Communications, 17*(1), 80–88. doi:10.1109/MWC.2010.5416354

Plenderleith, J. L. (2013). Clinical information systems in the intensive care unit. *Anaesthesia and Intensive Care Medicine, 14*(1), 19–21. doi:10.1016/j.mpaic.2012.11.003

Prasad, P. J., & Bodhe, G. L. (2012). Trends in laboratory information management system. *Chemometrics and Intelligent Laboratory Systems, 118*, 187–192. doi:10.1016/j.chemolab.2012.07.001

Rademakers, L., Coleman, D., & Reiny, S. (2013). Spinoff 2012. In *Dry Electrodes Facilitate Remote Health Monitoring* (pp. 42-43). Washington, DC: Government Printing Office.

Sahar, S. N., Shaikh, F. K., & Jokhio, I. A. (2013). P2P Data Management in Mobile Wireless Sensor Network. Mehran University Research Journal of Engineering and Technology, 32 (2), 339-352.

Shnayder, V., Chen, B. R., Lorincz, K., Jones, T. R. F., & Welsh, M. (2005, November). Sensor networks for medical care. SenSys, 5, 314-314.

Tongsiri, S. (2013). Electronic Health Records: Benefits and Contribution to Healthcare System. In Next-Generation Wireless Technologies (pp. 273-281). Springer.

Ullah, S., Higgins, H., Braem, B., Latre, B., Blondia, C., Moerman, I., & Kwak, K. S. (2012). A comprehensive survey of wireless body area networks. *Journal of Medical Systems, 36*(3), 1065–1094. doi:10.1007/s10916-010-9571-3 PMID:20721685

Wang, B., & Pei, Y. (2007). Body Area Networks. In B. Furht (Ed.), *Encyclopedia of Wireless and Mobile Communications*. Taylor & Francis.

Wang, S. J., Middleton, B., Prosser, L. A., Bardon, C. G., Spurr, C. D., & Carchidi, P. J. et al. (2003). A cost-benefit analysis of electronic medical records in primary care. *The American Journal of Medicine, 114*(5), 397–403. doi:10.1016/S0002-9343(03)00057-3 PMID:12714130

Wickramasinghe, N. (2013). Implicit and Explicit Knowledge Assets in Healthcare. In *Pervasive Health Knowledge Management* (pp. 15–26). Springer. doi:10.1007/978-1-4614-4514-2_3

Wu, S., Chaudhry, B., Wang, J., Maglione, M., Mojica, W., & Roth, E. et al. (2006). Systematic review: impact of health information technology on quality, efficiency, and costs of medical care. *Annals of Internal Medicine*, *144*(10), 742–752. doi:10.7326/0003-4819-144-10-200605160-00125 PMID:16702590

Yeh, J. Y., Wu, T. H., & Tsao, C. W. (2011). Using data mining techniques to predict hospitalization of hemodialysis patients. *Decision Support Systems*, *50*(2), 439–448. doi:10.1016/j.dss.2010.11.001

Yoo, I., Alafaireet, P., Marinov, M., Pena-Hernandez, K., Gopidi, R., Chang, J. F., & Hua, L. (2012). Data mining in healthcare and biomedicine: a survey of the literature. *Journal of Medical Systems*, *36*(4), 2431–2448. doi:10.1007/s10916-011-9710-5 PMID:21537851

ADDITIONAL READING

Afridi, M. J., & Farooq, M. (2011). OG-Miner: An intelligent health tool for achieving millennium development goals (MDGs) in m-health environments. *Proceedings of the 44th Hawaii International Conference on System Sciences (HICSS 2011)*, (pp. 1-10).

Antonelli, D., Baralis, E., Bruno, G., Cerquitelli, T., Chiusano, S., & Mahoto, N. (2013). Analysis of diabetic patients through their examination history. *Expert Systems with Applications*, *40*(11), 4672–4678. doi:10.1016/j.eswa.2013.02.006

Bell, D. S., Cima, L., Seiden, D. S., Nakazono, T. T., Alcouloumre, M. S., & Cunningham, W. E. (2012). Effects of laboratory data exchange in the care of patients with HIV. *International Journal of Medical Informatics*, *81*, e74–e82. doi:10.1016/j.ijmedinf.2012.07.012 PMID:22906370

Choi, K., Chung, S., Rhee, H., & Suh, Y. (2010). Classification and sequential pattern analysis for improving managerial efficiency and providing better medical service in public healthcare centers. *Journal of Korean Society of Medical Informatics*, *16*(2), 67–76. PMID:21818426

Chowdhry, N. P., Arain, A. A., Chowdhry, B. S., & Baloch, A. K. (2010). Grid for Post Operative Care through Wireless Sensor Network. In Handbook of Grid Technologies for e-Health: Applications for Telemedicine Services & Delivery, edited by Dr. Ekaterina Kldiashvili, Georgian Telemedicine Union (Association), Georgia. IGI Global publisher (USA)

Chowdhry, N. P., Ashraf, A., Chowdhry, B. S., Baloch, A. K., Ansari, A. W., & De Meer, H. (2010). Grid for Post Operative Care through Wireless Sensor Networks. *Grid technologies for e-Health*, 164.

Correal, N. S., & Patwari, N. (2001). Wireless sensor networks: Challenges and opportunities. In *Proceedings of the 2001 Virginia Tech Symposium on Wireless Personal Communications* (pp. 1-9)

Edwards, J. R., Pollock, D. A., Kupronis, B. A., Li, W., Tolson, J. S., & Peterson, K. D. et al. (2008). Making use of electronic data: The National Healthcare Safety Network eSurveillance Initiative. *American Journal of Infection Control*, *36*(3), S21–S26. doi:10.1016/j.ajic.2007.07.007 PMID:18374208

Hanson, M. A., Powell, H. C., Barth, A. T., Ringgenberg, K., Calhoun, B. H., Aylor, J. H., & Lach, J. (2009). Body area sensor networks: Challenges and opportunities. *Computer*, *42*(1), 58–65. doi:10.1109/MC.2009.5

Kazemzadeh, R. S., & Sartipi, K. (2006). Incorporating data mining applications into clinical guidelines. *Proceedings of the 19th IEEE Symposium on Computer-Based Medical Systems (CBMS'06)*.

Law, Y. W., Doumen, J., & Hartel, P. (2006). Survey and benchmark of block ciphers for wireless sensor networks. [TOSN]. *ACM Transactions on Sensor Networks, 2*(1), 65–93. doi:10.1145/1138127.1138130

Linder, J. A., Schnipper, J. L., & Middleton, B. (2012). Method of electronic health record documentation and quality of primary care. *Journal of the American Medical Informatics Association, 19*(6), 1019–1024. doi:10.1136/amiajnl-2011-000788 PMID:22610494

Mainwaring, A., Culler, D., Polastre, J., Szewczyk, R., & Anderson, J. (2002, September). Wireless sensor networks for habitat monitoring. In *Proceedings of the 1st ACM international workshop on Wireless sensor networks and applications* (pp. 88-97). ACM.

Marinkovic, S. J., Popovici, E. M., Spagnol, C., Faul, S., & Marnane, W. P. (2009). Energy-efficient low duty cycle MAC protocol for wireless body area networks. *IEEE Transactions on Information Technology in Biomedicine, 13*(6), 915–925. doi:10.1109/TITB.2009.2033591 PMID:19846380

Mohamudally, N., & Khan, D. M. (2011). Application of a unified medical data miner (umdm) for prediction, classification, interpretation and visualization on medical datasets: The diabetes dataset case. In *International conference on advances in data mining: Applications and theoretical aspects (ICDM)* (pp. 78–95). Berlin, Heidelberg: Springer-Verlag.

Omta, W. A., Egan, D. A., Spruit, M. R., & Brinkkemper, S. (2012). Information Architecture in High Throughput Screening. *Procedia Technology, 5*, 696–705. doi:10.1016/j.protcy.2012.09.077

Otto, C., Milenkovic, A., Sanders, C., & Jovanov, E. (2006). System architecture of a wireless body area sensor network for ubiquitous health monitoring. *Journal of Mobile Multimedia, 1*(4), 307–326.

Phanich, M., Pholkul, P., & Phimoltares, S. (2010). Food recommendation system using clustering analysis for diabetic patients. In *IEEE international conference on information science and applications* (pp. 1–8). ICISA. doi:10.1109/ICISA.2010.5480416

Ramli, S. N., Ahmad, R., Abdollah, M. F., & Dutkiewicz, E. (2013, January). A biometric-based security for data authentication in Wireless Body Area Network (WBAN). In *15th International Conference on Advanced Communication Technology (ICACT), 2013* (pp. 998-1001). IEEE.

Rossille, D., Cuggia, M., Arnault, A., Bouget, J., & Le Beux, P. (2008). Managing an emergency department by analysing HIS medical data: A focus on elderly patient clinical pathways. *Health Care Management Science, 11*, 139–146. doi:10.1007/s10729-008-9059-6

Ullah, S., Higgins, H., Braem, B., Latre, B., Blondia, C., & Moerman, I. et al. (2012). A comprehensive survey of wireless body area networks. *Journal of Medical Systems, 36*(3), 1065–1094. doi:10.1007/s10916-010-9571-3 PMID:20721685

Waheed, T., Shaikh, F. K., & Chowdhry, B. S. (2012). Fundamentals of Wireless Body Area networks. *Wireless Sensor Networks: Current Status and Future Trends, 79*.

Woeltje, K. F. (2013). Moving into the future: electronic surveillance for healthcare-associated infections. *The Journal of Hospital Infection, 84*(2), 103–105. doi:10.1016/j.jhin.2013.03.005 PMID:23643390

KEY TERMS AND DEFINITIONS

Association Rule: Implication between frequent items (antecedent and consequence) that measures dependency between the antecedent and the consequence by support and confidence values.

Data Mining: A process of extraction of knowledge from a large collection of data by using sophisticated methods.

Knowledge Base: Stored information such as facts, assumptions and rules that are available to access.

Quality of Service (QoS): Assessment of the characteristics that are used in services.

Wireless Body Area Networks (WBANs): A network of tiny sensor nodes (in-body or on-body) to monitor vital signs of the human body.

Wireless Sensor Networks (WSNs): A network of hundreds and thousands of constrained sensor nodes, which sense the environment and send data to a central base station.

Chapter 13
A Case Study of a Laboratory Information System Developed at the Institute for Cancer Research at Candiolo

Alessandro Fiori
Candiolo Cancer Institute – FPO, IRCCS, Italy

Emanuele Geda
Candiolo Cancer Institute – FPO, IRCCS, Italy

Alberto Grand
Candiolo Cancer Institute – FPO, IRCCS, Italy

Francesco Gavino Brundu
Politecnico di Torino, Italy

Piero Alberto
Candiolo Cancer Institute – FPO, IRCCS, Italy

Domenico Schioppa
Politecnico di Torino, Italy

Andrea Bertotti
Candiolo Cancer Institute – FPO, IRCCS, Italy & University of Torino, Italy

ABSTRACT

Research laboratories produce a huge amount of complex and heterogeneous data typically managed by Laboratory Information Management Systems (LIMSs). Although many LIMSs are available, it is often difficult to identify a product that covers all the requirements and peculiarities of a specific institution. To deal with this lack, the Candido Cancer Institute decided to start a project, named the Laboratory Assistant Suite (LAS), with the aim of developing a new software platform that assists researchers throughout diverse laboratory activities. The proposed system can track laboratory experiments even in problematic environments, support the integration of heterogeneous biomedical data, and help in decision-making tasks. In this chapter, the authors present the current architecture of the system, some real-use cases, as well as statistics about stored data and user feedback in order to provide an overview of the functionalities and show the effectiveness of the platform in supporting research in the molecular oncology field.

DOI: 10.4018/978-1-4666-6320-6.ch013

INTRODUCTION

Molecular oncology and biomedical processes produce a huge amount of heterogeneous and complex data, which is difficult to manage and analyze without a structured and well-organized system. The information embedded in the data needs to be made explicit, because data are usually not meaningful *per se*. This is especially true of oncological data, where different elements often cooperate together in multiple complex patterns. Genomic data decoding can be incredibly tricky, and this is why a supporting information system, equipped with state-of-the-art algorithms and data management tools, is a fundamental prerequisite.

A system that deals with this complexity is called a Laboratory Information Management System (LIMS). Some typical features offered by LIMSs include sample management, monitoring of laboratory activities, and recording of experimental results.. Sample management involves sample handling, registering and locating (to retrieve where a particular sample is stored). Analyses can also be defined through a workflow definition, and scheduled at a particular time. Data is stored securely and reliably, and can only be accessed by authorized users. In order to assure data quality, LIMSs usually comply with some standards, such as ISO/IEC 17025.

However, the definition of the tasks addressed by a LIMS can vary considerably from laboratory to laboratory, based on their different needs. In general, we can define a LIMS as a system that:

- Supports the rapid implementation of different workflows;
- Uses heterogeneous data;
- Has several built-in features to assist the users of a laboratory;
- Has several tools to support data import and export.

At the time of writing, several commercial LIMS solutions exist but they usually require a significant investment, in terms of either human or economic resources (sometimes both), in order to satisfy specific laboratory requirements (Haquin et al., 2008). Furthermore, if a closed-source project is discontinued, it may be impossible to either continue using the old platform, or seamlessly migrate to another project.

On the other hand, the research community has proven very active in this field, often releasing different LIMSs as free and open-source projects. For instance, LAMA (Milisavljevic et al., 2010) has been designed to support the tracking of different animal colonies.

However, since these systems are modeled to address the needs of a specific context, with a focus on few kinds of highly specialized data and sets of experiments, they might not suit the requirements of other research environments.

In 2004, the National Cancer Institute (NCI) started the Cancer Biomedical Informatics Grid (caBIG®) project (Kuhn et al., 2007), to develop an information infrastructure that enables the interdisciplinary collaboration for cancer research. Different tools have been developed under this project addressing both the management and the analysis of biomedical data. However, the adoption of caBIG® tools in research labs is not straightforward and presents many critical issues pointed out in London and Chatterjee (2010). In 2012, caBIG® was retired, and the NCI introduced the National Cancer Informatics Program (NCIP) as a successor.

As previously discussed, both open-source LIMS projects and commercial products may present issues, and their adoption is troublesome. For these reasons, the Institute for Cancer Research at Candiolo (Italy) started in 2011 to implement its own LIMS, named the Laboratory Assistant Suite (LAS) platform (Baralis et al., 2012). Its purpose is to assist researchers in different laboratory and research activities, allowing management of different kinds of raw data (e.g., biological, molecular) and tracking experimental data. Due to the pivotal role of integrated data analysis in discovering new knowledge related to tumors and improving medical treatments, the platform also supports the integration of different resources, and aids in performing a variety of analyses. Thanks to its modular architecture, the LAS platform can be easily extended to adapt to different needs and handle highly specific types of data, without compromising the other functionalities. In addition, the data models and procedures integrated in the platform try to comply with best practices and standards widely adopted by the research community at large. User interfaces have been designed in collaboration with the final users (technician and researchers) to ease data entry and management in hostile environments, where a limited interaction with the system is required (e.g., in sterile conditions).

The chapter presents a case study related to the development and the usage of the Laboratory Assistant Suite (LAS) in the research laboratories of the Institute for Cancer Research at Candiolo and its research partners. First, an overview of existing LIMS solutions, both commercial and opensource, is provided in the Background section. The Laboratory Assistant Suite section presents a functional analysis of the context in which the LAS project has been developed, by introducing the main procedures of the xenopatients experimental pipeline. Next, the architecture of the platform, and the software modules that currently make up the LAS suite are described. The Use cases section discusses some real usage scenarios to show how the system can effectively support daily laboratory activities, while the Usage statistics and system evaluation section presents statistics about the data and the activities currently tracked by the LAS suite, and the opinions of the users exploiting the system. Finally, future developments and research directions are presented in the Future Research Directions section.

BACKGROUND

Numerous efforts have been devoted to building management systems that assist researchers during laboratory activities. Many commercial Laboratory Information Management Systems (LIMS) solutions are available.

One of them is Clarity LIMS (Clarity LIMS, 2014) which provides workflow-tracking and integration, management reporting, and role-based interfaces. Its sample management functionalities include the capability to retrieve sample metadata, keep a detailed record of sample information, store samples in a secure location, and single out poor quality samples before analysis. Another feature is an extensive library of preconfigured workflows, in which each workflow template is designed with bioinformatics best practices in mind. A single-user version is available for free, while licensed versions are priced from about 1,000$ yearly per user.

Different alternatives are provided by LabLinx (2014) that makes available three LIMS products. ELab, formerly known as LabLinx LIMS, comes with over 30 different modules. webLIMS is a SaaS (software as a service) product, proposed as a more scalable solution. LIMStudio is a virtual desktop add-on for webLIMS-hosted applications, also providing a framework for users who need to develop their own applications. The features provided range from sample logging, accessioning, barcoding to workload and workflow management, scheduling, reporting, trending and control charting.

Qualoupe LIMS, developed by Two Fold Software Limited (Two Fold Software, 2014), is a system offering sample management, tracking and batching, project and document management, Quality Assessment/Control functions, configurable roles and security, data normalization and validation, reporting, modularity and a webbased interface. BioData Inc. provides LabGuru (LabGru, 2014), which is web-based and free for personal use. AgileBio proposes LabCollector (AgileBio, 2014), while BioMatters has different genome-related solutions (BioMatters, 2014). From RURO (2014), several products are available: ezColony (animal colony management), FreezerPro (frozen sample management), LIMS 24/7 (data management, security and analysis), Sciency (Electronic Laboratory Notebook – a scalable, integrated research environment).

LABVANTAGE (2014) offers a variety of features, such as information management and tracking for samples, consumables and experiments, integration with numerous third-party instruments and systems, graphical workflow design and process automation, and compliance with government regulations and other standards.

The research community has also proposed different tools focused on the management and the analysis of different biological data. For instance, MausDB (Maier et al., 2008) integrates standard mouse colony management, phenotyping workflow scheduling, and the management of mouse phenotyping results in a multi-user platform; it allows crosslinking mouse phenotype data with genotype data, metadata and external data such as public web databases. TreeSNPs (Clément, 2010) was a project that used to manage data generated through single nucleotide polymorphism (SNP) identification. Screensaver (Tolopko et al., 2010) supports the storage and the comparison of small molecule and RNA screening data. LAMA (Milisavljevic et al., 2010) has been designed to support the tracking of different animal colonies by means of user-friendly interfaces. It offers the possibility of tagging and grouping animals, managing projects and tracking breeding cages and weaning litters.

In 2005, Galaxy LIMS (Giardine et al., 2005; Blankenberg et al., 2010; Goecks et al., 2010) was proposed. Galaxy is a system for the integration of genomic sequences, their alignments, and functional annotation. It provides a key capability, the history system, which records each user operation. It is web-based (also cloud-based in the public

version) and, therefore, cross-platform. It is also highly interactive, allowing the user to inspect each analysis, input and results at any granularity level. Workflows can be shared between users and reused for different studies. Last but not least, Galaxy can annotate each analysis with metadata (dataset description, algorithm version etc.) in order to ensure the reproducibility of results.

Bika Labs (2014) has developed BIKA Lims, an open-source project with sample management and batching, data analysis, validation and query capabilities, results reporting, data export and a web-based client.

LabTrove (2014), proposed by the University of Southampton, provides web-based interfaces, API-enabled automated processing, metadata support, blog style with timeline views, document management, extensibility, LDAP, OpenID, username and password authentication. A support and consultancy service is also available.

In 2007, the first public version of openBIS (Bauch et al., 2011) was released. Mainly developed at the ETH Zurich, this system offers features such as high content screening, dataset management, data filtering and export, data integration through API, distributed storage support, proteomics-based functionality, metabolomics-based functionality and Illumina Next Generation Sequencing data management.

In (Nix et al., 2010), GNomeEx, a free open-source genomics LIMS and analysis project, is presented. It is oriented to organizing, annotating, tracking and distributing raw genomic data and their associated analysis.

Differently, SeqWare (O'Connor et al., 2010) is devoted to building analysis workflows for very large genomics datasets, such as those produced by next-generation sequencing (NGS) technology. It currently provides 5 main tools specifically designed to support massively parallel sequencing technologies. All tools can be used together or separately. MetaDB provides a common database to store metadata used by all components, while Portal is a LIMS-like web application to manage samples, record computational events, and present results back to end users. Differently, Pipeline is a workflow engine that is capable of wrapping and combining other tools (BFAST, BWA, SAMtools, etc) into complex pipelines, and recording metadata about the analysis. It facilitates automation of pipelines based on metadata. Web Service is a programmatic API that lets people build new tools on top of the project. Finally, Query Engine is a NoSQL database designed to store and query variants and other events inferred from sequence data.

caTissue Plus (2014) is a free open-source biobanking LIMS/LIS heavily modeled after the National Cancer Institute's caLIMS product. It offers role-based access, rapid data entry, annotations handling, data retrieval and reporting, and programmatic access using API.

Since 2004, several tools were developed under the Cancer Biomedical Informatics Grid (caBIG®) project (Kuhn et al., 2007). For example, VISDA (Wang et al., 2007) is an analytical tool focused on clustering approaches applied to high dimensional and complex biomedical datasets. However, the end user data accessibility in caBIG® tools could have been compromised by the object model complexity and overly generic terminologies (London and Chatterjee, 2010). Therefore, NCI replaced caBIG® with its successor NCIP, the National Cancer Informatics Program.

LabKey Server (Nelson et al., 2011) is another open-source solution, used to integrate and analyze large quantities of biomedical research data; it also provides secure, web-based query, reporting and collaboration services over a wide variety of data sources, such as gene sequences, specimens and proteomics data.

More LIMSs resources can be found at LIMSWiki (2014), which is constantly updated.

LABORATORY ASSISTANT SUITE

Context

Every day in research laboratories several procedures are performed to analyze different biological and medical aspects of tumors, with the aim of discovering new knowledge and improving the therapies. We started to analyze a subset of procedures developed and adopted in the research laboratories of our institution to model our environment. At the beginning, we focused our attention on the procedures that are involved in the xenopatient experimental pipeline (Bertotti et al., 2011). This approach is based on the serial transplantation of human tumor specimens in immunocompromised animals. The aim is to help in translating the correlative information emerging from data integration into clinically relevant and functionally validated biomarkers. After completing the main modules addressing the management of tumor specimen and xenopatient life cycle, we started to include additional elements to our environment in order to manage several research activities and exploit collected data. In the following, we describe the main activities of a research study including the xenopatients' approach.

Tumor specimens are initially collected from surgical interventions. From the individual patient-derived material, a set of aliquots is generated (i.e., vital, RNA Later and snap-frozen). According to the characteristics of the aliquots and the purpose of the research study in which they are collected, different operations can be performed: (i) storage in a dedicated container (e.g., freezers), (ii) extraction of derived aliquots such as DNA and RNA, and (iii) implantation in immunocompromised animals (i.e., xenopatients). Researchers can apply different experimental treatments on the implanted animals and monitor them. For instance, researchers can monitor the evolution of the tumor mass in an animal by means of measurements, and evaluate the response to drugs according to well-defined treatment protocols. Moreover, new tissue samples from these animals can be generated for further analyses. Indeed, all the (derived) aliquots can be exploited for experimental analyses with different technologies. For instance, the expression values of thousands of genes can be analyzed by means of the microarray technology, while Sanger sequencing experiments allow the identification of genetic mutations in target sequences.

To the aim of managing and integrating all this information, a robust but flexible data management platform is needed. In particular, different types of information (e.g., biological data, molecular data, procedure tracking data, sample tracking data), some of which can be highly complex, should be independently managed by the platform but, at the same time, interconnected to permit integrated analyses. User interfaces should be practical and intuitive on one side, and perfectly fit the actual procedures on the other, in order to avoid hindering the experimental pipeline. This is particularly relevant when working with biological samples, which implies that many data should be entered by the user in a hostile environment (e.g., working with gloves in sterile conditions with potentially infectious samples). To the best of our knowledge, the procedures adopted in our experimental pipeline are largely standardized, and they reflect common practice in the oncological research field. Thus, we believe that most functionalities offered by the system we are developing could be useful to other research institutes. The LAS software platform is freely available upon request to the authors.

Architecture

Since the laboratory-related procedures can be categorized into different levels according to data complexity and purpose, the LAS architecture has been modeled after the same rationale. Thus, it has been extensively based on a three-tier design pattern (Eckerson, 1995), both at the system-wide and the software module levels. This is a well-established architectural paradigm in software engineering, which targets flexibility and reusability by breaking up an application into tiers. Each tier addresses a specific issue and interacts with the other tiers by means of well-defined interfaces. We modeled the platform in the following tiers: (i) operative, (ii) integration, and (iii) analysis. In addition, a cross-tier software component regulates accesses to the system and enforces user privilege control for all LAS services. Figure 1 shows the current architecture and the modules belonging to each tier.

In the general architecture of LAS, each tier includes a set of fully-fledged applications, or modules. While the lower tier is mainly concerned with the collection of experimental data, the modules and data managed by the upper tiers are characterized by an increasing level of abstraction. Lower tiers can service requests generated by the upper tiers and provide the data needed to carry out complex tasks (e.g., data integration and/or analysis).

The operative tier is responsible for collecting, storing, and tracking raw experimental data. These include data from several sources, such as xenopatient management, microarray experiments, sequencing and tissue collection, each handled by a specific software module. Modules in this tier are meant to work in close interaction with the researchers in a laboratory setting. Thus, graphical user interfaces (GUIs) are explicitly tailored to ease data entry operations and assist the researchers throughout their experiments. The interaction is designed to be especially lean with the aid of special input devices, such as touch-screen notepads and barcode readers, available in the research institute.

The integration tier is aimed at integrating different types of raw experimental data by means of complex queries. Ad-hoc identifiers have been adopted throughout the databases, making it pos-

Figure 1. LAS architecture

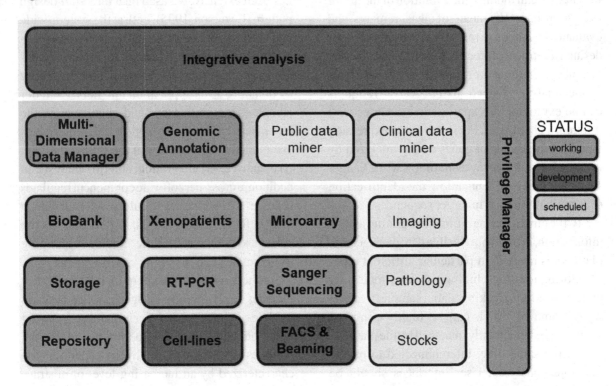

sible to correlate different biological entities. The integrated data can be browsed or visualized as graphs (e.g., genealogy trees). In addition, they can be fed to the analysis tier and enriched by means of annotations. For instance, the population of xenopatients can be annotated as responsive to a given drug according to statistical analyses. Moreover, aliquots used in molecular experiments can be identified by means of complex queries, and submitted to the appropriate operative modules to be managed.

The analysis tier allows the definition of a workflow for the analysis of integrated data. Like with popular data mining tools (e.g., Rapid Miner (Mierswa et al., 2006)), users can design their analysis session by selecting and cascading one or more analysis building blocks. The analysis process ultimately generates annotations, which are sent to the integration tier and stored in the database; it can optionally export data for visualization with external tools. Moreover, predefined

analysis flows can be directly exploited by some operative modules to perform analyses on data collected by the user during an experiment execution.

The access and privilege control system manages all user accesses to the software modules in each tier, according to their profile. The user profile is defined during user registration and can be updated as needed; it lists the LAS modules accessible by the user, together with the set of functionalities he/she is allowed to use in each module. Moreover, some users with special privileges can create groups of users, based on particular needs (e.g., research studies and/or laboratory activities carried out by a specific group of people). This system also provides a finer-grained control over the data by defining and enforcing user and/or group access privileges with a row-level granularity, in order to guarantee different security levels for confidential information.

Each LAS module is a web-based application implemented in Python and exploits Django, an open-source web application framework which follows the Model-View-Controller (Gamma et al., 2002) architecture. In this way, end users can access the applications from virtually any Internet-enabled device and with very limited system requirements. This aspect is fundamental to providing data access also in hostile environments (e.g. sterile conditions) with wireless devices. According to different types of data and data management needs a relational DBMS (MySQL), a non-relational database engine (MongoDB) and/or a graph database (Neo4j) are exploited to provide persistent storage for the experimental data and the annotations. Furthermore, all user activities within each module are tracked by means of audit trail procedures.

A set of APIs (Application Programming Interface) are provided to expose some of the functionalities offered by each application and permit data exchange among different applications. Finally, thanks to the modular architecture, different modules can be deployed on different server machines, so as to distribute the workload of the entire system. The integration of the LAS system with cloud computing environment is currently being designed, to increase the computational resources available for the analysis tasks.

Modules

Since one of the main purposes of the Laboratory Assistant Suite is to provide support to the most crucial laboratory activities, some modules, particularly those associated with the operative tier, have been implemented first, while others are still under development. This scenario is favored by the LAS architecture that was designed in the first place to be easily updatable when new laboratory or analysis activities need to be managed. To date, there are nine modules which are used every day in our institution: BioBanking, Storage, Xenopatients, Microarray, RealTime PCR (RT-PCR), SangerSequencing, Repository, Multi-Dimensional Annotation and Genomic Annotation

Managers. Even though these modules are already providing a wide set of functionalities, tracking several research procedures and providing useful support in laboratory activities, their development continues to add new features and perfect existing ones. Moreover, other modules have been planned, as pointed out in Figure 1, and some of them are in the first stages of development and/or testing. In the following, the main functionalities of each module used in our institution are described.

BioBanking Management Module

With the rapid advances in biomedical and genetic technologies, collections of biological materials have attracted increasing attention from the researcher community since they represent a fundamental resource for the research and the diagnosis of different pathologies, and the study of possible therapeutic applications. Such collections, named biobanks, are commonly divided into tissue and genetic biobanks according to the types of biological materials they store. The BioBanking Management Module (BBMM) addresses both issues.

The scope of this module spans a wide range of activities, including management of biological samples and associated pathological information, as well as support to a number of laboratory-related procedures. In particular, the module can currently handle the following activities and the corresponding data.

- Collection of biological material from surgical intervention and acquisition of aliquots from external laboratories. Aliquots stored in the system are characterized by features such as tumor type (e.g., colorectal), tissue type (e.g., liver metastasis), source hospital or laboratory, and pathological information.
- Measurement of aliquot physical characteristics, such as volume, concentration, purity and quality.

- Derivation of new biological materials (e.g., DNA, cDNA) from the aliquots stored in the biobank.
- Planning of experimental activities involving the aliquots stored in the BioBanking repository, such as microarray experiments.

Storage Management Module

Research laboratories make use of several types of containers (e.g., freezers, racks, plates, tubes) to store biological material. Their mutual interactions (i.e., which container can host another one) can change according to characteristics such as the layout and the laboratory procedure. For instance, a plate of a given manufacture and model may be able to host only some kind of tubes. Similarly, a research group may like to assign only one type of aliquot (e.g., RNA Later) to some plates. The Storage Management Module (SMM) allows managing any kind of container by defining and applying different rules to them. The functionalities provided by this module are the following.

- Management of all container information (e.g., manufacture, geometry) and aim (e.g., allowed aliquot types).
- Definition of the interaction among containers and management of user-defined constraints.
- Tracking of container usage and availability.
- Management of container shipment to external laboratories.

Xenopatients Management Module

In vivo experiments (e.g., xenopatients) allow testing different drug therapies and expanding the collection of biological samples. This kind of experiments in our institution are based on the model described in Bertotti et al. (2011). The Xenopatients Management Module (XMM) manages the immunocompromised animals and monitors the xenopatient life cycle, from their acquisition by the research institute to their death. The main functionalities provided by this module include the following.

- Acquisition of mice, characterized by different features (e.g., status, strain, age, source). The system promotes the use of barcode readers when mice are equipped with RFid tags, in order to speed up the identification of the animal and the retrieval of related information.
- Management of tumor tissue implants into the available xenopatients. The XMM effectively handles this operation by accessing the BioBanking and Storage modules (through the appropriate APIs) and retrieving the tumor aliquots currently stored in the source container (e.g., plate, tube), whose available quantity is updated accordingly.
- Monitoring of tumor growth within the xenopatients. Qualitative and quantitative measurements of the tumor mass are tracked for each mouse, and different operations can be assigned to measured mice, such as treatments, aimed at assessing the effectiveness of given drugs.
- Management of treatments, which are composed of several phases, each associated with different kinds of information. For instance, the drug, the administration mode, the dose, and the administration frequency can be defined.
- Management of tumor explants, marking the end of the xenopatient life cycle. A number of tumor tissue aliquots is generated and made available for future implants. Explant operations also cooperate with the BioBanking and Storage Management Modules, to display destination plates and transmit data about generated aliquots.
- Decision-making support for all the activities assigned to each mouse. The supervisors can monitor all experiment features

(e.g., tumor growth) and plan activities, which are tracked by the system. The decision process is supported by means of ad-hoc graphical utilities.

Microarray Management Module

With the advent of microarray technology, it is possible to analyze thousands of gene expression values with a single experiment to identify markers of a target phenotype (El Akadi et al, 2011; Golub et al., 1999). Thus, to assess the quality of the analyses and improve further integration tasks, it is fundamental to track both the biological information related to the sample source and the entire experimental process,. The Microarray Management Module (MMM) aims to track all the steps of a microarray experiment. The main functionalities it provides are the following.

- Plan microarray experiments by defining the position assigned to each sample on the microarray chips.
- Management of microarray chips and storage of related information (e.g., manufacturer, layout, target race).
- Tracking of hybridization procedures and support in preparing biological samples according to a predefined protocol.
- Management of scans and tracking of quality assessments.
- Inspection of scan results in order to identify candidate samples for further analyses.

The microarray raw data coming from the scans are remotely loaded in the Repository Manager, described in the following, and linked to the corresponding sample within MMM.

Molecular Analysis Module

Other molecular analyses can be done on aliquots besides microarray experiments. For instance, biologists may be interested in analyzing muta-tions for a target gene which is involved in tumor proliferation. For this purpose, several techniques can be exploited. In the Laboratory Assistant Suite, we have preliminarily included modules that manage data collection for the most frequently used techniques in our institution: Sanger sequencing and Real-time PCR. In the following, we briefly describe the main purpose of each technique and which data are tracked.

Sanger Sequencing Management Module

Sanger sequencing is a method of DNA sequencing based on the selective incorporation of chain-terminating dideoxynucleotides, named primers, by DNA polymerase during in vitro DNA replication. This technique was developed by Frederick Sanger and colleagues in 1977, and it is one of the most widely used sequencing methods. Since this approach can retrieve only a sequence of the target region delimited by the primers, in the last years the next-generation sequencing, named Next-gen, has become the most powerful method to sequence the entire genome. Despite the limited capability of sequencing, the Sanger sequencing procedure has some advantages. The cost of a Sanger sequencing experiment is cheaper than Next-gen, and, in many cases, researchers are only interested in analyzing few genes related to their research. Moreover, analyzing and extracting information from Next-gen results is still an issue. The Sanger sequencing module is aimed to track the experiments performed with this technology. In particular, it records data related to the planning of a sequencing experiment and its execution. For each sample included in the experiment, the target gene and the mutation, if any, are saved, using the genomic annotation facilities provided by the LAS. The electropherograms produced by the instruments can also be included to enrich the description of the experiment and reevaluate it in the future. These documents are managed by the repository module described in the next section.

RT-PCR Management Module

The real-time polymerase chain reaction (RT-PCR) is a laboratory technique of molecular biology based on the polymerase chain reaction (PCR). It is used to amplify and simultaneously quantify a targeted DNA molecule. For one or more specific sequences in a DNA sample, quantitative PCR enables both detection and quantification. The quantity can be either an absolute number of copies (CN) or a relative amount when normalized to DNA input or additional normalizing genes. Differently from classical PCR, the amplified DNA is detected during the reaction progress (i.e., in "real time") and not only at the end. The RT-PCR module manages and tracks this kind of experiments. A single experiment can include many aliquots analyzed for several mutations. The module stores the results for each analyzed sample, using the LAS genomic annotation facility, and the associated copy number. As in the case of Sanger sequencing, the experiment description can be enriched with the raw data extracted by the instrument.

Repository Manager

Heterogeneous digital resources can be associated with most laboratory activities. For instance, an experimental protocol can be described in details, in some text documents, while a machine (e.g., a microarray scanner) used in a molecular experiment can produce a large amount of data, including results and experimental settings. Managing this unstructured information is fundamental to tracking all research activities, but is a challenging task due to its heterogeneity. The Repository Manager serves this purpose by storing all the digital resources exploited by all the modules. The main functionalities of this module are the following.

- Storage of all the documents associated with experimental protocols.
- Storage of experimental raw data. According to the data complexity, different ad-hoc data management strategies are implemented. For instance, the output of microarray experiments is analyzed and decomposed to separate information related to each sample from that related to the scan event. Differently, Sanger sequencing results only include the electropherograms, describing the mutations occurring in a set of samples. In this case, the system only stores the instrument output, without processing its content.

Multi-Dimensional Data Manager

Tracking experimental procedures and recording all the data related to biological samples is fundamental to monitoring molecular and in vivo experiments. However, the research also aims at integrating such heterogeneous information to discover new knowledge related to tumors. The Multi-Dimensional Data Manger (MDDM) can extract all information of interest from the operative tier in a uniform way by exploiting graphical tools. To date, the MDDM includes the following functionalities.

- Query generator to perform queries and/or define templates representing frequent queries. The query set is defined as a workflow composed of blocks, named query blocks. Each query block defines the object that will be retrieved (e.g., aliquot, xenopatient), its related information of interest and the filtering conditions. Before retrieving the data from the corresponding modules, the workflow is analyzed to detect improperly defined operations (e.g., intersections among disjoint sets of objects) and define an optimal execution plan on the distributed databases.

- ◦ Wizards based on predefined workflows (i.e., templates) to allow unexperienced users to run most frequent queries.
- ◦ Graphical visualization (e.g., genealogy trees) of integrated data based on their relationships.
- ◦ Extraction of additional information starting from the query set, by means of predefined templates.

Genomic Annotation Manager

Thanks to a plethora of independent projects, maintained by universities and research institutions, nowadays genomic information is largely available in a number of public, freely accessible databases. On the other hand, such an abundance can make it hard to select a definitive and authoritative source of information. In addition, these databases are not always interchangeable, since data from one source may be missing, incomplete, or simply different in the other, so that finding a one-to-one correspondence is sometimes impossible. To address these issues, the Genomic Annotation Manager has been developed, which aims to integrate heterogeneous data sources and provide a uniform and non-redundant knowledge base for genomic annotation. For instance, genes, mutations and SNPs (single-nucleotide polymorphisms) can be unambiguously identified by all modules within the LAS system. So far, sequence mutations from COSMIC (2014) - Catalogue of somatic mutations in cancer - and gene transcript information from the UCSC Genome Browser (2014) database have been imported into the Genomic Annotation Manager. Furthermore, Blat, a fast alignment tool developed by J.W. Kent (Kent, 2002), has been integrated to support different molecular experiments and annotation procedures.

Privilege Manager

The management of data produced by different people and/or groups requires that access to functionalities and information be limited according to several aspects such as group and/or project membership, and user role. For these reasons, we developed a cross-tier module, named the Privilege Manager that manages users and their privileges. This module provides the following functionalities.

- Registration of new users. People who want to gain access to the LAS platform should send a subscription request by filling in the registration form with their personal details (e.g., affiliation, role), to allow the administrators to correctly process the registration.
- Management of working groups. A working group is defined as a group of people that work together under some specific rules. For instance, working groups can be matched to research or project groups within a given institution. The leaders of the working group, also named the principal investigators, can restrict the access to some functionalities and define sharing rules on the data. Data of a working group cannot be seen by other groups until an authorization has been approved by the principal investigators.
- Management of user privileges. The user privileges determine which functionalities are available to each user, according to their role and the restrictions enforced by the principal investigators of their working group.

USE CASES

The following sections illustrate how the LAS platform can concretely support laboratory research.

We present three real application scenarios we encountered in our laboratories, and describe how the LAS tools address these issues. Even though the idea and the design of such tools were based on the functional requirements of our laboratories, we believe they reflect common practice in the oncological research field and are general enough to be useful to other researchers from other institutions.

Use Case 1: Collection

The collection of new samples coming from a surgical intervention is the primary source of the biobank. To enable the employment of barcode readers and thus streamline data entry procedures, most pieces of experimental equipment (i.e., clinical folders, plates, tubes) are bar-coded by the institution prior to their use. Sample collection consists of two phases. In the first phase, the researcher inputs preliminary information about the collection event and selects one or more sample types. For instance, it is possible to insert an identifier for the patient and clinical parameters correlated with the surgical intervention. In the next phase, the researcher can add one or more samples for each of the sample types chosen. Figure 2 depicts the interface for the collection of biological samples, which is designed to closely match the physical working environment of the researcher. The collection plates are organized on screen into different tabs, so that types of aliquots that are usually collected together appear in the same tab. For instance, in Figure 2 is reported the panel containing the containers for viable, ffpe, RNA later, and snap-frozen aliquots that are usually collected for in-vivo and in-vitro experiments. It represents a physical working plate in which sample aliquots are stored. Plates or tubes can be loaded or created in the application by means of their barcode. Inserting an aliquot in a given plate position is done by simply clicking on the corresponding cell, which can be comfortably achieved on a touch-screen device without resort-

ing to a mouse. This results in a reduced number of lean interactions with the system, allowing the researcher to focus on the experimental task at hand, rather than on data entry operations.

Use Case 2: Experiment Review and Retrieval of Related Information

Immunocompromised mice that have been implanted with a tumor mass are regularly measured by laboratory technicians to monitor the growth of the tumor and assess the effectiveness of treatments. During this operation, technicians record the observed values and may propose a given course of action for each mouse (e.g., start/stop a treatment, explant). Such measurements and actions should be reviewed by the supervisor through the "Experiment review" screen (see Figure 3). In the left side of the window (block A) a list of all experimental groups for which new measurements exist is shown. When an experimental group is selected, its measurements and all associated pending actions are shown in the bottom table (block D). To ease the supervisor's task, any pending action awaiting approval is highlighted, while further information is available in the other tabs (e.g., historical measurement record for each mouse). Moreover, a plot showing the average variation of the tumor mass over time for each treatment arm (block C) provides a useful tool to support the supervisor in the decision-making process. The supervisor may accept the actions proposed by the technician for any measurement, or she may modify or reject them, by means of a set of buttons (block B). She may also add comments, such as explanations or future directions. Once the review is complete, a report is displayed, including all actions (both approved and rejected or modified ones), and sent to both the supervisor and the technician. After a few days, the supervisor may need check the aliquots explanted from a set of mice and find out where they are located within the storage system. For this purpose, she can exploit the query generator, reported in Fig-

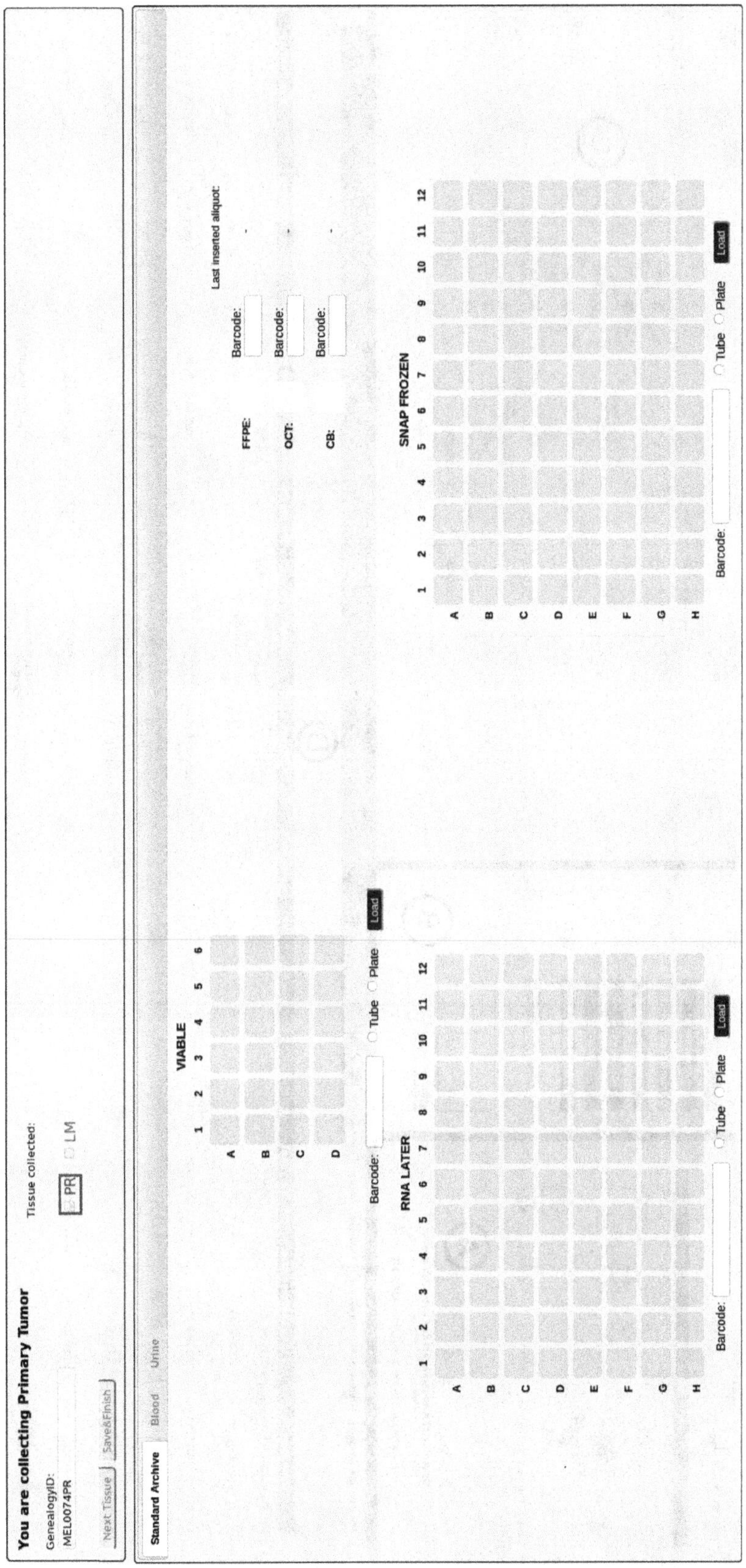

Figure 2. Collection interface

Figure 3. Experiment review interface

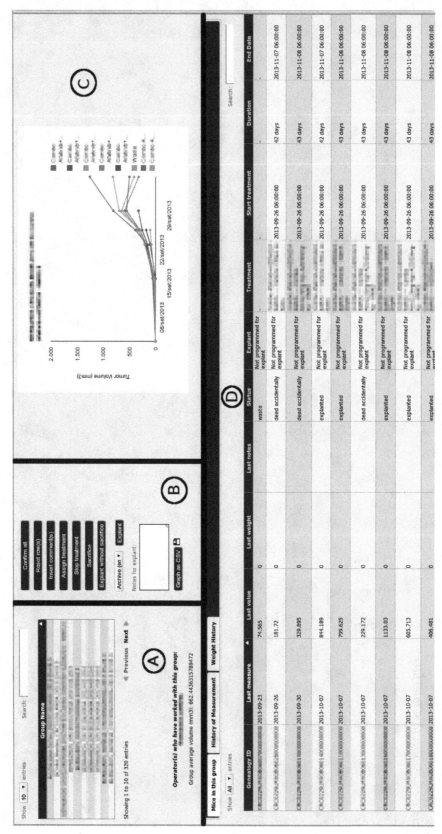

ure 4. The query blocks are shown on the left hand side of the editor (block A in Figure 4) and categorized according to the module from which the data are drawn (e.g., the flask icon for biobank data, the mouse icon for xenopatient data). The user can drag and drop the query blocks on the workflow editor (block B) and build the workflow of the query by connecting them. For instance, the query blocks used by the supervisor to design her query are the Mice and Explants block, belonging to the xenopatient category, the Aliquots block, drawn from the biobank category, and the Containers block, included in the storage category. Filtering conditions may be specified for each block by clicking the funnel icon. Set operators (union, intersection, difference) and special operators (group-count, template blocks, GenealogyID), listed in block C, can also be used in the workflow. The supervisor instantiates the GenealogyID block to quickly identify the mice of interest. Once the workflow has been defined, the user can assign a title and description to the query (block D). Finally, she can simply run the query or save it in the system to be reused in the future for different purposes.

Use Case 3: Derivation of Aliquot Collected from Target Patients

A collection is related to surgical intervention performed on a patient. However, the same patient may be subject to several surgical interventions that will produce independent collections. In some experimental procedures, it is very important to identify the aliquots coming from the same patient to compare possible mutations over time. To retrieve the target aliquots, researchers and technicians may choose one of two alternatives: (i) use the MDDM to build a query that retrieves the aliquots of interest, and (ii) use the patient interface in the BioBank. The first scenario is mainly targeted at more experienced users, who know the relationships among biological entities and which

entities contain the information relevant for search. To enhance the flexibility and the usability of the system, we introduced an ad-hoc interface in the BioBank module to identify aliquots related to the same patient. In this interface, reported in Figure 5, the user can set filtering parameters for the collections, and define security settings. According to the latter, the information in blocks B and C can be displayed in an anonymized form. Block B shows the list of patients satisfying the filtering criteria, while block C shows the aliquots related to the selected patient, along with their characteristics. At this point, the user can select one or more aliquots which are moved to the list in block D. When the selection of target aliquots is complete, different actions can be performed (e.g., derivation, molecular experiment). The system will automatically check if the aliquot types are consistent with the target action. For instance, suppose a researcher wishes to perform a molecular experiment, but no suitable aliquots are available for the patients of interest . Thus, it is necessary to create derivatives compatible with the target analysis (e.g., cDNA for microarray). In this case, the researcher will plan a derivation for the selected aliquots and assign this task to a user (e.g., a technician). The user in charge of this operation is prompted to select the aliquots, the protocol and the corresponding kit involved in the process. Next, she is taken to the interface driving the derivation process (Figure 6). In the top side of the interface, information related to the derivation protocol and the output is visualized. In block B, the details for each derivative are reported to guide the user through the preparation of the aliquots. Some parameters (e.g., volume and concentration) can be changed at will by the user for each aliquot, and the system will automatically update the values of the others to match the protocol rules. Once the technician has prepared the aliquots, she should position them in one or more containers. To inspect the layout, and the contents of each container (block C), the user must

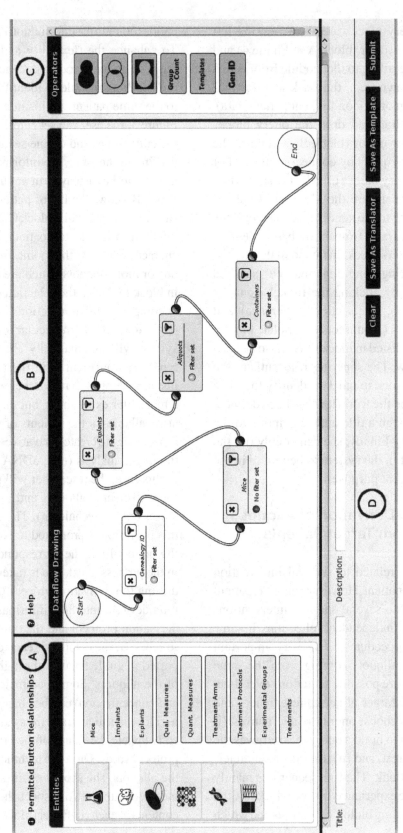

Figure 4. Query generator interface

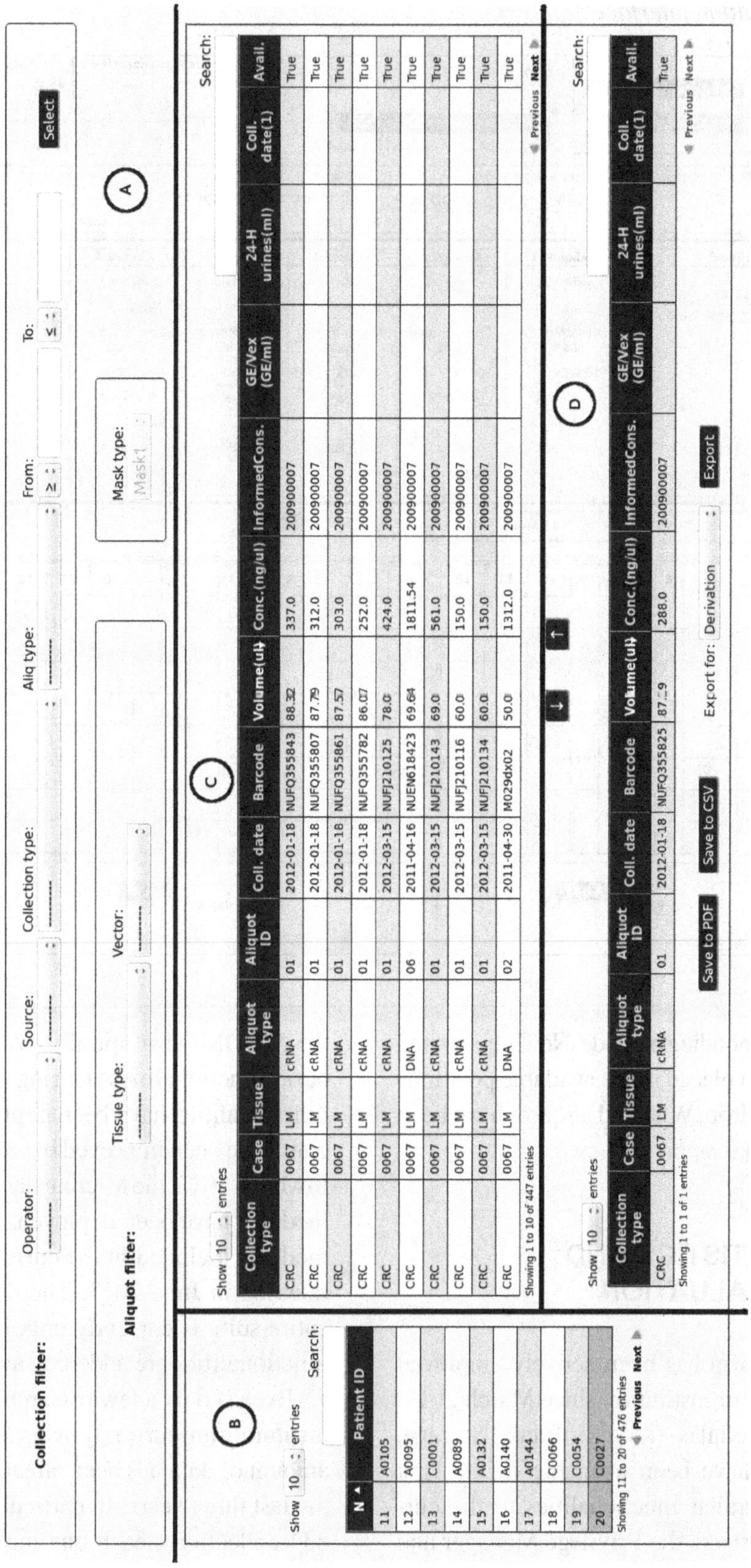

Figure 5. Patient-based filter interface

Collection filter: Operator: ——— Source: ——— Collection type: ——— Aliq type: ——— From: ——— To: ——— Select

Aliquot filter: Tissue type: ——— Vector: ——— Mask type: Mask1

(A)

(C)

Show 10 entries Search:

Collection type	Case	Tissue	Aliquot type	Aliquot ID	Coll. date	Barcode	Volume(ul)	Conc.(ng/ul)	InformedCons.	GE/Vex (GE/ml)	24-H urines(ml)	Coll. date(1)	Avail.
CRC	0067	LM	cRNA	01	2012-01-18	NUFQ355843	88.32	337.0	200900007				True
CRC	0067	LM	cRNA	01	2012-01-18	NUFQ355807	87.79	312.0	200900007				True
CRC	0067	LM	cRNA	01	2012-01-18	NUFQ355861	87.57	303.0	200900007				True
CRC	0067	LM	cRNA	01	2012-01-18	NUFQ355782	86.07	252.0	200900007				True
CRC	0067	LM	cRNA	01	2012-03-15	NUFj210125	78.0	424.0	200900007				True
CRC	0067	LM	DNA	06	2011-04-16	NUEN618423	69.64	1811.54	200900007				True
CRC	0067	LM	cRNA	01	2012-03-15	NUFj210143	69.0	561.0	200900007				True
CRC	0067	LM	cRNA	01	2012-03-15	NUFj210116	60.0	150.0	200900007				True
CRC	0067	LM	cRNA	01	2012-03-15	NUFj210134	60.0	150.0	200900007				True
CRC	0067	LM	DNA	02	2011-04-30	M029dx02	50.0	1312.0	200900007				True

Showing 1 to 10 of 447 entries Previous Next

(D)

Show 10 entries Search:

Collection type	Case	Tissue	Aliquot type	Aliquot ID	Coll. date	Barcode	Volume(ul)	Conc.(ng/ul)	InformedCons.	GE/Vex (GE/ml)	24-H urines(ml)	Coll. date(1)	Avail.
CRC	0067	LM	cRNA	01	2012-01-18	NUFQ355825	87 - 9	288.0	200900007				True

Showing 1 to 1 entries Previous Next

Export for: Derivation   Export   Save to PDF   Save to CSV

(B)

Show 10 entries Search:

N	Patient ID
11	A0105
12	A0095
13	C0001
14	A0089
15	A0132
16	A0140
17	A0144
18	C0066
19	C0054
20	C0027

Showing 11 to 20 of 476 entries Previous Next

Figure 6. Derivation interface

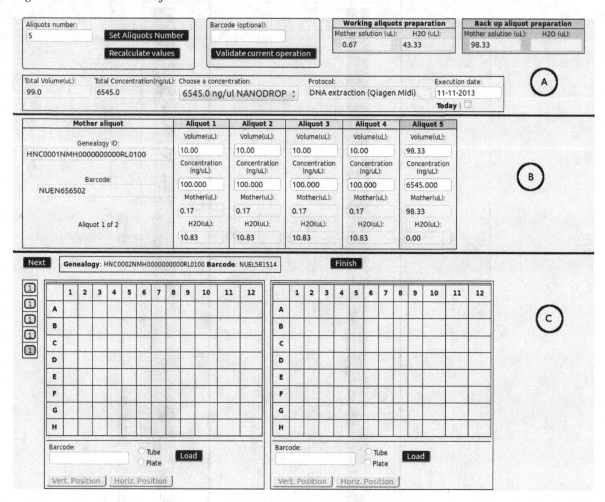

insert the corresponding barcode. Newly generated aliquots are then placed in the available positions using drag and drop. When all aliquots have been processed, a final report is shown.

USAGE STATISTICS AND SYSTEM EVALUATION

The LAS platform has been actively employed for research in our institution since March 2012. Only a few modules (i.e., BioBank, Storage, Xenopatients) have been available in the first release, with similar functionalities to the current version. Instead, the Privilege Manager and the MDDM have initially been restricted to the basic functionalities. During the first year, new functionalities have been deployed, and existing ones have been improved based on user feedback. In March 2013, the Microarray and the Repository modules have been deployed, while all the other modules included in the current suite have been released in June 2013. The development of the entire suite is currently ongoing, and additional functionalities are added on average every week.

Even if only a few research groups within our institution are currently using the platform, a large amount of data has been already stored related to the last three years. In particular, at the moment, 834 collections, each one including all the biological entities (i.e., aliquots, xenopatients) that share a common origin (i.e., the same collection event), are stored in the database. Each month, approximately 25 new collections are started. As of October 2013, the BioBank module includes approximately 84,000 aliquots, as pointed out in Table 1. On average, 2,400 aliquots are generated each month, including aliquots coming both from surgical interventions on human patients, and from xenopatients and derivation procedures. Since the most active user group works with xenopatients, approximately 85% of the aliquots stored in the BioBank are generated from mice. A detailed categorization of aliquots, based on their source, is reported in Table 2. Derived aliquots represent approximately 30% of the BioBank content, and most of them are DNA. On average, out of 590

derived aliquots extracted each month, 400 are DNA aliquots. The statistics on derived aliquot distribution is reported in Table 3. The BioBank module also tracks aliquot consumption according to the types of experiments. Over 70% are sent to external laboratories to perform special analyses such as fingerprinting, while all other molecular experiments are performed in our institution. As depicted in Table 4, the LAS modules cover a wide range of experiments performed in the institution. Figure 7 plots the number of performed experiments over time. On average, 125 aliquots are used each month for the experiments, except for the last month where over 1,000 aliquots were sent to an external laboratory for a particular analysis.

To date, the Storage module does not manage all the containers employed in our institution, but

Table 1. BioBank aliquots

	Stored		Available	
	#	%	#	%
Human	12,268	14.62	10,837	13.69
Xenopatients	71,621	85.38	68,351	86.31
Total	83,889		79,188	

Table 2. Categorization of stored and available aliquots according to the source

	Human				Xenopatients			
	Stored		*Available*		*Stored*		*Available*	
	#	%	#	%	#	%	#	%
RNALater	3,122	25.45	2,596	23.95	21,088	29.44	20,318	29.73
Snap frozen	142	1.16	141	1.30	18,591	25.96	18,499	27.06
DNA	4,704	38.34	4,576	42.23	10,196	14.24	10,089	14.76
Viable	1,425	11.62	926	8.54	8,663	12.10	6,508	9.52
Formalin fixed	0	0.00	0	0.00	6,782	9.47	6,756	9.88
RNA	135	1.10	135	1.25	4,928	6.88	4,851	7.10
Plasma	2,728	22.24	2,455	22.65	0	0.00	0	0.00
cRNA	12	0.10	8	0.07	1,236	1.73	1,208	1.77
OCTfrozen	0	0.00	0	0.00	82	0.11	72	0.11
cDNA	0	0.00	0	0.00	55	0.08	50	0.07
Total	12,268		10,837		71,621		68,351	

Table 3. Derivations

	#Derivatives created	DNA	RNA	cDNA	cRNA	#Derivation events
Total	19,438	13,271	4,867	52	1,248	5,051
Average	589.03	402.15	147.48	1.58	37.82	153.06

Table 4. Experiments

Experiment	# aliquots	% aliquots
Collaboration	1,666	72.09
Real time PCR	240	10.39
Microarray	177	7.66
Sanger sequencing	138	5.97
Histology-IHC	80	3.46
WesternBlots	10	0.43

only those used by the groups registered with the LAS system. Still, more than 80,000 containers belonging to different categories and with different characteristics are tracked. In Table 5, the categories of containers, with the current number of available units, are reported.

The Xenopatients module is one of the most currently used modules, since it manages the core research activity of most active users. As of October 2013, more than 11,000 mice have been tracked. Most of them are not alive due to programmed explants or accidental death (e.g., due to drug toxicity). Only 8% is currently alive and under treatment with experimental drugs. A detailed categorization of mice statuses is reported in Figure 8. On average, each month 313 implants and 160 explants are executed, where

each explant generates approximately 8 aliquots. Two main activities are performed on mice: measurement of implanted tumor size and application of experimental treatments. For the first activity, which can include both qualitative and quantitative measures, the monthly average of total measures is around 4,000 (equally distributed across both categories). For the second activity, to date, more than 3,200 treatments have been applied, and 80 are still under execution. On average, 170 treatments are started each month, while 165 are ended, and 3 are aborted due to some protocol constraints. In Figure 9, the number of monthly treatments tracked since the deployment of the LAS system is reported.

To evaluate the quality of the LAS platform, we asked the most active users (i.e., 12 users) to complete a questionnaire, to know their opinion about different aspects of the system and understand its impact on their daily work. As a general opinion, users agreed that the system is proving very useful in supporting their research, and plan to use it in the next future. However, they also met some difficulties in starting to use the platform, because of the way this has changed their working habits (e.g., users of the platform must follow predefined rules and procedures for each operation, and instantly report their activity) . Despite these difficulties, they noticed an improvement in the data quality and judge the platform very reliable. Moreover, they found the possibility to access the platform by using a simple web browser is a major benefit, since it allows the usage of tablet PCs which do not considerably reduce their working surface and can be comfortably used even in critical environments. Two critical aspects have emerged from the questionnaire:

Table 5. Containers

Container Type	# Units
Freezers	15
Racks	259
Plates	1,167
Tubes full or empty	79,137

Figure 7. Number of experiments per month

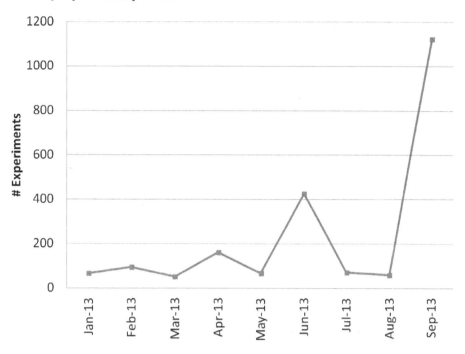

Figure 8. Mice status

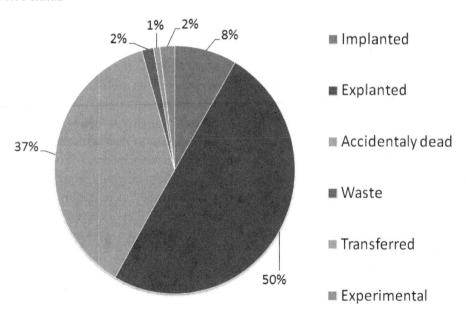

Figure 9. Number of treatments per month

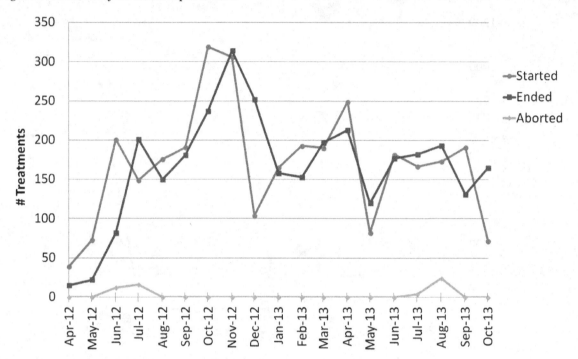

(i) some procedures and graphical interfaces are not very intuitive, and (ii) the retrieval of data is not always easy. To address the first issue, we are planning to improve some functionalities in order to simplify the operations. The second issue is mostly related to the MDDM module. Indeed, this module was primarily designed for principal investigators, whose querying needs are mainly exploratory and oriented to research purposes. For this reason, a wizard functionality, providing a standardized and less flexible way of querying the databases, was designed but not devoted as much attention. However, we noticed in many cases that even ordinary users do need to retrieve data and information to better plan their day-to-day work. Hence, as discussed in the Future work section, we are planning to improve the MDDM module with usability in mind.

The questionnaire submitted by the LAS users included opinions about the functionalities of each module, evaluated on a scale from 1 to 10 (where 1

is very bad, and 10 is excellent). The most widely used modules, i.e., Xenopatients, BioBank, Storage and Microarray, received an overall grade of about 9, while the MDDM was rated around 7, even though its usefulness was acknowledged by all users. As discussed above, the main reason is the lack of an easy-to-use wizard procedure, which forces users to deal with the complexity of the query generator interface. For the other modules, the questionnaire only requested a general opinion, since they were deployed few months ago. On average, they received a score of around 7, due to the reduced set of available functionalities.

FUTURE RESEARCH DIRECTIONS

The Laboratory Assistant Suite is a relatively young project that needs improvements and polishing to meet user requirements and expectations, and be able to compete with commercial LIMS under some aspects. In this direction, we are planning both different updates to the existing modules to broaden the set of offered functionalities, and the development of new modules addressing the management of other experimental procedures and data useful to daily work and research in our institution.

In particular, we are currently developing new functionalities in the Storage module, to load complex storage structures and provide more flexibility in the definition of the constraints associated with each container. The collection functionality will be redesigned to add several pieces of information related to the patient and the surgical event, and to allow the user to suspend and resume the operation at a different time. The graphical representation of containers will also be revised to improve the overall quality. The Microarray module will also be improved to allow the user to re-edit experimental plans and define datasets to be exported for further analyses. For a number of other operative modules, support will be added to track all steps of the experimental procedures. Finally, we are starting the development of a new module that will track all consumables involved in laboratory operations and manage the warehouse. A cell-line management module will also be developed to track the life cycle of cell lines and monitor the experimental conditions applied to each cell.

In the next month, the MDDM will receive an update to increase the query performance and improve its flexibility. The wizard functionality will be enhanced and made directly accessible from any other module if necessary. The Genomic Annotator will be expanded with other databases, and new functionalities will be included for managing and writing annotations associated with the biological entities stored in the system. We are also planning a new module that will exploit the MDDM capabilities to define complex experimental pipelines and monitor their execution.

Furthermore, we are introducing new security features related to user and data privileges, to increase the flexibility of the system in defining

restrictions. Finally, we are implementing an analysis library that will include state-of-the-art approaches from bioinformatics, statistics and data mining, allowing users to perform any kind of analysis on integrated data retrieved by the system. Architectural solutions are being investigated to increase the computational performance of the analysis processes.

CONCLUSION

The Laboratory Assistant Suite (LAS) platform is designed to assist researchers of biological and biomedical laboratories in all their activities. The modular architecture allows managing heterogeneous and complex data and performing different experimental procedures. Moreover, the graphical interfaces and the web-based architecture enable the researchers to use the platform in various environments, including hostile ones (e.g., in sterile conditions). Even though the software was deployed only 2 years ago, all core functionalities are available, and the users of the system found it useful in support to their daily work activities. The real use-cases presented in this chapter show the effectiveness of the proposed approach in modeling the research environments and managing laboratory-related procedures. We believe that future releases of the LAS system, besides offering new functionalities, will improve the overall reliability and usability of the platform, helping research laboratories deliver high-quality research.

REFERENCES

AgileBio. (2014). Retrieved from http://www.agilebio.com/

Baralis, E., Bertotti, A., Fiori, A., & Grand, A. (2012). LAS: a software platform to support oncological data management. *Journal of Medical Systems*, *36*(1), 81–90. doi:10.1007/s10916-012-9891-6 PMID:23117791

Bauch, A., Adamczyk, I., Buczek, P., Elmer, F. J., Enimanev, K., & Glyzewski, P. et al. (2011). openBIS: a flexible framework for managing and analyzing complex data in biology research. *BMC Bioinformatics*, *12*(1), 468. doi:10.1186/1471-2105-12-468 PMID:22151573

Bertotti, A., Migliardi, G., Galimi, F., Sassi, F., Torti, D., Isella, C., & Trusolino, L. (2011). A molecularly annotated platform of patient-derived xenografts ("xenopatients") identifies HER2 as an effective therapeutic target in cetuximab-resistant colorectal cancer. *Cancer Discovery*, *1*(6), 508–523. doi:10.1158/2159-8290.CD-11-0109 PMID:22586653

BioMatters. (2014). Retrieved from http://www.biomatters.com/

Blankenberg, D., Kuster, G. V., Coraor, N., Ananda, G., Lazarus, R., Mangan, M., & Taylor, J. (2010). Galaxy: A Web-Based Genome Analysis Tool for Experimentalists. *Current Protocols in Molecular Biology*, 19–10. PMID:20583098

caTissue Plus. (2014). Retrieved from http://www.catissueplus.org/

Clarity LIMS. (2014). Retrieved from http://genologics.com/claritylims

Clément, S., Fillon, J., Bousquet, J., & Beaulieu, J. (2010). TreeSNPs: A laboratory information management system (LIMS) dedicated to SNP discovery in trees. *Tree Genetics & Genomes*, *6*(3), 435–438. doi:10.1007/s11295-009-0261-6

COSMIC. (2014). Retrieved from http://cancer.sanger.ac.uk/cancergenome/projects/cosmic/

Eckerson, W. W. (1995). Three tier client/server architectures: Achieving scalability, performance, and efficiency in client/server applications. *Open Information Systems*, *3*(20), 46–50.

El Akadi, A., Amine, A., El Ouardighi, A., & Aboutajdine, D. (2011). A two-stage gene selection scheme utilizing MRMR filter and GA wrapper. *Knowledge and Information Systems*, *26*(3), 487–500. doi:10.1007/s10115-010-0288-x

UCSC Genome Browser. (2014). Retrieved from http://genome.ucsc.edu/

Giardine, B., Riemer, C., Hardison, R. C., Burhans, R., Elnitski, L., Shah, P., & Nekrutenko, A. (2005). Galaxy: A platform for interactive large-scale genome analysis. *Genome Research*, *15*(10), 1451–1455. doi:10.1101/gr.4086505 PMID:16169926

Goecks, J., Nekrutenko, A., Taylor, J., & Team, T. G. (2010). Galaxy: A comprehensive approach for supporting accessible, reproducible, and transparent computational research in the life sciences. *Genome Biology*, *11*(8), R86. doi:10.1186/gb-2010-11-8-r86 PMID:20738864

Golub, T. R., Slonim, D. K., Tamayo, P., Huard, C., Gaasenbeek, M., Mesirov, J. P., & Lander, E. S. (1999). Molecular classification of cancer: class discovery and class prediction by gene expression monitoring. *Science*, *286*(5439), 531–537. doi:10.1126/science.286.5439.531 PMID:10521349

Haquin, S., Oeuillet, E., Pajon, A., Harris, M., Jones, A. T., & van Tilbeurgh, H. et al. (2008). Data management in structural genomics: an overview. *Methods in Molecular Biology (Clifton, N.J.)*, *426*, 49. doi:10.1007/978-1-60327-058-8_4 PMID:18542857

Kent, W. J. (2002). BLAT—the BLAST-like alignment tool. *Genome Research*, *12*(4), 656–664. doi:10.1101/gr.229202. Article published online before March 2002 PMID:11932250

Kuhn, K. et al. (2007). The Cancer Biomedical Informatics Grid (caBIG™): Infrastructure and Applications for a Worldwide Research Community. *Medinfo*, *1*, 330.

LabGru. (2014). Retrieved from http://www.labguru.com/

LabLinx. (2014). Retrieved from http://www.lablynx.com/

Bika Labs. (2014). Retrieved from http://www.bikalabs.com/softwarecenter/bika

LabTrove. (2014). Retrieved from http://www.labtrove.org/

LABVANTAGE. (2014). Retrieved from http://www.labvantage.com/

LIMSWiki. (2014). Retrieved from http://www.limswiki.org/index.php?title=Main_Page

London, J. W., & Chatterjee, D. (2010). Using the Semantically Interoperable Biospecimen Repository Application, caTissue: End User Deployment Lessons Learned. In *Proceedings of 2010 IEEE International Conference on BioInformatics and BioEngineering (BIBE)* (pp. 316-317). IEEE.

Maier, H., Lengger, C., Simic, B., Fuchs, H., Gailus-Durner, V., & de Angelis, M. H. (2008). MausDB: An open source application for phenotype data and mouse colony management in large-scale mouse phenotyping projects. *BMC Bioinformatics*, *9*(1), 169. doi:10.1186/1471-2105-9-169 PMID:18366799

Mierswa, I., Wurst, M., Klinkenberg, R., Scholz, M., & Euler, T. (2006). Yale: Rapid prototyping for complex data mining tasks. In *Proceedings of the 12th ACM SIGKDD international conference on Knowledge discovery and data mining* (pp. 935-940). ACM.

Milisavljevic, M., Hearty, T., Wong, T. Y. T., Portales-Casamar, E., Simpson, E. M., & Wasserman, W. W. (2010). Laboratory Animal Management Assistant (LAMA): a LIMS for active research colonies. *Mammalian Genome*, *21*(5), 224–230. doi:10.1007/s00335-010-9258-6 PMID:20411264

Nelson, E. K., Piehler, B., Eckels, J., Rauch, A., Bellew, M., Hussey, P., & Igra, M. (2011). LabKey Server: An open source platform for scientific data integration, analysis and collaboration. *BMC Bioinformatics*, *12*(1), 71. doi:10.1186/1471-2105-12-71 PMID:21385461

Nix, D., Di Sera, T., Dalley, B., Milash, B., Cundick, R., Quinn, K., & Courdy, S. (2010). Next generation tools for genomic data generation, distribution, and visualization. *BMC Bioinformatics*, *11*(1), 455. doi:10.1186/1471-2105-11-455 PMID:20828407

O'Connor, B., Merriman, B., & Nelson, S. (2010). SeqWare Query Engine: storing and searching sequence data in the cloud. [Retrieved from: http://seqware.github.io/]. *BMC Bioinformatics*, *11*(Suppl 12), S2. doi:10.1186/1471-2105-11-S12-S2 PMID:21210981

Reich, M., Liefeld, T., Gould, J., Lerner, J., Tamayo, P., & Mesirov, J. P. (2006). GenePattern 2.0. *Nature Genetics*, *38*(5), 500–501. doi:10.1038/ng0506-500 PMID:16642009

RURO. (2014). Retrieved from http://www.ruro.com/

Tolopko, A., Sullivan, J., Erickson, S., Wrobel, D., Chiang, S., Rudnicki, K., & Shamu, C. (2010). Screensaver: an open source lab information management system (LIMS) for high throughput screening facilities. *BMC Bioinformatics*, *11*(1), 260. PMID:20482787

Two Fold Software. (2014). Retrieved from http://www.twofold-software.com/site/

Wang, J., Li, H., Zhu, Y., Yousef, M., Nebozhyn, M., & Showe, M. et al. (2007). VISDA: An open-source caBIG™ analytical tool for data clustering and beyond. *Bioinformatics (Oxford, England)*, *23*(15), 2024–2027. PMID:17540678

ADDITIONAL READING

Gibbon, G. A. (1996). A brief history of LIMS. *Laboratory Automation & Information Management*, *32*(1), 1–5. doi:10.1016/1381-141X(95)00024-K

Hemmer, M. (2003). Laboratory Information Management Systems (LIMS). Handbook of Chemoinformatics: From Data to Knowledge in 4 Volumes, 844-864.

Holovaty, A., & Kaplan-Moss, J. (2009). *The definitive guide to Django: Web development done right*. Apress. doi:10.1007/978-1-4302-1937-8

Jones, J. (2012). *The LIMS Book & Buyer's Guide*. Laboratory Informatics Institute, Inc.

Leclercq, É., & Savonnet, M. (2013). Enhancing scientific information systems with semantic annotations. In *Proceedings of the 28th Annual ACM Symposium on Applied Computing* (pp. 319-324). ACM.

Li, H., Gennari, J. H., & Brinkley, J. F. (2006). Model driven laboratory information management systems. In *AMIA Annual Symposium Proceedings* (p. 484).

McLelland, A. (1998). LIMS: A Laboratory Toy or a Critical IT Component?. *LIMS/Letter, 4*(2).

Myneni, S., & Patel, V. L. (2010). Organization of biomedical data for collaborative scientific research: A research information management system. *International Journal of Information Management*, *30*(3), 256–264. doi:10.1016/j.ijinfomgt.2009.09.005 PMID:20543892

O'Leary, K. M. (2008). Selecting the Right LIMS: Critiquing technological strengths and limitations. Retrieved from.http://www.scientificcomputing.com/articles/2008/08/selecting-right-lims

Palla, P., Frau, G., Vargiu, L., & Rodriguez-Tomé, P. (2012). QTreds: a flexible LIMS for omics laboratories. *EMBnet. journal, 18*(B), pp-41.

Pantanowitz, L., Henricks, W. H., & Beckwith, B. A. (2007). Medical laboratory informatics. *Clinics in Laboratory Medicine*, *27*(4), 823–843. doi:10.1016/j.cll.2007.07.011 PMID:17950900

Paszko, C., & Turner, E. (2001). *Laboratory information management systems*. CRC press.

Plant, C., & Böhm, C. (Eds.). (2010). *Database technology for life sciences and medicine* (Vol. 6). World Scientific.

Prasad, P. J., & Bodhe, G. L. (2012). Trends in laboratory information management system. *Chemometrics and Intelligent Laboratory Systems*. doi:10.1016/j.chemolab.2012.07.001

Rosenthal, A., Mork, P., Li, M. H., Stanford, J., Koester, D., & Reynolds, P. (2010). Cloud computing: A new business paradigm for biomedical information sharing. *Journal of Biomedical Informatics*, *43*(2), 342–353. doi:10.1016/j.jbi.2009.08.014 PMID:19715773

Royce, J. R. (2012). Industry Insights: Examining the Risks, Benefits and Trade-offs of Today's LIMS. *Scientific Computing Retrieved*, 7.

Silbermann, J., Weinert, S., Wernicke, C., & Frohme, M. (2011). Quality and information management in the laboratory. In *Logistics and Industrial Informatics (LINDI), 2011 3rd IEEE International Symposium on* (pp. 93-98).

Skobelev, D. O., Zaytseva, T. M., Kozlov, A. D., Perepelitsa, V. L., & Makarova, A. S. (2011). Laboratory information management systems in the work of the analytic laboratory. *Measurement Techniques*, *53*(10), 1182–1189. doi:10.1007/s11018-011-9638-7

Sparkes, A., & Clare, A. (2012). AutoLabDB: a substantial open source database schema to support a high-throughput automated laboratory. *Bioinformatics (Oxford, England)*, *28*(10), 1390–1397. doi:10.1093/bioinformatics/bts140 PMID:22467910

Triplet, T., & Butler, G. (2012). The EnzymeTracker: an open-source laboratory information management system for sample tracking. *BMC Bioinformatics*, *13*(1), 15. doi:10.1186/1471-2105-13-15 PMID:22280360

Van Rossum, T., Tripp, B., & Daley, D. (2010). SLIMS—a user-friendly sample operations and inventory management system for genotyping labs. *Bioinformatics (Oxford, England)*, *26*(14), 1808–1810. doi:10.1093/bioinformatics/btq271 PMID:20513665

Venco, F., Ceol, A., & Muller, H. (2013). SLIMS: a LIMS for handling next-generation sequencing workflows. *EMBnet. journal, 19*(B), 85.

Wood, S. (2007). Comprehensive laboratory informatics: A multilayer approach. *American Laboratory*, *39*(16), 20.

Yousef, A. F., Baggili, I. M., Bartlett, G., Kane, M. D., & Mymryk, J. S. (2011). LINA: A Laboratory Inventory System for Oligonucleotides, Microbial Strains, and Cell Lines. *Journal of the Association for Laboratory Automation*, *16*(1), 82–89. doi:10.1016/j.jala.2009.07.004 PMID:21609688

KEY TERMS AND DEFINITIONS

Biobank: A type of biorepository that stores biological samples for use in research.

Laboratory Information Management System (LIMS): Software-based laboratory and information management system that offers a set of key features that support a modern laboratory's operations.

Microarray: Technology used for rapid surveys of the expression of many genes simultaneously.

Molecular Oncology: A branch of oncology that leverages recent advances in molecular biology to define the changes affecting the control of cell growth, responsible for the rise and development of tumors, in molecular terms, and to trace the steps by which certain tumors evolve.

Real-Time Polymerase Chain Reaction (RT-PCR): Method for the detection and quantization of an amplified PCR product monitored at each cycle, "in real time".

Sanger Sequencing: Method of DNA sequencing based on the selective incorporation of chain-terminating dideoxynucleotides by DNA polymerase during in vitro DNA replication.

Xenopatient: Immunocompromised animal implanted with one or more tumor aliquots, used for research purposes in the oncological field.

Chapter 14
An Evaluation of Laboratory Information Systems in Medical Laboratories in Jamaica

Donovan McGrowder
The University of the West Indies, Jamaica

Romeo Bishop
The University of the West Indies, Jamaica

ABSTRACT

This chapter seeks to find out information on the functionalities of the laboratory information systems available in medical laboratories in Jamaica and their ease of use and the overall performance and satisfaction of medical technologists using them. A cross-sectional descriptive survey involving the use of a 48-item questionnaire was conducted among medical laboratories with a LIS. There were a total of 14 completed questionnaires out of 15, giving a response rate of 93.3%. The findings reveal that the majority of the laboratories have a LIS that provides multi-level security, allows password protection at different levels, maintains a patient database, and generates records. The majority of the medical technologists agree or strongly agree that it is easy to use the LIS and experience improved overall performance on the job. The medical technologists clearly understand the existing features and functionality of the LIS. Additional functional features of the LIS should be customized, and adequate funding is needed, especially for hospital-based laboratories.

INTRODUCTION

Laboratory medicine is the foundation on which the structure of scientific medicine is erected and is an integral component of the clinical diagnosis and management process. The clinical laboratory is increasingly integrated with patient care, assisting diagnosis, monitoring therapies and predicting clinical outcomes. Laboratories also provide essential public health information and disease surveillance (Dacombe et al., 2006). Due to this wide-ranging role, laboratories are an important part of many disease control programmes. Therefore, laboratory-based disciplines such as clinical

DOI: 10.4018/978-1-4666-6320-6.ch014

chemistry, haematology, histology, immunology and microbiology contribute significantly in effectively controlling infectious and non-infectious diseases.

Laboratory medicine has undergone marked changes during the 20th century and is likely to develop even more rapidly in the 21st century (Guidi & Lippi, 2006). Ongoing technological developments have considerably improved the productivity and efficiency of clinical laboratories, and there have been significant improvements in the provision and quality of diagnostic tests. Significant developments such as automation, commercially produced reagents and more powerful computers provide clinicians with an ever-increasing list of rapid and cost-effective tests. Furthermore, more efficient patient result verification has greatly improved laboratory test throughput while decreasing turn-around-times, enabling critical results to reach clinicians rapidly for better clinical outcomes. Advances in laboratory medicine have occurred in conjunction with analytical developments that measure many different analytes with specificity for pathological conditions and ever-increasing sensitivity. Such tests revolutionized clinical diagnosis in ways that were unimaginable even a decade ago (Herzlinger, 2006).

Information systems in pathology provide opportunities for clinical laboratory scientists and pathologists to impact both clinical care and research agendas adding value to the health care system, both at local and international levels. Pathology information systems can provide major databases for research in health services and new informatics-based approaches to database research. Databases are created through the archiving and organization of laboratory data through the laboratory information system (LIS), hospital information systems (HIS) or peripheral programs (Connelly, 1997). Databases of quantitative laboratory data can be used for data mining, rule discovery, retrospective analysis and other clinical research applications. Maintaining the integrity of databases is an im-

portant function of the laboratory diagnostician or information technology scientist (Friedman, 1990). Database support encompasses acquisition, coding, data classification, design, display, reporting standards, management, and query methods (Connelly, 1997; Friedman, 1990).

The last two decades have brought major advances in processing power and software engineering, many of which have had a direct impact in clinical laboratories. Laboratory information systems have revolutionized the storage and retrieval of information. They are used for assessing and improving quality in clinical laboratories, and patient management using decision support (Bates et al., 1999). The purchase and installation of a modern LIS module in clinical laboratories have significantly increased laboratory productivity in terms of quality and cost reductions, and improved turn-around-time as test results are produced faster (Pelegri et al., 1996).

There are approximately 83 medical and non-medical laboratories in Jamaica. As part of the Government of Jamaica's objective to prepare laboratories for accreditation, 25 non-medical laboratories between 2003 and 2006 received over 700 man-hours of consultancy from the Swedish Board for Accreditation and Conformity Assessment (SWEDAC) to assist them with their preparation for accreditation using ISO 17025:1999. In March 2007, the accreditation body in Jamaica, called the Jamaica National Agency for Accreditation (JANAAC), was legally incorporated and officially launched on June 9, 2009. JANNAC operates in conformity with ISO 17011:2004 entitled Conformity assessment - General requirements for accreditation bodies accrediting conformity assessment bodies. JANAAC is currently accepting applications from medical and non-medical laboratories that are prepared for accreditation. To date 6 non-medicals and one (1) medical laboratory received accreditation for various tests from JANAAC. This study sought to: (i) find out information on the functionalities and technical features of the laboratory information systems available in medical laboratories in Jamaica (ii) investigate their ease of use and effect on the efficiency and effectiveness of the medical technologist in completing daily tasks and (iii) assess the overall performance and satisfaction of medical technologists using the laboratory information systems.

BACKGROUND

This study was conducted in September 2013. A cross-sectional descriptive survey was used in this study. Following the design of the questionnaire, a pilot study was conducted involving two medical laboratories. A pilot study was conducted which resulted in important improvements to the questionnaire and a general increase in the efficiency of the study. The purpose of the pilot study was to identify any errors in the format, to determine whether or not the questions clearly reflected the information sought, to assess the adequacy of the questionnaire instructions, and to invite constructive comments from the participants. Amendments and adjustments were made to the questionnaire according to the results of the pilot study.

The reliability of results of this study was achieved through asking the medical technologist questions about the laboratory information system that they were familiar with and relevant to their day to day operations in the laboratory. The ethical issues in the study included confidentiality and anonymity. The completed questionnaire was sealed in an envelope and returned to me. It seemed that the medical technologists that participated in the study responded with openness and honesty, and there was a reasonably high degree of reliability. We requested that that the medical technologist filled out the questionnaire as soon as they could, and this was done in their own laboratory.

The questionnaire survey was distributed either by hand or sent electronically to medical laboratories who are members of the Laboratories Association of Jamaica (LAJ), and who possess a functioning laboratory information system. A medical technologist was randomly selected in each laboratory, and this individual was asked to complete the questionnaire. Before administration of the questionnaire, the purpose of the study was explained to each respondent and confidentiality of the information assured.

The questionnaire consisted of 48-items and Section A covered basic demographic information such as whether the laboratory is public or private and the number of years that the medical technologist who completed the questionnaire has been employed in the laboratory. Sections B, C and D looked at the functionalities and technical features of the laboratory information systems available in the medical laboratories and examined areas such as ease of use, effect on the efficiency and effectiveness of the medical technologist in completing daily tasks, as well as the overall performance and satisfaction of medical technologists using the laboratory information system.

Statistics were computed using the Statistical Package for Social Sciences, version 14.0 (SPSS Inc., Chicago, Illinois, United States). The results are given in percentages.

There was a total of 14 completed questionnaires out of 15 distributed among the medical laboratories that possess a LIS, giving a response rate of 93.3%.

RESULTS

Medical technologists from three public and eleven private medical laboratories completed the questionnaires. All the laboratories were located in Kingston and St. Andrew. The medical technologists who participated in the study were employed for 0 - 5 years (42.9%), 6 - 10 years (7.1%), 10 - 15 years (14.2%) and 16 years and over (35.8%). The vendors which provide the laboratory information systems to the participation laboratories in the study include SchuyLab,

CyberLAB, DISAlab and Lab Soft 2000. Most of the medical laboratories have SchuyLab.

The laboratory information systems in the participating medical laboratories comprised of internal modules primarily for clinical chemistry, haematology, microbiology and cytology. One laboratory had a module for anatomical pathology and other specialized sub-disciplines such as endocrinology and immunology. The key processes of the laboratory information systems in these medical laboratories were integrating chemistry, haematology, and microbiology reporting, result reporting, management/quality reporting, order entry, bar coding/label printing, trending of patient results and cumulative reporting across facility encounters. The processes which were least available in the medical laboratories were multi-site testing, outreach client services, specimen storage, specimen control work-list and work flow/staff scheduling

In terms of functionalities and technical features, the majority of the medical laboratories has a laboratory information system that: provide an outreach system that employs a centralized rational database (54.6%), provide a multi-level security system (92.7%), allow password protection at different levels (100.0%), maintain an audit trail for system entries (71.4%), allow analyzer interface (78.6%), allow compound ordering (86.7%), allow users to order tests by entering codes (85.7%), and provide release of results after they have been reviewed and approved by technical personnel (100.0%).

The majority of the medical technologists reported that the laboratory information systems were able to highlight abnormal results on patients' report (92.9%), maintain patient database and generate records (100.0%), allow users to graph patient results by tests to identify possible trends (76.9%), allow archiving of patient records (100.0%), allow implementation of Westgard quality control rules and flags (61.5%) and allow flagging of out-of-range quality control values (75.0%).

The study examined the ease of use and the how the laboratory information system affect the workflow and the ability of the medical technologist to complete their task in a more effective and efficient manner. The majority of the medical technologists agrees or strongly agree that: it was easy to use the laboratory information system, it was easy to find the information needed on the laboratory information system; the information on the laboratory information system was effective in assisting them in completing assigned tasks, the interface on the laboratory information system was attractive, the use of the laboratory information system allowed them to accomplish the task more quickly and enhance the effectiveness of the user on the job, feel comfortable using the laboratory information system, experience improved overall performance on the job and overall satisfied with how easy it was to use the system.

DISCUSSION

A laboratory information system is a highly organized electronic tool with adaptable application that has the capacity to receive, process and store laboratory information and data as well as various work-flow models at the same time (Biggs, 2001). Laboratory information systems have become a critical part of the operations of clinical laboratory, and their functionality goes beyond the transmission of orders and generation of results. They were important in the management of laboratory processes in the pre-analytical, analytical and post-analytical phases including communication of specimen collection, identification of specimen using bar coding, tracking of specimen, workload and volume data collection, test utilization management and monitoring of turnaround time (Lehmann and Cappello, 2003). It is critical that the laboratory information system be streamlined to meet the specific operational needs and key functions of each laboratory, end users and organization.

Private and public medical laboratories use laboratory information systems for the gathering and storage of laboratory data support and manage business practices. Less than one-quarter of medical laboratories in Jamaica possesses a laboratory information system. The purchase and implementation of laboratory information system can be costly, and validation of the requirements for the same can be difficult. In the selection of laboratory information system by a hospital or private clinical laboratory a number of parameters must be taken into consideration. These include: safety and security, cost of the module(s) and maintenance, scalability, reliability, functionality, technology, ease of use, training of personnel, customer support, and reputation of the vendor (Bilger, 1987). It is noted that there are more laboratory information systems in private compared with public medical laboratories. This may be due to a variety of factors such as budget constraints as there are inadequate financial resources, high cost of the laboratory information system and maintenance contracts, lack of or differences in communication between laboratory personnel and hospital/laboratory management. In instances where a public hospital decides to purchase a modern laboratory information system the consultation, decision and installation may take a long time (Brender and McNair, 2008). Less importance was given to the upgrade of the laboratory information system as more than one-half of the participating laboratories in this study did not provide a date of the most recent upgrade.

One of the features of laboratory information systems is that it can centralizes regulatory compliance procedures which have the advantage of improving and maximizing the level of responsibility and the reliability of data. It was observed that over one-half (54.6%) of the respondents did not have a laboratory information system that employs a centralized relational database. The laboratory information systems in the participating laboratories comprised of internal modules primarily for clinical chemistry, haematology, microbiol-ogy and cytology. One laboratory had a module for anatomical pathology and other specialized sub-disciplines such as endocrinology and immunology. There is a differentiation in laboratory workflow of these disciplines and sub-disciplines so the creation of different functionalities within the laboratory information system. Specialized targeted functionality in the laboratory information system such as the collection and receipt of specimen, tracking, work distribution in the pre-analytical, analytical and post-analytical phases in the disciplines and sub-disciplines may vary (Clifford, 2011).

The key processes of the laboratory information systems in these medical laboratories were chemistry, haematology, and microbiology reporting, result reporting, management/quality reporting, order entry, bar coding/label printing, trending of patient results and cumulative reporting across facility encounters. The processes which were least available in the laboratories were multi-site testing, outreach client services, specimen storage, specimen control work-list and work flow/staff scheduling.

Interfacing between the laboratory information system and the main auto-anayzers such as the Architect c8000 from the Abbott Diagnostics or the cobas 6000 analyzer from Roche Diagnostics (the main analyzers used in most of the medical laboratories) required compatibility of hardware and software which significantly improves productivity, and quality by reducing errors. It is important that the vendors customize the solutions such that the user-interface is easy to use and self-explanatory (McDowall, 1988). In this study, the majority of the medical technologists agrees or strongly agrees that they liked using the interface, and all agree or strongly agree that the information provided is easy to understand.

The laboratory information system should be secured from unauthorized access that can be internal or external and the confidentiality of the laboratory results of patients should be preserved according to local and international applicable laws and regulations without preventing staff personnel and other legitimate users from performing their job (Serdar et al., 2008). It is important that various levels of security be provided and in this study the majority of medical technologists reported that the laboratory information system provides a multi-system security system that ensure confidentiality of patient-related information. The ordering of tests by clinicians and other health care personnel along with systems which offer intelligent decision support will result in improved turnaround time offer guidance appropriation of tests and optimized utilization of laboratory tests (Westbrook et al., 2009). In its 2007 report, the American Hospital Association (AHA) stated that just under three-quarters (72%) of hospitals offered laboratory test electronic entry within the laboratory or by the clinician (AHA, 2007). The laboratory information systems allow the majority (85.7%) of medical technologists to order laboratory tests and select from a test menu. In order to optimize test utilization especially in a resource-limited setting such as ours, it is important to develop policies and procedures governing the utilization of laboratory resources.

All of the laboratories have a single laboratory information system which possesses multi-facility functions which rely on the computing hardware at a main data-centre, usually at the test processing site. One of the key functions of the laboratory information system is the ability of the system to track patients' samples location throughout the different testing phases comprised of pre-analytical, analytical and post-analytical. This includes transportation through the different sections of the laboratory at the testing site(s) and from other external sites, and the management and storage of such specimens (Emmerich et al., 1998). In this study just over one-half (53.9%) of the medical technologists indicated that the laboratory information system was able to provide tracking of patients samples through the different processes in the clinical laboratory. There should

also be a system that easily facilitates the retrieval of the specific specimen from various sections in the laboratory or external sites and proper management of storage and disposal of patient samples (Emmerich et al., 1988).

Data management is a critical function by laboratory information systems and there should be easy access to laboratory data and statistics. Laboratory information system modules should allow for the generation and integration of quality control algorithms including the Westgard rules and support the verification and validation of laboratory test results (Eggert et al., 1987). The findings of this study showed that the majority (61.5%) of the laboratory information system allow the implementation of Westgard rules and flags and allow flagging of out-of-range quality control values (76.9%). Most clinical laboratories have a modern quality control program which functions to enhance the reliability and accuracy of the results produced by decreasing to a minimum false rejection and maximizing the detection of errors (Westgard et al., 2004). The laboratory information system has a significant role in quality control and the majority of respondents in the study stated that the laboratory information system allows flagging of out-of-range quality control values.

The quality management module of the laboratory information system should support the accreditation requirements of ISO15189 and should be so designed that it is able to schedule automated performing of quality or giving alert to appropriate staff personnel regarding when quality control task must be completed (Yao et al., 2012). The laboratory information systems should guide the laboratory personnel in quality control rule selection and display quality control results including Levey-Jennings plots a well as any violation of Westgard quality control rules. The results of such should be easily interpreted by staff so that critical decisions about the acceptability of the test results can be made in a timely manner (Burnett, 2006).

Some laboratory information system has a thin-client browser interface whose use is intuitive and result in easier end-user adoption. With this feature, there is easier and quicker integration of the laboratory information system with the workflow and management operations of the clinical laboratory and enhanced productivity (Buffone et al., 1996). Laboratory information systems allow medical technologists and other laboratory personnel to improve scheduling of their work better schedule, assist in quality control checks, centralize laboratory data in a manner that is easily retrievable resulting in the laboratory being able to process more samples per hour worked.

Laboratory information systems are very complex, and a good understanding is required in order to operate them effectively and efficiently. The laboratory personnel are usually trained in the use of the laboratory information system while they are performing their day to day duties. All of the respondents stated that it was easy to learn how to use the laboratory information system and most were comfortable. The vendors offered extensive training to members of staff. In some cases, a few staff members were trained overseas and they subsequently on returning to the laboratory acted as trainers for other staff members. In other instances, the vendors trained the medical technologists locally. It is important that the medical technologists and other users are correctly trained so that they become proficient at using the system processes.

Laboratory technical personnel such as medical technologists and pathologists place significant emphasis on the efficient processing of tests, accuracy and timeliness of results (Donabedian et al., 1982). The laboratory information system is an important strategic tools at the disposal of laboratory personnel to improve and enable them to produce cost-effective and high quality service (Friedman, 1990). It is, therefore, important for the laboratory staff to understand the specific applications in order to reap the benefits that can be gained from the proper and efficient use of the laboratory information system. This requires that there is a cadre of highly trained and skilled personnel.

The laboratory information systems should enhance the efficiency and quality of work of health care professionals such as medical technologists and pathologists. In this study, the majority of the medical technologists reported that the LIS enhanced their effectiveness on the job and allowed them to efficiently complete their work. For most of the clinical laboratories the laboratory information system significantly assisted with the streamlining of the work flow of the laboratory so as to maximize the efficiency of the processing of clinical tests and availability of results in a timely manner, internal connectivity with analyzers and other laboratory equipments and delegation of work among laboratory personnel (Grandjean et al., 2011).

This study has a number of limitations. First the sample size, as there is not many medical laboratories in Jamaica with a laboratory information system. It would also be useful to include data from more medical technologist in the different laboratories, but this was limited by the time constraints and the medical technologist due to high work. It would also be useful to access the competence of other laboratory personnel users of the laboratory information systems such pathology consultants and medical laboratory assistants. These could be included in a future study. One of the areas that were not assessed in this study was the overall processing speed of the laboratory information system. This is important as medical technologists are not in favour of using an electronic device that is slow and difficult to handle. If the use of the laboratory information system is perceived to be beneficial to medical technologists and other laboratory personnel who take full advantage of its features, they will be more engaged in the process leading to full system optimization, greater productivity and greater job satisfaction.

It is important that staff at all levels have an input into the design and operational characteristics of the LIS especially during the implementation stage. The study did not assess the degree of participation of the medical technologists in the study in the process of the installation of the laboratory information system, and whether or not they were taught how to use the product overseas or on site. In addition, it is not known if medical technologist were given adequate time to learn and apply each feature of the laboratory information system in a stepwise implementation process or whether there was effective communication between the design team and staff. These factors will have a significant bearing of the job satisfaction.

Medical technologists should be taught by appropriate personnel of the vendor company or contracted trainers how to correctly use the features of the laboratory information system. They should be taught progressively so that they have the opportunity to use and apply the knowledge of the technology garnered in training and adjusted to new ways of working. Consistent training both from the vendor representatives and trainers can build team work and staff expertise and efficiency at different levels. Furthermore, there should be ongoing assessment or audit of the laboratory system with a well-developed feedback mechanism so that laboratory personnel present challenges that they are experiencing using the system and ways of a quick resolution identified and implemented.

CONCLUSION

The medical technologists in the participating medical laboratories clearly understand the existing features and functionality of the laboratory information system, and the majority is satisfied with its ease of use. However, they would like improvements in the ease at which information can be found, and there should be more features which makes their workload in the laboratory easier. Additional functional features of the laboratory information system should be customized in such a way that it optimizes their operational needs and improves the quality and cost-effectiveness

of service offered to clinicians and other users. There is also a major concern of the amount of medical laboratories that do not possess a laboratory information system. Adequate funding of the clinical laboratory by the stakeholders is needed especially hospital-based laboratories where test results are critical to in-patient diagnosis and care.

REFERENCES

American Hospital Association (AHA). (2007). Continued progress: Hospital use of information technology. Washington, DC: Author.

Bates, D. W., Pappius, E., Kuperman, G. J., Sittig, D., Burstin, H., & Fairchild, D. et al. (1999). Using information systems to measure and improve quality. *International Journal of Medical Informatics*, *53*, 115–124. doi:10.1016/S1386-5056(98)00152-X PMID:10193881

Bilger, M.P. (1987). Acquisition of a laboratory information system. *Health Comput. Commun.*, *4*(7), 44-46.

Brender, J., & McNair, P. (2008). Evaluation of robustness of a user requirements specification approach in a purchase context, a LIS case study. *Stud. Health Technol. Inform.*, *136*, 611-616.

Briggs, B. (2001). Planning for the future: the Department of Defense Laboratory Joint Working Group and Global Laboratory Information Transfer. *Health Data Management*, *9*(8), 22–24. PMID:11508063

Buffone, G.J., Moreau, D., & Beck, J.R. (1996). Work-flow computing: Improving management and efficiency of pathology diagnostic services. *Am. J. Clin. Pathol.*, *105*(4 Suppl 1), S17-S24.

Burnett, D. (2006). ISO 15189:2003-quality management, evaluation and continual improvement. *Clinical Chemistry and Laboratory Medicine*, *44*(6), 733–739. doi:10.1515/CCLM.2006.126 PMID:16729862

Clifford, L-J. (2011). *The evolving LIS needs to be everything for today's laboratories*. Medical Laboratory Observer. Retrieved October 31, 2013, from http://www.mlo-online.com/articles/201108/the-evolving-lis-needs-to-be-everything-for-todays-laboratories.php

Connelly, D. P., & Aller, R. D. (1997). Outcomes and informatics. *Archives of Pathology & Laboratory Medicine, 121*, 1176–1182. PMID:9372745

Dacombe, R. J., Aquire, S. B., Ramsay, A. R., Banda, H. J., & Bates, I. (2006). Essential medical laboratory services: Their role in delivering equitable health care in Malawi. *Malawi Medical Journal, 18*(2), 77–79.

Donabedian, A., Wheeler, R. R., & Wyszewianski, L. (1982). Quality, cost, and health: An integrative model. *Medical Care, 20*, 975–992. doi:10.1097/00005650-198210000-00001 PMID:6813605

Eggert, A.A., Westgard, J.O., Barrym, P.L., & Emmerich, K.A. (1987). Implementation of a multi-rule, multistage quality control program in a clinical laboratory computer system. *J. Med. Syst., 11*(6), 391-411.

Emmerich, K. A., Quam, E. F., Bowers, K. L., & Eggert, A. A. (1998). The combination of specimen tracking with an advanced AutoLog in a laboratory information system. *Journal of Medical Systems, 22*(3), 137–145. doi:10.1023/A:1022659631904 PMID:9604781

Friedman, B. A. (1990). Informatics as a separate section within a department of pathology. *American Journal of Clinical Pathology, 94*(Suppl 1), S2–S6. PMID:2220682

Grandjean, G., Graham, R., & Bartholomeusz, G. (2011). Essential attributes identified in the design of a laboratory information management system for a high throughput siRNA screening laboratory. *Comb. Chem. High. Throughput Screen., 14*(9), 766-771.

Guidi, G. C., & Lippi, G. (2006). Laboratory medicine in the 2000s: programmed death or rebirth? *Clinical Chemistry and Laboratory Medicine, 44*, 913–917. doi:10.1515/CCLM.2006.168 PMID:16879053

Herzlinger, R. E. (2006). Why innovation in health care is so hard. *Harvard Business Review, 84*, 58–66. PMID:16649698

Lehmann, C. A., & Cappello, S. C. (2003). Workflow analysis: an overview. In Clinical diagnostic technology: The total testing process (vol. 1). Washington, DC: American Association of Clinical Chemistry.

McDowall, R.D., Pearce, J.C., & Murkitt, G.S. (1988). Laboratory information management systems - Part 1 Concepts. *J. Pharm. Biomed. Anal., 6*(4), 339-359.

Pelegri, M. D., Garcia-Beltran, L., & Pascual, C. (1996). Improvement of emergency and routine turnaround time by data processing and instrumentation changes. *Clinica Chimica Acta, 248*(1), 65–72. doi:10.1016/0009-8981(95)06267-X PMID:8740571

Serdar, M. A., Turan, M., & Cihan, M. (2008). Rapid access to information resources in clinical biochemistry: medical applications of Personal Digital Assistants (PDA). *Clinical and Experimental Medicine*, 117–122. doi:10.1007/s10238-008-0166-y PMID:18618222

Westbrook, J. I., Georgiou, A., & Lam, M. (2009). Does computerized provider order entry reduce test turnaround times: a before-and-after study at four hospitals. *Studies in Health Technology and Informatics, 150*, 527–531. PMID:19745367

Westgard, J. O., & Darcy, T. (2004). The truth about quality: medical usefulness and analytical reliability of laboratory tests. *Clinica Chimica Acta, 346*(1), 3–11. doi:10.1016/j.cccn.2003.12.034 PMID:15234630

Yao, Q., Bai, Z., Zhu, L., Zhang, E., & Yuan, K. (2012). The rebuilding of LIS to pass the ISO15189. *Zhongguo Yi Liao Qi Xie Za Zhi, 36*(1), 59-60.

KEY TERMS AND DEFINITIONS

Accreditation: A voluntary process where medical laboratories are certified against an official international standard by an accreditation body to perform testing on human specimens.

Data Management: A key process in research where control is exercised over the information gathered in the different disciplines.

Database: The collection of data in an organized manner so that selected pieces of information can be retrieved quickly by a computer programme, thus increasing the efficiency and use of such information.

Functionalities: Usefulness.

Interface: The point of interconnection between the electronic data management system of an automated auto analyzer in the clinical laboratory, and the laboratory information system.

Laboratory Information System: A software-based information system that processes, manages and stores data from all the stages in the operations of the clinical laboratory.

Medical Laboratory: A laboratory where tests are performed on clinical specimens by medical technologists in order to obtain information about the health status of a patient, pertaining to the diagnosis, treatment, and prevention of disease.

Medical Technologist: An allied health professional who performs a number of technical and scientific functions in the clinical laboratory including complex analyses on body fluids, tissue and other substances.

Questionnaire: An instrument frequently used in quantitative research that comprises of a series of questions intended to gather information on a particular topic from respondents.

APPENDIX: QUESTIONNAIRE

Laboratory Information System Survey Questionnaire

This survey seeks to find out information on the functional and technical features of the laboratory information system (LIS) being currently employed by medical laboratories in Jamaica.

All of your responses will be kept strictly confidential, and your name or laboratory is not required. So, please use this opportunity to respond freely.

Section A

1. Is you laboratory: [ ] Public [ ] Private
2. Gender?

   Male [ ]
   Female [ ]

3. Is you laboratory located in:

   [ ] Kingston & St. Andrew [ ] Outside Kingston & St. Andrew
   Please state the parish: _____

4. How long have you been working in your laboratory?

   [ ] 0 - 5 years [ ] 6 - 10 years [ ] 10 - 15 years [ ] 16 years and over

Section B

5. What is the product name of your company's LIS?

   _____

6. What was the release date of its most recent version?

   _____

7. When was your first LIS installed and became operational?

   _____

8. What was the date of your most recent installation?

   _____

9.   Does your LIS handle any the following? (Please tick all that applies)

[ ] Bar coding/label printing
[ ] Charge capture/billing
[ ] Cumulative reporting across facility encounters
[ ] Image display within reports (for Anatomical Pathology)
[ ] Integrated chemistry, hematology, and microbiology reporting
[ ] Management/quality reporting
[ ] Multi-site blood banking
[ ] Blood bank multi-site inventory
[ ] Multi-site testing
[ ] Online test-utilization guidelines
[ ] Outreach client services
[ ] Patient scheduling
[ ] Preauthorization/coding validation
[ ] Order entry
[ ] Result reporting
[ ] Scanned entry of paper-based external results
[ ] Specimen storage
[ ] Specimen control worklist
[ ] Trending of patient results
[ ] Management reporting
[ ] Work flow/staff scheduling

10.   Which LIS functions are accessible via Web browser?

[ ] None
[ ] Some
[ ] All

11.   What internal modules (not interfaces) are available for, or included in, your LIS?

[ ] Blood banking
[ ] Chemistry
[ ] Cytology
[ ] Microbiology
[ ] Haematology
[ ] Anatomical Pathology
[ ] Other specialized applications (specify)
Other _____

12.   What is the operating system for your LIS (Unix, Windows, etc.)?

_____

13. Is your company ISO 9001:2000 certified? ISO 18189?

_____

Section C

Does your LIS:

14. Provide an outreach system that employs a centralized relational database?

    [ ] Yes
    [ ] No

15. Provide an operational environment that will ensure the security and integrity of the system and all its data?

    [ ] Yes
    [ ] No

16. Provide a multi-level security system that is separate from the LIS to ensure the confidentiality of patient-related information and to control access to outreach functions and features?

    [ ] Yes
    [ ] No

17. Allow password protection at different levels (i.e. system administrator, phlebotomy, nursing, provider, etc.)?

    [ ] Yes
    [ ] No

18. Maintain an audit trail for system entries including user code, date, and time of each system transaction?

    [ ] Yes
    [ ] No

19. Allow analyzer interfaces to operate so that result verification and reporting can be performed simultaneously at multiple station?

    [ ] Yes
    [ ] No

20. Allow compound test ordering: single header linked to multiple test result fields (e.g. CBC, lipid panel, and comprehensive metabolic panel)?

[ ] Yes
[ ] No

21. Allow users to order tests by entering codes and/or selecting from a test menu?

[ ] Yes
[ ] No

22. Provide intelligent sample labeling–groups samples in chemistry together and prints on labels, while hematology tests print on a separate label and microbiology prints separately?

[ ] Yes
[ ] No

23. Provide for release of results after they have been reviewed and approved by Technical personnel?

[ ] Yes
[ ] No

24. Ability to flag results based on criteria other than standard reference range to include testing location, drawing location, ordering provider, patient age, and priority of order?

[ ] Yes
[ ] No

25. Highlight abnormal results on patient reports without relying solely on colour
26. text?

[ ] Yes
[ ] No

27. Provide the ability to track patient samples throughout the testing process?

[ ] Yes
[ ] No

28. Provide identification of the individual who ordered the test, collected the sample, and released the test results, including the date and time of these occurrences so that this information is accessible throughout the process?

[ ] Yes
[ ] No

29. Maintain patient databases and provide ability to easily generate historical patient reports?

[ ] Yes
[ ] No

30. Allow the user to graph patient results by tests to identify possible trends?

[ ] Yes
[ ] No

31. Allow the user to easily access archived patient records?

[ ] Yes
[ ] No

32. Allow implementation of Westgard QC rules and flags?

[ ] Yes
[ ] No

33. Allow flagging of out-of-range QC values?

[ ] Yes
[ ] No

34. Provide ability to create billing summary reports by date?

[ ] Yes
[ ] No

Section D

Please circle or check that which best represents your response to each statement or question.

35. It was easy to learn how to use the LIS.

☐ Strongly agree ☐ Agree ☐ No opinion ☐ Disagree ☐ Strongly disagree

36. The LIS gives error messages that clearly tell me how to fix problems that arise.

   ☐ Strongly agree ☐ Agree ☐ No opinion ☐ Disagree ☐ Strongly disagree

37. The information (such as online help, on-screen messages, and other documentation) provided with the LIS is clear.

   ☐ Strongly agree ☐ Agree ☐ No opinion ☐ Disagree ☐ Strongly disagree

38. It is easy to find the information I need on the LIS.

   ☐ Strongly agree ☐ Agree ☐ No opinion ☐ Disagree ☐ Strongly disagree

39. The information provided by the LIS is easy to understand.

   ☐ Strongly agree ☐ Agree ☐ No opinion ☐ Disagree ☐ Strongly disagree

40. The information on the LIS is effective in helping me to complete my tasks.

   ☐ Strongly agree ☐ Agree ☐ No opinion ☐ Disagree ☐ Strongly disagree

41. The LIS has all the functions and capabilities I expect it to possess.

   ☐ Strongly agree ☐ Agree ☐ No opinion ☐ Disagree ☐ Strongly disagree

42. I like using the interface on the LIS

   ☐ Strongly agree ☐ Agree ☐ No opinion ☐ Disagree ☐ Strongly disagree

43. Using the LIS in my job enable me to accomplish tasks more quickly.

   ☐ Strongly agree ☐ Agree ☐ No opinion ☐ Disagree ☐ Strongly disagree

44. Using the system enhanced my effectiveness on the Job.

   ☐ Strongly agree ☐ Agree ☐ No opinion ☐ Disagree ☐ Strongly disagree

45. Using the system made it easier to do my work.

   ☐ Strongly agree ☐ Agree ☐ No opinion ☐ Disagree ☐ Strongly disagree

46. I am able to efficiently complete my work using the LIS.

☐ Strongly agree ☐ Agree ☐ No opinion ☐ Disagree ☐ Strongly disagree

47. I feel comfortable using the LIS.

☐ Strongly agree ☐ Agree ☐ No opinion ☐ Disagree ☐ Strongly disagree

48. Using the LIS improved my overall performance on the job.

☐ Strongly agree ☐ Agree ☐ No opinion ☐ Disagree ☐ Strongly disagree

49. Overall, I am satisfied with how easy it is to use the LIS.

☐ Strongly agree ☐ Agree ☐ No opinion ☐ Disagree ☐ Strongly disagree

Chapter 15
Laboratory Information Management Systems:
Role in Veterinary Activities

Patrizia Colangeli
*Istituto Zooprofilattico Sperimentale
dell'Abruzzo e del Molise "G. Caporale", Italy*

Francesca Cito
*Istituto Zooprofilattico Sperimentale
dell'Abruzzo e del Molise "G. Caporale", Italy*

Fabrizio De Massis
*Istituto Zooprofilattico Sperimentale
dell'Abruzzo e del Molise "G. Caporale", Italy*

Maria Teresa Mercante
*Istituto Zooprofilattico Sperimentale
dell'Abruzzo e del Molise "G. Caporale", Italy*

Lucilla Ricci
Istituto Zooprofilattico Sperimentale dell'Abruzzo e del Molise "G. Caporale", Italy

ABSTRACT

The Laboratory Information Management System (LIMS) is recognized as a powerful tool to improve laboratory data management and to report human health as well as veterinary public health. LIMS plays an essential role in public health surveillance, outbreak investigations, and pandemic preparedness. The chapter aims is to provide an overview of LIMS use in veterinary fields as well as to report 20 years of experience of a Veterinary Public Institute in working with LIMS, illustrating the features of the LIMS currently in use in the institute and highlighting the different aspects that should be considered when evaluating, choosing, and implementing a LIMS. In depth, the chapter illustrates how LIMS simplifies the accreditation path according to ISO IEC 17025 and the role in the epidemiology and veterinary public health. For this aspect, it is very important to collect clear data, and for this reason, a LIMS has to activate formal checks and controls on business rules. To facilitate this issue, an interconnection between LIMS and other applications (internal or external to laboratory) could be improved to allow automatic data exchange. At the same time, the unique data encoding at national/international level should be used.

DOI: 10.4018/978-1-4666-6320-6.ch015

INTRODUCTION

The Istituto Zooprofilattico Sperimentale dell'Abruzzo e del Molise "Giuseppe Caporale" (IZSAM) is a public health institute with administrative and managerial autonomy, which operates as a technical and scientific arm of the Italian State and the Abruzzo and Molise Regions, performing analytical work for the public veterinary services and providing the technical and scientific collaboration necessary to enable them to carry out their functions in the field of veterinary public health.

The main tasks of the Institute, as defined by the Italian legislation, are experimental research into the aetiology and pathogenesis of infectious diseases of domestic and wild animals; hygiene in animal breeding and livestock production; tests for laboratory diagnosis of animal diseases, tests for microbiological and chemical safety of food of animal origin destined for human consumption and livestock; epidemiological surveillance in the field of animal health and hygiene in the production of livestock and food of animal origin; production of vaccines, reagents and immunological products for the prophylaxis and diagnosis of animal diseases; consultancy, technical assistance and health information for breeders for the purpose of improving health standards and hygiene in livestock production; training for veterinarians and other operators in veterinary public health.

All the Institute's activities have been constantly certified and subjected to rigorous quality control since 1995, when the Institute became the first public veterinary body in Italy to be certified in accordance with international quality standards for performing laboratory tests in the chemical, microbiological, virological and serological fields (UNI CEI EN ISO/IEC 17025:2005– former 45001). Since 1991, the Institute uses a LIMS (named SILAB), which has the possibility to be constantly modified to suit the new health care needs and be adapted to the emerging technological innovations.

Taking advantage of these twenty years of experience, the chapter expresses some general considerations about the role played by LIMS in public health surveillance, outbreak investigations and pandemic preparedness.

The main objectives of chapter are to provide an overview of LIMS features, identify strengths, challenges and lessons learnt in terms of development, placement, use and maintenance as well as to illustrate the LIMS role in epidemiology and veterinary public health.

BACKGROUND

Veterinary services are essential to assure the health and welfare of both human and animal populations, as well as an optimal relationship between humans, animals and environment.

The slogan is ONE HEALTH - ONE MEDICINE. This approach recognized, already in the middle of the XX Century, that human and animals health are ONE and that it is more effective and efficient to prevent human disease working on animal population medicine. Moreover, it also led to the understanding that man and animals shared the same world and had a mutual influence with the environment they lived in (ONE PLANET).

The main missions of Veterinary services are to fight animal disease, including zoonosis, and to assure food security and safety worldwide with positive cost-benefit ratio for the international community, in particular:

- To reach the absence of diseases, including zoonosis, as well as food security and food safety, as primary factors for the welfare of human beings.
- To increase the availability and the quality of proteins for the human population and help to decrease crop waste.
- To prevent human affections.

Health and welfare of both humans and animals are closely interrelated. In Italy, the role of veterinary medicine in food security, food safety and prevention of human diseases, has been recognized since 1888 through first "Health Code" (Act December 22, 1888, n. 5849), establishing the role of the provincial veterinarian, in the context of public health. Since 1946 the General Directorate for veterinary services was included in the Ministry of Health.

The public veterinary laboratories, as the Institute's ones, are accredited in accordance with international quality standards UNI CEI EN ISO/IEC 17025:2005, for performing laboratory tests in different fields such as chemical, microbiological, virological and serological fields, while human health laboratories refer to ISO 15189 norm for accreditation. However, ISO 15189 meet the requirement of ISO/IEC 17025 and the principles of ISO 9001. ISO 17025 born from ISO guide 25 and from the experience in the use of EN ISO 45001 norm, which after became ISO/IEC 17025.

ISO IEC 17025 considers the processes related to the laboratory test results as well as the features of the system which support the analysis process itself. ISO 15189 deals with the processes inherent the pre-analysis activities, the processes inherent the analysis activities and those of the system in support of the analysis itself, as well as the processes concerning the post-analysis tasks (Montebelli & Pradella, 2010).

Accreditation according to the ISO 15189 specifies requirements for quality and competence in medical laboratories like ISO 17025 specifies requirements for quality and competence in all other labs.

Briefly, ISO 17025 meets the requirements of all ISO 15189 points that are referred to the management of laboratory activities, while the remaining points are covered with ISO 9001.

ISO 15189 includes additional requirements for the competence of medical laboratories, for example, in relation to the acceptance of patients, sampling and care of patients (including accommodation and environmental conditions), and considers also the post-examination processes. In addition, ISO 15189 is also more stringent than the ISO/IEC 17025 when requirements of other disciplines are considered, such as safety, security of the sensible data, environmental management.

LIMS BASIC FUNCTIONALITIES

A LIMS should not be simply a software-based laboratory and information management system oriented to collect all data related with samples and tests. It should also provide the following basic functionalities (Figure 1):

Entry Order and Sample Reception

During the process of samples acceptance, all requests about samples to be tested are recorded. Data concerning the testing purpose, the area of competence (human or animal health, food safety, feed analysis, environment), the customer and other information concerning the sample (such as geographical origin, animal species, number and type of material) are recorded into the system.

At this stage, additional information may be requested (referential number of authorities report, number of aliquots, condition of the sample, type of container, etc.), when they are necessary for sample's management and epidemiological purposes.

Specimen Processing and Distribution

After univocal identification of the sample by the generation of a label including barcode, samples are distributed to the different departments to undergo the tests requested by the customer.

In order to cut down working time, samples distribution by groups may be automatically performed: the operator can select a distribution

Figure 1. LIMS context and basic functionalities (© copyright 2013,Patrizia Colangeli, used with permission)

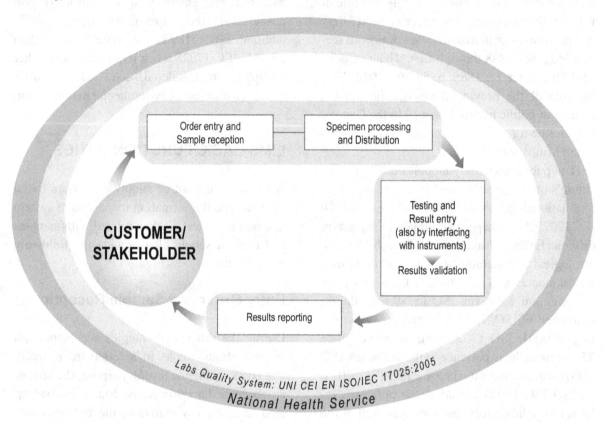

group (previously created on purpose), with which samples are distributed to all tests and laboratories included in the group.

Entered data and distributions are reported on electronic work-lists, which can be used both as data verification and as a working sheet.

Testing and Results Entry

The technician, after having received the coded samples, performs the required tests according to the assigned distributions and then enters results into the information system (data acquisition step). Where appropriate, he/she can insert interpretive comments.

In some cases, data acquisition is done directly by interfacing the instrument used for analysis. In instruments that allow it, this connection may also be at 2 ways (from LIMS to instrument and vice-versa). Integration with laboratory instruments increase quality of data and reduce time for typing results and their validation.

At this phase, the system produces work-lists to facilitate batch processing and resulting and 'pending result' lists to track remaining orders.

Results Validation

After results are entered, the head of the laboratory validates data in order to comply with general and specific requirements and satisfy customer needs. Results cannot be communicated to the customer until data are not validated.

Results Reporting

At the end of the diagnostic route of the sample, the test report is issued and sent to the customer requesting the diagnostic tests. The test report varies according to the kind of tests performed.

The report is dispatched by e-mail or ordinary mail after having been signed (with electronic signature) by the head of the department.

For notifiable diseases, electronic alerts may be sent to local, regional and national level.

Data Enquiries

It is possible to have progress reports on registered samples by enquiring at any time the system (number of samples accepted, distributed, validated, etc…).

Data Security and Integrity

The application manages different levels of security for users. Each user has username and password, a role that assigns functionalities as well as the area of competence.

Other important issues concerning security are firewalls, antivirus/malware software, which has to be installed in each PC's, Uninterruptible Power Supply (UPS) for server and system for data backup and disaster recovery. Disaster planning is also a critical function that all LIMSs need to consider.

Domain Tables Management

An "ideal" LIMS should be code-oriented, and internal codifications used should be linked to descriptions. All codes and relevant descriptions are entered into domain tables; for example, all species of interest are codified so that in the data

tables codes are reported, while in domain tables codes are linked to the relevant description and additional information. The management of domain tables is run by the application itself: some tables can be accessed by everyone (clients, users..); some others (tests, assays,…) only by departments heads or by Administrator role.

Management of Payment

The system needs to collect billing information, which may be different from those of the client, and interface with the billing system or directly issue the invoice.

OTHER FUNCTIONALITIES

In addition to the basic functionalities, a LIMS may also contain other features, such as:

- A management tool: LIMS may also be able to monitor customer service in terms of the gap between actual response and expected time, technical efficiency in terms of gaps between actual time requested to perform a diagnostic test and the same time predetermined in standard situations, as well as able to collect data on the frequency of acceptance of samples and, analyzing these data, allows to adjust the presence of personnel (Figure 2).
- From an epidemiological point of view, LIMS may be an essential instrument since it may collect a considerable amount of data in the context of research programs, surveys, clinical investigations, control, and eradication programs. Usually it is difficult to make use of these data for epidemiological considerations, since it is not always given that data will be representative of the event under study. In the case of clinical investigations for leishmaniasis, for example, inferences about the disease

Figure 2. Reception activity trend: reports and graphs 2012-2013 (© copyright 2013, Patrizia Colangeli, used with permission)

Reception Activity

IZSAM	2012 Acceptances Number	2012 Samples accepted	2012 % samples	2013 Acceptances Number	2013 Samples accepted	2013 % samples
All Facilities	83273	585658	7,03	78870	588077	7,46
Izsam – Biologia Delle Acque Marine E Pesca	1289	26296	20,40	1065	7986	7,50
Izsam – Sede Centrale	34734	170111	4,90	33063	189877	5,74
Izsam – Sezione Di Avezzano	7258	107980	14,88	6751	109740	16,26
Izsam – Sezione Di Campobasso	6941	16501	2,38	6937	26570	3,83
Izsam – Sezione Di Isernia	12415	156973	12,64	10263	135978	13,25
Izsam – Sezione Di Lanciano	4931	25665	5,20	6226	32403	5,20
Izsam – Sezione Di Pescara	15705	82132	5,23	14565	85523	5,87

Acceptances - monthly trend

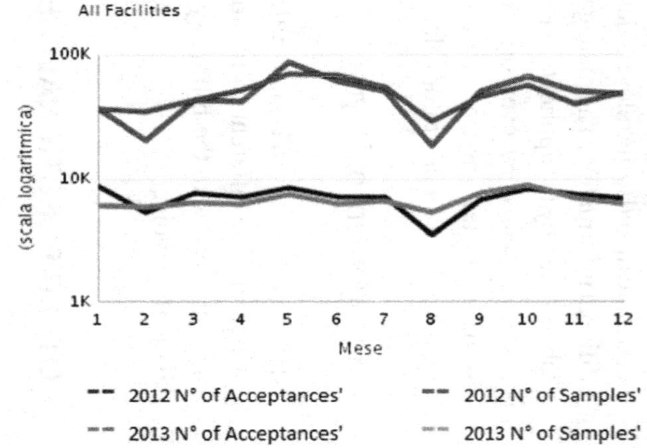

All Facilities

(scala logaritmica)

100K — 10K — 1K

Mese: 1 2 3 4 5 6 7 8 9 10 11 12

- 2012 N° of Acceptances'
- 2013 N° of Acceptances'
- 2012 N° of Samples'
- 2013 N° of Samples'

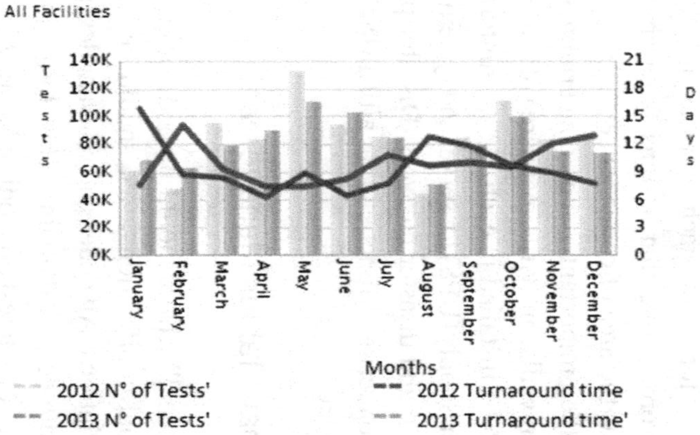

Acceptances per year and class

Year 2012 Class Standard

IZSAM Facilities	Acceptances	Samples	% Samples
Izsam - Biologia Delle Acque Marine E Pesca	76898	568446	7,39
Izsam - Sede Centrale	829	25267	30,48
Izsam - Sezione Di Avezzano	31516	160139	5,08
Izsam - Sezione Di Campobasso	7073	107515	15,20
Izsam - Sezione Di Isernia	5509	14189	2,58
Izsam - Sezione Di Lanciano	11835	154806	13,08
Izsam - Sezione Di Pescara	4749	24995	5,26
	15387	81535	5,30

Turnaround time - monthly trend

All Facilities

Tests: 140K 120K 100K 80K 60K 40K 20K 0K

Days: 21 18 15 12 9 6 3 0

Months: January February March April May June July August September October November December

- 2012 N° of Tests'
- 2013 N° of Tests'
- 2012 Turnaround time
- 2013 Turnaround time'

status of the canine population are derived through the serological diagnoses on specimens submitted under suspect. This sample represents only a subset of the real animal population and the probability that an animal sampled is conditioned by several aspects such as its apparent health status, the decision of the owner to undergo his pet to a clinical examination and the decision of the clinician to carry out a serological examination. In this scenario, the output of the system is largely biased by all these variables in data collection. An example of data generated by a LIMS and suitable for epidemiological analysis may be represented by those collected in the context of the Italian eradication program for bovine brucellosis which has the objective to test periodically all the bovine herds existing on the national territory. This means that blood samples are collected from all cattle every year in order to screen for brucellosis. In this case, the output of the system may be considered as representative of the real situation in the field, given that the investigation is extended to all the susceptible population. In this scenario, the performance of the system in terms of sensitivity and specificity are measurable and less biased, and data provided by the LIMS may be useful for epidemiological considerations.

However, a LIMS may also play a key role in disease monitoring and surveillance. In this case, the system is designed to collect data not only related to the specimens sampled and their origin, but also other data of epidemiological relevance and related to the disease under surveillance. In this case, the surveys are intentionally targeted and, even if not all the susceptible population is tested, however, the information provided may be considered as representative of the disease under study. Indeed to collect data useful for epidemio-

logical studies is necessary to clearly identify the aims of surveillance and define which data should be collected in which population.

An example of the application of LIMS to collect data concerning epidemiological surveillance is provided by the West Nile Virus (WNV) Italian surveillance program. The program includes operative procedures for collection of human, veterinary and entomological data, with the purpose to provide a surveillance system for early detection and monitoring of WNV circulation. The Italian national surveillance system for WNV includes data coming from active surveillance and data coming from passive surveillance. In particular, it collects data coming from:

- Screening of blood and hematopoietic stem cells donations in affected areas and screening of solid organ donations in the surveillance areas;
- Periodic blood testing of sentinel horses and chickens to check for seroconversion;
- Mosquito trapping;
- The collection of dead wild birds
- Periodic sampling of migratory birds found in humid areas.

In this context, the LIMS collects both laboratory data (as date of arrival of samples, type of samples, date of analysis, results of the analysis, analytical details) as well as epidemiological data as geographical coordinates of the sampling site, and relevant data concerning the animals (identification and age of the sampled animal, presence or absence of clinical signs etc.). In addition, in Italy, the information system for animal disease outbreaks notification called Animal Disease Notification System (SIMAN) is used to collect and dispatch to the competent Authorities data and information related to the WND outbreaks and to the surveillance activities (Colangeli, P., Iannetti, S., Cerella, A., Ippoliti, C., Di Lorenzo, A., Santucci, U., Simonetti, P., Calistri, P., & Lelli, R. 2011). SIMAN has useful epidemiological reporting tools to monitor, manage and analyze data generated by West Nile Disease (WND) surveillance activities. In particular, the section "Report West Nile Disease" allows downloading the list of registered sentinel farms and animals, as well as the sampling activities performed and the laboratory results. The data stored into the SIMAN WND database, together with the data on human cases weekly provided by the Ministry of Health, are the source of information for the weekly National Epidemiological bulletin on WND published by the National Reference Centre for Exotic Diseases (CESME) on the official national website dedicated to WND (http://sorveglianza. izs.it/emergenze/west_nile/emergenze_en.html [17/02/2014]).

Less timely and incomplete reporting of diseases may result in reduced ability in rapidly detect and monitoring outbreaks, which may cause delays in implementing action on conditions that may affect large numbers of people. Enhancing the capabilities of LIMS systems would provide a valuable tool making possible the electronic report of data and thus their timely availability. In the context of disease surveillance system, LIMS represents a powerful tool to identify and monitor the occurrence of infectious diseases and other conditions of public health importance.

- A tool to increase data quality, since a LIMS activates both formal checks (*i.e.* on dates) and, especially, controls on business rules (temporal progression of dates, check on the correctness of combination of tests-methods-matrix-species-department). For this reason, the system should supply tables containing parameters and truth tables, manageable through software only by authorized users with a appropriate role. A LIMS should be able to suggest default values for sample compliance (like "Negative" or "Absent", or "< 10", etc.), standard operative procedures, unit of measurement, and so on. The application should offer an extensive use of drop down lists to reduce data entry mistakes and minimize transcription errors. Integration with laboratory instruments increase data quality and reduce time necessary for typing results and their validation. In addition, the user obtains standardized reporting of laboratory data.

- Interconnection between LIMS and other applications (internal or external to laboratory) to allow information exchange. Through web services, a LIMS is able to obtain data from different veterinary information systems both public and private and automatically store them. In the context of animal health, information about breeding farms (code, address, owner, etc.) can be read directly from the National Farm Identification and Registration Animal Database (I&R system). The procedure also allows verifying the information about a single animal at sampling stage like ear-tag, age or sex. The same interconnection should be possible in the context of food safety where a "Food Business Operators (FBO) register" exists. This feature allows providing, in real time, the validated results of diagnostic tests to the connected information systems.

In this way, a LIMS may thoroughly satisfy information needs that the Ministry of Health and other body (National Reference Centers, an international organization) require for a public laboratory. The term "information needs" concerns the periodic demand to supply aggregated or single data about specific diseases, control plans or contaminants (for example, monthly dispatch of data on GMO or rabies, annual data on pesticides, daily data on West Nile Disease, Bluetongue, etc.). To share these information is, therefore, necessary to map codes of different systems and ensure that the exchanged data have the same meaning ("semantic interoperability").

Each information system should be always seen as part of a more complex system with which it should exchange data (Figure 3).

In addition, an "ideal" LIMS should allow automatically and independently adding specific information about each disease surveillance plan or for other purpose. These additional data are important for different actors in the context of Animal Health Information System, like the National Reference Centers.

- As a Thesaurus: The pillar for an efficient system cooperation is the use of unique data encoding as much as possible approved and shared at national/international level like, in the context of animal health, OIE codes for diseases. A centralized and unique I&R system exists in Italy; it col-

lects and univocally identifies each farm of main livestock species and each animal in the holding (only for cattle). A similar database, named "FBO register" is in progress for all other structures of interest (such as dairy factories, dealers, canteens, etc.). In the context of human medicine, standard terminology already exist (such as Logical Observation Identifiers Names and Codes (LOINC) and Systematized Nomenclature of Medicine - Clinical Terms (SNOMED-CT). The European Food Safety Authority (EFSA) is making the effort to unify and codify the variables involved in the food and feed sample identification (Standard Sample Description, currently at ver. 2.0) (http://www.efsa.europa.eu/en/efsajournal/pub/3424.htm [17/02/2014]) but the com-

Figure 3. Italian integrate veterinary information system (© copyright 2013, Patrizia Colangeli, used with permission)

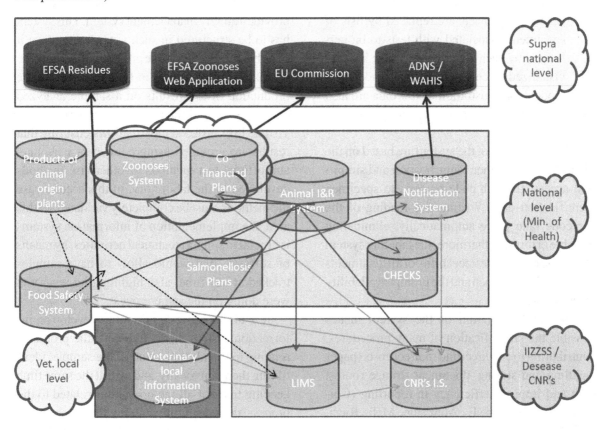

plete definition of a shared semantic and categorization in the veterinary field represent an effort to be still. The use of a thesaurus, starting from the necessity of the dialog among heterogeneous information systems allows managing the "knowledge" and simplifies its divulgation; moreover, it complies with the requirement to manage and maintain a set of sanitary codes aimed to allow all involved operators to use the same terms.

- As a tool for dematerialization. LIMS also may be a "paper-less" system, thus reducing paper and space needed for storing, as well as reducing fire risks. This means to remove sample reception register, all the paper support used to record raw data (register, technical notebook, worksheet, etc.), as well as test reports. Test reports are replaced by pdf files with digital signature, sent by e-mail and available also on line. Specimens are labeled with a bar code; paper working sheets are replaced by lists of specimens associated with tests to be performed by each department. These lists are visualized on computer screens, and digital models for registration of raw data are also available in all diagnostic departments.

The advantages of the system are based on the reliability of specimen identification and simplified access, through code readers, to specimen identification data. Writing and reading of the bar code take place automatically, eliminating possible errors. Furthermore, the labeling system allows the immediate traceability of all documents related to the specimen and the prompt availability of raw data.

The implementation of the system makes possible the simplification of many procedures, contributing to cut direct and indirect costs (paper handling and storing, document storage rooms, etc.) and improve efficiency in reporting (Colangeli, P., Ruggieri, E., Mercante, M.T., Ricci, L.,2013).

- As a support for the accreditation process: there is a worldwide trend for the progressive development of national and international veterinary laboratory networks. Central to this networking is the development of test standardization and harmonization, to ensure that test results from the participating laboratories are comparable.

A laboratory's fulfillment of the requirements of ISO/IEC 17025:2005 means that the laboratory meets both the technical competence requirements and management system requirements that are necessary to consistently deliver technically valid test results.

The need, for official laboratories, to respond to the requirements of ISO 17025, was determined by the obligation to implement the EEC Directive 93/99 and Regulation (EC) 882/2004. Then the public laboratories, like that of the Istituto Zooprofilattico Sperimentale, in order to meet the requirements of Community legislation have had to provide a quality management system. This system has to be structured in such a way as to make it possible to track the whole process concerning the sample, from its arrival in the laboratory to the production of test results on a sample analyzed and the issuing of the related test report.

The ISO 17025 standard allows ensuring that results are provided using competent personnel and official test methods or otherwise methods developed to the laboratory, in this second case the methods must be completely validated. In this area, the implementation of information systems is crucial to support technical activities, by means of software that would allow to have samples tracked at any time, also highlighting what you were doing on the same process.

It is in this sense important to develop an information system that could solve the problems relating to the identification of the sample, identifying them univocally, and also at the same time keeping track of all the operations related to the process, demonstrating not only the reliability of the result, but also the traceability of each step of the analysis process, including the different operators which have carried out each single step. For this reason the LIMS is a tool for traceability of sample and traceability of actions made on it ("who acted, how and when"), aspects which should be very difficult to keep under control only with a paper recording system. Moreover, the information system supports the sample activities, allowing you to keep all documentation for each sample and all the results relating to the tests carried out on a sample.

Solutions and Recommendations

LIMS is a fundamental component of lab management; however, there are major challenges to face in order to correctly implement it:

- Lack of funding to purchase and maintain a LIMS (commercial or developed), and/ or the hardware and network necessary to run it;
- Reluctance to improve knowledge in managing the LIMS, in particular by staff with low computer literacy;
- The frequent requests for customization made by the different users;
- Availability of skilled, motivated and trained personnel to manage the development and maintenance of LIMS.

The transitions to using a LIMS requires a highly-motivated staff, able to change old habits and accept a radical change in the methodological approach. The receptionist role becomes crucial to check sample conditions and to ensure the correct insertion of all data relating to accepted samples, pre-requisite of the entire flow of information. Indeed, an error in reception step has an impact on the whole process with effects that in some cases can have serious repercussions (management of disease outbreaks, incorrect billing etc.). For this reason, the interface between the LIMS and users should be as user-friendly as possible, in order to decrease the probability of input errors by operators.

An ideal LIMS should be web based to be accessible from different users at the same time, multi-language to avoid language barriers, and should offer a simple and intuitive user interface. Since different laboratories may not all operate in the same way, it is important that a LIMS matches the laboratory flow and has the flexibility to accommodate future changes in laboratory activities.

Appropriate network security policies are necessary to ensure that only authorized personnel have access to computing resources. These policies should encompass both users who work connected by local area network, as well as those who may be connected remotely. The ultimate purpose is to prevent unauthorized changes, deletions, or additions to customer data, as well as to prevent unauthorized disclosure of information.

Data integrity policies and procedures are important to ensure that the software that manages the data related to test and results of the laboratory would perform as expected and that changes are performed in a controlled and tested environment. The software should also record and track the changes made to the data by the operating laboratory personnel.

Frequent communications and engagement of end-users are very important not only during start-up, but also during LIMS's use. User manuals, available also on-line and provided with FAQ and suggestions, may obviously be useful, but also training could be important in order to increase trust and confidence in the software. In this context the role of a leader is also important that should be the referent for the management both of the technical and organizational aspects. Finally, the delivering of some incentives for the staff involved (money, awards, etc.) should not be excluded.

FUTURE RESEARCH DIRECTIONS

Since technological solutions are now available, the next efforts will all be geared up to improve the quality of data collected. The main objective is to limit the manual data entry; therefore the following steps may be necessary:

- Interoperability over a network with other application systems in order to read and capture what is already present in other systems (the same data is inserted only once);
- Interface with equipment used for analysis;
- Use of digital on-line forms to collect raw data;
- Use of standard data encodings and barcode labels;
- Use of checks and rules about syntactic and semantic meanings (truth tables);
- Use of a Thesaurus for standard codes.

CONCLUSION

A LIMS enables laboratories to track samples from submission to reporting and can facilitate the linkage between diagnostic results and response in the field. This would strengthen diagnostic capacities when these are directly related to the ability of the laboratory to report results rapidly.

Moreover, there is a direct temporary correlation among the celerity of the diagnosis, the beginning of the therapy and the possibility of limit the disease spread, with a consequent reduction of money loss.

LIMS is now a fair mature IT technology; however the active role in supporting disease detection, surveillance and response to disease outbreaks is the target to be reached in the near future.

With the decreasing hardware and software costs (using open tools) and the growing availability of internet connections and LAN, the pre-conditions for laboratories to leave the paper tracking systems are today fulfilled. While implementing a LIMS is not a short-term investment, however, it could produce a long-term effect on the vitality of the laboratory for many years following installation.

A LIMS can be a powerful tool that gives the laboratory a competitive advantage over other laboratories, saving time and money. Benefits of LIMS implementation include faster turnaround times, automation, increased productivity, higher quality of data, electronic reporting, and integration with other enterprise databases. In addition, you obtain standardized reporting of laboratory data.

Although it is recognized that epidemiology and Laboratory Information Management Systems may play a central role in monitoring animal diseases having public health importance, unfortunately not all countries are in a position to have enough resources available to implement complex disease surveillance programs involving LIMS.

REFERENCES

Colangeli, P., Iannetti, S., Cerella, A., Ippoliti,C., Di Lorenzo,A., Santucci, U., ... Lelli, R. (2011). The national information system for the notification of animal diseases in Italy. *Vet. Ital, 47*(3), 303-12.

Colangeli, P., Ruggieri, E., Mercante, M.T., & Ricci, L. (2013). *Un sistema integrato per la registrazione delle prove: Una esperienza di dematerializzazione (part one)*. Unificazione & Certificazione.

Guidance document 'Standard Sample Descriptionver. 2.0'. (n.d.). Retrieved February 2, 2013, from http://www.efsa.europa.eu/en/efsajournal/pub/3424.htm

Montebelli, G., & Pradella, M. (2010). *Le principali differenze tra i requisiti della norma UNI EN ISO 15189 e quelli della UNI CEI EN ISO/IEC 17025. UNINFORM group. 03 NOV 2010. ANGQ.*

ADDITIONAL READING

Caporale, V., Nannini, D., & Migliorati, G. (2000). L'accreditamento degli Istituti Zooprofilattici Sperimentali ed il mercato globale. *Bollettino delle Ricerche*, 2(1), 729–740.

Nannini, D., Giovannini, A., Fiore, G. L., Marabelli, R., & Caporale, V. (1999). Quality assurance of Veterinary Services at the International level: a proposed approach. *Revue Scientifique et Technique (International Office of Epizootics)*, 18(3), 571–584. PMID:10588001

Schwabe, C. W., Riemann, H. P., & Franti, C. E. (1977). *Epidemiology in veterinary practice*. Lea & FebigerEdagricole.

KEY TERMS AND DEFINITIONS

Animal Disease Surveillance: Aims to improve disease analysis, early warning and predicting disease emergence and spread. As a preventive measure, disease surveillance is aimed at reducing animal health-related risks and major consequences of disease outbreaks on food production and livelihoods.

Information System: The tool used to collect, filter, process, create, and distribute data. It consists of hardware, software, networks and operators.

Interconnection: Many organizations use multiple software systems for management. Different software systems often need to exchange data with each other. Interconnection is to link different systems to allows to exchange this data.

Laboratory Management System: A software-based laboratory and information management system that offers a set of key features that support a modern laboratory's operations.

Monitoring: Is the making of routine observations on health, productivity and environmental factors and the recording and transmission of these observations.

"Paper-Less" System: Is the work environment in which the use of paper is eliminated or greatly reduced. This is done by converting documents and other papers into digital form. Proponents claim that "going paperless" can save money, boost productivity, save space, make documentation and information sharing easier, keep personal information more secure, and help the environment. The concept can be extended to communications outside the office, as well.

Veterinary Epidemiology: Is principally concerned with the study of disease within populations (although it may also be used for investigation of issues such as animal welfare and productivity). Put simply, it involves the investigation of patterns of disease within a population, in relation to which animals are affected, the spatial distribution (i.e. location) of affected animals, and the temporal distribution of affected animals (i.e. animal disease surveillance patterns of disease through time).

Compilation of References

(1986). Management of a clinical pathology laboratory using a record system on personal computer data base. *Medica (Stuttgart)*, 77(9-10), 289–296.

Aarts, J., Ash, J., & Berg, M. (2007). Extending the understanding of computerized physician order entry: Implications for professional collaboration, workflow and quality of care. *International Journal of Medical Informatics*, 76(Supplement 1), S4–S13. doi:10.1016/j.ijmedinf.2006.05.009 PMID:16798068

Abdullah, M. M. B., Uli, J., & Tari, J. J. (2008). The influence of soft factors on quality improvement and performance: Perceptions from managers. *The TQM Journal*, 20(5), 436–452. doi:10.1108/17542730810898412

Abdullah, M. M. B., Uli, J., & Tari, J. J. (2009). The relationship of performance with soft factors and quality improvement. *Total Quality Management and Business Excellence*, 20(7), 735–748. doi:10.1080/14783360903037051

Abdul-Rahman, H. (1997). Some observations on the issues of quality cost in construction. *International Journal of Quality & Reliability Management*, 14(5), 464–481. doi:10.1108/02656719710170693

ABNT. (2005). *NBR ISO/IEC 27002 - Tecnologia da informação – Técnicas de segurança - Código de prática para a gestão da segurança da informação*. Rio de Janeiro: Associação Brasileira de Normas Técnicas.

ABNT. (2006). *ABNT-NBR ISO/IEC 27001 Tecnologia da informação – Técnicas de segurança – Sistema de Gestão de segurança da informação – Requisitos*. Rio de Janeiro: Associação Brasileira de Normas Técnicas.

Adam, B. (2004). *Time*. Cambridge, MA: Polity.

Adam, E. E., Corbett, L. M., Flores, B. E., Harrison, N. J., Lee, T. S., & Rho, B. H. et al. (1997). An international study of quality improvement approach and firm performance. *International Journal of Operations & Production Management*, 17(9), 842–873. doi:10.1108/01443579710171190

AgileBio. (2014). Retrieved from http://www.agilebio.com/

Agrawal, R., & Srikant, R. (1994). Fast algorithms for mining association rules. In *Proc. 20th Int. Conf. Very Large Data Bases, VLDB* (Vol. 1215, pp. 487-499). ACM.

Agrawal, R., & Srikant, R. (1995). Mining sequential patterns. In *Proceedings of Data Engineering*, (pp. 3-14). IEEE.

Agrawal, R., Imieliński, T., & Swami, A. (1993). Mining association rules between sets of items in large databases. *SIGMOD Record*, 22(2), 207–216. doi:10.1145/170036.170072

Agthong, S., & Wiwanitkit, V. (1999). Cyberspace in medicine. *Chulalongkorn Medical Journal*, 43(1), 5–14.

Aguilar, A. (2005, December). *Semantic Interoperability in the context of eHealth*. Paper presented at the HP/DERI/CIMRU Research Seminar. Galway, Ireland.

Ahire, S. L., & Dreyfus, P. (2000). The impact of design management and process management on quality: An empirical investigation. *Journal of Operations Management*, 18(5), 549–575. doi:10.1016/S0272-6963(00)00029-2

Ahire, S. L., Golhar, D. Y., & Waller, M. A. (1996). Development and validation of TQM implementation constructs. *Decision Sciences*, 27(1), 23–56. doi:10.1111/j.1540-5915.1996.tb00842.x

Ahire, S. L., & O'Shaughnessy, K. C. (1998). The role of top management commitment in quality management: An empirical analysis of the auto industry. *International Journal of Quality Science*, *3*(1), 5–37. doi:10.1108/13598539810196868

Ahire, S. L., & Ravichandran, T. (2001). An innovation diffusion model of TQM implementation. *IEEE Transactions on Engineering Management*, *48*(4), 445–464. doi:10.1109/17.969423

Albertin, A. L., & Pinochet, L. H. C. (2010). *Política de Segurança de Informações, página 275*. Rio de Janeiro: Elsevier Editora.

Alhere Healthpal. (2013). Retrieved from http://alereconnect.com/solutions/alere-healthpal/

Aller, R., Georgiou, A., & Pantanowitz, L. (2012). Electronic Health Records. In L. Pantanowitz, J. M. Tuthill, & U. G. Balis (Eds.), *Pathology Informatics Theory and Practice* (pp. 217–230). Canada: American Society for Clinical Pathology.

Al-Marri, K., Ahmed, A. M. M. B., & Zairi, M. (2007). Excellence in service: An empirical study of the UAE banking sector. *International Journal of Quality & Reliability Management*, *24*(2), 164–176. doi:10.1108/02656710710722275

American Hospital Association (AHA). (2007). Continued progress: Hospital use of information technology. Washington, DC: Author.

Anderson, J. C., Rungtusanatham, M., Schroeder, R. G., & Devaraj, S. (1995). A path analytic model of a theory of quality management underlying the Deming Management Method: Preliminary empirical findings. *Decision Sciences*, *26*(5), 637–658. doi:10.1111/j.1540-5915.1995.tb01444.x

Anonymous, . (1995). Understanding and implementing hospital information systems. *Health Devices*, *24*(2), 71–83. PMID:7737881

Antonelli, D., Baralis, E., Bruno, G., Cerquitelli, T., Chiusano, S., & Mahoto, N. A. (2013). Analysis of diabetic patients through their examination history. *Expert Systems with Applications*, *40*(11), 4672–4678. doi:10.1016/j.eswa.2013.02.006

Antonelli, D., Baralis, E., Bruno, G., Chiusano, S., Mahoto, N. A., & Petrigni, C. (2012). Analysis of diagnostic pathways for colon cancer. *Flexible Services and Manufacturing Journal*, *24*(4), 379–399. doi:10.1007/s10696-011-9095-2

Antonelli, D., Baralis, E., Bruno, G., Chiusano, S., Mahoto, N. A., & Petrigni, C. (2013). Extraction of Medical Pathways from Electronic Patient Records. In I. Association (Ed.), *Data Mining: Concepts, Methodologies, Tools, and Applications* (pp. 1004–1018). Hershey, PA: Information Science Reference.

Antony, J., Leung, K., Knowles, G., & Gosh, S. (2002). Critical success factors of TQM implementation in Hong Kong industries. *International Journal of Quality & Reliability Management*, *19*(5), 551–566. doi:10.1108/02656710210427520

Arawati, A. (2005). The structural linkages between TQM, product quality performance, and business performance: Preliminary empirical study in electronics companies. *Singapore Management Review*, *27*(1), 87–105.

Archondakis, S., Stathopoulou, A., & Sitaras, I. (2011). ISO 15189:2007: Implementation in a laboratory information system. In A. Moumtzoglou & A. Kastania (Eds.), E-Health Systems Quality and Reliability: Models and Standards (pp 64-72). Hershey, PA: IGI Global.

Archondakis, S., Georgoulakis, J., Stamataki, M., Anninos, D., Skagias, L., & Panayiotides, I. et al. (2009). Telecytology: a tool for quality assessment and improvement in the evaluation of thyroid fine-needle aspiration specimens. *Telemedicine Journal and e-Health*, *5*(7), 713–717. doi:10.1089/tmj.2009.0037 PMID:19694595

Arnold, K. L. (1994). *The manager's guide to ISO 9000*. New York, NY: Free Press.

Arumugam, V., Chang, H. W., Ooi, H. B., & Teh, P. L. (2009). Self-assessment of TQM practices: A case analysis. *The TQM Journal*, *21*(1), 46–58. doi:10.1108/17542730910924745

Arumugam, V., Ooi, K. B., & Fong, T. C. (2008). TQM practices and quality management performance – An investigation of their relationship using data from ISO 9001: 2000 firms in Malaysia. *The TQM Magazine*, *20*(6), 636–650. doi:10.1108/17542730810909383

Ash, J. S., Gorman, P. N., Seshadri, V., & Hersh, W. R. (2004). Computerized physician order entry in U.S. hospitals: Results of a 2002 survey. *Journal of the American Informatics Association, 11*, 95–99. doi:10.1197/jamia. M1427 PMID:14633935

Ash, J. S., Stavri, P. Z., Dykstra, R., & Fournier, L. (2003). Implementing Computerized Physician Order Entry: the importance of special people. *International Journal of Medical Informatics, 69*(2-3), 235–250. doi:10.1016/ S1386-5056(02)00107-7 PMID:12810127

Asif, M., De Bruijn, E. J., Douglas, A., & Fisscher, O. A. M. (2009). Why quality management programs fail: A strategic and operations management perspective. *International Journal of Quality & Reliability Management, 26*(8), 778–794. doi:10.1108/02656710910984165

Aspden, P., Corrigan, J. M., Wolcott, J., & Erickson, S. M. (Eds.). (2004). Patient safety: Achieving a new standard for care. National Academy Press.

ASQC. (1997). *Interpretive guidelines for the application of ANSI/ISO/ASQC Q9001-1994 or Q9002-1994 for owner's, designer's, and constructor's quality management systems*. Milwaukee, WI: ASQC Quality Press.

Asrilhant, B., Dyson, R. G., & Meadows, M. (2007). On the strategic project management process in the UK upstream oil and gas sector. *Omega, 35*(1), 89–103. doi:10.1016/j. omega.2005.04.006

Assarlind, M., & Gremyr, I. (2014). Critical factors for quality management initiatives in small- and medium-sized enterprises. *Total Quality Management & Business Excellence, 25*(3-4), 397–411. doi:10.1080/14783363.2 013.851330

Atkinson, H., & Brown, J. B. (2001). Rethinking performance measures: Assessing progress in UK hotels. *International Journal of Contemporary Hospitality Management, 13*(3), 128–135. doi:10.1108/09596110110388918

Austrian Standards Institute. (2013). *ÖNORM EN ISO 15189*. Medical Laboratories—Requirements for Quality and Competence. Retrieved September 21, 2013, from https://shop.austrian-standards.at/Preview.action;jsessi onid=99230A509647A240137A2C589CF5C872?previ ew=&dokkey=468411&selectedLocale=en

Axt-Adam, P., van der Woulden, J. C., & van der Does, E. (1993). Influencing behaviour of physicians ordering laboratory tests: a literature study. *Medical Care, 31*(9), 784–794. doi:10.1097/00005650-199309000-00003 PMID:8366680

Balloni, A. J. (2004). Why Management in System and Information Technology? In Virtual Enterprises and Collaborative Networks, (vol. 149, pp. 291-300). Springer. Retrieved October 15, 2013, from http://repositorio.cti. gov.br/repositorio/bitstream/10691/238/3/WHY%20 MANAGEMENT%20IN%20SYSTEM%20AND%20 INFORMATION%20TECHNOLOGY.pdf

Balloni, A. J. (2011). *GESITI Project, "An Evaluation of the Management Information System and Technology in Hospitals" (GESITI/HOSPITALS)*. Retrieved October 12, 2013, from http://repositorio.cti.gov.br/repositorio/ bitstream/10691/246/3/GESITI_Project_INGL_22.pdf

Balloni, A. J., & Holtz, S. V. (2008). *Aspectos sociotécnicos das TI & Relacionamento Humano & Sinergia*. Revista Iérica de Sistemas e Tecnologias de Informação (RISTI). Retrieved October 15, 2013, from http://repositorio.cti. gov.br/repositorio/bitstream/10691/250/1/Aspectos%20 sociot%c3%a9cnicos%20das%20TI%20%26%20Relac-ionamento.pdf

Balloni, A. J., Azevedo, A. M. M., & Silveira, M. A. (2012). Socio-technical management model for governance of an ecosystem. *International Journal of Managing Information Technology (IJMIT)*. Retrieved October 15, 2013, from http://airccse.org/journal/ijmit/papers/4312ijmit01.pdf

Balloni, A. J., Levy, S. N., Nemer, G. I. C. T., Freire, J. M. B., Júnior, J. C. L., Pereira, D. A., & Monteiro, B. L. F. (2014). *Por que GESITI? Gestão de Sistemas e Tecnologias da Informação em Hospitais: panorama, tendências e perspectivas em saúde*. Brasília, Brasil: Ministério da Saúde. Retrieved June 06, 2014,from bvsms.saude.gov. br/bvs/publicacoes/por_que_gesiti_gestao_sistemas.pdf

Balloni, A.J. (2006). *Por que GESITI? - Por que gestão em Sistemas e Tecnologias de Informação*. São Paulo: Editora Komedi. Retrieved October 15, 2013, from http://upload.wikimedia.org/wikipedia/commons/2/21/ LIVRO_POR_QUE_GESITI_CENPRA.pdf

Baralis, E., Bertotti, A., Fiori, A., & Grand, A. (2012). LAS: a software platform to support oncological data management. *Journal of Medical Systems*, *36*(1), 81–90. doi:10.1007/s10916-012-9891-6 PMID:23117791

Baralis, E., Bruno, G., Chiusano, S., Domenici, V. C., Mahoto, N. A., & Petrigni, C. (2010). Analysis of medical pathways by means of frequent closed sequences. In *Knowledge-Based and Intelligent Information and Engineering Systems* (pp. 418–425). Springer. doi:10.1007/978-3-642-15393-8_47

Barbará de Oliveira, S., Balloni, A. J., Barbará de Oliveira, F. N., & Toda, F. A. (2012). Information and Service-Oriented Architecture & Web Services: Enabling Integration and Organizational Agility. *Procedia Technology*, *5*, 141–151. Retrieved October 15, 2013 doi:10.1016/j.protcy.2012.09.016

Barbarito, F., Pinciroli, F., Mason, J., Marceglia, S., Mazzola, L., & Bonacina, S. (2012). Implementing standards for the interoperability among healthcare providers in the public regionalized Healthcare Information System of the Lombardy Region. *Journal of Biomedical Informatics*, *45*(4), 736–745. doi:10.1016/j.jbi.2012.01.006 PMID:22285983

Barclay, C. A. (1993). Quality strategy and TQM policies: Empirical evidence. *Management International Review*, *33*(2), 87–98.

Barman, S. (2002). *Writing Information Security Polices.* Indianapolis, IN: New Riders.

Bashshur, R. L. (1997). Telemedicine and the healthcare system. In R. L. Bashshur, J. H. Sanders, & G. W. Shannon (Eds.), Telemedicine theory and practice (pp. 5–36). Academic Press.

Bates, D. W., & Gawande, A. A. (2003). Improving safety with information technology. *The New England Journal of Medicine*, *348*(25), 2526–2534. doi:10.1056/NEJMsa020847 PMID:12815139

Bates, D. W., Pappius, E., Kuperman, G. J., Sittig, D., Burstin, H., & Fairchild, D. et al. (1999). Using information systems to measure and improve quality. *International Journal of Medical Informatics*, *53*, 115–124. doi:10.1016/S1386-5056(98)00152-X PMID:10193881

Bates, D., Kuperman, G., Rittenberg, M., Teich, J., Fiskio, J., & Ma'luf, N. et al. (1999). A randomized trial of a computer-based intervention to reduce utilization of redundant laboratory tests. *The American Journal of Medicine*, *106*(2), 144–150. doi:10.1016/S0002-9343(98)00410-0 PMID:10230742

Bauch, A., Adamczyk, I., Buczek, P., Elmer, F. J., Enimanev, K., & Glyzewski, P. et al. (2011). openBIS: a flexible framework for managing and analyzing complex data in biology research. *BMC Bioinformatics*, *12*(1), 468. doi:10.1186/1471-2105-12-468 PMID:22151573

Bayraktar, E., Tatiglu, E., & Zaim, S. (2008). An instrument for measuring the critical factor of TQM in Turkish higher education. *Total Quality Management and Business Excellence*, *19*(6), 551–574. doi:10.1080/14783360802023921

Beckwith, B.A., Aller, R.D., Brassel, J.H., Brodsky B.V., & Baca M.E. (2013). *Laboratory Interoperability Best Practices*. College of American Pathologists. Retrieved February 02, 2014, from http://www.cap.org/apps/docs/committees/informatics/cap_dihit_lab_interop_final_march_2013.pdf

Benčo, J., & Kuvíková, H. (Eds.). (2011). Economics of public services. Banská Bystrica: Ekonomická fakulta UMB, 333.

Bertotti, A., Migliardi, G., Galimi, F., Sassi, F., Torti, D., Isella, C., & Trusolino, L. (2011). A molecularly annotated platform of patient-derived xenografts ("xenopatients") identifies HER2 as an effective therapeutic target in cetuximab-resistant colorectal cancer. *Cancer Discovery*, *1*(6), 508–523. doi:10.1158/2159-8290.CD-11-0109 PMID:22586653

Bhatt, G. D., & Emdad, A. F. (2010). An empirical examination of the relationship between IT infrastructure, customer focus, and business advantages. *Journal of Systems and Information Technology*, *12*(1), 4–16. doi:10.1108/13287261011032625

Bika Labs. (2014). Retrieved from http://www.bikalabs.com/softwarecenter/bika

Bilger, M.P. (1987). Acquisition of a laboratory information system. *Health Comput. Commun.*, *4*(7), 44-46.

BioMatters. (2014). Retrieved from http://www.biomatters.com/

Birkmeyer, C. M., Lee, J., Bates, D. W., & Birkmeyer, J. D. (2002). Will electronic order entry reduce health care costs? *Effective Clinical Practice*, 5(2), 67–74. PMID:11990214

Bjorn-Andersen, N., Eason, K., & Robey, D. (1986). *Managing Computer Impact: An International Study of Management and Organization*. Norwood, NJ: Ablex.

Black, A., Car, J., Pagliari, C., Anandan, C., Cresswell, K., & Bokun, T. et al. (2011). The Impact of eHealth on the Quality and Safety of Health Care: A Systematic Overview. *PLoS Medicine*, 8(1). doi:10.1371/journal.pmed.1000387 PMID:21267058

Blackburn, R., & Rosen, B. (1993). Total quality and human resource management: Lessons learnt from Baldrige award-winning companies. *The Academy of Management Executive*, 7(3), 49–66.

Blankenberg, D., Kuster, G. V., Coraor, N., Ananda, G., Lazarus, R., Mangan, M., & Taylor, J. (2010). Galaxy: A Web-Based Genome Analysis Tool for Experimentalists. *Current Protocols in Molecular Biology*, 19–10. PMID:20583098

Bobb, A. M., Payne, T. H., & Gross, P. A. (2007). Viewpoint: controversies surrounding use of order sets for clinical decision support in Computerized Provider Order Entry. *Journal of the American Medical Informatics Association*, 14(1), 41–47. doi:10.1197/jamia.M2184 PMID:17068352

Bonini, P., Plebani, M., Ceriotti, F., & Rubboli, F. (2002). Errors in laboratory medicine. *Clinical Chemistry*, 48(5), 691–698. PMID:11978595

Boothe, J. F. (2000). Implementation of data security and data privacy provisions will bring sweeping changes to laboratory service providers. *Clinical Leadership & Management Review*, 14(6), 301–305. PMID:11210219

Bose, R. (2004). Knowledge management metrics. *Industrial Management & Data Systems*, 104(6), 457–468. doi:10.1108/02635570410543771

Bourouis, A., Feham, M., & Bouchachia, A. (2011). Ubiquitous Mobile Health Monitoring System for elderly (UMHMSE). *International Journal of Computer Science and Information Technology*, 3(3). doi:10.5121/ijcsit.2011.3306

Bowen, D. E., & Schneider, B. (1988). Services marketing and management: Implications for organizational behavior. *Research in Organizational Behavior*, 10, 43–80.

Brah, S. A., Serene, T. S. L., & Rao, B. M. (2002). Relationship between TQM and performance of Singapore companies. *International Journal of Quality & Reliability Management*, 19(4), 356–379. doi:10.1108/02656710210421553

Brah, S. A., Wong, J. L., & Rao, B. M. (2000). TQM and business performance in the service sector: A Singapore study. *International Journal of Operations & Production Management*, 20(11), 1293–1312. doi:10.1108/01443570010348262

Brender, J., & McNair, P. (2008). Evaluation of robustness of a user requirements specification approach in a purchase context, a LIS case study. *Stud. Health Technol. Inform.*, 136, 611-616.

Brerider-Jr-McNai, P. (1996). User requirements on the future laboratory information systems. *Computer Methods and Programs in Biomedicine*, 50(2), 87–93. doi:10.1016/0169-2607(96)01738-Q PMID:8875016

Briggs, B. (2001). Planning for the future: the Department of Defense Laboratory Joint Working Group and Global Laboratory Information Transfer. *Health Data Management*, 9(8), 22–24. PMID:11508063

Briscoe, C. (2011). Laboratory and software applications for clinical trials: the global laboratory environment. *Bioanalysis*, 3(21), 2381–2384. doi:10.4155/bio.11.246 PMID:22074278

Briscoe, D., Tellado, M. V., Buckner, S. B., Rosenthal, D. L., & O'Leary, T. J. (2000). Telecytologic diagnosis of breast fine needle aspiration biopsies. *Acta Cytologica*, 44, 175–180. doi:10.1159/000326357 PMID:10740603

Buczak, A. L., Moniz, L. J., Feighner, B. H., & Lombardo, J. S. (2009, March). Mining electronic medical records for patient care patterns. In *Proceedings of Computational Intelligence and Data Mining,* (pp. 146-153). IEEE.

Buffone, G.J., Moreau, D., & Beck, J.R. (1996). Workflow computing: Improving management and efficiency of pathology diagnostic services. *Am. J. Clin. Pathol.*, 105(4 Suppl 1), S17-S24.

Buntin, M., Burke, M., Hoaglin, M., & Blumenthal, D. (2011). The benefits of Health Information Technology: A review of the recent literature shows predominantly positive results. *Health Affairs, 30*(3), 464–471. doi:10.1377/hlthaff.2011.0178 PMID:21383365

Burati, J. L., Farrington, J. J., & Ledbetter, W. B. (1992). Causes of quality deviations in design and construction. *Journal of Construction Engineering and Management, 118*(1), 34–49. doi:10.1061/(ASCE)0733-9364(1992)118:1(34)

Burnett, D. (2006). ISO 15189:2003-quality management, evaluation and continual improvement. *Clinical Chemistry and Laboratory Medicine, 44*(6), 733–739. doi:10.1515/CCLM.2006.126 PMID:16729862

Bygstad, B. (2010). Generative mechanisms for innovation in information infrastructures. *Information and Organization, 20*(3-4), 156–168. doi:10.1016/j.infoandorg.2010.07.001

Cai, S. (2009). The importance of customer focus for organisational performance: A study of Chinese companies. *International Journal of Quality & Reliability Management, 26*(4), 369–379. doi:10.1108/02656710910950351

Callen, J. L., Braithwaite, J., & Westbrook, J. I. (2008). Contextual Implementation Model: A Framework for Assisting Clinical Information System Implementations. *Journal of the American Medical Informatics Association, 15*(2), 255–262. doi:10.1197/jamia.M2468 PMID:18096917

Callen, J., Paoloni, R., Georgiou, A., Prgomet, M., & Westbrook, J. (2010). The rate of missed test results in an Emergency Department. *Methods of Information in Medicine, 49*(1), 37–43. PMID:19893851

Camp, R. C. (1989). *Benchmarking: The search for industry best practices that lead to superior performance.* Milwaukee, WI: ASQ Quality Press.

Cannavo, M. J. (1990). Integrated information and image management systems for the 90s. *Hospital Technology Series, 9*(21), 1–11. PMID:10110925

CAP, College of American Pathologists, Commission on Laboratory Accreditation, Laboratory Accreditation Program. (2012, December 25). *Laboratory General Checklist.* Retrieved December 21, 2013, from http://www.pathologie-online.de/wordpress/wp-content/uploads/2012/11/laboratory_general_checklist.pdf

Carmona-Cejudo, J.M., Hortas, M.L., Baena-García, M., Lana-Linati, J., González, C., Redondo, M, & Morales-Bueno, R. (2012). DB4US: A Decision Support System for Laboratory Information Management. *Interactive journal of medical research, 1*(2), e16.

Carter, R. E., Lonial, S. C., & Raju, P. S. (2010). Impact of quality management on hospital performance: An empirical examination. *Quality Management Journal, 17*(4), 8–24.

Caruso, C., & Steffen, F. D. (1999). *Segurança em Informática e de Informações, página 49.* São Paulo: Editora SENAC.

Castka, P., & Balzarova, M. A. (2008). ISO 26000 and supply chains – On the diffusion of the social responsibility standard. *International Journal of Production Economics, 111*(2), 274–286. doi:10.1016/j.ijpe.2006.10.017

caTissue Plus. (2014). Retrieved from http://www.catissueplus.org/

Catley, C., & Frize, M. (2002, October). *Design of a health care architecture for medical data interoperability and application integration.* Paper presented at the Engineering in Medicine and Biology, 2002. New York, NY..

Center for Information Technology Leadership, Partners Healthcare System (CITL), Healthcare Information, & Management Systems Society. (2004). *The value of healthcare information exchange and interoperability.* Healthcare Information and Management Systems Society. Retrieved February 02, 2014, from http://www.partners.org/cird/pdfs/CITL_HIEI_Report.pdf

Chang, H. H. (2006). Development of performance measurement systems in quality management organizations. *The Service Industries Journal, 26*(7), 765–786. doi:10.1080/02642060600898286

Chassin, M. R., & Galvin, R. W. (1998). The urgent need to improve health care quality. *Journal of the American Medical Association, 280*(11), 1000–1005. doi:10.1001/jama.280.11.1000 PMID:9749483

Chaudhry, B., Wang, J., Wu, S., Maglione, M., Mojica, W., & Roth, E. et al. (2006). Systematic review: impact of health information technology on quality, efficiency, and costs of medical care. *Annals of Internal Medicine, 144*(10), 742–752. doi:10.7326/0003-4819-144-10-200605160-00125 PMID:16702590

Chen, G. Z., Chang, J. Y., Su, X. Y., & Cheng, P. H. (2013). Enterprise e-care package. *Transactions of Japanese Society for Medical and Biological Engineering, 51*(Supplement), U-15.

Cheng, P. H., Chen, H. S., Lai, F., & Lai, J. S. (2010). The strategic use of standardized information exchange technology in a university health system. *Telemedicine Journal and e-Health, 16*(3), 314–326. doi:10.1089/tmj.2009.0080 PMID:20406119

Cheng, P. H., Lin, B. S., Yu, C., Hu, S. H., & Chen, S. J. (2013). A seamless ubiquitous telehealthcare tunnel. *International Journal of Environmental Research and Public Health, 10*(6), 3246–3262. doi:10.3390/ijerph10083246 PMID:23917812

Chen, H. (1990). *Theory-driven evaluations.* Newbury Part, California: Sage Publications.

Chiavenatto, I. (2010). *Administração – Teoria, Processo e Prática, página 173.* Rio de Janeiro: Elsevier Editora.

Chien, T. N., Hsieh, S. H., Cheng, P. H., Chen, Y. P., Chen, S. J., & Luh, J. J. et al. (2012). Usability evaluation of mobile medical treatment carts: Another explanation by information engineers. *Journal of Medical Systems, 36*(3), 1327–1334. doi:10.1007/s10916-010-9593-x PMID:20852921

Chin, K. S., & Pun, K. F. (2002). A proposed framework for implementing TQM in Chinese organizations. *International Journal of Quality & Reliability Management, 19*(3), 272–294. doi:10.1108/02656710210415686

Chmura, A. (1987). Measurement of physician specimen-handling errors and its contribution to laboratory information system quality. *Journal of Medical Systems, 11*(2-3), 95–103. doi:10.1007/BF00992345 PMID:3668410

Choi, T. Y., & Eboch, K. (1998). The TQM paradox: Relations among TQM practices, plant performance, and customer satisfaction. *Journal of Operations Management, 17*(1), 59–75. doi:10.1016/S0272-6963(98)00031-X

Chou, D. (1996). Integrating instruments and the laboratory information system. *American Journal of Clinical Pathology, 105*(4 Suppl 1), S60-4.

Chousiadis, C., Georgiadis, C.K., & Pangalos, G. (2002). Integrating the lightweight authentication protocol (LAP) with access control mechanisms in wireless health care information systems. *Studies in Health Technology and Informatics, 90*, 697-701.

Chung, W. Y., Lee, Y. D., & Jung, S. J. (2008, August). A wireless sensor network compatible wearable u-healthcare monitoring system using integrated ECG, accelerometer and SpO< inf> 2</inf>. In *Proceedings of Engineering in Medicine and Biology Society*, (pp. 1529-1532). IEEE.

Cianciotto, J.P. (1990). On-line, on time: A centralized laboratory information system speeds the results. *Health Progress, 71*(8), 32-4.

Clarity LIMS. (2014). Retrieved from http://genologics.com/claritylims

Clegg, C., Axtell, C., Damodaran, L., Farbey, B., Hull, R., & Lloyd-Jones, R. et al. (1997). Information technology: a study of performance and the role of human and organizational factors. *Ergonomics, 40*(9), 851–871. doi:10.1080/001401397187694

Clément, S., Fillon, J., Bousquet, J., & Beaulieu, J. (2010). TreeSNPs: A laboratory information management system (LIMS) dedicated to SNP discovery in trees. *Tree Genetics & Genomes, 6*(3), 435–438. doi:10.1007/s11295-009-0261-6

Clifford, L-J. (2011). *The evolving LIS needs to be everything for today's laboratories.* Medical Laboratory Observer. Retrieved October 31, 2013, from http://www.mlo-online.com/articles/201108/the-evolving-lis-needs-to-be-everything-for-todays-laboratories.php

Coiera, E. (2004). Four rules for the reinvention of health care. *British Medical Journal, 328*(7449), 1197–1199. doi:10.1136/bmj.328.7449.1197 PMID:15142933

Colangeli, P., Iannetti, S., Cerella, A., Ippoliti,C., Di Lorenzo,A., Santucci, U., ... Lelli, R. (2011). The national information system for the notification of animal diseases in Italy. *Vet. Ital, 47*(3), 303-12.

Colangeli, P., Ruggieri, E., Mercante, M.T., & Ricci, L. (2013). *Un sistema integrato per la registrazione delle prove: Una esperienza di dematerializzazione (part one).* Unificazione & Certificazione.

College of American Pathology. (Ed.). (1965). *Laboratory management: Symposium on Computer-Assisted Pathology (1964 Miami).* Chicago: College of American Pathologists.

Committee on Patient Safety and Health Information Technology; Institute of Medicine. (2011). *Health IT and Patient Safety: Building Safer Systems for Better Care.* Washington, DC, USA: National Academies Press.

Conger, J. A., & Kanungo, R. (1988). The empowerment process: Integrating theory and practice. *Academy of Management Review, 13*(3), 471–482.

Connelly, D. P., & Aller, R. D. (1997). Outcomes and informatics. *Archives of Pathology & Laboratory Medicine, 121,* 1176–1182. PMID:9372745

Corbett, L., & Rastrick, K. (2000). Quality performance and organizational culture. *International Journal of Quality & Reliability Management, 17*(1), 14–26. doi:10.1108/02656710010300126

COSMIC. (2014). Retrieved from http://cancer.sanger.ac.uk/cancergenome/projects/cosmic/

CPA, Clinical Pathology Accreditation. (2012, December 12). Transition of CPA accredited medical laboratories to ISO 15189 accreditation by UKAS. *Clinical Pathology Accreditation News Letter.* Retrieved September 21, 2013, from http://www.cpa-uk.co.uk/files/CPA_News_28.pdf

Crosby, P. B. (1979). *Quality is free: The art of making quality certain.* New York, NY: McGraw-Hill.

Cua, K. O., Mc Kone, K. E., & Schroeder, R. G. (2001). Relationships between implementation of TQM, JIT, and TPM and manufacturing performance. *Journal of Operations Management, 19*(6), 675–694. doi:10.1016/S0272-6963(01)00066-3

Curkovic, C., Vickery, S., & Droge, C. (2000). Quality-related action programs: Their impact on quality performance and business performance. *Decision Sciences, 31*(4), 885–905. doi:10.1111/j.1540-5915.2000.tb00947.x

Curry, A., & Kadasah, N. (2002). Focusing on key elements of TQM – Evaluation for sustainability. *The TQM Magazine, 14*(4), 207–216. doi:10.1108/09544780210429816

Da Rin, G. (2009). Pre-analytical workstations: a tool for reducing laboratory errors. *Clinica Chimica Acta, 404*(1), 68–74. doi:10.1016/j.cca.2009.03.024

Dacombe, R. J., Aquire, S. B., Ramsay, A. R., Banda, H. J., & Bates, I. (2006). Essential medical laboratory services: Their role in delivering equitable health care in Malawi. *Malawi Medical Journal, 18*(2), 77–79.

Danilák, M. (2011). *Challenges for Health and possible eHealth solutions.* Košice: LYNX.

Dartmouth. (2008). *The PDCA Cycle.* Dartmouth Medical School - Office of Community-Based Education and Research - The Clinician's Black Bag of Quality Improvement Tools. Retrieved October 15, 2013, from http://www.aha.org/advocacy-issues/workforce/nww/nww-res-s5c.pdf

Das, A., Handfield, R. B., Calantone, R. J., & Ghosh, S. (2000). A contingent view of quality management – The impact of international competition on quality. *Decision Sciences, 31*(3), 649–690. doi:10.1111/j.1540-5915.2000.tb00938.x

Das, A., Kumar, V., & Kumar, U. (2011). The role of leadership competencies for implementing TQM: An empirical study of Thai manufacturing industry. *International Journal of Quality & Reliability Management, 28*(2), 195–219. doi:10.1108/02656711111101755

Davidson, E. J. (2005). *Evaluation Methodology Basics.* Thousand Oaks: Sage Publications.

De Ceiro, M. D. (2003). Quality management practices and operational performance: Empirical evidence for Spanish industry. *International Journal of Production Research, 41*(12), 2763–2786. doi:10.1080/0020754031000093150

Dean, J. W., & Bowen, D. E. (1994). Management theory and total quality: Improving research and practice through theory development. *Academy of Management Review, 19*(3), 392–418.

Deeble, J., & Lewis-Hughes, P. (1991). *Directions for pathology*. Melbourne: National Health Strategy.

Delic, M., Radlovacki, V., Kamberovic, B., Maksimovic, R., & Pecujlija, M. (2014). Examining relationships between quality management and organisational performance in transitional economies. *Total Quality Management & Business Excellence, 25*(3-4), 367–382. doi:10.1 080/14783363.2013.799331

Deming, W. E. (1982). *Quality, productivity, and competitive position*. Cambridge, MA: Center for Advanced Engineering Studies, Massachusetts Institute of Technology.

Deming, W. E. (1986). *Out of crisis*. Cambridge, MA: MIT Center for Advanced Engineering Study.

DeMuro, P.R., & Gantt, W.A. 3rd. (2001). HIPAA privacy standards raise complex implementation issues. *Health Financial Management, 55*(1), 42-7.

Deros, B.M., Yusof, S. M., & Salleh, A. M. (2006). A benchmarking implementation framework for automotive manufacturing SMEs. *Benchmarking: An International Journal, 13*(4), 396–430. doi:10.1108/14635770610676272

Dito, W.R., McIntire, S, & Leano, J. (1992). Bar codes and the clinical laboratory: adaptation perspectives. *Clinical Laboratory Management Review, 6*(1), 72-6, 78-80, 82-5.

Dixon, J. R., Nanni, A. J., & Vollman, T. E. (1990). *The new performance challenge: Measuring operations for world-class competition*. Homewood, IL: Business One Irwin.

Doll, W., & Vonderembse, M. A. (1991). The evolution of manufacturing systems: Towards the post-industrial enterprise. *Omega, 19*(5), 401–411. doi:10.1016/0305-0483(91)90057-Z

Donabedian, A., Wheeler, R. R., & Wyszewianski, L. (1982). Quality, cost, and health: An integrative model. *Medical Care, 20*, 975–992. doi:10.1097/00005650-198210000-00001 PMID:6813605

Douglas, T. J., & Judge, W. Q. (2001). Total quality management implementation and competitive advantage: The role of structural control and exploration. *Academy of Management Journal, 44*(1), 158–169. doi:10.2307/3069343

Dow, D., Samson, D., & Ford, S. (1999). Exploding the myth: Do all quality management practices contribute to superior quality performance? *Production and Operations Management, 8*(1), 1–27. doi:10.1111/j.1937-5956.1999. tb00058.x

DSIC. (2008). *Metodologia de gestão de segurança da informação e comunicações. 02/IN01/DSIC/GSIPR*. Brasília: Gabinete de Segurança Institucional da Presidência da República. Retrieved June 6, 2014, from http://dsic. planalto.gov.br/documentos/nc_2_metodologia.pdf

DSIC. (2009). *Diretrizes para elaboração de política de segurança da informação e comunicações nos órgão e entidades da administração pública federal. 03/IN01/DSIC/ GSIPR*. Brasília: Gabinete de Segurança Institucional da Presidência da República. Retrieved June 6, 2014, from http://dsic.planalto.gov.br/documentos/nc_3_psic.pdf

Easler, J. W., & Moore, J. F. (1999). Specimen information tracking system: information management in the laboratory support environment. *American Clinical Laboratory, 18*(9), 10. PMID:10623323

Easton, G. S., & Jarrell, S. L. (1998). The effects of total quality management on corporate performance: An empirical investigation. *The Journal of Business, 71*(2), 253–307. doi:10.1086/209744

Eckerson, W. W. (1995). Three tier client/server architectures: Achieving scalability, performance, and efficiency in client/server applications. *Open Information Systems, 3*(20), 46–50.

Eggert, A.A., Westgard, J.O., Barrym, P.L., & Emmerich, K.A. (1987). Implementation of a multi-rule, multistage quality control program in a clinical laboratory computer system. *J. Med. Syst., 11*(6), 391-411.

El Akadi, A., Amine, A., El Ouardighi, A., & Aboutajdine, D. (2011). A two-stage gene selection scheme utilizing MRMR filter and GA wrapper. *Knowledge and Information Systems, 26*(3), 487–500. doi:10.1007/s10115-010-0288-x

Eleftheriadou, M., & Tsimillis, K. C. (Eds.). (2013). *Accreditation for microbiological laboratories* (2nd ed.). Retrieved February 2, 2014, from www.eurachem.org

Emmerich, K. A., Quam, E. F., Bowers, K. L., & Eggert, A. A. (1998). The combination of specimen tracking with an advanced AutoLog in a laboratory information system. *Journal of Medical Systems*, *22*(3), 137–145. doi:10.1023/A:1022659631904 PMID:9604781

ENAC, Entidad Nacional de Acreditación. (March, 2011). *Survey on: Accreditation of medical laboratories within EA*. Retrieved November 1, 2013, from http://www.cskb.cz/res/file/zapisy-vyboru-cskb/2011/13/13-P7.pdf

Escrig-Tena, A. B. (2004). TQM as a competitive factor: A theoretical and empirical analysis. *International Journal of Quality & Reliability Management*, *21*(6-7), 612–637. doi:10.1108/02656710410542034

European cooperation for Accreditation. (2002). *EA-4/10 G: Accreditation for microbiological laboratories*. Retrieved February 2, 2014, from www.european-accreditation.org

European Cooperation for Accreditation. (2008). *EA-4/17 M: EA position paper on the description of scopes of accreditation of medical laboratories*. Retrieved February 2, 2014, from www.european-accreditation.org

Fayol, H. (1967). *General and Industrial Management*. London: Pitman.

Ferdows, K., Lewis, M. A., & Machuca, J. A. D. (2004). Rapid-fire fulfillment. *Harvard Business Review*, *82*(11), 104–110.

Fernando, S., Georgiou, A., Holdgate, A., & Westbrook, J. (2009). Challenges associated with electronic ordering in the emergency department: A study of doctors' experiences. *Emergency Medicine Australasia*, *21*(5), 373–378. doi:10.1111/j.1742-6723.2009.01214.x PMID:19840086

Fielder, F.G., Eleuteri, B.A., & Gross, E.M. (1993). Quality assurance responsibilities as defined by the EPA Good Automated Laboratory Practices (GALPs). *Quality Assurance*, *2*(1-2), 175-9.

Florida, R. (1996). Lean and green: The move to environmentally conscious manufacturing. *California Management Review*, *39*(1), 80–105. doi:10.2307/41165877

Flynn, B. B., & Flynn, E. J. (2005). Synergies between supply chain management and quality management: Emerging implications. *International Journal of Production Research*, *43*(6), 3421–3436. doi:10.1080/00207540500118076

Flynn, B. B., Schroeder, R. G., & Sakakibara, S. (1994). A framework for quality management research and an associated instrument. *Journal of Operations Management*, *11*(4), 339–366. doi:10.1016/S0272-6963(97)90004-8

Flynn, B. B., Schroeder, R. G., & Sakakibara, S. (1995). The impact of quality management practices on performance and competitive advantage. *Decision Sciences*, *26*(5), 659–691. doi:10.1111/j.1540-5915.1995.tb01445.x

Fontes, E. L. G., & Balloni, A. J. (2007). Security In Information Systems: Sociotechnical Aspects. In Innovations and Advanced Techniques in Computer and Information Sciences and Engineering (pp. 163-166). Springer. Retrieved October 15, 2013, from http://repositorio.cti.gov.br/repositorio/bitstream/10691/256/1/Security.pdf

Fontes, E. (2008). *Praticando a segurança da informação*. Rio de Janeiro: Editora Brasport.

Fontes, E. (2012). *Políticas e normas para a segurança da informação*. Rio de Janeiro: Editora Brasport.

Ford A. (2008 November). Labs on the brink of ISO 15189 approval. *CAP TODAY*. Retrieved September 22, 2013, from http://www.cap.org/apps/cap.portal?_nfpb=true&cntvwrPtlt_actionOverride=%2Fportlets%2FcontentViewer%2Fshow&cntvwrPtlt%7BactionForm.contentReference%7D=cap_today%2F1108%2F1108_ISO_15189_approval_02.html&_pageLabel=cntvwr

Forsman, R. W. (1996). Why is the laboratory an afterthought for managed care organizations? *Clinical Chemistry*, *42*(5), 813–816. PMID:8653920

Forza, C., & Flippini, R. (1998). TQM impact on quality conformance and customer satisfaction: A causal model. *International Journal of Production Economics*, *55*(1), 1–20. doi:10.1016/S0925-5273(98)00007-3

Fotopoulos, C. V., & Psomas, E. L. (2010). The structural relationships between total quality management factors and organizational performance. *The TQM Journal*, *22*(5), 539–552. doi:10.1108/17542731011072874

Freeman, R., Moore, L. S. P., García Álvarez, L., Charlett, A., & Holmes, A. (2013). Advances in electronic surveillance for healthcare-associated infections in the 21st century: A systematic review. *Journal of Hospital Infection, 84*(2), 106–119.

Freeman, K. P., Bauer, N., Jensen, A. L., & Thoresen, S. (2006). Introduction to ISO 15189: a blueprint for quality systems in veterinary laboratories. *Veterinarian Clinical Pathology, 35*(2), 157–171. doi:10.1111/j.1939-165X.2006.tb00109.x

Friedman, B.A., & Mitchell, W. (1992). The deployment of information technology in clinical laboratories and its impact on professional roles. *Clinical Laboratory Management Review, 6*(1), 87-8, 90-3.

Friedman, B. A. (1989). The laboratory information system as a tool for implementing a strategic plan. *American Journal of Clinical Pathology, 92*(4Suppl 1), S38–S43. PMID:2801622

Friedman, B. A. (1990). Informatics as a separate section within a department of pathology. *American Journal of Clinical Pathology, 94*(Suppl 1), S2–S6. PMID:2220682

Friedman, B. A. (1996). The challenge of managing laboratory information in a managed care environment. *American Journal of Clinical Pathology, 105*(4Suppl 1), S3–S9. PMID:8607459

Fuentes, M. M. F., Montes, F. J. L., & Fernandez, L. M. M. (2006). Total quality management, strategic orientation and organizational performance: The case of Spanish companies. *Total Quality Management, 17*(3), 303–323.

Gao, T., Massey, T., Selavo, L., Crawford, D., Chen, B. R., & Lorincz, K. et al. (2007). The advanced health and disaster aid network: A light-weight wireless medical system for triage. *IEEE Transactions on* Biomedical Circuits and Systems, *1*(3), 203–216.

Garcia-Bernal, J., & Garcia-Casarejos, N. (2014). Economic analysis of TQM adoption in the construction sector. *Total Quality Management & Business Excellence, 25*(3-4), 209–221. doi:10.1080/14783363.2012.728848

Garvin, D. (1988). *Managing quality: The strategic and competitive edge*. New York, NY: Free Press.

Gavurová, B., Šoltés, V., Kafková, K., & Černý, Ľ. (2013). *Selected aspects of the Slovak health efficiency. Day-healthcare and its development in the Slovak Republic. Košice.* Technical University.

Georgiou, A., Morse, W., Timmins, W., Ray, S., & Westbrook, J. I. (2008). The use of performance metrics to monitor the impact of CPOE on pathology laboratory services. In S. K. Andersen, G. O. Klein, S. Schulz, J. Aarts & M. Cristina Mazzoleni (Eds.), *eHealth Beyond the Horizon - Get IT There; Proceedings of MIE2008* (pp. 291-296). Amsterdam: IOS Press.

Georgiou, A., Westbrook, J., & Braithwaite, J. (2010). What effect does electronic ordering have on the organisation dynamics of a hospital pathology service?. In C. Safran, H. Marin & S. Reti (Eds.), *Partnerships for Effective eHealth Soultions 13th World Congress on Medical and Health Informatics (Medinfo 2010)* (pp. 223-227). Cape Town, South Africa: IOS Press.

Georgiou, A., Ampt, A., Creswick, N., Westbrook, J., & Braithwaite, J. (2009). Computerized provider order entry - what are health professionals concerned about? A qualitative study in an Australian hospital. *International Journal of Medical Informatics, 78*(1), 60–70. doi:10.1016/j.ijmedinf.2008.09.007 PMID:19010728

Georgiou, A., Greenfield, T., Callen, J., & Westbrook, J. (2009). Safety and efficiency considerations for the introduction of electronic ordering in a Blood Bank. *Archives of Pathology & Laboratory Medicine, 133*(6), 933–937. PMID:19492886

Georgiou, A., Lam, M., Allardice, J., Hart, G. K., & Westbrook, J. I. (2012). Troponin testing in the emergency department: a longitudinal study to assess the impact and sustainability of decision support strategies. *Journal of Clinical Pathology, 65*(6), 546–550. doi:10.1136/jclinpath-2011-200610 PMID:22412052

Georgiou, A., Lang, S., Alvaro, F., Whittaker, G., Westbrook, J. I., & Callen, J. (2007). Pathology's front line - a comparison of the experiences of electronic ordering in the Clinical Chemistry and Haematology departments. In J. Westbrook, E. Coiera, & J. Callen (Eds.), *Information Technology in Health Care; Socio-technical approaches* (pp. 121–132). Sydney, Australia: IOS Press.

Georgiou, A., Lang, S., Rosenfeld, D., & Westbrook, J. I. (2011). The Use of Computerized Provider Order Entry to Improve the Effectiveness and Efficiency of Coagulation Testing. *Archives of Pathology & Laboratory Medicine, 135,* 495–498. PMID:21466368

Georgiou, A., Prgomet, M., Paoloni, R., Creswick, N., Hordern, A., Walter, S., & Westbrook, J. (2013). The Effect of Computerized Provider Order Entry Systems on Clinical Care and Work Processes in Emergency Departments: A Systematic Review of the Quantitative Literature. *Annals of Emergency Medicine, 61*(6), 644–653. doi:10.1016/j.annemergmed.2013.01.028 PMID:23548404

Georgiou, A., Prgomet, M., Toouli, G., Callen, J., & Westbrook, J. (2011). What do physicians tell laboratories when requesting tests? A multi-method examination of information supplied to the Microbiology laboratory before and after the introduction of electronic ordering. *International Journal of Medical Informatics, 80*(9), 646–654. doi:10.1016/j.ijmedinf.2011.06.003 PMID:21757400

Georgiou, A., Tariq, A., & Westbrook, J. I. (2013). The temporal landscape of residential aged care facilities-implications for context-sensitive health technology. In M.-C. Beuscart-Zéphir, M. W. M. Jaspers, & C. Kuziemsky (Eds.), *Context Sensitive Health Informatics: Human and Sociotechnical Approaches* (Vol. 194, pp. 69–74). Amsterdam, Netherlands: IOS Press.

Georgiou, A., & Westbrook, J. I. (2007). Computerised Physician Order Entry systems and their effect on pathology laboratories. *Hospital Information Technology Europe, 2007*(Autumn), 40–41.

Georgiou, A., & Westbrook, J. I. (2007). Computerized order entry systems and pathology services — a synthesis of the evidence. *The Clinical Biochemist. Reviews / Australian Association of Clinical Biochemists, 27,* 79–87.

Georgiou, A., Westbrook, J. I., & Braithwaite, J. (2011). Time matters - a theoretical and empirical examination of the temporal landscape of a hospital pathology service and the impact of e-health. *Social Science & Medicine, 72,* 1603–1610. doi:10.1016/j.socscimed.2011.03.020 PMID:21497430

Georgiou, A., Westbrook, J. I., & Braithwaite, J. (2012). An empirically-derived approach for investigating health information technology: the elementally entangled organisational communication (EEOC) framework. *BMC Medical Informatics and Decision Making, 12*(1), 68. doi:10.1186/1472-6947-12-68 PMID:22788698

Georgiou, A., Westbrook, J. I., Braithwaite, J., Iedema, R., Ray, S., & Forsyth, R. et al. (2007). When requests become orders - A formative investigation into the impact of a Computerized Physician Order Entry system on a pathology laboratory service. *International Journal of Medical Informatics, 76*(8), 583–591. doi:10.1016/j.ijmedinf.2006.04.002 PMID:16702022

Georgiou, A., Westbrook, J. I., Callen, J. L., & Braithwaite, J. (2008). Electronic test management systems and hospital pathology laboratory services. In N. Wickramasinghe, & E. Geisler (Eds.), *Encyclopaedia of Healthcare Information Systems* (Vol. II, pp. 505–512). Hershey, PA: Medical Information Science Reference. doi:10.4018/978-1-59904-889-5.ch064

Georgiou, A., Westbrook, J., & Braithwaite, J. (2010). Computerized provider order entry systems–Research imperatives and organizational challenges facing pathology services. *Journal of Pathology Informatics, 1,* 11. doi:10.4103/2153-3539.65431 PMID:20805962

Georgiou, A., Westbrook, J., Braithwaite, J., & Iedema, R. (2005). Multiple perspectives on the impact of electronic ordering on hospital organisational and communication processes. *Health Information Management Journal, 34*(4), 130–134. PMID:18216417

Georgiou, A., Williamson, M., Westbrook, J., & Ray, S. (2007). The impact of computerised physician order entry systems on pathology services: a systematic review. *International Journal of Medical Informatics, 76*(7), 514–529. doi:10.1016/j.ijmedinf.2006.02.004 PMID:16567121

GESITI Health Repository of Indexed Scientific Publications. (n.d.). Retrieved October 15, 2013, from http://repositorio.cti.gov.br/repositorio/simple-search?query=hospital

GESITI. (2013). *Management of System and Information Technology in Hospitals (GESITI).* CTI Renato Acher – Campinas/SP – Brasila.

Ghobadian, A., & Gallear, D. (1997). TQM and organization size. *International Journal of Operations & Production Management, 17*(2), 121–163. doi:10.1108/01443579710158023

Giardine, B., Riemer, C., Hardison, R. C., Burhans, R., Elnitski, L., Shah, P., & Nekrutenko, A. (2005). Galaxy: A platform for interactive large-scale genome analysis. *Genome Research, 15*(10), 1451–1455. doi:10.1101/gr.4086505 PMID:16169926

Giddens, A. (1990). *The consequences of modernity*. Stanford, CA: Stanford University Press.

Giusca, C., & Leach, R. K. (2013). Calibration of the scales of areal surface topography measuring instruments: part 3. Resolution. *Measurement Science & Technology, 24*(10), 105010. doi:10.1088/0957-0233/24/10/105010

Gkatzikis, L., & Koutsopoulos, I. (2013). Migrate or not? Exploiting dynamic task migration in mobile cloud computing systems. *IEEE Wireless Communications, 20*(3), 24–32. doi:10.1109/MWC.2013.6549280

Global Risk. (2010). *A Global Risk Network Report*. World Economic Forum. Retrieved October 08, 2013, from http://www3.weforum.org/docs/WEF_Global-Risks_Report_2010.pdf

Godfrey, A. B. (1993). Ten areas for future research in total quality management. *Quality Management Journal, 1*(1), 47–70.

Goecks, J., Nekrutenko, A., Taylor, J., & Team, T. G. (2010). Galaxy: A comprehensive approach for supporting accessible, reproducible, and transparent computational research in the life sciences. *Genome Biology, 11*(8), R86. doi:10.1186/gb-2010-11-8-r86 PMID:20738864

Golub, T. R., Slonim, D. K., Tamayo, P., Huard, C., Gaasenbeek, M., Mesirov, J. P., & Lander, E. S. (1999). Molecular classification of cancer: class discovery and class prediction by gene expression monitoring. *Science, 286*(5439), 531–537. doi:10.1126/science.286.5439.531 PMID:10521349

Gore, E. W. (1999). Organizational culture, TQM, and business process reengineering: An empirical comparison. *Team Performance Management: An International Journal, 5*(5), 164–170. doi:10.1108/13527599910288993

Gorman, P. N., Lavelle, M. B., & Ash, J. S. (2003). Order creation and communication in healthcare. *Methods of Information in Medicine, 42*(4), 376–384. PMID:14534637

Gostin, L. O., Turek-Brezina, J., Powers, M., & Kozloff, R. (1995, Winter). Privacy and security of health information in the emerging health care system. *Health Matrix Clevel., 5*(1), 1–36. PMID:10141742

Grandjean, G., Graham, R., & Bartholomeusz, G. (2011). Essential attributes identified in the design of a laboratory information management system for a high throughput siRNA screening laboratory. *Comb. Chem. High. Throughput Screen., 14*(9), 766-771.

Grandjean, G., Graham, R., & Bartholomeusz, G. (2011). Essential attributes identified in the design of a Laboratory Information Management System for a high throughput siRNA screening laboratory. *Combinatorial Chemistry & High Throughput Screening, 14*(9), 766–771. doi:10.2174/138620711796957152 PMID:21631413

Grandzol, J. R., & Greshon, M. (1997). Which TQM practices really matter: An empirical investigation. *Quality Management Journal, 4*(4), 43–59.

Greenes, R. A., Pappalardo, A. N., Marble, C. W., & Barnett, G. O. (1969). Design and implementation of a clinical data management system. *Computers and Biomedical Research, an International Journal, 2*(5), 469–485. doi:10.1016/0010-4809(69)90012-3 PMID:11697375

Greenhalgh, T., & Russell, J. (2010). Why Do Evaluations of eHealth Programs Fail? An Alternative Set of Guiding Principles. *PLoS Medicine, 7*(11), e1000360. doi:10.1371/journal.pmed.1000360 PMID:21072245

Guidance document 'Standard Sample Descriptionver. 2.0'. (n.d.). Retrieved February 2, 2013, from http://www.efsa.europa.eu/en/efsajournal/pub/3424.htm

Guidi, G. C., & Lippi, G. (2006). Laboratory medicine in the 2000s: programmed death or rebirth? *Clinical Chemistry and Laboratory Medicine, 44*, 913–917. doi:10.1515/CCLM.2006.168 PMID:16879053

Gulla, V. (2010). How can telemedicine benefit from broadband technologies? In K. Khoumbati, Y. Dwivedi, A. Srivastava, & B. Lal (Eds.), *Handbook of Research on Advances in Health Informatics and Electronic Healthcare Applications: Global Adoption and Impact of Information Communication Technologies* (pp. 91–107). Hershey, PA: Medical Information Science Reference. doi:10.4018/978-1-60566-986-1.ch121

Guzel & Guner. (2009). ISO 15189 accreditation: Requirements for quality and competence of medical laboratories, experience of a laboratory. *Clinical Biochemistry, 42*(4-5), 274–278. PMID:19863920

Hackman, J. R., & Wageman, R. (1995). Total quality management: Empirical, conceptual, and practical issues. *Administrative Science Quarterly, 40*(2), 309–342. doi:10.2307/2393640

Hafeez, K., Malak, N., & Abdelmeguid, H. (2006). A framework for TQM to achieve business excellence. *Total Quality Management, 17*(9), 1213–1229. doi:10.1080/14783360600750485

Hales, D. N., & Chakravorty, S. S. (2006). Implementation of Deming's style of quality management: An action research study in a plastics company. *International Journal of Production Economics, 103*(1), 131–148. doi:10.1016/j.ijpe.2005.05.020

Hammond, W. E. (2008). *An Introduction to LOINC: Logical Observation Identifier Name and Codes.* Retrieved February 02, 2014, from http://www.hcup-us.ahrq.gov/datainnovations/clinicaldata/FL20LOINCIntroduction-Hammond.pdf

Haquin, S., Oeuillet, E., Pajon, A., Harris, M., Jones, A. T., & van Tilbeurgh, H. et al. (2008). Data management in structural genomics: an overview. *Methods in Molecular Biology (Clifton, N.J.), 426,* 49. doi:10.1007/978-1-60327-058-8_4 PMID:18542857

Harkovotová, S. (2011). *According to the OECD Slovaks are inefficient in healthcare.* Retrieved October 02, 2013, from http://aktualne.centrum.sk/domov/zdravie-skolstvospolocnost/clanek.phtml?id=1223847

Harvey, L., & Stensaker, B. (2008). Quality culture: Understandings, boundaries and linkages. *European Journal of Education, 43*(4), 427–442. doi:10.1111/j.1465-3435.2008.00367.x

Hasan, M., & Kerr, R. M. (2003). The relationship between TQM practices and organizational performance in service organization. *The TQM Magazine, 15*(4), 286–291. doi:10.1108/09544780310486191

Hawkins, R. C. (2007). Laboratory turnaround time. *The Clinical Biochemist. Reviews / Australian Association of Clinical Biochemists, 28,* 179–194. PMID:18392122

Healthcare Information and Management Systems Society (HIMSS). (2005). *Interoperability definition and background.* Retrieved July 25, 2013, from http://www.himss.org/files/HIMSSorg/content/files/AUXILIOHIMSSInteroperabilityDefined.pdf

Healthcare Information and Management Systems Society. (2013). *What is Interoperability.* Retrieved July 27, 2013, from http://www.himss.org/library/interoperability-standards/what-is

Hejduková, P., & Klepáková, A. (2013). *The Issue of Healthcare Financing in Selected Countries.* WSEAS Press.

Helms, M. M., Moore, R., & Ahmadi, M. (2011). Information Technology (IT) and the Healthcare Industry: A SWOT Analysis. In J. Tan (Ed.), *Developments in Healthcare Information Systems and Technologies: Models and Methods* (pp. 65–83). Hershey, PA: Medical Information Science Reference.

Hendricks, K. B., & Singhal, V. (2001). The long-run stock price performance of firms with effective TQM programs. *Management Science, 47*(3), 359–368. doi:10.1287/mnsc.47.3.359.9773

Herzlinger, R. E. (2006). Why innovation in health care is so hard. *Harvard Business Review, 84,* 58–66. PMID:16649698

Ho, D. C. K., Duffy, V. G., & Shih, H. M. (2001). Total quality management: An empirical test for mediation effect. *International Journal of Production Research, 39*(3), 529–548. doi:10.1080/00207540010005709

Hofmann, R. M. (2007). *Modeling medical devices for plug-and-play interoperability.* (Unpublished Doctoral Dissertation). Massachusetts Institute of Technology, Cambridge, MA.

HOKLAS, Hong Kong Laboratory Accreditation Scheme. (2013 April). *016 Assessment / Reassessment Questionnaire (Medical Laboratories) (based on HOKLAS 015 5th edition)*. Retrieved December 8, 2012, from http://www.itc.gov.hk/en/quality/hkas/doc/hoklas/HOKLAS016.pdf

Hong Kong Accreditation Service. (2004). Practical application of ISO 125189 by accreditation bodies. *EJIFCC*.

Hsieh, S. H., Hsieh, S. L., Cheng, P. H., & Lai, F. (2012). E-Health and healthcare enterprise information system leveraging service-oriented architecture. *Telemedicine Journal and e-Health, 18*(3), 205–212. doi:10.1089/tmj.2011.0100 PMID:22480301

Huang, Z., Lu, X., & Duan, H. (2012). On mining clinical pathway patterns from medical behaviors. *Artificial Intelligence in Medicine, 56*(1), 35-50

Hubca, A., Koniotou, R., Gligic, L., Noten, V., Zdilna, P., Kastrop, P., & Greven, I. (2013, June). *Comparison ISO 15189:2007 vs ISO 15189:2012*. Paper presented at the meeting of the EA WG "Healthcare". Frankfurt, Germany.

Hysong, S. J., Sawhney, M. K., Wilson, L., Sittig, D. F., Esquivel, A., Singh, S., & Singh, H. (2011). Understanding the management of electronic test result notifications in the outpatient setting. *BMC Medical Informatics and Decision Making, 11*, 22. doi:10.1186/1472-6947-11-22 PMID:21486478

IANZ, International Accreditation New Zealand. (n.d.). *Implementing ISO 15189:2012*. Retrieved September 21, 2013, from https://go.promapp.com/ianz/view/Documents/View/Open?displayType=document&documentId=e0196d0e-49e8-4962-94ee-b1b437d93970

ILAC, International Laboratory Accreditation Cooperation. (2012, October 26). *Adopted Resolutions 16th ILAC GA*. Retrieved November 1, 2013, from https://www.ilac.org/documents/Adopted%20Resolutions%2016th%20ILAC%20GA%2026%20Oct%202012.pdf doc

ILAC. (2011). *The ISO 15189 Medical Laboratory Accreditation*. Author.

INAP, Irish National Accreditation Board. (2013, April 10). *Summary of changes in ISO 15189:2012 compared to the 2007 version*. Retrieved September 21, 2013, from http://inab.ie/media/Summary%20of%20changes%20for%20ISO%2015189.pdf

Integrating the Healthcare Enterprise. (2013). Retrieved 27 June 2013 from http://www.ihe.net/Laboratory/

International Accreditation Forum - International Laboratory Accreditation Cooperation - International Organization for Standardization IAF-ILAC-ISO Joint communiqué on the management systems requirements of ISO 15189:2007. (2009). Retrieved February 2, 2014, from http://www.ilac.org

International Accreditation New Zealand. (2013). *Implementing ISO 15189:2012*. Retrieved 26 September, 2013 from https://go.promapp.com/ianz/view/Documents/View/Open?displayType=document&documentId=e0196d0e-49e8-4962-94ee-b1b437d93970.

International Health Terminology Standards Development Organization. (2013). *SNOMED CT® Editorial Guide July 2013 International Release*. Retrieved September 13 from http://ihtsdo.org/fileadmin/user_upload/doc/download/doc_EditorialGuide_Current-en-US_INT_20130731.pdf

International Laboratory Accreditation Cooperation. (2001). *ILAC B9: ISO 15189 Medical laboratory accreditation*. Retrieved February 2, 2014, from http://www.ilac.org

International Laboratory Accreditation Cooperation. (2010). *ILAC G18: Guideline for the formulation of scopes of accreditation for laboratories*. Retrieved February 2, 2014, from http://www.ilac.org

International Laboratory Accreditation Cooperation. (2012). *ILAC-G26: Guidance for the Implementation of a medical laboratory accreditation system*. Retrieved February 2, 2014, from http://www.ilac.org

International Laboratory Accreditation Cooperation. (2013). *ILAC B5: Securing testing, measurement or calibration services - The difference between accreditation and certification*. Retrieved February 2, 2014, from http://www.ilac.org

International Organization for Standardization / International Electrotechnical Committee. (2004). *ISO/IEC 17000: Conformity assessment- Vocabulary and general principles*. Geneva: ISO/IEC.

International Organization for Standardization / International Electrotechnical Committee. (2004). *ISO/IEC 17011: Conformity assessment - General requirements for accreditation bodies accrediting conformity assessment bodies*. Geneva: ISO/IEC.

International Organization for Standardization / International Electrotechnical Committee. (2005). *ISO/IEC 17025: General requirements for the competence of testing and calibration laboratories*. Geneva: ISO/IEC.

International Organization for Standardization / International Electrotechnical Committee. (2007). *ISO/IEC Guide 99: International vocabulary of metrology - Basic and general concepts and associated terms* (VIM 3rd ed). Retrieved February 2, 2014, from http://www.bipm.org/vim

International Organization for Standardization / International Electrotechnical Committee. (2010). *ISO/IEC 17043: Conformity assessment - General requirements for proficiency testing*. Geneva: ISO/IEC.

International Organization for Standardization. (2002) *ISO 19011: Guidelines for quality and/or environmental management systems auditing*. Geneva: ISO.

International Organization for Standardization. (2003). *ISO 15190: Medical laboratories – Requirements for safety*. Geneva: ISO.

International Organization for Standardization. (2004). *ISO 14001: Environmental management systems - Requirements with guidance for use*. Geneva: ISO.

International Organization for Standardization. (2005). *ISO 9000: Quality management systems - Fundamentals and vocabulary*. Geneva: ISO.

International Organization for Standardization. (2006). *ISO 22870: Point-of-care testing (POCT) - Requirements for quality and competence*. Geneva: ISO.

International Organization for Standardization. (2007). *ISO 15189: Medical laboratories - Particular requirements for quality and competence*. Geneva: ISO.

International Organization for Standardization. (2008). *ISO 9001: Quality management systems – Requirements*. Geneva: ISO.

International Organization for Standardization. (2012). *ISO 15189: Medical laboratories - Requirements for quality and competence*. Geneva: ISO.

Iroju, O., Soriyan, A., Gambo, I., & Olaleke, J. (2013). Interoperability in Healthcare: Benefits, Challenges and Resolutions. *International Journal of Innovation and Applied Studies, 3*(1), 262–270.

ISO 15189. (2013). In *Wikipedia*. Retrieved September 25, 2013, from http://en.wikipedia.org/wiki/ISO_15189

ISO 15189:2003. (2003). *Medical laboratories — Particular requirements for quality and competence. International Organization for Standards*. Geneva, Switzerland: ISO.

ISO 15189:2007. (2007). *Medical laboratories – Particular requirements for quality and competence. 2nd ed. International Organization for Standards*. Geneva, Switzerland: ISO.

ISO 15189:2012. (2012). *Medical laboratories – Requirements for quality and competence. 3rd ed. International Organization for Standards*. Geneva, Switzerland: ISO.

ISO 9001. (2008). *Quality management systems -- Requirements*. Geneva, Switzerland: ISO Press.

ISO IEC 15189. (2012). Medical laboratories -- Requirements for quality and competence. Geneva, Switzerland: ISO Press.

ISO IEC 17011. (2004). Conformity assessment — General requirements for accreditation bodies accrediting conformity assessment bodies. Geneva, Switzerland: ISO Press.

ISO IEC 17025. (2005). General requirements for the competence of testing and calibration laboratories. Geneva, Switzerland: ISO Press.

ISO/CEN. (2012). *Medical laboratories – Particular requirements for quality and competence* (EN ISO 15189:2012). Author.

ISO/CEN. (2012). *Medical laboratories – Requirements for quality and competence* (EN ISO 15189:2012). Author.

Ivančík, R. (2012). Globalization and the global economy. Vedecký Obzor, 4(1), 27-45.

Iversen, K.R., Heimly, V., & Lundgren, T.I. (1995). Implementing security in computer based patient records clinical experiences. *Medinfo, 8*(Pt 1), 657–660. PMID:8591292

Jani, I. V., & Peter, T. F. (2013). How point-of-care testing could drive innovation in global health. *The New England Journal of Medicine, 368*(24), 2319–2324. doi:10.1056/NEJMsb1214197 PMID:23758238

Janke, F., & Prídavok, M. (2012). B2B network performance: Practical Aspects Of Network Supply Adequacy Indicator. In *Proceedings of IDIMT-2012, ICT Support For Complex Systems*. Jindrichuv Hradec, Czech Republic: Schriftenreihe Informatik.

Jha, A. K., DesRoches, C. M., Campbell, E. G., Donelan, K., Rao, S. R., & Ferris, T. G. et al. (2009). Use of electronic health records in US hospitals. *The New England Journal of Medicine, 360*(16), 1628–1638. doi:10.1056/NEJMsa0900592 PMID:19321858

Jones, S. S., Rudin, R. S., Perry, T., & Shekelle, P. G. (2014). Health Information Technology: An Updated Systematic Review With a Focus on Meaningful Use. *Annals of Internal Medicine, 160*(1), 48–54. doi:10.7326/M13-1531 PMID:24573664

Juergensen, T. (2000). *Continuous improvement: Mindsets, capability, process, tools and results*. Indianapolis, IN: The Juergensen Consulting Group.

Jung, J. Y., Wang, Y. J., & Wu, S. (2009). Competitive strategy, TQM practice, and continuous improvement of international project management - A contingency study. *International Journal of Quality & Reliability Management, 26*(2), 164–183. doi:10.1108/02656710910928806

Jun, M., Cai, S., & Shin, H. (2006). TQM practice in Maquiladora: Antecedents of employee satisfaction and loyalty. *Journal of Operations Management, 24*(6), 791–812. doi:10.1016/j.jom.2005.09.006

Juran, J. M. (1994). The upcoming century for quality. *Quality Progress, 27*(8), 29–37.

Ju, T. J., Lin, B., Lin, C., & Kuo, H. J. (2006). TQM critical factors and KM value chain activities. *Total Quality Management, 17*(3), 373–393. doi:10.1080/14783360500451614

Kagadis, G. C., Langer, S. G., Sakellaropoulos, G. C., Alexakos, C., & Nagy, P. (2006). Overview of Medical Imaging Informatics. In A. B. Wolbarst, R. G. Zamenhof, W. R. Hendee, & I. P. Smith (Eds.), *Advances in Medical Physics* (pp. 160–169). Madison, WI: Medical Physics Publishing.

Kam, C. W., & Tang, S. L. (1997). Development and implementation of quality assurance in public construction works in Singapore and Hong Kong. *International Journal of Quality & Reliability Management, 14*(9), 909–928. doi:10.1108/02656719710186830

Kanji, G. K. (2001). Forces of excellence in Kanji's business excellence model. *Total Quality Management, 12*(2), 259–272. doi:10.1080/09544120120025311

Kanji, G. K., & Wallace, W. (2000). Business excellence through customer satisfaction. *Total Quality Management, 11*(7), 979–998. doi:10.1080/09544120050135515

Kaplan, B. (1991). Models of change and information systems research. In H.E. Nissen, H.K. Klein, & R. Hirschheim (Eds.), Information Systems Research: Contemporary Approaches and Emergent Traditions, (pp. 593–611). Academic Press.

Karia, N., & Asaari, M. H. A. H. (2006). The effects of total quality management practices on employees' work-related attitudes. *The TQM Magazine, 18*(1), 30–43. doi:10.1108/09544780610637677

Kataoka, H., Nishida, M., & Sugiura, T. (2000). Communications among components of automated clinical laboratory systems. *Rinsho Byori, 48*(Suppl 114), 59-65.

Kawai, T. (2007). Evaluation of clinical laboratories-assurance of their quality and competence. *Rinsho Byori, 55*(1), 59–62. PMID:17319492

Kawai, T. (2010). History of ISO 15189 and its future perspective. *Rinsho Byori, 58*(1), 64–68. PMID:20169946

Kawano. (2005). External quality assessment with reference to the certification/accreditation of medical laboratories. *Rinsho Byori, 53*(4), 319-23.

Kaynak, H. (2003). The relationship between total quality management practices and their effects on firm performance. *Journal of Operations Management, 21*(4), 405–435. doi:10.1016/S0272-6963(03)00004-4

Kent, W. J. (2002). BLAT—the BLAST-like alignment tool. *Genome Research, 12*(4), 656–664. doi:10.1101/gr.229202. Article published online before March 2002 PMID:11932250

Khurana, K. K. (2012). Telecytology and its evolving role in cytopathology. *Diagnostic Cytopathology, 40*(6), 498–502. doi:10.1002/dc.22822 PMID:22619124

Kim, D. Y., Kumar, V., & Kumar, U. (2012). Relationship between quality management practices and innovation. *Journal of Operations Management, 30*(4), 295–315. doi:10.1016/j.jom.2012.02.003

Kim, T. Y., Coenen, A., & Hardiker, N. (2012). Semantic mappings and locality of nursing diagnostic concepts in UMLS. *Journal of Biomedical Informatics, 45*(1), 93–100. doi:10.1016/j.jbi.2011.09.002 PMID:21951759

Kimura, M. (1999). Outline of Health Level Seven (HL7) standard. *Rinsho Byori, 47*(12), 1165-9.

Klein, C.S. (2003). LIMS user acceptance testing. *Quality Assurance, 10*(2), 91-106.

Klepáková, A. (2010). Information cluster for subjects of Slovak public health insurance market. In *Clusters, bi and global economy (international aspects)*. Poland: Serve & Bonus Liber.

Kling, R. (1980). Social analyses of computing: Theoretical perspectives in recent empirical research. *Computing Surveys, 12*, 61–110. doi:10.1145/356802.356806

Kohlbacher, M. (2010). The effects of process orientation: A literature review. *Business Process Management Journal, 16*(1), 135–152. doi:10.1108/14637151011017985

Koppel, R., Metlay, J. P., Cohen, A., Abaluck, B., Localio, A. R., Kimmel, S. E., & Strom, B. L. (2005). Role of computerized physician order entry systems in facilitating medication errors. *Journal of the American Medical Association, 293*(10), 1197–1203. doi:10.1001/jama.293.10.1197 PMID:15755942

Kristal, M. M., Huang, X., & Schroeder, R. G. (2010). The effect of quality management on mass customization capability. *International Journal of Operations & Production Management, 30*(9), 900–922. doi:10.1108/01443571011075047

Kubono. (2004). Quality management system in the medical laboratory-ISO15189 and laboratory accreditation. *Rinsho Byori, 52*(3), 274-8.

Kubono, K. (2007). Outline of the revision of ISO 15189 and accreditation of medical laboratory for specified health checkup. *Rinsho Byori, 55*(11), 1029–1036. PMID:18154036

Kuhn, K. et al. (2007). The Cancer Biomedical Informatics Grid (caBIG™): Infrastructure and Applications for a Worldwide Research Community. *Medinfo, 1*, 330.

Kull, T. J., & Narasimhan, R. (2010). Quality management and cooperative values: Investigation of multilevel influences on workgroup performance. *Decision Sciences, 41*(1), 81–113. doi:10.1111/j.1540-5915.2009.00260.x

Kumar, R., Garg, D., & Garg, T. K. (2011). Total quality management success factors in North Indian manufacturing and service industries. *The TQM Journal, 23*(1), 36–46. doi:10.1108/17542731111097470

Kumar, S., & Gupta, Y. (1991). Cross functional teams improve manufacturing at Motorola's Austin plant. *Industrial Engineering (American Institute of Industrial Engineers), 23*(5), 32–36.

Kumar, V., Choisne, F., De Grosfoir, D., & Kumar, U. (2009). Impact of TQM on company's performance. *International Journal of Quality & Reliability Management, 26*(1), 23–37. doi:10.1108/02656710910924152

Kushniruk, A. W., Bates, D. W., Bainbridge, M., Househ, M. S., & Borycki, E. M. (2013). National efforts to improve health information system safety in Canada, the United States of America and England. *International Journal of Medical Informatics, 82*(5), e149–e160.

Kuziemsky, C., Borycki, E., Purkis, M., Black, F., Boyle, M., & Cloutier-Fisher, D. et al. (2009). An interdisciplinary team communication framework and its application to healthcare'e-teams' systems design. *BMC Medical Informatics and Decision Making, 9*(1), 43. doi:10.1186/1472-6947-9-43 PMID:19754966

LabGru. (2014). Retrieved from http://www.labguru.com/

Lagrosen, S. (2003). Exploring the impact of culture on quality management. *International Journal of Quality & Reliability Management, 20*(4), 473–487. doi:10.1108/02656710310468632

Lakhal, L., Pasin, F., & Limam, M. (2006). Quality management practices and their impact on performance. *International Journal of Quality & Reliability Management, 23*(6), 625–646. doi:10.1108/02656710610672461

Lambert, G., & Ouedraogo, N. (2008). Empirical investigation of ISO 9001 quality management systems' impact on organisational learning and process performances. *Total Quality Management and Business Excellence, 19*(10), 1071–1085. doi:10.1080/14783360802264244

Laohavichien, T., Fredendall, L. D., & Cantrell, R. S. (2011). Leadership and quality management practices in Thailand. *International Journal of Operations & Production Management, 31*(10), 1048–1070. doi:10.1108/01443571111172426

Lascelles, D. M., & Dale, B. G. (1989). A review of the issues involved in quality improvement. *International Journal of Quality & Reliability Management, 5*(5), 76–94. doi:10.1108/eb002920

Latré, B., Braem, B., Moerman, I., Blondia, C., & Demeester, P. (2011). A survey on wireless body area networks. *Wireless Networks, 17*(1), 1–18. doi:10.1007/s11276-010-0252-4

Lawler, E. E. (1994). Total quality management and employee involvement: Are they compatible? *The Academy of Management Executive, 8*(1), 68–76.

Lawler, E. E., Mohrman, S. A., & Ledford, G. E. (1992). *Employee involvement and total quality management.* San Francisco, CA: Jossey-Bass.

Legg, M., & Cheong, I. (2004). *A Study of the Impact of the Use of General Practice Computer Systems on the Ordering of Pathology.* Retrieved from http://www.nhhrc.org.au/internet/main/publishing.nsf/Content/qupp-qupp-reports.htm

Lehmann, C. A., & Cappello, S. C. (2003). Workflow analysis: an overview. In Clinical diagnostic technology: The total testing process (vol. 1). Washington, DC: American Association of Clinical Chemistry.

Leifer, R., & McDonough, E. F. (1985). Computerization as a predominant technology effecting work unit structure. In *Proceedings 6th Annual Conference on Information Systems,* (pp. 238–248). Academic Press.

Lemak, D., Reed, R., & Satish, P. (1997). Commitment to quality management: Is there a relationship with firms' performance? *Journal of Quality Management, 2*(1), 77–86. doi:10.1016/S1084-8568(97)90022-5

Levine, D. I., & Toffel, M. W. (2010). Quality management and job quality: How the ISO 9001 standard for quality management systems affects employees and employers. *Management Science, 56*(6), 978–996. doi:10.1287/mnsc.1100.1159

Li, A. (2009). Laboratory quality regulations and accreditations standards in Canada: External quality assessment with reference to the certification/accreditation of medical laboratories. *Clinical Biochemistry, 42*(4-5), 249–255. doi:10.1016/j.clinbiochem.2008.09.006 PMID:19863915

Li, L., Su, Q., & Chen, X. (2011). Ensuring supply chain quality performance through applying the SCOR model. *International Journal of Production Research, 49*(1), 33–57. doi:10.1080/00207543.2010.508934

LIMSWiki. (2014). Retrieved from http://www.limswiki.org/index.php?title=Main_Page

Lockamy, A. (1998). Quality-focused performance measurement systems: A normative model. *International Journal of Operations & Production Management, 18*(8), 740–766. doi:10.1108/01443579810217440

London, J. W., & Chatterjee, D. (2010). Using the Semantically Interoperable Biospecimen Repository Application, caTissue: End User Deployment Lessons Learned. In *Proceedings of 2010 IEEE International Conference on BioInformatics and BioEngineering (BIBE)* (pp. 316-317). IEEE.

Luzon, M. D. M., & Pasola, J. V. (2011). Ambidexterity and total quality management: Towards a research agenda. *Management Decision, 49*(6), 927–947. doi:10.1108/00251741111143612

Madu, C. N., Kuei, C. H., & Lin, C. (1995). A comparative analysis of quality practice in manufacturing firms in the US and Taiwan. *Decision Sciences, 26*(5), 621–635. doi:10.1111/j.1540-5915.1995.tb01443.x

Mahoto, N. A. (2013). *Data mining techniques for complex application domains*. (Doctoral dissertation). Politecnico di Torino, Torino, Italy.

Maier, H., Lengger, C., Simic, B., Fuchs, H., Gailus-Durner, V., & de Angelis, M. H. (2008). MausDB: An open source application for phenotype data and mouse colony management in large-scale mouse phenotyping projects. *BMC Bioinformatics, 9*(1), 169. doi:10.1186/1471-2105-9-169 PMID:18366799

Maiga, A. S., & Jacobs, F. A. (2005). Antecedents and consequences of quality performance. *Behavioral Research in Accounting, 17*(1), 111–131. doi:10.2308/bria.2005.17.1.111

Mann, R., & Kehoe, D. (1994). An evaluation of the effects of quality improvement activities on business performance. *International Journal of Quality & Reliability Management, 11*(4), 29–44. doi:10.1108/02656719410057935

Markus, M. L. (1983). Power, politics, and MIS implementation. *Communications of the ACM, 26*, 430–444. doi:10.1145/358141.358148

Markus, M. L., & Robey, D. (1988). Information technology and organizational change: Causal structure in theory and research. *Management Science, 34*, 583–598. doi:10.1287/mnsc.34.5.583

Martínez, I., Escayola, J., Martínez-Espronceda, M., Serrano, L., Trigo, J., Led, S., & García, J. (2008, August). Standard-based middleware platform for medical sensor networks and u-health. In *Proceedings of Computer Communications and Networks*, (pp. 1-6). IEEE.

Martinez-Costa, M., Choi, T. Y., Martinez, J. A., & Martinez-Lorente, A. R. (2009). ISO 9000/1994, ISO 9001/2000 and TQM: The performance debate revisited. *Journal of Operations Management, 27*(6), 495–511. doi:10.1016/j.jom.2009.04.002

McDonald, C., Huff, S., Mercer, K., Hernandez, J. A., & Vreeman, D. J. (2004). *Logical observation identifiers names and codes (LOINC®) users' guide*. Retrieved February 02, 2014 from http://loinc.org/downloads/files/LOINCManual.pdf

McDonald, C.J., Wheeler L.A., Glazener, T., & Blevins, L. (1985). A data base approach to laboratory computerization. *American Journal Clinical Pathology, 83*(6), 707-15.

McDonald, J. M., & Smith, J. A. (1995). Value-added laboratory medicine in an era of managed care. *Clinical Chemistry, 41*(8 Pt 2), 1256–1262. PMID:7628116

McDowall, R.D. (1993). An update on laboratory information management systems. *Journal of Pharmaceutical and Biomedical Analysis, 11*(11 - 12), 1327 – 30.

McDowall, R.D., Pearce, J.C., & Murkitt, G.S. (1988). Laboratory information management systems - Part 1 Concepts. *J. Pharm. Biomed. Anal., 6*(4), 339-359.

McDowall, R. D. (1988). Laboratory Information Management Systems in practice. *Journal of Pharmaceutical and Biomedical Analysis, 6*(6-8), 547–553. doi:10.1016/0731-7085(88)80068-2 PMID:16867320

McGregor, C. (2013). Big data in neonatal intensive care. *Computer, 46*(6), 54–59. doi:10.1109/MC.2013.157

Mehra, S., & Agrawal, S. P. (2003). Total quality as a new global competitive strategy. *International Journal of Quality & Reliability Management, 20*(8-9), 1009–1026. doi:10.1108/02656710310500824

Mehra, S., Hoffmanm, J. M., & Sirias, D. (2001). TQM as a management strategy for the next millennia. *International Journal of Operations & Production Management, 21*(5-6), 855–876. doi:10.1108/01443570110390534

Mekhjian, H. S., Kumar, R. R., Kuehn, L., Bentley, T. D., Teater, P., & Thomas, A. et al. (2002). Immediate benefits realized following implementation of physician order entry at an academic medical center. *Journal of the American Medical Informatics Association, 9*(5), 529–539. doi:10.1197/jamia.M1038 PMID:12223505

Mellat Parast, M., Adams, S. G., Jones, E. C., Subba Rao, S., & Raghu-Nathan, T. S. (2006). Comparing quality management practices between the US and Mexico. *Quality Management Journal, 13*(4), 36–49.

Mellat-Parast, M., Adams, S. G., & Jones, E. C. (2007). An empirical study of quality management practices in the petroleum industry. *Production Planning and Control, 18*(8), 693–702. doi:10.1080/09537280701630759

Melo, R., Barreto, J. P., & Falcao, G. (2012). A New Solution for Camera Calibration and Real-Time Image Distortion Correction in Medical Endoscopy–Initial Technical Evaluation. *IEEE Transactions on Bio-Medical Engineering, 59*(3), 634–644. doi:10.1109/TBME.2011.2177268 PMID:22127990

Menou, M. J., & Taylor, R. D. (2006). A "grand challenge": Measuring information societies. *The Information Society, 22*(5), 261–267. doi:10.1080/01972240600903904

Mierswa, I., Wurst, M., Klinkenberg, R., Scholz, M., & Euler, T. (2006). Yale: Rapid prototyping for complex data mining tasks. In *Proceedings of the 12th ACM SIGKDD international conference on Knowledge discovery and data mining* (pp. 935-940). ACM.

Milenković, A., Otto, C., & Jovanov, E. (2006). Wireless sensor networks for personal health monitoring: Issues and an implementation. *Computer Communications, 29*(13), 2521–2533. doi:10.1016/j.comcom.2006.02.011

Milisavljevic, M., Hearty, T., Wong, T. Y. T., Portales-Casamar, E., Simpson, E. M., & Wasserman, W. W. (2010). Laboratory Animal Management Assistant (LAMA): a LIMS for active research colonies. *Mammalian Genome, 21*(5), 224–230. doi:10.1007/s00335-010-9258-6 PMID:20411264

Miller, H. G., & Veiga, J. (2009). Cloud Computing: Will Commodity Services Benefit Users Long Term? *IT Professional, 11*(6), 57–59. doi:10.1109/MITP.2009.117

Minato, H., Nojima, T., Nakano, M., & Yamazaki, M. (2011). Safety management in pathology laboratory: from specimen handling to confirmation of reports. *Rinsho Byori, 59*(3), 299–304. PMID:21560413

Modarress, B., & Ansari, A. (1989). Quality control techniques in US firms: A survey. *Production and Inventory Management Journal, 30*(2), 58–62.

Moehr, J. H. (2002). Special issue: Evaluation in health informatics. *Computers in Biology and Medicine, 32*, 11–236.

Mohrman, S. A., Tenkasi, R. V., Lawler, E. E., & Ledford, G. G. (1995). Total quality management: Practice and outcomes in the largest US firms. *Employee Relations, 17*(3), 26–41. doi:10.1108/01425459510086866

Mokhtar, S. S. M., & Yusof, R. Z. (2010). The influence of top management commitment, process quality management and quality design on new product performance: A case of Malaysian manufacturers. *Total Quality Management, 21*(3), 291–300. doi:10.1080/14783360903553198

Molina, L. M., Llorens-Montes, J., & Ruiz-Moreno, A. (2007). Relationship between quality management practices and knowledge transfer. *Journal of Operations Management, 25*(3), 682–701. doi:10.1016/j.jom.2006.04.007

Montebelli, G., & Pradella, M. (2010). *Le principali differenze tra i requisiti della norma UNI EN ISO 15189 e quelli della UNI CEI EN ISO/IEC 17025. UNINFORM group. 03 NOV 2010.* ANGQ.

Moraes, I. H. S. d., & Gomez, M. N. d. (2007). Informação e informática em saúde: Caleidoscópio contemporâneo da saúde. *Ciênc. Saúde Coletiva., 12*(3), 553-565.

Morvay, K. (2009). *"Relative price" of doctor in Slovakia is growing in a domestic and international scale.* Health Policy Institute. Retrieved from http://www.hpi.sk/hpi/sk/view/3536/relativna-cena-lekara-v-sr-rastie-v-nbsp-domacom-nbsp-aj-nbsp-medzinarodnom-meradle.html

Motwani, J. G. (2001). Critical factors and performance measures of TQM. *The TQM Magazine, 13*(4), 292–300. doi:10.1108/13683040010362300

Motwani, J. G., Mahmoud, E., & Rice, G. (1994). Quality practices of Indian organizations: An empirical analysis. *International Journal of Quality & Reliability Management, 1*(1), 38–52. doi:10.1108/02656719410049493

Nagy, G. K., & Newton, L. E. (2006). Cytopathology proficiency testing: Where do we go from here? *Diagnostic Cytopathology, 34*, 257–264. doi:10.1002/dc.20361 PMID:16544329

Najmi, M., & Kehoe, D. F. (2000). An integrated framework for post-ISO 9000 quality development. *International Journal of Quality & Reliability Management, 17*(3), 226–258. doi:10.1108/02656710010300117

Nararuk, N. (1998, May). Internet. *Chula Med J, 42*(5), 385–394.

NATA, National Association of Testing Authorities. (2013, May). *Gap analysis of ISO 15189:2012 and ISO 15189:2007 in the field of medical testing.* Retrieved September 21, 2013, from http://www.nata.asn.au/phocadownload/publications/Guidance_information/checklist-worksheets-site-notification-forms/Gap-analysis-15189.pdf

NATA. (2013). *Gap Analysis of ISO 15189:2012 and ISO 15189:2007 in the field of Medical Testing.* Australia Accreditation Body.

National Centre for Health Information. (2010). Retrieved October 12, 2013, from http://www.nczisk.sk/en/Statistical_Findings/Pages/default.aspx

National Coalition of Public Pathology. (2012). *Encouraging Quality Pathology Ordering in Australia's Public Hospitals.* National Coalition of Public Pathology.

National Library of Medicine (NLM). (2013). *SNOMED Clinical Terms.* Retrieved September 25, 2014 from http://www.nlm.nih.gov/research/umls/Snomed/snomed_main.html

National Library of Medicine (NLM). (2013). *Unified Medical Language System® (UMLS®).* Retrieved September 25, 2013 from http://www.nlm.nih.gov/research/umls/quickstart.html

Nelson, E. K., Piehler, B., Eckels, J., Rauch, A., Bellew, M., Hussey, P., & Igra, M. (2011). LabKey Server: An open source platform for scientific data integration, analysis and collaboration. *BMC Bioinformatics, 12*(1), 71. doi:10.1186/1471-2105-12-71 PMID:21385461

Nemec, J., Ochrana, F., & Šumpíková, M. (2008). Czech and Slovak Lessons for Public Administration Performance Evaluation, Management and Finance. *Ekonomicky Casopis, 56*(4), 353–369.

Neumann, M. (2013). Quality management in hospital laboratory. European Hospital, 22(3/13), 8-9.

Nix, D., Di Sera, T., Dalley, B., Milash, B., Cundick, R., Quinn, K., & Courdy, S. (2010). Next generation tools for genomic data generation, distribution, and visualization. *BMC Bioinformatics, 11*(1), 455. doi:10.1186/1471-2105-11-455 PMID:20828407

Nold, E. G. (1993). Preparing to implement an information system. *American Journal of Hospital Pharmacy, 50*(5), 958–964. PMID:8506877

North, K. (2009). *Healthcare's XML Heartbeat.* Retrieved September 23, 2013 from http://www.ibm.com/developerworks/data/library/dmmag/DMMag_2009_Issue2/Industry/

Nulan, C. (2001). HIPAA--a real world perspective. *Radiology Management, 23*(2),29-40.

O'Connor, B., Merriman, B., & Nelson, S. (2010). SeqWare Query Engine: storing and searching sequence data in the cloud.[Retrieved from: http://seqware.github.io/]. *BMC Bioinformatics, 11*(Suppl 12), S2. doi:10.1186/1471-2105-11 S12-S2 PMID:21210981

Oakland, J. S. (1993). *Total quality management.* Oxford, UK: Butterworth-Heineman.

OECD. (2010). OECD Health at Glance 2010. OECD Publishing.

Ogden, J. A., Wallin, C., & Foster, S. T. (2010). On Baldrige core values and commitment to quality. *Quality Management Journal, 17*(3), 21–34.

Okada, M. (2002). Future of laboratory informatics. *Rinsho Byori, 50*(7), 691–693. PMID:12187706

O'Kane, M. J. (2013). Observations from the archives: the evolution of point-of-care testing. *Annals of Clinical Biochemistry, 50*(1), 91–92. doi:10.1177/0004563212472794 PMID:23417446

Oliver, N. (1988). Employee commitment and total quality control. *International Journal of Quality & Reliability Management, 7*(1), 21–29.

Olson, M. H. (1982). New information technology and organizational culture. *Management Information Systems Quarterly, 6*, 71–92. doi:10.2307/248992

Ooi, K. B., Arumugam, V., Safa, M. S., & Bakar, N. A. (2007). HRM and TQM: Association with job involvement. *Personnel Review*, *36*(6), 939–962. doi:10.1108/00483480710822445

Ooi, K. B., Arumugam, V., Teh, P. L., & Chong, A. Y. L. (2008). TQM practices and its association with production workers. *Industrial Management & Data Systems*, *108*(7), 909–927. doi:10.1108/02635570810897991

Ooi, K. B., Bakar, N. A., Arumugam, V., Vellapan, L., & Loke, A. K. Y. (2007). Does TQM influence employees' job satisfaction? An empirical case analysis. *International Journal of Quality & Reliability Management*, *24*(1), 62–77. doi:10.1108/02656710710720330

Ooi, K. B., Cheah, W. C., Lin, B., & Teh, P. L. (2012). Total quality management practices and knowledge sharing: An empirical study of Malaysia's manufacturing organizations. *Asia Pacific Journal of Management*, *29*(1), 59–78. doi:10.1007/s10490-009-9185-9

Ooi, K. B., Lee, V. H., Chong, A. Y. L., & Lin, B. (2013). Does TQM improve employees' quality of work life? Empirical evidence from Malaysia's manufacturing firms. *Production Planning and Control*, *24*(1), 72–89. doi:10.1080/09537287.2011.599344

Organisation for Economic Co-operation Development. (2011). *OECD Guide to Measuring the Information Society 2011*. OECD.

Osmani, A. (2012). Design and Evaluation of New Intelligent Sensor Placement Algorithm to Improve Coverage Problem in Wireless Sensor Networks. *Journal of Basic and Applied Scientific Research*, *2*(2), 1431–1440.

Otter, M., & Domas, G., & membres des groupes de travail de la SFIL. (2013). Guidelines for quality management of laboratory information systems. *Annales de biologie clinique (Paris)*, *71*(1), 257-74.

Overhage, J. M., Tierney, W. M., Zhou, X.-H., & McDonald, C. J. (1997). A randomized trial of "corollary orders" to prevent errors of omission. *Journal of the American Medical Informatics Association*, *4*(5), 364–375. doi:10.1136/jamia.1997.0040364 PMID:9292842

Palamas, S., Kalivas, D., Panou-Diamandi, O., Zeelenberg, C., & van Nimwegen, C. (2001). Design and implementation of a portal for the medical equipment market. *MEDICOM*, *3*(4), E32.

Pannirselvam, G. P., & Ferguson, L. A. (2001). A study of the relationships between the Baldrige categories. *International Journal of Quality & Reliability Management*, *18*(1), 14–34. doi:10.1108/02656710110364468

Pantanowitz, L., Henricks, W. H., & Beckwith, B. A. (2007). Medical laboratory informatics. *Clinics in Laboratory Medicine*, *27*(4), 823–843. doi:10.1016/j.cll.2007.07.011 PMID:17950900

Pantanowitz, L., Hornish, M., & Goulart, R. A. (2009). The impact of digital imaging in the field of cytopathology. *CytoJournal*, *6*, 6. doi:10.4103/1742-6413.48606 PMID:19495408

Panteghini, M. (2009). Traceability as a unique tool to improve standardization in laboratory medicine. *Clinical Biochemistry*, *42*(4-5), 236–240. doi:10.1016/j.clinbiochem.2008.09.098 PMID:19863912

Parast, M. M., Adams, S. G., & Jones, E. C. (2011). Improving operational and business performance in the petroleum industry through quality management. *International Journal of Quality & Reliability Management*, *28*(4), 426–450. doi:10.1108/02656711111121825

Park, W.S., Yi, S.Y., Kim, S.A., Song, J.S., & Kwak, Y.H. (2005). Association between the implementation of a laboratory information system and the revenue of a general hospital. *Archive of Pathology and Laboratory Medicine*, *129*(6), 766-71.

Park, A. J., Kim, H. R., & Lee, M. K. (2006). Networking Experience of Point-of-Care Test Glucometer. *The Korean Journal of Laboratory Medicine*, *26*(4), 294–298. doi:10.3343/kjlm.2006.26.4.294 PMID:18156741

Parzinger, M. J., & Nath, R. (2000). A study of the relationships between total quality management implementation factors and software quality. *Total Quality Management*, *11*(3), 353–372. doi:10.1080/0954412006874

Patel, M., & Wang, J. (2010). Applications, challenges, and prospective in emerging body area networking technologies. *IEEE Wireless Communications, 17*(1), 80–88. doi:10.1109/MWC.2010.5416354

Pelegri, M. D., Garcia-Beltran, L., & Pascual, C. (1996). Improvement of emergency and routine turnaround time by data processing and instrumentation changes. *Clinica Chimica Acta, 248*(1), 65–72. doi:10.1016/0009-8981(95)06267-X PMID:8740571

Peltier, T. (2004). *Information Security Policies and Procedures*. Auerbach.

Peng, W. C., & Chen, M. S. (2005). Query processing in a mobile computing environment: exploiting the features of asymmetry. *IEEE Transactions on Knowledge and Data Engineering, 17*(7), 982–996. doi:10.1109/TKDE.2005.115

Perez-Arostegui, M. N., Benitez-Amado, J., & Tamayo-Torres, J. (2012). Information technology-enabled quality performance: An exploratory study. *Industrial Management & Data Systems, 112*(3), 502–518. doi:10.1108/02635571211210095

Peter, T. F., Rotz, P. D., Blair, D. H., Khine, A. A., Freeman, R. R., & Murtagh, M. M. (2010). Impact of Laboratory Accreditation on Patient Care and the Health System. *American Journal of Clinical Pathology, 134*, 550–555. doi:10.1309/AJCPH1SKQ1HNWGHF.

Peute, L. W. P., & Jaspers, M. W. M. (2007). The significance of a usability evaluation of an emerging laboratory order entry system. *International Journal of Medical Informatics, 76*(2-3), 157–168. doi:10.1016/j.ijmedinf.2006.06.003 PMID:16854617

Peute, L., Aarts, J., Bakker, P., & Jaspers, M. (2009). Anatomy of a failure: A sociotechnical evaluation of a laboratory physician order entry system implementation. *International Journal of Medical Informatics*. PMID:19640778

Pfeffer, J. (1982). *Organizations and Organization Theory*. Marshfield, MA: Pitman.

Phan, A. C., Abdallah, A. B., & Matsui, Y. (2011). Quality management practices and competitive performance: Empirical evidence from Japanese manufacturing companies. *International Journal of Production Economics, 133*(2), 518–529.

Phusavat, K., & Kanchana, R. (2008). Future competitiveness: Viewpoints from manufacturers and service providers. *Industrial Management & Data Systems, 109*(2), 191–207. doi:10.1108/02635570810847572

Picovsky, J. (2012). *Análise de Gestão de Riscos e Impactos da Tecnologia da Informação nos Negócios Hospitalares*. São Paulo: XIII – Congresso de Informática na Saúde.

Plenderleith, J. L. (2013). Clinical information systems in the intensive care unit. *Anaesthesia and Intensive Care Medicine, 14*(1), 19–21. doi:10.1016/j.mpaic.2012.11.003

Poole, M. S. (2004). Central Issues in the study of change and innovation. In M. Poole, & A. Van de Ven (Eds.), *Handbook of Organizational Change and Innovation* (pp. 3–31). New York: Oxford University Press.

Powell, T. C. (1995). Total quality management as competitive advantage: A review and empirical study. *Strategic Management Journal, 16*(1), 15–37. doi:10.1002/smj.4250160105

Power, D., & Sohal, A. S. (2000). Strategies and practices in Australian just-in-time environments. *International Journal of Operations & Production Management, 20*(8), 932–958. doi:10.1108/01443570010332953

Prajogo, D. I. (2005). The comparative analysis of TQM practices and quality performance between manufacturing and service firms. *International Journal of Service Industry Management, 16*(3), 217–228. doi:10.1108/09564230510601378

Prajogo, D. I., & Brown, A. (2004). The relationship between TQM practices and quality performance and the role of formal TQM programs: An Australian empirical study. *Quality Management Journal, 11*, 31–43.

Prajogo, D. I., & McDermott, C. M. (2005). The relationship between TQM practices and organizational culture. *International Journal of Operations & Production Management, 25*(11), 1101–1122. doi:10.1108/01443570510626916

Prajogo, D. I., & Sohal, A. S. (2003). The relationship between TQM practices, quality performance, and innovation performance: An empirical examination. *International Journal of Quality & Reliability Management, 20*(8), 901–918. doi:10.1108/02656710310493625

Prajogo, D. I., & Sohal, A. S. (2004). The multidimensionality of TQM practices in determining quality and innovation performance – An empirical examination. *Technovation, 24*(6), 443–453. doi:10.1016/S0166-4972(02)00122-0

Prasad, P. J., & Bodhe, G. L. (2012). Trends in laboratory information management system. *Chemometrics and Intelligent Laboratory Systems, 118,* 187–192. doi:10.1016/j.chemolab.2012.07.001

Price, C. P. (2003). Application of the principles of evidence-based medicine to laboratory medicine. *Clinica Chimica Acta, 333*(2), 147–154. doi:10.1016/S0009-8981(03)00179-7 PMID:12849898

PriceWaterhouseCoopers (PWC). (2010). *The price of excess: Identifying waste in healthcare spending.* London: PriceWaterhouseCoopers.

PriceWaterhouseCoopers (PWC). (2011). *Pharma (2020): Supplying the future.* London: PriceWaterhouseCoopers.

PriceWaterhouseCoopers. (2011). *Pesquisa Global de Segurança da Informação 2011.* São Paulo: PricewaterhouseCoopers.

Puffer, S. M., & McCarthy, D. J. (1996). A framework for leadership in a TQM context. *Journal of Quality Management, 1*(1), 109–130. doi:10.1016/S1084-8568(96)90008-5

Punter, L., & Gangneux, D. (1998). Social responsibility: The most recent element to ensure total quality management. *Total Quality Management, 9*(4-5), 197–199. doi:10.1080/0954412988893

Putnam, L., Nicotera, A., & McPhee, R. (2009). Introduction - Communication Constitutes Organization. In L. Putnam, & A. Nicotera (Eds.), *Building Theories of Organization - The Consitutive Role of Communication* (p. 222). New York: Routledge.

Qayoumi, M. (2000). Benchmarking and organizational change. Alexandria, VA: The Association of Higher Education Facilities Officers (APPA).

QMP-LS, Quality Management Program—Laboratory Services. (n.d.). *Gap analysis between ISO 15189:2007 and ISO 15189:2012– Items that affect laboratory practice.* Retrieved November 1, 2013, from http://www.qmpls.org/Portals/0/OLA/PDFs/Transition%20to%20ISO%2015189%202012.pdf

Rada, R. (2011). E-patients empower healthcare: discovery of adverse events in online communities. In J. Tan (Ed.), *Developments in Healthcare Information Systems and Technologies: Models and Methods* (pp. 232–240). Hershey, PA: Medical Information Science Reference.

Rademakers, L., Coleman, D., & Reiny, S. (2013). Spinoff 2012. In *Dry Electrodes Facilitate Remote Health Monitoring* (pp. 42-43). Washington, DC: Government Printing Office.

Radiological Society of North America. (2013). *Integrating the Healthcare Enterprise.* Retrieved 27 July 2013 from https://www.rsna.org/ihe.aspx

Rahman, S., & Bullock, P. (2005). Soft TQM, hard TQM, and organizational performance relationships: An empirical investigation. *Omega, 33*(1), 73–83. doi:10.1016/j.omega.2004.03.008

Rao, S. S., Solis, L. E., & Raghunathan, T. S. (1999). A framework for international quality management research: Development and validation of a measurement instrument. *Total Quality Management, 10*(7), 1047–1075. doi:10.1080/0954412997226

Ravichandran, T. (2000). Swiftness and intensity of administrative innovation adoption: An empirical investigation of TQM in information systems. *Decision Sciences, 31*(3), 691–724. doi:10.1111/j.1540-5915.2000.tb00939.x

Reed, R., Lemak, D., & Montgomery, J. (1996). Beyond process: TQM content and firm performance. *Academy of Management Review, 21*(1), 173–202.

Reich, M., Liefeld, T., Gould, J., Lerner, J., Tamayo, P., & Mesirov, J. P. (2006). GenePattern 2.0. *Nature Genetics, 38*(5), 500–501. doi:10.1038/ng0506-500 PMID:16642009

Roberts, B.I., Mathews, C.L., Walton, C.J, & Frazier, G. (2009). A computer-based maintenance reminder and record-keeping system for clinical laboratories. *Clinical Chemistry, 28*(9), 1917-21.

Romanová, D., Ivančová, L., & Klepáková, A. (2013). The requirements for competence for quality management entities. *Ekonomické spectrum, 8* (3), 4 - 13.

Rosenthal, A., Mork, P., Li, M. H., Stanford, J., Koester, D., & Reynolds, P. (2010). Cloud computing: a new business paradigm for biomedical information sharing. *Journal of Biomedical Informatics, 43*(2), 342–353. doi:10.1016/j.jbi.2009.08.014 PMID:19715773

Rungtusanatham, M., Forza, C., Koka, B. R., Salvadora, F., & Nie, W. (2005). TQM across multiple countries: Convergence hypothesis versus national specificity arguments. *Journal of Operations Management, 23*(1), 43–63. doi:10.1016/j.jom.2004.10.002

RURO. (2014). Retrieved from http://www.ruro.com/

RVA, Dutch Accreditation Council. (n.d.). *Comparison ISO 15189:2007 and ISO 15189:2012.* Retrieved September 21, 2013, from http://www.rva.nl/uri/?uri=AMGATE_10218_1_TICH_R121564070447 99&xsl=AMGATE_10218_1_TICH_L155999126

Sackett, D. L., Rosenberg, W. M., Gray, J. A., Haynes, R. B., & Richardson, W. S. (1996). Evidence based medicine: what it is and what it isn't. *British Medical Journal, 312*(7023), 71–72. doi:10.1136/bmj.312.7023.71 PMID:8555924

SADCAS. (2013, September 9). *Policy – ISO 15189:2012 Transition (Document No: SADCAS TR 10; Issue No: 2).* Retrieved September 21, 2013, from http://www.sadcas.org/doc/sadcas_tr10.pdf

Sadikoglu, E., & Zehir, C. (2010). Investigating the effects of innovation and employee performance on the relationship between TQM practices and firm performance: An empirical study of Turkish firms. *International Journal of Production Economics, 127*(1), 13–26. doi:10.1016/j.ijpe.2010.02.013

Sahar, S. N., Shaikh, F. K., & Jokhio, I. A. (2013). P2P Data Management in Mobile Wireless Sensor Network. *Mehran University Research Journal of Engineering and Technology, 32* (2), 339-352.

Salhieh, L., & Singh, N. (2003). A system dynamics framework for benchmarking policy analysis for university system. *Benchmarking: An International Journal, 10*(5), 490–498. doi:10.1108/14635770310495528

Sallis, E. (2002). *Total quality management in education.* London, UK: Kogan.

SAMM, Malaysian Accreditation Body. (2013). *ISO 15189:2012 Migration. SAMM Circular (NO.1 / 2013).* Retrieved September 21, 2013, from http://www.standardsmalaysia.gov.my/documents/10179/427212/SAMM%20Circular%20(No.%2012013)%20-%20Migration%20to%20ISO%2015189%2016072013%20(1).pdf

Samson, D., & Terziovski, M. (1999). The relationship between total quality management practices and operational performance. *Journal of Operations Management, 17*(4), 393–409. doi:10.1016/S0272-6963(98)00046-1

Sanchez-Rodriguez, C., Dewhurst, F. W., & Martinez-Lorente, A. R. (2006). IT use in supporting TQM initiatives: An empirical investigation. *International Journal of Operations & Production Management, 26*(5), 486–504. doi:10.1108/01443570610659874

Sanchez-Rodriguez, C., & Martinez-Lorente, A. R. (2004). Quality management practices in the purchasing function: An empirical study. *International Journal of Operations & Production Management, 24*(7), 666–687. doi:10.1108/01443570410541984

Santos-Vijande, M. L., & Alvarez-Gonzalez, L. I. (2007). Innovativeness and organizational innovation in total quality-oriented firms: The moderating role of market turbulence. *Technovation, 27*(9), 514–532. doi:10.1016/j.technovation.2007.05.014

Santos-Vijande, M. L., & Alvarez-Gonzalez, L. I. (2009). TQM's contribution to marketing implementation and firm's competitiveness. *Total Quality Management and Business Excellence, 20*(2), 171–196. doi:10.1080/14783360802622953

Scalfani, J., & Ramkissoon, R. A. (1993). Acquisition of a laboratory information system. *Medical Electronics, 14*(5), 97–109.

Schniederjans, M. J., Mellat Parast, M., Nabavi, M., Subba Rao, S., & Raghu-Nathan, T. S. (2006). Comparative analysis of Malcolm Baldrige National Quality Award criteria: An empirical study of India, Mexico, and the United States. *Quality Management Journal, 13*(4), 7–21.

Scholtes, P. R. (1988). *The team handbook: How to use teams to improve quality.* Madison, WI: Joiner Associates.

Schonberger, R. J. (1994). Human resource management lessons from a decade of total quality management and reengineering. *California Management Review, 36*(4), 109–123. doi:10.2307/41165769

Scriven, M. (1991). *Evaluation Thesaurus* (4th ed.). Newbury, CA: Sage.

Sepulveda, J. L., & Young, D. S. (2013). The ideal laboratory information system. *Archives of Pathology & Laboratory Medicine, 137*(8), 1129–1140. doi:10.5858/arpa.2012-0362-RA PMID:23216205

Serdar, M. A., Turan, M., & Cihan, M. (2008). Rapid access to information resources in clinical biochemistry: medical applications of Personal Digital Assistants (PDA). *Clinical and Experimental Medicine*, 117–122. doi:10.1007/s10238-008-0166-y PMID:18618222

Shabo, A., Rabinovici-Cohen, S., & Vortman, P. (2006). Revolutionary impact of XML on biomedical information interoperability. *IBM Systems Journal, 45*(2), 361–372. doi:10.1147/sj.452.0361

Sharabi, M. (2014). Today's quality is tomorrow's reputation (and the following day's business success). *Total Quality Management & Business Excellence, 25*(3-4), 183–197. doi:10.1080/14783363.2013.858877

Sharma, B., & Gadenne, D. (2008). An empirical investigation of the relationship between quality management factors and customer satisfaction, improved competitive position and overall business performance. *Journal of Strategic Marketing, 16*(4), 301–314. doi:10.1080/09652540802264181

Shenawy, E. E., Baker, T., & Lemak, D. J. (2007). A meta-analysis of the effect of TQM on competitive advantage. *International Journal of Quality & Reliability Management, 24*(5), 442–471. doi:10.1108/02656710710748349

Shnayder, V., Chen, B. R., Lorincz, K., Jones, T. R. F., & Welsh, M. (2005, November). Sensor networks for medical care. SenSys, 5, 314-314.

Siemens. (2013). *Integrating the Healthcare Enterprise.* Retrieved 27 July, 2013 from http://www.healthcare.siemens.com/services/it-standards/ihe-integrating-the-healthcare-enterprise

Sila, I. (2007). Examining the effects of contextual factors on TQM and performance through the lens of organizational theories: An empirical study. *Journal of Operations Management, 25*(1), 83–109. doi:10.1016/j.jom.2006.02.003

Sila, I., & Ebrahimpour, M. (2002). An investigation of the total quality management survey based research published between 1989 and 2000: A literature review. *International Journal of Quality & Reliability Management, 19*(7), 902–970. doi:10.1108/02656710210434801

Sila, I., & Ebrahimpour, M. (2003). Examination and comparison of the critical factors of total quality management (TQM) across countries. *International Journal of Production Research, 41*(2), 235–268. doi:10.1080/0020754021000022212

Sila, I., & Ebrahimpour, M. (2005). Critical linkages among TQM factors and business results. *International Journal of Operations & Production Management, 25*(11), 1123–1155. doi:10.1108/01443570510626925

Sila, I., Ebrahimpour, M., & Birkholz, C. (2006). Quality in supply chains: An empirical analysis. *Supply Chain Management: An International Journal, 11*(6), 491–502. doi:10.1108/13598540610703882

Sit, W. Y., Ooi, K. B., Lin, B., & Chong, A. Y. L. (2009). TQM and customer satisfaction in Malaysia's service sector. *Industrial Management & Data Systems, 109*(7), 957–975. doi:10.1108/02635570910982300

Sivic, S., Gojkovic, L., & Huseinagic, S. (2009). Evaluation of an information system model for primary health care. *Studies in Health Technology Informatics*, *150*, 106-10.

Snell, S. A., & Dean, J. W. (1992). Integrated manufacturing and human resources management: A human capital perspective. *Academy of Management Journal*, *34*(1), 60–85.

Soltani, E., Azadegan, A., Liao, Y., & Phillips, P. (2011). Quality performance in a global supply chain: Finding out the weak link. *International Journal of Production Research*, *49*(1), 269–293. doi:10.1080/00207543.2010.508955

Soltani, E., Pei-Chun, L., & Phillips, P. (2008). A new look at factors influencing total quality management failure: Work process control or workforce control? *New Technology, Work and Employment*, *23*(1-2), 125–142. doi:10.1111/j.1468-005X.2008.00207.x

Soltes, V., Gavurova, B., Balloni, A.J. & Pavlickova, V. (2012). *Website*. Retrieved October 12, 2013, from http://www.cti.gov.br/images/stories/cti/gesiti/relatorios_de_pesquisa/Research_report_Gavurova_TUKE_Eslovaquia_2012.pdf

Soltes, V., Gavurova, B., Balloni, A. J., & Pavlickova, V. (2013). *ICT in Medical Institutions in Selected Regions of the Slovak Republic. Research report of the GESITI Project: An Evaluation of the Management of the Information Systems (IS) and Technologies (IT) in Hospitals.* Brasil: Center for Information Technology Renato Archer – Ministry of Science, Technology and Innovation.

Sousa, R., & Voss, C. A. (2001). Quality management: Universal or context dependent. *Production and Operations Management*, *10*(4), 383–404. doi:10.1111/j.1937-5956.2001.tb00083.x

Sousa, R., & Voss, C. A. (2002). Quality management re-visited: A reflective review and agenda for future research. *Journal of Operations Management*, *20*(1), 91–109. doi:10.1016/S0272-6963(01)00088-2

Spencer, B. A. (1994). Models of organization and total quality management: A comparison and critical evaluation. *Academy of Management Review*, *19*(3), 446–471.

Spitzer, R. D. (1993). TQM: The only source of sustainable competitive advantage. *Quality Progress*, *26*(6), 59–65.

Srenger, V., Stavljenić-Rukavina, A., Cvorisćec, D., Brkljacić, V., Rogić, D., & Juricić, L. (2005). Development of laboratory information system--quality standards. *Acta Medica Croatica*, *59*(3), 233–239. PMID:16095197

Stading, G. L., & Vokurka, R. J. (2003). Building quality strategy content using the process from national and international quality awards. *TQM & Business Excellence*, *14*(8), 931–946. doi:10.1080/1478336032000090851

Štatistický Úrad Slovenskej Republiky (ŠÚ SR). (2013). *Regionálna databáza*. Retrieved October 22, 2013, from http://portal.statistics.sk/showdoc.do?docid=96

Stewart, J. III, Miyazaki, K., Bevans-Wilkins, K., Ye, C., Kurtycz, D. F., & Selvaggi, S. M. (2007). Virtual microscopy for cytology proficiency testing: are we there yet? *Cancer*, *111*(4), 203–209. doi:10.1002/cncr.22766 PMID:17580360

Strategic Objectives. (2012). Retrieved October 22, 2013, from http://www.ezdravotnictvo.sk/Documents/Strategicke_ciele/priloha_1.pdf

Sun, H. (2001). Comparing quality management practices in the manufacturing and service industries: Learning opportunities. *Quality Management Journal*, *8*(2), 53–71.

Su, Q., Li, Z., Zhang, S. X., Liu, Y. Y., & Dang, J. X. (2008). The impacts of quality management practices on business performance - An empirical investigation from China. *International Journal of Quality & Reliability Management*, *25*(8), 809–823. doi:10.1108/02656710810898621

Sutcliffe, K. M., Lewton, E., & Rosenthal, M. M. (2004). Communication failures: an insidious contributor to medical mishaps. *Academic Medicine*, *79*(2), 186. doi:10.1097/00001888-200402000-00019 PMID:14744724

Systematized Nomenclature of Medicine. (2013). In *Wikipedia*. Retrieved August 5, 2013, from http://en.wikipedia.org/wiki/Snomed

Szabo, K. Z., Šoltés, M., & Herman, E. (2013). Innovative Capacity & Performance of Transition Economies: Comparative Study at the Level of Enterprises. *E+M Ekonomie a Management, 16*(1), 52-69.

Szalay, T. (2009). *Ranking of health systems from a consumer perspective*. Retrieved from http://www.hpi.sk/hpi/sk/view/3703/slovensko-v-europe-sieste-od-konca.html

Talib, F., & Rahman, Z. (2010). Critical success factors of total quality management in service organization: A proposed model. *Services Marketing Quarterly, 31*(3), 363–380. doi:10.1080/15332969.2010.486700

Talib, F., Rahman, Z., & Qureshi, M. N. (2011). An interpretive structural modeling approach for modeling the practices of total quality management in service sector. *International Journal of Modeling in Operations Management, 1*(3), 223–250. doi:10.1504/IJMOM.2011.039528

Talib, F., Rahman, Z., & Qureshi, M. N. (2013). An empirical investigation of relationship between total quality management practices and quality performance in Indian service companies. *International Journal of Quality & Reliability Management, 30*(3), 280–318. doi:10.1108/02656711311299845

Tang, S. L., & Kam, C. W. (1999). A survey of ISO 9001 implementation in engineering consultancies in Hong Kong. *International Journal of Quality & Reliability Management, 16*(6), 562–574. doi:10.1108/02656719910249810

Tari, J. J. (2005). Components of successful total quality management. *The TQM Magazine, 17*(2), 182–194. doi:10.1108/09544780510583245

Tarkan, S., Plaisant, C., Shneiderman, B., & Hettinger, A. Z. (2011). Reducing missed laboratory results: defining temporal responsibility, generating user interfaces for test process tracking, and retrospective analyses to identify problems. In Proceedings of *AMIA* (pp. 1382–1391). AMIA.

Taylor, W. A., & Wright, G. H. (2006). The contribution of measurement and information infrastructure to TQM success. *Omega, 34*(4), 372–384. doi:10.1016/j.omega.2004.12.003

TCU. (2007). *Tribunal de Contas da União*. Brasília: Manual de Boas Práticas em Segurança da Informação.

TCU. (2010). Brasília: Tribunal de Contas da União, Levantamento de Governança de TI.

TCU. (2012). *Tribunal de Contas da União. Boas práticas em segurança da informação*. Brasília: TCU, Secretaria de Fiscalização de Tecnologia da Informação.

Teh, P. L., Ooi, K. B., & Yong, C. C. (2008). Does TQM impact on role stressors? A conceptual model. *Industrial Management & Data Systems, 108*(8), 1029–1044. doi:10.1108/02635570810904596

Teh, P. L., Yong, C. C., Arumugam, V., & Ooi, K. B. (2009). Does total quality management reduce employees' role conflict? *Industrial Management & Data Systems, 109*(8), 1118–1136. doi:10.1108/02635570910991337

Terra, J. C., & Bax, M. P. (2003). Portais corporativos: Instrumento de gestão de informação e de conhecimento. In *A Gestão da Informação e do Conhecimento*. Belo Horizonte.

Terziovski, M., & Samson, D. (1999). The link between total quality management practice and organizational performance. *International Journal of Quality & Reliability Management, 16*(3), 226–237. doi:10.1108/02656719910223728

Thallinger, G. G., Trajanoski, S., Stocker, G., & Trajanoski, Z. (2002). Information management systems for pharmacogenomics. *Pharmacogenomics, 3*(5), 651–667. doi:10.1517/14622416.3.5.651 PMID:12223050

The Occupational Health and Safety Advisory Services. (2007). *OSHAS 18001: Occupational Health and Safety Management*. London: OHSAS.

The World Alliance For Patient Safety Drafting Group. (2009). Towards an International Classification for Patient Safety: the conceptual framework. *International Journal for Quality in Health Care, 21*(1), 2–8. doi:10.1093/intqhc/mzn054 PMID:19147595

Thiagaragan, T., Zairi, M., & Dale, B. G. (2001). A proposed model of TQM implementation based on an empirical study of Malaysian industry. *International Journal of Quality & Reliability Management, 18*(3), 289–306. doi:10.1108/02656710110383539

Thrall, M., Pantanowitz, L., & Khalbuss, W. (2011). Telecytology: Clinical applications, current challenges, and future benefits. *Journal of Pathology Informatics*, *2*, 51. doi:10.4103/2153-3539.91129 PMID:22276242

Tilzer, L.L., & Jones, R.W. (1988). Use of bar code labels on collection tubes for specimen management in the clinical laboratory. *Archive Pathology and Laboratory Medicine*, *112*(12), 1200-2

Toffaletti, J. (2000). Wireless POCT data transmission. *Medical Laboratory Observer, 32*(6), 44-8, 50-1.

Tolk, A., Saikou, D., & Turnitsa, C. D. (2008). Applying the levels of conceptual interoperability model in support of integratability, interoperability, and composability for system-of-systems engineering. Journal of Systemics. *Cybernetics and Informatics.*, *5*(65), 65–74.

Tolopko, A., Sullivan, J., Erickson, S., Wrobel, D., Chiang, S., Rudnicki, K., & Shamu, C. (2010). Screensaver: an open source lab information management system (LIMS) for high throughput screening facilities. *BMC Bioinformatics*, *11*(1), 260. PMID:20482787

Tomlinson, J.J., Elliott-Smith, W., & Radosta, T. (2006). Laboratory information management system chain of custody: Reliability and security. *Journal of Automated Methods and Management in Chemistry,* 74907.

Tongsiri, S. (2013). Electronic Health Records: Benefits and Contribution to Healthcare System. In Next-Generation Wireless Technologies (pp. 273-281). Springer.

Tsimillis, K. C., & Michael, S. (2011, March). *Frequently occurring findings in the accreditation of medical laboratories*. Paper presented at the 5th Congress of Clinical Chemistry. Limassol, Cyprus.

Tsimillis, K. C. (2010). Accreditation or certification for laboratories? In B. W. Wenclawiak, M. Koch, & E. Hadjicostas (Eds.), *Quality assurance in Analytical Chemistry* (2nd ed., pp. 73–93). Heidelberg, Germany: Springer. doi:10.1007/978-3-642-13609-2_4

Turner, E., & Bolton, J. (2001). Required steps for the validation of a Laboratory Information Management System. *Quality Assurance*, *9*(3-4), 217-24.

Tutuncu, O., & Kucukusta, D. (2008). The role of supply chain management integration in quality management system for hospitals. *International Journal of Management Perspectives*, *1*(1), 31–39.

Two Fold Software. (2014). Retrieved from http://www.twofold-software.com/site/

Tzelepi, S., Pangalos, G., & Nikolacopoulou, G. (2002, September). Security of medical multimedia. *Medical Informatics and the Internet in Medicine, 27*(3), 169–184. doi:10.1080/14639230210153730 PMID:12507263

UCSC Genome Browser. (2014). Retrieved from http://genome.ucsc.edu/

UKAS, United Kingdom Accreditation Service. (n.d.). *Potential gap/difference in focus between CPA and UKAS assessment*. Retrieved November 13, 2013, from http://www.ukas.com/Library/Services/CPA/Assessment_Focus-Differences.pdf

UKAS, United Kingdom Accreditation Service. (n.d.). *Summary of ISO 15189 additional requirements*. Retrieved September 30, 2013, from http://www.ukas.com/Library/Services/CPA/Summary%20of%20Idifferences%20betwen%20ISO%2015189%20&%20CPA.pdf

Ulirsch, R.C., Ashwood, E.R., & Noce, P. (1990). Security in the clinical laboratory. Guidelines for managing the information resource. *Archives of Pathology & Laboratory Medicine*, *114*(1), 89–93. PMID:2294872

Ullah, S., Higgins, H., Braem, B., Latre, B., Blondia, C., Moerman, I., & Kwak, K. S. (2012). A comprehensive survey of wireless body area networks. *Journal of Medical Systems*, *36*(3), 1065–1094. doi:10.1007/s10916-010-9571-3 PMID:20721685

Ulma, W., & Schlabach, D.M. (2005). Technical Considerations in Remote LIMS Access via the World Wide Web. *Journal of Automated Methods and Management in Chemistry,* 217-22.

Vacata, V., Jahns-Streubel, G., Baldus, M., & Wood, W. G. (2007). Practical solution for control of the pre-analytical phase in decentralized clinical laboratories for meeting the requirements of the medical laboratory accreditation standard DIN EN ISO 15189. *Clinical Laboratory, 53*, 211–215. PMID:17447659 van Walraven, C., & Raymond, M. (2003). Population-based study of repeat laboratory testing. *Clinical Chemistry*, *49*(12), 1997–2005. doi:10.1373/clinchem.2003.021220 PMID:14633870

Vanichchinchai, A., & Igel, B. (2009). Total quality management and supply chain management: Similarities and differences. *The TQM Magazine*, *21*(3), 249–260. doi:10.1108/17542730910953022

Vasilakis, C., Lecnzarowicz, D., & Lee, C. (2010). Application of unified modelling language (UML) to the modelling of health care systems: An introduction and literature survey. In J. Rodrigues (Ed.), *Health Information Systems: Concepts, Methodologies, Tools, and Applications* (pp. 2179–2191). Hershey, PA: Medical Information Science Reference. doi:10.4018/978-1-61692-002-9.ch019

Vaught, J. B., & Henderson, M. K. (2011). Biological sample collection, processing, storage and information management. *IARC Scientific Publications*, (163): 23–42. PMID:22997855

Vecchi, A., & Brennan, L. (2011). Quality management: A cross-cultural perspective based on the GLOBE framework. *International Journal of Operations & Production Management*, *31*(5), 527–553. doi:10.1108/01443571111126319

Venkatraman, S. (2007). A framework for implementing TQM in higher education programs. *Quality Assurance in Education*, *15*(1), 92–112. doi:10.1108/09684880710723052

Vermeulen, W., & Crous, M. J. (2000). Training and education for TQM in the commercial banking industry of South Africa. *Managing Service Quality*, *10*(1), 61–67. doi:10.1108/09604520010307058

Vianez, M. S., Segobia, R.H., & Camargo, V. (2008). Segurança de Informação: Aderência à Norma ABNT NBR ISO/IEC N. 17.799:2005. *Revista de Informática Aplicada*, *4*(1).

Wajcman, J. (2008). Life in the fast lane? Towards a sociology of technology and time. *The British Journal of Sociology*, *59*(1), 59–77. doi:10.1111/j.1468-4446.2007.00182.x PMID:18321331

Waldman, D. A. (1994). The contributions of total quality management to theory of work performance. *Academy of Management Review*, *19*(3), 510–536.

Walker, J., Pan, E., Johnston, D., Adler-Milstein, J., Bates, D. W., & Middleton, B. (2005). The value of health care information exchange and interoperability. *Health Affairs*, *24*, W5. PMID:15659453

Wang, S., & Hom, V. (2004). Corrections of clinical chemistry test results in a laboratory information system. *Archives of Pathology and Laboratory Medicine*, *128*(8), 890-2

Wang, B., & Pei, Y. (2007). Body Area Networks. In B. Furht (Ed.), *Encyclopedia of Wireless and Mobile Communications*. Taylor & Francis.

Wang, J., Li, H., Zhu, Y., Yousef, M., Nebozhyn, M., & Showe, M. et al. (2007). VISDA: An open-source caBIG™ analytical tool for data clustering and beyond. *Bioinformatics (Oxford, England)*, *23*(15), 2024–2027. PMID:17540678

Wang, S. J., Middleton, B., Prosser, L. A., Bardon, C. G., Spurr, C. D., & Carchidi, P. J. et al. (2003). A cost-benefit analysis of electronic medical records in primary care. *The American Journal of Medicine*, *114*(5), 397–403. doi:10.1016/S0002-9343(03)00057-3 PMID:12714130

Weilert, M. (1991). Implementing information systems. *Clinics in Laboratory Medicine*, *11*(1), 41–51. PMID:2040148

Westbrook, J. I., Georgiou, A., & Rob, M. I. (2008). Computerised order entry systems: sustained impact on laboratory efficiency and mortality rates?. In S. Andersen, G. Klein, S. Schulz, J. Aarts & M. Mazzoleni (Eds.), *eHealth Beyond the Horizon Get IT There; Proceedings of MIE 2008 IOS Press Amsterdam* (pp. 345-350). Goteborg, Sweden: IOS Press.

Westbrook, J. I., Braithwaite, J., Georgiou, A., Ampt, A., Creswick, N., Coiera, E., & Iedema, R. (2007). Multimethod evaluation of information and communication technologies in health in the context of wicked problems and sociotechnical theory. *Journal of the American Medical Informatics Association*, *14*(6), 746–755. doi:10.1197/jamia.M2462 PMID:17712083

Westbrook, J. I., Georgiou, A., Dimos, A., & Germanos, T. (2006). Computerised pathology test order-entry reduces laboratory turnaround times and influences tests ordered by hospital clinicians: a controlled before and after study. *Journal of Clinical Pathology*, *59*(May), 533–536. doi:10.1136/jcp.2005.029983 PMID:16461564

Westbrook, J. I., Georgiou, A., & Lam, M. (2009). Does computerised provider order entry reduce test turnaround times? A before-and-after study at four hospitals. In K.-P. Adlassnig, B. Blobel, J. Mantas, & I. Masic (Eds.), *Medical informatics in a united and healthy Europe: proceedings of MIE 2009* (pp. 527–531). Amsterdam: IOS Press.

Westbrook, J. I., Georgiou, A., & Rob, M. (2009). Test turnaround times and mortality rates 12 and 24 months after the introduction of a computerised provider order entry system. *Methods of Information in Medicine*, *48*, 211–215. PMID:19283321

Westgard, J. O., & Darcy, T. (2004). The truth about quality: medical usefulness and analytical reliability of laboratory tests. *Clinica Chimica Acta*, *346*(1), 3–11. doi:10.1016/j.cccn.2003.12.034 PMID:15234630

Whetton, S., & Georgiou, A. (2010). Conceptual challenges for advancing the socio-technical underpinnings of health informatics. *The Open Medical Informatics Journal*, *4*, 221. doi:10.2174/1874325001004010221 PMID:21594009

Wickramasinghe, N. (2013). Implicit and Explicit Knowledge Assets in Healthcare. In *Pervasive Health Knowledge Management* (pp. 15–26). Springer. doi:10.1007/978-1-4614-4514-2_3

Wilson, D. D., & Collier, D. A. (2000). An empirical investigation of the Malcolm Baldrige National Quality Award causal model. *Decision Sciences*, *31*(2), 361–390. doi:10.1111/j.1540-5915.2000.tb01627.x

Winsten, D.I. (1992). Taking the risk out of laboratory information systems. *Clinical Laboratory Management Review*, *6*(1), 39-40, 42-4, 46-8.

Wiwanitkit, V. (2000). Laboratory information management system: an application of computer information technology. *Chulalongkorn Medical Journal*, *44*(11), 887–891.

Wiwanitkit, V. (2001). Types and frequency of preanalytical mistakes in the first Thai ISO 9002:1994 certified clinical laboratory, a 6 - month monitoring. *BMC Clinical Pathology*, *1*(1), 5. doi:10.1186/1472-6890-1-5 PMID:11696253

Wiwanitkit, V. (Ed.). (2011). *Medical laboratory information management system*. Bangkok: Chulalongkorn University.

Workman, R.D., Lewis, M.J., & Hill, B.T. (2000). Enhancing the financial performance of a health system laboratory network using an information system. *American Journal of Clinical Pathology*, *114*(1), 9-15.

World Health Organization. (2010). *The world health report: health systems financing: The path to universal coverage.* Geneva: World Health Organisation. Retrieved October 22, 2013, from http://www.who.int/health_financing/Health_Systems_Financing_Plan_Action.pdf

World Health Organization. (2011). *International Statistical Classification of Diseases and Related Health Problems 10th revision.* Retrieved September 01, 2013 from http://www.who.int/classifications/icd/ICD10Volume2_en_2010.pdf

World Health Organization. (2011). *World Health Statistics 2011.* Geneva: World Health Organisation. Retrieved October 22, 2013, from http://www.who.int/whosis/whostat/2011/en/

Yang, C. C. (2006). The impact of human resource management practices on the implementation of total quality management. *The TQM Magazine*, *18*(2), 162–173. doi:10.1108/09544780610647874

Yao, Q., Bai, Z., Zhu, L., Zhang, E., & Yuan, K. (2012). The rebuilding of LIS to pass the ISO15189. *Zhongguo Yi Liao Qi Xie Za Zhi*, *36*(1), 59-60.

Yates, J. K., & Aniftos, S. C. (1997). International standards and construction. *Journal of Construction Engineering and Management*, *123*(2), 127–137. doi:10.1061/(ASCE)0733-9364(1997)123:2(127)

Yeh, J. Y., Wu, T. H., & Tsao, C. W. (2011). Using data mining techniques to predict hospitalization of hemodialysis patients. *Decision Support Systems*, *50*(2), 439–448. doi:10.1016/j.dss.2010.11.001

Yeung, A. C. L., Edwin Cheng, T. C., & Lai, K. (2006). An operational and institutional perspective on total quality management. *Production and Operations Management, 15*(1), 156–170.

Yoo, E.H., Cho, H.J., Ki, C.S., & Lee, S.Y. (2006). Evaluation of COSMOsensor Glucose Monitoring System. *Korean Journal of Laboratory Medicine, 26*(1), 1-8.

Yoo, D. K., Rao, S. S., & Hong, P. (2006). A comparative study on cultural differences and quality practices: Korea, USA, Mexico and Taiwan. *International Journal of Quality & Reliability Management, 23*(6), 607–624. doi:10.1108/02656710610672452

Yoo, I., Alafaireet, P., Marinov, M., Pena-Hernandez, K., Gopidi, R., Chang, J. F., & Hua, L. (2012). Data mining in healthcare and biomedicine: a survey of the literature. *Journal of Medical Systems, 36*(4), 2431–2448. doi:10.1007/s10916-011-9710-5 PMID:21537851

Young, S. (1992). A framework for successful adoption and performance of Japanese manufacturing practices in the United States. *Academy of Management Review, 17*(4), 677–700.

Yusof, A. A., & Ali, J. (2000). Managing culture in organization. *Malaysian Management Review, 35*(2), 60–65.

Yusuf, Y., Gunasekaran, A., & Dan, G. (2007). Implementation of TQM in China and organizational performance: An empirical investigation. *Total Quality Management, 18*(5), 509–530. doi:10.1080/14783360701239982

Zákon č. 153. (2013). *O Národnom zdravotníckom informačnom systéme (NZIS)*. Retrieved October 22, 2013, from: http://epredpisy.sk/predpisy-vo-vlade/2520028-o-narodnom-zdravotnickom-informanom-systeme

Zakuan, N. M., Yusof, S. M., Laosirihongthong, T., & Shaharoun, A. M. (2010). Proposed relationship of TQM and organizational performance using structured equation modeling. *Total Quality Management, 21*(2), 185–203.

Závadská, Z., Závadský, J. & Sirotiaková, M. (2013). Process model and its real application in the selected management areas. *E+M Ekonomie a Management, 16*(1), 113-127.

Zhang, Z., Waszink, A., & Wijngaard, J. (2000). An instrument for measuring TQM implementation for Chinese manufacturing companies. *International Journal of Quality & Reliability Management, 17*(7), 730–755. doi:10.1108/02656710010315247

Zineldin, M., & Fonsson, P. (2000). An examination of the main factors affecting trust/commitment in supplier dealer relationships: An empirical study of the Swedish wood industry. *The TQM Magazine, 12*(4), 245–265. doi:10.1108/09544780010325831

Zisman, A. (2000). An overview of XML. *Computing & Control Engineering Journal, 11*(4), 165–167. doi:10.1049/cce:20000405

Zu, X. (2009). Infrastructure and core quality management practices: How do they affect quality? *International Journal of Quality & Reliability Management, 26*(2), 129–149. doi:10.1108/02656710910928789

Zu, X., Fredendall, L. D., & Douglas, T. J. (2008). The evolving theory of quality management: The role of Six Sigma. *Journal of Operations Management, 26*(5), 630–650. doi:10.1016/j.jom.2008.02.001

About the Contributors

Anastasius Moumtzoglou is an Executive Board Member of the European Society for Quality in HealthCare (ESQH) and President of the Hellenic Society for Quality & Safety in HealthCare (HSQSH). He holds a BA in Economics (National and Kapodistrian University of Athens), MA in Health Services Management (National School of Public Health), MA in Macroeconomics (The University of Liverpool), and PhD in Economics (National and Kapodistrian University of Athens). He works for 'P. & A. Kyriakou' Children's Hospital and teaches the module of quality at the graduate and postgraduate level. He has written three books, which are the only ones in the Greek references. He has also served as a scientific coordinator and researcher in Greek and European research programs. In 2004, he was declared "Person of Quality in Healthcare," with respect to Greece. His research interests include healthcare management, quality, knowledge management, pensions, and the dualism of the labor market.

Anastasia N. Kastania received her BSc in Mathematics and her PhD degree in Medical Informatics from the National and Kapodistrian University of Athens, Greece. She works in the Athens University of Economics and Business, Greece since 1987. Research productivity is summarized in various articles (monographs or in collaboration with other researchers) in international journals, international conference proceedings, international book series, and international book chapters. She has more than twenty years teaching experience in University programs and she is the writer of many didactic books. She also has ten years experience as Researcher in National and European Research Projects. Research interests are telemedicine and e-health, e-learning, bioinformatics, tele-epidemiology, mathematical modeling and statistics, web engineering, quality engineering, and reliability engineering.

Stavros Archondakis is a certified pathologist and director of the Cytopathology Department of 401 Athens Army Hospital. He graduated from Thessaloniki Medical School and National Military Medical School in 1996. Since 2007, he was appointed assessor of the Hellenic Accreditation System (ESYD) for the accreditation of medical laboratories according to ISO 15189:2012. He speaks English and French. He is a member of Hellenic Society of Clinical Cytopathology, Society of Medical Studies, and Society for Quality Management in the Health Sector. He is the author of 29 medical books, some of them awarded by the Greek Anticancer Society. He has participated with posters and oral presentations in more than 200 congresses and seminars, he has authored more than 25 articles in greek and foreign medical journals. He possesses more than 800 hours of teaching experience in medical and paramedical schools.

* * *

Piero Alberto received his Masters Degree in Computer Engineering in 2011 from Politecnico di Torino, Italy. He has been involved in the LAS (Laboratory Assistant Suite) project - a collaborative effort between IT specialists and biomedical researchers - since 2011. He started his work as a graduate candidate and pursued his activity as a software engineer at the Institute for Cancer Research and Treatment of Candiolo (IRCC). His research interests include biological data management systems. His core job focuses on the design and the development of software for managing and tracking in-vivo and in-vitro experiments in the context of the translational research pipeline based on xenopatients.

Antonio José Balloni received his MS and PhD from the Institute of Physics -Unicamp/Brazil-. In 1992,he was a Postdoctoral researcher at IMEC/Belgium. Since 1988, he has been a researcher at the Center for Information Technology Renato Archer -CTI/Brasil-. since 2005 has been an invited professor by the Institute of Economics/Unicamp, Extension Courses, lecturing about MIS. From 2003 to date he has created the GESITI Project (Management of System and Information Technology towards Organizations). From 2010 to 2012 he was a member of the Scientific Technical Council at CTI/MCTI. He has published 2 books and about 40 papers regarding information technology, political science and health management. He is the General Manager of eight editions of an international GESITI workshop. He is the author of GESITI/Health book which is in publication by the Ministry of Health. In 1995 he was the Brazilian champion in basketball -Master Category. He belongs to a beekeeper family an ecologically correct endeavor with technological innovation.

Andrea Bertotti has a background in cancer biology, with a focus on receptor tyrosine kinase (RTK) signal transduction, oncogene addiction, and targeted therapies. Following his PhD, in which he studied the biochemical mechanisms underlying the cooperation between RTKs and adhesion molecules during cancer progression, he worked on identifying molecular traits associated with oncogene addiction. Starting 2008, he focused his research activity on translational projects, by initiating and coordinating the generation of a preclinical platform for high-fidelity anticipation of clinical findings. This resulted in a large collection of liver metastases from colorectal carcinoma, which have been transplanted in immunocompromised mice, profiled for molecular characteristics and treated with approved or investigational compounds, leading to publications in major scientific journals.

Romeo Bishop holds a Bachelors of Science (Honours) in Biochemistry and Pure Chemistry from The University of the West Indies, Mona, Kingston, Jamaica. Mr. Bishop was a student Research Assistant in the Sub-Department of Chemical Pathology, Department of Pathology at the University of the West Indies. He worked on a number of projects including (i) a biochemical study of creatinine kinase and lactate dehydrogenase enzymes in patients with thyroid dysfunctions, and (ii) an audit of tumour marker requests in a teaching hospital. In 2011, Mr. Bishop participated in the Shaw University Jamaica MON Project, a summer research training programme for undergraduate students. The programme was held at the Mona Campus, The University of the West Indies, and he received the Most Outstanding Student Award. Mr. Bishop is a past student of Jamaica College and enjoys reading and playing cricket.

Francesco Gavino Brundu is currently a Computer Engineering PhD student at Politecnico di Torino, Italy. He obtained a Masters Degree in Computer Engineering from Politecnico di Torino in 2013. He worked as a research assistant at the Department of Control and Computer Engineering of Politecnico di Torino from June to December 2013. His research interests range from bioinformatics to computational biology, with a focus on class discovery problems, microarray data analysis, data preprocessing, and classification. He is currently working on class prediction algorithm designs and testing, making use of software engineering techniques and performance assessment.

Po-Hsun Cheng received a BSdegree in information and computer engineering from Chung Yuan Christian University, Taiwan, in 1988, an MS degree in electrical engineering from the University of Southern California, California, USA, in 1992, and a PhD degree in electronics engineering from National Taiwan University, Taiwan,in 2005. Since 2008, he has been a member of the faculty in the Department of Software Engineering, National Kaohsiung Normal University, Taiwan, where he is currently an associate professor. He was Deputy Director in the Information Systems Office, National Taiwan University Hospital, Taiwan. He was a visiting researcher in the Department of Computer Science and Engineering, University of California,Riverside, USA in 2000. He is a member of HL7, ACM, IEEE, IEICE, AMIA and CAMIT, a senior member of the TAMI, HL7 Taiwan and IICM. He is the Board Member of TAMI (2006-2015) and HL7 Taiwan (2006-2015). He was the Secretary General of HL7 Taiwan (2002-2006).

Bhawani Shankar Chowdhry is the Dean Faculty of Electrical, Electronics, and Computer Engineering at Mehran University of Engineering and Technology, Jamshoro (MUET), Pakistan. He did his BEng in 1983 from MUET and PhD in 1990 from School of ECS, University of Southampton, UK. He has more than 30 years of teaching, research, and administrative experience in the field of Information and Communication Technology. He is one of the editors of the books *Wireless Networks, Information Processing and Systems*, CCIS 20, *Emerging Trends and Applications in Information Communication Technologies*, CCIS 281, and *Wireless Sensor Networks for Developing Countries*, CCIS 366, published by Springer Verlag, Germany. His list of research publication crosses to over 60 in national and international journals, IEEE and ACM proceedings. Also, he has Chaired Technical Sessions in the USA, UK, China, UAE, Italy, Sweden, Finland, Switzerland, Pakistan, Ireland, Denmark, and Belgium. He is a member of various professional bodies including: Chairman of IEEE Communication Society (COM-SOC), Karachi Chapter, Region10 Asia/Pacific, Fellow IEP, Fellow IEEEP, Senior Member, IEEE Inc. (USA), and Senior Member ACM Inc. (USA).

Francesca Cito has a degree in Veterinary Medicine and a Specialization in Science and Medicine of Laboratory Animals from the University of Naples, Italy. From January to July 2011, she has been a veterinarian trainee assigned to the National Reference Centre for Epidemiology and Risk Analysis and the National Reference Centre for Epidemiology, Planning, Information, and Risk Analysis (COVEPI) to the Istituto Zooprofilattico dell'Abruzzo e del Molise (IZSAM). From October 2011 to date, she is working in contract at the COVEPI involved in epidemiological and risk assessment studies in food safety.

Patrizia Colangeli has a degree in Engineering from the University "La Sapienza" of Rome, Italy. She worked at a private company in the applied mathematics and economy sector in Rome and after in a Bank in Teramo. Since 1991, she has worked at the Istituto Zooprofilattico Sperimentale dell'Abruzzo e del Molise (IZSAM) where she is the head of "Information systems development and management" Unit. She managed the analysis and implementation of many information systems at enterprise, regional, national and sovra-national level among which: the Animal Health National Information System (i.e. Brucellosis, Bluetongue, West Nile Disease), Laboratory information management system, Administrative and Staff information management system, the Datawarehouse enterprise, National information system for the notification of animal diseases; Zoonoses National System, Web-based application for the international surveillance of bluetongue in the European Union, OIE Bluetongue Reference Laboratories network, and the SILAB for Africa: a LIMS for African Labs currently used in Namibia, Botswana, Zimbabwe, Zambia, and Tanzania.

Fabrizio De Massis has a degree in Veterinary Medicine from the University of Bologna, Italy, and a Specialization in Animal Health, Breeding, and Production of Animal Studies at the University of Teramo, Italy. From August 2001 to March 2006, he was a veterinarian incontract, epidemiologist assigned to the National Reference Centre for Epidemiology and Risk Analysis and the National Reference Centre for Brucellosis to the Istituto Zooprofilattico dell'Abruzzo e del Molise (IZSAM). From March 2006 to June 2009 he was the Seconded National Expert at the European Food Safety Authority to the Unit of Animal Health Welfare. He has been a permanent veterinary officer since April 2009. He directed the IZSAM laboratory of Isernia (from November 2009 to January 2011) and the IZSAM laboratory of Avezzano (from January to August 2011). He has been involved in the coordination and supervision of the activities of the laboratories of the above diagnostics sections. From August 2011 to October 2012, he directed the department of sample acceptance and control in the IZSAM's headquarters. From November 2012 to date, he is working at the National Reference Centre for Epidemiology, Planning, Information, and Risk Analysis (COVEPI) at IZSAM.

Alessandro Fiori holds a Masters Degree in Computer Engineering from Politecnico di Torino, and the European PhD degree from Politecnico di Torino, Italy. He has been project manager of the LAS (Laboratory Assistant Suite) project at the Institute for Cancer Research and Treatment of Candiolo (IRCC), Italy since January 2012. His research interests are in the field of data mining, in particular bioinformatics and text mining. His activity is focused on the development of information systems and analysis frameworks oriented to the management and integration of biological and molecular data. His research activities are also devoted to text summarization and social network analysis.

Edison Luiz Goncalves Fontes obtained an MS in Technology from Centro Paula Souza - San Paolo State, Brazil. Since 1988, he has been working as a professor and also as a manager and consultant in information security, risk management, business continuity, and fraud information prevention. He also worked as a Security Officer at Banorte Bank,Brazil, GTECH Brazil, and Royal Bank of Scotland,Brazil. He was manager of the Business Continuity Plan at PricewaterhouseCoopers. As a consultant, he developed the Information Security Policies which had been published as Law by the Republic of Cape Verde government. He has developed or reviewed over five hundred documents regarding policies and norms on information security. He is the author of five books on information security which has been referenced in scientific papers as well in specialized courses. His latest book, *Policies and Norms for an Information Security*, has about 30 practical examples of regulations. He is a columnist for Brazilian InformationWeek Magazine.

Beáta Gavurová works as an associate professor in the Faculty of Economics at the Technical University of Košice. In her science-research work, she focuses mainly on measuring and performing management in the organizations and process management. The results of her research are presented in various Professional and scientific journals, as well as in domestic and international conferences. Achieved results are being applied also in her pedagogical practice at all levels of education. She is an author and co- author of 5 scientific monographs, several chapters in monographs and a number of international publications. She participated in the solution of the VEGA project in the area of implementation and usage of Business intelligence in organizations in Slovakia, as well as in projects oriented on the measurement of efficiency and quality of healthcare facilities in Slovakia, in international projects: eBEST - "Empowering Business Ecosystems of Small Service Enterprises to face the economic crisis," 7th Framework Programme FP7-SME-2008-2 a DEN4DEK - "Digital Ecosystems Network of regions for DissEmination and Knowledge deployment," and Competitiveness and Innovation Framework Programme CIP-ICT-PSP-224976.

Emanuele Geda holds a Masters Degree in Computer Engineering from Politecnico di Torino, Italy. He has worked as a software engineer and developer at the Institute for Cancer Research and Treatment of Candiolo (IRCC), Italy since January 2012. He has been involved in the LAS (Laboratory Assistant Suite) project - a collaborative effort between IT specialists and biomedical researchers - since 2011. During his work, he has modeled and implemented complex database systems for the management of biological samples, laying the foundations for a biobanking software platform. Furthermore, he has designed and developed a system for managing the physical storage of biological materials within IRCC.

Andrew Georgiou is a Senior Research Fellow at the Centre for Health Systems and Safety Research, part of the Australian Institute of Health Innovation at the University of New South Wales. Andrew has worked extensively in the area of pathology IT systems, contributing over 40 papers and studies to the area. He was a member of the Scientific Program Committee of the first World Congress of Pathology Informatics held in Brisbane in 2007 and a member of the Scientific Program Committee for the 13th World Congress on Medical Informatics held in Cape Town, South Africa in 2011. Andrew is an Editorial Board member of the Open Medical Informatics Journal, Journal of Pathology Informatics, Health Care Informatics Review and the International Journal of Medical Informatics. He is currently the co-Chair of the International Medical Informatics Association Working Group on Technology Assessment and Quality Development (2013).

Alberto Grand holds a Masters Degree in Computer and Electrical Engineering from Politecnico di Torino and the University of Illinois at Chicago, and a PhD in Computer and Systems Engineering from Politecnico di Torino. His research interests are in the fields of data management systems and data mining, with a focus on large-scale data management, data integration, and biological and molecular data annotation. Since March 2013, he has been assistant coordinator in the development of an information system for the management, integration, and analysis of biological and molecular data at the Institute for Cancer Research and Treatment of Candiolo (IRCC), Italy.

Güney Gürsel was born in 1972 in İzmir, Turkey. He graduated from the Military Academy in 1994 as a systems engineer. He received his MSc degree in information systems field in 2003 from the Middle East Technical University (METU), and PhD in Medical Informatics field in 2012 again from METU. He is working in the Department of Medical Informatics, Gülhane Military Medical Academy, as medical informatics specialist. He speaks advanced English. He is working in the fields of Healthcare Information Systems (HIS), Evaluation of HIS, End user expectations from HIS, Fuzzy logic application in HIS, and Interoperability in HIS. He is married and has two kids.

Petros Karkalousos is a lecturer at the Technological and Educational Institute of Athens (TEI of Athens0. He teaches clinical chemistry, immunology and analysis of biological fluids. He is also a visiting professor to the Hellenic Open University where he teaches the lesson «special topics of quality». He is also an assessor of the Greek Accreditation Organisation, specialised in ISO 15189. He has studied Biomedical Science (Bsc), Biology (Bsc), Applied Statistics (Msc), and he has PhD in quality control. He has worked for sixteen years in the clinical laboratories of public hospitals. Apart from his work in the TEI of Athens, he is also a quality manager of a private clinical laboratory in Athens.

Kijpokin Kasemsap received his BEng degree in Mechanical Engineering from King Mongkut's University of Technology Thonburi, his MBA degree from Ramkhamhaeng University, and his DBA degree in Human Resource Management from Suan Sunandha Rajabhat University. He is a Special Lecturer at Faculty of Management Sciences, Suan Sunandha Rajabhat University based in Bangkok, Thailand. He is a Member of International Association of Engineers (IAENG), International Association of Engineers and Scientists (IAEST), International Economics Development and Research Center (IEDRC), International Association of Computer Science and Information Technology (IACSIT), International Foundation for Research and Development (IFRD), and International Innovative Scientific and Research Organization (IISRO). He also serves on the International Advisory Committee (IAC) for International Association of Academicians and Researchers (INAAR). He has numerous original research articles in top international journals, conference proceedings, and book chapters on business management, human resource management, and knowledge management published internationally.

Naeem A. Mahoto received his ME (CSN) from Mehran University of Engineering and Technology (MUET) Pakistan. He was awarded a PhD scholarship under UESTPs Project for higher studies and received his PhD (Computer Engineering) from Politecnico Di Torino, Italy. He is currently working as an Assistant Professor in the Department of Software Engineering, MUET Pakistan. He is a member of PEC, IEEE. Dr. Naeem is a co-author of several research articles published in national as well as international well-recognized journals. He also contributed in book chapters as a co-author. He works in the field of data mining and bioinformatics, and his research interests are focused on pattern extraction and classification of electronic records in the medical domain. His research activities are also devoted to the summarization of web documents and social network analysis.

Donovan McGrowder holds a Bachelor of Science (Honours) and Doctor of Philosophy (PhD) degree in Biochemistry and Chemistry and Biochemistry respectively from The University of the West Indies, Mona, Kingston, Jamaica. Dr. McGrowder also holds a Masters of Science degree from the University of Westminster, London, UK and a Masters of Arts in Psychology and Counseling from St. Stephens College, Alberta, Canada. He also has post-graduate training and experience in Clinical Biochemistry and Molecular Biology. Dr. McGrowder joined the staff of The University of the West Indies, Mona, in 2001 as a Research Fellow in the Department of Basic Medical Sciences – Biochemistry Section and was promoted to Lecturer in 2003 and Senior Lecturer in 2009. He is also Consultant of Chemical Pathology at the University Hospital of the West Indies. He is a Fellow of the Institute of Biomedical Science, UK, Fellow of the Royal Society of Tropical Medicine and Hygiene, UK, and a Member of the Institute of Health Promotion and Education, UK.

Maria Teresa Mercante is a biologist, graduate at the University of L'Aquila in 1988, and she has held the license to practice as a biologist since 1990. Since 1993, she has been employed as an executive at the Istituto Zooprofilattico Sperimentale dell'Abruzzo e del Molise (IZSAM). From 1993 to 1999, she worked at serology laboratory, and she carried out the production of monoclonal antibodies and the preparation of the registration dossier of vaccines. From 1999 to 2003, she worked at the quality assurance and control Unit, where she carried out the quality control and quality assurance in laboratory accreditation according to ISO/IEC 17025. From February 2003 to May 2004, she carried out the supervision and control of activities of the clinical biochemistry laboratory. She was employed as coordinator and supervisor of the serums and vaccines production laboratory from 2004 to 2009, in particular, from January 2006 to July 2009, she was Head of the viral vaccines, serums and diagnostics production department. Since July 2009, she has worked at the ReceptionUnit, where she is the reference person of the laboratory information system (SILAB).

Sappho Michael holds a BSc in Cell and Molecular Biology from Oxford Brookes University, UK, and an MSc in Human Reproductive Biology from Imperial College, UK. Returning to Cyprus, she first worked as a researcher at the Cyprus Institute of Neurology and Genetics, in the frame of a research programme on Thalassaemia A. She was then employed at the Haematology Laboratory of the Nicosia General Hospital and was later transferred to the Blood Establishment in Nicosia. There, she was responsible for the Quality Management programme. Since 2010, she has been working at the Ministry of Health as a member of the Competent Authority which regulates the activities of the Blood Services in Cyprus. She was trained in Quality Assurance and Accreditation and, since 2004, she is a Technical Expert at the Cyprus Accreditation Body.

Lucilla Ricci has a degree in Biological Sciences from the University of L'Aquila, Italy. From November 1985 to February 1989, she attended the Laboratory of Microbiology at the Faculty of Medicine and Surgery at the University of L' Aquila and acquired microbiological techniques dealing with the production of B- Iattamasi by Gram-negative, the bacterial resistance and techniques of in vitro mutagenesis by using mutagenic substances such as nitroso - guanidine. Later on, from 1989 to 1990, she dealt with cytological and bacteriological exams in the human field, microbiological exams of food, drinking water and wastewater. She taught from November 1989 to June 1992, mathematics, chemistry, biology, and astronomical geography, and since 1997, she is the chair of mathematics, chemical, and physical sciences. From 1992 to the 1993, she dealt with veterinary diagnostic bacteriology and food hygiene. Since December 1993, she has been working at the Quality Management Department at the Istituto Zooprofilattico Sperimentale dell'Abruzzo e Molise (IZSAM). From March 2005 to May 2007, she was Responsible for the Quality at the Italian Ministry of Health. She participated as an expert of ISO 17025, ISO 17020 ISO 19011 and ISO 9001 in several international projects.

Domenico Schioppa holds a Masters Degree in Computer Engineering from Politecnico di Torino, Italy. He has worked as a software engineer and developer at the Institute for Cancer Research and Treatment of Candiolo (IRCC), Italy since July 2013. His research interests include biological data management systems, with a focus on data security and role-based access control. In particular, he has contributed to the development of the LAS (Laboratory Assistant Suite) software – a collaborative effort between IT specialists and biomedical researchers – with the design and implementation of a data access control layer enforcing different privacy policies on a per-user basis.

Faisal K. Shaikh is currently completing his post doctorate at the University of Umm Al-Qura, Makkah, Kingdom of Saudi Arabia. He did his PhD at TU Darmstadt, Germany and is working as an Associate Professor at Mehran University of Engineering and Technology, Pakistan. He served as a Technical Program Committee (TPC) chair and TPC member for several National and International conferences. Dr. Shaikh investigates energy efficient communication protocols in wireless sensor networks (WSN) for mobile, ubiquitous, and pervasive applications. He is interested in environmental monitoring, vehicular adhoc networks, smart homes, telehealth (body area networks), and internet of things. He has published more than 30 refereed journals, conferences, and workshop papers. His research is financially supported by several grants and contracts, such as MUETRnD, ICTRnD, and PSF. He is a member of PEC, IEEE, and ACM.

Michal Šoltés is a researcher and lecturer with the Faculty of Economy at the Technical University in Košice, Slovakia. His main fields of research are investments focused on shares and new investment product developments, insurance market and actuarial science, and pension systems. He leads courses on Financial Investments, Actuarial Science, and Discussion Seminars. He published a number of articles in academic and scientific journals worldwide, several textbooks, and dozens of contributions on scientific conferences with many references. He was a member of research teams in several international scientific projects. He is a member of the editorial board of the scientific magazine *Creative Mathematics and Informatics* and is regularly a member of scientific committees in international conferences worldwide.

Vincent Šoltés is an expert in the field of financial derivatives, mainly on options and option strategies. He has been working as a dean of the Faculty of Economics at the Technical University in Kosice, Slovakia. His scientific field of interest is risk management and financial derivatives, hedging against interest and foreign exchange risks. He worked in a number of projects within the Slovakia and also several projects within 5th and 6th Framework programs. His research area is financial markets, financial derivatives, financial mathematics, quantitative methods in economics, portfolio analysis, and foreign direct investments. He is also interested in the issue of real and nominal convergence of Slovak´s economy in the view of the development of the EU countries. He teaches the subjects Financial Derivatives, Financial Markets, and Financial Mathematics. He is an author of a large number of books and articles in scientific journals.

Kyriacos Tsimillis holds a BSc and a PhD in Chemistry from the University of Athens. His post-graduate studies were carried out at the Nuclear Research Center "Demokritos." After a six-year period of lecturing at the Physical Chemistry Department of the University of Athens, he was involved in stan-dardization and certification activities in Cyprus for twenty years, followed by twelve years of active involvement in accreditation activities until his recent retirement (December 2013). In 2005, he became the Coordinator and in 2009 the Director of the Cyprus Accreditation Body. Since 1997, he represents Cyprus in Eurachem, including a two-year period as its Chair (2008-2010); he also represented Cyprus in Eurolab and the Euromed Quality Programme. He is the author of research papers and review articles and a co-author of books on Quality. He was an invited speaker in seminars, workshops and conferences. He organized a lot of training activities and awareness events.

Fikriye Uras is a professor of biochemistry and clinical chemistry at Marmara University, Istanbul, Turkey. She is a former director of the Clinical Biochemistry Laboratory at the International Hospital in Istanbul and Clinical Chemistry Department of Haseki Training and Research Hospital in Istanbul where she was active in teaching residents and fellows in Clinical Biochemistry. The International Hospital has been awarded accreditation by Joint Commission International (JCI) and Health Quality Service (HQS). The laboratory has been awarded ISO 15189 Accreditation. Her PhD is in biochemistry and she remains very active in professional organizations. She is the founder and former president of the Association of Clinical Biochemists (KBUD), Turkey. She organized the First International Symposium on Quality and Accreditation in Laboratory Medicine as the president. She was guest editor of *Clinical Biochemistry* based on this symposium. She has been president of 3 national symposia on accreditation and standardization of laboratories.

Viroj Wiwanitkit is currently working as a medical professor and Asian Scholar. He is also a visiting University Professor, Hainan Medical University, China and a visiting professorwith the Faculty of Medicine at the University of Nis, Serbia. His research interests include tropical medicine and public health, Laboratory medicine, clinical biochemistry, molecular biology, and microbiology.

Index

A

Accreditation 75-77, 123, 130, 136-142, 145, 147-152, 182, 184-185, 187, 199, 207, 209, 212, 214, 230, 234, 236, 281, 285, 289, 297, 299
Animal Disease Surveillance 309
Association Rule 240, 245, 250
Automated Selection and Reporting of Results 180, 203, 207

B

Backup Copy 112, 116
Biobank 264, 267, 270-271, 274, 279
Body/Personal Area Network (BAN 124, 134
Business Activity Monitoring (BAM) 116

C

Calibration 83, 85-92, 94, 137, 143-146, 152-153, 172, 185, 195-196, 199, 201, 211
Certification 136-141, 152, 156
Clinical Chemistry 138, 142, 207, 280, 283-284
Clinical Laboratory 72, 84, 183, 185, 199, 207, 209, 280-281, 283-287, 289
Cloud Computing 87, 94, 210, 215-216, 222-223, 229, 233-235, 259
Commercial System 66
Computerised Provider Order Entry 51-52, 66
Conformity Assessment 137-138, 140, 152, 281
Conformity Assessment Body 138, 152
Contingency Situations 95, 116
Conventional Environment 110, 116-117
Cytopathology 208-213, 215-216, 219-220, 222-226, 232-236

D

Data Management 72, 200, 208-209, 212, 216, 253, 255, 257, 259, 285, 289, 297
Data Mining 75-76, 211, 223, 237-241, 244-246, 251, 258, 275, 281
Digital Environment 110-113, 116-117

E

eHealth 32-34, 46, 48
Electronic Decision Support System 66
electronic medical record 50, 66, 241
Electronic Medical Record (EMR) 50, 66

F

Functionalities 87, 252, 254, 257-263, 270, 274-275, 280-284, 289, 299-301

G

Genomic Annotation 259, 261-263
Global information Collection 94

H

Harmonization 207
health informatics 54, 131
Home Area Network (HAN) 124, 134
Home-Grown System 66

I

Informatics and ICT Management 49
Information Confidentiality Level 117
Information Manager 109, 117